WELSH IN 12 WEEKS

Welsh in 12 Weeks

Phylip and Julie Brake

First published in 2020
Revised edition: 2021

© Phylip and Julie Brake / Gwasg Carreg Gwalch

© Gwasg Carreg Gwalch 2020

All rights reserved. No part of this publication
may be reproduced, stored in a retrieval system,
or transmitted in any form or by any means, electronic,
electrostatic, magnetic tape, mechanical, photocopying,
recording, or otherwise, without prior permission
of the authors of the works herein.

ISBN: 978-1-84527-724-6

Published with the financial support of the
Welsh Books Council.

Cover design: Eleri Owen

Published by Gwasg Carreg Gwalch,
12 Iard yr Orsaf, Llanrwst, Wales LL26 0EH
tel: 01492 642031
email: books@carreg-gwalch.cymru
website: www.carreg-gwalch.cymru

Mae'r llyfr hwn wedi ei gysegru i'm gwraig annwyl a'm cyd-awdur, a gymerwyd oddi wrthym ar ôl salwch byr, er y bydd ei hysbryd, ei llawenydd o fywyd, ei ffraethineb a'i hiwmor yn aros gyda ni am byth.

This book is dedicated to of my loving wife and co-author, who, after a short illness, was taken from us, although her spirit, her joy of life, her wit and her humour will remain with us forever.

Contents

Abbreviations vi

Preface vii

The Welsh Language viii

Further reading x

Week 1
1. Pronunciation 1
2. Nouns 6
3. Adjectives 8
4. The definite article 9
5. Mutation 10
6. Counting to 100 15
7. Recap exercises 18

Week 2
1. Affirmative forms of identification sentences 20
2. Negative forms of identification sentences 23
3. Interrogative forms of identification sentences 24
4. The use of identification verb forms after common interrogatives 27
5. Feminine numerals 28
6. Demonstrative phrases 30
7. Recap exercises 32

Week 3
1. Affirmative forms of the present tense of '**bod**' (to be) 36
2. Interrogative adverbs 46
3. Interrogative forms of present tense of '**bod**' 49
4. Negative forms of the present tense of '**bod**' 53
5. Locative adverbs 56
6. The weather and points of the compass 59
7. Recap exercises 65

Week 4
1. More adjectives 71
2. Expressing possession 73
3. Days of the week 86
4. Present relative form of '**bod**' 93
5. Genitive noun phrases 99
6. Nasal mutation 105
7. Recap exercises 109

Week 5
1. The prefixed possessive pronoun '**eich**' 113
2. Other prefixed possessive pronouns 118
3. Expressing '**self**' 123
4. Introduction to prepositions 125
5. The perfect aspect of '**bod**' 129
6. Telling the time 132
7. Recap exercises 137

Week 6
1. The past imperfect aspect of '**bod**' 140
2. The past perfect aspect of '**bod**' 148
3. That-clauses 149
4. Parts of speech followed by the that-clauses 152
5. The emphatic that-clause 155
6. Giving your age, and '**blwyddyn**', '**blwydd**' and '**blynedd**' 157
7. Recap exercises 160

Week 7
1. The imperative (giving a command) 163
2. Affirmative forms of the simple past (regular verbs) 170
3. Interrogative forms of the simple past tense (regular verbs) 173
4. Negative forms of the simple past tense (regular verbs) 176
5. The simple past tense of the '**mynd**','**dod**' and '**gwneud**' 180
6. The simple past tense of '**bod**' ... 184
7. Recap exercises 189

Week 8
1. The simple past tense of '**cael**' .. 193
2. Relative forms of '**bod**' 196
3. The preposition '**i**' and expressing 'I'd better' / 'I'd prefer' 199

4. Expressing obligation with '**rhaid**' 205
5. The equative and comparative forms of adjectives 211
6. The superlative form of adjectives 217
7. Recap exercises 221

Week 9
1. The future tense of '**bod**' 227
2. The simple future tense of regular verbs 234
3. The simple future tense of '**mynd**' and '**gwneud**' 243
4. The simple future tense of '**cael**' and asking permission 249
5. The simple future tense of '**dod**' 254
6. Dates, seasons, and months of the year 255
7. Recap exercises 262

Week 10
1. Expressing '**ever**' and '**never**' .. 267
2. Verb-nouns and related prepositions 271
3. Common prepositions 280
4. Illnesses, emotions, and idioms based on '**ar**' 288
5. The use of '**mo**' to negate simple past and future verb forms 296
6. Compound prepositions 300
7. Recap exercises 303

Week 11
1. The subjunctive mood 307
2. Conditional clauses with '**pe**' and '**os**' 315
3. Expressing 'should' and 'ought to' 318
4. The passive voice 319
5. The relative clause 323
6. The oblique relative clause 324
7. Recap exercises 329

Week 12
1. Defective verbs 334
2. '**Gwneud**' as an auxiliary verb .. 336
3. Emphatic sentences 339
4. The use of '**piau**' to indicate possession 343
5. Impersonal forms of the verb 345
6. Useful phrases 350
7. Recap exercises 354

Taking it Further 358

Reading Practice 361

Key to Exercises 365

A Brief Summary of the Modern Welsh Verb System 398

Mini-Dictionary 401

Index 428

v

Abbreviations

adv.	adverb
adj.	adjective
alt.	alternative
AM	aspirate mutation[1]
cf.	compare
cnj.	conjunction
e.g.	for example
f.	feminine
fam.	familiar
IPA	International Phonetics Association
interj.	interjection
irreg.	irregular
lit.	literally
m.	masculine
n.	noun
NM	nasal mutation
NW	North Wales
periph.	periphrastic
pers.	person
pl.	plural
pn	pronoun
prp.	preposition
sing.	singular
SM	soft mutation
SW	South Wales
vb	verb
vs	versus

---

[1] Also known as the spirant mutation.

Preface

Welsh in Twelve Weeks has been written by two people who are, and were, actively involved in teaching Welsh to a wide-ranging audience. Phylip Brake has vast experience organising Learn Welsh programmes at Aberystwyth University, including devising and developing intensive courses aimed at getting students fluent in the language in as short a period as possible. Until her untimely death in 2019, Julie Brake was a senior lecturer in Welsh at Wrexham Glyndŵr University in North Wales and had previously published on the subject of Wales and the Welsh language.

This book begins with an explanation of Welsh pronunciation. If you are working without a teacher, you will find that the use of the International Phonetic Association (IPA) symbols simplifies matters considerably. You will also find many pronunciation guides online to help you, including those on video sharing sites.

Welsh in Twelve Weeks introduces you to the essential vocabulary and main grammatical areas of Welsh. Constructions are clearly explained, and the order in which everything is presented takes into consideration the need for rapid progress. Each week of the course is divided into seven subsections or lessons, thereby providing you with an hour of study per day for twelve weeks. This is just a rough guide, and you should only do as much as you feel capable of doing at a time, as you are the best judge of whether you are assimilating new material. It is much better to learn a little at a time (and to learn it thoroughly) than to rush through the material while assimilating nothing. After most grammatical points have been covered, there are exercises for you to put what you have learned into practice. The seventh lesson in each week consists of exercises which you can use to decide whether you have assimilated the information introduced during that week and whether you are ready to proceed onto the next section. The answers to all the exercises can be found in a key at the end of the book.

Like most languages, Welsh has a standard written form which can be different from the spoken form. The form used in this book is *Cymraeg llafar ysgrifenedig*, 'written spoken Welsh', which is frequently used in newspapers, magazines, official documentation and websites. While there is no *one* form of standard spoken Welsh, the emergence of a Welsh mass media through platforms like *Radio Cymru* and *S4C* has meant that the seeds of a potential standard spoken language are being germinated, and developing remarkably quickly. Generally, Welsh is divided into North Welsh and South Welsh. These are broad terms and there are regional differences within them. Throughout this book, you will be presented with both South Welsh and North Welsh forms.

When you have completed the course, you should have a good understanding of Welsh, but remember that it is vital to continue to expand your vocabulary through reading. You may find that it helps to listen to radio programmes on *Radio Cymru* and watch Welsh television programmes on *S4C* (now available digitally), as many of these materials are produced specifically for Welsh learners. As we live in the Information Age, the 'Taking it Further' section at the ends of this book includes a list of useful websites for Welsh learners.

We hope you will enjoy *Welsh in Twelve Weeks*, and we wish you every success with your studies.

The Welsh Language

The emergence of Welsh as a distinct language is believed to have occurred by about 600 AD, with it having evolved from the language of the ancient Britons. Over time, Welsh became embedded in most aspects of life and society, including governance, law, learning and culture. However, its adoption into religious writing and practice was slower, and Latin texts were not translated into Welsh until the sixteenth century.

Wales was a Welsh-speaking country in the early Middle Ages, and even after its conquest by England in 1282, the Welsh language continued to hold official status. It was in the fifteenth century that English took a dominant role, and the number of spheres where Welsh was used declined. This was spurred, in part, by the Acts of Union (1535-42), which specified that English should be the only language heard in the courts and the use of Welsh would debar one from public office. Thankfully, Bishop William Morgan's 1588 translation of the Bible played a crucial role in preserving Welsh as a language of worship.

The Industrial Revolution transformed Welsh by causing its speakers to migrate into towns. By 1851, large numbers lived in them and enjoyed activities in Welsh which had not been possible in the sparsely populated rural areas. Among these activities were cultural societies, choirs, debating societies and *eisteddfodau* (Welsh-medium festivals of literature, music and performance). The language also started to be used for mass communication, with novels, essays, political leaflets, periodicals, newspapers and chronicles being published.

Despite the developments mentioned above, many still viewed Welsh as the language for religion and hearth, with English considered the language for every other sphere. Unfortunately, tables were set to turn even further, and from 1801 to 1901, the percentage of Welsh speakers in Wales fell from 80% to only 49.9%. One contributing factor is thought to have been the migration of non-Welsh speakers into Wales' industrialised areas, which happened at such a pace they could not be assimilated. Another obstacle for Welsh was the introduction of a state education system in the 1880s. This system had completely disregarded the language, both as a medium of education and as a subject.

Wales lost a generation of young Welsh-speaking men to the First World War, and the post-war depression in agriculture and industry led many more to migrate. By 1961, the Welsh-speaking population of Wales was 659,002, 26% of the total population. There were calls for the language to be protected and its status improved, culminating in a lecture by the academic, and playwright, Saunders Lewis entitled 'Tynged yr Iaith' (The Fate of the Language). Broadcast by the BBC in 1962, it called for direct action to protect Welsh, and led to the formation of *Cymdeithas yr Iaith Gymraeg* (The Welsh Language Society), which campaigned for the equal status of Welsh. This was achieved through the Welsh Language Act of 1967, which gave equal status to the Welsh language for the first time since 1536, thereby permitting the use of Welsh in courts and official documents.

Over the years, the status of Welsh has improved, particularly with the rise of Welsh-medium education like that encouraged by *Cymru'n Un* (One Wales), the vision of the Welsh government for a bilingual Wales. Additionally, *Mudiad Ysgolion Meithrin* was founded in 1971 to support the use of Welsh in education and nursery groups, and in 2011, *Y Coleg Cymraeg Cenedlaethol* started to work with universities to develop and coordinate Welsh-medium courses and resources for students, as well as fund scholarships, research, and lectureships.

Today, Welsh is spoken by around 20% of the population of Wales. It is visible everywhere, from street signs to official forms, as well as in the media and on social media. However, the only areas where substantial portions of the population speak Welsh are West and North West Wales, where there is a growing threat to the language from rural depopulation, migration, tourism and low social prestige. Starting at the end of the twentieth century, and continuing to the present day, the relatively cheap housing in Wales has attracted waves of incomers, mainly from South East England, leading to the anglicisation of rural, Welsh-speaking Wales. The strategy to strengthen Welsh as a community language has mainly been the responsibility of the *Mentrau Iaith* (language initiatives), and although they have had some success, the long-term prospects look bleak for a minority language which lacks a substantial and centralised community of speakers. With all of this said, the Welsh language is far from being a lost cause, and thousands of people continue to learn Welsh as adults, while increasing numbers of children become fluent in the language at school.

Further Reading

A History of Wales, John Davies, London: Penguin (1994).
Culture in Crisis: The Future of the Welsh Language, Clive Betts, Upton: Gwasg Ffynnon (1976).
Cymraeg 2050: A Million Speakers, Welsh Government (2018).
The Foundation of Modern Wales: Wales 1642-1780, Geraint Jenkins, Oxford University Press (1993).
The Mabinogion, Sioned Davies, Oxford University Press (2007) (translation and introductory notes by the author).
The Welsh Language 1961-81: An Independent Atlas, John Aitchison and Harold Carter, Cardiff: University of Wales Press (1985).
The Welsh Language and Its Social Domains, 1801-1911, Geraint Jenkins, Cardiff: University of Wales Press (2001).
The Welsh Language: A History, John Davies, Cardiff: University of Wales Press (2014).
Tynged yr Iaith, Saunders Lewis, Aberystwyth: Cymdeithas yr Iaith Gymraeg (1985) (translated as *The Fate of the Language* and available online: https://morris.cymru/testun/saunders-lewis-fate-of-the-language.html).
When was Wales?, Gwyn Alf Williams, London: Penguin (1985).

Week 1

Lesson 1: Pronunciation

The alphabet

a, b, c, ch, d, dd, e, f, ff, g, ng, h, i, j, l, ll, m, n, o, p, ph, r, rh, s, t, th, u, w, y

There are 29 letters in the Welsh alphabet. Letter combinations (digraphs) such as **ch**, **dd**, **ll**, etc., each represent one sound. This means that a word like **rhydd**, which means 'free' / 'liberated', consists of three letters: **rh + y + dd** [r̥iːð].

The stress accent
The stress accent in Welsh words is usually on the penult (the last but one syllable), with tonal stress on the last syllable. This double stress gives the impression that Welsh people 'sing'! Contrast the stress in 'problem', a word which occurs in both English and Welsh:

English: **PROB**lem   Welsh: **PROB***lem*.

There are exceptions to the above rule, especially in the case of recent English loanwords.

The stress accent is marked by the symbol ' in the IPA representation of words. Here are some examples: **siarad** 'to talk' [ˈʃɑrad], **polisi** 'policy' [ˈpɔlɪsi], **Cymraeg** 'Welsh' (language) [kəmˈraɪg].

Pronunciation of consonants
Welsh consonants are, overall, pronounced the same as in English. This is true of those below:

WELSH LETTER		IPA SYMBOL
b	is pronounced like **b** in English 'bat'.	/b/
d	is pronounced like **d** in English 'dash'.	/d/
ff	is pronounced like **ff** in English 'off'.	/f/
ng	is pronounced like **ng** in English 'bang'.	/ŋ/
j	is pronounced like **j** in English 'jam'.	/dʒ/
m	is pronounced like **m** in English 'man'.	/m/
n	is pronounced like **n** in English 'net'.	/n/
p	is pronounced like **p** in English 'pet'.	/p/
ph	is pronounced like **ph** in English 'philosophy'.	/f/
t	is pronounced like **t** in English 'ten'.	/t/
th	is pronounced like **th** in English 'thin'.	/θ/

The following consonants are pronounced differently than in English, or their pronunciation differs between North Welsh and South Welsh:

WELSH LETTER		IPA SYMBOL
c	is pronounced like **c** in English 'cap', *never* as in 'city'.	/k/
ch	is pronounced like **ch** in German 'bach' (stream).	/χ/
dd	is pronounced like **th** in English 'the'.	/ð/
f	is pronounced like **f** in English 'of'.	/v/
g	is pronounced like **g** in English 'get', *never* as in 'giant'.	/g/
	g can also be pronounced with rounded lips before a consonant, and this is represented in writing by **gw**, as in **gwlad** 'country' [gʷlɑːd].	/gʷ/
l	is pronounced like **l** in English 'lake'. It is always clear in South Welsh, with the tongue high in the mouth.	/l/
	In North Welsh, **l** is pronounced with the bottom of the tongue against the bottom of the mouth: /ɫ/, as in Southern English 'hello'.	/ɫ/
ll	is pronounced like **l** in English 'kettle'. It is a voiceless **l** produced by positioning the tongue to pronounce **l** and blowing.	/ɬ/
r	is pronounced like **r** in Scots 'run'. The Welsh **r** is usually trilled, especially at the beginning of a word, and *always* pronounced.	/r/
	After **t** and **d**, most Welsh speakers pronounce **r** as in the standard English 'red'.	/ɹ/
rh	is pronounced like **r** in standard English 'red', but pronounced without voice.	/ɹ̥/
s	is the same as in English.	/s/
	But, in South Welsh, **s** is usually pronounced **sh** after **i** in words of one syllable, and after the penult in longer words: **mis** 'month' [miːʃ], **bisi** 'busy' [ˈbiˑʃi], **bisgïen** 'biscuit' [biʃˈgiˑɛn]. Note this is *not* the case after **y**, which is pronounced like **i** in South Wales: **bys** 'finger' [biːs], **crys** 'shirt' [kriːs].	/ʃ/
t, d	in North Welsh, **t** and **d** are pronounced by placing the front of the tongue against the back of the teeth.	/t̪/, /d̪/

Diacritics

The following diacritics are used in the IPA representations of words and phrases:

DIACRITIC	
ˈ	indicates that the stress accent is on the syllable it precedes: **Cymraeg** 'Welsh' (language) [kəmˈraɪg].
¨	above a vowel means that it should be pronounced more centrally – almost like /ə/: **gynnau fach** 'just now' [ˈgənɛ väχ].

͏̺	below /t/ or /d/ means that the letter is pronounced with the tip of the tongue against the back of the upper front teeth (North Wales).	
̥	below or above a voiced consonant means it is pronounced without voice. In written Welsh, this unvoicing is represented by **h**, such as in: **rhan** 'part' [r̥an], **rhywbeth** 'something' [r̥ʊbɛθ], **(f)y nhad** 'my father' [(v)ə n̥ɑːd].	
h	although, not a diacritic as such, represents the unvoicing that often accompanies the movement of the stress accent, e.g. there is no **h** in **cymar** 'partner' ['kəmar], nor in **cyngor** 'advice' ['kəŋor], where the stress accent comes before the **m** and **ng**, but appears in **cymharu** 'to compare' [kəmˈhɑːri], and **cynghori** 'to advise' [kəŋˈhɔri], where the **m** and **ng** come at the beginning of the stress accent.	
ː	after a long vowel means that its length is full: **ffôn** 'telephone' [foːn], **cŵn** 'dogs' [kuːn].	
ˑ	after a long vowel means that its length is halved. This is particularly true in the penult: **canu** 'to sing' ['kɑˑni].	
̩	under a consonant means that the consonant is syllabic: **cefn** 'back' ['kɛvn̩].	
ʷ	in words like **gwlad** 'country' [gʷlɑːd] and **Wrecsam** 'Wrexham' [ʷrɛksam], indicates that the preceding or following consonant is pronounced with rounded lips. The technical term for this process is labialization.	
( )	indicates that the sound within isn't normally heard in everyday speech: **tre(f)** 'town' [tre̝ː(v)].	
.	indicates the boundary between two syllables with similar vowels: **deellir** 'is understood' [de.ˈɛɬɪr].	

Pronunciation of vowels

Welsh vowels are monophthong, which means they have a single perceived auditory quality. That being the case, the equivalents given below are approximate:

WELSH LETTER		IPA SYMBOL
a (short)	is pronounced like **a** in Northern English 'cat'.	/a/
á	is pronounced like **a** in Northern English 'cat'.	/a/
a (long)	is pronounced like **a** in English 'father'.	/ɑː/
â	is pronounced like **a** in English 'father'.	/ɑː/
e (short)	is pronounced like **e** in English 'let'.	/ɛ/
e (long)	is pronounced like **ea** in English 'bear'.	/eː/
ê	is pronounced like **ea** in English 'bear'.	/eː/
i (short)*	is pronounced like **i** in English 'pin'.	/ɪ/
ì	is pronounced like **i** in English 'pin'.	/ɪ/
i (long)*	is pronounced like **ee** in English 'peel'.	/iː/
î	is pronounced like **ee** in English 'peel'.	/iː/
o (short)**	is pronounced like **o** in English 'pot'.	/ɔ/
ò	is pronounced like **o** in English 'pot'.	/ɔ/
o (long)**	is pronounced like **oe** in Northern English 'toe'.	/oː/

ô	is pronounced like oe in Northern English 'toe'.	/oː/
u (short)***	is pronounced like i in English 'pin'.	/ɪ/
u (long)***	is pronounced like ee in English 'peel'.	/iː/
û***	is pronounced like ee in English 'peel'.	/iː/
w (short)	is pronounced like oo in Southern English 'hook'.	/ʊ/
w (long)	is pronounced like oo in English 'moon'.	/uː/
ŵ	is pronounced like oo in English 'moon'.	/uː/
y (short)***	is pronounced like i in English 'pin'.	/ɪ/
y (long)***	is pronounced like ee in English 'peel'.	/iː/
ŷ***	is pronounced like ee in English 'peel'.	/iː/
y****	is pronounced like u in Southern English 'bus'.	/ə/

* When **i** appears in the final unstressed syllable of a word, it should be pronounced approximately halfway between /iː/ and /ɪ/. This will appear as /ɪ/ in the IPA transcriptions.

** When **o** appears in the final unstressed syllable of a word, it should be pronounced approximately halfway between /oː/ and /ɔ/. This will appear as /o/ in the IPA transcriptions.

*** In North Welsh, these vowels are produced by lifting the middle of the tongue towards the roof of the mouth: /ɨː/. There is no similar sound in English.

**** Usually, **y** is pronounced /ə/ when it occurs in the accented penult.

All vowels are long in words of one syllable not ending in a consonant: **te** 'tea' [teː], **ti** 'you' (*fam.*) [tiː], **llw** 'oath' [ɬuː].

Diphthongs (vowel combinations)
A diphthong is a combination of two vowels pronounced one after the other in one breath or 'syllable'. As we have seen, some Welsh vowels, like **i** and **u**, sound the same (especially in South Welsh), and diphthongs like **ai** and **au** also sound the same.

DIPHTHONG		IPA SYMBOL
ai, ae, au, áu, âu	are all pronounced like ie in Northern English 'pie'.	/aɪ/
aw	is pronounced like ow in English 'cow'.	/aʊ/
ei, eu, ey	are all pronounced either like a centralised ie in English 'tie' or like ey in English 'prey'. From now on, it will be represented in the IPA transcriptions as /əɪ/.	/əɪ/, /eɪ/
ew	is pronounced like ow Western English 'cow'.	/ɛʊ/
iw, yw	are both produced by pronouncing i in English 'bit', followed immediately by oo in English 'book'.	/ɪʊ/
oi, oe, ou	are all produced by pronouncing o in English 'got', followed immediately by i in English 'bit'.	/ɔɪ/
wy, ŵy	are both produced by pronouncing oo in Southern English 'book', followed immediately by i in English 'bit'.	/ʊɪ/

Pronunciation of semivowels
A semivowel is a vowel sound that can function as a consonant, usually before a true vowel. For example, the letter **y** in the English word 'yet' is a semivowel, as is the **w** in

'water'. We have already seen that the Welsh **w** is pronounced like the English **oo**, and the Welsh **i** is pronounced like the English **ee**, but they can also function as semivowels. In the case of **w** /w/, this usually happens after the letters **g** /g/ and **ch** /χ/. An example involving **g** would be **Gwent** 'Gwent' [gwɛnt] (a revived ancient name that corresponds to the old Monmouthshire), and an example involving **ch** would be **chwech** 'six' [χweːχ]. It is also important to remember that the consonant preceding **w** is pronounced with rounded lips. Often, **i** /j/ is a semivowel at the beginning of a diphthong, as in **iach** 'healthy' [jɑːχ], **ionawr** 'january' ['jɔnaʊr].

WELSH LETTER		IPA SYMBOL
w	**gwên** 'smile' [gweːn], with **w** as in English 'water'.	/w/
i	**iâr** 'hen' [jɑːr], with **y** as in English 'yet'.	/j/

Accents

There are three accents in Welsh that affect the quality of the vowel they are associated with:

- The acute (ascending) accent (´) is usually found on the letter **a** /a/ to indicate that the stress accent is on the last syllable, as in **casáu** 'to hate' [kasˈaɪ].
- The grave (descending) accent (`) is usually found on **i** /ɪ/ and **o** /ɔ/ to show that the vowel is short, as in **sgìl** 'skill' [sgɪl], **clòs** 'close' (in relation to the weather) [klɔs].
- The circumflex (^) is found on any vowel to show that it is long, as in **trên** 'train' [t̪reːn], **dŵr** 'water' [duːr].

Accents are diacritical marks. The diaeresis (¨) is another diacritical mark, and it is used to show that a particular vowel is pronounced separately rather than forming a diphthong with the vowel next to it. The vowel sound itself does not change, as can be seen by comparing **stori** 'story' ['stɔri] to **storïau** 'stories' [stɔrɪ̈ɛ]. Note that the IPA transcription does *not* become ['stɔrjɛ].

Pronunciation of the Welsh alphabet

Letters of the Welsh alphabet are words in their own right, and their pronunciation is a close approximation to their phonetic quality. The Welsh alphabet below should be read from left to right:

A	(a)	[ɑː]	B	(bi)	[biː]	C	(èc)	[ɛk]
CH	(èch)	[ɛχ]	D	(di)	[diː]	DD	(èdd)	[ɛð]
E	(e)	[eː]	F	(èf)	[ɛv]	FF	(èff)	[ɛf]
G	(èg)	[ɛg]	NG	(èng)	[ɛŋ]	H	(aitsh)	[aɪtʃ]
I	(i-dot)	[iː dɔt]	J	(je)	[dʒeː]	L	(èl)	[ɛl]
LL	(èll)	[ɛɬ]	M	(èm)	[ɛm]	N	(èn)	[ɛn]
O	(o)	[oː]	P	(pi)	[piː]	PH	(ffi)	[fiː]

R	(èr)	[ɛr]	RH	(rhi)	[r̥iː]	S	(ès)	[ɛs]
T	(ti)	[tiː]	TH	(èth)	[ɛθ]	U	(i-bedol)	[iːˈbedol]
W	(w)	[uː]	Y	(like English 'her' without the **h**)				[əː]

Lesson 2: Nouns

What is a noun?
All languages have nouns. These can be people, places, things, and concepts or ideas:

- (i) A person: **postmon** 'postman' [ˈpɔstmon], **athro** 'male teacher' [ˈaθro].
- (ii) A place: **Cymru** 'Wales' [ˈkəmri], **siop** 'shop' [ʃɔp], **tre(f)*** 'town' [ˈtre̝ː(v)].
- (iii) A thing: **ci** 'dog' [kiː], **pêl** 'ball' [peːl], **afal** 'apple' [ˈɑval].
- (iv) A concept or idea: **harddwch** 'beauty' [ˈharðʊχ], **nerfusrwydd** 'nervousness' [nɛrvˈɪsrʊɪð].

* *The final f in some words is generally not pronounced in everyday speech. To reflect this, we have placed the final f in brackets where this holds true.*

In Welsh, all nouns are either masculine or feminine. Nouns which denote something biologically male are always masculine, and nouns which denote something biologically female are always feminine:

MASCULINE NOUN	ENGLISH	IPA
tarw	bull	[ˈtɑrʊ]
bachgen	boy	[ˈbäχgen]
tad	father	[tɑːd]

FEMININE NOUN	ENGLISH	IPA
buwch	cow	[bɪʊχ]
merch	girl	[mɛrχ]
mam	mother	[mam]

Unfortunately, there are few other rules that can help determine the gender of Welsh nouns. It is therefore a good idea to learn the noun and its gender at the same time. Nouns in this book are classified according to their gender, including those listed in the mini dictionary at the end.

Noun plurals
Unlike in English, there is no regular way of forming a noun plural in Welsh. The most common way is by adding an ending such as **-au** /aɪ/ (usually pronounced /ɛ/ in everyday speech), but as you can see from the table below, sometimes (as in the case of **tŷ** 'house' [tiː] and **ci** 'dog' [kiː]) the plural form is quite different from the singular.

MASCULINE NOUN	ENGLISH	IPA	PLURAL FORM	IPA
tŷ*	house	[tiː]	tai	[taɪ]
ci	dog	[kiː]	cŵn	[kuːn]

dyn	man	[diːn]	dynion	['dənjon]
pentre(f)	village	['pɛntrɛ(v)]	**pentrefi**	[pɛn'tr̥ɛvi]

* **Tŷ** is pronounced [t̪iː] in North Welsh.

FEMININE NOUN	ENGLISH	IPA	PLURAL FORM	IPA
siop	shop	[ʃɔp]	**siopau**	['ʃɔpɛ]
merch	girl	['mɛrχ]	**merched**	['mɛrχɛd]
tre(f)	town	[tr̥eː(v)]	**trefi**	['tr̥evi]
esgid	shoe	['ɛsɡɪd]	**esgidiau**	[ɛs'ɡɪdjɛ]

There is no indefinite article (such as the English 'a' and 'an') in Welsh. This means a word like **ci** [kiː] is both 'dog' and 'a dog'; **tre(f)** [tr̥eː(v)] is 'town' and 'a town'; **tarw** ['tɑrʊ] is 'bull' and 'a bull'.

These first exercises should allow you to test yourself on the vocabulary introduced thus far.

Exercise 1

*Match the noun under **A** with its plural form under **B**.*

A
1) tŷ (a house)
2) siop (a shop)
3) tref (a town)
4) dyn (a man)
5) pentre(f) (a village)
6) merch (a girl)
7) esgid (a shoe)
8) ci (a dog)

B
a) merched
b) cŵn
c) pentrefi
d) trefi
e) tai
f) esgidiau
g) siopau
h) dynion

Exercise 2

Write down the English equivalent of the following Welsh nouns.

1) merch _____   2) dyn _____
3) cŵn _____   4) esgidiau _____
5) siop _____   6) ci _____
7) pentre(f) _____   8) tŷ _____

Exercise 3

Write down the Welsh equivalent of the following English nouns.

1) a dog _____ 2) men _____
3) a house _____ 4) a town _____
5) shops _____ 6) shoes _____
7) a girl _____ 8) a village _____

Exercise 4

Write down the plurals of the following Welsh nouns.

1) tŷ _____ (house) 2) siop _____ (shop)
3) dyn _____ (man) 4) tref _____ (town)
5) esgid _____ (shoe) 6) pentre(f) _____ (village)
7) ci _____ (dog) 8) merch _____ (girl)

Exercise 5

Write down the singular form of the following nouns.

1) tai _____ 2) pentrefi _____
3) merched _____ 4) esgidiau _____
5) cŵn _____ 6) dynion _____
7) trefi _____ 8) siopau _____

Exercise 6

For each of the following words, note whether they are masculine (m.) or feminine (f.).

1) tre(f) ____ 2) tŷ ____ 3) merch ____
4) siop ____ 5) dyn ____ 6) tarw ____
7) pentre(f) ____ 8) mam ____ 9) ci ____
10) esgid ____

Lesson 3: Adjectives

An adjective is a word which describes a noun. Examples include **bach** 'small' [bɑːχ], **hen** 'old' [heːn], **tal** 'tall' [tal].

Welsh adjectives with their English counterpart(s):

ADJECTIVE	ENGLISH	IPA
bach	small / little	[bɑːχ]
da	good	[dɑː]
drwg	bad / naughty	[druːg]
mawr	big / large	[maʊr]
tal	tall	[tal]

In Welsh, an adjective generally comes after the noun it is describing:

NOUN + ADJECTIVE	ENGLISH	IPA
bachgen da	a good boy	[ˈbäχgɛn dɑː]
siopau bach	small shops	[ˈʃɔpɛ bɑːχ]
trefi mawr	large towns	[ˈtrɛvi maʊr]
dyn da	a good man	[diːn dɑː]

Exercise 1

Write and say the following in Welsh.

1) a large house _____
2) tall girls _____
3) small villages _____
4) good men _____
5) large shoes _____
6) good shops _____
7) a tall man _____
8) good dogs _____
9) small towns _____
10) a large bull _____

Lesson 4: The definite article

In Welsh, the definite article* 'the' in Welsh has three forms:

i.) The full form is **yr** 'the' [ər], and this occurs before a vowel (**a, e, i, o, u, w, y**) and before **h**, such as in: **yr afal** 'the apple' [ər ˈɑval], **yr heol** 'the road' [ər ˈheˑol]**.
ii.) Before consonants, **y** is used, such as in: **y dyn** 'the man' [ə diːn].
iii.) After vowels, **yr** contracts to **'r**, such as in: **ci'r dyn** 'the man's dog' [kiːr diːn], **i'r tŷ** 'to the house' [iːr tiː].

* *Remember there is no indefinite article (like 'a' and 'an' in English) in Welsh.*

** ***Heol*** *is usually pronounced **hewl** [heʊl] in everyday speech.*

Exercise 1

*Place **y**, **yr** or **'r** in front of the following nouns.*

1) _____ tarw (the bull)
2) _____ siop (to the shop)
3) _____ oren (the orange)
4) _____ merched (the girls)
5) _____ pentre(f) (from the village)
6) _____ hufen (the cream)
7) _____ ci (the dog)
8) _____ trefi (the towns)

Lesson 5: Mutation

A characteristic which is common to all living Celtic languages (including Irish, Scots Gaelic, Breton, Cornish, Manx and Welsh), is that certain consonants change at the beginning of some words. These changes, known as mutations, are governed by the grammatical context in which they occur.

Mutation is an integral part of the Welsh language, but don't let that worry you. Many Welsh speakers make mutations unconsciously and haven't any idea of the rules governing the consonantal changes – in much the same way that English speakers pronounce the **s** in the singular noun **house** [haʊs] differently to how they pronounce it in the equivalent plural **houses** ['haʊzɪz], without understanding why.

Some people learn better if they have an overview of a topic, whereas others require a context. There is no need to assimilate all the knowledge in this section, as it is merely an introduction to mutation. That being said, the words and grammatical contexts which cause mutation should be learnt in the same way as vocabulary.

To begin with, it will help if you have a general idea of the principles of mutation. There are three types of mutations in Welsh, and these are classified roughly according to the type of phonetic change which occurs:

(i)   soft mutation
(ii) nasal mutation
(iii) aspirate mutation*

MUTABLE CONSONANT	IPA	SOFT MUTATION	IPA	NASAL MUTATION	IPA	ASPIRATE MUTATION	IPA
p	/p/	**b**	/b/	**mh**	/m̥/	**ph**	/f/
t	/t/	**d**	/d/	**nh**	/n̥/	**th**	/θ/

c	/k/	**g**	/g/	**ngh**	/ŋ̊/	**ch**	/χ/
b	/b/	**f**	/v/	**m**	/m/		
d	/d/	**dd**	/ð/	**n**	/n/		
g	/g/	_**		**ng**	/ŋ/		
m	/m/	**f**	/v/				
ll	/ɬ/	**l**	/l/				
rh	/r̥/	**r**	/r/				

* Also called the spirant mutation.
** In modern Welsh, the soft mutation causes **g** to simply vanish. An underscore is used to represent this in examples.

By referring to the section on pronunciation, you should have little difficulty in pronouncing the majority of the mutated forms listed above, although the nasal forms may present some problems; **m**, **n** and **ng** are pronounced the same as in English, while the **h** in **mh**, **nh** and **ngh** merely denotes that these nasal sounds are produced without voice (in the same way that **rh** is a voiceless **r**).

(i) The soft mutation is the most common. If you have travelled into Wales, you may have seen the sign: **Croeso i Gymru** 'Welcome to Wales' [ˈkrɔɪso iː ˈgəmri]. **Gymru** is an example of a word which has undergone soft mutation. The soft mutation is caused in a number of ways, such as after certain prepositions like **i** 'to, for' [iː]:

MUTATED PHRASE	ENGLISH	IPA	NOUN PRE-MUTATION	ENGLISH	IPA
i Gymru	to Wales	[i ˈgəmri]	**Cymru**	Wales	[ˈkəmri]
i bentre(f)	to a village	[i ˈbɛntɹɛ(v)]	**pentre(f)**	village	[ˈpɛntɹɛ(v)]

Soft mutation also occurs in grammatical contexts. For example, a feminine singular noun will cause an adjective describing it to mutate softly:

FEMININE NOUN + ADJECTIVE	ENGLISH	IPA
merch dda	a good girl	[mɛrχ ðaː]
tre(f) fawr	a large town	[tɹɛː(v) vaʊr]

(ii) Like the soft mutation, the aspirate mutation occurs after certain words, such as the conjunction **a** 'and' [ä]:

MUTATED PHRASE	ENGLISH	IPA
pentre(f) a thre(f)	a town and a village	[ˈpɛntɹɛ(v) ä θreː(v)]

(iii) The nasal mutation is the least common mutation, occurring only after **fy** 'my' [və] and **yn** 'in' [ən], as well as with **blynedd** 'year' [ˈblənɛð] after certain numerals:

MUTATED PHRASE	ENGLISH	IPA	NOUN PRE-MUTATION	ENGLISH	IPA
fy mhentre(f) i	my village	[və ˈm̥ɛntɹɛ(v) iː]	**pentre(f)**	village	[ˈpɛntɹɛ(v)]
yng Nghymru	in Wales	[ə(ŋ) ˈŋ̊əmri]	**Cymru**	Wales	[ˈkəmri]
pum mlynedd	five years	[pɪ(m) ˈmlənɛð]	**blynedd**	year	[ˈblənɛð]

> **IMPORTANT**
> Now you have had an overview of mutation, we will look at some of the words and grammatical contexts we have learnt so far and apply the soft mutation rules.

As we saw when we looked at adjectives, there is no change to an adjective that follows a masculine noun. However, adjectives preceded by feminine nouns undergo soft mutation:

MASCULINE NOUN + ADJECTIVE	ENGLISH	IPA
dyn da	a good man	[diːn dɑː]
ci mawr	a big dog	[kiː maʊr]
pentre(f) bach	a small village	[ˈpentɹɛ(v) bɑːχ]

ADJECTIVE PRE-MUTATION	ENGLISH	IPA	FEMININE NOUN + ADJECTIVE	ENGLISH	IPA
da	good	[dɑː]	merch dda	a good girl	[mɛrχ ðɑː]
mawr	big	[maʊr]	cath fawr	a big cat	[kɑːθ vaʊr]
bach	small	[bɑːχ]	tre(f) fach	a small town	[tɹeː(v) vɑːχ]

After plural nouns the original, unmutated form occurs:

MASCULINE NOUN (pl.) + ADJECTIVE	ENGLISH	IPA
bechgyn da	good boys	[ˈbɛχgɪn dɑː]
cŵn mawr	big dogs	[kuːn maʊr]
pentrefi bach	small villages	[penˈtɹɛvi bɑːχ]

FEMININE NOUN (pl.) + ADJECTIVE	ENGLISH	IPA
merched da	good girls	[ˈmɛrχɛd dɑː]
cathod mawr	big cats	[ˈkaθod maʊr]
trefi bach	small towns	[ˈtɹɛvi bɑːχ]

Vocabulary

MASCULINE NOUN	ENGLISH	IPA	PLURAL FORM	IPA
bore	morning	[ˈbɔrɛ]	boreau	[borˈəɪɛ]
prynhawn	afternoon	[prɪnˈhaʊn]	prynhawniau	[prɪnˈhaʊnjɛ]

FEMININE NOUN	ENGLISH	IPA	PLURAL FORM	IPA
noswaith	evening	[ˈnɔswɛθ]	nosweithiau	[nɔsˈwəɪθjɛ]

The pattern **noun + adjective**, together with the mutation after a feminine singular noun, can be seen in greetings:

GREETING	ENGLISH	IPA
bore da	good morning	[ˈboːrɛ dɑː]
prynhawn da	good afternoon	[prɪnˈhaʊn dɑː]
noswaith dda	good evening	[ˈnɔswɛθ ðɑː]

There is also another greeting which is less formal than the ones given above: **sut mae?** 'how are things?' [sɪt maɪ].

Exercise 1

How would you greet someone at the following times?

a) 8.30 a.m. _____ b) 2 p.m. _____ c) 7.30 p.m. _____
d) 10 a.m. _____ e) 6 p.m. _____ f) 3.30 p.m. _____
g) 9.20 p.m. _____

Vocabulary

MASCULINE NOUN	ENGLISH	IPA	PLURAL FORM	IPA
mynydd	mountain	[ˈmənɪð]	**mynyddoedd**	[mənˈəðɔɪð]

FEMININE NOUN	ENGLISH	IPA	PLURAL FORM	IPA
gwlad	country	[gʷlɑːd]	**gwledydd**	[ˈgʷlɛdɪð]
cadair	chair	[ˈkɑdɛr]	**cadeiriau**	[kadˈəɪrjɛ]

ADJECTIVE	ENGLISH	IPA
cryf	strong	[kriːv]*
melyn	yellow	[ˈmɛlɪn]
prysur	busy	[ˈprəsɪr]
gwyrdd	green	[gwɪrð]
lleol	local	[ˈɬeˑol]
rhad	cheap	[ɹɑːd]
du	black	[diː]

* *Pronounced* [kriː(v)] *in North Welsh.*

Exercise 2

Rewrite the Welsh word in brackets in the preceding space, mutating it softly if necessary.

For example:

Question: merch ____ (bach)
Answer: merch <u>f</u>ach

For example:

Question: dyn ____ (bach)
Answer: dyn <u>b</u>ach

1) pentre(f) _____ (prysur) (a busy village)
2) esgidiau _____ (gwyrdd) (green shoes)
3) gwlad _____ (mawr) (a large country)
4) tref _____ (lleol) (a local town)
5) mam _____ (balch) (a proud mother)
6) tarw _____ (da) (a good bull)
7) cath _____ (du) (a black cat)
8) cadair _____ (rhad) (a cheap chair)
9) bachgen _____ (cryf) (a strong boy)
10) mamau _____ (balch) (proud mothers)

Remember that adjectives which follow a feminine singular noun undergo soft mutation.

Mutating after the definite article

The first letter of a singular feminine noun undergoes soft mutation after the definite article (except when the noun begins with **ll** or **rh**), whereas the first letters of masculine nouns do not:

DEFINITE ARTICLE + FEMININE NOUN	ENGLISH	IPA	NOUN PRE-MUTATION	ENGLISH
y ferch	the girl	[ə vɛrχ]	**merch**	girl
y gath	the cat	[ə ɡɑːθ]	**cath**	cat
y gegin	the kitchen	[ə ɡɛɡɪn]	**cegin**	kitchen
y dre(f)	the town	[ə drɛː(v)]	**tre(f)**	town

DEFINITE ARTICLE + FEMININE NOUN (*pl.*)	ENGLISH	IPA
y merched	the girls	[ə ˈmɛrχɛd]
y cathod	the cats	[ə ˈkaθod]
y ceginau	the kitchens	[ə kɛɡˈiːnɛ]
y trefi	the towns	[ə ˈtrɛvi]

DEFINITE ARTICLE + MASCULINE NOUN	ENGLISH	IPA
y dyn	the man	[ə diːn]
y ci	the dog	[ə kiː]
y car	the car	[ə kar]

y pentre(f)	the village	[ə 'pɛntɹɛ(v)]

DEFINITE ARTICLE + MASCULINE NOUN (pl.)	ENGLISH	IPA
y dynion	the men	[ə 'dənjon]
y cŵn	the dogs	[ə kuːn]
y ceir	the cars	[ə kəɪr]
y pentrefi	the villages	[ə pɛn'tɹɛvi]

Vocabulary

MASCULINE NOUN	ENGLISH	IPA	PLURAL FORM	IPA
blodyn	flower	['blɔdɪn]	blodau	['bloˑdɛ]

FEMININE NOUN	ENGLISH	IPA	PLURAL FORM	IPA
desg	desk	[dɛsg]	desgiau	['dɛsgjɛ]
ffenest(r)	window	['fɛnɛst(ɹ)]	ffenestri	[fɛnɛs'tɹi]
llaw	hand	[ɬaʊ]	dwylo	['dʊɪlo]
pont	bridge	[pɔnt]	pontydd	['pɔntɪð]

Exercise 3

Place the Welsh word in brackets after the definite article, mutating where necessary.

1) Y _____ (mam) (the mother)
2) Y _____ (pont) (the bridge)
3) Y _____ (gwlad) (the country)
4) Y _____ (blodyn) (the flower)
5) Y _____ (merched) (the girls)
6) Y _____ (desg) (the desk)
7) Y _____ (ffenestr) (the window)
8) Y _____ (cadair) (the chair)
9) Y _____ (llaw) (the hand)
10) Y _____ (tad) (the father)

Lesson 6: Counting to 100

Don't let the heading put you off. Once you know the numerals 0-10, you can count to 100, as the modern Welsh counting system is decimal:

NUMERAL	WELSH	IPA
0	**dim**	[dɪm]
1	**un**	[iːn]
2	**dau**	[daɪ]
3	**tri**	[tr̝iː]
4	**pedwar**	['pɛdwar]
5	**pump***	[pɪmp]
6	**chwech****	[χweːχ]
7	**saith**	[saɪθ]
8	**wyth**	[ʊɪθ]
9	**naw**	[naʊ]
10	**deg**	[deːg]

*   *This becomes **pum** [pɪm] before nouns in formal Welsh.*

** *This becomes **chwe** [χweː] before nouns in formal Welsh.*

Unlike in English, numerals in Welsh are followed by the singular form of the noun. For example, when the noun 'girl' follows a numeral in English, one says 'nine girls' rather than 'nine girl'. In Welsh, **merch** 'girl' [mɛrχ] does *not* become **merched** 'girls' [mɛrχɛd]:

WELSH PHRASE	ENGLIS	IPA
naw merch	nine girls (*lit.* nine girl)	[naʊ mɛrχ]
saith cadair	seven chairs (*lit.* seven chair)	[saɪθ ˈkaˑdɛr]

Exercise 1

Translate the following phrases.

1) eight dogs _____
2) one village _____
3) three mornings _____
4) two names _____
5) three flowers _____
6) ten cats _____
7) seven fathers _____
8) four men _____
9) five bridges _____
10) nine countries _____

Vocabulary

MASCULINE NOUN	ENGLISH	IPA	PLURAL FORM	IPA
enw	name	['ɛnʊ]	enwau	['ɛnwɛ]

After ten, there are two ways of counting in Welsh. The traditional, vigesimal counting system has **ugain** 'twenty' ['i·gɛn] as the base (as in French and the other Celtic languages), whereas the more modern, decimal counting system has **deg** 'ten' [de:g] (as in English). The decimal system is simpler and is widely used in schools, and this is the system we will mainly use in this book. However, the vigesimal system is still used when telling time and discussing dates, which we will cover later. Here are some more numerals in both systems:

NUMERAL	DECIMAL NUMERAL	IPA	VIGESIMAL NUMERAL	IPA
11	un deg un	[iːn deːg iːn]	un ar ddeg	[iːn ar ðeːg]
12	un deg dau	[iːn deːg daɪ]	deuddeg	['dəɪðeg]
13	un deg tri	[iːn deːg t̪ɾiː]	tri ar ddeg	[t̪ɾiː ar ðeːg]
14	un deg pedwar	[iːn deːg 'pɛdwar]	pedwar ar ddeg	['pɛdwar ar ðeːg]
15	un deg pump	[iːn deːg pɪmp]	pymtheg	['pəmθeg]
16	un deg chwech	[iːn deːg χweːχ]	un ar bymtheg	[iːn ar 'bəmθeg]
17	un deg saith	[iːn deːg saɪθ]	dau ar bymtheg	[daɪ ar 'bəmθeg]
18	un deg wyth	[iːn deːg ʊɪθ]	deunaw	['dəɪnaʊ]
19	un deg naw	[iːn deːg naʊ]	pedwar ar bymtheg	['pɛdwar ar 'bəmθeg]
20	dau ddeg	[daɪ ðeːg]	ugain	['i·gɛn]
21	dau ddeg un	[daɪ ðeːg iːn]	un ar hugain	[iːn ar 'hi·gɛn]
22	dau ddeg dau	[daɪ ðeːg daɪ]	dau ar hugain	[daɪ ar 'hi·gɛn]
23	dau ddeg tri	[daɪ ðeːg t̪ɾiː]	tri ar hugain	[t̪ɾiː ar 'hi·gɛn]
30	tri deg	[t̪ɾiː deːg]	deg ar hugain	[deːg ar 'hi·gɛn]
31	tri deg un	[t̪ɾiː deːg iːn]	un ar ddeg ar hugain	[iːn ar ðeːg ar 'hi·gɛn]
40	pedwar deg	['pɛdwar deːg]	deugain	['dəɪgɛn]
41	pedwar deg un	['pɛdwar deːg iːn]	un a deugain	[iːn a 'dəɪgɛn]
50	pum deg	[pɪm deːg]	hanner cant	['häner kant]
60	chwe deg	[χweː deːg]	trigain	['t̪ɾi·gɛn]
70	saith deg	[saɪθ deːg]	deg a thrigain	[deːg a 'θɾi·gɛn]
80	wyth deg	[ʊɪθ deːg]	pedwar ugain	['pɛdwar 'i·gɛn]
90	naw deg	[naʊ deːg]	deg a phedwar ugain	[deːg a 'fɛdwar 'i·gɛn]
100	cant	[kant]	cant	[kant]

You can see that the decimal system follows the pattern '(...) ten (...)', so 'thirty-four' is **tri deg pedwar** [t̪ɾiː deːg 'pɛdwar] (*lit*. three ten four). You will also notice that **dau** 'two' (*m*.) [daɪ] causes a soft mutation. Remember that the singular form of a noun is used after numerals:

WELSH PHRASE	ENGLISH	IPA
tri deg buwch	thirty cows	[tɹi deːg bɪʊχ]

Exercise 2

Write the following figures in Welsh.

a) 25 _____

b) 86 _____

c) 37 _____

d) 91 _____

e) 65 _____

f) 24 _____

Lesson 7: Recap exercises

Exercise 1

Write the plural form of the following nouns.

1) ci _____ 2) siop _____
3) merch _____ 4) pentref _____
5) cath _____ 6) desg _____
7) tŷ _____ 8) dyn _____
9) tre(f) _____ 10) esgid _____

*If you have difficulty with this exercise, refer to **Week 1, Lesson 2**.*

Exercise 2

Complete the following by translating the adjective in brackets.

a) tarw   _____ (big)   (a big bull)
b) dyn   _____ (tall)   (a tall man)
c) gwlad   _____ (small)   (a small country)
d) cath   _____ (bad)   (a bad cat)
e) merch   _____ (busy)   (a busy girl)
f) cegin   _____ (cheap)   (a cheap kitchen)
g) ffenestr _____ (strong) (a strong window)
h) caseg   _____ (black)   (a black mare)
i) blodyn _____ (yellow) (a yellow flower)

j) pont _____   (good)   (a good bridge)

*Remember that if an adjective follows a feminine singular noun, it undergoes the soft mutation. If you have difficulty with this exercise, refer to **Week 1, Lesson 5**.*

Exercise 3

Translate the following phrases.

a) the shop _____   b) the morning _____
c) the apple _____   d) the orange   _____
e) the shoes _____   f) the one   _____
g) the chair _____   h) the desk   _____
i) the hand _____   j) the name   _____

*If you have difficulty with this exercise, refer to **Week 1, Lesson 4** and **Lesson 5**.*

Exercise 4

*Match up the Welsh phrases under **A** to the correct English translations under **B**.*

A
1) y fuwch fawr
2) hufen da
3) pont enwog
4) bechgyn cryf
5) y mynydd llwm
6) y wlad
7) y tri thad
8) y fam brysur
9) y blodau
10) ffenestri rhad

B
a) strong boys
b) the desolate mountain
c) the country
d) the busy mother
e) the flowers
f) a famous bridge
g) the large cow
h) cheap windows
i) the three fathers
j) good cream

Exercise 5

Write the following numerals using full words and the decimal system.

a) thirty-one   _____
b) forty-nine   _____
c) eighty-six   _____
d) twenty-seven _____
e) fifty-eight   _____

*If you have difficulty with this exercise, refer to **Week 1, Lesson 4**.*

Week 2

Lesson 1: Affirmative forms of identification sentences

> **IMPORTANT**
> **Definitions**
> **Verb:** A verb describes an action, such as 'to kick'; a condition, such as 'is'; or an experience, such as 'to happen'. In Welsh, a verb also tells you who did the action and when it occurred. The verb form **wyt ti** [ʊɪ(t) tiː], which we will meet below, tells us the person is the second person singular (**ti** 'you' [tiː]) and that the action is in the present tense.
>
> **Subject:** The subject of a sentence performs the action of the verb. In the sentence which you will shortly read below, 'Rhys' is performing the action of the verb ('kicked'), and so 'Rhys' is the subject. In the sentence 'I ate the cake', the subject is 'I'.
>
> **Object:** The object of a sentence receives the action of the verb. In the sentence below, the ball is the object as it is receiving the action (the kicking) of the verb.
>
> **Adverbial:** An adverbial is a word or phrase which describes or gives more information about a verb, adjective or phrase. It usually describes the manner (how), place (where), time (when), frequency (how often), etc. In the sentence below, **yn uchel** 'high' [ən ˈiːχɛl] is an adverbial phrase which tells us the manner in which the ball is kicked.

In English, it is the subject which normally comes first in a sentence:

SUBJECT	VERB	OBJECT	ADVERBIAL
Rhys	kicked	the ball	high.

As we will see in **Week 3**, the verb normally comes first in a Welsh sentence. However, in an identification sentence in Welsh, when you are stating what something is, the predicate comes first.

	PREDICATE	COPULA	SUBJECT
WELSH	**Rhys**	ydy	'r athro.
ENGLISH	Rhys	is	the teacher.
IPA	[r̥iːs	ədi	raθro]

> **IMPORTANT**
> **Definitions**
> **Copula:** A copula is a connecting word or words, usually a form of the verb '**to be**' (**is, was, will be**, etc.), which connects the predicate to the subject. It functions as an equals sign in a sentence: **Rhys = 'r athro**.
>
> **Predicate:** The predicate is the part of a sentence or phrase which says something about the subject.

Here are examples of identification sentences:

IDENTIFICATION SENTENCE	ENGLISH	IPA
Bachgen ydy Rhys.	Rhys is a boy.	['bäχɡɛn 'ədi ɹiːs]
Ci ydy Fflos.	Fflos is a dog.	[kiː 'ədi flɔs]
Dinas ydy Wrecsam.	Wrexham is a city.	['diːnas 'ədi ʷrɛksäm]
Pentre(f) ydy Llanddewi.	Llanddewi is a village.	['pɛntɹɛ(v) 'ədi ɬan'ðɛʊi]

Just as the forms of the verb change according to the subject in English, such as in 'I am', 'you are', 'he is', etc., there is also a specific present tense form according to the subject in Welsh. The forms for the present tense can be found in the table below:

IDENTIFICATION SENTENCE	ENGLISH	IPA
Rhys ydw i.	I am Rhys.	[ɹiːs 'ədʊ iː]
Rhys wyt ti.*	You are Rhys. (*fam.*)	[ɹiːs ʊɪ(t) tiː]
Rhys ydy e.*	He is Rhys. (South Wales)	[ɹiːs 'ədi eː]
Rhys ydy o.*	He is Rhys. (North Wales)	[ɹiːs 'ədi oː]
Rhiannon ydy hi.	She is Rhiannon.	[ɹi'anon 'ədi hiː]
Cymry ydyn ni.	We are Welsh.	['kəmri 'ədɪ(n) niː]
Cymry ydych chi.*	You are Welsh.	['kəmri 'ədɪ(χ) χiː]
Cymry ydyn nhw.	They are Welsh.	['kəmri 'ədɪ(n) n̥uː]

* *You will have noticed that there are two words in Welsh for 'you',* **ti** [ti] *(as in* **wyt ti**) *and* **chi** [χiː] *(as in* **ydych chi**)*. Like many Indo-European languages, Welsh uses an informal form,* **ti***, which is used when addressing people who you know very well, animals, a deity or children. The pronoun* **chi** *is the formal or polite form, as well as being the plural 'you' form.* **Chi** *is used to address people you don't know very well or at all, more than one person, and anyone to whom you wish to show respect. There is some variation among speakers as to which form of 'you' they use. Younger people tend to be more informal, using* **ti** *more frequently than older people do. In a school setting, a teacher would address the individual child using* **ti** *and the class as a whole using the plural form* **chi***.*

** *One of the main differences between the Welsh spoken in North Wales and in South Wales is the word for 'he'. In North Wales, the pronoun which corresponds to the English 'he' is* **o** [oː]*, whereas in South Wales* **e** [eː] *is used. We will use both forms in this book, and these will either receive their own marked entries in tables, or* **e** *and* **o** *will be separated by a slash (/). Decide which variation of Welsh will be most useful to you and concentrate on its forms.*

'It'

Welsh does not have a word for 'it'; the pronouns **e** (SW) / **o** (NW) or **hi** are used depending on the gender of the noun, as can be seen in the examples below:

MASCULINE IDENTIFICATION SENTENCE	ENGLISH	IPA
Blodyn ydy o. (NW)	It is a flower.	['bɫɔdɪn 'ədi oː]
Blodyn ydy e. (SW)	It is a flower.	['blɔdɪn 'ədi eː]
Ci ydy e. (SW)	It is a dog.	[kiː 'ədi eː]
Ci ydy o. (NW)	It is a dog.	[kiː 'ədi oː]

FEMININE IDENTIFICATION SENTENCE	ENGLISH	IPA
Cadair ydy hi.	It is a chair.	[ˈkɑːdɛr ˈədi hiː]
Cath ydy hi.	It is a cat.	[kɑːθ ˈədi hiː]

In spoken Welsh, the diphthongs **ae**, **ai** and **au** (all /aɪ/ in South Wales) are pronounced as **e** /ɛ/ in unaccented final syllables:

WORD WITH DIPHTHONG	ENGLISH	IPA
gwahaniaeth	difference	[gwaˈhanjɛθ]
cyfraith	law	[ˈkəvrɛθ]
ceffylau	horses	[kɛfəlɛ]

In Welsh, sentences like 'I am Welsh', 'I am English', etc., are expressed by using the identification sentence pattern: **Cymro ydw i** [ˈkəmro ˈədʊ i]. This literally means 'I am a Welshman'.

IDENTIFICATION SENTENCE	ENGLISH	IPA
Cymro ydw i.	I am Welsh. (*lit*. I am a Welshman.)	[ˈkəmro ˈədʊ iː]
Cymraes ydw i.	I am Welsh. (*lit*. I am a Welsh woman.)	[kəmˈrais ˈədʊ iː]
Cymry ydyn ni.	We are Welsh. (*lit*. We are Welsh people.)	[ˈkəmri ˈədɪ(n) niː]

> **IMPORTANT**
> Note that the third person singular **ydy** is used when the subject is a plural noun:
>
> **Cymry ydy'r dynion.**   The men are Welsh.   [ˈkəmri ˈədir ˈdənjon]
> **Pobl dda ydy'r Cymry.** The Welsh (people) are good people. [ˈpobol ða: ˈədir ˈkəmri]

Exercise 1

Fill in the gaps in the following sentences.

1) Siopau da _____ nhw.   (They are good shops.)
2) Dyn enwog ydw _____.   (I am a famous man.)
3) Mamau balch ydyn _____.   (We are proud mothers.)
4) Ci _____ e (SW) / o (NW).   (It is a dog.)
5) Athro da _____ ti.   (You are a good teacher.)
6) Cadair ydy _____.   (It is a large chair.)
7) Hufen ydy _____.   (It is cream.)
8) Dynion tal _____ chi.   (You are tall men.)

Exercise 2

Translate the following:

1) I am a teacher. _____
2) He is a father. _____
3) She is a doctor. _____
4) I am Gareth _____
5) We are doctors. _____
6) You are Welsh (people). (*pl.*) _____
7) It is a village. _____
8) They are girls. _____
9) You are a mother. (*fam.*) _____
10) It is a small country. _____

Lesson 2: Negative forms of identification sentences

A negative identification sentence is expressed by putting **nid** [nɪd] at the beginning:

	SENTENCE	IPA
AFFIRMATIVE	**Ci ydy e.** (SW)	[kiː ədi eː]
NEGATIVE	**Nid ci ydy e.** (SW)	[nɪd kiː ədi eː]

	SENTENCE	IPA
AFFIRMATIVE	**Ci ydy o.** (NW)	[kiː ədi oː]
NEGATIVE	**Nid ci ydy o.** (NW)	[nɪd kiː ədi oː]

Here are some more negative identification sentences:

SENTENCE	ENGLISH	IPA
Nid Alun ydw i.	I'm not Alun.	[nɪd ˈɑːlɪn ˈədʊ iː]
Nid Alun wyt ti.	You're not Alun. (*fam.*)	[nɪd ˈɑːlɪn ʊɪ(t) tiː]
Nid Siôn ydy e. (SW)	He's not Siôn.	[nɪd ʃoːn ˈədi eː]
Nid Siôn ydy o. (NW)	He's not Siôn.	[nɪd ʃoːn ˈədi oː]
Nid Siân ydy hi.	She's not Siân.	[nɪd ʃɑːn ˈədi hiː]
Nid Cymry ydyn ni.	We are not Welsh.	[nɪd ˈkəmri ˈədɪ(n) niː]
Nid Cymry ydych chi.	You are not Welsh.	[nɪd ˈkəmri ˈədɪ(χ) χiː]
Nid Cymry ydyn nhw.	They're not Welsh.	[nɪd ˈkəmri ˈədɪ(n) n̥uː]

IMPORTANT
As in the affirmative, the third person singular **ydy** is used when the subject is a plural noun:

Nid meddygon ydy'r dynion.	The men are not doctors.	[nɪd mɛðˈəgon ˈədɪr ˈdənjon]
Nid nyrsys ydy'r merched.	The girls are not nurses.	[nɪd ˈnərsɪs ˈədɪr ˈmɛrχed]

Vocabulary

MASCULINE NOUN	ENGLISH	IPA	PLURAL FORM	IPA
meddyg	doctor	[ˈmɛðɪg]	**meddygon**	[mɛˈðəgon]
plentyn	child	[ˈplɛntɪn]	**plant**	[plant]
hufen	cream	[ˈhiˑvɛn]		

FEMININE NOUN	ENGLISH	IPA	PLURAL FORM	IPA
nyrs	nurse	[nərs]	**nyrsys**	[ˈnərsɪs]
pobl	people	[ˈpoˑbol]	**pobloedd**	[ˈpɔblɔɪð]

PLACE NAME	ENGLISH	IPA
Caerdydd	Cardiff	[kaɪrˈdiːð]

Exercise 1

Translate the following sentences.

1) I am not a teacher.
2) They are not cats.
3) Cardiff is not a town.
4) They aren't children.
5) We aren't doctors.
6) Meg is not a cat.
7) She is not a doctor.
8) It is not a small country.
9) We are not busy people.
10) He is not a nurse.

Lesson 3: Interrogative forms of identification sentences

An interrogative identification sentence can be expressed simply by inflecting the corresponding affirmative sentence, i.e. by making it sound like a question:

INTERROGATIVE IDENTIFICATION SENTENCE	ENGLISH	IPA
Rhys ydw i?	Am I Rhys?	[r̥iːs ˈədʊ iː]
Rhys wyt ti?	Are you Rhys? (*fam.*)	[r̥iːs ʊɪ(t) tiː]
Rhys ydy e? (SW)	Is he Rhys?	[r̥iːs ˈədi eː]
Rhys ydy o? (NW)	Is he Rhys?	[r̥iːs ˈədi oː]
Rhiannon ydy hi?	Is she Rhiannon?	[r̥iˈanon ˈədi hiː]

Cymry ydyn ni?	Are we Welsh (people)?	[ˈkəmri ˈədɪ(n) niː]
Cymry ydych chi?	Are you Welsh (people)?	[ˈkəmri ˈədɪ(χ) χiː]
Cymry ydyn nhw?	Are they Welsh (people)?	[ˈkəmri ˈədɪ(n) n̩uː]

In formal contexts, **ai** [aɪ] is used as an interrogative particle with identification sentences:

INTERROGATIVE IDENTIFICATION SENTENCE	ENGLISH	IPA
Ai Cymry ydyn nhw?	Are they Welsh (people)?	[aɪ ˈkəmri ˈədɪ(n) n̩uː]

> **IMPORTANT**
> As in the affirmative and the negative, the third person singular **ydy** is used when the subject is a plural noun:
> **Meddygon ydy'r dynion?** Are the men doctors? [mɛðəgon ˈədɪr ˈdənjon]
> **Nyrsys ydy'r merched?** Are the girls nurses? [ˈnərsɪs ˈədɪr ˈmɛrχed]

Vocabulary

MASCULINE NOUN	ENGLISH	IPA	PLURAL FORM	IPA
Cymro	Welshman	[ˈkəmro]	**Cymry**	[ˈkəmri]
Sais	Englishman	[saɪs]	**Saeson**	[ˈsəɪson]
Almaenwr	German man	[alˈməɪnʊr]	**Almaenwyr**	[alˈməɪnwɪr]
Albanwr	Scottish man	[ˈalbanʊr]	**Albanwyr**	[alˈbanwɪr]
Americanwr	American man	[amɛrikˈɑːnʊr]	**Americanwyr**	[amɛrikˈanwɪr]
Ffrancwr	Frenchman	[ˈfraŋkʊr]	**Ffrancwyr**	[ˈfraŋkwɪr]
gwas sifil	civil servant	[ˈgwɑːs ˈsɪvɪl]	**gweision sifil**	[ˈgwəɪʃon ˈsɪvɪl]

FEMININE NOUN	ENGLISH	IPA	PLURAL FORM	IPA
postmones	postwoman	[postˈmonɛs]	**postmonesau**	[postmonˈɛsɛ]
Cymraes	Welsh woman	[kəmˈraɪs]	**Cymraesau**	[kəmˈraɪsɛ]
Saesnes	English woman	[ˈsəɪsnɛs]	**Saesnesau**	[səɪsˈnɛsɛ]
Almaenes	German woman	[alˈməɪnɛs]	**Almaenesau**	[alməɪnˈɛsɛ]
Albanes	Scottish woman	[alˈbɑːnɛs]	**Albanesau**	[albanˈɛsɛ]
Americanes	American woman	[amɛrikˈɑːnɛs]	**Americanesau**	[amɛrikanˈɛsɛ]
Ffrances	French woman	[ˈfraŋkɛs]	**Ffrancesau**	[fraŋˈkɛsɛ]

The replies to questions in this structure are **ie** 'yes' [ˈiˑɛ] (pronounced as *two* syllables: *ee-eh*, not like the **yeah** in the famous Beatles' song!) and **nage** 'no' [ˈnɑˑgɛ]:

QUESTION	ENGLISH	IPA
Rhys ydych chi?	Are you Rhys?	[ɹiːs ˈədɪχ χiː]

REPLY	ENGLISH	IPA
Ie, Rhys ydw i.	Yes, I'm Rhys.	[ˈiˑe r̝iːs ˈədʊ iː]
Nage, nid Rhys ydw i.	No, I'm not Rhys.	[ˈnɑˑge nɪd r̝iːs ˈədʊ iː]

Exercise 1

Translate the following sentences.

1) Are you a nurse? (*fam.*) _____
2) Is he a postman? _____
3) Are they English? _____
4) Are they French? _____
5) Am I a good teacher? _____
6) Are we good people? _____
7) Is he a famous German man? _____
8) Are you a civil servant? (*formal*) _____
9) Are they cheap chairs? _____
10) Is she Scottish? _____

Exercise 2

Respond to the questions below.

For example:

Question: Cymraes ydych chi? (✓)
Answer: Ie, Cymraes ydw i.

For example:

Question: Ffrancwr wyt ti? (✗)
Answer: Nage, nid Ffrancwr ydw i.

1) Siop dda ydy hi? (✓) _____
2) Blodyn melyn ydy e (SW)/o (NW)? (✗)

_____

3) Meddygon ydyn nhw? (✗) _____
4) Mr a Mrs Williams ydyn nhw? (✓)

_____

5) Merch enwog ydw i? (✗) _____

6) Almaenwyr ydyn ni? (✓)

7) Nyrs dda ydy e (SW)/o (NW)? (✓)

8) Albanes wyt ti? (✓)

9) Plentyn tal ydy e (SW)/o (NW)? (✗)

10) Pobl leol ydyn nhw? (✓)

The use of 'a' and 'ac'

CONJUNCTION	ENGLISH	IPA
a (AM)	and	[ä]
ac	and [used before a vowel]	[äg]

As you can see below, **a** causes an **aspirate mutation**. This means following **a**, t becomes **th**; c becomes **ch**; and p becomes **ph**:

ASPIRATE MUTATION	PHRASE	ENGLISH	IPA
t > th	buwch a <u>th</u>arw	a cow and a bull	['bɪʊχ ä 'θɑrʊ]
c > ch	cathod a <u>ch</u>ŵn	cats and dogs	['kaθod ä χuːn]
p > ph	tre(f) a <u>ph</u>entre(f)	a town and a village	[tɹeː(v) ä 'fɛntɹe(v)]

The conjunction **a** 'and' [ä] becomes **ac** [äg] before a vowel:

PHRASE	ENGLISH	IPA
blodau ac esgidiau	flowers and shoes	['bloˑdɛ äg ɛs'gɪdjɛ]

Lesson 4: The use of identification verb forms after common interrogatives

The verb forms we have been using which were introduced in **Week 2, Lesson 3** are also used after the following question forms:

QUESTION FORM	ENGLISH	IPA
beth	what	[beːθ]
pwy	who	[pʊɪ]
faint	how much	[vaɪnt]
faint o (SM)	how many	[vaɪnt oː]
faint o'r gloch	what time	[vaɪnt oːr gloːχ]

Here are some example questions:

QUESTION	ENGLISH	IPA
Faint o'r gloch ydy hi?	What time is it?	[vaɪnt ɔɪr glɔːχ 'ədi hiː]
Beth ydy e? (SW)	What is it?	[beːθ 'ədi eː]
Beth ydy o? (NW)	What is it?	[beːθ 'ədi ɔː]
Pwy ydyn nhw?	Who are they?	[pʊɪ 'ədɪ(n) n̥uː]
Faint ydy'r hufen?	How much is the cream?	[vaɪnt 'ədir 'hiˑven]

Vocabulary

MASCULINE NOUN	ENGLISH	IPA	PLURAL FORM	IPA
pris	price	['priːs]	**prisiau**	['prɪʃɛ]

Exercise 1

Fill in the blanks using the appropriate form of the verb.

For example:

Question: Pwy ___ hi?
Answer: Pwy ydy hi?

1) Beth _____ nhw?
2) Pwy _____ 'r postmon?
3) Pwy _____ ti?
4) Faint _____ 'r cadeiriau?
5) Pwy _____ 'r merched?
6) Pwy _____ 'r athro?
7) Beth _____ 'r pris?
8) Pwy _____ chi?
9) Pwy _____ e (SW)/o (NW)?

Lesson 5: Feminine numerals

As we saw in **Week 1, Lesson 2**, Welsh singular nouns are either masculine or feminine. By now you will be familiar with Welsh numerals, which were introduced in **Week 1, Lesson 6**. Some numerals (2, 3 and 4) change their form when they precede a feminine noun:

MASCULINE FORM	IPA	FEMININE FORM	IPA
dau	[daɪ]	**dwy**	[dʊɪ]
tri	[tɹiː]	**tair**	[taɪr]
pedwar	['pedwar]	**pedair**	['peˑder]

For example:

PHRASE	ENGLISH	IPA
dwy wlad	two countries (*lit.* two country)	[dʊɪ ʷlɑːd]
tair mam	three mothers (*lit.* three mother)	[taɪr mam]
pedair cadair	Four chairs (*lit.* four chair)	[ˈpeˑdɛr ˈkɑˑdɛr]

A few numerals cause a mutation. The following reference chart shows all the forms, both masculine and feminine, and the mutation caused (if any).

NUMERAL	MASCULINE FORM	MUTATION CAUSED	FEMININE FORM	MUTATION CAUSED
0	dim		dim	
1	un		un	soft
2	dau	soft	dwy	soft
3	tri	aspirate	tair	
4	pedwar		pedair	
5	pum		pum	
6	chwe	aspirate	chwe	aspirate
7	saith		saith	
8	wyth		wyth	
9	naw		naw	
10	deg		deg	

Exercise 1

Translate the following phrases, remembering that numerals are followed by a singular noun, and that feminine singular nouns will take the feminine form, as in **dwy** *(2),* **tair** *(3) and* **pedair** *(4).*

1) two Englishmen
2) three nurses
3) four flowers
4) three countries
5) four towns
6) three doctors
7) two mountains
8) three bridges
9) four chairs
10) two Welsh women

Vocabulary

FEMININE NOUN	ENGLISH	IPA	PLURAL FORM	IPA
doler ($)	dollar ($)	[ˈdɔlɛr]	**doleri**	[dɔlˈɛri]
punt (£)	pound (£)	[pɪnt]	**punnoedd**	[ˈpɪnɔɪð]

We have seen that singular nouns follow a numeral. A plural noun can only follow a numeral if **o** 'of' [oː] (SM) is placed between them. This method is used:

(i) When the items are thought of as individual units:

PHRASE	ENGLISH	IPA
tri o blant	three children	[tɹiː oː blant]
pump o ddefaid	five sheep	[pɪmp oː ðeˑvɛd]

(ii) When large numbers are involved:

PHRASE	ENGLISH	IPA
dau gant o ddoleri	two hundred dollars	[daɪ gant o ðɔlˈɛri]
mil o bunnoedd	a thousand pounds	[miːl oː ˈbɪnɔɪð]

Lesson 6: Demonstrative phrases

In spoken Welsh, demonstrative phrases like 'this book' and 'that book' are expressed by the use of the locative adverbs **yma** 'here' [ˈəmä], **yna** 'there' [ˈənä], acw 'yonder' [ˈäkʊ]:

PHRASE	ENGLISH	IPA
y llyfr yma	this book (*lit.* the book here)	[ə ɬəvr̪ ˈəmä]
y llyfr yna	that book (*lit.* the book there)	[ə ɬəvr̪ ˈənä]
y llyfr acw	yon book (*lit.* the book yonder)	[ə ɬəvr̪ ˈäkʊ]

This is the same for both singular and plural nouns:

PHRASE	ENGLISH	IPA
y llyfrau yma	these books	[ə ɬəvrɛ ˈəmä]
y llyfrau yna	those books	[ə ɬəvrɛ ˈənä]
y llyfrau acw	yon books	[ə ɬəvrɛ ˈäkʊ]

In everyday speech, **yma** and **yna** are respectively contracted to **'ma** and **'na**. This can be seen in the examples below:

PHRASE	ENGLISH	IPA
y llyfr 'ma	this book	[ə ɬəvr̪ mä]
y llyfr 'na	that book	[ə ɬəvr̪ nä]

Vocabulary

MASCULINE NOUN	ENGLISH	IPA	PLURAL FORM	IPA
papur	paper	[ˈpäpɪr]	**papurau**	[papˈiˑrɛ]
peth	thing	[peːθ]	**pethau**	[ˈpeθe]
teimlad	feeling	[ˈtəimlad]	**teimladau**	[təimˈlɑˑdɛ]
llyfr	book	[ɬəvr̩]	**llyfrau**	[ˈɬəvrɛ]

FEMININE NOUN	ENGLISH	IPA	PLURAL FORM	IPA
menyw	woman	[ˈmɛnɪʊ]	**menywod**	[mɛnˈɪʊod]
gwers	lesson	[gwɛrs]	**gwersi**	[ˈgwɛrsi]

Exercise 1

Translate the following demonstrative phrases.

1) this man _____ 2) that girl _____
3) these women _____ 4) this lesson _____
5) that book _____ 6) this house _____
7) those papers _____ 8) these things _____
9) this feeling _____

Vocabulary

MASCULINE NOUN	ENGLISH	IPA	PLURAL FORM	IPA
hanes	history	[ˈhanɛs]	**hanesion**	[hanˈɛʃon]
croeso	welcome	[ˈkrɔɪso]		
diolch	thanks	[ˈdiˑɔlχ]	**diolchiadau**	[diɔlχˈjɑˑdɛ]

FEMININE NOUN	ENGLISH	IPA	PLURAL FORM	IPA
Saesneg	English	[ˈsəɪsnɛg]		
ysgol	school	[ˈəsgol]	**ysgolion**	[əsˈgɔljon]
myfyrwraig	student	[məvˈərʷraɪg]	**myfyragedd**	[məvˈərʷrɑˑgɛð]
dinas	city	[ˈdiˑnas]	**dinasoedd**	[dinˈasɔɪð]
Cymraeg	Welsh (language)	[kəmˈraɪg]		

PLACE NAME	ENGLISH	IPA
Cymru	Wales	[ˈkəmri]

PREPOSITION	ENGLISH	IPA	EXAMPLE PHRASE	ENGLISH
gyda (SW)	with	[ˈgədä]	**te gyda llaeth**	te with milk
efo (NW)	with	[ˈeˑvo]	**coffi efo hufen**	coffee with cream
i (SM)	to	[iː]	**mynd i Gaerdydd**	to go to Cardiff
o (SM)	of / from	[oː]	**dod o Lundain**	to come form London
yn (NM)	in	[ən]	**byw yng Nghymru**	to live in Wales

ADJECTIVE	ENGLISH	IPA
newydd	new	[ˈnɛʊɪð]
arall	other	[ˈɑˑrał]

ADVERBIAL	ENGLISH	IPA
rŵan (NW)	now	[ˈruˑan]
nawr (SW)	now	[naʊr]
wrth gwrs	of course	[ʊrθ gʊrs]

Dialogue

Welsh Dialogue

Richard: Bore da
Ann: Bore da. Mr Williams ydych chi? Yr athro hanes newydd?
Richard: Nage, nage. Nid Mr Williams ydw i. Richard Davies ydw i, yr athro Saesneg newydd.
Ann: Croeso i'r ysgol, Richard. Ann Jones ydw i, un o'r athrawon Cymraeg yn yr ysgol. Mae dwy athrawes Cymraeg arall yn yr ysgol ac un athro Saesneg. Mae tri athro Saesneg yn yr ysgol rŵan – a saith cant o blant, wrth gwrs! Coffi?
Richard: Diolch, coffi gyda llaeth, os gwelwch yn dda.

English Translation

Richard: Good morning!
Ann: Good morning! Are you Mr Williams? The new history teacher?
Richard: No, no. I'm not Mr Williams. I am Richard Davies, the new English teacher.
Ann: Welcome to the school, Richard. I am Ann Jones, one of the Welsh teachers at the school. There are two other (female) Welsh teachers at the school and one (male) English teacher. There are three English teachers at the school now – and seven hundred children, of course! Coffee?
Richard: Thanks, coffee with milk, please.

Lesson 7: Recap exercises

Exercise 1

Translate the following sentences.

1) I'm Welsh (a Welshman). _____
2) We're good boys. _____
3) They're famous people. _____
4) She's Scottish. _____
5) Wales is a small country.* _____
6) Cardiff is a busy city. _____
7) He is a teacher. _____
8) You are a child. (*fam.*) _____
9) We are nurses. _____
10) They are Americans. _____

* You should start with the phrase 'small country'.

If you have difficulty completing this exercise, refer to **Week 2, Lesson 1**.

Exercise 2

Translate the following sentences.

1) He's not Siôn. _____
2) They're not teachers. _____
3) Gareth isn't a policeman. _____
4) I'm not a Scottish man. _____
5) Ffido isn't a dog. _____
6) We are not local people. _____
7) You are not a nurse. (*fam.*) _____
8) You are not French. (*pl.*) _____
9) She is not a civil servant. _____
10) It is not a big problem. _____

If you have difficulty completing this exercise, refer to **Week 2, Lesson 2**.

Exercise 3

Translate the following sentences.

1) Am I a Welshman? _____
2) Are you Rhiannon? (*formal*) _____
3) Are we famous people? _____

4) Are you a doctor? (*fam.*) _____
5) Are the children German? _____
6) Are they Welsh? _____
7) Is she a student? _____
8) Is he French? _____

If you have difficulty completing this exercise, refer to **Week 2, Lesson 3**.

Exercise 4

Answer the questions below in Welsh.

For example:

Question: Cymraes ydych chi? (✓)
(Are you Welsh [a Welsh woman]?)
Answer: Ie, Cymraes ydw i.
(Yes, I'm Welsh.)

For example:

Question: Gareth ydych chi? (✗)
(Are you Gareth?)
Answer: Nage, nid Gareth ydw i.
(No, I'm not Gareth.)

1) Alun ydych chi? (✓) _____
2) Siôn ydy e (SW)/o (NW)? (✗) _____
3) Dinas ydy Aberystwyth? (✗) _____
4) Ffrancwr ydy Pierre? (✓) _____
5) Albanwyr ydyn nhw?___ (✗) _____
6) Hufen ydy o? (✓) _____
7) Gweision sifil ydyn ni? (✗) _____
8) Meddygon ydy'r dynion 'na? (✓) _____

If you have difficulty completing this exercise, refer to **Week 2, Lesson 3**.

Exercise 5

Translate the following questions.

1) What time is it? _____
2) How much is this chair? _____

3) Who are they? _____
4) Who are the doctors? _____
5) Who is he? _____
6) What is the feeling? _____
7) What is the problem? _____
8) How much are those windows? _____

*If you have difficulty completing this exercise, refer to **Week 2, Lesson 4**.*

Exercise 6

Translate the following noun phrases.

1) three sisters _____
2) twenty-nine people _____
3) ten children _____
4) four bridges _____
5) twenty-three Frenchmen _____
6) a hundred dollars _____
7) three thousand pounds (£) _____
8) fifty houses _____
9) two hundred countries _____
10) those two girls _____

*If you have difficulty completing this exercise, refer to **Week 2, Lesson 5** and **Lesson 6**.*

Exercise 7

Translate the following demonstrative phrases:

1) this man _____ 2) that girl _____
3) these women _____ 4) this problem _____
5) that book _____ 6) this house _____
7) those things _____ 8) these things _____
9) this feeling _____

Week 3

Lesson 1: Affirmative forms of the present tense of 'bod' (to be)

In **Week 2** we learnt that sentences like 'I am a (female) teacher' have a special construction in that the predicate comes first: **Athrawes ydw i** [aθ'raʊɛs 'ədʊ iː]. The same construction is used with inanimate objects. For example: **Dinas ydy Caerdydd** 'Cardiff is a city' ['dɪnas 'ədi kaɪr'diːð]. However, the usual order of a Welsh sentence is **verb + subject + object** (VSO):

	VERB	SUBJECT	OBJECT	ADVERBIAL
WELSH	Rhedodd	Siân	filltir	ddoe.
IPA	['ʝɛ·dɔð]	ʃaːn	'vɪɬtɪr	ðoɪ]

	SUBJECT	VERB	OBJECT	ADVERBIAL
ENGLISH	Siân	ran	a mile	yesterday.

There are two ways of forming a verb in Welsh:

(i) In the sentence above, **rhedodd** is an example of an inflected form of the verb. It consists of the stem **rhed-** ['ʝɛd] (< **rhedeg** 'to run') and the inflection **-odd** [oð] ('he did' / 'she did'). We will look at this in more detail in **Week 7, Lesson 2**. In Welsh, inflected verbs are used to form the simple past tense and the simple future tense in the indicative mood, the conditional in the subjunctive mood, as well as in the imperative mood (giving commands). (If you are confused by these grammatical terms, please refer to the chapter entitled **A Brief Summary of the Modern Welsh Verb System** at the end of this course.)

(ii) Periphrastic, or long, forms of the verb are formed by combining the personal forms of **'bod'** with a verb-noun, namely the unchanged form of the verb. In spoken Welsh, these forms are used to express the imperfect and perfect aspects of the present, future and past tenses, and the conditional. For example, the pattern used to form the present imperfect is: **present tense of bod + subject + yn + verb-noun**:

	VERB (is)	SUBJECT	ASPECTUAL MARKER	VERB-NOUN	OBJECT	ADVERBIAL
WELSH	Mae	Siân	yn	rhedeg	milltir	nawr.
IPA	[maɪ	ʃaːn	ən	'ʝɛ·dɛg	'mɪɬtɪr	naʊr]

The above sentence (**Mae Siân yn rhedeg milltir nawr.**) translates as:

	SUBJECT	VERB	VERB	ARTICLE	OBJECT	ADVERBIAL
ENGLISH	Siân	is	running	a	mile	now.

The use of 'yn' as an aspectual marker

You will have noticed the **yn** [ən] between the subject (**Siân**) and the verb-noun (**rhedeg**) in the example above. It is called an 'imperfect aspectual marker' (No need to learn this term!), and it is there to join the subject (**Siân**) to the verb-noun (**rhedeg**) 'to run'. Note also that **yn rhedeg** can be translated as 'running' or 'runs'. On housing estates in Wales, you will often see a sign saying: **Plant yn chwarae** [plant ən ˈχwaːrɛ]. This warns you that there are children playing. After a vowel, **yn** becomes **'n**.

Here are some other examples of present tense Welsh sentences:

	VERB	SUBJECT	YN	VERB-NOUN	ENGLISH
SENTENCE	Mae	Siân	yn	rhedeg.	Siân is running.
IPA	[maɪ	ʃaːn	ən	ˈr̥eˑdeg]	
SENTENCE	Mae	Gareth	yn	gweithio.	Gareth is working.
IPA	[maɪ	ˈgaˑrɛθ	ən	ˈgwəɪθjo]	
SENTENCE	Mae	Siân	yn	dysgu Cymraeg.	Siân is learning Welsh.
IPA	[maɪ	ʃaːn	ən	ˈdəsgi kəmˈraɪg]	
SENTENCE	Mae	Gareth	yn	gyrru Volvo.	Gareth is driving a Volvo.
IPA	[maɪ	ˈgaˑrɛθ	ən	ˈgəri ˈvɔlvo]	
SENTENCE	Mae	'r athro	yn	dysgu Saesneg.	The teacher is teaching English.
IPA	[maɪ	r aθro	ən	ˈdəsgi ˈsəɪsnɛg]	
SENTENCE	Mae	Gareth a Siân	yn	chwarae.	Gareth and Siân are playing.
IPA	[maɪ	ˈgaˑrɛθ a ʃaːn	ən	ˈχwaˑrɛ]	
SENTENCE	Mae	'r plant	yn	rhedeg.	The children are running.
IPA	[maɪ	r plant	ən	ˈr̥eˑdeg]	

Notice that **mae** is also used with plural subjects such as **Gareth a Siân** and **y plant** (**'r** after the vowel).

Vocabulary

VERB-NOUN	ENGLISH	IPA
dysgu	to learn / to teach	[ˈdəsgi]
gweithio	to work	[ˈgwəɪθjo]
gyrru	to drive	[ˈgəri]
rhedeg	to run	[ˈr̥eˑdeg]
chwarae	to play	[ˈχwaˑrɛ]

Exercise 1

Translate the following sentences.

1) Gareth is running.
2) The doctors are working.
3) Tom is teaching Welsh.
4) Ann is learning.
5) The dogs are running.
6) Gareth and Siân are working.
7) Tom is driving.
8) The boy is playing.
9) Gareth is playing.
10) Siân is working.

The use of 'wedi' as an aspectual marker

The preposition **wedi** [ˈwɛdi] means 'after', and **wedi wyth** [ˈwɛdi ʊɪθ] means 'after eight'. It can also work as a perfect aspectual marker. (Again, no need to remember the grammatical term!) This means that when placed in front of a verb-noun in the present tense, it expresses 'has' (done something). **Wedi** simply takes the place of **yn**:

	VERB	SUBJECT	WEDI	VERB-NOUN	OBJECT
WELSH	Mae	Siân	wedi	rhedeg	milltir.
IPA	[maɪ	ʃɑːn	ˈwɛdi	ˈr̩ɛˈdɛg	ˈmɪɫtɪr]

	SUBJECT	VERB	VERB	ARTICLE	OBJECT
ENGLISH	Siân	has	run	a	mile.

Here are further examples of the use of **wedi**:

SENTENCE	ENGLISH	IPA
Mae Gareth wedi dysgu Cymraeg.	Gareth has learnt Welsh.	[maɪ ˈgɑrɛθ ˈwɛdi ˈdəsgi kəmˈraɪg]
Mae Tom wedi gyrru tractor.	Tom has driven a tractor.	[maɪ tɔm ˈwɛdi ˈgəri ˈtɹaktor]

We will discuss **wedi** in more detail in **Week 5, Lesson 5**.

> **IMPORTANT**
> Neither aspectual marker, **yn** nor **wedi**, causes mutation.

So far, we have only seen the third person singular form, **mae**.

(i) with personal names:

SENTENCE	ENGLISH	IPA
Mae Gareth yn gyrru.	Gareth is driving.	[maɪ 'gɑːreθ ən 'gəri]

(ii) with plural nouns as the subject:

SENTENCE	ENGLISH	IPA
Mae'r plant yn darllen.	The children are reading.	[maɪr plant ən 'darɬen]
Mae'r merched yn canu.	The girls are singing.	[maɪr 'mɛrχed ən 'kɑːni]
Mae'r bechgyn yn chwarae.	The boys are playing.	[maɪr 'bɛχgɪn ən 'χwɑːre]

The verb form **mae** is used with the pronouns **e** (SW) / **o** (NW) and **hi**:

SENTENCE	ENGLISH	IPA
Mae e'n dysgu Cymraeg. (SW)	He is learning Welsh.	[maɪ eːn 'dəsgi kəm'raɪg]
Mae o'n dysgu Cymraeg. (NW)	He is learning Welsh.	[maɪ oːn 'dəsgi kəm'raɪg]
Mae hi'n dysgu Cymraeg.	She is learning Welsh.	[maɪ hiːn 'dəsgi kəm'raɪg]

We will now look at the present tense of '**bod**' in its entirety:

The affirmative forms of the present tense of 'bod'

SENTENCE	ENGLISH	IPA
Dw i'n dysgu.	I am learning. / I learn.	[dwiːn 'dəsgi]
Rwyt ti'n dysgu.	You are learning. / You learn. (*fam.*)	[rʊɪ(t) tiːn 'dəsgi]
Mae e'n dysgu. (SW)	He is learning. / He learns.	[maɪ eːn 'dəsgi]
Mae o'n dysgu. (NW)	He is learning. / He learns.	[maɪ oːn 'dəsgi]
Mae hi'n dysgu.	She is learning. / She learns.	[maɪ hiːn 'dəsgi]
Dyn ni'n dysgu.	We are learning. / We learn.	[də(n) niːn 'dəsgi]
Dych chi'n dysgu.	You are learning. / You learn. (*pl.*) (*sing. formal*)	[də(χ) χiːn 'dəsgi]
Maen nhw'n dysgu.	They are learning. / They learn.	[maɪ(n) n̥uːn 'dəsgi]

IMPORTANT

This construction is also used to denote the present habitual, the tense used to describe an action which occurs repeatedly or regularly:

Dw i'n mynd i'r dre(f) bob dydd   I go to town every day.
   [dwiːn mɪnd ir dɹeː(v) boːb diːð]

Dw i'n mynd can be translated into English as 'I am going' or 'I go'.

Vocabulary

VERB-NOUN	ENGLISH	IPA
byw	to live	[bɪʊ]
darllen	to read	['darɬɛn]
meddwl	to think	['mɛðʊl]
cerdded	to walk	['kɛrðɛd]
ysgrifennu	to write	[əsgrɪv'ɛni]
ysgrifennu at (SM)	to write to	[əsgrɪv'ɛni at]
paentio	to paint	['pəɪntjo]
gwisgo	to dress / to get dressed	['gwɪsgo]
ymolchi	to wash (oneself)	[əm'ɒlχi]
codi	to get up	['kɔdi]
breuddwydio	to dream	[brəɪð'ʊɪdjo]
mynd	to go	[mɪnd]

Exercise 2

*Pair the sentences from **A** with those from **B**.*

A
1) Dw i'n ysgrifennu at Gareth.
2) Mae o'n rhedeg. (NW)
3) Dyn ni'n ymolchi.
4) Maen nhw'n gwisgo.
5) Mae hi'n meddwl.
6) Rwyt ti'n cerdded.
7) Dych chi'n gweithio.
8) Mae'r plant yn chwarae bob dydd.
9) Mae e'n darllen. (SW)
10) Maen nhw'n breuddwydio.

B
a) You are working./You work.
b) She is thinking./She thinks.
c) They are dreaming./They dream.
d) You are walking./You walk.
e) He is reading./He reads.
f) He is running./He runs.
g) They are getting dressed./They get dressed.
h) I am writing./I write to Gareth.
i) We are getting washed./We get washed.
j) The children play every day.

Exercise 3

*Fill in the blanks using the appropriate form of the present tense of '**bod**'.*

For example:

Question: ____ e'n rhedeg.
Answer: Mae e'n rhedeg.

1) _____ i'n siarad Cymraeg.

(I speak Welsh./I am speaking Welsh.)

2) _____ ni'n gyrru.
(We drive./We are driving.)

3) _____ nhw'n gweithio.
(They work./They are working.)

4) _____ ti'n rhedeg.
(You run./You are running.)

5) _____ hi'n paentio.
(She paints./She is painting.)

6) _____ ni'n gweithio.
(We work./We are working.)

7) _____ 'n rhedeg.
(I run./I am running.)

8) _____ e'n (SW)/o'n (NW) breuddwydio.
(He dreams./He is dreaming.)

9) _____ 'r bobl yn darllen.
(The people read./The people are reading.)

10) _____ chi'n cerdded.
(You walk./You are walking.)

Vocabulary

ADVERBIAL	ENGLISH	IPA
heddiw	today	['hɛðɪʊ]
heno	tonight	['hɛno]
y bore 'ma	this morning	[ə 'bɔrɛ̈ mä]
y prynhawn 'ma	this afternoon	[ə prɪn'haʊn mä]
bob dydd	everyday	[bob 'dɪð]
bob bore	every morning	[boːb 'bɔrɛ̈]
yn y bore	in the morning	[ən ə 'bɔrɛ̈]
yn y nos	in the evening / at night	[ən ə 'noːs]
yn y prynhawn	in the afternoon	[ən ə prɪn'haʊn]
allan	out	['äɫan]
yn y tŷ	at home (*lit.* in the house)	[ən ə tiː]
yn y gwaith	at work	[ən ə gwaɪθ]
yn y dre(f)	in town (*lit.* in the town)	[ən ə dɹeː(v)]
i'r dre(f)	to town (*lit.* to the town)	[iːr dɹeː(v)]

Exercise 4

Translate the following sentences.

1) The boys are playing at home today. _____
2) I work in the house in the morning. _____
3) She is driving to town today. _____
4) They read at night _____
5) We speak Welsh _____
6) He is going out tonight. _____
7) You are painting at home today. (*fam.*)
   _____
8) The children are getting dressed. _____
9) I walk to town every morning. _____
10) You run in the afternoon (*pl.*) (*sing. formal*)
    _____

Vocabulary

MASCULINE NOUN	ENGLISH	IPA	PLURAL FORM	IPA
dosbarth	class	[ˈdɔsbarθ]	**dosbarthiadau**	[dɔsbarθjɑˑdɛ]
dim	no	[dɪm]		
rygbi	rugby	[ˈrəgbi]		

FEMININE NOUN	ENGLISH	IPA	PLURAL FORM	IPA
gêm	game	[geːm]	**gemau**	[ˈgeˑmɛ]
problem	problem	[ˈprɔblɛm]	**problemau**	[prɔbˈlɛmɛ]

VERB-NOUN	ENGLISH	IPA
hoffi	to like	[ˈhɔfi]
ymlacio	to relax	[əmˈlakjo]

PREPOSITION	ENGLISH	IPA
i (SM)	to / for	[iː]
am (SM)	about	[am]

CONJUNCTION	ENGLISH	IPA
ond	but	[ɔnd]

ADVERBIAL	ENGLISH	IPA
hefyd	too / also	[ˈhɛvɪd]
wedyn	afterwards / after / then	[ˈwɛdɪn]
yn fawr iawn	very much	[ən vaʊr jaʊn]

MISCELLANEOUS	ENGLISH	IPA
diolch yn fawr iawn	thank you very much	[ˈdiɔlχ ən vaʊr jaʊn]
diolch am	thanks for	[ˈdiɔlχ am]

You will see **dim** 'no' / 'zero' [dɪm] in public notices such as:

PUBLIC NOTICE	ENGLISH	IPA
dim parcio	no parking	[dɪm ˈparkjo]
dim ysmygu*	no smoking	[dɪm əsˈməgi]

* ***Ysmygu*** *is a more formal form of **smocio**, and is used on public notices and official documentation.*

Dialogue

Welsh Dialogue

Richard: Diolch am y coffi. Dw i'n hoffi coffi'n fawr iawn.
Ann: Dim problem. Mae'r plant yn chwarae rygbi yn Llanbedr heddiw. Maen nhw'n hoffi chwarae rygbi'n fawr iawn. Dw i'n mynd i Lanbedr hefyd. Dw i'n gyrru yno gyda'r merched. Dyn ni'n rhedeg yn y parc bob nos. Dw i'n hoffi bod allan.
Richard: Dw i'n hoffi rygbi hefyd, a dw i'n hoffi rhedeg. Dw i'n cerdded i'r gwaith bob bore. Dw i'n chwarae rygbi hefyd. Gêm dda! Dw i'n breuddwydio am chwarae dros Gymru.
Ann: Dw i wedi chwarae rygbi, ond dim rŵan. Rhedeg gyda'r merched ac wedyn, dw i'n mynd i baentio'r gegin. Dw i'n breuddwydio am ymlacio yn y nos!
Richard: Prysur iawn!

English Translation

Richard: Thanks for the coffee. I like coffee very much.
Ann: No problem. The children are playing rugby in Llanbedr today. They like playing rugby very much. I am going to Llanbedr as well. I'm driving there with the girls. We run in the park every evening. I like being outside.
Richard: I like rugby as well, as I like running. I walk to work every morning. I also play rugby. Good game! I dream about playing for Wales.
Ann: I have played rugby, but not now. Run with the girls, and then I'm going to paint the kitchen. I dream about relaxing in the evening.
Richard: Very busy!

Exercise 5

We saw examples of the soft mutation after **i** in the dialogue above. Here is a quick exercise to remind you of the soft mutation. Place the word in brackets in the gap provided, remembering to mutate if necessary.

1) Croeso i _____ (Cymru).
   (Welcome to Wales.)
2) Diolch am _____ (gweithio) heno.
   (Thanks for working tonight.)
3) Maen nhw'n rhedeg i _____ (Bangor).
   (They are running to Bangor.)
4) Mae hi'n meddwl am _____ (darllen) llyfr.
   (She is thinking about reading a book.)
5) Dw i'n mynd i _____ (paentio)'r gegin.
   (I am going to paint the kitchen.)
6) Mae o'n cerdded i _____ (Maesteg).
   (He is walking to Maesteg.)
7) Dyn ni'n mynd i _____ (Rhos).
   (We are going to Rhos.)
8) Mae e'n mynd i _____ (Llanelli) heddiw. (SW)
   (He is going to Llanelli today.)
9) Dw i'n cerdded i _____ (Tremadog).
   (I am walking to Tremadog.)
10) Maen nhw'n mynd i _____ (dosbarth) Cymraeg.
    (They are going to a Welsh class.)

If you would like to refresh your memory of the letters which undergo soft mutation, refer to **Week 1, Lesson 5**.

The grammatical functions of 'yn' (in)

In Welsh, the word **yn** 'in' [ən] has four grammatical functions:

(i) As an aspectual marker in the periphrastic construction of **'bod'** (see **Week 3, Lesson 1**):

SENTENCE	ENGLISH	IPA
Mae Siân yn darllen.	Siân is reading. / Siân reads.	[maɪ ʃɑːn ən ˈdarlen]
Mae'r plant yn canu.	The children are singing. / The children sing.	[maɪr plant ən ˈkɑːni]

(ii) As a predicative marker*, which causes the soft mutation:

SENTENCE	WORD BEFORE SOFT MUTATION	ENGLISH	IPA
Mae Siôn yn **blismon**. (*n.*)	**plismon**	Siôn is a policeman.	[maɪ ʃoːn ən ˈblɪsmon]
Mae Siôn yn **dda**. (*adj.*)	**da**	Siôn is good.	[maɪ ʃoːn ən ðɑː]

* The **predicative** expresses a property that is assigned to the 'subject', **Siôn** in this case, who is a **policeman** (noun) in the first example, and **good** (adjective) in the second.

The letters which are mutated in this case are:

p > b   **b > f**   **m > f**
t > d   **d > dd**
c > g   **g > -**

(iii) As an adverbial marker, turning an adjective into an adverbial, which causes the soft mutation as in (ii) above:

SENTENCE	ENGLISH	IPA	ADJECTIVE PRE-MUTATION	ENGLISH
Mae'r plant yn darllen **yn gyflym**.	The children read quickly.	[maɪr plant ən ˈdarɬɛn ən ˈgəvlɪm]	**cyflym**	quick
Mae'r bws yn symud **yn araf**.	The bus is moving slowly.	[maɪr bəs ən ˈsəmɪd ən ˈɑrav]	**araf**	slow

(iv) As a preposition which corresponds to 'in', and which causes the nasal mutation (see **Week 3, Lesson 1**):

SENTENCE OR PHRASE	ENGLISH	IPA
Dw i'n byw **yng Nghymru**.	I live in Wales.	[dwiːn bɪʊ ə(ŋ) ˈŋ̊əmri]
tad-**yng-nghyfraith**	father-in-law	[tɑːd ə(ŋ) ˈŋ̊əvrɛθ]

Vocabulary

ADJECTIVE	ENGLIS	IPA
tal	tall	[tal]
byr	short	[bɪr]
sâl	ill	[sɑːl]
prysur	busy	[ˈprəsɪr]
diflas	miserable	[ˈdɪvlas]
siriol	cheerful	[ˈsɪrjol]
hapus	happy	[ˈhäpɪs]
trist	sad	[tɹɪst]
twym (SW)	warm	[tʊɪm]
cynnes (NW)	warm	[ˈkənɛs]
oer	cold	[ɔɪr]

Exercise 6

Translate the following sentences.

1) I'm ill. _____
2) He is tall. _____
3) They are short. _____
4) Siân is busy. _____
5) She is warm. _____
6) We are miserable. _____
7) The children are naughty. _____
8) You are cheerful. _____
9) The girls are sad. _____
10) I'm happy. _____

Lesson 2: Interrogative adverbs

An interrogative adverb is a question word which asks about:

(i) time: **pryd** 'when' [priːd]
(ii) place: **ble** 'where' [bleː]
(iii) reason: **pam** 'why' [pam]
(iv) manner, time, quantity, amount and degree: **sut** 'how' [sɪt].

Interrogative adverbs are followed by the affirmative forms of '**bod**', as we saw in **Week 3, Lesson 1** above.

INTERROGATIVE ADVERB	ENGLISH	IPA
ble	where	[bleː]
pam	why	[pam]
sut	how	[sɪt]
pryd	when	[priːd]

Here are some examples:

	QUESTION
WELSH	**Ble dych chi'n byw?**
ENGLISH	Where do you live?
IPA	[bleː də(χ) χiːn bɪʊ]

WELSH	**Pam dych chi'n cerdded i'r dre(f)?**
ENGLISH	Why are you walking to town?

IPA	[pam də(χ) χiːn 'kɛrðɛd iːr dɹɛː(v)]
WELSH	**Sut dych chi'n dysgu Cymraeg?**
ENGLISH	How are you learning Welsh?
IPA	[sɪt də(χ) χiːn 'dəsgi kəm'raɪg]
WELSH	**Pryd dych chi'n ysgrifennu yn y gwaith?**
ENGLISH	When do you write at work?
IPA	[priː(d) dəχ χiːn əsgrɪv'ɛni ən ə gwaɪθ]

Exercise 1

*Match the questions under **A** to the appropriate answers under **B**.*

A
1) Ble mae'r plant yn chwarae?
2) Ble dych chi'n byw?
3) Pam mae o'n cerdded heddiw?
4) Sut rwyt ti'n dysgu Cymraeg?
5) Pryd dyn ni'n rhedeg?
6) Ble dw i'n gweithio y prynhawn 'ma?

B
a) Dw i'n dysgu Cymraeg gyda llyfr.
b) Dych chi'n rhedeg y bore 'ma.
c) Dw i'n byw yn Waun-fawr.
d) Rwyt ti'n gweithio yn Llanelli.
e) Maen nhw'n chwarae yn y parc.
f) Mae o'n hoffi cerdded.

Vocabulary

MASCULINE NOUN	ENGLISH	IPA	PLURAL FORM	IPA
gwaith	work	[gwaɪθ]	**gweithiau**	['gwəɪθjɛ]

VERB-NOUN	ENGLISH	IPA
cwrdd â (AM)	to meet	[kʊrð ä]

ADJECTIVE	ENGLISH	IPA
gwych	excellent / brilliant	[gwiːχ]

PREPOSITION	ENGLISH	IPA
mewn	in a	[mɛʊn]
llawer o (SM)	lots of, many	['ɬaʊɛr oː]

ADVERBIAL	ENGLISH	IPA
o hyn ymlaen	from now on	[oː hɪn əm'laɪn]
hwyl* am y tro	bye for now	[hʊil am ə tɹoː]

* ***Hwyl*** *'bye'* [hʊil] *is the short form of **hwyl fawr** 'goodbye'* [hʊil vaʊr]. *The word **hwyl** literally means 'sail'. **Hwyl fawr** translates literally as 'big sail', and the origin of using this as a means of saying farewell dates back to a time when long journeys would have meant travel by boat. Another common phrase using **hwyl** is **pob hwyl** 'all the best'* [poːb hʊil].

Dialogue

Welsh Dialogue

Richard: Dw i'n dysgu Cymraeg.
Ann: Da iawn chi. Ble dych chi'n dysgu Cymraeg?
Richard: Dw i'n dysgu Cymraeg mewn dosbarth yn y dref. Dw i'n hoffi dysgu Cymraeg, dw i wedi cwrdd â llawer o ffrindiau newydd.
Ann: Da iawn chi. Dyn ni'n mynd i siarad Cymraeg bob tro o hyn ymlaen.
Richard: Gwych! Dw i'n mynd i ddysgu'r dosbarth nawr, neis cwrdd â chi.
Ann: Iawn. Dw i'n mynd i ddysgu dosbarth rŵan hefyd. Plant dosbarth chwech. Hwyl am y tro.

English Translation

Richard: I'm learning Welsh.
Ann: Well done (very good) you. Where do you learn Welsh?
Richard: I'm learning Welsh in a class in town. I like learning Welsh, I have met lots of new friends.
Ann: Well done (very good) you. We are going to speak Welsh all the time from now on.
Richard: Excellent! I'm going to teach the class now, nice to meet you.
Ann: OK. I'm going to teach a class now as well. The class 6 children. Bye for now.

The preposition 'yn' / 'mewn'

Yn [ən] and **mewn** [mɛʊn] can both be thought of as meaning 'in'. **Yn** is used with definite nouns.

A definite noun is:

(i) A specific name, such as 'Cardiff', 'Tom', 'Mary', etc.
(ii) A noun following the definite article of **y**; **yr**; or **'r**. Examples of this include: **y wlad** 'the country' [ə ʷlɑːd], **y llyfr** 'the book' [ə ɬəvr̩], **yr esgidiau** 'the shoes' [ər ɛsˈɡɪdjɛ].
(iii) A genitive phrase, such as **car Tom** 'Tom's car' [kar tɔm], **eu coffi nhw** 'their coffee' [iː ˈkɔfi n̥uː].

We will look at the genitive noun phrase in **Week 4, Lesson 5**.

Here are examples of the use of **yn** and **mewn**:

SENTENCE	ENGLISH	IPA
Dw i'n gweithio mewn ysgol.	I work in a school.	[dwiːn ˈɡwəɪθjo mɛʊn ˈəsɡol]
Dw i'n gweithio yn yr ysgol.	I work at / in the school.	[dwiːn ˈɡwəɪθjo ən ər ˈəsɡol]
Mae e'n byw mewn tre(f).	He lives in a town.	[maɪ eːn bɪʊ mɛʊn tɹeː(v)]
Mae o'n byw yn Llanelli.	He lives in Llanelli.	[maɪ oːn bɪʊ ən ɬanˈɛɬi]

| Mae hi'n cerdded mewn parc. | She is walking in a park. | [maɪ hiːn ˈkɛrðɛd mɛʊn park] |
| Mae hi'n cerdded yn y parc. | She is walking in the park. | [maɪ hiːn ˈkɛrðɛd ən ə park] |

Exercise 2

*Fill in the gaps below using either **yn** or **mewn** where appropriate.*

1) Mae hi'n ymlacio _____ y gadair.
2) Dyn ni'n gyrru _____ car.
3) Maen nhw wedi darllen yr hanes _____ llyfr.
4) Dw i'n byw _____ pentre(f) bach.
5) Mae o'n cerdded _____ parc.
6) Rwyt ti'n byw _____ y dre(f).
7) Dych chi'n gyrru _____ y car.
8) Mae hi'n chwarae _____ gêm rygbi.

Lesson 3: Interrogative forms of present tense of 'bod' (to be)

INTERROGATIVE SENTENCE	ENGLISH	IPA
Ydw i'n dysgu?	Am I learning? / Do I learn?	[ˈədʊ iːn ˈdəsgi]
Wyt ti'n dysgu?	Are you learning? / Do you learn? (*fam.*)	[ʊɪ(t) tiːn ˈdəsgi]
Ydy e'n dysgu? (SW)	Is he learning? / Does he learn?	[ˈədi ɛːn ˈdəsgi]
Ydy o'n dysgu? (NW)	Is he learning? / Does he learn?	[ˈədi oːn ˈdəsgi]
Ydy hi'n dysgu?	Is she learning? / Does she learn?	[ˈədi hiːn ˈdəsgi]
Ydyn ni'n dysgu?	Are we learning? / Do we learn?	[ˈədɪ(n) niːn ˈdəsgi]
Ydych chi'n dysgu?	Are you learning? / Do you learn? (*pl.*) (*sing. formal*)	[ˈədɪ(χ) χiːn ˈdəsgi]
Ydyn nhw'n dysgu?	Are they learning? / Do they learn?	[ˈədɪ(n) n̥uːn ˈdəsgi]

Remember that a plural subject takes the third person singular **ydy** [ˈədi] form:

> **IMPORTANT**
> The third person singular form **ydy** is also used with common and proper nouns, both singular and plural:
>
> **Singular**
>
> **Ydy'r plentyn yn rhedeg?** Response: **Ydy.** **Nac ydy.**
> Is the child running?   Yes.   No.
> [ˈədiːr plɛntɪn ən ˈr̥ɛˑdɛg]   [ˈədi] [nɑːg ˈədi]
>
> **Ydy'r ferch yn canu?** Response: **Ydy.** **Nac ydy.**
> Is the girl singing?   Yes.   No.
> [ˈədiːr ˈdəsbarθ ən ˈkɑˑni]   [ˈədi] [nɑːg ˈədi]

IMPORTANT (CONTINUATION)
Plural

Ydy'r merched yn canu?	*Response:*	**Ydyn.**	**Nac ydyn.**
Are the girls singing?		Yes.	No.
[ˈədir ˈmerχed ən ˈkani]		[ˈədɪn]	[nɑːg ˈədɪn]
Ydy'r plant yn rhedeg?	*Response:*	**Ydyn.**	**Nac ydyn.**
Are the children running?		Yes.	No.
[ˈədir ˈplant ən ˈr̥edeg]		[ˈədɪn]	[nɑːg ˈədɪn]

This applies to *all* verbs, not just '**bod**'.

Exercise 1

Translate the following sentences.

1) Are we walking to town?
2) Are you reading? (*pl.*)
3) Am I famous?
4) Is the other teacher working?
5) Are the flowers in the kitchen?
6) Is she in a Welsh class?
7) Does he live in a village?
8) Do you sing every morning? (*fam.*)
9) Are the children getting dressed?
10) Is she playing rugby in the afternoon?

Saying 'yes' and 'no' in Welsh

There is no single word for 'yes' and 'no' in Welsh. In **Week 2, Lesson 3**, we saw the affirmative answer **ie** [ˈiˑɛ]* and the negative answer **nage** [ˈnɑgɛ]. These are used to respond to a question which uses the 'identification' structure:

QUESTION	ENGLISH	IPA
Dyn lleol ydy e? (SW)	Is he a local man?	[diːn ˈɬeˑol ˈədi eː]
Dyn lleol ydy o? (NW)	Is he a local man?	[diːn ˈɬeˑol ˈədi oː]

REPLY	ENGLISH	IPA
Ie, dyn lleol ydy e. (SW)	Yes, he is a local man.	[ˈiˑɛ diːn ˈɬeˑol ˈədi eː]
Ie, dyn lleol ydy o. (NW)	Yes, he is a local man.	[ˈiˑɛ diːn ˈɬeˑol ˈədi oː]

QUESTION	ENGLISH	IPA
Athrawes ydy hi?	Is she a teacher?	[aθrauɛs 'ədi hi]

REPLY	ENGLISH	IPA
Nage, nid athrawes ydy hi.	No, she is not a teacher.	['nɑːgɛ nɪd aθrauɛs 'ədi hi]

* Remember that **ie** is pronounced in two syllables: *ee-eh*, not like the *yeah* in the famous Beatles' song!

The replies **ie** and **nage** are only used when the sentence does not start with a verb, as is the case in the sentences we saw in **Week 2, Lesson 2**. When a question begins with a verb, it is answered with the appropriate personal form of the verb. This is like the way questions are answered in some parts of England and Ireland, in that a question like 'Are you going?' is answered with 'I am' rather than 'yes' or 'no'.

The response forms for the present tense are as follows:

AFFIRMATIVE REPLY	ENGLISH	IPA
Ydw.	Yes, I am / do.	['ədʊ]
Wyt.	Yes, you are / do. (*fam.*)	['ʊit]
Ydy.	Yes, he / she / it is / does.	['ədi]]
Ydyn.	Yes, we are / do	['ədɪn]
Ydych.	Yes, you are / do.	['ədɪχ]
Ydyn.	Yes, they are / do.	['ədɪn]

NEGATIVE REPLY	ENGLISH	IPA
Nac ydw.	No, I am not / don't.	[nɑːg 'ədʊ]
Nac wyt.	No, you are not / don't. (*fam.*)	[nɑːg ʊit]
Nac ydy.	No, he / she / it is not / doesn't.	[nɑːg 'ədi]
Nac ydyn.	No, we are not / don't.	[nɑːg 'ədɪn]
Nac ydych.	No, you are not / don't.	[nɑːg 'ədɪχ]
Nac ydyn.	No, they are not / don't.	[nɑːg 'ədɪn]

Very often the affirmative replies are repeated to show emphasis:

	QUESTION	REPLY
WELSH	**Ydych chi'n gweithio nawr?**	**Ydw, ydw.**
ENGLISH	Are you working now?	Yes, yes.
IPA	['ədɪ(χ) χiːn 'gwəɪθjo naʊr]	['ədʊ 'ədʊ]

Here are some further examples of questions and responses:

	QUESTION	REPLY
WELSH	**Ydy'r plant yn chwarae?**	**Nac ydyn.**
ENGLISH	Are the children playing?	No, they're not.

IPA	[ˈədir plant ən ˈχwɑːrɛ]	[nɑːg ˈədɪn]
WELSH	**Wyt ti'n dysgu Cymraeg?**	**Ydw.**
ENGLISH	Are you learning Welsh?	Yes, I am.
IPA	[ʊi(t) tiːn ˈdəsgi kəmˈraig]	[ˈədʊ]
WELSH	**Ydyn ni'n mynd allan heno?**	**Ydyn.**
ENGLISH	Are we going out tonight?	Yes, we are.
IPA	[ˈədɪ(n) n̥uːn mɪnd ˈaɬan ˈhɛno]	[ˈədɪn]

Exercise 2

*Pair the questions below **A** with the appropriate answers from **B**.*

A
1) Ydy'r athrawes arall yn dysgu? (✗)
2) Ydw i'n cwrdd â'r athro wedyn? (✓)
3) Ydyn ni'n cerdded i'r gwaith heddiw? (✓)
4) Ydych chi'n rhedeg yn y parc bob dydd? (✗)
5) Wyt ti'n dysgu Cymraeg? (✓)
6) Ydy o'n siarad Cymraeg o hyn ymlaen? (✓)
7) Ydy pawb yn gyrru i'r dre(f)? (✗)
8) Ydyn nhw'n enwog? (✓)

B
a) Wyt.
b) Nac ydw.
c) Nac ydyn.
d) Ydy.
e) Ydyn.
f) Nac ydy.
g) Ydw.
h) Ydych.

Exercise 3

Answer the following questions affirmatively in full sentences.

For example:

Question: Ydy hi'n gweithio yn y dre(f)?
Answer: Ydy. Mae hi'n gweithio yn y dre(f).

1) Ydy'r ci'n breuddwydio? _____
2) Ydy'r plant yn ysgrifennu yn yr ysgol?
  _____
3) Wyt ti'n ymolchi bob bore? _____
4) Ydyn ni'n rhedeg tair milltir?
  _____ *
5) Ydy Richard yn dysgu Cymraeg?
  _____
6) Ydych chi'n gwisgo het? _____
7) Ydy hi'n siarad â'r postmon? _____
8) Ydych chi'n hoffi llaeth? _____ *

9) Ydw i'n gwisgo esgidiau gwyrdd? _____ *

10) Ydyn nhw'n ymlacio nawr? _____

Each of these questions has two possible answers.

Vocabulary

MASCULINE NOUN	ENGLISH	IPA	PLURAL FORM	IPA
cawod	shower	['kaʊod]	**cawodydd**	[kaʊ'ɔdɪð]

FEMININE NOUN	ENGLISH	IPA	PLURAL FORM	IPA
het (*b.*)	hat	[hɛt]	**hetiau**	['hɛtjɛ]

Exercise 4

Translate the following sentences.

1) Am I working today?
2) Do they walk to school?
3) Do you sing in the shower?
4) Does she play rugby every day?
5) Are you getting up now?
6) Do I teach today?
7) Is the woman thinking?
8) Are we going to speak to a policeman?
9) Are you reading the paper?
10) Is he running?

Lesson 4: Negative forms of the present tense of 'bod'

SENTENCE	ENGLISH	IPA
Dw i ddim yn dysgu.	I am not learning. / I don't learn.	[dwi: ðɪm ən 'dəsgi]
Dwyt ti ddim yn dysgu.	You are not learning. / You don't learn.	[dʊɪ(t) ti: ðɪm ən 'dəsgi]
Dydy e ddim yn dysgu. (SW)	He is not learning. / He doesn't learn.	['dədi e: ðɪm ən 'dəsgi]
Dydy o ddim yn dysgu. (NW)	He is not learning. /	['dədi o: ðɪm ən 'dəsgi]

	He doesn't learn.	
Dydy hi ddim yn dysgu.	She is not learning. / She doesn't learn.	[ˈdədi hiː ðɪm ən ˈdəsgi]
Dyn ni ddim yn dysgu.	We are not learning. / We don't learn.	[də(n) niː ðɪm ən ˈdəsgi]
Dych chi ddim yn dysgu.	You are not learning. / You don't learn.	[də(χ) χiː ðɪm ən ˈdəsgi]
Dyn nhw ddim yn dysgu.	They are not learning. / They don't learn.	[də(n) n̪u: ðɪm ən ˈdəsgi]

Exercise 1

Answer the following questions negatively.

For example:

Question: Ydy hi'n gweithio yn y dre(f)?
Answer: Nac ydy, dydy hi ddim yn gweithio yn y dre(f).

1) Ydy hi'n gwylio'r gêm?
_____

2) Ydy o'n ysgrifennu llyfr?
_____

3) Ydyn ni'n chwarae rygbi heno?
_____

4) Ydy'r plant yn bwyta yn y gegin?
_____

5) Ydych chi'n hoffi'r nyrs?
_____

6) Wyt ti'n parcio'r car?
_____

7) Ydyn nhw'n darllen y papur?
_____

8) Ydw i'n mynd i Fangor gyda (SW)/efo (NW) chi?
_____

Vocabulary

ADJECTIVE	ENGLISH	IPA
hapus	happy	[ˈhäpɪs]

MASCULINE NOUN	ENGLISH	IPA	PLURAL FORM	IPA
maes parcio	car park	[maɪs ˈparkjo]	**meysydd parcio**	[ˈməɪsɪð ˈparkjo]

FEMININE NOUN	ENGLISH	IPA	PLURAL FORM	IPA
brechdan	sandwich	[ˈbrɛχdan]	**brechdanau**	[brɛχˈdɑːnɛ]

VERB-NOUN	ENGLISH	IPA
bwyta	to eat	[ˈbʊɪtä]
gwylio	to watch	[ˈgwɪljo]
parcio	to park	[ˈparkjo]

Exercise 2

Negate the following affirmative sentences.

For example:

Question: Mae o'n hoffi gwylio rygbi.
Answer: Dydy o ddim yn hoffi gwylio rygbi.

1) Rwyt ti'n gwylio'r gêm.

2) Mae hi'n enwog.

3) Dw i'n bwyta brechdan.

4) Dyn ni'n gweithio mewn siop.

5) Mae'r athro'n dysgu heddiw.

6) Dw i'n parcio'r car yn y maes parcio.

7) Mae e'n breuddwydio.

8) Dych chi'n darllen llyfr.

9) Mae'r ceffyl yn cicio.

10) Mae'r plant yn canu yn yr ysgol.

Exercise 3

Translate the following sentences.

1) I'm not in the car park.

2) We don't like sandwiches.

3) The boy isn't getting dressed.

4) She isn't watching the rugby game.

5) You don't go every day.

6) I don't speak Welsh.

7) You aren't getting up.

8) The teachers are happy.

9) They aren't meeting the class this afternoon.

10) He doesn't like the new bridge.

Lesson 5: Locative adverbs

In Welsh, there are special words which locate one or more objects in relation to the speaker. They are called locative adverbs:

LOCATIVE ADVERB	ENGLISH	IPA
dyma	here is / are; this is	['dəmä]
dyna	there is / are; that is	['dənä]
dacw	yonder is / are*	['däkʊ]

* In spoken English, **dacw** translates as, 'There is / are (...) over there.'

LOCATIVE SENTENCE	ENGLISH	IPA
Dyma'r maes parcio.	Here's the car park.	['dəmär maɪs 'parkjɔ]
Dyna'r lorri.	There's the lorry.	['dənär 'lɔri]
Dacw'r bachgen.	Yonder is the boy.	['däkʊr 'bäχgɛn]

When used with an indefinite noun, all three locative adverbs cause the soft mutation (which includes **rh** > **r** and **ll** > **l**):

LOCATIVE SENTENCE	ENGLISH	IPA	NOUN PRE-MUTATION
Dyma raw.	Here is a spade.	['dəmä raʊ]	**rhaw**
Dyna lwy.	There is a spoon.	['dənä lʊɪ]	**llwy**

| Dacw <u>fachgen</u>. | Yonder is a boy. | [ˈdäkʊ ˈväχɡɛn] | **bachgen** |

Vocabulary

ADJECTIVE	ENGLISH	IPA
balch	proud / glad	[balχ]
diddorol	interesting	[dɪðˈoˑrol]
hyfryd	lovely	[ˈhəvrɪd]

MASCULINE NOUN	ENGLISH	IPA	PLURAL FORM	IPA
rheswm	reason	[ˈɹɛsʊm]	**rhesymau**	[ɹɛsˈəmɛ]
gwir	truth	[gwiːr]		

FEMININE NOUN	ENGLISH	IPA	PLURAL FORM	IPA
rheilffordd	railway	[ˈɹəɪlfɔrð]	**rheilffyrdd**	[ˈɹəɪlfɪrð]
rhaw	spade	[ɹaʊ]	**rhawiau**	[ˈɹaʊjɛ]
llwy	spoon	[ɬʊɪ]	**llwyau**	[ˈɬʊɪ.ɛ]
lorri	lorry	[ˈlɔri]	**lorïau**	[lɔrˈi.ɛ]
ffordd	way / road	[fɔrð]	**ffyrdd**	[fɪrð]

Exercise 1

Complete the following sentences by using the Welsh word in brackets, remembering to mutate if necessary.

1) Dyma _____. (blodau) (Here are flowers.)
2) Dacw _____. (ceffyl) (There is a horse over there.)
3) Dyna _____. (llyfr da) (That's a good book.)
4) Dyma _____. (ffenest[r] fach) (This is a small window.)
5) Dyna _____. (tŷ mawr) (That's a big house.)
6) Dacw _____. (maes parcio prysur) (Over there is a busy car park.)
7) Dyma _____. (desg fawr) (This is a large desk.)
8) Dyna _____. (pentref bach) (That's a small village.)
9) Dacw _____. (rheilffordd) (Over there is a railway.)
10) Dyna _____. (gwaith da) (That is good work.)

For a reminder of which letters undergo soft mutation, refer to **Week 1, Lesson 5**.

Dyna can also mean 'that's' or 'how' in phrases like:

PHRASE	ENGLISH	IPA	ADJECTIVE PRE-MUTATION
Dyna <u>falch</u> ydy e! (SW)	How proud he is!	['dənä valχ 'ədi eː]	**balch**
Dyna <u>falch</u> ydy o! (NW)	How proud he is!	['dənä valχ 'ədi oː]	**balch**
Dyna hyfryd!	That's nice/lovely!	['dənä 'həvrɪd]	

It can often translate into English as 'What a ...', as in **Dyna groeso!** 'What a welcome!' ['dənä 'grɔɪso].

Exercise 2

Translate the following sentences.

1) That's strong. _____
2) That's interesting. _____
3) What a man! _____
4) What a morning! _____
5) That's naughty. _____
6) That's new. _____
7) What people! _____
8) That's small. _____
9) What a problem! _____

In spoken Welsh, **dyma** ['dəmä], **dyna** ['dənä] and **dacw** ['däkʊ] are usually shortened to **'ma** [mä], **'na** [nä] and **'co** [koː], respectively. To turn statements with **dyma**, **dyna** or **dacw** into questions, **ai** [aɪ] is placed in front of the locative adverb:

QUESTION	ENGLISH	IPA
Ai dyma'r rheswm?	Is this the reason?	[aɪ 'dəmär 'ɹɛsʊm]
Ai dyna'r gwir?	Is that the truth?	[aɪ 'dənär gwiːr]
Ai dacw Gaerdydd?	Is that Cardiff (in the distance)?	[aɪ 'däkʊ gaɪr'diːð]

Ai is usually dropped in spoken Welsh, leaving the rising tone as the only clue a question is being asked:

Dyma'r ffordd? Is this the way? ['dəmär fɔrð]

The answers to such questions are **ie** 'yes' ['iˑɛ] or **nage** 'no' ['nɑˑgɛ].

To negate a statement with **dyma**, **dyna** or **dacw** in it, **nid** [nɪd] is placed in front of the pronoun:

SENTENCE	ENGLISH	IPA
Nid dyma'r ffordd.	This isn't the way.	[nɪd ˈdəmär fɔrð]
Nid dyna'r gwir.	That's not the truth.	[nɪd ˈdənär gwiːr]
Nid dacw Gaerdydd.	That's not Cardiff (in the distance).	[nɪd ˈdäkʊ gairˈdiːð]

Dim [dɪm] or **ddim** [ðɪm] can take the place of **nid** in spoken Welsh.

Exercise 3

Translate the following sentences.

1) Is that the reason? _____
2) No, that's not Bangor over there. _____
3) Yes, this is the truth. _____
4) No, that's not the spoon. _____
5) Yes, this is the woman. _____
6) This isn't the mountain. _____
7) Is this the city? _____
8) That's not the reason. _____
9) No, that's not the feeling. _____
10) Is that the house over there? _____

Lesson 6: The weather and points of the compass

The weather

Being so changeable in Wales, the weather is often discussed somewhere or other in a Welsh conversation. When referring to the weather, as there is no word for 'it' in Welsh, **hi** 'she' [hi] is used:

STATEMENT	ENGLISH	IPA
Mae hi'n oer heddiw.	It is cold today.	[maɪ hiːn ɔɪr ˈheðɪʊ]
Mae hi'n niwlog heno.	It is foggy tonight.	[maɪ hiːn ˈnɪʊlog ˈheðɪʊ]

As can be seen above, **mae hi'n** 'it is' [maɪ hiːn] is usually contracted to **mae'n** 'it's' [maɪn] in everyday speech:

STATEMENT	ENGLISH	IPA
Mae'n oer heddiw.	It is cold today.	[maɪn ɔɪr ˈheðɪʊ]
Mae'n niwlog heno.	It is foggy tonight.	[maɪn ˈnɪʊlog ˈheðɪʊ]

Vocabulary

ADJECTIVE	ENGLISH	IPA
braf*	fine	[brɑːv]
cymylog	cloudy	[kəmˈəlog]
gwyntog	windy	[ˈgwɪntog]
gwlyb	wet	[gʷliːb]
niwlog	foggy / misty	[ˈnɪʊlog]
stormus	stormy	[ˈstɔrmɪs]

* *Braf* does not mutate.

Soft mutation after the predicative marker 'yn'

Adjectives and nouns undergo soft mutation after the predicative marker **yn** [ən] / **'n** [n] (see **Week 3, Lesson 1**). The exceptions to this rule are:

(i) words beginning with the letters **ll** and **rh**:

SENTENCE	ENGLISH	IPA
Mae hi'n rhad.	It is cheap.	[maɪ hiːn r̥ɑːd]
Dydy hi ddim yn lleol.	She isn't local.	[ˈdədi hi ðɪm ən ɬeˑol]

(ii) the adjective **braf**:

QUESTION	ENGLISH	IPA
Ydy hi'n braf?	Is it fine? (weather)	[ˈədi hiːn ˈbrɑːv]

Here are some examples where **yn** causes the soft mutation. The mutated letter is underlined, and _ is used to indicate the mutated **g**:

IT IS / IT'S	ADJECTIVE	ENGLISH
Mae hi'n / Mae'n	**gymylog.**	It is / It's cloudy.
Mae hi'n / Mae'n	**_wyntog.**	It is / It's windy.
Mae hi'n / Mae'n	**_wlyb.**	It is / It's wet.
Mae hi'n / Mae'n	**gynnes.** (NW)	It is / It's warm.
Mae hi'n / Mae'n	**dwym.** (SW)	It is / It's warm.

Asking about the weather

Questions about the weather which correspond to 'Is it ...?' in English are constructed as follows:

QUESTION	ENGLISH	IPA
Ydy hi'n oer?	Is it cold?	[ˈədi hiːn ˈɔɪr]

REPLY	ENGLISH	IPA
Ydy, mae hi'n oer.	Yes, it is cold.	[ˈədi maɪ hiːn ˈɔɪr]
Nac ydy, dydy hi ddim yn oer.	No, it isn't cold.	[nɑːg ədi ˈdədi hi ˈðɪm ən ˈɔɪr]

Exercise 1

Translate the following sentences.

1) No, it isn't fine.

2) It is going to be windy this afternoon.

3) It isn't warm.

4) It is stormy.

5) It is misty.

6) Is it warm?

7) It is cloudy

8) Yes, it is cloudy

9) Is it wet?

10) It isn't foggy today, it is lovely.

Vocabulary

VERB-NOUN	ENGLISH	IPA
bwrw* (glaw)	to rain	[ˈbuːru (glau)]
bwrw eira	to snow	[ˈbuːru ˈəɪra]
bwrw cesair	to hail	[ˈbuːru ˈkɛsɛr]
bwrw eirlaw	to sleet	[ˈbuːru ˈəɪrlau]
rhewi	to freeze	[ˈɹɛui]

* *Rain is so common in Wales that people normally say* **mae'n bwrw** [maɪn ˈbuːru] *for 'It's raining.', with* **glaw** *'rain' being understood without being said.*

Remember, verb-nouns never mutate after **yn / 'n**:

IT IS / IT'S	VERB-NOUN	ENGLISH	IPA
Mae hi'n / Mae'n	bwrw glaw.	It is / It's raining.	[maɪ hiːn 'buru (glau)]
Mae hi'n / Mae'n	bwrw eira.	It is / It's snowing.	[maɪ hiːn 'buru 'əɪra]
Mae hi'n / Mae'n	rhewi.	It is / It's freezing.	[maɪ hiːn 'r̥ɛui]
Mae hi'n / Mae'n	bwrw cesair.	It is / It's hailing.	[maɪ hiːn 'buru 'kɛsɛr]

Exercise 2

*Mutate the Welsh word in brackets if necessary, remembering that verb-nouns do not mutate after **yn**, and neither does **braf**.*

1) Dydy hi ddim yn _____.   (cymylog)   (It isn't cloudy.)
2) Mae hi'n _____.   (cynnes)   (It is warm.)
3) Ydy hi'n _____? (NW)   (bwrw eirlaw)   (Is it sleeting?)
4) Mae hi'n _____.   (gwyntog)   (It is windy.)
5) Ydy hi'n _____.   (braf)   (Is it fine?)
6) Dydy hi ddim yn _____. (SW) (twym)   (It isn't warm.)
7) Mae'n _____.   (gwlyb)   (It's wet.)
8) Mae'n _____.   (rhewi)   (It's freezing.)

'Iawn'

Iawn [jaun] means 'very' and is used after the adjective it is describing:

PHRASE	ENGLISH	IPA
oer iawn	very cold	[ɔɪr jaun]
cynnes iawn	very warm	['kənɛs jaun]
gwyntog iawn	very windy	['gwɪntɔg jaun]
cryf iawn	very strong	[kriːv jaun]

Exercise 3

Translate the following sentences.

1) He is very busy.   _____
2) They are very warm.   _____
3) I am very strong.   _____
4) He isn't very bad.   _____
5) The chair is very small. _____

6) I'm not very tall. _____
7) She isn't very warm. _____
8) Are they very big? _____
9) It (*f.*) is very cheap. _____
10) Are we very good? _____

Points of the compass

Here are the four main points of the compass in Welsh:

DIRECTION	ENGLISH	IPA
gogledd	north / northern	[ˈgɔglɛð]
de	south / southern	[deː]
dwyrain	east / eastern	[ˈdʊɪraɪn]
gorllewin	west / western	[gɔrɬɛʊɪn]

For example:

	SENTENCE
WELSH	**Mae hi'n stormus yn y de heddiw.**
ENGLISH	It is stormy in the south today.
IPA	[maɪ hiːn ˈstɔrmɪs ən ə deː ˈheðɪʊ]

	QUESTION
WELSH	**Ydych chi'n byw yn y gorllewin?**
ENGLISH	Do you live in the west?
IPA	[ˈədɪ(χ) χiːn bɪʊ ən ə gɔrɬɛʊɪn]

Compass points are placed in front of the word they are describing:

PHRASE	ENGLISH	IPA
Gogledd Cymru	North Wales	[ˈgɔglɛð ˈkəmri]
Gorllewin Cymru	West Wales	[gɔrɬɛʊɪn ˈkəmri]
Dwyrain Timor	East Timor	[ˈdʊɪraɪn ˈtiˈmor]
De Affrica	South Africa	[deː ˈafrɪkä]

Before a place name, **gogledd**, **de**, etc., can translate as 'northern' 'southern', etc.

PHRASE	ENGLISH	IPA
Gogledd Iwerddon	Northern Ireland	[ˈgɔglɛð ɪʊˈɛrðon]
De Transvaal	Southern Transvaal	[deː tranzˈvɑːl]

And they can also translate as 'the north of', 'the south of', etc., before a place name:

PHRASE	ENGLISH	IPA
Gogledd yr Alban	the North of Scotland	[ˈgɔgleð ər ˈalban]
De Lloegr	the South of England	[ˈgɔgleð ˈɬɔɪgɛr]

Vocabulary

MASCULINE NOUN	ENGLISH	IPA
trueni	pity	[tɹiˈɛni]

ADVERBIAL	ENGLISH	IPA
ar hyn o bryd	at the moment	[ar hɪn o briːd]
o leia(f)	at least	[o ˈləɪä(v)]
yn nes ymlaen	later on	[ən nes əmˈlaɪn]
o gwbl	at all	[o ˈguˑbʊl]

ADJECTIVE	ENGLISH	IPA
trwm	heavy	[tɹʊm]

PLACE NAME	ENGLISH	IPA
Lloegr	England	[ˈɬɔɪgɛr]
Iwerddon	Ireland	[iˈwɛrðon]

Dialogue

Welsh Dialogue

Ann: Helo!
Megan: Helo! Sut wyt ti heddiw?
Ann: Da iawn, diolch! A ti?
Megan: Wedi blino, ond dw i'n edrych ymlaen at redeg heno. Mae hi'n oer iawn y prynhawn 'ma, ond o leiaf, dydy hi ddim yn wlyb. Dw i ddim yn hoffi'r glaw.
Ann: Ydy, ydy, oer iawn iawn. Dw i'n edrych ymlaen hefyd.
Megan: Mae hi'n mynd i fwrw glaw yn nes ymlaen. Dyn ni'n mynd i gael cawodydd trwm.
Ann: Ach a fi! Dw i ddim yn hoffi rhedeg yn y glaw o gwbl. A! Dyma'r merched eraill.
Mari: Helo.
Beth: Sut mae pawb?
Ann: Helo 'na. Dyn ni'n siarad am y tywydd. Mae glaw mawr ar y ffordd.
Mari: Ach a fi! Dyna drueni.
Beth: Wel, mae hi'n sych iawn mewn tafarn, wrth gwrs.
Ann: Dyna syniad da. Beth am fynd i'r dafarn?
Mari: Syniad gwych.
Megan: Syniad gwych iawn.

English Translation

Ann:	Hello!
Megan:	Hello! How are you today?
Ann:	Very well, thanks! And you?
Megan:	Tired, but I'm looking forward to running tonight. It is very cold this afternoon, but at least it isn't wet. I don't like the rain.
Ann:	Yes, yes. Very, very cold. I'm looking forward, too.
Megan:	It is going to rain later on. We are going to have heavy showers.
Ann:	Yuk! I don't like running in the rain at all. Ah! Here are the other girls.
Mari:	Hello.
Beth:	How is everyone?
Ann:	Hello there. We are talking about the weather. There is a lot of rain on the way.
Mari:	Yuk! That's a pity.
Beth:	Well, it is very dry in a pub, of course.
Ann:	That's a good idea. What about going to the pub?
Mari:	A great idea.
Megan:	A very great idea.

Lesson 7: Recap exercises

Exercise 1

Fill in the blanks using the correct pronouns.

1) Mae _____ gyrru adref. (He is driving home.)
2) Sut rwyt _____ 'r prynhawn 'ma? (How are you this afternoon?)
3) Maen _____ 'n ymolchi bob bore. (They get washed every morning.)
4) Ydych _____ 'n breuddwydio? (Do you dream? / Are you dreaming?)
5) Dyn _____ ddim yn rhedeg heno. (We aren't running tonight.)
6) Mae _____ 'n darllen yn y gadair. (She is reading in the chair.)
7) Dw _____ 'n gweithio mewn ysgol. (I work at a school.)
8) Ydy _____ 'n hoffi dysgu yn yr ysgol? (Does he like teaching at the school.)

If you have trouble completing this exercise, review **Week 3, Lesson 1** *to* **Lesson 4**.

Exercise 2

Turn the following imperfect aspect sentences into perfect aspect sentences.

For example:

Imperfect: Dw i'n rhedeg milltir. (I am running a mile.)
Perfect: Dw i wedi rhedeg milltir. (I have run a mile.)

1) Mae'r plant yn canu.

2) Mae o'n paentio'r ffenestr.

3) Rwyt ti'n gwisgo.

4) Dyn ni'n ymlacio.

5) Dych chi ddim yn cwrdd â'r athro.

6) Dw i'n gyrru tractor gwyrdd.

7) Maen nhw'n parcio'r car.

8) Ydych chi'n ysgrifennu at yr athrawes?

9) Dw i'n gwylio'r gêm.

10) Mae hi'n dysgu Cymraeg.

If you have trouble completing this exercise, review **Week 3, Lesson 2**.

Exercise 3

Fill in the blanks with the appropriate form of the present tense verb.

1) _____ i'n ymlacio heno. (I am relaxing tonight.)
2) Pryd _____ nhw'n codi? (When do they get up?)
3) _____ nhw'n siarad Cymraeg? (Do they speak Welsh?)
4) _____ hi ddim yn gyrru. (She doesn't drive.)
5) _____ ti'n hoffi brechdanau. (You like sandwiches.)
6) Ble _____ e'n chwarae? (Where is he playing?)
7) _____ chi'n mynd heno? (Are you going tonight?)
8) _____ ni'n breuddwydio? (Are we dreaming?)
9) _____ nhw ddim yn brysur. (They aren't busy.)
10) _____ hi'n gymylog? (Is it cloudy?)

If you have trouble completing this exercise, review **Week 3, Lesson 1** *to* **Lesson 4**.

Exercise 4

Translate the following sentences.

1) I don't like walking and I am not happy.

2) No idea.

3) Where do they live? They don't live in the North.

4) Is she warm?

5) When are you getting up?

6) Are they thinking about going to work?

7) We like horses.

8) Thank you very much.

9) How are you going to work.

10) Are we meeting tomorrow?

If you have trouble completing this exercise, review **Week 3, Lesson 1** *to* **Lesson 4**.

Exercise 5

*Connect the questions under **A** to the appropriate answers under **B**.*

A
1) Ble dych chi'n chwarae rygbi?
2) Diolch am weithio heno.
3) Wyt ti'n falch?
4) Ble dych chi'n dysgu Cymaeg?
5) Sut mae'r tywydd heddiw?
6) Pam mae hi'n dysgu Cymraeg?
7) Ydy hi'n wyntog?
8) Ydych chi'n byw yn y Gogledd?
9) Ble mae'r llwy?

B
a) Nac ydyn, yn y De.
b) Dw i'n dysgu mewn dosbarth nos.
c) Mae'r plant yn mynd i ysgol Gymraeg.
d) Dim problem.
e) Nac ydy, mae'n braf
f) Maen nhw'n gyrru.
g) Mae hi'n rhewi.
h) Dyn ni'n chwarae yn y parc.
i) Ydw, yn falch iawn.

10) Sut mae'r athrawon yn mynd i'r ysgol?   j)   Dyma hi yn y gegin.

If you have trouble completing this exercise, review **Week 3, Lesson 3**.

Exercise 6

Fill in the blanks using the word(s) in brackets, remembering to mutate where appropriate:

1) Dw i'n mynd i _____. (Betws Garmon)
2) Maen nhw'n mynd i _____. (Dinas Powys)
3) Dyn ni'n mynd i _____. (Llangollen)
4) Mae o'n mynd i _____. (NW) (Pontypridd)
5) Mae hi'n mynd i _____. (Gorseinon)
6) Rwyt ti'n mynd i _____. (Rhuthun)
7) Mae pawb yn mynd i _____. (Maesteg)
8) Dych chi'n mynd i _____. (Ffwrnais)
9) Dw i'n mynd i _____. (Tonypandy)
10) Mae Ann a Richard yn mynd i _____. (Caernarfon)

Vocabulary

ADVERBIAL	ENGLISH	IPA
eto	yet	['ɛto]

NOUN *(pl.)*	ENGLISH	IPA
newyddion	news	[nɛʊˈəðjon]

VERB-NOUN	ENGLISH	IPA
cysgu	to sleep	['kəsgi]
disgwyl	to expect	['dɪsgʊɪl]

Exercise 7

Fill in the gaps using either **yn** *'in' or* **mewn** *'in'.*

1) Dw i wedi darllen newyddion _____ y papur.
2) Ydy o'n dysgu _____ dosbarth?
3) Mae hi'n cwrdd â chi _____ siop.
4) Maen nhw'n chwarae _____ Llandudno.

5) Mae hi wedi parcio'r car _____ maes parcio.
6) Mae'r llyfr _____ y ddesg.
7) Mae'r gwas sifil yn cysgu _____ cadair.
8) Dyn ni'n byw _____ tŷ melyn.
9) Dw i wedi darllen am y ddinas _____ llyfrau hanes.
10) Ydych chi'n cwrdd â Megan _____ Aber-soch?

If you have trouble completing this exercise, review **Week 3, Lesson 2**.

Exercise 8

Give the correct 'yes' or 'no' response to the following questions.

For example:

Question: Ydy pawb yn hapus? (✓)
Answer: Ydyn.

For example:

Question: Ydw i'n parcio yn y maes parcio? (✗)
Answer: Nac wyt. / Nac ydych.

1) Ydy o'n gwisgo het felen? (✓) _____
2) Ydw i yn y newyddion? (✓) _____ *
3) Ydy hi'n wyntog heddiw? (✗) _____
4) Ydy'r cŵn yn cysgu? (✗) _____
5) Ydych chi'n ymolchi yn y cawod? (✓) _____ *
6) Ydy Elen yn siarad â'r bachgen tal? (✗) _____
7) Ydyn ni'n gwylio'r gêm heno? (✗) _____ *
8) Almaenwr ydy o? (✓) _____
9) Ydyn nhw'n hoffi brechdanau? (✓) _____
10) Wyt ti'n falch? (✗) _____

* *Each of these questions has two possible answers.*

If you have trouble completing this exercise, review **Week 3, Lesson 3**.

Exercise 9

Translate the following sentences.

1) Here are the local people. _____

2) Over there is the new bridge. _____
3) What a price! _____
4) This is a good spade. _____
5) Is this the way? _____
6) There is the package. _____
7) That's not the reason. _____
8) Is that the truth? _____
9) That's the problem. _____
10) That's a good book. _____

*If you have trouble completing this exercise, review **Week 3, Lesson 5**.*

Exercise 10

Fill in the blanks in the weather forecast by translating the word in brackets.

Heddiw mae hi'n _____ (dry) iawn yn y gogledd, ond mae hi'n _____ (misty) iawn yn y mynyddoedd ac mae hi'n mynd i _____ (sleet) yn y prynhawn. Yn y _____ (west), mae hi'n _____ (wet) iawn ar hyn o bryd ac yn y prynhawn mae hi'n mynd i _____ (snow). Dyn ni ddim yn disgwyl tywydd braf tan heno. Yn y dwyrain, dydy hi ddim yn _____ (wet) eto, ond mae _____ (rain) ar y ffordd. Mae hi'n mynd i _____ (freeze) heno. Dyn ni'n disgwyl tywydd _____ (windy) yn y de, ac mae hi'n mynd i fod yn _____ (stormy) iawn y prynhawn 'ma.

Week 4

Lesson 1: More adjectives

As we saw in **Week 1, Lesson 3**, adjectives generally come after nouns in Welsh:

NOUN + ADJECTIVE	ENGLISH	IPA
bachgen da	a good boy	[ˈbæχɡɛn dɑː]
ci mawr	a big dog	[kiː maʊr]
pentre(f) bach	a small village	[ˈpɛntɹe(v) bɑːχ]

You will also remember, and see from the above examples, that no change occurs to an adjective when it follows a masculine noun or a plural noun (see **Week 1, Lesson 5**):

MASCULINE NOUN (pl.) + ADJECTIVE	ENGLISH	IPA
bechgyn da	good boys	[ˈbɛχɡɪn dɑː]
cŵn mawr	big dogs	[kuːn maʊr]
pentrefi bach	small villages	[pɛnˈtɹevi bɑːχ]

FEMININE NOUN (pl.) + ADJECTIVE	ENGLISH	IPA
merched da	good girls	[ˈmɛrχɛd dɑː]
cathod mawr	big cats	[ˈkaθod maʊr]
trefi bach	small towns	[ˈtɹevi bɑːχ]

However, remember that adjectives preceded by feminine nouns undergo soft mutation:

FEMININE NOUN + ADJECTIVE	ENGLISH	IPA
merch dda	a good girl	[mɛrχ ðɑː]
cath fawr	a big cat	[kɑːθ vaʊr]
tre(f) fach	a big cat	[tɹeː(v) vaːχ]

Most adjectives nearly always come after the noun they are describing. But, when an adjective comes before a noun, the noun undergoes soft mutation. Here are some of the most common adjectives that precede the noun they describe:

ADJECTIVE	ENGLISH	IPA
hen	old	[heːn]
gwir	true / real	[gwiːr]
unig	only	[iˈnɪg]
prif	main / chief / head	[priːv]
annwyl	dear	[ˈänʊɪl]
hoff	favourite	[hoːf]

And here are some examples of the mutations they cause:

PHRASE	ENGLISH	IPA	NOUN PRE-MUTATION	ENGLISH
hen **dŷ**	old house	[heːn diː]	**tŷ**	house
annwyl **blentyn**	dear child	[ˈanʊɪl ˈblɛntɪn]	**plentyn**	child
gwir **reswm**	real reason	[gwiːr ˈrɛsʊm]	**rheswm**	reason
prif **ferch**	head girl	[priː(v) vɛrχ]	**merch**	girl
prif **reswm**	main reason	[priːv ˈrɛsʊm]	**rheswm**	reason
hoff **lyfr**	favourite book	[hoːf ˈləvr̩]	**llyfr**	book

The word **gwahanol** 'different' [gwäˈhɑnɔl] is often placed in front of the noun.

PHRASE	ENGLISH	IPA	NOUN PRE-MUTATION	ENGLISH
gwahanol **bethau**	different things	[gwäˈhɑnɔl ˈbɛθɛ]	**pethau**	things

The adjective **unig** [ˈiːnɪg] changes the meaning of the phrase in which it occurs, depending on whether it comes before or after the noun:

PHRASE OR QUESTION	ENGLISH	IPA
unig blentyn	only child	[ˈiːnɪg ˈblɛntɪn]
plentyn unig	lonely child	[ˈplɛntɪn ˈiːnɪg]

QUESTION	ENGLISH	IPA
Ai dyna'r unig reswm?	Is that the only reason'	[aɪ ˈdənar ˈiːnɪg ˈrɛsʊm]

Exercise 1

Complete the following, mutating the word in brackets if appropriate.

1) annwyl _____ (plant)   (dear children)
2) gwahanol _____ (cadair)   (a different chair)
3) hoff _____ (gwlad)   (favourite country)
4) y brif _____ (gwers)   (the main lesson)
5) hen _____ (dafad)   (an old sheep)
6) y gwir _____ (problem)   (the real problem)
7) yr unig _____ (rheswm)   (the only reason)
8) hen _____ (ffenestr)   (an old window)
9) gwir _____ (teimladau)   (true feelings)
10) yr unig _____ (newyddion) (the only news)

The adjective **prif** 'main' [priːv] mutates after the definite article **y** 'the' [ə] when it is describing a feminine singular noun:

Y + PRIF + FEMININE NOUN	ENGLISH	IPA
y brif ferch	the head girl	[ə briː(v) vɛrχ]

Remember that this is not the case with masculine singular nouns:

Y + PRIF + MASCULINE NOUN	ENGLISH	IPA
y prif fachgen	the head boy	[ə priː(v) ˈvaχgɛn]

Exercise 2

Translate the following phrases.

1) a lonely girl _____
2) old books _____
3) true north _____
4) the only spoon _____
5) the only boy _____
6) the main car park _____
7) the old country _____
8) a main road _____

IMPORTANT
In Welsh, like nouns, many adjectives have plural forms, and although the use of plural adjectives is rare in both spoken and written Welsh, they are used as collective nouns. Here are some of the most common:

enwog	famous	[ˈɛnwog]	**yr enwogion**	the famous	[ər ɛnˈwɔgjon]
marw	dead	[ˈmaru]	**y meirwon**	the dead	[ə ˈmeɪrwon]
gorau	best	[ˈgoːrɛ]	**y goreuon**	the best	[ə gorəɪon]
dall	blind	[daɬ]	**y deillion**	the blind	[ə ˈdəɪʎjon]

Lesson 2: Expressing possession

The use of 'mae' with definite and indefinite nouns

To express possession, in an affirmative statement in the present tense, **mae** [maɪ] is the form of '**bod**' which precedes:

(i) an indefinite noun which normally translates as 'there is' / 'there are'.
(ii) a definite noun, such as the name of a person or place.
(iii) an ordinary noun which is immediately preceded by 'the'.
(iv) a genitive noun phrase (see **Week 4, Lesson 5**).

Below are some examples of **mae** with indefinite nouns:

SENTENCE	ENGLISH	IPA
Mae llaeth yn y cwpan.	There is (some)* milk in the cup.	[maɪ ɬaɪθ ən ə ˈkʊpan]
Mae ci yn yr ystafell.	There is a dog in the room.	[maɪ kiː ən ər əsˈtaˑvɛɬ]
Mae blodau ar y ddesg.	There are flowers on the desk.	[maɪ ˈbloˑdɛ ar ə ðɛsg]

* *There is no Welsh word for 'some' or 'any' in expressions such as 'Is there **any** milk left?', 'Do you want **some** ice cream?'.*

Below are some examples of **mae** with definite nouns:

SENTENCE	ENGLISH	IPA
Mae'r llaeth yn y cwpan.	The milk is in the cup.	[maɪr ɬaɪθ ən ə ˈkʊpan]
Mae'r ci yn yr ystafell.	The dog is in the room.	[maɪr kiː ən ər əsˈtaˑvɛɬ]
Mae'r blodau ar y ddesg.	The flowers are on the desk.	[maɪr ˈbloˑdɛ ar ə ðɛsg]

Vocabulary

MASCULINE NOUN	ENGLISH	IPA	PLURAL FORM	IPA
cwpan	cup	[ˈkʊpan]	cwpanau	[kʊpˈɑˑnɛ]
ffôn	phone	[foːn]	ffonau	[ˈfoˑnɛ]
cae	field	[kaɪ]	caeau	[ˈkəɪɛ]

FEMININE NOUN	ENGLISH	IPA	PLURAL FORM	IPA
ystafell	room	[əsˈtaˑvɛɬ]	ystafelloedd	[əstavˈɛɬɔɪð]
llyfrgell	library	[ˈɬəvrgɛɬ]	llyfrgelloedd	[ɬəvrˈgɛɬɔɪð]
fflasg	flask	[flasg]	fflasgiau	[ˈflasgjɛ]

Exercise 1

Translate the following sentences.

1) There is strong coffee in the flask. _____

2) There are people reading in the library.
_____

3) There is a cat sleeping in the chair.
_____

4) There are classes this afternoon. _____

5) Richard is on the phone. _____

Asking a question about an indefinite noun

When asking a question, **oes** [ɔɪs] is the form used with indefinite nouns:

QUESTION	ENGLISH	IPA
Oes llaeth yn y cwpan?	Is there (some) milk in the cup?	[ɔɪs ɬaɪθ ən ə ˈkʊpan]
Oes ci yn yr ystafell?	Is there a dog in the room?	[ɔɪs kiː ən ər əsˈtaˑvɛɬ]
Oes blodau ar y ddesg?	Are there flowers on the desk?	[ɔɪs ˈbloˑdɛ ar ə ðɛsg]

Exercise 2

Translate the following questions.

1) Is there a German (man) in the class? _____
2) Is there a bull in the field? _____
3) Are there desks in the library? _____
4) Is there a book in the room? _____
5) Are there lots of cars in the car park? _____

The answer to all questions beginning with **oes** is either **oes** 'yes' [ɔɪs] or **nac oes** 'no' [naːg ɔɪs].

	QUESTION	REPLY
WELSH	**Oes llaeth yn y cwpan?**	**Oes.**
ENGLISH	Is there milk in the cup?	Yes.
IPA	[ɔɪs ɬaɪθ ən ə ˈkʊpan]	[ɔɪs]
WELSH	**Oes ci yn yr ystafell?**	**Nac oes.**
ENGLISH	Is there a dog in the room?	No.
IPA	[ɔɪs kiː ən ər əsˈtaˑvɛɬ]	[naːg ɔɪs]

Asking a question about a definite noun

When asking a question, **ydy** [ˈədi] is the form used with definite nouns:

QUESTION	ENGLISH	IPA
Ydy'r llaeth yn y cwpan?	Is the milk in the cup?	[ˈədir ɬaɪθ ən ə ˈkʊpan]
Ydy'r ci yn yr ystafell?	Is the dog in the room?	[ˈədir kiː ən ər əsˈtaˑvɛɬ]
Ydy'r blodau ar y ddesg?	Are the flowers on the desk?	[ˈədir ˈbloˑdɛ ar ə ðɛsg]

The answers to the questions above, as we saw in **Week 3, Lesson 3**, are **ydy** 'yes, it is' [ˈədi] and **ydyn** 'yes, they are' [ˈədɪn]:

Exercise 3

Translate the following questions.

1) Is Mr Williams in the class? _____
2) Is the bull in the field? _____
3) Are the desks in the library? _____
4) Is the book in the room? _____
5) Are the cars in the car park? _____

The negative form and indefinite nouns
The negative form used with indefinite nouns is **does dim** [dɔɪs dɪm]:

SENTENCE	ENGLISH	IPA
Does dim llaeth yn y cwpan.	There is no milk in the cup	[dɔɪs dɪm ɬaɪθ ən ə ˈkʊpan]
Does dim ci yn yr ystafell.	There is no dog in the roon	[dɔɪs dɪm kiː ən ər əsˈtɑːvɛɬ]

In spoken Welsh, the negative is often shortened to **'sdim** [sdɪm]:

SENTENCE	ENGLISH	IPA
'Sdim llaeth yn y cwpan.	There is no milk in the cup.	[sdɪm ɬaɪθ ən ə ˈkʊpan]
'Sdim ci yn yr ystafell.	There is no dog in the room.	[sdɪm kiː ən ər əsˈtɑːvɛɬ]

Vocabulary

MASCULINE NOUN	ENGLISH	IPA	PLURAL FORM	IPA
bwyd	food	[bʊɪd]	**bwydydd**	[ˈbʊɪdɪð]
bara	bread	[ˈbɑːra]		
te	tea	[teː]		

FEMININE NOUN	ENGLISH	IPA	PLURAL FORM	IPA
oergell	fridge	[ˈɔɪrgɛɬ]	**oergelloedd**	[ɔɪrˈgɛɬɔɪð]

ADJECTIVE	ENGLISH	IPA
glân	clean	[glɑːn]

Exercise 4

Translate the following negative sentences.

1) There aren't any lorries in the car park.

_____

2) There isn't any milk in the fridge.
___

3) There aren't any clean spoons.
___

4) There isn't a mountain in the country.
___

5) There aren't any prices on the things in the shop.
___

The negative form and definite nouns
The negative form used with definite nouns is **dydy (...) ddim** [ˈdədi (...) ðɪm]:

SENTENCE	ENGLISH	IPA
Dydy'r llaeth ddim yn y cwpan.	The milk isn't in the cup.	[ˈdədir ɬaɪθ ðɪm ən ə ˈkʊpan]
Dydy'r ci ddim yn yr ystafell.	The dog isn't in the room.	[ˈdədir kiː ðɪm ən ər əsˈtɑˑvɛɬ]

Exercise 5

Translate the following negative sentences.

1) The lorries aren't in the car park. ___

2) The milk isn't in the fridge. ___

3) The spoons aren't clean. ___

4) Mr Williams isn't in the country. ___

5) The food isn't cheap. ___

Exercise 6

*Fill in the gaps with the appropriate forms of **bod**:*

For example:

Question: ___ papur yn y ddesg?
Answer: Oes papur yn y ddesg?

1) ___   cawod yn y tŷ?   Is there a shower in the house?
2) ___   dim bwyd yn yr oergell.   There's no food in the fridge.
3) ___   Siân yna?   Is Siân there.

4) _____	bara yn y gegin.	There's some bread in the kitchen.
5) _____	desg yn yr ystafell?	Is there a desk in the room?
6) _____	dim te yma.	There's no tea here.
7) _____	'r bechgyn ddim yna.	The boys are not here.

Vocabulary

MASCULINE NOUN	ENGLISH	IPA	PLURAL FORM	IPA
bwrdd (NW)	table	[bʊrð]	**byrddau**	[ˈbərðɛ]
teledu	television	[telˈɛdi]	**setiau teledu**	[ˈsɛtjɛ tɛlˈɛdi]

FEMININE NOUN	ENGLISH	IPA	PLURAL FORM	IPA
bord (SW)	table	[bɔrd]	**bordydd**	[ˈbɔrdɪð]

Exercise 7

Answer the following according to the example given below.

For example:

Question: Oes llaeth yn yr oergell? (✓)
Answer: Oes, mae llaeth yn yr oergell.

1) Oes newyddion yn y papur? (✗) _____

2) Oes buwch yn y cae? (✓) _____

3) Oes llyfrau yn y llyfrgell? (✓) _____

4) Oes Cymry yn yr ysgol? (✗) _____

5) Oes meddyg yn yr ystafell? (✓) _____

6) Oes esgidiau ar y bwrdd? (✗) _____

7) Oes cath yn y ffenestr? (✗) _____

8) Oes gêm ar y teledu heno? (✓) _____

One of the main differences between the Welsh spoken in North Wales and the language spoken in South Wales is the way possession ('I have a car', 'they have a large house', 'he hasn't got a dog', etc.) is expressed. We will look at each version separately.

Expressing possession in South Wales

Possession is expressed in South Welsh by using the conjuction **gyda** 'with' ['gədä], followed by an independent pronoun. The verb form used is the third person singular form of '**bod**':

SENTENCE	ENGLISH	IPA
Mae car gyda fi.	I have a car. (*lit.* [There] is [a] car with me.)	[maɪ kar 'gədä viː]

As you can see, the object owned is placed between **mae** and **gyda**:

	MAE	OBJECT	GYDA FI
SENTENCE	Mae	rheswm	gyda fi.
IPA	[maɪ	'r̥ɛsʊm	'gədä viː]
ENGLISH	I have a reason.		

	MAE	OBJECT	GYDA FI
SENTENCE	Mae	teimlad da	gyda fi.
IPA	[maɪ	'təɪmlad dɑː	'gədä viː]
ENGLISH	I have a good feeling.		

	MAE	OBJECT	GYDA FI
SENTENCE	Mae	newyddion	gyda fi.
IPA	[maɪ	nɛʊ'əðjon	'gədä viː]
ENGLISH	I have some news.		

The tense can be altered by changing the verb form:

SENTENCE	ENGLISH	IPA
Roedd car gyda fi.	I had a car. (*lit.* [There] was [a] car with me.)	[rɔɪð kar 'gədä viː]

Roedd [rɔɪð] implies the past imperfect. We will see this again in **Week 6, Lesson 1**.

Below are the personal forms in the present tense:

SENTENCE	ENGLISH	IPA
Mae car gyda fi.	I have a car.	[maɪ kar 'gədä viː]
Mae car gyda ti.	You have a car. (*fam.*)	[maɪ kar 'gədä tiː]
Mae car gyda fe.	He has a car.	[maɪ kar 'gədä veː]
Mae car gyda hi.	She has a car.	[maɪ kar 'gədä hiː]
Mae car gyda ni.	We have a car.	[maɪ kar 'gədä niː]
Mae car gyda chi.	You have a car. (*pl.*) (*sing. formal*)	[maɪ kar 'gədä χiː]
Mae car gyda nhw.	They have a car.	[maɪ kar 'gədä n̥uː]

You will have noticed, while studying possession, that the **i** previously seen in **dw i** 'I am' [dwiː] and the **e** [eː] seen in **mae e** [maɪ eː] have become **fi** [viː] and **fe** [veː], respectively. **I** [iː] and **e** [eː] are the forms used after a verb, and are called auxiliary pronouns because they are dependent on the verb that precedes them. **Fi** and **fe** are used when not following a verb, as they are independent pronouns, called such because they stand independently of a verb.

Vocabulary

MASCULINE NOUN	ENGLISH	IPA
arian (SW)	money	['arjän]
pres (NW)	money	[preːs]

Exercise 8

Translate the following sentences expressing possession.

1) I have some money.
2) We have a lot of time.
3) He has a new shower.
4) The cat has some cream.
5) You have a big dog.
6) The town has a large car park.
7) The lorry has clean windows.
8) She has some good friends.
9) You have a lovely house. (*fam.*)
10) They have an old spade.

Expressing possession in North Wales

A lot of Welsh prepositions decline, i.e. they possess different forms depending on number and person, similar to verbs. In North Welsh, possession is expressed using the declined preposition **gan** 'by' [gan], which causes the soft mutation (see **Week 1, Lesson 5**), in conjunction with the third person singular form of **bod** 'to be' [boːd]. **Gen i** is the first person singular form of **gan**:

SENTENCE	ENGLISH	IPA
Mae gen i gar.	I have a car. (*lit.* [There] is by me [a] car.)	[maɪ gɛn iː gar]

The tense can be altered by changing the verb form:

SENTENCE	ENGLISH	IPA
Roedd gen i gar.	I had a car. (*lit.* [There] was by me [a] car.)	[rɔɪð gɛn iː gar]

Below are the declined personal forms in the present tense:

SENTENCE	ENGLISH	IPA
Mae gen i gar.	I have a car.	[maɪ gɛn iː gar]
Mae gen ti gar.	You have a car. (*fam.*)	[maɪ gɛn ţi: gar]
Mae ganddo fo gar.	He has a car.	[maɪ 'gändo voː gar]
Mae ganddi hi gar.	She has a car.	[maɪ 'gänði hiː gar]
Mae ganddon ni gar.	We have a car.	[maɪ 'gändo(n) niː gar]
Mae ganddoch chi gar.	You have a car. (*pl.*) (*sing. formal*)	[maɪ 'gändo(χ) χiː gar]
Mae ganddyn nhw gar.	They have a car.	[maɪ 'gänðɪ(n) ŋuː gar]

We will deal with declining prepositions in more detail in **Week 10, Lesson 2**

Exercise 9

Translate the following sentences expressing possession, using the personal forms of ***gan***.

1) I have some money.
2) We have a lot of time.
3) He has a new shower.
4) The cat has some cream.
5) You have a big dog.
6) The town has a large car park.
7) The lorry has clean windows.
8) She has some good friends.
9) You have a lovely house. (*fam.*)
10) They have an old spade.

Asking and responding to a question involving a singular indefinite noun

As we saw earlier, **oes** is substituted for **mae** when asking a question involving an indefinite noun (subject):

QUESTION	ENGLISH	IPA
Oes car gyda chi? (SW)	Have you got a car?	[ɔɪs kar 'gədä χiː]
Oes ganddoch chi gar? (NW)	Have you got a car?	[ɔɪs 'gändo(χ) χiː gar]

The response to the above are **oes** 'yes' [ɔɪs] and **nac oes** 'no' [nɑːg ɔɪs]:

REPLY	ENGLISH	IPA
Oes.	Yes.	[ɔɪs]
Nac oes.	No.	[nɑːg ɔɪs]

Vocabulary

MASCULINE NOUN	ENGLISH	IPA	PLURAL FORM	IPA
newid	change	[ˈnɛʊɪd]	**newidiadau**	[nɛʊɪdˈjɑˑdɛ]
anifail anwes	pet	[anˈiˑvɛl ˈanwɛs]	**anifeiliaid anwes**	[anɪˈvəɪljɛd ˈanwɛs]

ADVERBIAL	ENGLISH	IPA
digon o (SM)	enough	[ˈdiˑgon oː]

Exercise 10

Translate the following sentences using either North Welsh or South Welsh forms.

1) Have you got any strong coffee? *(fam.)* _____

2) Have I got enough time? _____

3) Does the cat have some milk? _____

4) Has she got a flask? _____

5) Does he have any children? _____

6) Does the postman have a package for us? _____

7) Have you got enough food? _____

8) Have we got any clean spoons? _____

9) Do they have any pets? _____

10) Have you got any change? _____

Asking and responding to a question involving a singular definite noun

Take the following question about the definite subject **y car** 'the car' [ə kar]:

QUESTION	ENGLISH	IPA
Ydy'r car gyda chi? (SW)	Have you got the car?	[ˈədɪr kar ˈgədä χiː]
Ydy'r car ganddoch chi? (NW)	Have you got the car?	[ˈədɪr kar ˈgänðo(χ) χiː]

The responses to such questions are **ydy** 'yes' [ˈədi] and **nac ydy** 'no' [nɑːg ˈədi]:

REPLY	ENGLISH	IPA
Ydy.	Yes.	[ˈədi]
Nac ydy.	No.	[nɑːg ˈədi]

Asking a question involving a plural indefinite noun

Below are examples of questions with a plural indefinite subject:

QUESTION	ENGLISH	IPA
Oes plant gyda chi? (SW)	Do you have children?	[ɔɪs plant ˈgədä χiː]
Oes ganddoch chi blant? (NW)	Do you have children?	[ɔɪs ˈgänðo(χ) χiː blant]

As in the case of an indefinite singular noun, the response to the above are **oes** 'yes' [ɔis] and **nac oes** 'no' [nɑːg ɔɪs]:

REPLY	ENGLISH	IPA
Oes.	Yes.	[ɔɪs]
Nac oes.	No.	[nɑːg ɔɪs]

Asking and responding to a question involving a plural definite noun

Below are examples of questions with a plural definite subject:

QUESTION	ENGLISH	IPA
Ydy'r plant gyda chi?* (SW)	Are *the* children with you?	[ˈədir plant ˈgədä χiː]
Ydy'r plant efo chi? (NW)	Are *the* children with you?	[ˈədir plant ˈevo χiː]

* This sentence can also mean 'Do you have the children'.

The responses to questions about plural definite subjects are **ydyn** 'yes' [ˈədɪn] and **nac ydyn** 'no' [nɑːg ˈədɪn]:

REPLY	ENGLISH	IPA
Ydyn.	Yes.	[ˈədɪn]
Nac ydyn.	No.	[nɑːg ˈədɪn]

Exercise 11

Translate the following using either North Welsh or South Welsh possessive forms.

1) Does she have the things? Yes. _____
2) Do you have the time? No. _____
3) Do they have the money? Yes. _____
4) Does the postman have the parcel? No.
_____

5) Do we have the flask? No. _____
6) Does he have the spoon? No. _____
7) Do you have the change? Yes. _____
8) Does he have the spade? No. _____
9) Do they have the flowers? Yes. _____
10) Do you have the desk? No. _____

Forming the negative with an indefinite noun

In order to form the negative with an indefinite noun, **does dim** is substituted for **mae**.

SENTENCE	ENGLISH	IPA
Does dim car gyda fi. (SW)	I haven't got a car.	[dɔɪs dɪm kar ˈgədä viː]
Does gen i ddim car. (NW)	I haven't got a car.	[d̪ɔɪs gɛn iː ðɪm kar]
Does dim ceir gyda fi. (SW)	I haven't got any cars.	[dɔɪs dɪm kəɪr ˈgədä viː]
Does gen i ddim ceir. (NW)	I haven't got any cars.	[d̪ɔɪs gɛn iː ðɪm kəɪr]

Forming the negative with a definite noun

If the subject is definite, then the corresponding forms would be **dydy (...) ddim** [ˈdədi (...) ðɪm].

Below are some South Welsh examples:

SENTENCE	ENGLISH	IPA
Dydy'r car ddim gyda fi.	I haven't got the car.	[ˈdədir kar ðɪm ˈgədä viː]
Dydy'r car ddim gyda'r dyn.	The man doesn't have the car.	[ˈdədir kar ðɪm ˈgədär diːn]
Dydy'r ceir ddim gyda fi.	I haven't got the cars.	[ˈdədir kəɪr ðɪm ˈgədä viː]
Dydy'r ceir ddim gyda'r dyn.	The man doesn't have the cars.	[ˈdədir kəɪr ðɪm ˈgədär diːn]

The following are the North Welsh forms:

SENTENCE	ENGLISH	IPA
Dydy'r car ddim gen i.	I haven't got the car.	[ˈd̪ədir kar ðɪm gɛn iː]
Dydy'r car ddim gen ti.	You haven't got the car. (fam.)	[ˈd̪ədir kar ðɪm gɛn t̪iː]
Dydy'r car ddim ganddo fo.	He hasn't got the car.	[ˈd̪ədir kar ðɪm ˈgänðo voː]
Dydy'r car ddim ganddi hi.	She hasn't got the car.	[ˈd̪ədir kar ðɪm ˈgänði hiː]
Dydy'r car ddim gan y dyn.	The man doesn't have the car.	[ˈd̪ədir kar ðɪm gan ə d̪iːn]

Exercise 12

Turn the following sentences into negative ones, choosing either SW or NW forms or both.

1) Mae'r arian gyda fi. (SW)/Mae gen i'r pres. (NW)

2) Mae rheswm da gyda ti. (SW)/Mae gen ti reswm da. (NW)

3) Mae'r teledu gyda Mr Jones. (SW)/Mae gan Mr Jones y teledu. (NW)

4) Mae'r blodau gyda ni. (SW)/Mae ganddon ni'r blodau. (NW)

5) Mae fflasg dda gyda hi. (SW)/Mae ganddi hi fflasg dda. (NW)

6) Mae ffôn newydd gyda nhw. (SW)/Mae ganddyn nhw ffôn newydd. (NW)

7) Mae cwpan mawr gyda chi. (SW)/Mae ganddoch chi gwpan mawr. (NW)

8) Mae llawer o fwyd gyda'r ci. (SW)/Mae gan y ci lawer o fwyd. (NW)

9) Mae'r newid gyda hi. (SW)/Mae ganddi hi'r newid. (NW)

10) Mae hen gar gyda fe. (SW)/Mae ganddo fo hen gar. (NW).

Idioms with 'gyda' / 'gan'

Gyda and **gan** are used in some idiomatic expressions.

Below are South Welsh examples:

EXPRESSION	ENGLISH	IPA
Mae'n dda gyda fi.	I'm glad.	[maɪn ðɑː ˈgədä viː]
Mae'n ddrwg gyda fi.	I'm sorry.	[maɪn ðruːg ˈgədä viː]
Mae'n gas gyda fi.	I hate.	[maɪn gɑːs ˈgədä viː]
Mae pen tost gyda fi.	I've got a headache.	[maɪ pɛn tɔst ˈgədä viː]

Here are their North Welsh equivalents:

EXPRESSION	ENGLISH	IPA
Mae'n dda gen i.	I'm glad.	[maɪn ðɑː gɛn iː]
Mae'n ddrwg gen i.	I'm sorry.	[main ðruːg gɛn iː]
Mae'n gas gen i.	I hate.	[main gɑːs gɛn iː]

| Mae gen i gur pen. | I've got a headache. | [maɪ gɛn iː gɪːr pɛn] |

We will learn more of how to talk about illness in **Week 10, Lesson 4**.

Parenthesis

Parenthesis is a word, or words, inserted into a sentence or passage. The phrases **gyda fi** and **gen i**, are adverbial. Adverbials usually come at the end of a sentence in Welsh, but they can also occur in the middle of a sentence as parenthesis which, in turn, causes the soft mutation (see **Week 4, Lesson 2**). Here is an example without mutation:

SENTENCE WITHOUT MUTATION	ENGLISH
Mae car gyda fi.	I've got a car.

Below, the adverbial is placed in the middle of the sentence, thereby causing a soft mutation which changes **car** to **gar**:

SENTENCE WITH MUTATION	ENGLISH
Mae gyda fi <u>gar</u>.	I've got a car.

As we have seen, in North Wales **gen i** is placed after **mae** to express possession, thus triggering soft mutation:

SENTENCE WITH MUTATION	ENGLISH	IPA
Mae gen i <u>broblem</u>.	I've got a problem.	[maɪ gɛn i ˈbrɔblɛm]

In idioms like 'I'm glad', 'I hate', etc., **gyda fi** and **gen i** always come in the middle of the sentence, and so they cause soft mutation:

MUTATED SENTENCE	ENGLISH	IPA	PHRASE PRE-MUTATION
Mae'n dda gyda fi <u>gwrdd</u> â chi. (SW)	I'm glad to meet you.	[maɪn ðaː ˈgədä viː gʊrð ä χiː]	cwrdd â chi
Mae'n gas ganddo fo <u>ddinasoedd</u>. (NW)	He hates cities.	[maɪn gaːs ˈgänðo voː ðinˈasɔɪð]	dinasoedd
Mae'n ddrwg gen i <u>glywed</u> hynny. (NW)	I'm sorry to hear that.	[maɪn ðrug gɛn iː ˈgləʊɛd ˈhəni]	clywed hynny

---

Vocabulary

VERB-NOUN	ENGLISH	IPA
clywed	to hear	[ˈkləʊɛd]

Lesson 3: Days of the week

Although Welsh is a Celtic language, as in French and other Romance languages based on Latin, certain days of the week are named after Roman gods:

ROMAN GOD	ENGLISH	IPA
Mawrth	Mars	[maʊrθ]
Mercher	Mercury	[ˈmɛrχer]
Iau	Jove (Jupiter)	[jaɪ]
Gwener	Venus	[ˈgwɛnɛr]
Sadwrn	Saturn	[ˈsɑˑdʊrn]

The above means that **dydd Mawrth** 'Tuesday' [diːð maʊrθ] is also 'Mars' day', and that **dydd Gwener** 'Friday' [diːð ˈgwɛnɛr] is also 'Venus' day', etc.

Here are the days of the week in Welsh:

DAY OF THE WEEK	ENGLISH	IPA
dydd Sul	Sunday	[diːð siːl]
dydd Llun	Monday	[diːð ɬiːn]
dydd Mawrth	Tuesday	[diːð maʊrθ]
dydd Mercher	Wednesday	[diːð ˈmɛrχer]
dydd Iau	Thursday	[diːð jaɪ]
dydd Gwener	Friday	[diːð ˈgwɛnɛr]
dydd Sadwrn	Saturday	[diːð ˈsɑˑdʊrn]

In North Welsh, remember that:

(i) **u** is pronounced [ɨ];
(ii) **d** is pronounced [d̪]; &
(iii) **ll** is is pronounced [ɬ].

(See **Week 1, Lesson 1**)

For Example: [d̪iːð siːɬ], [d̪iːð ɬiːn] and [d̪iːð jaɪ]

Dydd Llun, **dydd Mawrth**, etc., are the names of the days of the week. If you want to describe a specific day of the week, **dydd** [diːð] undergoes soft mutation. There is no word which is the equivalent to the English word 'on' in this context.

	SENTENCE
WELSH	**Dw i'n mynd i Aberystwyth _ddydd_ Llun.**
ENGLISH	I am going to Aberystwyth on Monday.
IPA	[dwiːn mɪnd iː abɛrˈəstwɪθ ðiːð ɬiːn]
WELSH	**Mae'r parti _ddydd_ Gwener.**
ENGLISH	The party is on Friday.
IPA	[maɪr ˈparti ðiːð ˈgwɛnɛr]
WELSH	**Maen nhw'n paentio'r tŷ _ddydd_ Sul.**

ENGLISH	They are painting the house on Sunday.
IPA	[mae(n) ŋuːn ˈpəɪntjor tiː ðiːð siːl]

Vocabulary

MASCULINE NOUN	ENGLISH	IPA	PLURAL FORM	IPA
parti	party	[ˈparti]	**partïon**	[partiˑon]

PREPOSITION	ENGLISH	IPA
ar (SM)	on	[ar]

If you wish to talk about an event which occurs 'on Mondays' or 'on Fridays', etc., the preposition **ar** 'on' [ar] is used:

	SENTENCE
WELSH	**Dyn ni'n mynd i'r dosbarth Cymraeg ar ddydd Iau.**
ENGLISH	We go to the Welsh class on Thursdays.
IPA	[də(n) niːn mɪnd iːr ˈdɔsbarθ kəmˈraɪg ar ðiːð jaɪ]

	SENTENCE
WELSH	**Maen nhw'n chwarae rygbi ar ddydd Sadwrn.**
ENGLISH	They play rugby on Saturdays.
IPA	[maɪ(n) ŋuːn ˈχwaˑre ˈrəgbi ar ðiːð ˈsaˑdʊrn]

The word for 'night' is **nos** [noːs]. As it is a feminine noun, adjectives following it undergo soft mutation:

NIGHT OF THE WEEK	ENGLISH	IPA
nos Sul	Sunday evening / night	[noːs siːl]
nos Lun	Monday evening / night	[noːs liːn]
nos Fawrth	Tuesday evening / night	[noːs vaʊrθ]
nos Fercher	Wednesday evening / night	[noːs ˈvɛrχɛr]
nos Iau	Thursday evening / night	[noːs jaɪ]
nos Wener	Friday evening / night	[noːs ˈwɛnɛr]
nos Sadwrn	Saturday evening / night	[noːs ˈsaˑdʊrn]

Following the same pattern, **bore** and **prynhawn** come before the day of the week to express 'Wednesday morning', 'Monday afternoon', etc.:

	SENTENCE
WELSH	**Dw i'n mynd i Abertawe bore dydd Iau.**
ENGLISH	I am going to Swansea on Thursday morning.
IPA	[dwiːn mɪnd iː abɛrˈtaʊɛ ˈboˑrɛ diːð jaɪ]

WELSH	**Maen nhw'n mynd i'r pwll nofio prynhawn dydd Iau.**
ENGLISH	They are going to the swimming pool on Thursday afternoon.
IPA	[maɪ(n) n̪ʊːn mɪnd iːr pʊːɬ 'nɔvjo prɪn'haʊn diːð jaɪ]

If you want to emphasise that you do an activity regularly, you can use **pob** 'every' [poːb] in front of the day of the week. This mutates to **bob** when used adverbially, as below:

	SENTENCE
WELSH	**Dw i'n mynd i'r gwely <u>bob</u> nos am ddeg o'r gloch.**
ENGLISH	I go to bed every night at ten o'clock.
IPA	[dwiːn mɪnd ir 'gwɛly boːb noːs am ðeːg oːr gloːχ]

Vocabulary

MASCULINE NOUN	ENGLISH	IPA	PLURAL FORM	IPA
gwely	bed	['gwɛli]	**gwelyau**	[gwɛl'iˑɛ]
capel	chapel	['käpɛl]	**capeli**	[kä'pɛli]
sglodyn	chip	['sglɔdɪn]	**sglodion**	['sglɔdjon]
penwythnos	weekend	[pɛn'ʊɪθnos]	**penwythnosau**	[pɛnʊɪθ'nɔsɛ]

FEMININE NOUN	ENGLISH	IPA	PLURAL FORM	IPA
campfa	gym	['kampva]	**campfeydd**	[kamp'vəɪð]
eglwys	church	['ɛglʊɪs]	**eglwysi**	[ɛg'lʊɪsi]

VERB-NOUN	ENGLISH	IPA
cael	to get / to have / to obtain	[kaɪl]
bod	to be	[boːd]
gwneud	to do / to make	[gʷnəɪd]
siopa	to shop / to do the shopping	['ʃɔpä]

PREPOSITION	ENGLISH	IPA
ar ôl	after	[ar oːl]
dros (SM)	over	[drɔs]

ADJECTIVE	ENGLISH	IPA
parod	ready	['pɑˑrod]

MISCELLANEOUS	ENGLISH	IPA
wedi blino	tired	['wɛdi 'bliˑno]
iawn	all right	[jaʊn]
pob	every	[poːb]

Dialogue

Welsh Dialogue

Ann:	Prynhawn da.
Gareth:	Prynhawn da. Sut dych chi?
Ann:	Iawn diolch, a chi?
Gareth:	Wedi blino, ond yn barod am y penwythnos.
Ann:	Mae gen i lawer o bethau i'w gwneud dros y penwythnos. Dw i'n mynd i fod yn brysur iawn.
Gareth:	Beth dych chi'n mynd i'w wneud?
Ann:	Dw i'n mynd i'r gampfa ddydd Gwener ar ôl yr ysgol.
Gareth:	Beth dych chi'n mynd i'w wneud ar ôl mynd i'r gampfa?
Ann:	Dw i'n mynd i siopa. Dw i'n gwneud y siopa bob prynhawn dydd Gwener ar ôl yr ysgol. Dw i'n mynd i'r siop sglodion wedyn; dyn ni'n cael sglodion i de bob nos Wener.
Gareth:	Sglodion? Ar ôl mynd i'r gampfa?

English Translation

Ann:	Good afternoon.
Gareth:	Good afternoon. How are you?
Ann:	Fine, thanks, and you?
Gareth:	Tired but ready for the weekend.
Ann:	I have a lot of thing to do over the weekend. I'm going to be very busy.
Gareth:	What are you going to do?
Ann:	I'm going to the gym on Friday after school.
Gareth:	What are you going to do after going to the gym?
Ann:	I'm going to shop. I do the shopping every Friday afternoon after school. I go to the chip shop afterwards; we have chips for tea every Friday evening.
Gareth:	Chips? After going to the gym?

Exercise 1

Complete the following sentences by translating and using the words in brackets.

1) Dw i'n mynd i'r gampfa _____.
   (on Friday evenings)

2) Mae e'n (SW)/o'n (NW) mynd i Langollen _____.
   (on Sunday)

3) Dyn ni'n mynd adref _____.
   (Thursday night)

4) Maen nhw'n siopa _____.
   (on Saturdays)

5) Mae hi'n canu yn yr eglwys _____.
   (every Sunday morning)

6) Dyn ni'n cael coffi _____.
   (every Friday afternoon)

7) Mae e'n (SW)/o'n (NW) cwrdd â Siân _____.
   (on Tuesdays)

8) Dych chi'n cael ffenestri newydd _____.
   (on Wednesday)

9) Dydy hi ddim yn gweithio _____.
   (every Monday)

10) Mae hi'n gwylio'r gêm _____.
    (on Saturdays)

'Dw i'n mynd i'r eglwys'

We have already seen **i'r** 'to the' [iːr]. The definite article is used before places you go to regularly, like work, places of worship, town, bed, etc.:

	SENTENCE
WELSH	**Dw i'n mynd i'r gwely.**
ENGLISH	I am going to bed. (*lit.* I am going to the bed.)
IPA	[dwiːn mɪnd iːr 'gwɛli]
WELSH	**Dw i'n mynd i'r gwaith.**
ENGLISH	I am going to work. (*lit.* I am going to the work.)
IPA	[dwiːn mɪnd iːr gwaɪθ]
WELSH	**Dw i'n mynd i'r ysgol.**
ENGLISH	I am going to school. (*lit.* I am going to the school.)
IPA	[dwiːn mɪnd iːr 'əsgol]
WELSH	**Dw i'n mynd i'r capel.**
ENGLISH	I am going to chapel. (*lit.* I am going to the chapel.)
IPA	[dwiːn mɪnd iːr 'kapel]
WELSH	**Dw i'n mynd i'r dre(f).**
ENGLISH	I am going to town. (*lit.* I am going to the town.)
IPA	[dwiːn mɪnd iːr drɛː(v)]

Vocabulary

MASCULINE NOUN	ENGLISH	IPA	PLURAL FORM	IPA
pwll nofio	swimming pool	[puɬ 'nɔvjo]	**pyllau nofio**	['pəɬɛ 'nɔvjo]
ysbyty	hospital	[əs'bəti]	**ysbytai**	[əs'bətai]

FEMININE NOUN	ENGLISH	IPA	PLURAL FORM	IPA
sinema	cinema	['sɪnɛma]	**sinemâu**	[sɪnɛm'ai]

ADVERBIAL	ENGLISH	IPA
trwy'r dydd	all day	[tr̥ʊɪr diːð]

Dialogue

Welsh Dialogue

Gareth: Dw i'n mynd i'r sinema nos Wener, ond does dim llawer o bethau eraill gyda fi i'w gwneud dros y penwythnos.
Ann: Bore dydd Sadwrn, dyn ni'n mynd i siopa yn y dref. Dw i eisiau cael het newydd.
Gareth: Ydych chi'n mynd i siopa trwy'r dydd?
Ann: Nac ydyn. Dim trwy'r dydd. Yn y prynhawn, dyn ni'n mynd i'r pwll nofio.
Gareth: Ac yn cael sglodion wedyn?
Ann: Nage!

English Translation

Gareth: I'm going to the cinema Friday evening, but I don't have a lot of other things to do over the weekend.
Ann: Saturday morning, we are going to shop in town. I want to get a new hat.
Gareth: Are you going to shop all day?
Ann: No, not all day. In the afternoon, we are going to the swimming pool.
Gareth: And having chips afterwards?
Ann: No!

'Trwy'r dydd'

The preposition **trwy** [tɾʊɪ] means 'through' / 'throughout', and it is used in many adverbial expressions to mean 'all' / 'throughout'.

ADVERBIAL	ENGLISH	IPA
trwy'r nos	all night	[tɾʊɪr noːs]
trwy'r bore	all morning	[tɾʊɪr ˈboːrɛ]

Exercise 2

Translate the following sentences.

1) He is shopping on Wednesday afternoon.

2.) Do you run on a Friday?

3) Are you going to town on Tuesday night?

4) I am expecting to work Wednesday night.

5) They are eating chips in the park.
   _____

6) We have a shower every day.
   _____

7) I am going to the swimming pool on Monday morning.
   _____

8) We aren't walking to school on Tuesday.
   _____

9) It is going to snow all night on Saturday.
   _____

10) They go to chapel on Sunday.
    _____

IMPORTANT
Note the difference between:

Mae cawod gyda hi. / Mae ganddi hi gawod.
She has a shower. (She owns a shower.)

[maɪ 'kaʊod 'gədä hiː] / [maɪ 'gänði hiː 'gaʊod̪]

Mae hi'n cael cawod.
She has a shower. (She bathes in a shower regularly.)

[maɪ hiːn kail 'kaʊod]

Lesson 4: The present relative form of 'bod' (to be)

Vocabulary

MASCULINE NOUN	ENGLISH	IPA
rhywun	someone	['r̥ʊɪn]
radio	radio	['radjo]

FEMININE NOUN	ENGLISH	IPA	PLURAL FORM	IPA
iaith	language	[jaɪθ]	**ieithoedd**	['jəɪθɔɪð]

ADJECTIVE	ENGLISH	IPA
blin	angry	[bliːn]
dig	angry	[diːg]

VERB-NOUN	ENGLISH	IPA
gweld	to see	[gwɛld]
(ad)nabod*	to know (a person, place)	[(ad)'nɑˈbod]

gwybod	to know (a fact)	[ˈgwiːbod]
digwydd	to happen	[ˈdɪgwɪð]
ennill	to win / to gain	[ˈɛnɨɬ]
adeiladu	to build	[adəɪˈlɑːdi]
siarad â (AM)	to speak to	[ˈʃɑrad ä]

* **Adnabod** is usually pronounced **nabod** [ˈnɑːbod] in everyday speech, and so **ad** has been placed in brackets to reflect this.

'Faint'

We have already seen the word **pwy** 'who' [pʊɪ]. **Pwy** is an interrogative pronoun and is only used to ask questions:

QUESTION	ENGLISH	IPA
Pwy ydych chi?	Who are you?	[pʊɪ ˈədɪ(χ) χiː]

In Welsh, **sydd** [siːð] corresponds to 'who is' / 'who are' and 'which is' / 'which are'. It is usually contracted to **sy** [siː] before **yn** and written as **sy'n**:

	SENTENCE
WELSH	**Dyma'r ferch sy'n gweithio yn Iwerddon.**
ENGLISH	Here / This is the girl who works / is working in Ireland.
IPA	[ˈdəmär vɛrχ siːn ˈgwəɪθjo ən ɪʊˈɛrðon]

WELSH	**Dyma'r merched sy'n gweithio yn Iwerddon.**
ENGLISH	Here are/these are the girls who work / are working in Ireland.
IPA	[ˈdəmär ˈmɛrχed siːn ˈgwəɪθjo ən ɪʊˈɛrðon]

WELSH	**Dyna'r ceffyl sy'n ennill.**
ENGLISH	That is the horse which is winning / wins.
IPA	[ˈdənär ˈkɛfɪl siːn ˈɛnɨɬ]

WELSH	**Dyna'r ceffylau sy'n ennill.**
ENGLISH	There are the horses which are winning / which win.
IPA	[ˈdənär kɛfələ siːn ˈɛnɨɬ]

WELSH	**Ble mae'r ferch sy'n gweithio yn y dre(f)?**
ENGLISH	Where is the girl who works in town?
IPA	[ble maɪr vɛrχ siːn ˈgwəɪθjo ən ə dɹɛː(v)]

WELSH	**Dw i'n ffonio'r cwmni sy'n adeiladu'r bont.**
ENGLISH	I am phoning the company that is building the bridge.
IPA	[dwiːn ˈfonior ˈkʊmni siːn adəɪˈlɑːdir bɔnt]

The present perfect is expressed by substituting **wedi** for **yn**:

	SENTENCE
WELSH	**Dyma'r bachgen sydd wedi rhedeg marathon.**
ENGLISH	Here is the boy who has run a marathon.
IPA	[ˈdəmär ˈbaχɡɛn siːð ˈwɛdi ˈɹɛˑdɛɡ ˈmaräθɔn]
WELSH	**Dyna'r ceffyl sydd wedi ennill.**
ENGLISH	That is the horse which has won.
IPA	[ˈdənar ˈkɛfɪl siːð ˈwɛdi ˈɛnɪɬ]
WELSH	**Dyma'r bechgyn sydd wedi ennill.**
ENGLISH	Here are the boys who have won.
IPA	[ˈdənär ˈbɛχɡɪn siːð ˈwɛdi ˈɛnɪɬ]
WELSH	**Dyna'r merched sydd wedi rhedeg marathon.**
ENGLISH	Those are the girls who have run a marathon.
IPA	[ˈdəmär ˈmɛrχɛd siːð ˈwɛdi ˈɹɛˑdɛɡ ˈmaräθɔn]
WELSH	**Dyna'r ceir sydd wedi ennill.**
ENGLISH	There are the cars which have won.
IPA	[ˈdənar keir siːð ˈwɛdi ˈɛnɪɬ]

The following sentences may help to prepare you for the next exercise:

	SENTENCE
WELSH	**Ydych chi wedi gweld y dyn sy'n darllen y newyddion ar y radio?**
ENGLISH	Have you seen the man who reads the news on the radio?
IPA	[ˈədɪ(χ) χi ˈwɛdi ɡwɛld ə diːn siːn ˈdarɬɛn ə nɛʊˈəðjon ar ə ˈradjo]
WELSH	**Dw i'n (ad)nabod rhywun sy'n siarad wyth iaith.**
ENGLISH	I know someone who speaks eight languages.
IPA	[dwiːn (ad)ˈnɑˑbod ˈɹɪʊɪn siːn ˈʃarad ʊɪθ jaɪθ]

Exercise 1

Complete the following by translating the clause in italics.

1) **Dyna'r ffordd** *which goes to Bangor.*

   _____

2) **Dw i wedi clywed am rywun** *who is writing a book about Wales.*

   _____

3) **Ai dyna'r dyn** *who has built a house in the village?*

   _____

4) **Ydych chi'n adnabod rhywun** *who lives in the west?*
　_____

5) **Dyna'r fenyw** (SW)/**ddynes** (NW) *who walks seven miles to work.*
　_____

6) **Ble mae'r bobl** *who do the flowers in church every Sunday?*
　_____

7) **Mae pawb** *who work on a Saturday* yn cael arian (SW)/pres (NW) da.
　_____

8) **Mae'r plant** *who walk to school* yn yr ystafell acw.
　_____

Exercise 2

*Match the words under **A** with the correct definitions under **B**.*

A	B
1) bara	a) pobl sy'n dysgu
2) athro	b) rhywun sy'n gweithio mewn eglwys
3) Saesnes	c) rhywbeth sy'n gyrru ar y ffordd
4) glaw	d) bwyd sy'n gwneud brechdanau
5) dosbarth	e) rhywun sy'n cerdded milltiroedd
6) ficer	f) tywydd sy'n gwneud pobl yn wlyb
7) car	g) rhywun sy'n gweithio mewn ysgol
8) postmon	h) dynes/benyw sy'n dod o Loegr

'Sy' after 'pwy', 'faint', 'pa fath o', and 'beth'

Sy [siː] is used after **pwy** 'who' [pʊɪ], **faint** 'how much' / 'how many' [vaɪnt] and **beth** 'what' [beːθ] in front of:

(i) a verb-noun

QUESTION	ENGLISH	IPA
Pwy sy'n siarad?	Who is speaking?	[pʊɪ siːn 'ʃɑrad]
Beth sy'n digwydd?	What is happening?	[beːθ siːn 'dɪgwɪð]
Pwy sydd wedi ennill?	Who has won?	[pʊɪ siː(ð) 'wedi 'ɛnɪɬ]

(ii) an indefinite noun

QUESTION	ENGLISH	IPA
Pwy sy'n athro?	Who is a teacher?	[pʊɪ siːn 'aθro]

(iii) an adjective

QUESTION	ENGLISH	IPA
Faint sy'n hapus?	How many are happy?	[vaɪnt siːn ˈhapɪs]

(iv) a preposition

	QUESTION
WELSH	**Faint o anifeiliaid anwes sy(dd) gyda chi?** (SW)
ENGLISH	How many pets do you have?
IPA	[vaɪnt o anivˈəɪlje̞d ˈanwɛs siː(ð) ˈgədä χiː]
WELSH	**Faint o anifeiliaid anwes sy ganddoch chi?** (NW)
ENGLISH	How many pets do you have?
IPA	[vaɪnt o anivˈəɪlje̞d ˈanwɛs siː(ð) ˈgänðo(χ) χiː]
WELSH	**Beth sydd ar y ford** (SW) / **bwrdd** (NW)?
ENGLISH	What is on the table?
IPA	[beːθ siːð ar ə vɔrd / burð]

Vocabulary

QUESTION FORM	ENGLISH	IPA
pa fath o (SM)	what type of	[pa vaːθ oː]
faint o (SM)	how much / how many	[vaɪnt oː]

Exercise 3

Translate the following sentences.

1) What has happened?
2) Who is having coffee with me?
3) What type of car does he have?
4) Who has watched the game?
5) Who is in hospital?
6) How many have arrived?
7) Who is ready?
8) How many of those people are Scottish?

The spoken negative form
In spoken Welsh, the negative form is **sydd ddim** [siː(ð) ðɪm]:

	SENTENCE WITH NEGATIVE FORM
WELSH	**Dyma'r bachgen sydd ddim yn mynd.**
ENGLISH	Here is the boy who isn't going.
IPA	[ˈdəmär ˈbäχgɛn siː(ð) ðɪm ən mɪnd]
WELSH	**Dyna'r car sydd ddim yn gweithio.**
ENGLISH	That is the car which doesn't work.
IPA	[ˈdənär kar siː(ð) ðɪm ən ˈgwəɪθjo]
WELSH	**Dyna'r ceir sydd ddim wedi ennill.**
ENGLISH	There are the cars which haven't won.
IPA	[ˈdənär keir siː(ð) ðɪm ˈwɛdi ˈɛnɨl]
WELSH	**Pwy ydy'r dyn sydd ddim yn siarad â chi?**
ENGLISH	Who is the man who doesn't talk to you?
IPA	[pʊɪ ˈədir diːn siː(ð) ðɪm ən ˈʃaˑrad ä χi]
WELSH	**Ble mae'r bobl sydd ddim yn hapus?**
ENGLISH	Where are the people who aren't happy?
IPA	[bleː maɪr ˈboˑbol siː(ð) ðɪm ən ˈhapɪs]
WELSH	**Dw i wedi gweld rhywun sydd ddim yn barod.**
ENGLISH	I have seen someone who isn't ready.
IPA	[dwiː ˈwɛdi gwɛld ˈr̥ɪʊɪn siː(ð) ðɪm ən ˈbɑˑrod]

Exercise 4

Make the following italicized clauses, negative.

1) Ble mae'r bobl *sydd wedi ennill*?
   (Where are the people who have won?)

_____

2) Ydych chi'n adnabod rhywun *sy'n mynd* i'r parti?
   (Do you know someone who is going to the party?)

_____

3) Mae'r blodau *sydd ar y ddesg* yn mynd i'r eglwys.
   (The flowers that are on the desk are going to the church.)

_____

4) Dw i'n hoffi pobl *sy'n ffonio* yn y bore.
   (I like people who phone in the morning.)

_____

Exercise 5

Translate the following sentences.

1) That's the old man who swims every day.
   _____

2) Everyone who wins is getting money.
   _____

3) He has a friend who is a vicar.
   _____

4) How many people eat white bread?
   _____

5) I prefer pets which sleep all night.
   _____

6) Who is angry?
   _____

7) I know someone who makes bread every day.
   _____

8) She is writing a book for children who are starting to read.
   _____

9) How much change do you have?
   _____

10) We are speaking to the woman who is walking from Land's End to John O'Groats.
    _____

Vocabulary

MASCULINE NOUN	ENGLISH	IPA	PLURAL FORM	IPA
ffrind	friend	[frɪnd]	**ffrindiau**	[ˈfrɪndjɛ]

ADJECTIVE	ENGLISH	IPA
gwyn	white	[gwɪn]

VERB-NOUN	ENGLISH	IPA
ffonio	to telephone	[ˈfɔnjo]
nofio	to swim	[ˈnɔvjo]
dechrau	to start / to begin	[ˈdɛχrɛ]

Lesson 5: Genitive noun phrases

In English, as in other languages, there are two ways of expressing that something belongs to someone (or something):

(i) **the + object + of + owner**:

THE	OBJECT	OF	OWNER
The	house	of	Megan

(ii) **owner + case-inflection + object**:

OWNER	CASE-INFLECTION	OBJECT
Megan	's	house

In Welsh, on the other hand, the pattern is as follows:

OBJECT	OWNER
tŷ	**Megan**

The above translates to 'Megan's house'. Below are some more examples which follow the same pattern:

OBJECT + OWNER	ENGLISH	IPA
plant Ann	Ann's children	[plant an]
bwyd y ci	the dog's food	[bʊɪd ə kiː]
teimladau pawb	everyone's feelings	[tɔɪmˈlɑdɛ paʊb]

This same **object + owner** pattern can be translated as 'the [object] of [owner]':

OBJECT + OWNER	ENGLISH	IPA
mynyddoedd Cymru	the mountains of Wales	[mənˈəðɔɪð ˈkəmri]
Banc Lloegr	the Bank of England	[baŋk ˈɬɔɪgɛr]
pris petrol	the price of petrol	[priːs ˈpɛtɹol]
tre(f) Wrecsam	the town of Wrexham	[tɹeː(v) ˈʷrɛksäm]
ystyr y gair	the meaning of the word	[ˈəstɪr ə gaɪr]
prifddinas Lloegr	the capital (city) of England / the English capital	[ˌprivˈðiːnas ˈɬɔɪgɛr]

Vocabulary

MASCULINE NOUN	ENGLISH	IPA	PLURAL FORM	IPA
banc	bank	[baŋk]	**banciau**	[ˈbaŋkjɛ]
ystyr	meaning	[ˈəstɪr]	**ystyron**	[əsˈtəron]

FEMININE NOUN	ENGLISH	IPA	PLURAL FORM	IPA
prifddinas	capital city	[ˌprivˈðiːnas]	**prifddinasoedd**	[ˌprivðiːnˈasɔɪð]

Exercise 1

Translate the following genitive phrases.

1) the city of Cardiff   _____

2) the meaning of the word 'mynydd' _____
3) the price of bread _____
4) Gareth's friend _____
5) the Welsh anthem (the anthem of Wales)
   _____
6) Gareth's friend's dog _____
7) the school library (the library of the school)
   _____
8) the sound of the sea _____
9) Ifan's tea _____
10) the head of the school _____

'Coeden achau' (family tree)

Vocabulary

MASCULINE NOUN	ENGLISH	IPA	PLURAL FORM	IPA
teulu	family	['tɔɪli]	**teuluoedd**	[tɔɪl'i·ɔɪð]
tad	father	[tɑːd]	**tadau**	['tɑ·de]
tad-cu (SW)	grandfather	[täd'kiː]		
taid (NW)	grandfather	[ṭaɪd]	**teidiau**	['ṭəɪdje]
llystad	stepfather	[ɬɪ'stɑːd]	**llystadau**	[ɬis'tɑ·de]
llysfab	stepson	[ɬɪ'svɑːb]	**llysfeibion**	[ɬi'svəɪbjon]
hanner	half	['hänɛr]	**haneri**	[hän'ɛri]
hanner brawd	half-brother	['hänɛr braʊd]	**hanner brodyr**	['hänɛr 'brɔdɪr]
hen dad-cu (SW)	great-grandfather	[heːn däd'kiː]		
hen daid (NW)	great-grandfather	[heːn daɪd]	**hen deidiau**	[heːn 'dəɪdje]
brawd	brother	[braʊd]	**brodyr**	['brɔdɪr]
cymar	partner (emotional)	['kəmar]	**cymheiriaid**	[kəm'həɪrjed]
partner	partner (business)	['partnɛr]	**partneriaid**	[part'nɛrjed]
ewyrth	uncle	['ɛʊɪrθ]	**ewyrthod**	[ɛʊ'ərθod]
cefnder	cousin (male)	['kɛvndɛr]	**cefnderoedd**	[kɛvn'dɛrɔɪð]
mab	son	[mɑːb]	**meibion**	['məɪbjon]
gŵr	husband	[guːr]	**gwŷr**	[gwiːr]
nai	nephew	[naɪ]	**neiaint**	['nəɪaɪnt]
sŵn	sound	[suːn]	**synau**	['sənɛ]

FEMININE NOUN	ENGLISH	IPA	PLURAL FORM	IPA
mam	mother	[mam]	**mamau**	['mamɛ]
llysfam	stepmother	[ɬɪ·svam]	**llysfamau**	[ɬis'vamɛ]

Welsh	English	IPA	Welsh (pl.)	IPA (pl.)
llysferch	stepdaughter	[ɬisˈvɛrχ]	**llysferched**	[ɬisˈvɛrχɛd]
mam-gu (SW)	grandmother	[mämˈgiː]		
nain (NW)	grandmother	[naɪn]	**neiniau**	[ˈnəɪnjɛ]
hen fam-gu (SW)	great-grandmother	[heːn vämˈgiː]		
hen nain (NW)	great-grandmother	[heːn naɪn]	**hen neiniau**	[heːn ˈnəɪnjɛ]
chwaer	sister	[χwaɪr]	**chwiorydd**	[χwiˈɔrɪð]
modryb	aunt	[ˈmɔdɹɪb]	**modrybedd**	[mɔdˈɹəbɛð]
cyfnither	cousin (female)	[kəvˈniˈθɛr]	**cyfnitheroedd**	[kəvniθˈɛrɔɪð]
merch	daughter	[mɛrχ]	**merched**	[ˈmɛrχɛd]
gwraig	wife	[gʷraig]	**gwragedd**	[ˈgʷrɑˈgɛð]
nith	niece	[niːθ]	**nithod**	[ˈniˈθod]
coeden	tree	[ˈkɔɪdɛn]	**coed**	[kɔɪd]

Below is Sam's family tree:

Coeden Achau Sam

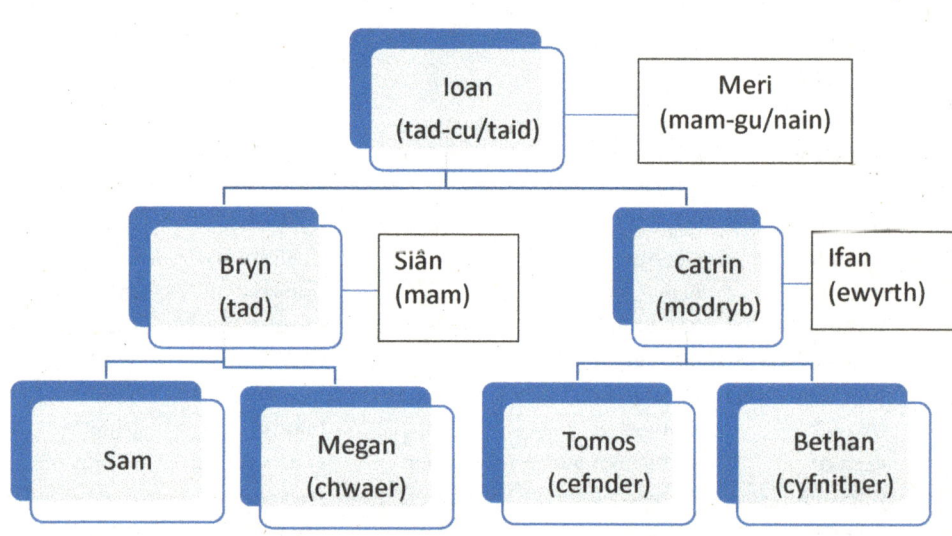

Below are some example observations we can make by using it:

WELSH	ENGLISH	IPA
Ioan ydy tad-cu Sam. (SW)	Ioan is Sam's grandfather.	[ˈjoˑan ˈədi tädˈki sam]
Ioan ydy taid Sam. (NW)	Ioan is Sam's grandfather.	[ˈjoˑan ˈədi taɪd sam]
Catrin ydy modryb Sam.	Catrin is Sam's aunty.	[ˈkatɹɪn ˈədi ˈmɔdɹɪb sam]

Exercise 2

Answer the following questions based on Sam's family tree.

For example:

Question: Pwy ydy mam-gu Megan?
Answer: Meri ydy mam-gu Megan

1) Pwy ydy chwaer Sam? _____
   (Who is Sam's sister?)

2) Pwy ydy cefnder Sam? _____
   (Who is Sam's cousin [*m*.]?)

3) Pwy ydy chwaer Bryn? _____
   (Who is Bryn's sister?)

4) Pwy ydy mab Ioan? _____
   (Who is Ioan's son?)

5) Pwy ydy merch Meri? _____
   (Who is Meri's daughter?)

6) Pwy ydy brawd Catrin? _____
   (Who is Catrin's brother?)

7) Pwy ydy plant Ifan _____
   (Who are Ifan's children?)

8) Pwy ydy ewythr Bethan? _____
   (Who is Bethan's uncle?)

Exercise 3

Answer the following questions:

For example:

Question: Bethan ydy chwaer Sam?
Answer: Nage, Megan ydy chwaer Sam.

For example:
Question: Meri ydy gwraig Ioan?
Answer: Ie, Meri ydy gwraig Ioan.

1) Siân ydy gwraig Bryn? _____
   (Is it Siân who is Bryn's sister?)

2) Bryn ydy tad Tomos? _____
   (Is it Bryn who is Tomos' father?)

3) Tomos ydy brawd Bethan? _____
   (Is it Tomos who is Bethan's brother?)

4) Catrin ydy mam Megan? _____
   (Is it Catrin who is Megan's mother?)
5) Ioan ydy taid Tomos? _____
   (Is it Ioan who is Tomos' grandfather?)
6) Meri ydy nain Sam? _____
   (Is it Meri who is Sam's grandmother?)
7) Bethan ydy chwaer Bryn? _____
   (Is it Bethan who is Bryn's sister?)
8) Ifan ydy gŵr Catrin? _____
   (Is it Ifan who is Catrin's husband?)

The partitive genitive

When the object owned is part of the whole, the prepostion **o** 'of' [oː], which causes soft mutation, is employed:

PARTITIVE GENITIVE PHRASE	ENGLISH	IPA
y rhan ucha(f) o'r mynydd	the upper part of the mountain	[ə ɹan ˈiχa(v) oːr ˈmənɪð]
un o blant y mans	one of the children of the manse	[iːn oː blant ə mans]

Vocabulary

MASCULINE NOUN	ENGLISH	IPA	PLURAL FORM	IPA
oed	age	[ɔɪd]	**oedrannau**	[ɔɪdˈɹanɛ]
cwmni	company	[ˈkʊmni]	**cwmnïau**	[kʊmˈniˈɛ]
ficer	vicar	[ˈvɪkɛr]	**ficeriaid**	[vɪkˈerjed]

VERB-NOUN	ENGLISH	IPA
mynd â (AM)	to take	[mɪnd äː]
astudio	to study	[asˈtɪdjo]

Dialogue

Welsh Dialogue

Ann: Yn y nos, ar ôl bwyd, dyn ni'n mynd â'r plant i'r sinema. Oes ganddoch chi blant?

Richard: Nac oes, nac oes. Ond mae llawer o anifeiliaid anwes gyda fi.

Ann: Mae gen i ddau o blant. Mae ganddon ni ddau fab o'r enw Tomos a Gethin. Mae Tomos yn un deg dwy flwydd oed, ac mae Gethin yn ddeg mlwydd oed.

Richard: A dyna'r bechgyn sy'n hoffi rygbi?

Ann: Ie, dyna chi. Dyna i chi ddau fachgen sy'n hoffi bod yn brysur. Ddydd Sul, wedyn, dyn ni'n mynd i'r eglwys yn y bore, ac wedyn, mae gen i lawer o bethau i'w gwneud yn y tŷ.

Richard: Penwythnos prysur iawn!

Ann:	Oes gen ti deulu arall?
Richard:	Oes, oes. Mae brawd gyda fi sy'n gweithio i gwmni yn Abertawe, ac mae dwy chwaer gyda fi. Mae un yn astudio'r gyfraith yn y brifysgol yn Aberystwyth ac mae'r un arall yn gweithio yn Llanelli. Ficer ydy hi.
Ann:	Diddorol iawn.

English Translation

Ann:	In the evening, after food, we are taking the children to the cinema. Do you have any children?
Richard:	No, no. But I have a lot of pets.
Ann:	I have two children. We have two sons called Tomos and Gethin. Tomos is twelve years old and Gethin is ten years old.
Richard:	And those are the boys who like rugby?
Ann:	Yes, there you are. There are two boys who like to be busy for you. On Sunday, then, we are going to church in the morning, and afterwards I have lots of things to do in the house.
Richard:	A very busy weekend!
Ann:	Have you other family?
Richard:	Yes, yes. I have a brother who works for a company in Swansea, and I have two sisters. One is studying law at the university in Aberystwyth, and the other one works in Llanelli. She's a vicar.
Ann:	Very interesting.

Vocabulary

MASCULINE NOUN	ENGLISH	IPA
bara	bread	['bɑːra]

FEMININE NOUN	ENGLISH	IPA	PLURAL FORM	IPA
cacen	cake	['kakɛn]	**cacennau**	[kak'ɛnɛ]

Lesson 6: Nasal mutation

Six mutatable consonants undergo nasal mutation:

MUTABLE CONSONANT	NASAL MUTATION	IPA
p	mh	/m̥/
t	nh	/n̥/
c	ngh	/ŋ̊/
b	m	/m/
d	n	/n/
g	ng	/ŋ/

This mutation may look a little strange. What happens is that plosives (consonants formed by breath 'exploding' out of the mouth, such as the unvoiced plosives **p**, **t**, **c**; and the voiced plosives **b**, **d**, **g**) are replaced by their nasal equivalents: **m**, **n** and **ng** are pronounced the same as in English, while the **h** in **mh**, **nh** and **ngh** merely denotes that these nasal sounds are produced without voice (in the same way that **rh** is a voiceless **r**).

The nasal mutation is the least common of the mutations in Welsh, occurring only after **fy** 'my' [və] and **yn** 'in' [ən], and with **blynedd** 'year' ['blənɛð] after certain numerals:

MUTATED PHRASE	ENGLISH	IPA	NOUN PRE-MUTATION	ENGLISH
yng **Nghymru**	in Wales	[ə(ŋ) 'ŋ̊əmri]	Cymru	Wales
fy **nghi**	my dog	[(v)ə ŋ̊i]	ci	dog
pum **mlynedd**	five years	[pɪ(m) 'mlənɛð]	blynedd	year

We will look at each of these separately.

'Fy ... i'

To say 'my car', 'my money', 'my pets', etc., the prefixed possessive pronoun **fy** [və] is placed in front of the word, and the affixed pronoun **i** is placed after it:

MUTATED PHRASE	ENGLISH	IPA	NOUN PRE-MUTATION	MUTATION
fy **mhapur** i	my paper	[(v)ə 'm̥apɪr iː]	papur	p > mh
fy **nhad** i	my father	[(v)ə n̥aːd iː]	tad	t > nh
fy **nghadair** i	my chair	[(v)ə ŋ̊aˑdɛr iː]	cadair	c > ngh
fy **mlodau** i	my flowers	[(v)ə 'mloˑdɛ iː]	blodau	b > m
fy **nosbarth** i	my class	[(v)ə 'nɔsbarθ iː]	dosbarth	d > n
fy **ngwaith** i	my work	[(v)ə ŋwaiθ iː]	gwaith	g > ng

In spoken Welsh, **fy** is usually pronounced as **yn** 'in' [ən] and causes the same nasal mutation. In the examples above, the written form is used but the initial /v/ is shown in brackets in the IPA transcription.

Exercise 1

*Place the pronoun **fy** in front of the words below, making any changes necessary to the word which follows.*

1) prif reswm i   _____   (my main reason)
2) teledu i   _____   (my television)
3) bwyd i   _____   (my food)
4) ffrindiau i   _____   (my friends)
5) pres i (NW)   _____   (my money)
6) cwpan i   _____   (my cup)
7) teimladau i   _____   (my feelings)
8) desg i   _____   (my desk)
9) ystafell i   _____   (my room)
10) gwely i   _____   (my bed)

Vocabulary

PLACE NAME	ENGLISH	IPA
Dinbych	Denbigh	[ˈdɪnbɪχ]/[ˈdɪmbɪχ]
Penfro	Pembroke	[ˈpɛnvro]
Rhiwabon	Ruabon	[ɹɪʊˈaˑbon]

'Yn'

The preposition **yn** 'in' [ən] (before a definite or proper noun) causes the nasal mutation (see **Week 3, Lesson 2**). Additionally, the written form of **yn** changes, being assimilated by the mutation it causes:

NASAL MUTATION	YN	NOUN PRE-MUTATION	YN + NOUN	IPA
c > ngh	yn	Caerdydd	yng Nghaerdydd	[ə(ŋ) ŋ̊aɪrˈdiːð]
p > mh	yn	Penfro	ym Mhenfro	[ə(m) ˈm̥ɛnvro]
t > nh	yn	Tremadog	yn Nhremadog	[ə(n) n̥rɛˈmɑˑdog]
g > ng	yn	Gorseinon	yng Ngorseinon	[ə(ŋ) ŋɔrˈsəɪnon]
b > m	yn	Boncath	ym Moncath	[ə(m) ˈmɔŋkaθ]
d > n	yn	Dinbych	yn Ninbych	[ə(n) ˈnɪnbɪχ]

IMPORTANT
In place names consisting of more than one word, only the first letter mutates:

ym Metws Bledrws   in Betws Bledrws   [ə(m) ˈmɛtʊs ˈblɛdɾʊs]

Non-Welsh place-names do not usually mutate:

yn Paraguay   in Paraguay   [ən ˈpɑrəgwaɪ]
yn Torquay   in Torquay   [ən toˈkiː]

Exercise 2

Translate the following adverbial phrases.

1) In Porthmadog   _____
2) In Brymbo   _____
3) In Gwynedd   _____
4) In Tregaron   _____
5) In Rhiwabon   _____
6) In Dolgellau   _____
7) In Caernarfon   _____

8) In Pentre Bach

'Diwrnod', 'blwydd', 'blynedd'

The words **diwrnod** [ˈdɪʊrnod], **blwydd** [blʊɪð] and **blynedd** [ˈblənɛð] mutate after the numerals **pump*** [pɪmp], **saith** [saɪθ], **wyth** [ʊɪθ], **naw** [naʊ], **deg** [deːg], **deuddeg** [ˈdəɪðɛg], **pymtheg** [ˈpəmθɛg], **deunaw** [ˈdəɪnaʊ], **ugain** [ˈiˈgɛn] and **cant*** [kant]. The nasal mutation in **diwrnod** is a feature of the literary language. We will see **blwydd** and **blynedd** again in **Week 6, Lesson 5**.

** Before other words, **pump** becomes **pum** and **cant** becomes **can**.*

MUTATED PHRASE	ENGLISH	IPA
pum <u>niwrnod</u>	five days	[pɪm ˈnɪʊrnod]
saith <u>mlynedd</u>	seven years (time)	[saɪθ ˈmlənɛð]
naw <u>mlwydd</u>	nine years (old)	[naʊ mlʊɪð]

Diwrnod refers to the 24-hour period (as opposed to **dydd** [diːð], which is used to refer to the daylight hours). **Diwrnod** is used:

(i) after numerals:

PHRASE	ENGLISH	IPA
tri diwrnod	three days	[tɹi ˈdɪʊrnod]

(ii) when referring to the whole day:

PHRASE	ENGLISH	IPA
diwrnod du	a black day	[ˈdɪʊrnod diː]
diwrnod allan	a day out	[ˈdɪʊrnod ˈälan]
diwrnod o waith	a day's work	[ˈdɪʊrnod oː waiθ]
diwrnod braf	a fine day	[ˈdɪʊrnod braːv]

Dydd [diːð] is used:

(i) to refer to a specific day:

SPECIFIC DAY	ENGLISH	IPA
dydd Llun	Monday	[diːð ɬiːn]
dydd Nadolig	Christmas Day	[diːð nadˈɔlɪg]

(ii) in adverbial phrases:

ADVERBIAL	ENGLISH	IPA
trwy'r dydd	all day	[tɹʊɪr diːð]

| bob dydd | everyday | [boːb diːð] |

There are also two words for 'night'. These are **noson** [ˈnɔson] and **nos** [noːs], and they are used in the same way. The 'night' equivalent of **diwrnod** is **noson**:

PHRASE	ENGLISH	IPA
tair noson	three nights	[tair ˈnɔson]
pum noson	five nights	[ˈpeˑdɛr ˈnɔson]
noson dda o gwsg	a good night's sleep	[ˈnɔson ðaː oː gʊsg]
noson stormus	a stormy night	[ˈnɔson ˈstɔrmɪs]

The equivalent of **dydd** [diːð] is **nos** [noːs]:

SPECIFIC NIGHT	ENGLISH	IPA
nos Lun	Monday night	[noːs liːn]

ADVERBIAL	ENGLISH	IPA
trwy'r nos	all night	[tɹʊɪr noːs]
bob nos	every night	[boːb noːs]

Vocabulary

MASCULINE NOUN	ENGLISH	IPA	PLURAL FORM	IPA
diwrnod	day	[ˈdɪʊrnod]	diwrnodau	[dɪʊrˈnoˑdɛ]
cwsg	sleep	[kʊsg]		

FEMININE NOUN	ENGLISH	IPA	PLURAL FORM	IPA
noson	night	[ˈnɔson]	nosweithiau	[nɔsˈwəɪθjɛ]

Lesson 7: Recap exercises

Exercise 1

Answer according to the examples given.

For example:

Question: Oes ganddoch chi gwmni? (NW)/Oes cwmni gyda chi? (SW) (✓)
Answer: Oes, mae gen i gwmni. (NW)/Oes, mae cwmni gyda fi. (SW)

For example:

Question: Oes ganddoch chi gwmni? (NW)/Oes cwmni gyda chi? (SW) (✗)
Answer: Nac oes, does gen i ddim cwmni. (NW)/Nac oes, does dim cwmni gyda fi. (SW)

1) Oes ganddoch chi hen gar? (NW)/Oes hen gar gyda chi? (SW) (✓)

2) Oes gan y tŷ ffenestri mawr? (NW)/Oes ffenestri mawr gyda'r tŷ? (SW) (✗)

3) Oes ganddo fo gawod yn y tŷ? (NW)/Oes cawod gyda fe yn y tŷ? (SW) (✓)

4) Oes ganddi hi ddigon o arian? (NW)/Oes digon o arian gyda hi? (SW) (✓)

5) Oes gen ti frawd? (NW)/Oes brawd gyda ti? (SW) (✗)

6) Oes ganddon ni ddigon o amser? (NW)/Oes digon o amser gyda ni? (SW) (✓)

7) Oes gen ti hoff lyfr? (NW)/Oes hoff lyfr gyda ti? (SW) (✗)

8) Oes ganddoch chi deulu sy'n byw yng Ngogledd Cymru? (NW)/Oes teulu gyda chi sy'n byw yng ngogledd Cymru? (SW) (✓)

If you have difficulty completing this exercise, refer to **Week 4, Lesson 1** *and* **Lesson 2**.

Vocabulary

ADVERBIAL	ENGLISH	IPA
tu allan i (SM)	outside	[tiː ˈaɬan iː]

Exercise 2

Translate the following sentences.

1) I have a brother who builds houses.

2) He is learning Welsh for different reasons.

3) Are they going on Tuesday?

4) She hates smoking outside shops.

5) I am getting a new car on Friday.

6) She goes to the swimming pool on a Wednesday evening.

7) We prefer eating chips.

8) What is the real problem?

9) Are you working over the weekend?

10) What is happening at the school?

Exercise 3

*Complete **Coeden Achau Seren** using the clues provided below.*

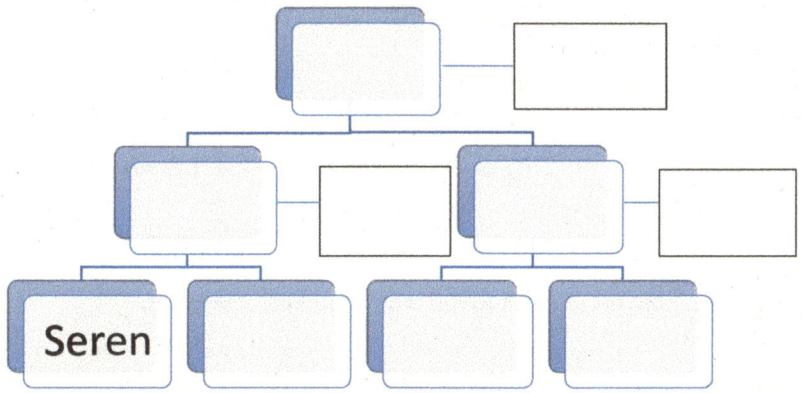

1) Angharad ydy nain (NW) / mam-gu (SW) Seren.
2) Dan ydy cymar Angharad.
3) Meri ydy mam Seren. Nid merch Dan ydy Meri.
4) Megan ydy merch Dan a modryb Seren.
5) Ben ydy brawd Megan.
6) Meri ydy modryb Dewi.
7) Gareth ydy tad Dewi.
8) Efa ydy cyfnither Seren.
9) Ifan ydy nai Megan.

*If you have difficulty completing this exercise, refer to **Week 4, Lesson 5**.*

Vocabulary

ADJECTIVE	ENGLISH	IPA
brwnt (SW)	dirty	[brʊnt]
budr (NW)	dirty	['bɨ·dɪr]

Exercise 4

Translate the following sentences.

1) Do you know what the price of bread is?

2) The village chapels (chapels of the village) are very old.

3) What is the main language of the country?

4) When is the children's party?

5) Who is the church vicar (vicar of the church)?

6) The windows of the house are very dirty.

If you have difficulty completing this exercise, refer to **Week 4, Lesson 5**.

Exercise 5

Connect the English phrases under A to the Welsh equivalent under B:

A
1) my money
2) my bed
3) my cousin (*f.*)
4) my bread
5) my television
6) my bank
7) my tables
8) my class
9) my partner (emotional)

B
a) fy nghyfnither i
b) fy nosbarth i
c) fy mara i
d) fy nghymar i
e) fy manc i
f) fy nheledu i
g) fy arian i (SW); fy mhres i (NW)
h) fy ngwely i
i) fy myrddau i

If you have difficulty completing this exercise, refer to **Week 4, Lesson 6**.

Week 5

Lesson 1: The prefixed possessive pronoun 'eich'

In **Week 4**, we saw that **fy** 'my' [və] causes nasal mutation:

MUTATED PHRASE	ENGLISH	IPA
fy* **ngwallt** i	my hair	[(v)ə ŋwałt iː]
fy* **nannedd** i	my teeth	[(v)ə 'näneð iː]

* *Remember that the f in fy isn't pronounced in everyday speech.*

In Welsh, phrases like 'help me' and 'see me' are expressed by placing the verb-noun, or the unchanged form of the verb (see **Week 3, Lesson 1**), namely 'help' and 'see', between **fy** and **i**:

QUESTION	ENGLISH	IPA
Ydych chi'n gallu (f)y **ngweld** i?	Can you see me?	['ədɪ(χ) χiːn 'gäłi (v)ə ŋwɛld i]
Ydych chi'n gallu (f)y **nghlywed** i?	Can you see me?	['ədɪ(χ) χiːn 'gäłi (v)ə 'n̥ləuɛd i]
Ydych chi'n gallu (f)y **neall** i?	Can you understand me?	['ədɪ(χ) χiːn 'gäłi (v)ə 'neˑał i]

This same pattern is used with the other personal pronouns.

Vocabulary

MASCULINE NOUN	ENGLISH	IPA	PLURAL FORM	IPA
gwallt	hair	[gwałt]	**gwalltiau**	['gwałtjɛ]
dant	tooth	[dant]	**dannedd**	['däneð]
eisiau*	want	[əɪʃɛ]		
rhif ffôn	phone number	[ɹiːv foːn]	**rhifau ffôn**	['ɹiˑvɛ foːn]
lliw	colour	[ɬɪʊ]	**lliwiau**	['ɬɪʊjɛ]

* *Eisiau operates as a verb-noun, but, as it is a noun, it is not preceded by an aspectual marker. Compare the sentences in the table below:*

SENTENCE	ENGLISH	IPA
Dw i eisiau mynd.	I want to go.	[dwiː 'əɪʃɛ mɪnd]
Dw i'n bwriadu mynd.	I intend to go.	[dwiːn bʊrˈjɑˑdi mɪnd]

FEMININE NOUN	ENGLISH	IPA	PLURAL FORM	IPA
wythnos	week	['ʊɪθnɔs]	**wythnosau**	[ʊɪθnɔsɛ]

VERB-NOUN	ENGLISH	IPA
gallu	to be able	[ˈgałi]
deall	to understand	[ˈdeˑał]
ceisio	to try	[ˈkəɪʃo]
helpu	to help	[ˈhelpi]

Gallu can translate as the English 'can' when used with the present tense:

SENTENCE	ENGLISH	IPA
Dw i'n gallu.	I can. (*lit.* I am able to.)	[dwiːn ˈgałi]
Ydych chi'n gallu?	Can you? (*lit.* Are you able to?)	[ˈədɪ(χ) χiːn ˈgałi]

Exercise 1

Complete the following sentences.

1) Mae e eisiau _____.
   (He wants to telephone me.)

2) Ydych chi'n gallu _____.
   (Can you help me?)

3) Mae'r cwmni'n _____ bob wythnos.
   (The company pays me every week.)

4) Ydych chi'n gallu _____?
   (Can you understand me?)

5) Mae e'n (SW)/o'n (NW) ceisio _____.
   (He is trying to kick me.)

6) Ydyn nhw'n _____?
   (Do they know me?)

7) Dych chi ddim yn gallu _____.
   (You can't lift me.)

8) Ydy hi'n _____?
   (Is she expecting me?)

9) Mae hi'n ceisio _____.
   (She is trying to hit me.)

10) Pwy sy'n _____?
    (Who is teaching me?)

To express 'your' when using the polite or plural form, place **eich** [əχ] in front of the noun/verb-noun and **chi** after it:

SENTENCE	ENGLISH	IPA
eich gwallt chi	your hair	[əχ gwaɬt χiː]
eich dannedd chi	your teeth	[əχ ˈdäneð χiː]

Remember that [əχ] is the colloquial pronunciation and [əɪχ] is the pronunciation in formal Welsh. As you can see, **eich** does not cause any mutation:

SENTENCE	ENGLISH	IPA
Beth ydy eich enw chi?	What is your name?	[beːθ ˈədi əχ ˈenʊ χiː]
Beth ydy eich rhif ffôn chi?	What is your telephone number?	[beːθ ˈədi əχ ɹiːv foːn χiː]
Dw i'n gallu eich clywed chi.	I can hear you.	[dwiːn ˈgäɬi əχ ˈkləʊɛd χiː]
Dw i ddim yn eich deall chi.	I don't understand you.	[dwiː ðɪm ən əχ ˈdeˑaɬ χiː]
Dw i eisiau eich gweld chi.	I want to see you.	[dwiː ˈəɪʃɛ əχ gwɛld χiː]

Exercise 2

Translate the following sentences.

1) Does your partner have family in North Wales?

2) We can't phone you tonight.

3) Have they paid you?

4) Where is your son working now?

5) He wants to hear you singing.

6) Can I see you?

7) Your hair is different today.

8) I am trying to understand you.

9) How is your tooth?

10) Everyone is expecting you.

Exercise 3

Respond according to the question, using the information in bold.

For example:

Question: Beth ydy eich enw chi?   **Ifan**
Answer: Ifan ydy fy enw i.

1) Beth ydy lliw eich car chi?　　　　　　　　　　　　　　　　**gwyn**
   (What is the colour of your car?)　　　　　　　　　　　　　**(white)**

---

2) Beth ydy eich hoff liw chi?　　　　　　　　　　　　　　　**gwyrdd**
   (What is your favourite colour?)　　　　　　　　　　　　　**(green)**

---

3) Beth ydy enw eich brawd chi?　　　　　　　　　　　　　　**Siôn***
   (What is your brother's name?)　　　　　　　　　　　　　　**(Siôn)**

---

4) Beth ydy rhif eich tŷ chi?　　　　　　　　　　　　　　**un deg saith**
   (What is the number of your house?)　　　　　　　　　　　**(17)**

---

5) Beth ydy oedran eich plant chi?　　　　　　　　　　　**chwech ac wyth**
   (What are the ages of your children?)　　　　　　　　　　**(6 and 8)**

---

6) Beth ydy eich hoff wlad chi?　　　　　　　　　　　　　　**Cymru**
   (What is your favourite country?)　　　　　　　　　　　　**(Wales)**

---

* **Siôn** is the cymricized form of **John**. The Earlier version, directly from the Latin **Ioannes**, is **Ieuan** [ˈjɔɪ.an]. Variations include **Iwan** [ˈɪʊan], **Ifan** [ˈi·van], **Ioan** [ˈjo·an] and **Ian** [jan].

Vocabulary

MASCULINE NOUN	ENGLISH	IPA	PLURAL FORM	IPA
pennaeth	head / chief	[ˈpɛnaɪθ]	**penaethiaid**	[pɛnˈəɪθjed]
cwestiwn	question	[ˈkwɛstʃʊn]	**cwestiynau**	[kwɛsˈtʃəne]
amser	time	[ˈämsɛr]	**amserau**	[ämˈsɛrɛ]

ADJECTIVE	ENGLISH	IPA
cyfleus	convenient	[kəvˈləɪs]
anodd	difficult	[ˈɑ·noð]

hir	long	[hiːr]

VERB-NOUN	ENGLISH	IPA
gwrando ar (SM)	to listen to	[ˈgʷrando ar]
gofyn i (SM)	to ask	[ˈgɔvɪn iː]
cofio	to remember	[ˈkɔvjo]
cymryd	to take	[ˈkəmrɪd]

PREPOSITION	ENGLISH	IPA
(gwrando) arna i	(listen) to me	[(ˈgʷrändo) arna iː]
cyn	before	[kɪn]

ADVERBIAL	ENGLISH	IPA
hyd yn hyn	up to now / so far	[hid ən hɪn]
wrth ei fodd*	delighted	[ʊrθ iː voːð]
yn anffodus	unfortunately	[ən anˈfɔdɪs]
dyna i gyd	that's all	[dəna iː giːd]
cyn bo hir	before long	[kɪn boː hiːr]

* **Wrth fodd** (< **bodd** 'contentment' [boːð]) means delighted. The form changes depending on who you are talking about:

SENTENCE	ENGLISH	IPA
Dw i wrth fy modd.	I am delighted.	[dwiː ʊrθ (v)ə moːð]
Dych chi wrth eich bodd.	You are delighted.	[də(χ) χiː ʊrθ əχ boːð]

As you can see above, different prefixed (possessive) pronouns (see **Week 5, Lesson 2**) are used between **wrth** and **bodd**.

Dialogue

Welsh Dialogue

Richard: Ers faint dych chi'n gweithio yma, Ann?
Ann: Ers deg mlynedd. Dw i wrth fy modd yn gweithio yn yr ysgol. Mae'r plant yn dda iawn, ac mae fy nhŷ i'n agos i'r ysgol. Felly, mae'n gyfleus iawn. Mae pennaeth yr ysgol yma ers deg mlynedd hefyd.
Richard: Mae fy ngwersi i wedi mynd yn dda hyd yn hyn. Dw i'n falch iawn cael gweithio yma. Dw i'n deall pam dych chi wrth eich bodd yn dysgu yma. Mae'r plant yn gwrando arna i ac yn gofyn llawer o gwestiynau. Dw i'n ceisio cofio eu henwau nhw. Mae'n anodd iawn.
Ann: Dw i ddim yn gallu eich helpu chi i gofio enwau'r plant yn anffodus. Mae hi'n cymryd amser i gofio'r enwau, dyna i gyd, ond cyn bo hir, byddwch chi'n adnabod y plant yn dda ac yn gwybod eu henwau nhw i gyd.

English Translation

Richard: For how long have you been working here, Ann?
Ann: For ten years. I love working at the school. The children are very good, and my house is very near to the school. It is therefore very convenient. The school head has been here ten years as well.
Richard: My lessons have gone very well so far. I am very glad to get to work here. I understand why you love teaching here. The children listen to me and ask lots of questions. I try to remember their names. It is very difficult.
Ann: I can't help you to remember the names of the children, unfortunately. It takes time to remember the names, that's all, but before long you will know the children very well and know all their names.

Lesson 2: Other prefixed possessive pronouns

We have so far seen the prefixed possessive pronouns **fy** 'my' [(v)ə] and **eich** 'your' [əχ]. Below is a complete list of the personal prefixed possessive pronouns and the mutations they cause:

PRONOUN	ENGLISH	IPA	MUTATION	EFFECT ON VOWEL
fy	my	[(v)ə]	(+ Nasal Mutation)	
dy	your (*fam.*)	[də]	(+ Soft Mutation)	
ei	his	[iː]	(+ Soft Mutation)	
ei	her	[iː]	(+ Aspirate Mutation)	(+ **h** before a vowel)
ein	our	[ən]		(+ **h** before a vowel)
eich	your	[əχ]		
eu	their	[iː]		(+ **h** before a vowel)

We will go through each of the pronouns.

The familiar, singular form of 'your'
When you are addressing a child or someone who you know very well, the form for 'your' is **dy** in front of a word and **di** after it. It is **dy** which causes the soft mutation.

PHRASE	ENGLISH	IPA
dy wallt di	your hair	[də waɫt diː]
dy ddannedd di	your teeth	[də 'ðanɛð diː]

QUESTION	ENGLISH	IPA
Beth ydy dy enw di?	What is your name?	[beːθ 'ədi də 'ɛnʊ diː]
Beth ydy dy rif ffôn di?	What is your telephone number?	[beːθ 'ədi də riːv foːn diː]

SENTENCE	ENGLISH	IPA
Mae'n ddrwg gyda fi dy boeni di. (SW)	I'm sorry to trouble you.	[main ðruːg 'gədä viː də 'bɔɪni diː]
Mae'n ddrwg gen i dy boeni di. (NW)	I'm sorry to trouble you.	[main ðruːg gɛn iː də 'bɔɪni diː]

Expressing 'his' [ei (...) e (SW) / ei (...) o (NW)]

To express 'his' in Welsh, the personal prefixed possessive pronoun **ei** [iː] is placed in front of the possessed item. Remember that [iː] is the colloquial pronunciation of **ei**; and [əɪ] is the pronunciation in formal Welsh. **Ei** causes a soft mutation, and it is followed by **e** in South Wales and **o** in North Wales:

PHRASE	ENGLISH	IPA
ei gefnder e (SW)	his [male] cousin	[iː ˈgɛvndɛr eː]
ei gefnder o (NW)	his [male] cousin	[iː ˈgɛvndɛr oː]

QUESTION	ENGLISH	IPA
Pam rwyt ti'n ei boeni e? (SW)	Why are you bothering him?	[pam rʊɪ(t) tiːn iː ˈbɔɪni eː]
Pam rwyt ti'n ei boeni o? (NW)	Why are you bothering him?	[pam rʊɪ(t) tiːn iː ˈbɔɪni oː]
Ydych chi wedi ei weld o? (NW)	Have you seen him / it?	[ˈədɪ(χ) χi ˈwedi iː wɛld oː]
Pwy sy'n ei (ad)nabod e? (SW)	Who knows him?	[pʊɪ siːn iː (ad)ˈnɑːbod eː]

Ei is contracted to **i** after the words **a** and **o**, and to **'w** after the preposition **i**:

PHRASE	ENGLISH	IPA
a'i dad e (SW)	and his father	[aɪ dɑːd eː]
a'i dad o (NW)	and his father	[aɪ dɑːd eː]
o'i dŷ e (SW)	from his house	[ɔɪ diː eː]
o'i dŷ o (NW)	from his house	[ɔɪ diː oː]
i'w dŷ e (SW)	to his house	[ɪʊ diː eː]
i'w dŷ o (NW)	to his house	[ɪʊ diː oː]

Vocabulary

MASCULINE NOUN	ENGLISH	IPA	PLURAL FORM	IPA
ŵyr	grandson	[ʊɪr]	**wyrion**	[ˈʊɪrjon]

FEMININE NOUN	ENGLISH	IPA	PLURAL FORM	IPA
afal	apple	[ˈɑval]	**afalau**	[(a)ˈvɑlɛ]
wyres	grand-daughter	[ˈʊɪrɛs]	**wyresau**	[ʊɪˈrɛsɛ]
ystafell wely (SW)	bedroom	[əsˈtɑvɛɬ ˈwɛli]	**ystafelloedd gwely**	[əsˈtɑvɛɬɔɪð ˈgwɛli]
llofft (NW)	bedroom	[ɬɔft]	**llofftydd**	[ˈɬɔftɪð]

VERB-NOUN	ENGLISH	IPA
poeni	to bother / to worry	[ˈpɔɪni]

ADJECTIVE	ENGLISH	IPA
cyfeillgar	friendly	[kəˈvəɪɬgar]

Exercise 1

Translate the following genitive phrases.

1) Your work (*fam.*) _____
2) His table _____
3) Your problem (*fam.*) _____
4) His cups _____
5) Your aunt (*fam.*) _____
6) His bed _____
7) Your partner (*fam.*) _____
8) His wife _____
9) We want to pay you now. (*fam.*)
   _____
10) Who is going to paint it (*m.*)? _____

Expressing 'her' [ei (…) hi]

To express 'her' in Welsh, the possessed item is placed between the personal prefixed possessive pronoun **ei** [iː] and the affixed pronoun **hi** [hiː]. (Remember that [iː] is the colloquial pronunciation of **ei**; [əɪ] is the pronunciation in formal Welsh.) **Ei** causes an aspirate mutation when it precedes a singular feminine noun:

ASPIRATE MUTATION	MUTATED PHRASE	ENGLISH	IPA
t > th	ei <u>th</u>eulu hi	her family	[iː ˈθəɪli hiː]
c > ch	ei <u>ch</u>yfnither hi	her (female) cousin	[iː χəvˈniˑθɛr hiː]
p > ph	ei <u>ph</u>roblem hi	her problem	[iː ˈfrɔblɛm hiː]

If the word following **ei** 'her' begins with a vowel, the letter **h** is placed in front of the word.

PHRASE	ENGLISH	IPA
ei afal e (SW)	his apple	[iː ˈɑˑval eː]
ei afal o (NW)	his apple	[iː ˈɑˑval oː]
ei hafal hi	her apple	[iː ˈhɑˑval hiː]
ei hŵyr hi	her grandson	[iː hʊɪr hiː]
ei hystafell wely hi	her bedroom	[iː həsˈtɑˑvɛɬ ˈwɛli hiː]

Ei is contracted to **'i** after the words **a** 'and' and **o** 'from' / 'of':

PHRASE	ENGLISH	IPA
a'i thad hi	and her father	[aɪ θɑːd hiː]
o'i thŷ hi	from her house	[ɔi θiː hiː]

Ei is contracted to **'w** after the preposition **i**:

PHRASE	ENGLISH	IPA
i'w thŷ hi	to her house	[ɪʊ θiː hiː]

Exercise 2

Translate the following sentences.

1) Have you heard her? _____
2) Am I troubling her? _____
3) I am trying to help her. _____
4) Where is her money? _____
5) Who goes to her church? _____
6) Her chairs are dirty. _____
7) Her grandfather writes for the newspaper.
_____
8) Her dogs and her cats are very friendly.
_____

'Our' [ein (...) ni] and 'their' [eich (...) chi]
To express 'our', **ein** [ən] is placed before the possessed item and **ni** [niː] is placed after it. Remember that [ən] is the colloquial pronunciation, and [əɪn] is the pronunciation in formal Welsh.

PHRASE	ENGLISH	IPA
ein chwiorydd ni	our sisters	[ən χwiˈɔrɪð niː]
ein llyfrau ni	our books	[ən ˈɬəvre niː]

Ein contracts to **'n** after the words **a**, **i** and **o**.

SENTENCE OR PHRASE	ENGLISH	IPA
a'n brodyr a'n chwiorydd ni	and our brothers and our sisters	[än ˈbrɔdɪr än χwiˈɔrɪð niː]
Mae hi'n dod i'n tŷ ni.	She is coming to our house.	[maɪ hiːn dod iːn tiː niː]
Mae hi'n gofyn i'n tad ni am lifft.	She asks our father for a lift.	[maɪ hiːn ˈɡɔvɪn iːn tɑːd niː am lɪft]

To express 'their', **eu** [iː] is placed before the possessed item and **nhw** [n̥uː] is placed after it. Remember that [iː] is the colloquial pronunciation; [əɪ] is the pronunciation in formal Welsh.

PHRASE	ENGLISH	IPA
eu garej nhw	their garage	[iː ˈgɑrɛdʒ n̥uː]
eu drws nhw	their door	[iː druːs n̥uː]

After the words **a** and **o**, **eu** contracts to **'u**:

SENTENCE OR PHRASE	ENGLISH	IPA
a'u brodyr a'u chwiorydd nhw	and their brothers and their sisters	[aɪ ˈbrɔdɪr aɪ χwiˈɔrɪð n̥uː]
Mae hi'n gofyn i'n tad ni am lifft.	She asks our father for a lift.	[maɪ hiːn ˈgɔvɪn iːn tɑːd niː am lɪft]

After the preposition **i**, **eu** becomes **'w**:

SENTENCE	ENGLISH	IPA
Mae hi'n dod i'w tŷ nhw.	She is coming to their house.	[maɪ hiːn doːd ɪʊ tiː n̥uː]

After **ein** and **eu**, words beginning with a vowel will have **h** added to them at the beginning:

PHRASE	ENGLISH	IPA
ein hiaith ni	our language	[ən hjaɪθ niː]
eu hewyrth nhw	their uncle	[iː ˈhɛʊɪrθ n̥uː]

Vocabulary

MASCULINE NOUN	ENGLISH	IPA	PLURAL FORM	IPA
garej	garage	[ˈgɑrɛdʒ]	**garejys**	[ˈgɑrɛdʒɪz]
drws	door	[druːs]	**drysau**	[ˈdrəsɛ]
lifft	lift	[lɪft]	**lifftiau**	[ˈlɪftjɛ]

Exercise 3

Translate the following sentences.

1) Our tables and our chairs are in their garage.
   _____

2) I don't understand their language at all.
   _____

3) He wants to see us today.
   _____

4) Can you lift (raise) them?
___

5) Who is speaking to their family?
___

6) Who is expecting us?
___

7) I can't eat them.
___

8) Our shoes are clean.
___

Affixed pronouns
In Welsh, affixed pronouns come after the word which follows a prefixed possessive pronoun. This can be seen with the **i** in **fy nghar i** 'my car' [(v)ə ŋ̊ar iː].

PHRASE	ENGLISH	IPA	AFFIXED PRONOUN	IPA
fy nghar i	my car	[(v)ə ŋ̊ar iː]	**i**	[iː]
dy gar di	your car (*fam.*)	[də gar diː]	**di / ti**	[diː] / [tiː]
ei gar e (SW)	his car	[iː gar eː]	**e / fe** (after a vowel) (SW)	[eː] / [veː]
ei gar o (NW)	his car	[iː gar oː]	**o / fo** (after a vowel) (NW)	[oː] / [voː]
ei char hi	her car	[iː χar hiː]	**hi**	[hiː]
ein car ni	our car	[ən kar niː]	**ni**	[niː]
eich car chi	your car (*pl.*) (*sing. formal*)	[əχ kar χiː]	**chi**	[χiː]
eu car nhw	their car	[iː kar n̥uː]	**nhw**	[n̥uː]

In spoken Welsh, affixed pronouns also occur with inflected forms of the verb (see **Week 7**) and declined prepositions (see **Week 10**). For example:

SENTENCE	ENGLISH	IPA
Gweithiais *i* yn galed.	I worked hard.	[ˈgwəɪθjes iː ən ˈgɑːled]
Does dim byd ynddo *fe*.	There's nothing in it.	[dɔɪs dɪm biːd ˈənðo veː]

Lesson 3: Expressing 'self'

'Hunan'
The Welsh word for 'self' is **hunan** [ˈhiˑnan] (**hun** [hiːn] in North Wales). The reflexive pronouns 'myself', 'yourself', 'himself', etc., are formed by putting the appropriate prefixed pronoun in front of **hunan**, the plural of which is **hunain** [ˈhiˑnɛn]:

REFLEXIVE PRONOUN	ENGLISH	IPA
fy hunan*	myself	[və ˈhiˑnan]
dy hunan	yourself (*fam.*)	[də ˈhiˑnan]

ei hunan	himself / herself / itself	[iː ˈhiˑnan]
ein hunain	ourselves	[ən ˈhiˑnɛn]
eich hunan	yourself (*pl.*) (*sing. formal*)	[əχ ˈhiˑnan]
eu hunain	themselves	[iː ˈhiˑnɛn]

The Welsh word for 'by' is **wrth** [ʊrθ] (SM). It is used in the idiom **wrth fy hunan** 'by myself' [ʊrθ və ˈhiˑnan̥]*. You will also hear the idiom **ar fy mhen fy hunan** 'on my own' [ar (v)ə m̥ɛn və ˈhiˑnan]:

	SENTENCE OR PHRASE
WELSH	**Mae e'n cerdded wrth ei hunan.** (SW)
ENGLISH	He is walking by himself.
IPA	[ˈmaɪ ein ˈkɛrðed ʊrθ iː ˈhiˑnan]
WELSH	**Mae o'n cerdded wrth ei hunan.** (NW)
ENGLISH	He is walking by himself.
IPA	[ˈmaɪ oːn ˈkɛrðed ʊrθ iː ˈhiˑnan]
WELSH	**eu llyfrau nhw eu hunain**
ENGLISH	their own books
IPA	[iː ɬəvre n̥uː iː ˈhiˑnɛn]
WELSH	**Oes gen ti dy gar di dy hunan?** (NW)
ENGLISH	Have you got your own car?
IPA	[ɔɪs ˈɡɛn ti də gar di də ˈhiˑnan]
WELSH	**fy mhroblemau i fy hunan**
ENGLISH	my own problems
IPA	[(v)ə m̥rɔbˈlɛme iː və ˈhiˑnan]
WELSH	**Oes ganddo fo ei gar ei hunan?** (NW)
ENGLISH	Has he got his own car?
IPA	[ɔɪs ˈɡänðo voː iː gar eː iː ˈhiˑnan]

* *Remember that, in spoken Welsh,* ***fy*** *is usually pronounced* ***yn*** *[ən]. This is particularly true before a vowel or* ***h***.

Exercise 1

Translate the following sentences.

1) They are walking by themselves.

_____

2) We are going in our own cars.

_____

3) He prefers his own company.

_____

4) They have their own way of doing things.

5) She is building her house by herself.

Independent pronouns

As their name implies, independent pronouns can be used on their own, unlike the prefixed possessive pronouns (**fy**, **dy**, etc.) that we saw in **Week 5, Lesson 1** above, which must be followed by something else:

INDEPENDANT PRONOUN	ENGLISH	IPA
fi	me	[viː]
ti	you (*fam.*)	[tiː]
fe (SW)	him	[veː]
fo (NW)	him	[voː]
hi	she	[hiː]
ni	us	[niː]
chi	you (*pl.*) (*sing. formal*)	[χiː]
nhw	them	[n̥uː]

QUESTION	ENGLISH	IPA
Pwy sydd eisiau dod?	Who wants to come?	[puɪ siːð ˈəɪʃɛ doːd]

REPLY	ENGLISH	IPA
Fi!	Me!	[viː]

Lesson 4: Introduction to prepositions

There are three types of prepositions in Welsh:

(i) Those which are followed directly by nouns or independent pronouns:

PREPOSITION	ENGLISH	PHRASE	ENGLISH	IPA
â (AM)	with (by means of)	**â chyllell**	with a knife	[ä ˈχəɬɛɬ]
ers	since	**ers wythnos**	for (since) a week	[ɛrs ˈʊɪθnos]
gyda (SW)	with	**gyda fi**	with me	[ˈgədä viː]
efo (NW)	with	**efo fi**	with me	[ˈeˑvo viː]
heblaw	besides	**heblaw Ifan**	besides Ifan	[hɛbˈlau̯ ˈiˑvan]
mewn	in a	**mewn pentre(f)**	in a village	[mɛʊn ˈpɛntɹ̩ɛ(v)]
tua	about / approximately	**tua phedwar**	about four	[ˈtiˑa ˈfɛdwar]
erbyn	by	**erbyn deg**	by ten	[ˈɛrbɪn deːg]

	SENTENCE
WELSH	**Dw i'n byw ym Mhenfro ers pum mlynedd.**
ENGLISH	I have been living in Pembroke for five years.
IPA	[dwiːn bɪʊ ə(m) ˈm̥ɛnvro ɛrs pɪm ˈmlənɛð]

	QUESTION
WELSH	**Ydych chi'n gallu cyrraedd erbyn wyth o'r gloch?**
ENGLISH	Can you arrive by eight o'clock?
IPA	[ˈədɪ(χ) χiːn ˈgaɬi ˈkəra(ɪ)ð ˈɛrbɪn ʊɪθ oːr gloːχ]

As you can see from the above, **â**, **gyda** and **efo** mean 'with'. The preposition **â** [ä] 'with' is used to convey the meaning 'by means of', or 'containing':

	SENTENCE
WELSH	**Mae hi'n torri'r bara â chyllell.**
ENGLISH	She is cutting the bread with a knife.
IPA	[maɪ hiːn ˈtɔrir ˈbɑra ä ˈχəɬɛɬ]

	PHRASE
WELSH	**te â llaeth**
ENGLISH	tea with milk
IPA	[teː ä ɬaɪθ]

The preposition **gyda** 'with' [ˈgədä] is used to convey 'in the company of' or 'together with':

SENTENCE	ENGLISH	IPA
Dw i'n mynd gyda Siôn	I am going with Siôn.	[dwiːn iːn mɪnd ˈgədä ʃoːn]

and a feeling, wish or response:

PHRASE	ENGLISH	IPA
gyda chydymdeimlad	with sympathy	[ˈgədä ˌχidəmˈdəɪmlad]
gyda'n dymuniadau gorau	with our best wishes	[ˈgədän dəmɪnˈjɑˑdɛ ˈgoˑrɛ]

(ii) Those which are declined when followed by a pronoun (see **Week 10**):

PREPOSITION	ENGLISH	PHRASE	ENGLISH	IPA
am (SM)	about / for	**amdana i**	about me	[amˈdɑna iː]
ar (SM)	on	**arno fe** (SW) / **fo** (NW)	on him	[ˈärno veː / voː]
at (SM)	to (a person)	**atoch chi**	to you	[ˈato(χ) χi]
gan (SM)	by	**gen i**	by me	[gɛn iː]
i (SM)	to / for	**i fi**	to me / for me	[iː viː]
(o) dan (SM)	under	**o dano fe** (SW) / **fo** (NW)	under it	[oˈdɑno veː / voː]

rhwng	between	**rhyngddon ni**	between us	[ˈr̥əŋðo(n) niː]
trwy (SM)	through	**trwyddyn nhw**	through them	[ˈtr̥ʊɪðo(n) ni]
wrth (SM)	by (near)	**wrtho fe** (SW) / **fo** (NW)	by him	[ˈʊrθo veː / voː]
yn (NM)	in	**ynddyn nhw**	in them	[ˈənðɪ(n) n̥uː]

	SENTENCE
WELSH	**Dw i'n ysgrifennu atoch chi heno.**
ENGLISH	I am writing to you tonight.
IPA	[ˈdwiːn əsgrɪvˈeni ˈato(χ) χiː ˈhɛno]
WELSH	**Mae gen i lyfr gan Kate Roberts.**
ENGLISH	I have a book by Kate Roberts.
IPA	[maɪ gɛn iː ˈləvr̥ gan keːt̬ ˈrɔbət̬s]
WELSH	**Dw i ddim yn mynd hebddoch chi.**
ENGLISH	I'm not going without you.
IPA	[ˈdwiː ðɪm ən mɪnd ˈhɛbðo(χ) χi]

Vocabulary

FEMININE NOUN	ENGLISH	IPA	PLURAL FORM	IPA
wythnos	week	[ˈʊɪθnos]	**wythnosau**	[ʊɪθˈnɔsɛ]

VERB-NOUN	ENGLISH	IPA
torri	to break / to cut	[ˈtɔri]

(iii) Those which are declined by placing a personal prefixed possessive pronoun between their respective elements and are followed, especially in spoken Welsh, by an affixed pronoun (see **Week 10, Lesson 6**):

PREPOSITION	ENGLISH	PHRASE	ENGLISH	IPA
ar bwys (SW)	near	**ar fy mhwys i**	near me	[ar (v)ə m̥ʊis iː]
yn ymyl (NW)	near	**yn ei ymyl o**	near him	[ən iː ˈəmɪl oː]
ar draws	across	**ar eu traws nhw**	across them	[ar iː tr̥aʊs n̥uː]
ar gyfer	for	**ar ei gyfer e** (SW) / **o** (NW)	for him	[ar iː ˈgəvɛr eː / oː]
ar ôl	behind / after	**ar fy ôl i**	behind me / after me	[ar və oːl iː]
er mwyn	for the sake of	**er dy fwyn di**	for your sake (*fam.*)	[ɛr də vʊɪn diː]
o amgylch	around	**o'n hamgylch ni**	around us	[oːn ˈhamgɪlχ niː]
wrth ochr	by the side of	**wrth ei hochr hi**	by her side	[ʊrθ iː ˈhoχor hiː]
ymysg	amongst	**yn eu mysg nhw**	amongst them	[ən iː mɪsg n̥uː]

yn lle	instead	yn ein lle ni	instead of us	[ən ən ɬeː niː]
ynghylch	concerning	yn eich cylch chi	concerning you	[ən əχ kɪlχ χiː]

	SENTENCE
WELSH	Mae e'n eistedd ar fy mhwys i. (SW)
ENGLISH	He is sitting near me.
IPA	[maɪ eːn ˈeɪsteð ar (v)ə m̥ʊis iː]
WELSH	Mae o'n eistedd ar fy mhwys i. (NW)
ENGLISH	He is sitting near me.
IPA	[maɪ oːn ˈeɪsteð ar (v)ə m̥ʊis iː]
WELSH	Dyn ni'n sefyll wrth ei hochr hi.
ENGLISH	We are standing by her side.
IPA	[dən niːn ˈsɛvɨɬ ʊrθ iː ˈhoχor hiː]

The following simple prepositions cause the soft mutation:

PREPOSITION	ENGLISH	PHRASE	ENGLISH	IPA	WORD PRE-MUTATION
ar	on	ar gadair	on a chair	[ar ˈgɑdɛr]	cadair
at	to	at rywun	to someone	[at ˈrɪʊɪn]	rhywun
gan	by	gan bobl	by people	[gan ˈboˑbol]	pobl
heb	without	heb feddwl	without thinking	[heːb ˈvɛðʊl]	meddwl
i	to (a place)	i Loegr	to England	[iː ˈlɔɪgɛr]	Lloegr
(o) dan	under	(o) dan bont	under a bridge	[(oː) dan bɔnt]	pont
trwy	through	trwy Gymru	through Wales	[tɻʊɪ ˈgəmri]	Cymru
wrth	by (near)	wrth fynydd	by a mountain	[ʊrθ ˈvənɨð]	mynydd

The following simple prepositions cause the aspirate mutation:

PREPOSITION	ENGLISH	PHRASE	ENGLISH	IPA	WORD PRE-MUTATION
â	with (by means of)	â chyllell	with a knife	[ä ˈχəɬeɬ]	cyllell
tua	about	tua phump	about four	[ˈtiˑa fɪmp]	pump

The conjunction **gyda** 'with' [ˈgədä] also causes the aspirate mutation:

CONJUNCTION	ENGLISH	PHRASE	ENGLISH	IPA	WORD PRE-MUTATION
gyda	with	gyda phobl	with people	[ˈgədä ˈfoˑbol]	pobl

Vocabulary

MASCULINE NOUN	ENGLISH	IPA	PLURAL FORM	IPA
llythyr	letter (correspondence)	[ˈɬəθɪr]	**llythyron**	[ɬəˈθəron]
cerdyn	card	[ˈkɛrdɪn]	**cardiau**	[ˈkardjɛ]

VERB-NOUN	ENGLISH	IPA
anfon at (SM)	to send to	[ˈanvon at]

Exercise 1

Fill in the blanks using the appropriate preposition from the choices given in brackets.

1) Mae o'n astudio hanes _____ mis. (rhwng/ers/ymysg)
   (He has been studying history for a month.)

2) Beth maen nhw'n ei feddwl _____ 'r adeilad newydd? (am/ar/o)
   (What do they think of the new building?)

3) Dyn ni wedi anfon dau becyn _____ 'n mab ni. (ar ôl/wrth/at)
   (We have sent two packages to our son.)

4) Dw i ddim yn gallu torri'r bara _____ gyllell. (heblaw/heb/gan)
   (I can't cut the bread without a knife.)

5) Pwy sy'n eistedd _____ dy dad yng nghyfraith di? (wrth ochr/yn lle/o amgylch)
   (Who is sitting by the side of your father-in-law?)

6) Mae _____ un deg naw o bobl yn dod i'r parti. (erbyn/gan/tua)
   (About nineteen people are coming to the party.)

7) Mae'r siop fara _____ y ffordd. (ar draws/at/ymysg)
   (The bread shop is across the road.)

8) _____ anfon y pecyn, beth am fynd â fe ein hunain. (yn lle/ar gyfer/rhwng)
   (Instead of sending the parcel, why not take it ourselves.)

9) Maen nhw'n mynd _____ Brestatyn. (heb/i/ar)
   (They are going to Prestatyn.)

Lesson 5: The perfect aspect of 'bod'

The perfect aspect (see **Week 3, Lesson 1**) of the verb views the event it describes as a completed whole rather than from within the event as it unfolds. For example, 'she has eaten' (perfect) as opposed to 'she is eating' (imperfect).

Imperfect aspect vs perfect aspect

Here are some examples of the use of **yn** and **wedi** as aspectual markers in the present tense:

	SENTENCE WITH IMPERFECT ASPECT	SENTENCE WITH PERFECT ASPECT
WELSH	Mae hi'<u>n</u> mynd.	Mae hi <u>wedi</u> mynd.
ENGLISH	She is going.	She has gone.
IPA	[mai hiːn mɪnd]	[mai hiː ˈwɛdi mɪnd]
WELSH	Maen nhw'<u>n</u> gwneud brechdanau.	Maen nhw <u>wedi</u> gwneud brechdanau.
ENGLISH	They are making sandwiches.	They have made sandwiches.
IPA	[mai(n) n̥uːn gʷnəɪd brɛχˈdɑnɛ]	[mai(n) n̥uː ˈwɛdi gʷnəɪd brɛχˈdɑnɛ]
WELSH	Ydych chi'<u>n</u> anfon cerdyn?	Ydych chi <u>wedi</u> anfon cerdyn?
ENGLISH	Are you sending a card?	Have you sent a card?
IPA	[ˈədɪ(χ) χiːn ˈanvon ˈkɛrdɪn]	[ˈədɪ(χ) χiː ˈwɛdi ˈanvon ˈkɛrdɪn]

The aspectual marker **wedi** also conveys the past perfect when combined with the periphrastic past tense of '**bod**' (see **Week 6**):

	PRESENT PERFECT	PAST PERFECT
WELSH	<u>Mae</u> Carys wedi ffonio.	<u>Roedd</u> Carys wedi ffonio.
ENGLISH	Carys <u>has</u> phoned.	Carys <u>had</u> phoned.
IPA	[mai ˈkɑrɪs ˈwɛdi ˈfɔnjo]	[rɔɪð ˈkɑrɪs ˈwɛdi ˈfɔnjo]

Exercise 1

Translate the following sentences.

1) Has it rained today?

2) They haven't tried to speak to their grandfather.

3) Has she met him?

4) We have reached Swansea.

5) Who has started to make breakfast?

6) I have sent my father an email.

7) What has happened in his bedroom?

8) He hasn't seen that film.
___

9) Has she painted her room again?
___

10) Have you had breakfast yet?
___

Vocabulary

MASCULINE NOUN	ENGLISH	IPA	PLURAL FORM	IPA
brecwast	breakfast	[ˈbrɛkwast]	**brecwastau**	[brɛkˈwastɛ]
e-bost	email	[ˈeˑbɔst]	**e-byst**	[ˈeˑbɪst]
ffôn clyfar	smartphone	[ffoːn ˈkləvar]	**ffonau clyfar**	[ˈffoˑnɛ ˈkləvar]
poced	pocket	[ˈpɔkɛd]	**pocedi**	[pɔkˈɛdi]

FEMININE NOUN	ENGLISH	IPA	PLURAL FORM	IPA
ffilm	film	[fɪlm]	**ffilmiau**	[ˈfɪlmjɛ]

VERB-NOUN	ENGLISH	IPA
cyrraedd	to arrive / to reach	[ˈkəra(ɪ)ð]

Dialogue

Welsh Dialogue

Ann: Oes rhywun wedi gweld fy ffôn clyfar newydd i?
Gethin: Mae o ar bwys y teledu yn y lolfa, dw i'n meddwl.
Tomos: Nac ydy. Dw i wedi ei weld o. Mae o ar y bwrdd bach yn ein hystafell fwyta ni.
Ann: Dw i wedi edrych ar bwys y teledu ac ar y bwrdd bach. Dim golwg ohono.
Gethin: Beth am edrych yn eich ystafell wely chi? Weithiau mae o ar y cwpwrdd bach wrth eich gwely chi. Dw i wedi ei weld o sawl gwaith.
Tomos: Neu wrth ochr y cloc yn yr ystafell fwyta? Yn lle mynd i chwilio yn yr ystafell wely beth am fynd i'r ystafell fwyta i chwilio?
Ann: Syniad gwych!
Gethin: Ydych chi wedi dod o hyd i'ch ffôn chi?
Ann: Ydw, yn fy mhoced i roedd o trwy'r amser.

English Translation

Ann: Has anyone seen my new smartphone?
Gethin: It is near the television in the lounge, I think.
Tomos: No, it isn't. I have seen it. It is on the small table in our dining room.
Ann: I have looked near the television and on the small table. No sign of it.
Gethin: What about looking in your bedroom? Sometimes it is on the small cupboard next to your bed. I have seen it many times.

Tomos:	Or by the side of the clock in the dining room? Instead of going to look in the bedroom, what about going to the dining room to look?
Ann:	Great idea!
Gethin:	Have you found your phone?
Ann:	Yes, it was my in pocket all the time.

Lesson 6: Telling the time

In English, there are two main ways of telling the time:

(i) half past one
(ii) one thirty

In Welsh, however, there is only one, which follows pattern (i) above:

SENTENCE	ENGLISH	IPA
hanner awr wedi un	half past one (*lit.* half [an] hour after one)	[ˈhaner aʊr ˈwedi iːn]

The feminine **hi** is used when talking about the time. Just as we saw when we discussed the weather in **Week 3, Lesson 6**, **mae hi'n** 'it is' [maɪ hiːn] contracts to **mae'n** 'it's' [maɪn] in everyday conversation.

On the hour
To tell time on the hour, **o'r gloch** 'o'clock' [oːr gloːχ] (*lit.* 'of the bell') is used. Here are some examples:

SENTENCE	ENGLISH	IPA
Mae'n un o'r gloch.	It's one o'clock.	[maɪn iːn oːr gloːχ]
Mae'n ddau o'r gloch.	It's two o'clock.	[maɪn ðaɪ oːr gloːχ]
Mae'n dri o'r gloch.	It's three o'clock.	[maɪn dɹiː oːr gloːχ]
Mae'n bedwar o'r gloch.	It's four o'clock.	[maɪn ˈbedwar oːr gloːχ]
Mae'n un ar ddeg o'r gloch.	It's eleven o'clock.	[maɪn iːn ar ðeːg oːr gloːχ]
Mae'n ddeuddeg o'r gloch.	It's twelve o'clock.	[maɪn ˈðəɪðeg oːr gloːχ]

Traditional numerals
Note that the traditional numerals for 11, 12, 20 and 25 which we saw in **Week 1, Lesson 6** are used when telling the time: **un ar ddeg** (11), **deuddeg** (12), **ugain** (20), **pump ar hugain** (25).

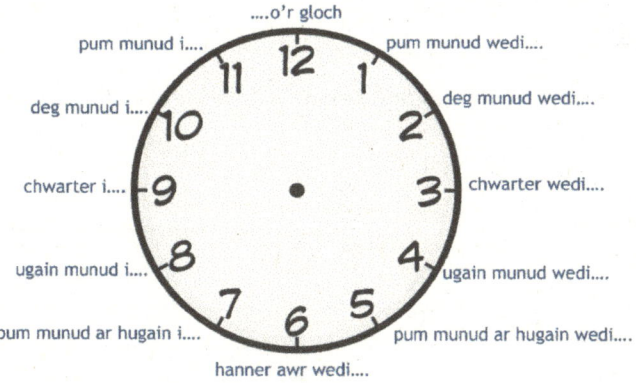

Past the hour
To tell time *past* the hour, **wedi** 'after' [ˈwedi] followed by the masculine form of the numeral is used:

SENTENCE	ENGLISH	IPA
Mae'n ddeg munud wedi dau.	It's ten past two.	[maɪn ðeːg ˈmɪnɪd ˈwedi daɪ]
Mae'n chwarter wedi dau.	It's quarter past two.	[maɪn ˈχwarter ˈwedi daɪ]
Mae'n ugain munud wedi dau.	It's twenty past two.	[maɪn ˈɪgen ˈmɪnɪd ˈwedi daɪ]
Mae'n hanner awr wedi dau.	It's half past two.	[maɪn ˈhäner aʊr ˈwedi daɪ]

To the hour
To tell time *to* the hour, **i** 'to' [iː], followed by the masculine form of the numeral, is used. (Remember that **i** causes the soft mutation). For example:

SENTENCE	ENGLISH	IPA
Mae'n chwarter i dri.	It's quarter to three.	[maɪn ˈχwarter iː dɹiː]
Mae'n bum munud ar hugain i ddau.	It's twenty-five to two.	[maɪn bɪm ˈmɪnɪd ar ˈhigen iː ðaɪ]
Mae'n ddeg munud i bump.	It's ten to five.	[maɪn ðeːg ˈmɪnɪd iː bɪmp]

Am [am] is used to express 'at' in the context of time. (Remember that **am** causes the soft mutation). For example:

PHRASE	ENGLISH	IPA
am ddeg o'r gloch yn y bore	at ten o'clock in the morning	[am ðeːg oːr gloːχ ən ə ˈboːre]
am ddeg o'r gloch yn y nos	at ten o'clock at night	[am ðeːg oːr gloːχ ən ə noːs]
am dri o'r gloch yn y prynhawn	at three o'clock in the afternoon	[am dɹiː oːr gloːχ ən ə prɪnˈhaʊn]

Exercise 1

Write the following time in full. Denote whether it is in the morning, afternoon or night.

a) 9.45 p.m. _____

b) 10.15 a.m. _____

c) 6.05 p.m. _____

d) 3.35 p.m. _____

e) 2.50 a.m. _____

f) 1.20 p.m. _____

g) 4.40 a.m. _____

h) 9.55 p.m. _____

Asking the time

QUESTION	ENGLISH	IPA
Faint o'r gloch ydy hi?	What time is it?	[vaɪnt oːr gloːχ ˈədi hi]
Am faint o'r gloch?	At what time?	[am vaɪnt oːr gloːχ]

Vocabulary

MASCULINE NOUN	ENGLISH	IPA	PLURAL FORM	IPA
cloc	clock	[klɔk]	**clociau**	[ˈklɔkjɛ]

FEMININE NOUN	ENGLISH	IPA	PLURAL FORM	IPA
cloch	bell	[kloːχ]	**clychau**	[ˈkləχɛ]
awr	hour	[aʊr]	**oriau**	[ˈɔrjɛ]
eiliad	second (time)	[ˈəɪljad]	**eiliadau**	[əɪlˈjɑːdɛ]

Amser 'time' [ˈämsɛr] can also be used to describe specific periods during the day:

PHRASE	ENGLISH	IPA
amser coffi	coffee time	[ˈämsɛr ˈkɔfi]
amser te	tea time	[ˈämsɛr teː]
amser brecwast	breakfast time	[ˈämsɛr ˈbrɛkwast]
amser chwarae	play time	[ˈämsɛr ˈχwɑrɛ]
amser cinio	dinner time	[ˈämsɛr ˈkɪnjo]

'Munud'

The word **munud** 'minute' [ˈmɪnɪd] is masculine in North Wales and feminine in South Wales:

MASCULINE & FEMININE NOUN	ENGLISH	IPA	PLURAL FORM	IPA
munud	minute	[ˈmɪnɪd]	**munudau**	[mɪnˈiˑdɛ]

Here is a list of words commonly used when discussing time, along with examples:

WORD	ENGLISH	PHRASE	ENGLISH
erbyn	by	**erbyn dau o'r gloch**	by two o'clock
bron	almost	**bron yn ddau**	almost two
tua (AM)	about / approximately	**tua thri o'r gloch**	about three o'clock
am (SM)	at	**am ddeg o'r gloch**	at ten o'clock
ar ei ben	exactly	**chwech o'r gloch ar ei ben**	six o'clock exactly
newydd droi	just turned	**newydd droi un**	just turned one
hanner dydd	midday		
canol nos	midnight		

Below are some more examples:

	SENTENCE
WELSH	**Maen nhw'n dod rywbryd ar ôl hanner awr wedi saith.**
ENGLISH	They are coming sometime after half past seven.
IPA	[maɪ(n) ŋuːn doːd ˈrɪʊbrɪd ar oːl häner aʊr ˈwedi saɪθ]
WELSH	**Dw i eisiau i ti ddod erbyn wyth.**
ENGLISH	I want you to come by eight.
IPA	[dwiː ˈəɪʃe iː tiː ðoːd ˈɛrbɪn ʊɪθ]
WELSH	**Maen nhw'n cyrraedd cyn naw fel arfer.**
ENGLISH	They usually arrive before nine.
IPA	[maɪ(n) ŋuːn ˈkəra(ɪ)ð kɪn naʊ vɛl ˈarvɛr]
WELSH	**Mae'r siop yn agor am hanner awr wedi wyth.**
ENGLISH	The shop opens at 8.30.
IPA	[maɪr ʃɔp ən ˈaˑgor am ˈhäner aʊr ˈwedi ʊɪθ]
WELSH	**Mae'n ddeg o'r gloch ar ei ben.**
ENGLIS	It is 10.00 exactly.
IPA	[maɪn ðeːg or gloːχ ar iː bɛn]
WELSH	**Mae hi newydd droi pum munud wedi un.**
ENGLIS	It has just turned 1.05.
IPA	[maɪ hiː ˈneʊɪð dɪɔɪ pɪm ˈmɪnɪd ˈwedi iːn]

'Newydd'

The adjective **newydd** 'new' [ˈnɛʊɪð] conveys the meaning 'just' when used after a verb:

SENTENCE	ENGLISH	IPA
Dw i newydd fynd.	I have just gone.	[dwiː ˈnɛʊɪð vɪnd]
Dw i newydd gyrraedd.	I have just arrived.	[dwiː ˈnɛʊɪð ˈɡəra(ɪ)ð]

When used in this way, **newydd** causes a soft mutation.

Vocabulary

FEMININE NOUN	ENGLISH	IPA	PLURAL FORM	IPA
ffon	stick	[fɔn]	**ffyn**	[fɪn]
ffon gerdded	walking stick	[fɔn ˈɡɛrðɛd]	**ffyn cerdded**	[fɪn ˈkɛrðɛd]
damwain	accident	[ˈdamwain]	**damweiniau**	[damˈwəɪnjɛ]

Dialogue

Welsh Dialogue

Gethin: Mam, ydych chi'n gallu rhoi llfft i fi i dŷ Garmon y bore 'ma? Dyn ni eisiau gweithio ar brosiect i'r ysgol.

Ann: Mae'n dibynnu. Faint o'r gloch wyt ti eisiau mynd? Dw i eisiau bod yn y dref erbyn un ar ddeg y bore 'ma, dw i'n gadael y tŷ ymhen hanner awr. Mae hi newydd droi deg rŵan, a dwyt ti ddim wedi gwisgo eto. Mae'n well i ti frysio os wyt ti eisiau lifft.

Gethin: Os wyt ti'n gallu mynd â fi i'r pentref a fy ngadael i wrth waelod y bryn wrth y cloc dw i'n gallu cerdded i fyny'r bryn i dŷ Garmon. Mae hi'n cymryd hanner awr i gerdded yno, felly bydda i'n cyrraedd y tŷ erbyn un ar ddeg.

Ann: Iawn, syniad da.

English Translation

Gethin: Mum, can you give me a lift to Garmon's house this morning? We want to work on a project for school.

Ann: It depends. What time do you want to go? I want to be in town by eleven o'clock this morning. I'm leaving the house in half an hour. It has just turned ten now, and you haven't got dressed yet. You'd better hurry if you want a lift.

Gethin: If you can take me to the village and leave me at the bottom of the hill by the clock, I can walk up the hill to Garmon's house. It takes half an hour to walk there, so I will reach the house by eleven o'clock.

Ann: All right, good idea.

Lesson 7: Recap exercises

Exercise 1

Complete the sentences below by using the word in brackets, remembering to mutate if necessary.

1) Ble dych chi wedi ei _____ o. (gadael)
   (Where have you left it?)
2) Maen nhw'n ceisio eich _____ chi. (ateb)
   (They are trying to answer you.)
3) Beth ydy ei _____ hi? (cwestiwn)
   (What is her question?)
4) Dw i'n mynd i ofyn i fy _____ i. (pennaeth)
   (I'm going to ask my head [boss].)
5) Dw i ddim yn gallu dod o hyd i fy arian, wyt ti wedi ei _____ o? (gweld)
   (I can't find my money. Have you seen it?)
6) Ble mae dy _____ di'n byw? (teulu)
   (Where do your family live?)
7) Dw i ddim yn gallu cofio ei _____ hi. (enw)
   (I can't remember her name.)
8) Mae hi'n bwrw glaw. Mae ein _____ ni i gyd yn wlyb iawn. (dillad)
   (It's raining. Our clothes are all very wet.)
9) Dyn ni eisiau newid ein _____ ni. (oergell)
   (We want to change our fridge.)
10) Wyt ti wedi eu _____ nhw? (helpu)
    (Have you helped them?)

If you have any difficulty answering these questions, review **Week 5, Lesson 1** *and* **Lesson 2**.

Exercise 2

Complete the sentences using the most appropriate preposition from the list in brackets. You will not use all the prepositions.

(â, ers, heblaw, tua, erbyn, ar, heb, o dan, rhwng, trwy, ar draws, ar ôl, wrth ochr, yn lle.)

1) Dyn ni'n astudio'r Gymraeg _____ tri mis.
   (We have studied Welsh for three months.)
2) Mae'r banc wrth ochr y llyfrgell, _____ y llyfrgell a'r ysgol.
   (The bank is by the library, between the library and the school.)

3) Roedd _____ phump o geir yn y ddamwain.
   (There were about five cars in the accident.)

4) Does dim llawer o fwyd yn yr oergell _____ caws ac wyau.
   (There's not much food in the fridge besides cheese and eggs.)

5) Mae hi wedi bwrw'r ffenest(r) _____ ffon.
   (She has hit the window with a stick.)

6) Mae hi'n braf siopa _____ boeni am y car.
   (It's lovely shopping without worrying about the car.)

7) Beth dyn ni'n mynd i'w wneud _____ cinio.
   (What are we going to do after lunch/dinner?)

8) Mae o'n (e'n [SW]) gyrru _____ 'r dref yn ei gar coch newydd.
   (He is driving to town in his new red car.)

9) Beth am gerdded yno _____ gyrru.
   (What about walking there instead of driving?)

10) Maen nhw'n rhedeg _____ y ffordd.
    (They are running across the road.)

*If you have any difficulty answering these questions, review **Week 5, Lesson 4**.*

Exercise 3

Translate the following sentences.

1) They have come to town by themselves.

2) Has he left on his own?

3) She has cut her own hair.

4) Have you remembered to get cheese and milk?

5) We have left our grand-daughter with her father.

6) Who has eaten it? (*m.*)

7) She has sent a letter and card to her brother.

8) I haven't walked up the hill yet and I am tired.

*If you have any difficulty answering these questions, review **Week 5, Lesson 3** and **Lesson 5**.*

Exercise 4

Answer the following questions.

For example:

Question: Am faint o'r gloch mae Mair yn codi?   (7.00 a.m.)
(What time does Mair get up?)
Answer: Mae Mair yn codi am saith o'r gloch.
(Mair gets up at seven o'clock.)

1) Am faint o'r gloch mae Mair yn cael brecwast?   (8.00 a.m.)

_____

2) Am faint o'r gloch mae hi'n cyrraedd y gwaith?   (9.00 a.m.)

_____

3) Am faint o'r gloch mae hi'n cael coffi   (10.30 a.m.)

_____

4) Am faint o'r gloch mae hi'n cael cinio?   (12.25 p.m.)

_____

5) Am faint o'r gloch mae hi'n mynd adref?   (4.45 p.m.)

_____

If you have any difficulty answering these questions, review **Week 5, Lesson 6**.

Week 6

Lesson 1: The past imperfect aspect of 'bod'

'I was' can be translated into Welsh as either **bues i** [ˈbiˑɛs iː] or **roeddwn i** [ˈrɔɪðʊn iː]. They are known respectively as the simple past tense of '**bod**' and the past imperfect aspect of '**bod**':

The simple past tense of 'bod'
The simpe past tense of '**bod**' refers to a specific period of time in the past:

SENTENCE	ENGLISH	IPA
Bues i'n siopa ddoe.	I was shopping yesterday.	[ˈbiˑɛs iːn ˈʃɔpa ðɔɪ]
Bues i yn y dafarn neithiwr.	I was in the pub last night.	[ˈbiˑɛs iː ən ə ˈdavarn ˈnəɪθjʊr]

The past imperfect aspect of 'bod'
The past imperfect aspect of '**bod**' indicates that an action was ongoing or continuous:

	SENTENCE
WELSH	**Roeddwn i'n chwarae rygbi trwy'r bore.**
ENGLISH	I was playing (I played) rugby all morning.
IPA	[ˈrɔɪðʊn iːn ˈχwaˑrɛ ˈrəgbi tɾʊɪr ˈbɔˑrɛ]
WELSH	**Roeddwn i'n rhedeg gyda Siôn.**
ENGLISH	I was running with Siôn.
IPA	[ˈrɔɪðʊn iːn ˈr̥ɛdɛg ˈgədä ʃoːn]

We will meet **bues i** in **Week 7, Lesson 6**. For now, we will concentrate on the past imperfect:

PAST IMPERFECT	ENGLISH	IPA
roeddwn i	I was	[ˈrɔɪðʊn iː]
roeddet ti	you were (*fam.*)	[ˈrɔɪðɛ(t) tiː]
roedd e (SW)	he was	[rɔɪð eː]
roedd o (NW)	he was	[rɔɪð oː]
roedd hi	she was	[rɔɪð hiː]
roedden ni	we were	[ˈrɔɪðɛ(n) niː]
roeddech chi	you were	[ˈrɔɪðɛ(χ) χiː]
roedden nhw	they were	[ˈrɔɪðɛ(n) n̥uː]

> **IMPORTANT**
> Note that the third person singular **roedd** [rɔɪð] is used when the subject is a singular or plural noun. For example:
>
> **Roedd Siôn yn mynd.**   Siôn was going.   [rɔɪð ʃoːn ən mɪnd]
> **Roedd y plant yn mynd.** The children were going.   [rɔɪð ə plant ən mɪnd]

The **roedd** forms are also used with adjectives:

SENTENCE	ENGLISH	IPA
Roedd y dyn yn falch.	The man was glad.	[rɔɪð ə diːn ne valχ]
Roedd y gwynt yn gryf.	The wind was strong.	[rɔɪð ə gwɪnt ən griːv]
Roedd y bwyd yn flasus.	The food was delicious	[rɔɪð ə bʊɪd ən 'vlasɪs]
Roedd y gwaith yn anodd.	The work was difficult.	[rɔɪð ə gwaɪθ ən 'ɑnoð]
Sut roedd eich tad chi?	How was your father?	[sɪt rɔɪð əχ taɪd χiː]

> **IMPORTANT**
> In spoken Welsh, the **roedd** forms are usually shortened to **(r)o'n i** [(r)oːn iː], **(r)o't ti** [(r)oː(t) tiː], **(r)oedd e** [(r)ɔɪð eː], **(r)oedd hi** [(r)ɔɪð hiː], **(r)o'n ni** [(r)oː(n) niː], **(r)o'ch chi** [(r)oː(χ) χiː], **(r)o'n nhw** [(r)oː(n) n̥uː], etc.

Vocabulary

MASCULINE NOUN	ENGLISH	IPA	PLURAL FORM	IPA
dyn	man	[diːn]	dynion	['dənjon]
gwynt	wind	[gwɪnt]	gwyntoedd	['gwɪntɔɪð]

ADJECTIVE	ENGLISH	IPA
blasus	tasty / delicious	['blasɪs]

ADVERBIAL	ENGLISH	IPA
neithiwr	last night	['nəɪθjʊr]

Other uses of the past imperfect
(i) In spoken Welsh, the following verb-nouns usually occur only with the past imperfect:

VERB-NOUN	ENGLISH	PHRASE	ENGLISH	IPA
credu	to believe / to think	roeddwn i'n credu	I believed	['rɔɪðʊn iːn 'krɛdi]
meddwl	to think	roeddwn i'n meddwl	I thought	['rɔɪðʊn iːn 'mɛðʊl]

deall	to understand	roeddwn i'n deall	I understood	[ˈrɔɪðʊn iːn ˈdeˑaɫ]
gwybod	to know (a fact)	roeddwn i'n gwybod	I knew	[ˈrɔɪðʊn iːn ˈgwiˑbod]
adnabod	to know (a person or place)	Roeddwn i'n (ad)nabod ei dad e.	I knew his father.	[ˈrɔɪðʊn iːn (ad)ˈnɑˑbod iː daːd eː]
gobeithio	to hope	roeddwn i'n gobeithio	I hoped	[ˈrɔɪðʊn iːn goˈbəiθjo]
hoffi	to like	roeddwn i'n hoffi	I liked	[ˈrɔɪðʊn iːn ˈhɔfi]
perthyn	to belong / to be related	roedd e'n perthyn (i)	he belonged /was related (to)	[rɔɪð eːn ˈpɛrθɪn (iː)]

These verbs are sometimes referred to as the 'verbs of mental state'.

The past imperfect aspect of '**bod**' is also used in conjunction with the noun **eisiau** 'need' [ˈəɪʃɛ] (pronounced **isio** [ˈiˑʃo] in North Wales) and the preposition **am** 'for' [am] when describing events in the past:

SENTENCE	ENGLISH	IPA
Roeddwn i eisiau mynd.	I wanted to go. (*lit.* I needed to go.)	[ˈrɔɪðʊn iː ˈəɪʃɛ mɪnd]

(ii) The past imperfect forms, together with the verb-noun **arfer** 'to use' [ˈarvɛr] correspond to the English 'I used to':

SENTENCE	ENGLISH	IPA
Roedden ni'n arfer byw yn y wlad.	We used to live in the country.	[ˈrɔɪðɛ(n) niːn ˈarvɛr bɪʊ ən ə ʷlaːd]
Roeddwn i'n arfer chwarae rygbi.	I used to play rugby.	ˈrɔɪðɛ(n) niːn ˈarvɛr ˈχwɑˑrɛ ˈrəgbi]

Another exception is the weather; **roedd** is always used when referring to weather in the past:

SENTENCE	ENGLISH	IPA
Roedd hi'n braf ddoe.*	It was fine yesterday.	[rɔɪð hiːn braːv ðoi]
Roedd hi'n stormus neithiwr.	It was stormy last night.	[rɔɪð hiːn ˈstərmɪs ˈnəiθjʊr]

* Unlike other adjectives, **braf** *never mutates (see* **Week 3, Lesson 6**).

Vocabulary

MASCULINE NOUN	ENGLISH	IPA	PLURAL FORM	IPA
coleg	college	[ˈkɔlɛg]	**colegau**	[kɔlˈɛgɛ]
rhiant	parent	[ˈr̝iant]	**rhieni**	[r̝iˈɛni]

FEMININE NOUN	ENGLISH	IPA	PLURAL FORM	IPA
tafarn	pub	[taˑvarn]	**tafarnau**	[tavˈarnɛ]

ADJECTIVE	ENGLISH	IPA
ifanc	young	[ˈiˑvaŋk]
enwog	famous	[ˈɛnwog]

ADVERBIAL	ENGLISH	IPA
yn y coleg	at college	[ən ə ˈkɔlɛg]
yn yr ysgol	at school	[ən yr ˈəsgol]
yn y dre(f)	in town	[ən ə ˈdreː(v)]
ddoe	yesterday	[ðɔɪ]
echdoe	the day before yesterday	[ˈɛχdɔɪ]
echnos	the night before last	[ˈɛχnos]

VERB-NOUN	ENGLISH	IPA
sefyll	to stand	[ˈsɛvɨɫ]
gadael	to leave	[ˈgaˑdɛl]

Exercise 1

Translate the following sentences.

1) He hoped to run in the marathon.

2) He was writing a letter in his bedroom.

3) We were talking all night.

4) I used to work in a busy cinema.

5) People were beginning to leave.

6) It was very foggy.

7) My aunt used to live in Llandegla.

8) They were standing between my parents.

9) I knew the way.

10) She used to go to the gym every night.

The interrogative forms

To ask a question, the initial **r** in the **roedd** forms is dropped. So, in spoken Welsh, it is important to inflect the voice (raise its pitch) to signify that you are asking a question. Below are the personal interrogative forms of **roedd**:

QUESTION	ENGLISH	IPA
Oeddwn i?	Was I?	[ˈɔɪðʊn iː]
Oeddet ti?	Were you? (*fam.*)	[ˈɔɪðɛ(t) tiː]
Oedd e? (SW)	Was he?	[ɔɪð eː]
Oedd o? (NW)	Was he?	[ɔɪð ɔː]
Oedd hi?	Was she?	[ɔɪð hiː]
Oedden ni?	Were we?	[ˈɔɪðɛ(n) niː]
Oeddech chi?	Were you?	[ˈɔɪðɛ(χ) χiː]
Oedden nhw?	Were they?	[ˈɔɪðɛ(n) n̥uː]

> **IMPORTANT**
> Note that the third person singular **oedd** [ɔɪð] is used when the subject is a singular or a plural noun.

Exercise 2

Translate the following sentences.

1) Was the milk cold?

2) Did you believe him? (*informal*) (*lit.* Were you believing him?)

3) Did they understand?

4) Was it cloudy yesterday?

5) Did you used to live with her parents?

6) Was the letter long?

7) Did he understand my question?

8) Were you hoping to arrive last night? (*formal*)

9) Were they expecting to see us?

10) Was she very angry?

The negative forms

SENTENCE	ENGLISH	IPA
Doeddwn i ddim.	I wasn't.	[ˈdɔɪðʊn iː ðɪm]
Doeddet ti ddim.	You weren't. (*fam.*)	[ˈdɔɪðɛ(t) tiː ðɪm]
Doedd e ddim. (SW)	He wasn't.	[dɔɪð eː ðɪm]
Doedd e ddim. (NW)	He wasn't.	[dɔɪð oː ðɪm]
Doedd hi ddim.	She wasn't.	[dɔɪð hiː ðɪm]
Doedden ni ddim.	We weren't.	[ˈdɔɪðɛ(n) niː ðɪm]
Doeddech chi ddim.	You weren't.	[ˈdɔɪðɛ(χ) χiː ðɪm]
Doedden nhw ddim.	They weren't.	[ˈdɔɪðɛ(n) n̥uː ðɪm]

> **IMPORTANT**
> Note that the third person singular **doedd (...) ddim** [dɔɪð (...) ðɪm] is used when the subject is a singular or a plural noun.

Exercise 3

Translate the following sentences.

1) I wasn't standing for a long time.

2) We didn't recognise her.

3) Did they like history at school?

4) The flowers weren't in the room.

5) He didn't used to eat meat.

6) They weren't friendly.

7) We didn't learn Welsh at school. (*lit.* We didn't learn Welsh in the school.)

8) My uncle wasn't famous.

9) The class wasn't very interesting.

10) It wasn't sleeting, it was snowing.

Responses

The replies to closed questions in the past imperfect are as follows:

AFFIRMATIVE REPLY	ENGLISH	IPA
Oeddwn.	Yes, I was.	[ˈɔɪðʊn]
Oeddet.	Yes, you were. (*fam.*)	[ˈɔɪðɛt]
Oedd.	Yes, he / she / it was.	[ɔɪð]
Oedden.	Yes, we were.	[ɔɪðɛn]
Oeddech.	Yes, you were.	[ˈɔɪðɛχ]
Oedden.	Yes, they were.	[ˈɔɪðɛn]

NEGATIVE REPLY	ENGLISH	IPA
Nac oeddwn.	No, I wasn't.	[nɑːg ˈɔɪðʊn]
Nac oeddet.	No, you weren't.	[nɑːg ˈɔɪðɛt]
Nac oedd.	No, he / she / it wasn't.	[nɑːg ɔɪð]
Nac oedden.	No, we weren't.	[nɑːg ˈɔɪðɛn]
Nac oeddech.	No, you weren't.	[nɑːg ˈɔɪðɛχ]
Nac oedden.	No, they weren't.	[nɑːg ˈɔɪðɛn]

The shortened forms used in everyday speech are:

NEGATIVE REPLY	ENGLISH	IPA
Nac o'n.	No, I wasn't.	[nɑːg oːn]
Nac o't.	No, you weren't.	[nɑːg oːt]
Nac oedd.	No, he / she / it wasn't.	[nɑːg ɔɪð]
Nac o'n.	No, we weren't.	[nɑːg oːn]
Nac o'ch.	No, you weren't.	[nɑːg oːχ]
Nac o'n.	No, they weren't.	[nɑːg oːn]

Exercise 4

Answer the following questions in the affirmative or negative depending on the symbol given in brackets at the end of the sentence.

For example:

Question: Oeddech chi'n arfer byw yn Ninbych? (✓)
(Did you used to live in Denbigh?)
Answer: Oeddwn, roeddwn i'n byw yn Ninbych.
(Yes, I used to live in Denbigh.)

For example:

Question: Oeddech chi'n ei chredu hi? (✗)
(Did you believe her?)
Answer: Nac oeddwn, doeddwn i ddim yn ei chredu hi.
(No, I didn't believe her.)

1) Oedden ni'n meddwl am adael? (✓)

2) Oedd hi'n oer ddoe? (✗)

3) Oedden nhw eisiau gweithio heno? (✓)

4) Oedd Gareth yn gwybod y ffordd? (✗)

5) Oedd y wers yn ddiddorol? (✗)

6) Oeddet ti'n arfer gyrru lorri? (✓)

7) Oedd llawer o bobl yn y llyfrgell? (✓)

8) Oedd y plant yn deall? (✗)

9) Oeddet ti'n meddwl am eich tad chi? (✓)

10) Oedden nhw'n arfer chwarae rygbi yn yr ysgol? (✗)

Lesson 2: The past perfect aspect of 'bod'

As we saw in **Week 5, Lesson 5**, in Welsh, the present perfect is expressed by substituting **wedi** ['wɛdi] for **yn** [ən] in the present tense of **'bod'**:

	PRESENT IMPERFECT	PRESENT PERFECT
WELSH	Mae Gareth <u>yn</u> mynd.	Mae Gareth <u>wedi</u> mynd.
ENGLISH	Gareth is going.	Gareth has gone.
IPA	[maɪ 'gaːrɛθ ən mɪnd]	[maɪ 'gaːrɛθ 'wɛdi mɪnd]

Similarly, the past perfect aspect (sometimes referred to as the pluperfect) of **'bod'** is expressed by substituting **wedi** for **yn**:

	PAST IMPERFECT	PAST PERFECT
WELSH	Roedd Gareth yn mynd.	Roedd Gareth wedi mynd.
ENGLISH	Gareth was going.	Gareth had gone.
IPA	[rɔɪð 'gaːrɛθ ən mɪnd]	[rɔɪð 'gaːrɛθ 'wɛdi mɪnd]

Vocabulary

MASCULINE NOUN	ENGLISH	IPA	PLURAL FORM	IPA
môr	sea	[moːr]	moroedd	['mɔrɔɪð]

VERB-NOUN	ENGLISH	IPA
newid	to change	['nɛʊɪd]

Exercise 1

Translate the following sentences.

1) I hadn't written the letter to my parents by 5 o'clock.

2) Had he read the books?

3) He hadn't thought about the news at all.

4) We had changed our car.

5) Had she swum in the sea?

6) Had you put the milk in the fridge?

7) I had given the television to the children.

8) My mother had painted the chair green.

9) The policeman had seen the accident.

10) Had someone eaten all the bread?

Lesson 3: That-clauses

In the present and periphrastic past tenses of '**bod**', the that-clause is represented by **bod** itself:

	SENTENCE
WELSH	**Dw i'n gwybod bod y dre(f) yn brysur.**
ENGLISH	I know that the town is busy.
IPA	[dwiːn 'gwiˑbod boːd y dɹeː(v) ən 'brəsɪr]
WELSH	**Roeddwn i'n gwybod bod y dre(f) yn brysur.**
ENGLISH	I knew that the town is busy.
IPA	['rɔɪðʊn iːn 'gwiˑbod boːd y dɹeː(v) ən 'brəsɪr]

> **IMPORTANT**
> In other moods and tenses, it is represented by the the particle **y** [ə] followed by a personal form of the verb. Don't worry about this now. We will with deal with all the verb forms in Welsh throughout this course.

However, one shouldn't think of **bod** as being a direct translation of 'that'. It is possible to leave the 'that' out of the English sentence and it will still make sense, as in 'I know the town is busy.' But **bod** is an integral part of the corresponding Welsh sentence, taking the place of the personal form **mae**:

	CLAUSE		CLAUSE		SENTENCE
WELSH	**Dw i'n gwybod**	+	**mae'r dre(f) yn brysur.**	=	**Dw i'n gwybod bod y dre(f) yn brysur.**
ENGLISH	I know	+	the town is busy	=	I know (that) the town is busy.
IPA	[dwiːn 'gwiˑbod]		[maɪr dɹeː(v) ən 'brəsɪr]		[dwiːn 'gwiˑbod boːd y dɹeː(v) ən 'brəsɪr]

Personal forms of the 'that' clause are formed by combining prefixed possessive pronouns (see **Week 5, Lesson 2**):

	SENTENCE
WELSH	**Dw i'n gwybod fy mod i'n mynd.**
ENGLISH	I know that I'm going.
IPA	[dwiːn 'gwiˑbod (və) moːd iːn mɪnd]

WELSH	**Mae e'n gwybod ei fod e'n mynd.** (SW)
ENGLISH	He knows that he is going.
IPA	[maɪ eːn ˈgwiˑbod iː voːd eːn mɪnd]

WELSH	**Mae o'n gwybod ei fod o'n mynd.** (NW)
ENGLISH	He knows that he is going.
IPA	[maɪ oːn ˈgwiˑbod iː voːd oːn mɪnd]

Often, the prefixed possessive pronoun itself (**fy** and **ei** in our examples) isn't heard in spoken Welsh, but the mutation it causes remains:

SENTENCE	IPA
Dw i'n gwybod mod i'n mynd	[dwiːn ˈgwiˑbod moːd iːn mɪnd]
Mae e'n gwybod fod e'n mynd. (SW)	[maɪ eːn ˈgwiˑbod voːd eːn mɪnd]
Mae e'n gwybod fod o'n mynd. (NW)	[maɪ eːn ˈgwiˑbod voːd oːn mɪnd]

The personal forms are as follows:

PHRASE	ENGLISH	IPA
(fy) mod i	that I am / was	[(və) moːd iː]
dy fod ti	that you are / were (*fam.*)	[də voː(d) tiː]
ei fod e (SW)	that he is / was	[(iː) voːd eː]
ei fod o (NW)	that he is / was	[(iː) voːd oː]
ei bod hi	that she is / was	[(iː) boːd hiː]
ein bod ni	that we are / were	[(ən) boːd niː]
eich bod chi	that you are / were (*pl.*) (*sing. formal*)	[(əχ) boːd χiː]
eu bod nhw	that they are / were	[(iː) boːd n̦uː]

Vocabulary

MASCULINE NOUN	ENGLISH	IPA
pawb	everyone	[paʊb]

VERB-NOUN	ENGLISH	IPA
cystadlu	to compete	[kəsˈtadli]
credu	to believe	[ˈkrɛdi]
dod	to come	[doːd]

ADJECTIVE	ENGLISH	IPA
cynnar	early	[ˈkənar]
iawn	right / correct	[jaʊn]

Exercise 1

*Fill the following gaps with the appropriate forms of **bod**.*

1) Dw i'n gwybod eich _____ chi'n falch.
   (I know that you are glad.)
2) Dyn ni'n gwybod ei _____ e'n (SW)/o'n (NW) cystadlu.
   (We know that he is competing.)
3) Dw i'n gwybod ein _____ ni'n codi'n gynnar.
   (I know that we are getting up early.)
4) Maen nhw'n gwybod ei _____ hi'n eu credu nhw.
   (They know that she believes them.)
5) Dyn ni'n gwybod _____ y plant yn dod.
   (We know that the children are coming.)
6) Maen nhw'n gwybod eu _____ nhw'n cystadlu.
   (They know that they are competing)
7) Mae pawb yn gwybod dy _____ ti'n deall.
   (Everyone knows that you understand.)
8) Dych chi'n gwybod fy _____ i'n iawn.
   (You know that I'm right.)
9) Dw i'n credu _____ Alun yn dda.
   (I think that Alun is good.)
10) Dw i wedi clywed _____ damwain wedi digwydd.
    (I have heard that an accident has happened.)

Exercise 2

Translate the following sentences.

1) He knows that he is right.

2) I think (believe) that he knows.

3) We hope that the house is ready.

4) I believe that everyone is coming.

5) They know that they are in the way.

6) We believe that you are right.

7) Everyone knows that she is competing

---

8) I understand that the railway is very old.

In everyday speech, a that-clause is negated simply by adding the negative particle **ddim** [ðɪm]:

SENTENCE	IPA
Dw i'n gwybod (fy) mod i ddim yn mynd.	[dwiːn ˈgwiˑbod (və) moːd iː ðɪm ən mɪnd]
Mae e'n gwybod ei fod e ddim yn mynd. (SW)	[maɪ eːn ˈgwiˑbod iː voːd eː ðɪm ən mɪnd]
Mae o'n gwybod ei fod o ddim yn mynd. (NW)	[maɪ oːn ˈgwiˑbod iː voːd oː ðɪm ən mɪnd]

Lesson 4: Parts of speech followed by that-clauses

The verb-noun '**bod**' itself is used after certain prepositions, conjunctions, adverbials and expressions:

Prepositions

PREPOSITION	ENGLISH	IPA
er	although	[ɛr]
am (SM)	because	[am]
gan (SM)	since (because)	[gan]

Here are some example sentences:

	SENTENCE
WELSH	**Dw i'n mynd i lan y môr er ei bod hi'n bwrw glaw.**
ENGLISH	I am going to the seaside although it is raining.
IPA	[dwiːn mɪnd iː lan ə moːr er (iː) boːd hiːn ˈburʊ glaʊ]
WELSH	**Dw i'n dysgu Cymraeg am fy mod i wedi symud i Gymru.**
ENGLISH	I'm learning Welsh because I have moved to Wales.
IPA	[dwiːn ˈdəsgi kəmˈraɪg am (və) moːd iː ˈwedi ˈsəmɪd i ˈgəmri]
WELSH	**Gallwch chi fynd gan ein bod ni yma.**
ENGLISH	You can go since we are here.
IPA	[ˈgaɫʊ(χ) χiː vɪnd gan (ən) boːd niː ˈəmä]

Vocabulary

FEMININE NOUN	ENGLISH	IPA
glan y môr	seaside	[glan ə moːr]

VERB-NOUN	ENGLISH	IPA
symud	to move	[ˈsəmɪd]

(o) achos

The masculine noun **achos** 'case' [ˈäχos] is often used as a preposition meaning 'because'

PREPOSITION	ENGLISH	IPA
(o) achos	because	[(oː) ˈäχos]

Here is an example:

	SENTENCE
WELSH	**Dyn ni'n canu bob dydd (o) achos (ein) bod ni'n cystadlu (yr) wythnos nesa(f).**
ENGLISH	We sing every day because we are competing next week.
IPA	[də(n) niːn kɑˈni boːb diːð (oː) ˈäχos (ən) boːd niːn kəsˈtadli (ər) ˈʊɪθnos ˈnɛsa(v)]

Vocabulary

MISCELLANEOUS	ENGLISH	IPA
nesa(f)	next	[ˈnɛsa(v)]
(yr) wythnos nesa(f)	next week	[ər ˈʊɪθnos ˈnɛsa(v)]

Adverbials

ADVERBIAL	ENGLISH	IPA
(e)fallai (SW)	perhaps	[(ɛ)ˈväɬɛ]
hwyrach (NW)	perhaps	[ˈhʊɪraχ]
oni bai	unless / were it not for the fact	[ˌɔniˈbaɪ]

Here are some examples:

	SENTENCE
WELSH	**Efallai bod hynny'n iawn.**
ENGLISH	Perhaps that is correct.

IPA	[(ɛ)ˈväɫɛ boːd ˈhənin jaʊn]
WELSH	**Oni bai fy mod i'n gyrru.**
ENGLISH	If it wasn't for the fact that I was driving.
IPA	[ˌɔniˈbaɪ (və) moːd iːn ˈgəri]
WELSH	**Efallai fy mod i wedi cwrdd â fe, ond dw i ddim yn cofio.**
ENGLISH	Perhaps I have met him, I don't remember.
IPA	[(ɛ)ˈväɫɛ (və) moːd iː ˈwɛdi kʊrð ä veː ɔnd dwiː ðɪm ən ˈkɔvjo]
WELSH	**Hwyrach ei fod o eisiau mynd.** (NW)
ENGLISH	Perhaps he wants to go.
IPA	[(ɛ)väɫɛ (iː) voːd oː əɪʃɛ mɪnd]
WELSH	**Oni bai dy fod ti eisiau mynd, dw i ddim yn mynd.**
ENGLISH	Unless you want to go, I am not going.
IPA	[ˌɔniˈbaɪ də voː(d) ti əɪʃɛ mɪnd dwiː ðɪm ən mɪnd]

Adverbial phrases

Here are some adverbial phrases commonly used in front of that-clauses:

PHRASE	ENGLISH	IPA
mae'n debyg	it seems	[maɪn ˈdɛbɪg]
mae'n drueni	it's a pity	[maɪn driˈɛni]
wrth gwrs	of course	[ʊrθ gʊrs]
mae'n amlwg	it's obvious	[maɪn ˈamlʊg]
mae'n bosib	it's possible	[maɪn ˈbɔsɪb]

Here are some examples of them in sentences:

	SENTENCE
WELSH	**Mae'n bosib (ei) bod hi'n gadael.**
ENGLISH	It's possible that she is leaving.
IPA	[maɪn ˈbɔsɪb (iː) boːd hiːn ˈgɑˈdɛl]
WELSH	**Mae'n amlwg (eu) bod nhw'n sâl.**
ENGLISH	It's obvious that they are ill.
IPA	[maɪn ˈamlʊg (iː) boːd n̥uːn saːl]

Exercise 1

Translate the following sentences.

1) Of course I am glad.

2) It's a pity that they don't remember their grandfather.

_____

3) Perhaps he is sleeping.

_____

4) Although it is freezing we are going.

_____

5) I am studying in Caernarfon because I have a cousin (*m.*) who lives there.

_____

6) I'm not going since it is very stormy.

_____

Lesson 5: The emphatic that-clause

In a sentence like 'Gareth is a postman', 'Gareth' is the subject and 'a postman' is the identifying predicate, as this describes what 'Gareth' is. In Welsh, there are two ways of expressing such a statement:

(i) **Mae Gareth yn bostmon.**
(ii) **Postmon ydy Gareth.**

The first statement above is neutral. However, the second statement emphasises the fact that Gareth is a postman rather than a policeman or a teacher, etc. However, if we wish to turn these sentences into that-clauses, the **mae** [maɪ] in the first sentence is replaced by **bod** [boːd], while the emphatic conjunction **mai** [maɪ] (**taw** [tau] in informal contexts in South Wales) is placed in front of the second sentence:

	SENTENCE
WELSH	**Dw i'n gwybod bod Enfys yn athrawes.**
ENGLISH	I know that Enfys is a teacher.
IPA	[dwiːn ˈgwiˑbod boːd ˈɛnvɪs ən aˈθrauɛs]
WELSH	**Dw i'n gwybod mai *athrawes* ydy Enfys.**
ENGLISH	I know that Enfys is a *teacher* (and not in a different job).
IPA	[dwiːn ˈgwiˑbod maɪ aˈθrauɛs ədi ˈɛnvɪs]
WELSH	***Chwiorydd* ydyn nhw.**
ENGLISH	They are *sisters*. (not just friends)
IPA	[χwiˈɔrɪð ˈədɪ(n) n̥u]
WELSH	**Dw i'n gwybod mai *chwiorydd* ydyn nhw.**
ENGLISH	I know that they are *sisters*.
IPA	[dwiːn ˈgwiˑbod maɪ χwiˈɔrɪð ˈədɪ(n) n̥uː]

We will learn more about emphasising elements of a Welsh sentence in **Week 12, Lesson 3**.

Vocabulary

MASCULINE NOUN	ENGLISH	IPA	PLURAL FORM	IPA
tîm	team	[tiːm]	**timau**	[ˈtiːmɛ]
athro	teacher	[ˈaθro]	**athrawon**	[aθrauon]

FEMININE NOUN	ENGLISH	IPA	PLURAL FORM	IPA
athrawes	teacher	[aθraues]	**athrawesau**	[aθrauˈɛsɛ]

VERB-NOUN	ENGLISH	IPA
dweud wrth (SM)	to tell / to say to	[ˈdwəɪd urθ]
mynd i ennill	going to win	[mɪnd iː ˈɛnił]

ADJECTIVE	ENGLISH	IPA
gwir	true	[gwiːr]
gorau	best	[ˈgo·rɛ]

PRONOUN	ENGLISH	IPA
hynny	that (abstract)	[ˈhəni]

ADVERBIAL	ENGLISH	IPA
(e)fallai (SW)	perhaps	[(ɛ)ˈvałɛ]
hwyrach (NW)	perhaps	[ˈhʊ(ɪ)raχ]

Exercise 1

*Fill the gaps in the following sentences with either **bod** or **mai**.*

1) Dw i'n gwybod _____ Alun yn athro da.
   (I know that Alun is a good teacher.)

2) Dw i'n credu _____ Mair ydy'r athrawes orau.
   (I think that *Mair* is the best teacher.)

3) Efallai _____ pawb yn dod.
   (Perhaps everyone is coming.)

4) Maen nhw'n dweud _____ Llanelli yn mynd i ennill.
   (They say that Llanelli is going to win.)

5) Mae pawb yn gwybod _____ Caerdydd ydy'r tîm gorau.
   (Everyone knows that Cardiff is the best team.)

6) Dw i'n credu eu _____ nhw wedi mynd.

(I believe that they have gone.)

7) Mae e'n dweud _____ ni sy'n iawn.
(He say's that *we* are right.)

8) Dw i'n gwybod ei _____ hi'n niwlog.
(I know that it's foggy.)

Lesson 6: Giving your age, and 'blwyddyn', 'blwydd' and 'blynedd'

In Welsh, there are three forms of the feminine noun **blwyddyn** 'year' [ˈblʊɪðɪn]:

(i) **Blwyddyn** [ˈblʊɪðɪn] is used:

(a) on its own:

	SENTENCE
WELSH	**Bues i'n byw yn Iwerddon am flwyddyn.**
ENGLISH]	I lived in Ireland for a year.
IPA	[ˈbiˑes iːn bɪʊ ən ɪʊˈɛrðon am ˈvlʊɪðɪn]

(b) with the numeral **un** 'one' [iːn]:

	SENTENCE
WELSH	**Bues i'n athro am un flwyddyn.**
ENGLISH	I was a teacher for one year.
IPA	[ˈbiˑes iːn ˈaθro am iːn ˈvlʊɪðɪn]

(c) with all ordinals (See **Week 9, Lesson 6**):

PHRASE	ENGLISH	IPA
y flwyddyn gynta(f)	the first year.	[ə ˈvlʊɪðɪn ˈgənta(v)]

(ii) **Blwydd** [blʊɪð] is used with age:

PHRASE	ENGLISH	IPA
un flwydd oed	one year old	[iːn vlʊɪð ɔɪd]
tair blwydd oed	three years old	[tair blʊɪð ɔɪd]

Blwydd is often omitted in such phrases, but **oed** 'age' remains:

PHRASE	ENGLISH	IPA
pump oed	five (years old)	[pɪmp ɔɪd]
deuddeg oed	twelve (years old)	[ˈdəɪðɛg ɔɪd]

(iii) **Blynedd** [ˈblənɛð] is used with numerals (except **un**):

PHRASE	ENGLISH	IPA
dwy flynedd yn ôl	two years ago	[dʊɪ ˈvlənɛð ən oːl]
ymhen chwe blynedd	in six years time	[əmˈhen χweː ˈblənɛð]

The mutations are the same for both **blynedd** and **blwydd**, so we'll concentrate on the former:

NUMERAL	MUTATION	FORM	IPA
1	soft	**un flwyddyn**	[iːn ˈvlʊɪðɪn]
2	soft	**dwy flynedd**	[dʊɪ ˈvlənɛð]
3		**tair blynedd**	[taɪr ˈblənɛð]
4		**pedair blynedd**	[ˈpedɛr ˈblənɛð]
5	nasal	**pum mlynedd**	[pɪ(m) ˈmlənɛð]
6		**chwe blynedd**	[χweː ˈblənɛð]
7	nasal	**saith mlynedd**	[saɪθ ˈmlənɛð]
8	nasal	**wyth mlynedd**	[ʊɪθ ˈmlənɛð]
9	nasal	**naw mlynedd**	[naʊ ˈmlənɛð]
10	nasal	**deg (deng)* mlynedd**	[deːg ˈmlənɛð]

* **Deng** [deŋ] *is an alternative form of* **deg** [deːg] *used before* **diwrnod** [ˈdɪʊrnod], **blwydd** [blʊɪð] *and* **blynedd** [ˈblənɛð], *mainly in formal written contexts.*

After 10, **blynedd** mutates according to the numeral it follows. This is true of both the decimal and the vigesimal systems:

NUMERAL	DECIMAL	VIGESIMAL
11	**un deg un mlynedd**	**un mlynedd ar ddeg**
12	**un deg dwy flynedd**	**deuddeg mlynedd**
15	**un deg pum mlynedd**	**pymtheg mlynedd**
16	**un deg chwe blynedd**	**un mlynedd ar bymtheg**
20	**dau ddeg mlynedd**	**ugain mlynedd**
31	**tri deg un mlynedd**	**un mlynedd ar ddeg ar hugain**
50	**pum deg mlynedd**	**hanner can mlynedd**
100	**can mlynedd**	**can mlynedd**

Exercise 1

Give the appropriate form of **blynedd** *after the following numerals.*

a) 2 _____ b) 11 _____ c) 8 _____

d) 20 _____ e) 3 _____ f) 17 _____

g) 6 _____ h) 36 _____ i) 50 _____

j) 18 _____ k) 19 _____ l) 21 _____

Vocabulary

MASCULINE NOUN	ENGLISH	IPA	PLURAL FORM	IPA
cyfnod	period	[ˈkəvnod]	cyfnodau	[kəvˈnoˑdɛ]
côr	choir	[koːr]	corau	[ˈkoˑrɛ]
ffermwr	farmer	[ˈfɛrmʊr]	ffermwyr	[ˈfɛrmwɪr]

FEMININE NOUN	ENGLISH	IPA	PLURAL FORM	IPA
swydd	job	[sʊɪð]	swyddi	[ˈsʊɪði]
ardal	area	[ˈardal]	ardaloedd	[arˈdɑˑlɔɪð]

ADJECTIVE	ENGLISH	IPA
twp	stupid	[tʊp]
gwirion	silly	[ˈgwɪrjon]
pell	far	[peɬ]
cyntaf	first	[ˈkəntɑ(v)]
siŵr	sure / certain	[ʃuːr]

VERB-NOUN	ENGLISH	IPA
cynnig	to try / to apply	[ˈkənɪg]
mwynhau	to enjoy	[mʊɪnˈhaɪ]
canu	to sing / to ring	[ˈkɑˑni]
dweud	to say / to tell	[dwəɪd]

ADVERB	ENGLISH	IPA
gartre(f)	at home	[ˈgartɹɛ(v)]
dim ond	only	[dɪm ɔnd]
yma	here	[ˈəmä]

MISCELLANEOUS	ENGLISH	IPA
mor (SM)	so / as	[moːr]
yn ôl	back / backwards / ago	[ən oːl]
ers faint	for how long	[ɛrs vaɪnt]

Dialogue

Welsh Dialogue

Richard: Ers faint dych chi'n gweithio yn yr ysgol, Ann?
Ann: Ers deg mlynedd. Bues i'n dysgu mewn ysgol yng Ngorllewin Cymru am gyfnod, ond roedd fy ngŵr i a fi eisiau symud yn ôl i'r Gogledd i fyw. Ers faint dych chi'n athro?

Richard:	Dim ond ers blwyddyn. Dyma fy swydd gyntaf i. Roeddwn i wedi cynnig am sawl swydd cyn dod yma. Roeddwn i'n falch iawn i gael y swydd.
Ann:	Gobeithio eich bod chi'n mwynhau'r gwaith yn yr ysgol.
Richard:	Ydw, yn fawr iawn. Roedd pawb gartref yn meddwl fy mod i'n dwp iawn i symud mor bell, ond dw i'n falch iawn fy mod i wedi dod yma.
Ann:	Dim yn wirion o gwbl! Roeddwn i wedi clywed eich bod chi'n mynd i helpu efo côr yr ysgol. Dw i'n siŵr bod Mrs Williams yn falch iawn.
Richard:	Ydy. Dw i'n mwynhau canu'n fawr iawn, felly dyn ni'n gobeithio cystadlu yn yr Eisteddfod y flwyddyn nesaf. Mae'n drueni bod dim eisteddfod leol yn yr ardal.

English Translation

Richard:	How long have you worked at the school, Ann?
Ann:	Ten years. I taught in a school in West Wales for a time, but my husband and I wanted to move back to the North to live. How long have you been a teacher?
Richard:	Only for a year. This is my first job. I had applied for many jobs before coming here. I was very glad to get the job.
Ann:	I hope you enjoy the work at the school.
Richard:	Yes, very much. Everyone at home thought I was very stupid to move so far, but I'm very glad that I have come here.
Ann:	Not silly at all! I had heard that you were going to help with the school choir. I'm sure that Mrs Williams is very glad.
Richard:	Yes. I enjoy singing very much, so we hope to compete in the Eisteddfod next year. It's a pity that there isn't a local eisteddfod in the area.

Lesson 7: Recap exercise

Exercise 1

Fill the gaps in the following sentences.

For example:

Question: ___ hi'n heulog ddoe.
Answer: Roedd hi'n heulog ddoe.

1) _____ i eisiau cystadlu.
   (I wanted to compete.)
2) _____ hi'n wyntog echdoe.
   (It was windy the day before yesterday.)
3) _____ chi'n arfer byw yn yr ardal?
   (Did you used to live in the area?)
4) _____ ti ddim yn wirion.
   (You weren't silly.)
5) _____ ni'n hoffi gwrando ar y côr.

(We liked listening to the choir.)
6) _____ nhw ddim eisiau gadael.
(They didn't want to leave.)
7) _____ hi ddim yn braf y bore 'ma.
(It wasn't fine this morning.)
8) _____ i'n meddwl bod hynny'n iawn.
(I thought that was all right.)
9) _____ e (SW)/o (NW) ddim eisiau mynd allan.
(He didn't want to go out.)
10) _____ chi'n ei adnabod e (SW)/o (NW)?
(Did you know him?)

If you have difficulty completing this exercise, review **Week 6, Lesson 1**.

Exercise 2

Translate the following sentences.

1) It was windy yesterday. _____
2) They didn't want to go out. _____
3) I had driven. _____
4) Everyone had understood us. _____
5) Had she applied? _____
6) I thought that was true. _____
7) Of course he had believed her. _____
8) They had moved house. _____
9) Had you eaten your breakfast? _____
10) I hadn't seen the accident. _____

If you have difficulty completing this exercise, review **Week 6, Lesson 2** *and* **3**.

Exercise 3

Translate the following sentences.

1) He says that we are silly.

_____

2) Of course I am listening.

_____

3) I think that we are early.

_____

4) I had heard that there is an eisteddfod next week.

_____

5) They say that she has written another letter.

_____

6) It's a pity that it is so windy.

_____

7) We thought that he is a *policeman*.

_____

8) Although it is snowing, we are going to walk.

_____

If you have difficulty completing this exercise, review **Week 6, Lesson 3, Lesson 4,** *and* **Lesson 5**.

Exercise 4

Fill in the blanks with the correct form of **blwyddyn, blynedd,** *and* **blwydd,** *remembering to mutate where necessary:*

1) Bues i'n gweithio i'r cwmni 'na am naw _____.
2) Mae gen i gi sy'n ddeg _____ oed.
3) Dw i'n byw yn fy nhŷ i ers un deg chwe _____.
4) Mae o'n cynnig am swydd newydd bob dwy _____.
5) Dyn ni'n mynd i Iwerddon y _____ nesaf.
6) Roedd 1990 yn _____ wael i ffermwyr.

If you have difficulty completing this exercise, review **Week 6, Lesson 6**.

Week 7

Lesson 1: The imperative (giving a command)

The imperative is a grammatical mood which is used to express commands, instructions or requests. Examples of verbs in the imperative mood in English are 'be' and 'open' in the phrases 'Be quiet!' and 'Open the window!'

In English, there is only one way to express the imperative, irrespective of person. For example, when we say 'Sit (down)!', we could be talking to one person, more than one person, or a third person. Welsh, on the other hand, differentiates between *five* types of imperative depending on person:

PERSON	ENGLISH FORM	WELSH COMMAND	ENGLISH EQUIVALENT	IPA
second person singular	you (*fam.*)	**Eistedd!**	Sit!	[ˈəɪsteð]
second person plural	you (*sing. formal, pl.*)	**Eisteddwch!**	Sit!	[əɪsˈteðʊχ]
third person singular	he, she	**Eistedded!**	Let him / her / it sit!	[əɪsˈteðed]
first person plural	we	**Eisteddwn!**	Let us stand!	[əɪsˈteðʊn]
third person plural	they	**Eisteddent!**	Let them stand!	[əɪsˈteðent]

Only the second person singular and second person plural forms are common in spoken Welsh; the third person singular and first person plural are used occasionally, especially by older people and in formal contexts, e.g. **gweddïwn** 'let us pray' [gweˈðiːʊn]); third person plural is purely a literary form. We will only deal with second person singular and second person plural in detail in this section.

Verb-nouns and verb stems

Before proceeding, we need to know a little more about verb-nouns and verb stems. A verb-noun is usually said to consist of a 'stem' and a verbal ending. Different verb-nouns form their stem in different ways:

(i) The stem is usually the part of the verb-noun which remains after the last vowel has been removed:

VERB-NOUN	ENGLISH	IPA	STEM	IPA
canu	to sing / to ring	[ˈkɑːni]	**can-**	[kɑn]
gweithio	to work	[ˈgwəɪθjo]	**gweithi-**	[gwəɪθj]

(ii) Verb-nouns ending in **-ed** [ed] and **-eg** [eg] will drop those endings to form the stem:

VERB-NOUN	ENGLISH	IPA	STEM	IPA
rhedeg	to run	[ˈr̥eˑdeg]	**rhed-**	[r̥ed]
cerdded	to walk	[ˈkɛrðed]	**cerdd-**	[kɛrð]

(iii) Some verb-nouns remain intact:

VERB-NOUN	ENGLISH	IPA	STEM	IPA
eistedd	to sit	['əɪstɛð]	**eistedd-**	[əɪs'tɛð]
darllen	to read	['darɬɛn]	**darllen-**	[dar'ɬɛn]

However, remember that the stress syllable moves to the penult (the last but one syllable).

(iv) Some verb-nouns undergo a slight change in their stem:

VERB-NOUN	ENGLISH	IPA	STEM	IPA
gofyn	to ask	['gɔvɪn]	**gofynn-**	[gɔ'vən]
cyrraedd	to arrive	['kəra(ɪ)ð]	**cyrhaedd-**	[kər'həɪð]
newid	to change	['nɛʊɪd]	**newidi-**	[nɛʊ'ɪdj]
meddwl	to think	['mɛðʊl]	**meddyli-**	[mɛ'ðəlj]

The familiar 'you' command (second person singular)
The familiar 'you' command usually corresponds to to stem of the verb-noun:

VERB-NOUN	ENGLISH	IPA	STEM	IPA	IMPERATIVE	IPA
sefyll	to stand	['sɛvɪɬ]	**saf-**	[sɑ·v]	**saf**	[sɑːv]
galw	to call	['galʊ]	**galw-**	[ga·lw]	**galw**	['galʊ]
eistedd	to sit	['əɪstɛð]	**eistedd-**	['əɪstɛð]	**eistedd**	['əɪstɛð]
edrych	to look	['ɛdɪχ]	**edrych-**	[ɛd'ɹəχ]	**edrych**	['ɛdɪχ]
rhedeg	to run	['ɹɛ·dɛg]	**rhed-**	[ɹɛ·d]	**rhed**	[ɹɛːd]
darllen	to read	['darɬɛn]	**darllen-**	[dar'ɬɛn]	**darllen**	['darɬɛn]
clywed	to hear	['kləʊɛd]	**clyw-**	[kləʊ]	**clyw**	[klɪʊ]

If the verb-noun is formed from a noun or an adjective (usually ones that end in **-i** [i], **-io** [jo] or **-u** [i] (SW) / [ɨ] (NW)), such as **ffonio** ['fɔnjo] < **ffôn** ['foːn], **-a** [ä] is added to the stem to form the familiar 'you' command:

VERB-NOUN	ENGLISH	IPA	STEM	IPA	IMPERATIVE	IPA
ffonio	to telephone	['fɔnjo]	**ffoni-**	[fɔnj]	**ffonia**	['fɔnjä]
ysgrifennu	to write	[əsgrɪv'ɛni]	**ysgrifenn-**	[əsgrɪv'ɛn]	**ysgrifenna**	[əsgrɪv'ɛnä]
gweithio	to work	['gwəɪθjo]	**gweithi-**	[gwəɪθj]	**gweithia**	['gwəɪθjä]
meddwl	to think	['mɛðʊl]	**meddyli-**	[mɛð'əlj]	**meddylia**	[mɛð'əljä]
stopio	to stop	['stɔpjo]	**stopi-**	[stɔpj]	**stopia**	['stɔpjä]
dihuno (SW)	to wake up	[di'hi·no]	**dihun-**	[di'hiːn]	**dihuna**	[di'hiːnä]
neidio	to jump	['nəɪdjo]	**neidi-**	[nəɪdj]	**neidia**	['nəɪdjä]

There are a few irregular forms which are so common they should be learnt thoroughly:

VERB-NOUN	ENGLISH	FAMILIAR 'YOU' COMMAND	IPA
mynd	to go	**cer** (SW)	[kɛr]
mynd	to go	**dos** (NW)	[dɔːs]
dod	to come	**dere** (SW)	[ˈdeˑrɛ]
dod	to come	**ty(r)d** (NW)	[tɪ(r)d]
peidio*	don't	**paid**	[paɪd]
codi	to lift / to get up	**cwyd**	[kʊɪd]
cysgu	to sleep	**cwsg**	[kʊsg]
gwneud	to do / to make	**gwna**	[gʷnɑː]
bod	to be	**bydd**	[biːð]

*You will also hear **peidio â** (AM) [ˈpeɪdjo ɑ̃]. This is considered more formal.*

Vocabulary

FEMININE NOUN	ENGLISH	IPA	PLURAL FORM	IPA
cot (SW)	coat	[kɔt]	**cotiau**	[ˈkɔtjɛ]
côt (NW)	coat	[koːt]	**cotiau**	[ˈkɔtjɛ]

VERB-NOUN	ENGLISH	IPA	STEM	IPA
prynu	to buy	[ˈprəni]	**pryn-**	[prən]
peidio â (AM)	to refrain from	[ˈpəɪdjo ɑ̃]	**peidi-**	[pəɪdj ɑ̃]

ADJECTIVE	ENGLISH	IPA
tawel	quiet	[ˈtaʊɛl]
distaw	quiet	[ˈdɪstaʊ]

Exercise 1

*Fill in the blanks by forming a second person singular **ti** command using one of the verb-nouns listed in brackets below.*

(siarad, bod, meddwl, ysgrifennu, mynd, sefyll, peidio, eistedd, cofio, codi)

1) _____! Mae'n saith o'r gloch. (Get up! It's seven o'clock!)
2) _____ at eich rhieni! (Write to your parents.)
3) _____ Gymraeg! (Speak Welsh!)
4) _____ yn dawel/ddistaw! (Be quiet!)
5) _____ am bobl eraill. (Think of other people.)
6) _____ ar dy draed! (Stand on your feet!)
7) _____ wisgo dy got. (Remember to wear your coat.)

8) _____ i'r siop i brynu llaeth.   (Go to the shop to buy milk.)
9) _____ yn y gadair 'na   (Sit in that chair.)
10) _____ â phoeni!   (Don't worry!)

The formal 'you' command (second person plural)
The more formal 'you' command is formed by adding **-wch** [ʊχ] to the stem of the verb-noun. It is used when addressing strangers, older people (as a mark of respect), and more than one person directly:

VERB-NOUN	ENGLISH	IPA	STEM	IPA	IMPERATIVE	IPA
sefyll	to stand	['sɛvɨl]	saf-	[saːv]	safwch	['saːvʊχ]
galw	to call	['ɡɑlu]	galw-	[ɡɑlw]	galwch	['ɡɑlʊχ]
eistedd'	to sit	['ɔɪstɛð]	eistedd-	[ɔɪstɛð]	eisteddwch	[ɔɪs'tɛðʊχ]
edrych	to look	['ɛdɹɨχ]	edrych-	[ɛd.ɹəχ]	edrychwch	[ɛd.ɹəχʊχ]
rhedeg	to run	['r̥ɛdɛɡ]	rhed-	[r̥ɛd]	rhedwch	['r̥ɛdʊχ]
darllen	to read	['darɬɛn]	darllen-	[darɬɛn]	darllenwch	[darɬɛnʊχ]
clywed	to hear	['kləvɛd]	clyw-	[kləu]	clywch	[klɪʊχ]
ffonio	to phone	['fɔnjo]	ffoni-	[fɔnj]	ffoniwch	['fɔnjʊχ]
ysgrifennu	to write	[əsɡrɪv'ɛni]	ysgrifenn-	[əsɡrɪv'ɛn]	ysgrifennwch	[əsɡrɪv'ɛnʊχ]
gweithio	to work	['ɡwəɪθjo]	gweithi-	['ɡwəɪθj]	gweithiwch	['ɡwəɪθjʊχ]
meddwl	to think	['mɛðʊl]	meddyli-	[mɛðəlj]	meddyliwch	[mɛðəljʊχ]
stopio	to stop	['stɔpjo]	stopi-	[stɔpj]	stopiwch	['stɔpjʊχ]
dihuno	to awake	[dɪ'hiːno]	dihun-	[dɪ'hiːn]	dihunwch	[dɪ'hiːnʊχ]
neidio	to jump	['nɔɪdjo]	neidi-	[nɔɪdj]	neidiwch	['nɔɪdjʊχ]

Here are the irregular forms:

VERB-NOUN	ENGLISH	FORMAL 'YOU' COMMAND	IPA
mynd	to go	**cerwch** (SW)	['kɛrʊχ]
mynd	to go	**ewch** (NW)	[ɛʊχ]
dod	to come	**dewch** (SW)	[dɛʊχ]
dod	to come	**dowch** (NW)	[doʊχ]
gwneud	to do / to make	**gwnewch**	[ɡʷnɛʊχ]
bod	to be	**byddwch**	['bəðʊχ]

The direct object (see **Week 2, Lesson 1**) of a command undergoes soft mutation:

IMPERATIVE SENTENCE	ENGLISH	IPA
Anghofiwch bopeth.	Forget everything.	[aŋ'hɔvjʊχ 'bɔpɛθ]
Bwytwch lysiau bob dydd.	Eat vegetables every day.	['bʊitʊχ 'ləʃɛ boːb diːð]

Vocabulary

MASCULINE NOUN	ENGLISH	IPA	PLURAL FORM	IPA
llysieuyn	vegetable	[ɬəˈʃɔɪ.ɪn]	llysiau	[ˈɬəʃɛ]
rhywbeth	something	[ˈrɪʊbɛθ]		

VERB-NOUN	ENGLISH	IPA	STEM	IPA
cau	to close / to shut	[kaɪ]	cae-	[kəɪ]

Exercise 2

Turn the familiar imperatives in the sentences below into formal **chi** imperatives. The verb to be changed is in italics.

1) *Bydd* yn ofalus! _____ (Be careful!)
2) *Gwna* rywbeth! _____ (Do something!)
3) *Cwsg* yn dawel. _____ (Sleep soundly.)
4) *Cer* i'r gwely. (SW) / *Dos* i'r gwely. (NW) _____ (Go to bed.)
5) *Saf* wrth y drws. _____ (Stand by the door.)
6) *Rhed* i'r dref. _____ (Run to town.)
7) *Dere* yma. (SW) / *Tyrd* yma. (NW) _____ (Come here.)
8) *Symud* y car. _____ (Move the car.)
9) *Yf* ddigon o ddŵr. _____ (Drink plenty of water.)
10) *Cae'*r drws. _____ (Close the door.)

The 'he' / 'she' command (third person singular)

This is a command given to a third person who isn't in earshot of the speaker. It is formed by adding **-ed** [ɛd] to the stem of the verb. It can be loosely translated as 'let him (...)' / 'let her (...)':

IMPERATIVE SENTENCE	ENGLISH	IPA
Caned yr anthem!	Let him / her sing the anthem.	[ˈkɑnɛd ər ˈanθɛm]
Safed ar ei draed!	Let him stand on his feet.	[ˈsɑvɛd ar i draɪd]

The 'we' command (first person plural)

This is a command given to a group of people of which the speaker is a member. It is formed by adding the **-wn** [ʊn] to the stem of the verb:

VERB-NOUN	IPA	STEM	IPA	IMPERATIVE	IPA
sefyll	[ˈsɛvɪɫ]	saf-	[saˑv]	Safwn!	[ˈsaˑvʊn]
eistedd	[ˈəɪstɛð]	eistedd-	[əɪsˈtɛð]	Eisteddwn!	[əɪsˈtɛðʊn]
edrych	[ˈɛdɪχ]	edrych-	[ɛdˑɹəχ]	Edrychwn!	[ɛdˑɹəχʊχ]
meddwl	[ˈmɛðʊl]	meddyli-	[mɛðˈəlj]	Meddyliwn!	[mɛðˈəljʊn]
stopio	[ˈstɔpjo]	stopi-	[stɔpj]	Stopiwn!	[ˈstɔpjʊn]
peidio	[ˈpəɪdjo]	peidi-	[pəɪdj]	Peidiwn!	[ˈpəɪdjʊn]

The 'they' command (third person plural)
The 'they' command is given to more than one person when they aren't in earshot of the speaker. It is formed by adding **-ent** [ɛnt] to the stem of the verb, and can be loosely translated as 'let them':

IMPERATIVE SENTENCE	ENGLISH	IPA
Canent yr anthem.	Let them sing the anthem.	[ˈkanɛnt ər ˈänθɛm]
Safent ar eu traed.	Let them stand on their feet.	[ˈsaˑvɛnt ar əɪ tɹaɪd]

Vocabulary

MASCULINE NOUN	ENGLISH	IPA	PLURAL FORM	IPA
dŵr	water	[duːr]	**dyfroedd**	[ˈdəvrɔɪð]
chwith	left	[χwiːθ]		
cyfeiriad	address / direction	[kəvˈəɪrjad]	**cyfeiriadau**	[kəvəɪrˈjɑˑdɛ]
tro	turn / turning / time	[tɹoː]	**troeon**	[ˈtɹɔɪon]
adeilad	building	[adˈəɪlad]	**adeiladau**	[adəɪlˈɑˑdɛ]

FEMININE NOUN	ENGLISH	IPA	PLURAL FORM	IPA
swyddfa bost	post office	[ˈsʊɪðvä bɔst]	**swyddfeydd post**	[sʊɪðvəɪð post]
acen	accent	[ˈakɛn]	**acenion**	[akˈɛnjon]
troed	foot	[tɹɔɪd]	**traed**	[tɹaɪd]
heol	road	[ˈheˑol]	**heolydd**	[heˑoˈlɪð]
siop fara	bakery / bread shop	[ʃɔp ˈvɑˑra]	**siopau bara**	[ˈʃɔpɛ ˈbɑˑra]
de	right	[deː]		
croesffordd	crossroads	[ˈkrɔɪsfɔrð]	**croesffyrdd**	[ˈkrɔɪsfɪrð]
croesfan	pedestrian crossing	[ˈkrɔɪsvan]	**croesfannau**	[ˈkrɔɪsvänɛ]
cornel	corner	[ˈkɔrnɛl]	**corneli**	[kɔrˈnɛli]
stryd	street	[stɹiːd]	**strydoedd**	[ˈstɹədɔɪð]
anthem	anthem	[ˈanθɛm]	**anthemau**	[anˈθɛmɛ]
ysgol uwchradd	secondary school	[ˈəsgol ˈɪʊχrað]	**ysgolion uwchradd**	[əsˈgoljon ˈɪʊχrɑ...]

VERB-NOUN	ENGLISH	IPA	STEM	IPA
esgusodi	to excuse	[ɛsgɪsˈɔdi]	**esgusod-**	[ɛsgɪsˈɔd]
troi	to turn	[tjɔɪ]	**troi-**	[tjɔɪ]
croesi	to cross	[ˈkrɔɪsi]	**croes-**	[krɔɪs]

PLACE NAME	ENGLISH	IPA
Caerfyrddin	Carmarthen	[kaɪrˈvərðɪn]

ADJECTIVE	ENGLISH	IPA
teg	fair	[teːg]

ADVERBIAL	ENGLISH	IPA
ar goll	lost	[ar gɔɬ]
ar droed	on foot	[ar drɔɪd]
i lawr	down	[iː laʊr]

MISCELLANEOUS	ENGLISH	IPA
i gyfeiriad	in the direction of	[iː gəvˈəɪrjad]

Dialogue

Welsh Dialogue

Richard: Esgusodwch fi. Dw i'n credu fy mod i ar goll. Ydych chi'n gwybod ble mae'r swyddfa bost?

Mr Williams: Ydw, ydw. Dych chi ddim yn bell o gwbl. Dim ond deg munud ar droed. Un o'r De ydych chi wrth eich acen chi.

Richard: Dych chi'n iawn, dw i'n dod o Gaerfyrddin. Dw i wedi symud i'r Gogledd i fyw achos fy mod i wedi cael swydd yn yr ysgol uwchradd.

Mr Williams: Chwarae teg. Wel, ewch i lawr y lôn yma, ac wedyn, trowch i'r chwith, i Stryd y Dŵr. Mae siop fara ar y dde. Mae ganddyn nhw gacennau blasus iawn. Ewch i lawr Heol y Dŵr, i'r groesffordd. Croeswch y lôn ar y groesfan. Mae'r ffordd yn brysur iawn. Mae'r ceir yn mynd yn gyflym iawn. Byddwch yn ofalus iawn wrth groesi. Wedyn, ewch i gyfeiriad yr eglwys. Mae'r eglwys ar y dde. Cymerwch y tro cyntaf wedyn. Mae siop gamerâu ar y gornel. Mae swyddfa bost hanner ffordd i lawr y stryd. Mae'n adeilad mawr iawn.

Richard: Diolch yn fawr.

English Translation

Richard: Excuse me. I think I'm lost. Do you know where the post office is?

Mr Williams: Yes, yes. You are not far at all. Only ten minutes on foot. You are from the South, judging by your accent.

Richard: That's (You are) right. I come from Carmarthen. I've moved to the North to live because I've got a job in the secondary school.

Mr Williams: Fair play. Well, go down this road and then turn to the left, into Water Street. There's a bread shop on the right. They have very tasty cakes. Go down Water Street. The cars go very quickly. Be very careful crossing. Then go in the direction of the church. The church is on the right. Take the first turning then. There's a camera shop on the corner. The post office is half way down the street. It's a very big building.

Richard: Thanks very much.

Lesson 2: Affirmative forms of the simple past tense (regular verbs)

There are two types of verb construction in Welsh:

(i) The periphrastic or 'long' forms, where personal forms of **'bod'** are combined with a verb-noun:

Here is an example in the present imperfect:

SENTENCE	ENGLISH	IPA
Mae Alun yn dysgu.*	Alun is learning.	[maɪ 'ɑ:lɪn ən 'dəsgi]

* Remember that **dysgu** can also mean 'to teach'.

For more on this topic, see **Week 3, Lesson 1** to **Lesson 5**.

Here is an example in the past imperfect:

SENTENCE	ENGLISH	IPA
Roeddwn i'n sefyll.	I was standing.	['rɔɪðʊn iːn 'sɛvɪɬ]

We saw this pattern used in the past imperfect when we looked at the 'verbs of mental state' (see **Week 6, Lesson 1**):

PHRASE	ENGLISH	IPA
roeddwn i'n credu	I believed	['rɔɪðʊn iːn 'krɛdi]

(ii) With regular verbs, the simple past is formed by adding a personal inflection, or ending, which denotes person and tense, to the stem of the verb:

dysg- + **odd**   he / she learnt
⇑   ⇑
stem   inflection

-**odd** [oð] is the third person singular (3 pers. sing.) ending in the simple past.

In spoken Welsh, the inflected forms are generally accompanied by affixed pronouns (see **Week 5, Lesson 2**):

Dysgodd { **e** / **hi** } { he / she } learnt

Below is the past tense conjugation of the verb **dysgu** (to learn / to teach):

SENTENCE	ENGLISH	IPA
Dysgais i.	I learnt. / I taught	['dəsgɛs iː]
Dysgaist ti.	You learnt. / You taught (*fam.*)	['dəsgɛs(t) tiː]
Dysgodd e. (SW)	He learnt. / He taught.	['dəsgoð eː]
Dysgodd o. (NW)	He learnt. / He taught.	['dəsgoð oː]
Dysgodd hi.	She learnt. / She taught.	['dəsgoð hiː]
Dysgon ni.	We learnt. / We taught.	['dəsgo(n) niː]
Dysgoch chi.	You learnt. / You taught. (*pl.*) (*sing. formal*)	['dəsgo(χ) χiː]
Dysgon nhw.	They learnt. / They taught.	['dəsgo(n) n̥uː]

Vocabulary

VERB-NOUN	IPA	STEM	IPA	SENTENCE	ENGLISH	IPA
sefyll	['sɛvɨɬ]	**saf-**	[saːv]	**safais i.**	I stood.	['saːvɛs i]
codi	['kɔdi]	**cod-**	[kɔd]	**codon nhw.**	they got up.	['kɔdo(n) n̥u]

FEMININE NOUN	ENGLISH	IPA	PLURAL FORM	IPA
gwers	lesson	[gwɛrs]	**gwersi**	['gwɛrsi]

ADVERBIAL	ENGLISH	IPA
yn dda	well	[ən ðaː]

As we saw with the imperative in **Week 7, Lesson 1**, the direct object of inflected verbs undergoes soft mutation:

	VERB	SUBJECT	DIRECT OBJECT	DIRECT OBJECT PRE-MUTATION
WELSH	**Dysgodd**	**Gareth**	*Gymraeg*.	**Cymraeg**
ENGLISH	Gareth learnt Welsh.			
IPA	['dəsgoð]	'gareθ	gəm'raɪg]	

> **IMPORTANT**
> The 3 pers. sing. form, **dysgodd** ['dəsgoð], is used when the subject is a singular or plural noun.

	SENTENCE
WELSH	**Dysgodd y plant y wers yn dda.**
ENGLISH	The children learnt the lesson well.
IPA	['dəsgoð ə plant ə wɛrs ən ðaː]

Often, a preverbal particle (**mi** [miː] in North Wales and **fe** [veː] in South Wales) is placed in front of the affirmative form of an inflected verb. Both **mi** and **fe** cause the first letter of the verb they precede to undergo soft mutation:

fe ⎫
    ⎬ ddysgodd Gareth Gymraeg   Gareth learnt Welsh
mi ⎭

The preverbal particle is usually omitted in everyday speech, but the mutation in clauses remains:

	SENTENCE
WELSH	**'Ddysgodd Gareth Gymraeg.**
ENGLISH	Gareth learnt Welsh.
IPA	[ˈðəsgoð ˈɡɑːrɛθ gəmˈraɪg]

The **fe** (SW) / **mi** (NW) forms have been noted for reference but are not used in this book.

Exercise 1

Fill in the blanks by making a past tense verb using the verb-noun in brackets.

For example:

Question: ____ hi wneud y cinio.   (dechrau)
Answer: Dechreuodd hi wneud y cinio.

1) _____ i wyau i frecwast.   (bwyta)
2) _____ Richard gyda'r côr neithiwr. (canu)
3) _____ y plant ar eu hiPod.   (gwrando)
4) _____ ti'n gynnar.   (gadael)
5) _____ hi'r gwaith yn hwyr.   (cyrraedd)
6) _____ ni yn y pwll nofio.   (nofio)
7) _____ nhw i'r dref.   (cerdded)
8) _____ chi'r hanes yn y papur.   (darllen)

Vocabulary

MASCULINE NOUN	ENGLISH	IPA	PLURAL FORM	IPA
arogl	smell / aroma	[ˈɑːrogl]	**aroglau**	[arˈɔglɛ]
stamp	stamp	[stamp]	**stampiau**	[ˈstampjɛ]

FEMININE NOUN	ENGLISH	IPA	PLURAL FORM	IPA
taith	journey	[taɪθ]	**teithiau**	[ˈtəɪθjɛ]
torth	loaf	[tɔrθ]	**torthau**	[ˈtɔrθɛ]

ADJECTIVE	ENGLISH	IPA
ffres	fresh	[frɛʃ]

MISCELLANEOUS	ENGLISH	IPA
yng nghanol	in the middle of	[ə(ŋ) ˈŋ̊ɑˈnol]

Dialogue

Welsh Dialogue

Gareth: Rwyt ti'n hwyr. Ble rwyt ti wedi bod?
Richard: Cerddais i i'r dref. Roeddwn i eisiau mynd i'r swyddfa bost.
Gareth: Dyna daith hir i brynu stamp!
Richard: Ie, doeddwn i ddim yn gwybod bod y swyddfa'r bost yng nghanol y dref. Roeddwn i'n meddwl ei bod hi yn Stryd y Bont.
Gareth: Mae arogl da yma.
Richard: Oes. Prynais i dorth o fara ffres a dwy gacen fach yn y siop fara.
Gareth: Diddorol. Dwy gacen fach ddwedaist ti?

English Translation

Gareth: You are late. Where have you been?
Richard: I walked to the town. I wanted to go to the post office.
Gareth: That's a long journey to buy a stamp!
Richard: Yes, I didn't know that the post office was in the middle of town. I thought it was in Bridge Street.
Gareth: There's a good smell here.
Richard: Yes. I bought a loaf of fresh bread and two small cakes in the bread shop.
Gareth: Interesting. Two small cakes, did you say?

Lesson 3: Interrogative forms of the simple past tense (regular verbs)

To ask a question, simply softly mutate the first letter of the verb:

QUESTION	ENGLISH	IPA
Ddysgoch chi?	Did you learn?	[ˈðəsgo(χ) χiː]
Fwytodd e?	Did he eat?	[ˈvʊɪtoð eː]

As in English, Welsh is characterised by rising and falling intonation in questions:

Ddysgoch chi?

Here are the personal inflected forms:

QUESTION	ENGLISH	IPA
Ddysgais i?	Did I learn?	['ðəsgɛs iː]
Ddysgaist ti?	Did you learn? (fam.)	['ðəsgɛs(t) tiː]
Ddysgodd e? (SW)	Did he learn?	['ðəsgoð eː]
Ddysgodd o? (NW)	Did he learn?	['ðəsgoð oː]
Ddysgodd hi?	Did she learn?	['ðəsgoð hiː]
Ddysgon ni?	Did we learn?	['ðəsgo(n) niː]
Ddysgoch chi?	Did you learn? (pl.) (sing. formal)	['ðəsgo(χ) χiː]
Ddysgon nhw?	Did they learn?	['ðəsgo(n) n̥uː]

> **IMPORTANT**
> The 3 pers. sing. form, **ddysgodd** ['dəsgoð], is used when the subject is a singular or plural noun.

The response to closed questions in the simple past is **do** 'yes' [doː] and **naddo** 'no' ['naˑðo].

	WELSH	ENGLISH	IPA
QUESTION	Gymeroch chi'r llaeth o'r oergell?	Did you take the milk from the fridge?	[gəm'ɛro(χ) χiːr ɬaiθ or 'ɔirgɛɬ]
REPLY	Do.	Yes.	[doː]
QUESTION	Ddwedon nhw wrth Siôn?	Did they tell Siôn?	['ðwɛdo(n) n̥uː urθ ʃoːn]
REPLY	Naddo.	No.	['naˑðo]

Vocabulary

MASCULINE NOUN	ENGLISH	IPA	PLURAL FORM	IPA
cwpwrdd	cupboard	['kupurð]	cypyrddau	[kəp'ərðɛ]
ymarfer	exercise / practice	[əm'arvɛr]	ymarferion	[əmar'vɛrjon]
pysgodyn	fish	[pəs'gɔdɪn]	pysgod	['pəsgod]
hyfforddwr	trainer	[həf'ɔrðʊr]	hyfforddwyr	[həf'ɔrðwɪr]
larwm	alarm	['lɑrʊm]	larymau	[lɑˑr'əmɛ]

VERB-NOUN	ENGLISH	IPA	STEM	IPA
talu	to pay	['tɑˑli]	tal-	[tɑl]
colli	to lose / to miss	['kɔɬi]	coll-	[kɔɬ]
sgorio	to score	['sgɔrjo]	sgori-	[sgɔrj]
ymarfer	to practise	[əm'arvɛr]	ymarfer-	[əmar'vɛr]
aros	to stay / to wait	['ɑˑros]	arhos-	[ar'hɔs]

ADJECTIVE	ENGLISH	IPA
lwcus	lucky	['lʊkɪs]
mwy	more	[mʊɪ]

ADVERBIAL	ENGLISH	IPA
digon	enough	['dɪˑgon]
yn ôl	back(wards) / according to / ago	[ən oːl]
rhywle	somewhere	['ɲʊlɛ]
eto	again	['ɛto]

Dialogue

Welsh Dialogue

Ann: Brynaist ti laeth ar y ffordd yn ôl o'r gêm?
Tomos: Do, rhoiais i fe yn yr oergell.
Ann: Diolch, gofiaist ti gael bara?
Tomos: Do. Rhoiais i'r bara yn y cwpwrdd yn y gegin.
Ann: Enilloch chi?
Tomos: Naddo. Collon ni eto. Tair i un.
Ann: Dyna drueni ar ôl eich holl ymarfer chi. Gobeithio bod y tîm yn fwy lwcus yr wythnos nesaf. Sgoriaist ti?
Tomos: Do, fi sgoriodd ein hunig gôl ni. Chwaraeon ni'n dda iawn, ond dim yn ddigon da i ennill yn anffodus.
Ann: Arhosoch chi rywle ar y ffordd yn ôl i gael bwyd?
Tomos: Do. Arhoson ni yn Nhre-maen i gael pysgod a sglodion. Blasus iawn.
Ann: Dalodd yr hyfforddwr eto?
Tomos: Naddo. Y tro 'ma, talon ni dros ein hunain.

English Translation

Ann: Did you buy milk on the way home from the game?
Tomos: Yes. I put it in the fridge.
Ann: Thanks, did you remember to get bread?
Tomos: Yes. I put the bread in the cupboard in the kitchen.
Ann: Did you win?
Tomos: No. We lost again. 3-1.
Ann: That's a pity after all your practice. I hope the team are luckier next week. Did you score?
Tomos: Yes. I scored our only goal. We played very well, but not good enough to win, unfortunately.
Ann: Did you stop somewhere on the way back to get food?
Tomos: Yes. we stopped in Tre-maen to get fish and chips. Very tasty.
Ann: Did the coach pay again?
Tomos: No. This time we paid for ourselves.

Exercise 1

Fill in the blanks by forming a past tense interrogative verb using the verb-noun in brackets. Remember to mutate if necessary.

1) _____ chi'r ffilm neithiwr? (gwylio)
   (Did you see the film last night?)
2) _____ hi ei hoergell hi yn y siop newydd? (prynu)
   (Did she buy her fridge in the new shop?)
3) _____ ti'r car? (*fam.*) (symud)
   (Did you move the car?)
4) _____ o yn ei ystafell wely ei hunan? (cysgu)
   (Did he sleep in his own bedroom?)
5) _____ nhw'r larwm? (clywed)
   (Did they hear the alarm?)
6) _____ nhw chi? (dysgu)
   (Did they teach you?)
7) _____ yr athrawes yn y wers? (siarad)
   (Did the teacher speak in the lesson?)
8) _____ y plant i'r ysgol. (rhedeg)
   (Did the children run to school?)

Lesson 4: Negative forms of the simple past tense (regular verbs)

To form the negative in the simple past tense, **ddim** is placed after the verb. Also, if the initial consonant of begins with **p**, **t** or **c**, it will undergo aspirate mutation, while, if the initial consonant of begins with one of the other six other letters subject to mutation (see **Week 1, Lesson 5**), it will undergo soft mutation.

Here are some examples:

SENTENCE	ENGLISH	IPA	MUTATION
Phaentiais i ddim.	I didn't paint.	[ˈfəɪntjɛs iː ðɪm]	aspirate
Throiodd e ddim.	He didn't turn.	[ˈθrɔɪɔð eː ðɪm]	aspirate
Cherddodd hi ddim.	She didn't walk.	[ˈχɛrðɔð hiː ðɪm]	aspirate
Fwyton ni ddim.	We didn't eat.	[ˈvʊɪtɔn ni ðɪm]	soft
Ddarllenoch chi ddim.	You didn't read.	[ðarɬɛnɔ(χ) χiː ðɪm]	soft
Weithiodd e ddim.	He didn't work.	[ˈwəɪθjɔð eː ðɪm]	soft
Fentrais i ddim.	I didn't venture.	[ˈvɛntɹɛs iː ðɪm]	soft
Lanwon nhw ddim.	They didn't fill.	[ˈlanwɔ(n) n̥uː ðɪm]	soft
Redaist ti ddim.	You didn't run. (*fam.*)	[ˈrɛˑdɛs(t) tiː ðɪm]	soft

The initial mutations (particularly the aspirate mutation) are not that common in spoken Welsh – the **ddim** being enough to show that the verb is negative.

When the direct object of a negative inflected verb is indefinite (for example, in English: 'a paper', 'papers'), it is not mutated:

SENTENCE	ENGLISH	IPA
Welais i ddim papur.	I didn't see any paper / a paper.	[ˈwɛles i ðɪm ˈpapɪr]
Welais i ddim papurau.	I didn't see any papers.	[ˈwɛles i ðɪm papˈɪrɛ]

Vocabulary

MASCULINE NOUN	ENGLISH	IPA	PLURAL FORM	IPA
dilledyn	a garment	[dɪlʲedɪn]	**dillad**	[ˈdɪɬad]

VERB-NOUN	ENGLISH	IPA	STEM	IPA
teithio	to travel	[ˈtəɪθjo]	**teithi-**	[təɪθj]
mentro	to venture	[ˈmentro]	**mentr-**	[mentr̥]
llenwi	to fill	[ˈɬenwi]	**llenw-**	[ɬenw]

Exercise 1

Translate the following sentences.

1) I didn't write a letter to the police. _____
2) They didn't drive to Denbigh. _____
3) We didn't walk home. _____
4) No-one saw anything. _____
5) I didn't drink any coffee. _____
6) We didn't travel together. _____
7) You didn't buy any clothes. _____
8) They didn't phone yesterday. _____

When the direct object of an inflected verb is definite (for example: 'the paper', 'the papers', 'Huw') **ddim o** [ðɪm oː] is used:

	SENTENCE
WELSH	**Welais i ddim o'r papur.**
ENGLISH	I didn't see the paper. (*lit.* I saw nothing of the paper.)
IPA	[ˈwɛles iː ðɪm oːr ˈpapɪr]

WELSH	Welais i ddim o'r papurau.
ENGLISH	I didn't see the papers. (*lit.* I saw nothing of the papers.)
IPA	[ˈwɛlɛs iː ðɪm oːr papˈiːrɛ]

WELSH	Welais i ddim o Huw.
ENGLISH	I didn't see Huw. (*lit.* I saw nothing of Huw.)
IPA	[ˈwɛlɛs iː ðɪm oː hɪʊ]

O 'of' / 'from' [oː] is a declined preposition (see **Week 10, Lesson 5**):

PHRASE	ENGLISH	IPA
ohona i	[oˈhɔna iː]	of me
ohonot ti	[oˈhɔno(t) tiː]	of you (*fam.*)
ohôno fe (SW)	[oˈhɔno vɛː]	of him
ohono fo (NW)	[oˈhɔno voː]	of him
ohoni hi	[oˈhɔni hiː]	of her
ohonon ni	[oˈhɔno(n) niː]	of us
ohonoch chi	[oˈhɔno(χ) χiː]	of you (*pl.*) (*sing. formal*)
ohonyn nhw	[oˈhɔnɪ(n) n̥uː]	of them

Therefore, 'I didn't see him' is translated as: **Welais i ddim ohono fe** [ˈwɛlɛs iː ðɪm oˈhɔno vɛː].

This can be shortened to: **Welais i mohono fe** [ˈwɛlɛs iː moˈhɔno vɛː].

The word **neb** 'no one' [nɛːb] is itself negative, and so does not need **ddim**:

SENTENCE	ENGLISH	IPA
Welais i neb.	I didn't see anyone. (*lit.* I saw no-one.)	[ˈwɛlɛs iː nɛːb]

Vocabulary

MASCULINE NOUN	ENGLISH	IPA	PLURAL FORM	IPA
clwb	club	[klʊb]	**clybiau**	[ˈkləbjɛ]
carped	carpet	[ˈkarpɛd]	**carpedi**	[karˈpɛdi]
ffôn	telephone	[foːn]	**ffonau**	[ˈfonɛ]
trên	train	[t͡ʃeːn]	**trenau**	[ˈt͡ʃenɛ]

FEMININE NOUN	ENGLISH	IPA	PLURAL FORM	IPA
gwobr	prize	[ˈgwoˑbor]	**gwobrau**	[ˈgwɔbrɛ]

VERB-NOUN	ENGLISH	IPA	STEM	IPA
canu	to sing / to ring	[ˈkɑni]	**can-**	[kɑn]
colli	to miss / to lose / to spill	[ˈkɔɬi]	**coll-**	[kɔɬ]

galw	to call	['ɡɑ·lʊ]	**galw-**	[ɡɑ·lw]
gadael	to leave	[ɡɑ·dɛl]	**gadaw-**	[ɡad·aʊ]

ADVERBIAL	ENGLISH	IPA
adre(f)	home(wards)	['adɹɛ(v)]
gartre(f)	at home	['ɡartɹɛ(v)]

Exercise 2

Translate the following sentences.

1) The phone rang.
2) I didn't read the paper.
3) Did Siôn win a prize?
4) We ran home.
5) Did you write a letter?
6) You didn't wash the carpet.
7) He left the club.
8) She didn't miss the train.
9) Did Mair call?
10) Did you hear the news?

Lesson 5: The simple past tense forms of 'mynd', 'dod' and 'gwneud'

The verbs '**mynd**', '**dod**', '**gwneud**', '**cael**' and '**bod**' are all irregular in that they are not formed by inflection, i.e. by adding an personal ending to a stem. We will see the past tense of '**bod**' in **Week 7, Lesson 6** and the past tense of '**cael**' in **Week 8**. In this lesson, we will deal only with '**mynd**', '**dod**' and '**gwneud**', which as you can see from the lists below are very similar in appearance.

Affirmative forms of the simple past tense of 'mynd'

PHRASE	ENGLISH	IPA
es i	I went	[eːs iː]
est ti	you went (*fam.*)	[eːs(t) tiː]
aeth e (SW)	he went	[aɪθ eː]
aeth o (NW)	he went	[aɪθ oː]
aeth hi	she went	[aɪθ hiː]
aethon ni	we went	['əɪθo(n) niː]
aethoch chi	you went (*pl.*) (*sing. formal*)	['əɪθo(χ) χiː]
aethon nhw	they went	['əɪθo(n) n̥uː]

Affirmative forms of the simple past tense of 'dod'

PHRASE	ENGLISH	IPA
des i	I came	[deːs iː]
dest ti	you came (*fam.*)	[deːs(t) tiː]
daeth e (SW)	he came	[daɪθ eː]
daeth o (NW)	he came	[daɪθ oː]
daeth hi	she came	[daɪθ hiː]
daethon ni	we came	[ˈdəɪθo(n) niː]
daethoch chi	you came (*pl.*) (*sing. formal*)	[ˈdəɪθo(χ) χiː]
daethon nhw	they came	[ˈdəɪθo(n) n̥uː]

Affirmative forms of the simple past tense of 'gwneud'

PHRASE	ENGLISH	IPA
gwnes i	I did / made	[gʷneːs iː]
gwnest ti	you did / made (*fam.*)	[gʷneːs(t) tiː]
gwnaeth e (SW)	he did / made	[gʷnaɪθ eː]
gwnaeth o (NW)	he did / made	[gʷnaɪθ oː]
gwnaeth hi	she did / made	[gʷnaɪθ hiː]
gwnaethon ni	we did / made	[ˈgʷnəɪθo(n) niː]
gwnaethoch chi	you did / made (*pl.*) (*sing. formal*)	[ˈgʷnəɪθo(χ) χiː]
gwnaethon nhw	they did / made	[ˈgʷnəɪθo(n) n̥uː]

> **IMPORTANT**
> Note that the third person singular **aeth** [aɪθ], **daeth** [daɪθ] and **gwnaeth** [gʷnaɪθ] are used when the subject is a singular or plural noun.

Grammatically, the irregular verbs operate in exactly the same way as regular verbs, and so their interrogative and negative forms, together with the mutations they undergo, follow the same rules as those of the regular verbs (see **Week 7, Lesson 2** and **Lesson 3**):

Interrogative forms of the simple past tense of irregular verbs (SM)

The initial consonant of interrogative verb forms undergoes soft mutation, including **ll** and **rh** (see **Week 1, Lesson 5**). Soft mutation also occurs after the interrogative pronouns **beth** 'what' [beːθ] and **pwy** 'who' [pʊɪ]:

QUESTION	ENGLISH	IPA
Aethon ni?	Did we go?	[ˈəɪθo(n) niː]
Ddaeth y plant?	Did the children come?	[ðaɪθ ə plant]
Wnaeth Dafydd yn dda?	Did Dafydd do well?	[ʷnaɪθ ˈdavɪð ən ðaː]
Gawsoch chi frecwast?	Did you have breakfast?	[ˈgaʊso(χ) χiː ˈvrɛkwast]

Beth <u>wn</u>aethoch chi?	What did you do?	[beːθ ˡʷnəɪθo(χ) χiː]
Beth <u>g</u>awsoch chi?	What did you have?	[beːθ ˈgaʊso(χ) χiː]
Ble <u>a</u>ethoch chi?	Where did you go?	[ble: ˈəɪθo(χ) χiː]

Negative forms of the simple past tense of irregular verbs (SM & AM)

The initial consonant of the negative verb forms undergoes the aspirate mutation in the case of **p, t,** and **c** (**see Week 1, Lesson 5**), and the soft mutation in the case of all other mutable consonants (**see Week 1, Lesson 5**):

SENTENCE	ENGLISH	IPA
Aethon nhw ddim.	They didn't go.	[ˈəɪθo(n) n̥uː ðɪm]
<u>Dd</u>aeth y plant ddim.	The children didn't come.	[ðaɪθ ə plant ðɪm]
<u>W</u>naeth Dafydd ddim yn dda.	Dafydd didn't do well.	[ʷnaɪθ ˈdaˑvɪð ðɪm ən ðɑː]
<u>Ch</u>awsoch chi ddim brecwast.	You didn't have breakfast.	[ˈχaʊso(χ) χiː ðɪm ˈbrɛkwast]

Expressing 'to take' (mynd â) and 'to bring' (dod â)

In Welsh, 'to take' and 'to bring' are expressed as **mynd â** (*lit.* 'to go with') [mɪnd ä] and **dod â** (*lit.* 'to come with') [doːd ä], respectively:

	SENTENCE
WELSH	**Es i â'r ci am dro.**
ENGLISH	I took the dog for a walk.
IPA	[eːs i är kiː am dɹoː]

WELSH	**Dw i'n mynd â'r arian i'r banc.**
ENGLISH	I'm taking the money to the bank.
IPA	[dwiːn mɪnd är ˈärjan iːr baŋk]

WELSH	**Roedden ni'n mynd i ddod â llaeth.**
ENGLISH	We were going to bring some milk.
IPA	[ˈrɔɪðɛ(n) niːn mɪnd iː doːd ä ɬaɪθ]

Â [ä] causes the first letter of the following word to undergo aspirate mutation: **p > ph; t > th; c > ch.**

SENTENCE	ENGLISH	IPA	MUTATED WORD
Dewch â <u>ph</u>otel.	Bring a bottle.	[dɛʊχ ä ˈfɔtɛl]	potel
Aethon nhw â <u>th</u>eledu.	They took a television.	[ˈəɪθo(n) n̥uː ä θɛlˈedi]	teledu
Daeth hi â <u>ch</u>wpan.	She bought a cup.	[daɪθ hiː ä ˈχʊpan]	cwpan

Ag [äg] is the form of **â** before a vowel:

	SENTENCE
WELSH	**Des i ag afal.**
ENGLISH	I brought an apple.
IPA	[deːs iː äg 'ɑval]

WELSH	**Cofiwch eich bod chi'n mynd ag arian.**
ENGLISH	Remember (that you are) to take money.
IPA	['kɔvjʊχ əχ boːd χiːn mɪnd äg 'ärjan]

The verb **cymryd** 'to take' ['kəmrɪd] is used in expressions like 'to take medicine', 'to take advice'. For example:

	SENTENCE
WELSH	**Dw i'n cymryd moddion at yr annwyd.**
ENGLISH	I'm taking medicine for the cold.
IPA	[dwiːn 'kəmrɪd 'mɔðjon at ər 'änʊɪd]

WELSH	**Cymerais i gyngor (f)y nhad.**
ENGLISH	I took my father's advice.
IPA	[kəm'ɛrɛs iː 'gəŋor (v)ə n̥ɑːd]

Exercise 1

Translate the following sentences.

1) I came to the gym in the car. _____
2) What did you get for your birthday? _____
3) Did he make the bread? _____
4) Where did she have food? _____
5) We made coffee in the kitchen. _____
6) Did you make the bed? _____
7) We came yesterday morning. _____
8) Did she do her work? _____
9) Did we bring coats? _____
10) They didn't take the money. _____

Vocabulary

MASCULINE NOUN	ENGLISH	IPA	PLURAL FORM	IPA
annwyd	cold (illness)	['änʊɪd]	**anwydau**	[än'ʊɪdɛ]
cyngor	advice	['kəŋor]	**cynghorion**	[kəŋ'hɔrjon]

haul	sun	[haɪl]	**heuliau**		[ˈhəɪljɛ]
eli haul	sun cream	[ˈɛli haɪl]			
lledr	leather	[ɬɛdɛr]	**lledrau**		[ɬɛdrɛ]
persawr	perfume	[ˈpɛrsaʊr]	**persawrau**		[pɛrˈsaʊrɛ]
tywod	sand	[ˈtəʊod]	**tywodydd**		[təɪˈɔdɪð]
popeth	everything	[ˈpɔpɛθ]			
pythefnos	fortnight	[pəθˈɛvnos]	**pythefnosau**		[pəθɛvˈnɔsɛ]

FEMININE NOUN	ENGLISH	IPA	PLURAL FORM	IPA
potel	bottle	[ˈpɔtɛl]	**poteli**	[pɔtˈɛli]
tegan	toy	[ˈtɛˈgan]	**teganau**	[tɛgˈɑˈnɛ]

NOUN (pl.)	ENGLISH	IPA
moddion	medicine	[ˈmɔðjon]
gwyliau	holidays	[ˈgwɪljɛ]

VERB-NOUN	ENGLISH	IPA	STEM	IPA
gwisgo	to put on / to wear	[ˈgwɪsgo]	**gwisg-**	[gwɪsg]
mynd am dro	to go for a walk	[mɪnd am drɔ]		
yfed	to drink	[ˈɔvɛd]	**yf-**	[əv]
hedfan	to fly	[ˈhɛdvan]	**hedfan-**	[hɛdˈvɑˈn]

ADJECTIVE	ENGLISH	IPA
lliwgar	colourful	[ɬɪʊgar]
bendigedig	splendid / brilliant	[bɛndɪgˈɛdɪg]
poeth	hot	[pɔɪθ]
diwetha(f)	last	[dɪʊˈɛθa(v)]

ADVERBIAL	ENGLISH	IPA
rhy (SM)	too	[ɹiː]

PLACE NAME	ENGLISH	IPA
Yr Aifft	Egypt	[ər aɪft]

Dialogue

Welsh Dialogue

Richard: Ble aethoch chi ar eich gwyliau diwethaf?
Ann: Aethon ni i'r Aifft, i Sharm El Sheik.
Richard: Roedd hi'n boeth iawn yno, dw i'n siŵr.
Ann: Oedd, oedd. Ond roedden ni'n yfed digon o ddŵr potel ac yn gwisgo digon o eli haul. Roedd popeth yn iawn.
Richard: Am faint aethoch chi?

Ann:	Aethon ni am bythefnos. Hedfanon ni. Dyna oedd y tro cyntaf i ni hedfan gyda'r plant. Daethon ni â llawer o bethau adref gyda ni – teganau, bagiau lledr, tywod lliwgar, persawr. Roedd ein bagiau'n llawn.
Richard:	Beth wnaethoch chi yno? Aethoch chi i rywle diddorol?
Ann:	Aethon ni ar daith i Alexandria. Mae gen i ddiddordeb mawr yn hanes yr Aifft.

English Translation

Richard:	Where did you go on your last holidays?
Ann:	We went to Egypt, to Sharm El Sheik.
Richard:	It was really hot there, I'm sure.
Ann:	Yes, yes. But we drank enough bottled water and wore enough sun cream. Everything was fine.
Richard:	For how long did you go?
Ann:	We went for a fortnight. We flew. That was the first time for us to fly with the children. We brought a lot of things home with us – toys, leather bags, coloured sand, perfume. Our bags were full.
Richard:	What did you do there? Did you go anywhere interesting?
Ann:	We went on a trip to Alexandria. I'm interested in Egyptian history.

Lesson 6: The simple past tense of 'bod'

In **Week 6, Lesson 1**, we learnt that 'I was' can be translated into Welsh as either **bues i** [ˈbiˑɛs i] or **roeddwn i** [ˈrɔɪðʊn i], and that **bues i** refers to a specific period of time, while **roeddwn i** expresses a condition or an unspecified, continuous period of time. We will now consider the simple past of '**bod**'.

Affirmative forms of the simple past tense forms of 'bod'

PHRASE	ENGLISH	IPA
bues i	I was	[ˈbiˑɛs iː]
buest ti	you were (*fam.*)	[ˈbiˑɛs(t) tiː]
buodd e (SW)	he was	[ˈbiˑoð eː]
buodd o (NW)	he was	[ˈbiˑoð oː]
buodd hi	she was	[ˈbiˑoð hiː]
buon ni	we were	[ˈbiˑo(n) niː]
buoch chi	you were (*pl.*) (*sing. formal*)	[ˈbiˑo(χ) χiː]
buon nhw	they were	[ˈbiˑo(n) n̥uː]

> **IMPORTANT**
> Remember that the third person singular **buodd** [ˈbiˑoð] is used when the subject is a singular or plural noun.

For example:

	SENTENCE
WELSH	**Buest ti'n lwcus iawn.**
ENGLISH	You were very lucky.
IPA	[ˈbiˑes(t) tiːn ˈlʊkɪs jaʊn]

WELSH	**Ble buoch chi echdoe?**
ENGLISH	Where were you the day before yesterday?
IPA	[bleː ˈbiˑo(χ) χiː ˈɛχdɔɪ]

WELSH	**Bues i yn y dre(f) neithiwr.**
ENGLISH	I was in town last night.
IPA	[ˈbiˑes i ən ə dɹeː(v) ˈnəɪθjʊr]

Interrogative forms of the simple past tense of 'bod'

The interrogative is formed by mutating the initial consonant softly and inflecting the voice:

QUESTION	ENGLISH	IPA
Fues i?	Was I?	[ˈviˑes iː]
Fuest ti?	Were you? (*fam.*)	[viˑes(t) tiː]
Fuodd e (SW)	Was he?	[ˈviˑoð eː]
Fuodd o (NW)	Was he?	[ˈviˑoð oː]
Fuodd hi?	Was she?	[ˈviˑoð hiː]
Fuon ni?	Were we?	[ˈviˑo(n) niː]
Fuoch chi?	Were you? (*pl.*) (*sing. formal*)	[ˈviˑo(χ) χiː]
Fuon nhw?	Were they?	[ˈviˑo(n) n̥uː]

> **IMPORTANT**
> Remember that the third person singular **fuodd** [ˈviˑoð] is used when the subject is a singular or a plural noun.

For example:

	QUESTION
WELSH	**Fuest ti allan neithiwr?**
ENGLISH	Did you go out last night? (*lit.* Were you out last night?)
IPA	[ˈviˑes(t) tiː ˈaɬan ˈnəɪθjʊr]

WELSH	**Fuoch chi yn y gampfa neithiwr?**
ENGLISH	Were you at the gym last night?
IPA	[ˈviˑo(χ) χiː ən ə ˈgampvä ˈnəɪθjʊr]

WELSH	**Fuon nhw yn y siop fara y prynhawn 'ma?**

ENGLISH	Were they at the bread shop this afternoon?
IPA	[ˈviːo(n) n̦uː ən ə ʃɔp ˈvɑrra ə prɪnˈhaʊn mä]

As we saw in **Week 7, Lesson 3**, the replies to questions in the past are **do** 'yes' [doː] and **naddo** 'no' [ˈnɑðoː].

Vocabulary

MASCULINE NOUN	ENGLISH	IPA	PLURAL FORM	IPA
llun	picture	[ɬiːn]	**lluniau**	[ˈɬɪnjɛ]
cefn	back (of body)	[ˈkɛvn̦]	**cefnau**	[ˈkɛvnɛ]
gwesty	hotel	[ˈgwɛsti]	**gwestai**	[ˈgwɛstaɪ]
parc	park	[park]	**parciau**	[ˈparkjɛ]
camel	camel	[ˈkamɛl]	**camelod**	[kamˈɛlod]

FEMININE NOUN	ENGLISH	IPA	PLURAL FORM	IPA
marchnad	market	[ˈmarχnad]	**marchnadoedd**	[marχnɑˈdɔɪð]
diod	drink	[ˈdiːod]	**diodydd**	[diˈɔdɪð]
taith	trip / journey	[taɪθ]	**teithiau**	[ˈtəɪθjɛ]

VERB-NOUN	ENGLISH	IPA	STEM	IPA
hwylio	to sail	[ˈhʊɪljo]	**hwyli-**	[hʊɪlj]

ADJECTIVE	ENGLISH	IPA
cenedlaethol	national	[kɛnɛdˈləɪθol]

ADVERBIAL	ENGLISH	IPA
gormod	too much	[ˈgɔrmod]
rhywbryd	sometime	[ˈr̦ʊbrɪd]
gyda'n gilydd	together	[ˈgədän giˈlɪð]

Dialogue

Welsh Dialogue

Richard: Sut roedd y bwyd?
Ann: Roedd y bwyd yn y gwesty'n fendigedig. Bwyton ni ormod o fwyd, ac yfon ni ormod. Dyn ni eisiau mynd yn ôl i'r Aifft rywbryd.
Richard: Fuoch chi ar daith camel?
Ann: Naddo, nid fi, ond aeth y plant gyda'r gŵr. Mwynhaon nhw'n fawr iawn. Mae gen i lun hyfryd. Bues i'n siopa mewn hen farchnad pan oedden nhw ar y camel. Buon ni'n hwylio gyda'n gilydd. Diwrnod bendigedig. Aethon ni i barc cenedlaethol a gweld llawer o bethau diddorol iawn fel hen eglwysi. Buon ni ar y traeth hefyd, wrth gwrs.

English Translation

Richard:	How was the food?
Ann:	The food in the hotel was splendid. We ate too much food, and we drank too much. I want to go back to Egypt sometime.
Richard:	Did you go on a camel tour?
Ann:	No, not me, but the children went with my husband. They enjoyed it very much. I have a lovely picture. I went shopping in an old market when they were on the camel. We went sailing with each other. A wonderful day. We went to a national park and saw a lot of interesting things like old churches. We went to the beach as well, of course.

Negative forms of the simple past tense of 'bod'

The negative past tense of **bod** is formed by softly mutating the initial consonant and adding **ddim** after the verb.

PHRASE	ENGLISH	IPA
fues i ddim	I wasn't	['viˑes iː ðɪm]
fuest ti ddim	you weren't (*fam.*)	['viˑes(t) tiː ðɪm]
fuodd e ddim (SW)	he wasn't	['viˑoð eː ðɪm]
fuodd o ddim (NW)	he wasn't	['viˑoð oː ðɪm]
fuodd hi ddim	she wasn't	['viˑoð hiː ðɪm]
fuon ni ddim	we weren't	['viˑo(n) niː ðɪm]
fuoch chi ddim	you weren't (*pl.*) (*sing. formal*)	['viˑo(χ) χiː ðɪm]
fuon nhw ddim	they weren't	['viˑo(n) n̥u ðɪm]

> **IMPORTANT**
> Remember that the third person singular **fuodd (...) ddim** ['viˑoð (...) ðɪm] is used when the subject is a singular or a plural noun.

For example:

	SENTENCE
WELSH	**Fuodd y plant ddim yn yr ysgol ddoe.**
ENGLISH	The children weren't at school yesterday.
IPA	['viˑoð ə plant ðɪm ən ər 'əsgol ðoɪ]

Vocabulary

MASCULINE NOUN	ENGLISH	IPA	PLURAL FORM	IPA
digwyddiad	event	[dɪg'wɪðjad]	**digwyddiadau**	[dɪgwɪðˈjɑˈdɛ]
bachgen	boy	['bäχgen]	**bechgyn**	['beχgɪn]
diwedd	end	['dɪʊɛð]		

meddwl	mind / thought	['mɛðʊl]	**meddyliau**	[mɛðˈəljɛ]
llanast	mess	[ɬaˈnast]		

FEMININE NOUN	ENGLISH	IPA	PLURAL FORM	IPA
neges	message	[ˈnɛgɛs]	**negeseuon**	[nɛgɛsˈəɪɔn]
sianel	channel	[ˈʃanɛl]	**sianeli**	[ʃanˈɛli]

VERB-NOUN	ENGLISH	IPA	STEM	IPA
cynnal	to hold (an event, etc.)	[ˈkənal]	**cynhali-**	[kənˈhal-]
holi am (SM)	to ask (about)	[ˈhɔli am]	**hol-**	[ˈhɔl-]
codi arian at (SM)	to raise money for	[ˈkɔdi ˈärian at]		

ADJECTIVE	ENGLISH	IPA
drud	expensive / dear	[driːd]
sawl	several	[saʊl]

ADVERBIAL	ENGLISH	IPA
eitha(f)	quite	[ˈəɪθa(v)]
gynnau fach	just now	[ˈgənɛ väχ]
i gyd	all	[iː giːd]

Dialogue

Welsh Dialogue

Richard: Ble buest ti neithiwr? Bues i'n dy ffonio di. Gadawais i dair neges.
Gareth: Mae'n ddrwg gen i. Bues i allan gyda bechgyn y clwb rygbi. Dyn ni'n codi arian at ein taith i Ganada. Buon ni yno dair blynedd yn ôl. Mae'n eithaf drud i hedfan yno, felly dyn ni'n cynnal digwyddiadau codi arian.
Richard: Bues i yng Nghanada ar daith rygbi pan oeddwn i yn yr ysgol. Enillon ni sawl gêm, ond collon ni'r gêm fawr ar ddiwedd y daith. Buodd y tîm arall yn lwcus iawn.

English Translation

Richard: Where were you last night? I phoned you. I left three messages.
Gareth: I'm sorry. I went out with the boys from the rugby club. We are raising money for our trip to Canada. We went there three years ago. It's pretty expensive to fly there, so we are holding events to raise money.
Richard: I went to Canada on a rugby trip when I was at school. We won a number of games, but we lost the big game at the end of the trip. The other team was very lucky.

Exercise 1

Fill the gaps in the following sentences.

For example:
Question: _____ hi yn y dafarn ddoe.
Answer: Buodd hi yn y dafarn.

1) _____ i ddim allan o'r tŷ.
   (I wasn't out of the house.)

2) _____ rhywun yn holi am Ifan gynnau fach.
   (Someone was inquiring about Ifan just now.)

3) _____ ti yn y dref echdoe?
   (Were you in town the day before yesterday?)

4) _____ y teulu i gyd yn sâl echnos.
   (All the family were ill the night before last.)

5) _____ hi ddim yn lwcus o gwbl.
   (She wasn't lucky at all.)

6) _____ nhw yn y gwesty ddoe?
   (Were they in the hotel last night.)

7) _____ i ddim yn Yr Aifft yr haf diwethaf.
   (I wasn't in Egypt last summer.)

8) _____ e ddim eisiau mynd allan.
   (He didn't want to go out.)

IMPORTANT

Just as some verb-nouns are used exclusively with the past imperfect aspect of **bod**, so **byw** 'to live' [bɪʊ] and **marw** 'to die' ['mɑrʊ] are used exclusively with the simple past tense of '**bod**' when they express a completed action:

Buodd fy mam-gu i fyw nes ei bod hi'n naw deg oed
My grandmother lived until she was ninety (years of age).
['bɪ·oð (v)ə mäm'gi: i: vɪʊ nɛs i: boːd hiːn naʊ deːg ɔɪd]

Buodd fy nhad i farw llynedd
My father died last year.
['bɪ·oð (v)ə n̥aːd i: vɑrʊ 'ɬənɛð]

It should also be noted that in such sentences, **byw** and **marw** are not preceded by aspectual marker **yn** (see **Week 3, Lesson 2**), and that they undergo soft mutation

---

Lesson 7: Recap exercises

Exercise 1

Translate the following commands.

1) Take the dog for a walk. _____

2) Stand on the corner. (*fam.*) _____
3) Wake up. _____
4) Don't worry. (*fam.*) _____
5) Change the channel. _____
6) Do something. _____
7) Bring your dirty clothes. _____
8) Take (go with) medicine for your cold. _____

9) Inquire about the weather. _____
10) Be quiet. (*fam.*) _____

If you have difficulty completing this exercise, review **Week 7, Lesson 1**.

Exercise 2

Answer the questions according to the example given.

For example:

Question: Weloch chi bethau diddorol? (✓)
Answer: Do, gwelais i/gwelon ni bethau diddorol.

For example:

Question: Glywodd hi larwm? (✗)
Answer: Naddo, chlywodd hi ddim larwm.

1) Ganodd o'r anthem genedlaethol? (✓)
   (Did he sing the national anthem?)
   _____

2) Ofynnon nhw gwestiwn? (✗)
   (Did they ask a question?)
   _____

3) Newidiaist ti dy feddwl? (✓)
   (Did you change your mind? [*fam.*])
   _____

4) Ddihunon ni'n gynnar? (✗)
   (Did we wake up early?)
   _____

5) Brynon nhw gar newydd? (✗)
   (Did they buy a new car?)
   _____

6) Weithiodd pawb yn galed? (✘)
   (Did everyone work hard?)
   _____

7) Adawoch chi'r gwaith yn gynnar? (✓)
   (Did you leave work early?)
   _____

8) Fwyton ni'r caws i gyd? (✓)
   (Did we eat all the cheese?)
   _____

*If you have difficulty completing this exercise, review **Week 7, Lesson 2, Lesson 3**, and **Lesson 4**.*

Exercise 3

Translate the following sentences.

1) What did we do? _____
2) Did she bring a knife? _____
3) I didn't go to the supermarket. _____
4) Did you make enough sandwiches? (*fam.*) _____
5) They made their own clothes. _____
6) He took the dog for a walk. _____
7) Did you go for a fortnight? _____
8) What time did she go? _____
9) Who made the cakes? _____
10) We didn't make a mess _____

*If you have difficulty completing this exercise, review **Week 7, Lesson 5** and **Lesson 6**.*

Exercise 4

Translate the following sentences.

1) Were they sailing last weekend?
   _____

2) Where was he last night?
   _____

3) I was at the chapel.
   _____

4) She wasn't at the event.

5) Were you in Cardiff over the weekend? (*fam.*)
_____

6) We were watching the play.
_____

7) They weren't at school.
_____

8) Were you in the city?
_____

If you have difficulty completing this exercise, review **Week 7, Lesson 6**.

Week 8

Lesson 1: The simple past tense of 'cael'

Here are the personal forms of the simple past tense of **'cael'**:

PHRASE	ENGLISH	IPA
ces i	I got / had	[keːs iː]
cest ti	you got / had (*fam.*)	[keːs(t) tiː]
cafodd e (SW)	he got / had	[ˈkɑvoð eː]
cafodd o (NW)	he got / had	[ˈkɑvoð oː]
cafodd hi	she got / had	[ˈkɑvoð hiː]
cawson ni	we got / had	[ˈkaʊso(n) niː]
cawsoch chi	you got / had (*pl.*) (*sing. formal*)	[ˈkaʊso(χ) χiː]
cawson nhw	they got / had	[ˈkaʊso(n) n̥uː]

> **IMPORTANT**
> Remember that the third person singular **cafodd** [ˈkɑvoð] is used when the subject is a singular or a plural noun.

You will note that while **ces i** and **cest ti** follow the same pattern as the simple past tense of the other irregular verbs that we saw in **Week 7, Lesson 5**, the remaining personal forms are slightly different.

The interrogative and negative forms of **'cael'**, together with the mutations they undergo, follow the same rules as those of the regular verbs (see **Week 7, Lesson 3** and **Lesson 4**) and the other irregular verbs (see **Week 7, Lesson 5**).

Interrogative forms of the simple past tense of 'cael' (SM)

As with all other verbs in the simple past tense, to form a question in the simple past tense of **'cael'**, the verb undergoes soft mutation, and the responses are **do** 'yes' and **naddo** 'no'. Here are a few examples:

	QUESTION	REPLY
WELSH	**Gawsoch chi frecwast?**	**Do, ces i frecwast.**
ENGLISH	Did you have breakfast?	Yes, I had breakfast.
IPA	[ˈgaʊso(χ) χiː ˈvrɛkwast]	[doː keːs iː ˈvrɛkwast]
WELSH	**Gawsoch chi wyau i frecwast?**	**Do, ces i wyau i frecwast.**
ENGLISH	Did you have eggs for breakfast?	Yes, I had eggs for breakfast.
IPA	[ˈgaʊso(χ) χiː ˈʊɪ.ɛ iː ˈvrɛkwast]	[do keːs iː ˈʊɪ.ɛ iː ˈvrɛkwast]

WELSH	Gafodd hi lawer o anrhegion ar ei phen-blwydd hi?	Do, llawer iawn.
ENGLISH	Did she get lots of presents on her birthday?	Yes, very many.
IPA	['gɑˑvoð hiː 'lauɛr o anˈɹɛgjon ar iː fɛnˈblʊɪð hiː]	[doː 'kɑˑvoð hiː 'lauɛr]

Negative forms of the past tense of 'cael' (AM)

To form the negative, the verb undergoes aspirate mutation if it begins with **p**, **t**, **c** (see **Week 1, Lesson 5**):

SENTENCE	ENGLISH	IPA	PERSONAL VERB FORM PRE-MUTATION
Chawsoch chi ddim brecwast.	You didn't have breakfast.	['χauso(χ) χiː ðɪm 'brɛkwast]	cawsoch chi
Ches i ddim anrhegion.	I didn't get any presents.	[χeːs i ðɪm anˈɹɛgjon]	ces i
Chawson nhw ddim gwobr.	They didn't get a prize.	['χauso(n) n̥uː ðɪm 'gwoˑbor]	cawson nhw

Epenthesis

Overall, Welsh is written phonetically, as one letter represents one sound, but there are exceptions. One is 'epenthesis': repeating the vowel in the penult (the last but one syllable) in the last syllable of a word which ends in two consonants. **Gwobr** 'prize' ['gwoˑbor] is an example of this. Other examples are **ochr** 'side' ['oˑχor] and **pobl** 'people' ['poˑbol]. This is the standard way to pronounce **gwobr**, **ochr** and **pobl** throughout Wales. However, epenthesis is very common in South Welsh. Here are some examples:

WELSH	ENGLISH	SW PRONUNCIATION	STANDARD PRONUNCIATION
cefn	back	['kɛˑvɛn]	['kɛvn̩]
lledr	leather	['ɬɛˑdɛr]	['ɬɛdr̩]
llyfr	book	['ɬəvɪr]	['ɬəvr̩]
ofn	fear	['oˑvon]	['ɔvn̩]
rhestr	list	['ɹɛstɛr]	['ɹɛstr̩]
storm	storm	['stoˑrom]	['stɔrm]
trefn	order	['tɹ̥ɛˑvɛn]	['tɹ̥ɛvn̩]

Vocabulary

MASCULINE NOUN	ENGLISH	IPA	PLURAL FORM	IPA
wy	egg	[ʊɪ]	wyau	['ʊɪ.ɛ]
pwdin	dessert / pudding	['pʊdɪn]	pwdinau	[pʊdˈiˑnɛ]
pen-blwydd	birthday	[pɛnˈblʊɪð]	penblwyddi	[pɛnˈblʊɪði]
pâr	pair	[paːr]	parau	['pɑˑrɛ]
dewis	choice	['dɛʊɪs]	dewisiadau	[dɛʊɪsˈjɑˑdɛ]
syniad	idea	['sənjad]	syniadau	[sənˈjɑˑdɛ]

mis	month	[miːs]	**misoedd**	[mɪˈsɔɪð]	

FEMININE NOUN	ENGLISH	IPA	PLURAL FORM	IPA
anrheg	present (gift)	[ˈanɾɛg]	**anrhegion**	[anˈɾɛgjɔn]
priodas	wedding / marriage	[priˈɔdas]	**priodasau**	[priˈɔdäsɛ]
siwt	suit	[sɪʊt]	**siwtiau**	[ˈsɪʊtjɛ]
het	hat	[hɛt]	**hetiau**	[ˈhɛtjɛ]
ffrog	dress / frock	[frɔg]	**ffrogiau**	[ˈfrɔgjɛ]

ADJECTIVE	ENGLISH	IPA
del (NW)	pretty	[dɛl]
pert (SW)	pretty	[pɛrt]
nesa(f)	next	[ˈnɛsa(v)]

VERB-NOUN	ENGLISH	IPA	STEM	IPA
chwilio	to search	[ˈχwɪljo]	**chwili-**	[χwɪlj]
chwilio am (SM)	to look for / to search for	[ˈχwɪljo am]		

MISCELLANEOUS	ENGLISH	IPA
ar-lein	online	[arˈləɪn]
dim byd	nothing	[dɪm biːd]
ond	but	[ɔnd]
dros y penwythnos	over the weekend	[drɔs ə pɛnˈʊɪθnos]

Dialogue

Welsh Dialogue

Ann: Gest ti ddillad ar gyfer y briodas fawr y mis nesaf?
Mari: Naddo. Es i i'r dref ddydd Sadwrn diwethaf, ond welais i ddim byd roeddwn i eisiau ei brynu. Buon ni yno trwy'r dydd hefyd.
Ann: Dim byd o gwbl?
Mari: Wel, roedd pâr o esgidiau roeddwn i'n ei hoffi'n fawr iawn, ond dw i ddim eisiau prynu esgidiau cyn y dillad!
Ann: Aeth Mari a fi i lawr i Gaerdydd i gael ein dillad ni.
Mari: Gawsoch chi bopeth?
Ann: Do. Ces i bopeth roeddwn i ei eisiau, siwt, esgidiau a het. Cafodd Mari ffrog fach ddel hefyd. Mae llawer o ddewis yn y brifddinas.
Mari: Ond mae'n rhy bell i fynd i brynu dillad. Bydd rhaid i fi fynd i chwilio am ddillad ar-lein, dw i'n meddwl.
Ann: Beth am fynd dros y penwythnos. Gadael prynhawn dydd Gwener ar ôl yr ysgol, siopa dydd Sadwrn, noson allan yn y brifddinas a dod yn ôl dydd Sul.
Mari: Syniad gwych.

English Translation

Ann: Did you get clothes for the big wedding next month?
Mari: No. I went to town on Saturday, but I didn't see anything I wanted to buy. We were there all day as well.
Ann: Nothing at all?
Mari: Well, there was a pair of shoes I liked very much, but I don't want to buy the shoes before the clothes!
Ann: Mari and I went down to Cardiff to get our clothes.
Mari: Did you get everything?
Ann: Yes. I got everything I needed: suit, shoes and a hat. Mari got a nice pretty dress also. There's a lot of choice in the capital.
Mari: But it's too far to go to buy clothes. I will have to search for clothes online, I think.
Ann: What about going over the weekend? Leave on Friday afternoon after school, shop on Saturday, a night out in the capital and return on Sunday.
Mari: A great idea!

Exercise 1

Translate the following sentences.

1) Did you get some apples from the shop?
2) The school got new carpets.
3) What time did we have coffee?
4) He had an accident last night.
5) Did she have a shower this morning?
6) Did you get any new clothes? (*fam.*)
7) They didn't get any food.
8) Did you get another coat in town.
9) The Welsh class had a good time in France.
10) I didn't have any dessert.

Lesson 2: Relative forms of 'bod'

We have already seen that **sydd** is the relative form of **'bod'** in the present tense (see **Week 4, Lesson 4**). In formal Welsh, the relative particle **a** [ä] (which causes the soft mutation) is used with all other tenses to introduce a relative clause, i.e. to express the English 'which', 'who' or 'that' used before the relative clause describing the antecedent.

Statement
Here is an example of the past imperfect aspect of **'bod'**:

	SENTENCE
WELSH	**Roedd y dyn yn poeni.**
ENGLISH	The man was worrying.
IPA	[rɔɪð ə diːn ən ˈpɔɪni]

Here is an example of the simple past tense of '**bod**':

	SENTENCE
WELSH	**Buodd y dyn yn gweithio ddoe.**
ENGLISH	The man was working yesterday.
IPA	[ˈbɪˑoð ə diːn ən ˈgwəɪθjo ðɔɪ]

Here are those two sentences transformed into relative clauses describing an antecedent:

	ANTECEDENT	RELATIVE PARTICLE	RELATIVE CLAUSE
WELSH	**y dyn**	**a**	**oedd yn poeni**
ENGLISH	the man	who	was worrying
IPA	[ə diːn]	ä	ɔɪð ən ˈpɔɪni]
WELSH	**y dyn**	**a**	**oedd yn gweithio ddoe**
ENGLISH	the man	who	was working yesterday
IPA	[ə diːn]	ä	ɔɪð ən ˈgwəɪθjo ðɔɪ]

Here are a few more examples with the regular verbs '**gweld**', '**dysgu**' and '**bwyta**':

	ANTECEDENT	RELATIVE PARTICLE	RELATIVE CLAUSE
WELSH	**y ferch**	**a**	**welodd y ddamwain**
ENGLISH	the girl	who	saw the accident
IPA	[ə vɛrχ]	ä	ˈwɛloð ə ˈðamwaɪn]
WELSH	**yr athrawes**	**a**	**ddysgodd (f)y mam**
ENGLISH	the teacher	who	taught my mother
IPA	[ər aθˈraʊɛs]	ä	ˈðəsgoð (v)ə mam]
WELSH	**y bwyd**	**a**	**fwytais i**
ENGLISH	the food	which	I ate
IPA	[ə bʊɪd]	ä	ˈvʊɪtɛs i]

Negating the relative clause

In spoken Welsh, relative clauses in the present imperfect or past imperfect are negated by adding **ddim**:

	CLAUSE
WELSH	**y dyn sydd ddim yn gweithio**

ENGLISH	the man who isn't working	
IPA	[ə diːn siː(ð) ðɪm ən ˈgwəiθjo]	
WELSH	**y dyn oedd ddim yn gweithio**	
ENGLISH	the man who wasn't working	
IPA	[ə diːn ɔi(ð) ðɪm ən ˈgwəiθjo]	

However, in the simple past tense, **a** is replaced by **na** [nɑː], which causes the aspirate mutation with **p, t** and **c**, and the soft mutation with the other mutable consonants (see **Week 1, Lesson 5**):

	CLAUSE
WELSH	**y ferch na welodd y ddamwain**
ENGLISH	the girl who didn't see the accident
IPA	[ə vɛrχ nɑː ˈwɛloð ə ˈðamwain]
WELSH	**y bwyd na fwytais i**
ENGLISH	the food which I didn't eat
IPA	[ə bʊɪd nɑː ˈvʊɪtɛs i]
WELSH	**yr athrawes na ddysgodd fy mam i**
ENGLISH	the teacher who did not teach my mother
IPA	[ər aθˈraʊɛs nɑː ðəsgoð (v)ə mam iː]

Vocabulary

MASCULINE NOUN	ENGLISH	IPA	PLURAL FORM	IPA
tocyn	ticket	[ˈtɔkɪn]	**tocynnau**	[tɔkˈənɛ]

FEMININE NOUN	ENGLISH	IPA	PLURAL FORM	IPA
drama	play	[ˈdrɑːma]	**dramâu**	[dramˈaɪ]
neuadd	hall	[ˈnəɪað]	**neuaddau**	[nəɪˈɑːðɛ]

VERB-NOUN	ENGLISH	IPA	STEM	IPA
derbyn	to accept / to receive	[ˈdɛrbɪn]	**derbyni-**	[dɛrˈbənj]

ADJECTIVE	ENGLISH	IPA
gofalus	careful	[govˈɑːlɪs]

Exercise 1

Translate the underlined English phrase in the sentences below.

1) Pwy oedd y dyn <u>who built</u> bont y dref?

2) Fe (SW)/Fo (NW) oedd yr unig un <u>who believed you</u>.
___

3) Derbyniodd pob plentyn <u>who wrote a letter</u> wobr.
___

4) Roedd pawb <u>who had left</u> cyn diwedd y ddrama wedi prynu tocyn.
___

5) Hi yw'r ferch <u>who sang</u> yr anthem genedlaethol.
___

6) Roedd pawb <u>who were watching</u> 'r gêm yn oer iawn.
___

7) Mae pawb <u>who went to the play</u> yn dweud ei bod hi'n wych.
___

8) Pwy oedd y bobl <u>who came</u> yn hwyr?
___

9) Roedd pawb <u>who wanted a ticket</u> yn aros tu allan i'r neuadd.
___

10) Oeddech chi'n nabod y ferch <u>who had an accident</u> yesterday?
___

Lesson 3: The preposition 'i' and expressing 'I'd better' / 'I'd prefer'

In Welsh, 'I'd better (...)' is expressed by the idiomatic use of the preposition **i** 'to' / 'for' [iː]. Quite a number of Welsh prepositions are declined (see **Week 10, Lesson 2**), and **i** is such a preposition. You can see how **i** declines or changes when it is used with different pronouns below. We will discuss prepositions in more detail in **Week 10**.

'i'

PHRASE	ENGLISH	IPA
i fi	to me / for me	[iː viː]
i ti	to you / for you (*fam.*)	[iː tiː]
iddo fe (SW)	to him / for him	[ˈɪðo veː]
iddo fo (NW)	to him / for him	[ˈɪðo voː]
iddi (hi)	to her / for her	[ˈɪði hiː]
i ni	to us / for us	[iː niː]
i chi	to you / for you	[iː χiː]
iddyn nhw	to them / for them	[ˈɪðɪ(n) n̥uː]

The phrase **mae'n well i fi** [maɪn weːɬ iː viː] is used to express 'I'd better' (*lit.* 'It is better for me'). The preposition **i** declines or changes according to the person, as in the list above, and this can be seen in the examples below:

	SENTENCE
WELSH	**Mae'n well i fi fynd.**
ENGLISH	I'd better go.
IPA	[maɪn weːɬ iː viː vɪnd]
WELSH	**Mae'n well iddi hi benderfynu.**
ENGLISH	She'd better decide.
IPA	[maɪn weːɬ 'iði hiː bɛndɛr'vəni]
WELSH	**Mae'n well iddyn nhw ddweud.**
ENGLISH	They'd better say.
IPA	[maɪn weːɬ 'iðɪ(n) n̥uː ðwəɪd]

To express 'better not', the verb-noun **peidio** 'to refrain (from)' ['pəɪdjo] is used:

	SENTENCE
WELSH	**Mae'n well i fi beidio mynd.**
ENGLISH	I'd better not go.
IPA	[maɪn weːɬ iː viː 'bəɪdjo mɪnd]
WELSH	**Mae'n well i ni beidio croesi'r ffordd.**
ENGLISH	We'd better not cross the road.
IPA	[maɪn weːɬ iː niː 'bəɪdjo 'krɔɪsir fɔrð]

As you can see, the pattern **mae'n well i fi** causes a soft mutation:

	SENTENCE
WELSH	**Mae'n well i bawb fod yn ofalus.**
ENGLISH	Everyone had better be careful.
IPA	[maɪn weːɬ iː baʊb voːd ən ov'ɑːlɪs]

Exercise 1

Translate the following sentences.

1) I'd better buy a ticket.
   _____

2) She had better sing the national anthem. She sings better than me.
   _____

3) We'd better not stay too long.
   _____

4) They'd better decide now.

5) You'd better be quiet.

6) He'd better not swim in the sea.

7) I'd better not talk to them.

8) The family had better travel by aeroplane.

Vocabulary

FEMININE NOUN	ENGLISH	IPA	PLURAL FORM	IPA
awyren	aeroplane	[auˈərɛn]	**awyrennau**	[auərˈɛnɛ]

VERB-NOUN	ENGLISH	IPA	STEM	IPA
penderfynu	to decide	[pɛndɛrˈvəni]	**penderfyn-**	[pɛndɛrˈvən]

Expressing a preference

'I prefer (...)', on the other hand, is expressed by the idiomatic use of the conjunction **gyda** in South Wales and by the preposition **gan** in North Wales (see **Week 4, Lesson 2**). For example:

	PHRASE
WELSH	**Mae'n well gyda fi fynd.** (SW)
ENGLISH	I'd prefer to go.
IPA	[maɪn wɛːɬ ˈgədä viː vɪnd]
WELSH	**Mae'n well gen i fynd** (NW)
ENGLISH	I'd prefer to go.
IPA	[maɪn wɛːɬ gɛn iː vɪnd]
WELSH	**Mae'n well gyda nhw ddweud.** (SW)
ENGLISH	They'd prefer to say.
IPA	[maɪn wɛːɬ ˈgədä n̥uː ðwəɪd]
WELSH	**Mae'n well ganddyn nhw ddweud.** (NW)
ENGLISH	They'd prefer to say.
IPA	[maɪn wɛːɬ ˈgänðɪ(n) n̥uː ðwəɪd]
WELSH	**Mae'n well gyda fi beidio mynd.** (SW)
ENGLISH	I'd prefer not to go.
IPA	[maɪn wɛːɬ ˈgədä viː bəɪdjo mɪnd]

WELSH	Mae'n well gen i beidio mynd. (NW)
ENGLISH	I'd prefer not to go.
IPA	[maɪn weɬ gɛn iː ˈbəidjo mɪnd]

Oes well [ɔis weɬ] is used to ask 'Do (you) prefer?':

QUESTION	ENGLISH	IPA
Oes well gen ti goffi? (NW)	Do you prefer coffee?	[ɔis weɬ gɛn ti̥ː ˈgɔfi]
Oes well gyda ti goffi? (SW)	Do you prefer coffee?	[ɔis weɬ ˈgədä tiː ˈgɔfi]

To express 'I preferred' / 'I used to prefer', substitute **roedd** for **mae**:

QUESTION	ENGLISH	IPA
Roedd hi'n well gen i hanes.	I preferred history.	[rɔɪð hiːn weɬ gɛn iː ˈhanɛs]

Vocabulary

MASCULINE NOUN	ENGLISH	IPA	PLURAL FORM	IPA
myfyriwr	student	[məˈərjʊr]	**myfyrwyr**	[məˈərwɪr]
tywydd	weather	[ˈtəʊɪð]		

FEMININE NOUN	ENGLISH	IPA	PLURAL FORM	IPA
archfarchnad	hypermarket, supermarket	[ˌarχˈvarχnad]	**archfarchnadoedd**	[ˌarχvarχˈnaˈdɔɪð]
myfyrwraig	student	[məˈərʷraig]	**myfyrwragedd***	[məvərʷraˈgeð]

* Where gender is not specified, the masculine plural is used.

Exercise 2

1) I prefer not to say.
___

2) We prefer to buy our tickets in a local shop.
___

3) He prefers to shop in the large supermarket.
___

4) Do you prefer hot weather?
___

5) She prefers the red carpet.
___

6) They prefer the other company.

7) The students prefers to study in the library.

8) Does he prefer to walk?

The colours in Welsh

COLOUR	ENGLISH	IPA
oren	orange	[ˈɔrɛn]
pinc	pink	[pɪŋk]
brown	brown	[broʊn]
gwyrdd	green	[gwɪrð]
glas	blue	[glɑːs]
du	black	[diː]*
porffor	purple	[ˈpɔrfor]
melyn	yellow	[ˈmɛlɪn]
llwyd	grey	[ɬʊɪd]
coch	red	[koːχ]

* [d̜iː] *in North Wales.*

Vocabulary

MASCULINE NOUN	ENGLISH	IPA	PLURAL FORM	IPA
math	type	[mɑːθ]	mathau	[ˈmɑˑθɛ]
wyneb	face	[ˈwiˑnɛb]	wynebau	[wɪnˈɛbɛ]
dim byd	nothing	[dɪm biːd]		

FEMININE NOUN	ENGLISH	IPA	PLURAL FORM	IPA
sgert	skirt	[sgɛrt]	sgertiau	[ˈsgɛrtjɛ]
siwt	suit	[sɪʊt]	siwtiau	[ˈsɪʊtjɛ]
siwmper	jumper	[ˈdʒʊmpɛr]*	siwmperi	[dʒʊmˈpɛri]
ysgol gynradd	primary school	[ˈəsgol ˈgənrað]	ysgolion cynradd	[əsˈgɔljon ˈcənrað]
ysgol uwchradd	secondary school	[ˈəsgol ˈɪʊχrað]	ysgolion uwchradd	[əsˈgɔljon ˈɪʊχrað]

* *Usually, in Welsh,* **si** *represents the English* **sh** */ʃ/, but here it represents the English* **j** */dʒ/.*

CONJUNCTION	ENGLISH	IPA
neu (SM)	or	[nəɪ]

VERB-NOUN	ENGLISH	IPA	STEM	IPA
edrych ymlaen at (SM)	to look forward to	[ˈɛdɹɪχ əmˈlaɪn at]	**edrych-**	[ɛdˈɹəχ əmˈlaɪn at]
trïo	to try	[ˈtɹiˈo]	**trï-**	[tɹi]
siwtio	to suit	[ˈsɪʊtjo]	**siwti-**	[sɪʊtj]
sylwi	to notice	[ˈsəlwi]	**sylw-**	[səlw]
dod o hyd i (SM)	to find	[doːd oː hiːd iː]		
arfer	to use	[ˈarvɛr]		
tynnu	to draw / to pull	[ˈtəni]	**tynn-**	[tən]

PRONOUN	ENGLISH	IPA
y rheiny	those	[ə ˈɹəɪni]

ADJECTIVE	ENGLISH	IPA
rhesymol	reasonable	[ɹɛsˈəmol]
gwael	bad	[gwaɪl]
tywyll	dark	[ˈtəʊɬ]
perffaith	perfect	[ˈpɛrfɛθ]
arbennig	special / particular	[arˈbɛnɪg]
unrhyw (SM)*	any	[ˈɪnɹɪʊ]
hoff o (SM)	fond of	[hoːf oː]

* ***Unrhyw*** *precedes the noun it is describing and causes a soft mutation.*

MISCELLANEOUS	ENGLISH	IPA
mewn golwg	in view / in mind	[mɛʊn ˈgɔlʊg]
heblaw	besides	[hɛbˈlaʊ]
ers hynny	since then	[ɛrs ˈhəni]
rhywsut	somehow	[ˈɹɪʊsɪt]
na (AM)	nor	[nä]

Dialogue

Welsh Dialogue

Mari: Roedd pris y tocynnau'n rhesymol iawn. Dw i wedi bod yn edrych ymlaen at fynd i Gaerdydd trwy'r wythnos. Mae hi wedi bod yn wythnos brysur iawn.

Ann: Fi hefyd. Ie, roedd y tocynnau'n eithaf rhesymol. Wyt ti wedi penderfynu beth wyt ti eisiau ei wisgo yn y briodas – sgert, ffrog, siwt?

Mari: Nac ydw. Dw i wedi bod yn trïo pob math o ddillad, ond dw i ddim wedi gweld dim byd dw i eisiau ei brynu eto, a dw i'n chwilio ers amser hir.

Ann: Dw i'n meddwl dy fod ti'n edrych yn dda mewn siwt. Oes gen ti liw arbennig mewn golwg?

Mari: Unrhyw liw heblaw gwyrdd neu frown. Roedden ni'n arfer gwisgo sgertiau brown a siwmperi brown yn yr ysgol gynradd. Yn yr ysgol uwchradd, roedden ni'n gwisgo dillad gwyrdd, a dw i ddim wedi gwisgo dillad gwyrdd na brown ers

Ann:	hynny. Dw i'n eithaf hoff o borffor, coch a glas. Mae'n gas gen i hetiau mawr, felly dw i ddim yn mynd i wisgo un o'r rheiny.
	Mae glas yn dy siwtio di, ond mae llawer o ddillad melyn a du yn y siopau, sylwais i ar hynny y tro diwethaf y bues i'n siopa.
Mari:	Oes, a dw i'n edrych yn wael mewn melyn. Mae'n tynnu'r lliw o fy wyneb i rywsut. Mae'n well gen i liwiau tywyll.
Ann:	Dyn ni'n mynd i ddod hyd i'r dillad perffaith i ti, Mari. Paid poeni!

English Translation

Mari:	The ticket prices were very reasonable. I have been looking forward to going to Cardiff all week. It has been a very busy week.
Ann:	Me as well. Yes, the tickets were pretty reasonable. Have you decided what you want to wear at the wedding – a skirt, dress, suit?
Mari:	No. I have been trying all sorts of clothes, but I haven't seen anything I want to buy yet, and I have been searching for a long time.
Ann:	I think you look good in a suit. Have you got a particular colour in mind?
Mari:	Any colour except green or brown. We used to wear brown skirts and brown jumpers at primary school. In secondary school, we wore green clothes, and I haven't worn green or brown clothes since then. I'm pretty fond of purple, red and blue. I hate big hats, so I'm not going to wear one of those.
Ann:	Blue suits you, but there are a lot of yellow and black clothes in the shops. I noticed that the last time I went shopping.
Mari:	Yes, and I look bad in yellow. It draws the colour from my face somehow. I prefer dark colours.
Ann:	We are going to find perfect clothes for you, Mari. Don't worry!

Lesson 4: Expressing obligation with 'rhaid'

In Welsh 'I must' / 'I have to' is expressed by combining **rhaid** 'necessity' [ˌraɪd] with one of the personal forms of the preposition **i** 'to' / 'for' [iː] (see **Week 8, Lesson 3**):

	SENTENCE
WELSH	**Mae rhaid i fi fynd.**
ENGLISH	I must go. (*lit.* 'There is a necessity for me to go.')
IPA	[maɪ ˌraɪd iː viː vɪnd]
WELSH	**Mae rhaid i chi wrando.**
ENGLISH	You must listen.
IPA	[maɪ ˌraɪd iː χiː ˈwrändo]

Note that the first letter of the verb-noun ('**mynd**' and '**gwrando**') is mutated. This remains the case even if a noun, which itself is mutated, intervenes:

PHRASE	ENGLISH	IPA	MUTATED WORD	ENGLISH
Mae rhaid i <u>rywun</u> fynd.	Someone must go.	[maɪ ɹaɪd i 'rıʊın vınd]	rhywun	someone

In everyday speech, the **mae** is often dropped, as in: **Rhaid i rywun fynd.**

Passive sentences like 'The cost must be considered', are expressed by getting rid of **i** altogether:

SENTENCE	ENGLISH	IPA
Rhaid ystyried y gost.	The cost must be considered	[ɹaɪd əs'tərjɛd ə gɔst]
Rhaid bwydo'r ci.	The dog must be fed.	[ɹaɪd 'bʊɪdor kiː]

Because **rhaid** is indefinite, **oes** is used in questions:

QUESTION	ENGLISH	IPA
Oes rhaid i fi fynd?	Do I have to go?	[ɔɪs ɹaɪd iː viː vınd]
Oes rhaid i fi wrando?	Do I have to listen?	[ɔɪs ɹaɪd iː viː 'ʷrändo]

For the same reason, **does dim** [dɔɪs dım] is used in negative sentences:

SENTENCE	ENGLISH	IPA
Does dim rhaid i chi wrando.	You don't have to listen.	[dɔɪs dım ɹaɪd iː χiː 'ʷrändo]
Does dim rhaid i mi fynd.	I don't have to go.	[dɔɪs dım ɹaɪd iː viː vınd]

The verb-noun **peidio** 'to refrain (from)' ['pəɪdjo] is used in expressions which correspond to 'you mustn't':

SENTENCE	ENGLISH	IPA
Rhaid i fi beidio mynd.	I mustn't go.	[ɹaɪd iː viː 'bəɪdjo mınd]
Rhaid i chi beidio gwrando.	You mustn't listen.	[ɹaɪd iː χiː 'bəɪdjo 'gʷrändo]

To change tense, **mae** is replaced by the appropriate third person singular form of '**bod**':

SENTENCE	ENGLISH	IPA
Roedd rhaid i mi fynd.	I had to go.	[rɔɪð ɹaɪd iː viː vınd]

Vocabulary

FEMININE NOUN	ENGLISH	IPA	PLURAL FORM	IPA
cost	cost	[kɔst]	**costau**	['kɔstɛ]

ADVERBIAL	ENGLISH	IPA
erbyn hyn	by now	['ɛrbın hın]

VERB-NOUN	ENGLISH	IPA	STEM	IPA
ystyried	to consider	[əsˈtərjɛd]	**ystyri-**	[əsˈtərj]
bwydo	to feed	[ˈbuɪdo]	**bwyd-**	[əsˈtərj]
smocio	to smoke	[ˈsmɔkjo]	**smoci-**	[smɔkj]

ADJECTIVE	ENGLISH	IPA
caled	hard	[ˈkɑˑlɛd]

Exercise 1

Translate the following sentences.

1) I must go to the supermarket on the way home.

2) Does he have to stay in the hotel?

3) He mustn't drink too much.

4) We don't have to accept the prize.

5) You mustn't smoke.

6) Everyone has to decide.

7) They must have heard by now.

8) She has to get up early.

9) You must drive carefully.

10) I don't have to go by aeroplane.

Expressing 'must be' / 'must have'

In Welsh, a sentence like 'The family must be happy', is expressed as follows:

(Mae) rhaid + that-clause (bod) + yn + adjective

For a reminder of that-clauses, see **Week 6, Lesson 3**.

Given the above, 'The family must be happy', in Welsh is:

(Mae) rhaid + bod y teulu yn hapus.

Here are some more examples:

	SENTENCE
WELSH	**Rhaid bod Alun yn hapus.**
ENGLISH	Alun must be happy.
IPA	[ɹaɪd boːd 'ɑˈlɪn ən 'häpɪs]
WELSH	**Rhaid bod Siân yn gweithio'n galed.**
ENGLISH	Siân must be working hard.
IPA	[ɹaɪd boːd ʃɑːn ən 'gwəɪθjon 'gɑːlɛd]
WELSH	**Rhaid eich bod chi wedi clywed.**
ENGLISH	You must have heard.
IPA	[ɹaɪd əχ boːd χiː 'wɛdi 'klɔʊɛd]

Exercise 2

Translate the following sentences.

1) You must remember.
2) He must be warm.
3) Everyone must be angry.
4) They must be famous.
5) I must be hearing things.

Prepositional clauses

In Welsh, 'before going' is expressed as **cyn mynd** [kɪn mɪnd]. However, to show who is going, personal forms of **i** 'to' / 'for' [iː] (as seen in **Week 8, Lesson 3**) are employed:

PHRASE	ENGLISH	IPA
cyn i fi fynd	before I go	[kɪn iː viː vɪnd]
cyn i ti anghofio	before you forget	[kɪn iː tiː aŋˈhɔvjo]

Prepositions cannot show tense, and so the exact meaning of **cyn i fi fynd** depends on the preceding main clause:

	SENTENCE
WELSH	**Rhaid i fi gloi'r drws cyn i fi fynd.**
ENGLISH	I must lock the door before I go.
IPA	[ɹaɪd iː viː glɔɪr druːs kɪn iː viː vɪnd]
WELSH	**Roedd rhaid i fi gloi'r drws cyn i fi fynd.**
ENGLISH	I had to lock the door before I went.
IPA	[rɔɪð ɹaɪd iː viː glɔɪr druːs kɪn iː viː vɪnd]

Here are some of the more common prepositional clauses:

	PREPOSITION	PREPOSITIONAL CLAUSE
WELSH	**cyn**	**cyn i fi fynd**
ENGLISH	before	before I go / went
IPA	[kɪn]	[kɪn iː viː vɪnd]
WELSH	**ar ôl**	**ar ôl iddo fe** (SW) / **fo** (NW) **orffen**
ENGLISH	after	after he finishes / finished
IPA	[ar oːl]	[ar oːl 'iðo veː / voː ˈɔrfen]
WELSH	**erbyn**	**erbyn i bawb fwyta**
ENGLISH	by	by the time everyone eats / ate
IPA	[ˈɛrbɪn]	[ˈɛrbɪn iː baʊb ˈvʊɪtä]
WELSH	**ers**	**ers i ti ymddeol**
ENGLISH	since	since you retired
IPA	[ɛrs]	[ɛrs iː tiː əmˈðeˑol]
WELSH	**wrth**	**wrth iddyn nhw adael**
ENGLISH	as	as they leave / left
IPA	[ʊrθ]	[ʊrθ ˈiˑðɪ(n) ņuː ˈɑˑdɛl]
WELSH	**rhag ofn**	**rhag ofn i chi anghofio**
ENGLISH	in case	in case you forget / forgot
IPA	[ɹag ˈɔvn]	[ɹag ˈɔvn iː χiː aŋˈhɔvjo]
WELSH	**hyd nes**	**hyd nes iddyn nhw gyrraedd**
ENGLISH	until	until they arrive / arrived
IPA	[hiːd nɛs]	[hiːd nɛs ˈiˑðɪ(n) ņuː ˈgəra(ɪ)ð]

Exercise 3

Translate the following sentences.

1) We'd better go before it snows.

2) She has learnt Welsh since she moved to Wales.

3) They had left by the time we arrived.

4) Take an umbrella in case it rains

5) As we sat on the chair it broke.

6) Before he parked the car he looked in the mirror.

7) They came after we arrived.

8) He wants to go to Egypt before he retires.

Vocabulary

MASCULINE NOUN	ENGLISH	IPA	PLURAL FORM	IPA
ymbarél	umbrella	[əmbaˈrɛl]	ymbarelau	[əmbaˈrɛlɛ]
drych	mirror	[dɹiːχ]	drychau	[ˈdɹəχɛ]
syched	thirst / dryness	[ˈsəχɛd]		

VERB-NOUN	ENGLISH	IPA	STEM	IPA
ymddeol	to retire (from work)	[əmˈðeˑol]	ymddeol-	[əmˈðeˑɔl]
anghofio	to forget	[aŋˈhɔvjo]	anghofi-	[aŋˈhɔvj]
marw	to die*	[ˈmaɾʊ]	marw-	[ˈmaɾw]
trafod	to discuss	[ˈtɹaˑvod]	trafod-	[tɹaˈvɔd]
dewis	to choose	[ˈdɛʊɪs]	dewis-	[dɛʊˈɪs]
atgoffa	to remind	[atˈgɔfä]	atgoff-	[atˈgɔf]
cloi	to lock	[klɔɪ]	cloi-	[klɔɪ]
gorffen	to finish	[ˈgɔrfɛn]	gorffenn-	[gɔrˈfɛn]

* Not conjugated in standard Welsh.

FEMININE NOUN	ENGLISH	IPA	PLURAL FORM	IPA
rhestr	list	[ˈɹ̥ɛstɹ̥]*	rhestrau	[ˈɹ̥ɛstrɛ]
rhestr fer	short list	[ˈɹ̥ɛstɹ̥ vɛr]	rhestrau byrion	[ˈɹ̥ɛstrɛ ˈbərjon]

* [ˈɹ̥ɛstɛr] is the pronunciation in South Welsh (see **Week 8, Lesson 1**).

ADJECTIVE	ENGLISH	IPA
tyn*	tight	[tɪn]

* Spelled **tynn** if it mutates.

PRONOUN	ENGLISH	IPA
rhai	those / ones	[ɹai]
hwn (*m.*)	this	[hʊn]
hon (*f.*)	this	[hɔn]

VERB	ENGLISH	IPA
bydd	will be	[biːð]

Dialogue

Welsh Dialogue

Ann: Oes, rhaid i ti drïo'r siwt ymlaen. Dych chi ddim eisiau ei gwisgo hi bore'r briodas a gweld ei bod hi'n rhy dynn neu'n rhy fawr.

Mari: Iawn, ond rhaid i ni gael coffi wedyn – cyn i fi farw o syched.

Ann: Iawn, coffi i drafod beth dyn ni wedi ei weld hyd yn hyn yn y caffi ar ôl i ti wisgo hon.

Mari: Syniad da. Dyn ni wedi gweld llawer o ddillad bendigedig. Mae hi'n anodd iawn dewis. Mae gen i restr fer o'r rhai gorau dw i wedi eu gweld.

Ann: Wel mae'n well i ti benderfynu cyn hir, neu bydd y siopau wedi cau erbyn i ti ddewis. Cofia fod rhaid cael esgidiau a het hefyd.

Mari: Dw i'n cofio – rwyt ti wedi bod yn fy atgoffa i ers i ni ddod i'r brifddinas!

English Translation

Ann: Yes, you must try the suit on. You don't want to wear it the morning of the wedding and see that it's too tight or too big.

Mari: All right, but we must have a coffee afterwards – before I die of thirst.

Ann: All right, a coffee to discuss what we have seen up to now in the café after you put this on.

Mari: Good idea. We have seen a lot of splendid clothes. It's very difficult to choose. I have a shortlist of the best ones I've seen.

Ann: Well, you had better decide before long, or the shops will close by the time you have chosen. Remember, you have to get shoes and a hat as well.

Mari: I remember; you have been reminding me since we came to the capital!

Lesson 5: The equative and comparative forms of adjectives

Equative

The construction of the equative comparison of adjectives in Welsh is very similar to that of English:

Welsh:	**mor** (SM)	+	**adjective**	+	**â** (AM)
English:	**as**	+	**adjective**	+	**as**

For example:

PHRASE	ENGLISH	IPA
mor goch â	as red as	[moːr goːχ ä]
mor ddrud â	as expensive as	[moːr ðriːd ä]

The equative particle **mor** causes a soft mutation, with the exception of adjectives beginning **ll** or **rh**:

PHRASE	ENGLISH	IPA
mor llawn â	as full as	[moːr ɬaʊn ä]
mor rhad â	as cheap as	[moː(r) ɹɑːd ä]

The preposition **â** 'with' / 'as' causes the aspirate mutation (see **Week 1, Lesson 5**):

PHRASE	ENGLISH	IPA	PREMUTATED WORD
mor goch â *thân*	as red as fire	[moːr goːχ ä θɑːn]	**tân**
mor bell â *Chaerdydd*	as far as Cardiff	[moːr beːɬ ä χaɪrˈdiːð]	**Caerdydd**

Â becomes **ag** before a noun:

PHRASE	ENGLISH	IPA
mor wyn ag eira	as white as snow	[moːr wɪn ag ˈəɪrä]

The equative forms can be used adverbially:

	SENTENCE
WELSH	**Mae'r tywydd mor braf.**
ENGLISH	The weather is so fine.
IPA	[mair ˈtəʊɪð moːr brɑːv]

	SENTENCE
WELSH	**Canodd y plant mor bert.**
ENGLISH	The children sang so prettily.
IPA	[ˈkɑˑnoð ə plant moːr bɛrt]

Here are some common comparisons:

PHRASE	ENGLISH	IPA
mor dywyll â bola buwch	as dark as a cow's stomach	[moːr ˈdəʊɬ ä ˈboˑla bɪʊχ]
mor falch â phaun	as proud as a peacock	[moːr valχ ä faɪn]
mor ddu â'r frân	as black as the crow	[moːr ðiː är brɑːn]*

* Remember that **du** is pronounced [ɖiː] in North Welsh.

Irregular adjectives

Not all adjectives follow the **mor (...) â** pattern. The most common irregular adjectives are listed below.

ADJECTIVE	IPA	PHRASE	ENGLISH	IPA
mawr	[maʊr]	cymaint â	as large as / as great as / as much as	['kəmaɪnt ä]
bach	[baːχ]	cyn lleied â	as small as	[kɪn ɬəɪed ä]
da	[daː]	cystal â	as good as / as well as	['kəstal ä]
drwg	[druːg]	cynddrwg â	as bad as	['kənðrug ä]

Here are some examples:

	SENTENCE
WELSH	**Dydy archfarchnad y dre(f) ddim cymaint ag archfarchnadoedd Wrecsam.**
ENGLISH	The town supermarket isn't as big as Wrexham's supermarkets.
IPA	['dədi ˌarχ'varχnad ə dɹɛː(v) ðɪm 'kəmaɪnt ag ˌarχvarχ'naˈdɔɪð ʷˈrɛksam]

WELSH	**Roedd e'n gwneud cyn lleied â phosib.**
ENGLISH	He did as little as possible.
IPA	[rɔɪð eːn gʷnəɪd kɪn ɬəɪed ä 'fɔsɪb]

WELSH	**Wnaeth tîm Twm ddim chwarae cystal â'r tîm arall.**
ENGLISH	Twm's team didn't play as well as the other team.
IPA	[ʷnaɪθ tiːm tʊm ðɪm 'χwaːre 'kəstal är tiːm 'araɬ]

The irregular forms can undergo soft mutation when used adverbially. For example:

	SENTENCE
WELSH	**Does dim eisiau bwyta gymaint.**
ENGLISH	There's no need to eat so much.
IPA	[dɔɪs dɪm 'əɪʃe 'bʊɪta 'gəmaɪnt]

WELSH	**Dw i ddim yn cofio gweld yr ardd yn edrych gystal.**
ENGLISH	I don't remember seeing the garden look so good.
IPA	['dwiː ðɪm ən 'kɔvjo gwɛld ər arð ən 'edɹɪχ 'gəstal]

Exercise 1

Translate the following sentences.

1) Twm isn't as tall as Ifan.

_____

2) Swansea isn't as big as Cardiff.

_____

3) He doesn't run as slow as Elen.

_____

4) My coat isn't as warm as her coat.

_____

5) Siôn isn't as strong as Ceri.

_____

6) It is not as windy today.

_____

7) The book I am reading is not as interesting as the one which I read last week.

_____

8) She is as bad as him.

_____

Vocabulary

MASCULINE NOUN	ENGLISH	IPA	PLURAL FORM	IPA
tân	fire	[tɑːn]	tanau	[ˈtɑˑnɛ]

MASCULINE NOUN	ENGLISH	IPA	PLURAL FORM	IPA
gardd	garden	[garð]	gerddi	[ˈgɛrði]

ADJECTIVE	ENGLISH	IPA
araf	slow	[ˈɑrav]
drwg	bad / naughty	[druːg]
llawn	full	[ɬaʊn]
diolchgar	grateful	[diˈɔlχgar]

Comparative (-er than)

The comparative pattern in Welsh is as follows:

Welsh: **adjective** + **-ach** + **na** (AM)
English: **adjective** + -er   + than

There are two ways of forming the comparative in Welsh, and they depend on the length of the adjective used:

(i) In most cases, the ending **-ach** [aχ] is added to the adjective:

PHRASE	ENGLISH	IPA
cochach na	redder than	[ˈkoˑχaχ næ]
talach na	taller than	[ˈtalaχ næ]
henach na	older than	[ˈheˑnaχ næ]

> **IMPORTANT**
> As we saw in **Week 5, Lesson 2**, the prefixed possessive pronouns **ei** 'his' / 'her', **ein** 'our', **eich** 'your' and **eu** 'their' can be respectively shortened to **'i**, **'n**, **'ch** and **'u**. We will see in this Lesson that this occurs after **â** and **na**. For example:
>
> **Mae e mor dal â'i dad**
> He is as tall as his father.
> [maɪ eː moːr dal äɪ daːd]
>
> **Mae e'n dalach na'i dad**
> He is taller than his father.
> [maɪ eːn 'daˑlaχ näɪ daːd]
>
> **Na** causes the aspirate mutation:
>
> **Na** becomes **nag** before a vowel:
>
> **yn gochach na thân**
> redder than fire
> [ən 'goˑχaχ nä θaːn]
>
> **yn wynnach nag eira**
> whiter than snow
> [ən 'wənaχ nag 'əɪrä]

(ii) With longer words (usually words of more than one syllable), **mwy** [mʊɪ] is used to form the comparative, in the same way that English uses 'more':

PHRASE	ENGLISH	IPA
mwy diolchgar	more grateful	[mʊɪ diˈɔlχgar]
mwy cyfleus	more convenient	[mʊɪ kəvˈləɪs]

Adjectives can be used in their comparative form:

PHRASE	ENGLISH	IPA
tŷ henach*	an older house	[tiː ˈheˑnaχ]

* *Remember that **tŷ** is pronounced* [tiː] *in North Welsh.*

Irregular adjectives

RADICAL	ENGLISH	IPA	COMPARATIVE	ENGLISH	IPA
mawr	big	[maʊr]	**yn fwy na**	bigger than / more than	[ən vʊɪ nä]
bach	small	[baːχ]	**yn llai na**	less than / fewer than	[ən ɬaɪ nä]
da	good	[daː]	**yn well na**	better than	[ən weːɬ nä]
drwg	bad	[druːg]	**yn waeth na**	worse than	[ən waɪθ nä]
cynnar	early	[ˈkənar]	**yn gynt na**	earlier than / sooner than	[ən gɪnt nä]
uchel	high / loud	[ˈiˑχel]	**yn uwch na**	higher than / louder than	[ən ɪʊχ nä]
isel	low	[ˈiˑsɛl]	**yn is na**	lower than	[ən iːs nä]

If an adjective ends with **b**, **d** or **g**, they respectively become **p**, **t** or **c** in the comparative and superlative forms (see **Week 8, Lesson 6**):

RADICAL	ENGLISH	IPA	COMPARATIVE	ENGLISH	IPA
gwlyb	wet	[gʷliːb]	**gwlypach**	wetter	[ˈgʷləpaχ]
rhad	cheap	[ɹaːd]	**rhatach**	cheaper	[ˈɹataχ]
teg	fair	[teːg]	**tecach**	fairer	[ˈtɛkaχ]

Note the following changes:

RADICAL	ENGLISH	IPA	COMPARATIVE	ENGLISH	IPA
gwyn	white	[gwɪn]	**gwynnach**	whiter	[ˈgwənaχ]
trwm	heavy	[tɾʊm]	**trymach**	heavier	[ˈtɾəmaχ]
byr	short	[bɪr]	**byrrach**	shorter	[ˈbəraχ]
glân	clean	[glɑːn]	**glanach**		[ˈglɑnaχ]

Llai 'less' [ɬai] can be used with adjectives to express 'less interesting', 'less convenient'. For example:

PHRASE	ENGLISH	IPA
llai diddorol	less interesting	[ɬai dɪðˈoˑrol]
llai cyfleus	less convenient	[ɬai kəvˈləis]

Exercise 2

Complete the following sentences by changing the Welsh word in brackets in to its comparative form. Remember to mutate if necessary.

1) Dw i'n credu bod y gwynt yn _____ heddiw na ddoe. (cryf)
   (I think that the wind is stronger today than yesterday.)
2) Mae'n rhaid i ti fod yn _____. (gofalus)
   (You must be more careful.)
3) Mae'r caws 'na'n _____ na'r caws 'ma. (rhad)
   (That cheese is cheaper than this cheese.)
4) Rwyt ti'n edrych yn _____ heddiw. (hapus)
   (You look happier today.)
5) Gwnes i'n _____ na'r disgwyl. (da)
   (I did better than expected.)
6) Mae'r tywydd yn _____ ym mis Hydref. (stormus)
   (The weather is stormier in October.)
7) Mae'n well gen i siopa yn y siop leol; mae'r staff yn _____. (cyfeillgar)
   (I prefer shopping in the local shop; the staff are friendlier.)
8) Does dim byd _____ na rhedeg allan o laeth. (drwg)
   (There is nothing worse than running out of milk.)
9) Mae pawb eisiau cymdeithas _____. (teg)
   (Everyone wants a fairer society.)

10) Mae'r drych hwn yn _____ na'r hen un.   (trwm)
    (This mirror is heavier than the old one.)

Vocabulary

MASCULINE NOUN	ENGLISH	IPA
mis Hydref	October	[miːs 'hədrɛv]

FEMININE NOUN	ENGLISH	IPA	PLURAL FORM	IPA
cymdeithas	society	[kəm'dəɪθas]	cymdeithasau	[kəmdəɪθ'asɛ]

MISCELLANEOUS	ENGLISH	IPA
na'r disgwyl	than expected	[nar 'dɪsɡʊɪl]

Lesson 6: The superlative form of adjectives

As with the comparative (See **Week 8, Lesson 5**), there are two ways of forming the superlative form of adjectives in Welsh. These depend on the length of the adjective:

(i) If the word is short (normally one syllable), the ending **–a(f)** [a(v)] is attached. The final **f** is often dropped in everyday speech.

Welsh: **adjective + -a(f)**
English: **adjective + -est**

For example:

ADJECTIVE	ENGLISH	IPA
cocha(f)	reddest	['koχa(v)]
hira(f)	longest	['hiːra(v)]

As was the case with the comparative, if an adjective ends in **b**, **d** or **g**, it respectively becomes **p**, **t** or **c**:

RADICAL	ENGLISH	IPA	COMPARATIVE	ENGLISH	IPA
gwlyb	wet	[ɡʷliːb]	gwlypa(f)	wettest	['ɡʷləpa(v)]
rhad	cheap	[ɹaːd]	rhata(f)	cheapest	['ɹɑta(v)]
teg	fair	[teːɡ]	teca(f)	fairest	['tɛka(v)]

(ii) With adjectives of more than one syllable, **mwya(f)** ['mʊɪa(v)] is used:

PHRASE	ENGLISH	IPA
mwya(f) diolchgar	most grateful	['mʊɪa(v) di'ɔlχgar]
mwya(f) cyfleus	most convenient	['mʊɪa(v) kəv'ləɪs]

Irregular adjectives

The same adjectives we saw in the comparative also have an irregular superlative:

RADICAL	ENGLISH	COMPARATIVE	IPA
mawr	big	**mwya(f)**	[ˈmʊɪa(v)]
bach	small	**lleia(f)**	[ˈɬəɪa(v)]
da	good	**gorau**	[ˈgoˑrɛ]
drwg	bad	**gwaetha(f)**	[ˈgwəɪθa(v)]
cynnar	early	**cynta(f)**	[ˈkənta(v)]
uchel	high / loud	**ucha(f)**	[ˈiˑχa(v)]
isel	low	**isa(f)**	[ˈiˑsa(v)]

Lleia(f) [ˈɬəɪa(v)] can be used to express 'least':

PHRASE	ENGLISH	IPA
lleia(f) diddorol	least interesting	[ˈɬəɪa(v) dɪðˈoˑrol]
lleia(f) cyfleus	least convenient	[ˈɬəɪa(v) kəvˈleɪs]

Using the superlative

The emphatic construction (see **Week 12, Lesson 3**) is used when the sentence does not start with a verb. This is like the identification structure we saw in **Week 2, Lesson 1** to **Lesson 4**.

	SENTENCE
WELSH	**Caerdydd ydy'r ddinas fwya(f).**
ENGLISH	Cardiff is the biggest city.
IPA	[kaɪrˈdiːð ədir ðiˑnas ˈvʊɪa(v)]
WELSH	**Tyddewi ydy'r ddinas leia(f).**
ENGLISH	St Davids is the smallest city.
IPA	[tiˈðɛʋi ədir ðiˑnas ləɪa(v)]

Vocabulary

PLACE NAME	ENGLISH	IPA
Tyddewi	St Davids (Pembrokeshire)	[tiˈðɛʋi]

MASCULINE NOUN	ENGLISH	IPA	PLURAL FORM	IPA
gwregys	belt	[ˈgʷrɛgɪs]	**gwregysau**	[gʷrɛgˈəsɛ]
patrwm	pattern	[ˈpatɹʊm]	**patrymau**	[patɹˈəmɛ]
tipyn	a bit	[ˈtɪpɪn]		
anifail	animal	[anˈiʋɛl]	**anifeiliaid**	[anɪvˈəɪljɛd]

FEMININE NOUN	ENGLISH	IPA	PLURAL FORM	IPA
sach	sack	[sɑːχ]	**sachau**	[ˈsɑˑχɛ]

VERB-NOUN	ENGLISH	IPA	STEM	IPA
gwerthu	to sell	[ˈgwɛrθi]	**gwerth-**	[gwɛrθ]

ADJECTIVE	ENGLISH	IPA
golau	light	[ˈgoˑlɛ]
llawn	full	[ɬaʊn]

ADVERBIAL	ENGLISH	IPA
o'r diwedd	at last	[oːr ˈdɪʊɛð]
ofnadwy o (SM)	awfully	[ɔvˈnɑˑdʊɪ oː]
o bell ffordd	by a long way	[oː beːɬ fɔrð]

PRONOUN	ENGLISH	IPA
hwnna (*m.*)	that one	[ˈhʊna]
honna (*f.*)	that one	[ˈhɔna]

Dialogue

Welsh Dialogue

Mari: Coffi o'r diwedd. Hyfryd iawn.
Ann: Iawn. Beth sydd ar y rhestr fer 'ma?
Mari: Y ffrog las.
Ann: Yr un las tywyll neu'r un las golau?
Mari: Glas golau. Roedd hi'n hirach na'r un las tywyll.
Ann: Roedd hi dipyn yn ddrutach hefyd.
Mari: Oedd, oedd. ond nid mor ddrud â'r un borffor.
Ann: Digon gwir, dyna'r ffrog ddrutaf i ni ei gweld – yn ofnadwy o ddrud.
Mari: Roedd cymaint o ddillad du a melyn, ond roeddwn i'n hoffi'r ffrog hufen a du – yr un gyda'r gwregys du. Roedd hi'n fyrrach na'r dillad eraill a'r sgert yn llawnach, ond roeddwn i'n ei hoffi'n fawr iawn.
Ann: Fi hefyd, ond efallai ei bod hi ddim yn iawn ar gyfer priodas. Dw i'n siŵr bod y siwt binc ddim ar dy restr fer di.
Mari: Dim o gwbl, dyna'r siwt waethaf i ni ei gweld, o bell ffordd. Roeddwn i'n edrych fel cath mewn sach!
Ann: Doedd hi ddim cynddrwg â hynny, ond roedd llawer o bethau gwell. Roedd y ffrog hufen gyda'r patrwm coch a gwyrdd yn un dda.
Mari: Oedd. Roeddwn i'n hoffi honna, dyna'r un orau. Ie, dw i'n meddwl mai dyna'r un dw i'n mynd i'w phrynu.
Ann: Gwell i ni fynd yn ôl i'r siop i'w phrynu hi cyn iddyn nhw ei gwerthu hi.

English Translation

Mari: Coffee at last. Very nice.
Ann: All right. What's on this shortlist?

Mari:	The blue dress.
Ann:	The dark blue one or the light blue one?
Mari:	Light blue. It was longer than the dark blue one.
Ann:	It was a bit more expensive as well.
Mari:	Yes, yes, but not as expensive as the purple one.
Ann:	True enough, that's the most expensive dress we have seen – awfully expensive.
Mari:	There were so many black and yellow clothes, but I liked the cream and black dress – the one with the black belt. It was shorter than the other clothes and the skirt fuller, but I liked it very much.
Ann:	Me too, but perhaps it isn't right for a wedding. I'm sure that the pink suit isn't on your shortlist.
Mari:	Not at all; that's the worse suit we saw, by a long way. I looked like a cat in a sack!
Ann:	It wasn't as bad as that, but there were a lot of better things. The cream dress with the red and green pattern was a good one.
Mari:	Yes. I liked that one, that's the best one. Yes, I think that's the one I'm going to buy.
Ann:	We'd better go back to the shop and buy it before they sell it.

Mutating superlative forms

Superlative forms of adjectives, that follow the definite article **y**, undergo soft mutation when they describe feminine singular nouns.

Below is an example of the masculine:

SENTENCE	ENGLISH	IPA
Dewi ydy'r cryfa(f).	Dewi is the strongest.	[ˈdɛʊi ˈədir ˈkrəva(v)]

And here is an example of the feminine, complete with soft mutation:

SENTENCE	ENGLISH	IPA
Ann ydy'r gryfa(f).	Ann is the strongest	[ˈan ˈədir ˈgrəva(v)]

Exercise 1

Complete the following sentences by filling in the gaps using the word in brackets. Remember to mutate if necessary.

1) Dyna'r rheilffordd _____ yng Nghymru.   (hir)
   (That is the longest railway in Wales.)

2) Pwy ydy'r Cymro _____?   (enwog)
   (Who is the most famous Welshman?)

3) Nos Sul oedd y noson _____.   (stormus)
   (Sunday night was the stormiest night.)

4) Pwy ydy'r ferch _____?   (teg)

(Who is the fairest girl?)

5) P'un yw'r bag _____ ? (trwm)
   (Which is the heaviest bag?)

6) Pa anifail ydy'r _____ ? (cyflym)
   (Which animal is the fastest?)

7) Fe (SW)/Fo (NW) ydy'r _____ yn y dosbarth. (tal)
   (He is the tallest in the class.)

8) Dyna'r coffi _____ dw i wedi'i flasu erioed. (da)
   (That is the best coffee I have ever tasted.)

9) Dydd Llun oedd y diwrnod _____ . (gwlyb)
   (Monday was the wettest day.)

10) Beth oedd y ffilm _____ eleni? (drwg)
    (What was the worst film this year?)

Lesson 7: Recap exercises

Exercise 1

Complete the following sentences in the dialogue by filling the gaps with forms of the past tense of the verb-noun **'cael'**.

For example:

Question: _____ ni ein harian yn ôl?
Answer: Cawson ni ein harian yn ôl?

1) _____ chi amser da neithiwr?

2) Do. _____ ni amser da iawn. Aethon ni allan am bryd o fwyd yn y bwyty newydd. Roedd y bwyd yn fendigedig, _____ i bysgod fel arfer. _____ Steffan gyw iâr gyda thatws a llysiau. _____ ni ddim gwin achos bod Siôn yn gyrru ac mae llawer o win gyda ni yn y tŷ.

3) Beth _____ y plant?

4) _____ Siôn a Teleri fwyd oddi ar fwydlen arbennig i blant. _____ nhw sglodion fel arfer.

5) Beth _____ ti, Siôn?

6) _____ i sglodion a selsig. _____ Teleri yr un peth, ond _____ hi ddim ffa pob.

Translation
1) Did you have a good time last night?

2) Yes. We had a really good time. We went out for a meal at the new restaurant. The food was wonderful, I had fish as usual. Steffan had chicken with potatoes and vegetables. We didn't have wine because Sion was driving and we have a lot of wine in the house.
3) What about the children?
4) Siôn and Teleri had food off a special children's menu. They had chips as usual.
5) What about you, Siôn?
6) I had chips and sausages. Teleri had the same (thing), but she didn't have baked beans.

If you have difficulty completing this exercise, review **Week 8, Lesson 1**.

Vocabulary

MISCELLANEOUS	ENGLISH	IPA
ffa pob	baked beans	[fɑː poːb]
yr un	the same	[ər iːn]

Exercise 2

Translate the following sentences.

1) Where is the man who was considering buying her house?

2) We spoke to someone who knew the doctor well.

3) Do you know the teacher who used to play international rugby?

4) I met the people who lost all the money.

5) Have they named the woman who drove her car up Snowdon?

6) Everyone who had heard the alarm left the building.

7) Everyone who had eaten the sausages felt ill afterwards.

8) The children who had had a shower early were very lucky. The water was hot.

If you have difficulty completing this exercise, review **Week 8, Lesson 2**.

Vocabulary

ADJECTIVE	ENGLISH	IPA
rhyngwladol	international	[ɹəŋˈwlɑːdol]

VERB-NOUN	ENGLISH	IPA	STEM	IPA
enwi	to name	[ˈɛnwi]	**enw-**	[ˈɛnw]

PLACE NAME	ENGLISH	IPA
Yr Wyddfa	Mount Snowdon	[ər ˈʊɪðvä]

Exercise 3

Translate the following sentences.

1) He'd better decide now.

2) You'd better not take all the paper. (*fam.*)

3) She prefers chips.

4) Do they prefer to give money or to buy a present?

5) I'd better be ready in time.

6) Do you prefer to go up in the lift?

7) We'd better not worry about the accident.

8) I'd better not cut the bread now.

If you have difficulty completing this exercise, review **Week 8, Lesson 3**.

Vocabulary

ADVERBIAL	ENGLISH	IPA
mewn pryd	in time	[mɛʊn priːd]

Exercise 4

Fill in the blanks by translating the English phrase in brackets.

1) _____ beth mae hi'n mynd i'w wisgo yn y briodas.
   (She has to choose)

2) Golchais i fy ngwallt _____.
   (after I watched the film).

3) Cofiais i fy mag i _____ y tŷ.
   (as I left)

4) _____ i'w rhieni nhw?
   (Do they have to ask)

5) _____ ddechrau cyn deg o'r gloch.
   (We have to)

6) Rho'r gyllell yn y cwpwrdd _____ ddamwain.
   (before you have)

7) _____ tan 9.30 p.m.
   (He doesn't have to arrive)

8) Ysgrifennais i nodyn _____.
   (in case I forgot)

9) Mae hi wedi cynnig am sawl swydd _____.
   (since she retired)

10) _____ y gwesty roedd y briodas wedi gorffen.
    (By the time Marc reached)

Vocabulary

MASCULINE NOUN	ENGLISH	IPA	PLURAL FORM	IPA
nodyn	note	['nɔdɪn]	**nodiadau**	[nɔdˈjaˑdɛ]

Exercise 5

Translate according to the example.

For example:

Question: Siôn is as tall as Mair.
Answer: Mae Siôn mor dal â Mair.

1) This area is not as pretty as West Wales.

2) I'm as tall as my father.

3) Siwan is not as punctual as Megan.

4) The film is as silly as the play.

5) She's as thin as her husband.

If you have difficulty with this exercise, review **Week 8, Lesson 5** *and* **Lesson 6**.

Exercise 6

Translate the following sentences according to the example.

For example:

Question: Siôn is taller than Mair.
Answer: Mae Siôn yn dalach na Mair.

1) I go to Cardiff more often than my parents.

2) I hope the fish is fresher today.

3) The weather is sunnier in the South.

4) Food is cheaper today.

5) Her suit is darker than the dress.

If you have difficulty with this exercise, review **Week 8, Lesson 5** *and* **Lesson 6**.

Exercise 7

Translate the following sentences according to the example.

For example:

Question: Siôn is the tallest (one).
Answer: Siôn yw'r talaf.

1) Meri is the fairest.
   _____

2) He is the worst teacher.
   _____

3) Anthony Hopkins is the most famous.
   _____

4) Blaenau Ffestiniog is the wettest village.
   _____

5) She is the shortest.
   _____

If you have difficulty with this exercise, review **Week 8, Lesson 5** *and* **Lesson 6**.

Week 9

Lesson 1: The future tense of 'bod'

The affirmative forms
In Welsh, 'I will be' is expressed as **bydda i** ['bəða i]. Here are all the personal forms:

SENTENCE	ENGLISH	IPA
Bydda i'n hwyr.	I will be late.	['bəða iːn huɪr]
Byddi di'n hwyr.	You will be late. (*fam.*)	['bəði diːn huɪr]
Bydd e'n hwyr. (SW)	He will be late.	[biːð eːn huɪr]
Bydd o'n hwyr. (NW)	He will be late.	[biːð oːn huɪr]
Bydd hi'n hwyr.	She will be late.	[biːð hiːn huɪr]
Byddwn ni'n hwyr.	We will be late	['bəðʊ(n) niːn huɪr]
Byddwch chi'n hwyr.	You will be late (*pl.*) (*sing. formal*)	['bəðʊ(χ) χiːn huɪr]
Byddan nhw'n hwyr.	They will be late	['bəða(n) ŋuːn huɪr

> **IMPORTANT**
> Remember that the third person singular **bydd** [biːð] is used when the subject is a singular or plural noun.

For example:

SENTENCE	ENGLISH	IPA
Bydda i'n falch.	I will be glad.	['bəða iːn valχ]
Byddi di'n hwyr.	You will be late. (*fam.*)	['bəði diːn huɪr]
Bydd hi'n braf yfory.	It will be fine tomorrow.	[biːð hiːn braːv 'vɔri]

As in the present tense (see **Week 3, Lesson 1**), the future personal forms of '**bod**' are combined with verb-nouns to form the future imperfect and perfect aspects:

SENTENCE	ENGLISH	IPA	ASPECT
Bydd Siôn *yn* mynd.	Siôn will be going.	[biːð ʃoːn ən mɪnd]	Imperfect
Bydd Siôn *wedi* mynd.	Siôn will have gone.	[biːð ʃoːn 'wedi mɪnd]	Perfect

As in the present tense (see **Week 3, Lesson 1**), the affirmative forms of the future tense of '**bod**' come after interrogative adverbs such as **pryd** 'when' [priːd], **sut** 'how' [sɪt], **pam** 'why' [pam], **ble** 'where' [bleː], **faint o'r gloch** 'what time' [vaɪnt oːr gloːχ], etc.:

	SENTENCE
WELSH	**Pryd byddwch chi'n mynd?**
ENGLISH	When will you be going?
IPA	[priːd 'bəðʊ(χ) χiːn mɪnd]
WELSH	**Sut byddwch chi'n teithio yno?**
ENGLISH	How will you be travelling there?
IPA	[sɪt 'bəðʊ(χ) χiːn 'təɪθjo 'əno]
WELSH	**Pam byddwch chi'n gadael?**
ENGLIS	Why will you be leaving?
IPA	[pam 'bəðʊ(χ) χiːn 'gɑːdɛl]
WELSH	**Ble bydd y plant yn mynd ar ôl yr ysgol?**
ENGLISH	Where will the children be going after school?
IPA	[bleː biːð ə plant ən mɪnd ar oːl ər 'əsgol]

Vocabulary

ADVERBIAL	ENGLISH	IPA
(y)fory	tomorrow	[(ə)'vɔri]

VERB-NOUN	ENGLISH	IPA	STEM	IPA
cysylltu â (AM)	to contact	[kəsˈəɬti ã]	**cysyllt-**	[kəsˈəɬt]

Exercise 1

*Complete the following sentences by using the correct future tense form of '**bod**'.*

For example:

Question: Pryd _____ ni'n gadael?
Answer: byddwn

1) Faint o'r gloch _____ chi'n gadael?
2) _____ i'n gynnar yfory.
3) Pam _____ e'n (SW)/o'n (NW) brysur yfory?
4) _____ nhw'n gobeithio teithio yn y bore.
5) _____ ni'n clywed cyn hir.
6) _____ hi'n gymylog yfory.
7) Ble _____ y plant yn mynd i'r ysgol?
8) Sut _____ di'n cysylltu â hi?

The interrogative forms

The first letter of of the interrogative future forms of 'bod' undergoes soft mutation. The rules governing the usage of the future tense of **'bod'** (how to form the interrogative and negative, etc.) are similar to the present (see **Week 3, Lesson 1**) and past imperfect aspect of **'bod'** (see **Week 6, Lesson 1**). To form the interrogative, the verb undergoes soft mutation (see **Week 1, Lesson 5**):

QUESTION	ENGLISH	IPA
Fydda i'n hwyr?	Will I be late?	['vəða iːn huɪr]
Fyddi di'n hwyr?	Will you be late? (*fam.*)	['vəði diːn huɪr]
Fydd e'n hwyr? (SW)	Will he be late?	[viːð eːn huɪr]
Fydd o'n hwyr? (NW)	Will he be late?	[viːð oːn huɪr]
Fydd hi'n hwyr?	Will he be late?	[viːð hiːn huɪr]
Fyddwn ni'n hwyr?	Will we be late?	['vəðʊ(n) niːn huɪr]
Fyddwch chi'n hwyr?	Will you be late? (*pl.*) (*sing. formal*)	['vəðʊ(χ) χiːn huɪr]
Fyddan nhw'n hwyr?	Will they be late?	['vəða(n) n̥uːn huɪr]

> **IMPORTANT**
> Remember that the third person singular **fydd** [viːð] is used when the subject is a singular or plural noun.

For example:

	QUESTION
WELSH	**Fydd e'n (SW) / o'n (NW) cael cinio yn yr ysgol heddiw?**
ENGLISH	Will he be having dinner at school today?
IPA	[viːð eːn / oːn kaɪl 'kɪnjo ən ər 'əsgol 'heðɪʊ]
WELSH	**Fydd y plant yn gwisgo dillad du?**
ENGLISH	Will the children be wearing black clothes?
IPA	[viːð ə plant ən 'gwɪsgo 'dɪɬad diː]

Giving a 'yes' or 'no' response to a question which begins with a verb in the future tense of 'bod'

The personal replies are as follows:

REPLY	ENGLISH	IPA
Bydda.	Yes, I will be.	['bəðä]
Byddi.	Yes, you will be. (*fam.*)	['bəði]
Bydd.	Yes, he /she / it will be.	[biːð]
Byddwn.	Yes, we will be.	['bəðʊn]
Byddwch.	Yes, you will be. (*pl.*) (*sing. formal*)	['bəðʊχ]
Byddan.	Yes, they will be.	['bəðan]

For example:

	QUESTION	REPLY
WELSH	**Fyddwch chi'n gadael cyn wyth?**	**Byddwn**
ENGLISH	Will you leave before eight? (*pl.*)	Yes, we will.
IPA	['vəðʊ(χ) χiːn 'gaːdɛl kɪn ʊɪθ]	['bədʊn]
WELSH	**Fydd hi'n stormus (y)fory?**	**Bydd**
ENGLISH	Will it be stormy tomorrow?	Yes, it will.
IPA	[viːð hiːn 'stɔrmɪs (ə)'vɔri]	[biːð]

'No' is expressed by placing the negative particle **na** [naː] in front of the appropriate personal response. **Na** causes a soft mutation:

	QUESTION	REPLY
WELSH	**Fyddwch chi'n edrych ar y teledu?**	**Na fydda.**
ENGLISH	Will you be watching the television?	No, I won't.
IPA	['vəðʊ(χ) χiːn 'ɛdrɪχ ar ə tɛl'ɛdi]	[naː 'vəðä]
WELSH	**Fyddan nhw'n cael anrhegion?**	**Na fyddan.**
ENGLISH	Will they be getting presents?	No, they won't.
IPA	['vəða(n) n̥uːn kaɪl an'r̥ɛgjon]	[naː 'vəðan]

> **IMPORTANT**
>
> The interrogative pronouns **pwy** and **beth** cause the soft mutation:
>
> **Pwy fydd yn mynd?**   Who will go?   [pʊɪ viːð ən mɪnd]
> **Beth fydd yn digwydd?**   What will happen?   [beːθ viːð ən 'dɪgwɪð]
>
> **Pryd**, **sut** and **pam** (interrogative adverbs) do not cause soft mutation:
>
> **Pryd bydd y parti?**   When will the party be?   [priːd biːð ə 'parti]

Exercise 2

Complete the following sentences using an interrogative form of the future tense of **'bod'**.

For example:

Question: _____ chi'n mynd i'r briodas?
Answer: Fyddwch chi'n mynd i'r briodas?

1) _____ hi'n bwrw glaw yfory?	(Will it rain tomorrow?)
2) _____ chi eisiau aros yma?	(Will you want to stay here.)
3) _____ Meri'n ddiolchgar?	(Will Meri be thankful?)
4) _____ di'n ddigon cynnes?	(Will you be warm enough?)
5) _____ ni'n gallu gyrru i'r dref?	(Will we be able to drive to town?)
6) _____ i'n adnabod rhywun yno?	(Will I know anyone there?)
7) _____ nhw'n cofio'r llaeth?	(Will they remember the milk?)
8) _____ e'n (SW)/o'n (NW) deall?	(Will he understand?)

The negative forms

The negative forms of the future tense of 'bod' are formed by mutating the initial consonant of the verb and adding **ddim** [ðɪm] after the subject:

SENTENCE	ENGLISH	IPA
Fydda i ddim yn hwyr.	I will be not late.	[ˈvəða iː ðɪm ən hʊɪr]
Fyddi di ddim yn hwyr.	You will not be late. (*fam.*)	[ˈvəði diː ðɪm ən hʊɪr]
Fydd e ddim yn hwyr. (SW)	He will not be late.	[viːð eː ðɪm ən hʊɪr]
Fydd o ddim yn hwyr. (NW)	He will not be late.	[viːð oː ðɪm ən hʊɪr]
Fydd hi ddim yn hwyr.	She will not be late.	[viːð hiː ðɪm ən hʊɪr]
Fyddwn ni ddim yn hwyr.	We will not be late.	[ˈvəðʊ(n) niː ðɪm ən hʊɪr]
Fyddwch chi ddim yn hwyr.	You will not be late.	[ˈvəðʊ(χ) χiː ðɪm ən hʊɪr]
Fyddan nhw ddim yn hwyr.	They will not be late.	[ˈvəða(n) n̥uː ðɪm ən hʊɪr]

> **IMPORTANT**
> Remember that the third person singular **fydd ... ddim** [viːð (...) ðɪm] is used when the subject is a singular or plural noun.

For example:

	SENTENCE
WELSH	**Fydda i ddim yn deall popeth.**
ENGLISH	I won't understand everything.
IPA	[ˈvəða iː ðɪm ən ˈdeˑaɬ ˈpɔpɛθ]

WELSH	**Fyddwn ni ddim yn anghofio.**
ENGLISH	We won't forget.
IPA	[ˈvəðʊ(n) niː ðɪm ən aŋˈhɔvjo]

'Byth'

The adverb **byth** 'ever' / 'never' [bɪθ] takes the place of **ddim** in a negative sentence. We will see **byth** in more detail in **Week 10**.

For example:

SENTENCE	ENGLISH	IPA
Fydda i byth yn enwog.	I will never be famous.	[ˈvəða iː bɪθ ən ˈɛnwog]
Fydd hi byth yn cofio.	She will never remember.	[viːð hiː bɪθ ən ˈkɔvjo]

'Neb'

Whereas in English the affirmative is used with 'no one' / 'nobody', in Welsh the indefinite pronoun **neb** 'no one' [neːb] takes the place of **ddim** in the sentence:

SENTENCE	ENGLISH	IPA
Fydd neb yn dod.	No one will come.	[viːð neːb ən doːd]

Exercise 3

Respond to the following questions in full sentences which include an appropriate 'yes' or 'no' response.

For example:

Question: Fyddi di'n cyrraedd cyn chwech? (✓)
Answer: Bydda, bydda i'n cyrraedd cyn chwech.

For example:

Question: Fydda i'n ddigon cynnes? (✗)
Answer: Na fyddi, fyddi di ddim yn ddigon cynnes

1) Fydd o'n cytuno â chi? (✓)

___

2) Fydd y plant yn cloi'r drws? (✗)

___

3) Fyddi di'n cwrdd â fe (SW)/cyfarfod â fo (NW) yfory? (✓)

___

4) Fydda i'n cerdded yno? (✓)

___

5) Fydd hi'n stormus yfory? (✗)

___

6) Fyddan nhw'n credu'r meddyg? (✓)

___

7) Fyddwch chi'n galw heibio? (✗)

___

8) Fyddwn ni'n cael brecwast cyn mynd? (✗)

Vocabulary

MASCULINE NOUN	ENGLISH	IPA	PLURAL FORM	IPA
priodfab	bridegroom	[pri'ɔdvɑb]	**priodfeibion**	[priɔd'vəɪbjon]
diwrnod	day	['dɪʊrnod]	**diwrnodau**	[dɪʊr'nodɛ]
neb	nobody / no-one	[neːb]		

FEMININE NOUN	ENGLISH	IPA	PLURAL FORM	IPA
priodas	wedding	[pri'ɔdas]	**priodasau** (*llu.*)	[priɔd'asɛ]
hwyl	fun	[hʊɪl]		

MISCELLANEOUS	ENGLISH			IPA
y	that [with the future tense]			[ə]
i gyd	all [used after the word it is qualifying]			[iː giːd]
pob lwc	good luck			[poːb lʊk]

VERB-NOUN	ENGLISH	IPA	STEM	IPA
croesawu	to welcome	[krɔɪs'aʊi]	**croesaw-**	
edrych ymlaen (at)	to look forward (to)	['ɛdrɪχ əm'laɪn (at)]		
galw heibio	to call by	['gɑ'lʊ 'həɪbjo]		
cychwyn	to set out / to start	['kəχwɪn]	**cychwynn-**	[kəχ'wən]
dymuno	to wish	[dəm'iːno]	**dymun-**	[dəm'iːn]

ADJECTIVE	ENGLISH	IPA
neis	nice	[nəɪs]

Dialogue

Welsh Dialogue

Ann: Fyddi di yn y parti ffarwél i Geraint prynhawn dydd Gwener, Richard?
Richard: Na fydda. Bydda i ar y ffordd i Dde Cymru. Mae fy chwaer i'n priodi ddydd Sadwrn, a dw i eisiau cyrraedd erbyn wyth. Mae'n rhaid i fi gychwyn am dri. Dw i wedi siarad â Geraint ac wedi dymuno pob lwc iddo fe.
Ann: Wrth gwrs, dw i'n cofio rŵan, roeddwn i wedi anghofio am y briodas. Wyt ti'n edrych ymlaen?
Richard: Ydw ac nac ydw. Dw i ddim yn hoffi mynd i briodasau, ond bydd hi'n neis gweld y teulu i gyd. Byddwn ni'n cael parti bach nos Wener i groesawu teulu Ifan, y priodfab. Byddan nhw'n cyrraedd y pentref yn hwyr yn y prynhawn.
Ann: Diwrnod hir i chi, fydd neb yn mynd i'r gwely'n gynnar, dw i'n siŵr.
Richard: Na fydd. Dyn ni'n deulu sy'n hoff iawn o siarad a chael hwyl.
Ann: Wel, gobeithio y bydd pawb yn iawn dydd Sadwrn ac y bydd y tywydd yn braf.
Richard: Dw i'n siŵr bydd popeth yn iawn.

English Translation

Ann:	Will you be at the farewell party for Geraint on Friday afternoon, Richard?
Richard:	No. I will be on the way to South Wales. My sister is getting married on Saturday and I want to arrive by eight. I have to start out at three. I have spoken to Geraint and wished him good luck.
Ann:	Of course, I remember now. I had forgotten about the wedding. Are you looking forward?
Richard:	Yes and no. I don't like going to weddings but it will be nice to see all the family. We will be having a small party on Friday night to welcome Ifan, the bridegroom's, family. They will reach the village late in the afternoon.
Ann:	A long day for you, no one will go to bed early, I'm sure.
Richard:	No. We are a family who is very fond of talking and having fun.
Ann:	Well, I hope everyone will be all right on Saturday and that the weather will be fine.
Richard:	I'm sure everything will be all right.

Lesson 2: The simple future tense of regular verbs

The future affirmative forms

As with the simple past tense (see **Week 7, Lesson 2**), a inflected personal ending is added to the stem of a verb-noun to form the simple future tense. Below are the future personal forms of the regular inflected verbs. We will use **dysgu** 'to learn' / 'to teach' ['dəsgi] as the example. The future endings are underlined:

SENTENCE	ENGLISH	IPA
Dysga i.	I will learn / teach.	['dəsga iː]
Dysgi di.	You will learn / teach. (*fam.*)	['dəsgi diː]
Dysgith e. (SW)	He will learn / teach.	['dəsgɪθ eː]
Dysgith o. (NW)	He will learn / teach.	['dəsgɪθ oː]
Dysgith hi.	She will learn / teach.	['dəsgɪθ hiː]
Dysgwn ni.	We will learn / teach.	['dəsgʊ(n) niː]
Dysgwch chi.	You will learn / teach. (*pl.*) (*sing. formal*)	['dəsgʊ(χ) χiː]
Dysgan nhw.	They will learn / teach.	['dəsga(n) n̥uː]

> **IMPORTANT**
> Remember that the third person singular **dysgith** ['dəsgɪθ] is used when the subject is a singular or plural noun.

For example:

SENTENCE	ENGLISH	IPA
Caea i'r drws.	I will close the door.	['kəɪa iːr dɹuːs]
Ffonith hi eto yfory	She will phone again tomorrow.	['fɔnɪθ hiː 'eto (ə)'vɔri]

Arhosan nhw gartre(f).   They will stay at home.   [arˈhɔsan nuː ˈgartɹ̠ɛ(v)]

Vocabulary

MASCULINE NOUN	ENGLISH	IPA	PLURAL FORM	IPA
gliniadur	laptop	[glɪnˈjɑˑdɪr]	**gliniaduron**	[glɪnjadˈiˑrɔn]
staff	staff	[staf]		
môr	sea	[moːr]	**moroedd**	[ˈmoˑrɔɪð]

ADVERBIAL	ENGLISH	IPA
rywbryd arall	some other time	[ˈrɪʊbrɪd ˈɑˑraɬ]

VERB-NOUN	ENGLISH	IPA	STEM	IPA
cytuno â (AM)	to agree with	[kətˈiˑno ä]	**cytun-**	[kətˈiˑn ä]
anghytuno	to disagree	[aŋhətˈiˑno]	**anghytun-**	[aŋhətˈiˑn]

Exercise 1

Complete the following sentences by filling in the gaps using the verb-noun given in brackets.

1) _____ i'r llofft rywbryd arall.   (paentio)
2) _____ ni'r carped y flwyddyn nesaf.   (newid)
3) _____ nhw yn y pwll nofio heno.   (nofio)
4) Pryd _____ ni â'r staff?   (siarad)
5) _____ e'r (SW)/o'r (NW) larwm o'i ystafell wely. (clywed)
6) Ble _____ ni yn y dref?   (bwyta)
7) _____ ni liniadur newydd y mis nesaf.   (prynu)
8) _____ hi dy ffonio di heno.   (ceisio)
9) _____ o wrth y staff yfory.   (dweud)
10) _____ ni i anghytuno.   (cytuno)

'Bydda i'n dysgu' and 'Dysga i'

Note the difference between the future imperfect aspect of '**bod**' we saw in **Week 9, Lesson 1** and the simple future tense we are studying now. The simple future expresses a more specific, definite intent. These two patterns are also known as the periphrastic (or 'long') and inflected (or 'short') constructions (see **Week 3, Lesson 1**) respectively.

Here is a reminder of the periphrastic construction:

SENTENCE	ENGLISH	IPA
Bydda i'n gadael.	I will be leaving (sometime).	['bəða iːn 'gaˈdɛl]
Bydda i'n dysgu.	I will be learning (at an unspecified time).	['bəða iːn 'dəsgi]

Here are some examples of the simple future:

SENTENCE	ENGLISH	IPA
Gadawa i.	I will leave (now).	[gadˈaʊa iː (naʊr)]
Dysga i.	I will learn /teach (at an specified time).	['dəsga iː]

However, this is not a hard and fast rule, and it is quite common for Welsh speakers to use the long **bydda i'n gadael** form to express specific situations.

The future tense of 'gallu'
The future tense of the **'gallu'** ['gäɬi] translates as 'can' in English:

PERSONAL FORM	ENGLISH	IPA
galla i	I can	['gäɬa iː]
gelli di	you can (*fam.*)	['gɛɬi diː]
gallith e (SW)	he can	[gaɬ eː]
gallith o (NW)	he can	[gaɬ oː]
gallith hi	she can	[gaɬ hiː]
gallwn ni	we can	['gäɬʊ(n) niː]
gallwch chi	you can (*plu.*) (*formal*)	['gäɬʊ(χ) χiː]
gallan nhw	they can	['gäɬa(n) ṉuː]

> **IMPORTANT**
> Remember that the third person singular **gall** [gaɬ] is used when the subject is a singular or a plural noun.

For example:

SENTENCE	ENGLISH	IPA
Galla i weld y môr.	I can see the sea.	['gäɬa iː wɛld ə moːr]
Allwch chi (f)y nghlywed i?	Can you hear me?	['äɬʊ(χ) χiː (v)ə 'ŋ̊ləʊɛd iː]

The future interrogative forms
The mutational rules governing the interrogative and negative forms are the same as the simple past tense of regular verbs (see **Week 7, Lesson 3**):

For the interrogative, there is a soft mutation to the initial consonant of the verb:

	QUESTION	VERB-NOUN PRE-MUTATION
WELSH	**Welwn ni chi eto?**	**gweld**
ENGLISH	Will we see you again?	to see
IPA	['wɛlʊ(n) niː χiː 'ɛto]	[gwɛld]
WELSH	**Gymerwch chi sêt?**	**cymryd**
ENGLISH	Will you take a seat?	to take
IPA	[gəm'ɛrʊ(χ) χiː 'seːt]	['kəmrɪd]
WELSH	**Alla i helpu?**	**gallu**
ENGLISH	Can I help?	to be able
IPA	['aɬa iː 'hɛlpi]	['gäɬi]

The others are usually expressed by the future imperfect aspect of '**bod**' (see **Week 9, Lesson 1**):

	QUESTION
WELSH	**Fyddwch chi'n mynd i'r gêm heno?**
ENGLISH	Will you (be) go(ing) to the game tonight?
IPA	['vəðʊ(χ) χiːn mɪnd iːr geːm 'hɛno]
WELSH	**Fyddan nhw'n galw heibio yfory?**
ENGLISH	Will they (be) call(ing) by tomorrow?
IPA	['vəða(n) n̥uːn 'gɑˑlʊ 'həɪbjo (ə)'vɔri]
WELSH	**Fydd Cymru yn ennill?**
ENGLISH	Will Wales (be) win(ning)?
IPA	[viːð 'kəmri ən 'ɛnɪɬ]

Here are some useful interrogatives:

	QUESTION
WELSH	**Beth gymerwch chi?**
ENGLISH	What will you have? (*lit.* What will you take?)
IPA	[beːθ gəm'ɛrʊ(χ) χiː]
WELSH	**Allwch chi helpu?**
ENGLISH	Can you help?
IPA	['äɬʊ(χ) χiː 'hɛlpi]
WELSH	**Pwy welwch chi?**
ENGLISH	Who will you see?
IPA	[pʊɪ 'wɛlʊ(χ) χiː]

Vocabulary

MASCULINE NOUN	ENGLISH	IPA	PLURAL FORM	IPA
adroddiad	report	[adˈrɔðjad]	**adroddiadau**	[adrɔðˈjɑ·dɛ]

FEMININE NOUN	ENGLISH	IPA	PLURAL FORM	IPA
sêt	seat	[seːt]	**seti**	[seˈti]
gêm	game	[geːm]	**gemau**	[ˈge·mɛ]

ADVERBIAL	ENGLISH	IPA
heibio	by / past	[ˈhəɪbjo]

VERB-NOUN	ENGLISH	IPA	STEM	IPA
ffonio	to telephone	[ˈfɔnjo]	**ffoni-**	[fɔnj]
edrych ar (SM)	to look at / to watch	[ˈɛdrɪχ ar]	**edrych-**	[ɛdˈrəχ ar]

ADJECTIVE	ENGLISH	IPA
nesa(f)	next	[ˈnɛsa(v)]

Exercise 2

Translate the following sentences using the the simple future tense for those verbs which are underlined, and the future imperfect aspect of 'bod' for all other verbs.

For example:
Question: Will he understand?
Answer: Fydd e'n deall? (SW)
Answer: Fydd o'n deall? (NW)

For example:
Question: Will he <u>see</u> the doctor?
Answer: Welith e'r meddyg? (SW)
Answer: Welith o'r meddyg? (NW)

1) Will I <u>see</u> you tomorrow?

2) <u>Can</u> she see the sea from her window?

3) Will the doctor call?

4) Will they sell the house?

5) <u>Can</u> they help?

6) Will they read the report?

7) Will Emyr (be) watch(ing) the game tonight?

8) Will you <u>take</u> another (one)? (*formal*)

9) Who will we <u>see</u> next?

10) Will you <u>take</u> (have) a cuppa? (*informal*)

Responses
When answering questions in everyday conversation, the future inflected verb forms follow the general rule of employing the appropriate personal form:

	QUESTION	AFFIRMATIVE REPLY	NEGATIVE REPLY
WELSH	**Welwch chi Siôn yfory?**	**Gwela.**	**Na wela.**
ENGLISH	Will you see Siôn tomorrow?	Yes, I will see.	No, I won't see.
IPA	[weˈlʊ(χ) χiː ʃoːn (ə)ˈvɔri]	[ˈgweˑla]	[naː ˈweˑla]
WELSH	**Gymerwch chi wy i frecwast?**	**Cymera.**	**Na chymera.**
ENGLISH	Will you have an egg for breakfast?	Yes.	No.
IPA	[gəmˈɛrʊ(χ) χiː ʊi iː ˈvrɛkwast]	[kəmˈɛra]	[naː χəmˈɛra]
WELSH	**Allith hi alw heibio yfory?**	**Gallith.**	**Na allith.**
ENGLISH	Can she call by tomorrow?	Yes.	No.
IPA	[ˈaɬiθ hiː ˈaˑlʊ ˈhəɪbjo (ə)ˈvɔri]	[ˈgaɬiθ]	[ˈnaː ˈaɬiθ]

Exercise 3

*For the questions listed under **A**, select the appropriate responses from under **B**.*

A **B**
1) Alla i dy weld di?
2) Welan nhw hi heno?
3) Allith hi fynd nawr?
4) Gymerwch chi goffi?
5) Allwn ni adael yn gynnar?
6) Allwch chi ei ddarllen e (SW)/o (NW)?
7) Allith y staff gael gwyliau?
8) Welwch chi'r ddrama heno?
9) Gymerith y plant wydraid o laeth?

a) Gwela
b) Gallwn
c) Cymeran
d) Gwelan
e) Gelli
f) Gallwch
g) Gallith
h) Cymera
i) Galla

Vocabulary

MASCULINE NOUN	ENGLISH	IPA	PLURAL FORM	IPA
gwydraid	a glassful	[ˈgwɪdrɛd]	**gwydreidiau**	[gwɪdˈrəɪdjɛ]
gwin	wine	[gwiːn]	**gwinoedd**	[ˈgwiˑnɔɪð]
siocled	chocolate	[ˈʃɔklɛd]	**siocledi**	[ʃɔkˈlɛdi]
bocs	box	[bɔks]	**bocsys**	[ˈbɔksɪz]

VERB-NOUN	ENGLISH	IPA
lliwio	to colour in	[ˈɬɪʊjo]

The ending '-aid'

The suffix **-aid** [ɛd] is added to a noun in order to convey that the noun is 'full'.

	NOUN	PHRASE
WELSH	**potel***	**potelaid o ddŵr***
ENGLISH	a bottle	a bottle of water
IPA	[ˈpɔtɛl]	[pɔtˈɛlɛd oː ðuːr]
WELSH	**sach**	**sachaid o datws**
ENGLISH	a sack	a sack of potatoes
IPA	[saːχ]	[ˈsaˑχɛd o ˈdatʊs]
WELSH	**cwpan**	**cwpanaid** o de**
ENGLISH	a cup	a cup of tea
IPA	[ˈkʊpan]	[kʊpˈaˑnɛd oː deː]

* Note the difference between **potel dŵr** 'a water bottle' and **potelaid o ddŵr** 'a bottle of water'.

** This is normally shortened to **paned** [ˈpaˑnɛd] (SW) or **panad** [ˈpaˑnad̥] (NW) in everyday conversation.

The gender of the resultant word agrees with that of the original. For example, both **potel** and **potelaid** are feminine, whereas **cwpan** and **cwpanaid** are masculine.

Exercise 4

Translate the following phrases.

1) a spoonful of sugar _____
2) a bag of books _____
3) a bottle of wine _____
4) a basket of flowers _____
5) a cup of hot chocolate _____

6) a box of chocolates   _____

For all other verbs, the response given is the personal forms of the future tense of the verb **gwneud** 'to do' / 'to make' [gʷnəɪd] (see **Week 9, Lesson 3**):

AFFIRMATIVE REPLY	ENGLISH	NEGATIVE REPLY	ENGLISH
Gwnaf.	Yes, I will.	**Na wnaf.**	No, I won't.
Gwnei.	Yes, you will. (*fam.*)	**Na wnei.**	No, you won't. (*fam.*)
Gwneith.	Yes, he / she / it will.	**Na wneith.**	No, he / she / it won't.
Gwnawn.	Yes, we will.	**Na wnawn.**	No, we won't.
Gwnewch.	Yes, you will.	**Na wnewch.**	No, you won't. (*pl.*) (*formal*)
Gwnân.	Yes, they will.	**Na wnân.**	No, they won't.

Exercise 5

Match the questions under A with the correct answers from under B.

A
1) Ddysgan nhw Gymraeg yn yr ysgol?
   (Will they learn Welsh at school?)

2) Ganwn ni yn yr eisteddfod?
   (Will we sing at the Eisteddfod?)

3) Ofynnwn ni i'r staff?
   (Will we ask the staff?)

4) Chwaraei di yn y parc?
   (Will you [*fam.*] play in the park?)

5) Gerddith hi i'r theatr?
   (Will she walk to the theatre?)

6) Nofiwch chi yn y môr
   (Will you swim in the sea?)

7) Brynith y plant ginio yn y siop fara?
   (Will the children buy lunch in the bread shop?)

8) Anfonith e anrhegion i'r plant?
   (Will he send the children presents?)

B
a) Gwneith

b) Gwnân

c) Gwnaf

d) Gwnewch

e) Gwnawn

f) Gwnei

The future negative forms
The initial consonant of the negative verb forms undergoes the aspirate mutation in the case of **p**, **t**, and **c** (see **Week 1, Lesson 5**), and the soft mutation in the case of all other mutable consonants (**see Week 1, Lesson 5**).

Here is an example of the aspirate mutation:

	SENTENCE
WELSH	**Theithian nhw ddim dros y penwythnos.**
ENGLISH	They won't travel over the weekend.
IPA	[ˈθəɪθja(n) n̬uː ðɪm drɔs ə pɛnˈʊɪθnos]

Here is an example of the soft mutation:

	SENTENCE
WELSH	**_Welwn ni ddim pobl.**
ENGLISH	We won't see any people.
IPA	[ˈwɛlʊ(n) niː ðɪm ˈpoˑbol]

Exercise 6

Turn the following negative future imperfect sentences into their corresponding simple future forms.

For example:

Question: Fydda i ddim yn cofio agor y ffenest(r).
Answer: Chofia i ddim agor y ffenestr.

1) Fyddi di ddim yn dysgu.
   (You won't learn.)

2) Fydda i ddim yn clywed.
   (I won't listen.)

3) Fydd hi ddim yn gwylio'r gêm.
   (She won't be watching the game.)

4) Fydda i ddim yn deall.
   (I won't understand.)

5) Fyddwch chi ddim yn rhedeg.
   (You won't run.)

6) Fyddwn ni ddim yn cysgu yn y car.
   (We won't sleep in the car.)

7) Fydd e (SW)/o (NW) ddim yn gadael.
   (He won't leave.)

8) Fydd y meddygon ddim yn gweithio yfory.
   (The doctors won't be working tomorrow.)

9) Fyddwn ni ddim yn gofyn.
   (We won't ask.)

10) Fydd y plant ddim yn lliwio amser chwarae.
(The children won't be colouring in at play time.)

Lesson 3: The simple future tense of 'mynd' and 'gwneud'

The future forms of the irregular verbs '**mynd**' and '**gwneud**' are very similar. The future forms of '**dod**', which we will see in **Week 9, Lesson 5**, are a little different.

Like the regular verbs (see **Week 9, Lesson 2**), the future tense of the irregular verbs originally denoted the present tense, and they can still used in this way in literary Welsh.

In this lesson, we will focus on the inflected future forms of '**mynd**' and '**gwneud**':

The affirmative forms

Here are the affirmative forms of '**mynd**':

SENTENCE	ENGLISH	IPA
af fi	I will go	[ɑː(v) viː]
ei di	you will go (*fam.*)	[əɪ diː]
eith e (SW)	he will go	[əɪθ eː]
eith o (NW)	he will go	[əɪθ oː]
eith hi	she will go	[əɪθ hiː]
awn ni	we will go	[aʊ(n) niː]
ewch chi	you will go (*pl.*) (*sing. formal*)	[ɛʊ(χ) χiː]
ân nhw	they will go	[ɑː(n) n̥uː]

Here are the affirmative forms of '**gwneud**':

SENTENCE	ENGLISH	IPA
gwnaf fi	I will do / make	[gʷnɑː(v) viː]
gwnei di	you will do / make (*fam.*)	[gʷnəɪ diː]
gwneith e (SW)	he will do / make	[gʷnəɪθ eː]
gwneith o (NW)	he will do / make	[gʷnəɪθ oː]
gwneith hi	she will do / make	[gʷnəɪθ hiː]
gwnawn ni	we will do / make	[gʷnaʊ(n) niː]
gwnewch chi	you will do / make (*pl.*) (*sing. formal*)	[gʷnɛʊ(χ) χiː]
gwnân nhw	they will do / make	[gʷnɑː(n) n̥uː]

For example:

	SENTENCE
WELSH	**Af fi i'r gwaith (y)fory.**
ENGLISH	I will go to work tomorrow.
IPA	[ɑː(v) viː iːr gwaith (ə)'vɔri]

WELSH	**Gwneith o'r llestri.**
ENGLISH	He will do the dishes.
IPA	[gʷnəiθ eːr 'ɬestɹ̥i]

The interrogative forms

To form a question using the future tense of '**mynd**', it is only necessary to inflect the sentence:

	QUESTION
WELSH	**Ewch chi i'r parti?**
ENGLISH	Will you go to the party?
IPA	[ɛʊ(χ) χiː iːr 'parti]

To form a question using the future tense of '**gwneud**', the initial consonant of the verb undergoes the soft mutation, just as in the case of simple past tense verbs, and the future tense of '**bod**' (see **Week 9, Lesson 1** and **Week 1, Lesson 5**):

	QUESTION
WELSH	**Wnewch chi olchi'r llestri?**
ENGLISH	Will you wash the dishes?
IPA	[ʷnɛʊ(χ) χiː 'ɔlχir 'ɬestɹ̥i]

Vocabulary

MASCULINE NOUN	ENGLISH	IPA
llanast(r)	mess	['ɬɑˈnast(ɹ̥)]

NOUN (*pl.*)	ENGLISH	IPA
llestri	dishes	['ɬestɹ̥i]

The negative forms

To form the negative of the future tense of '**mynd**', **ddim** is added after the verb (and the affixed pronoun):

	SENTENCE
WELSH	**Awn ni ddim yfory.**
ENGLISH	We won't go tomorrow.
IPA	[aʊn niː ðɪm (ə)'vɔri]

To form the negative of the future tense of '**gwneud**', the initial consonant of the verb is mutated and **ddim** placed after it:

	SENTENCE
WELSH	**Wnân nhw ddim byd.**
ENGLISH	They won't do anything. (*lit.* They won't do nothing.)
IPA	[ʷnɑː(n) n̥uː ðɪm biːd]

Exercise 1

Fill the blank spaces in the exercise below with the simple future form of the verb, remembering to mutate questions and negatives where necessary.

1) Ble _____ chi yfory? (Where will you go tomorrow?)
2) _____ hi i weld y meddyg yfory? (Will she go to see the doctor tomorrow?)
3) _____ nhw ddim byd. (They won't do anything.)
4) Beth _____ ni wedyn? (What will we do afterwards?)
5) _____ i i'r parti ffarwél nos Wener. (I will go to the farewell party on Friday night.)
6) _____ di i'r briodas? (Will you go to the wedding?)
7) _____ ni ddim wrth ein hunain. (We won't go on our own.)
8) _____ dy fam y gacen briodas? (Will your mother make the wedding cake?)
9) _____ i ddim byd. (I won't do anything.)
10) _____ o ddim llanastr. (He won't make a mess.)

'Gwneud' as an auxiliary verb in the future tense

'**Gwneud**' is often used as an auxiliary verb in the future tense, especially with interrogatives and negatives. (We will discuss the role of '**gwneud**' as an auxiliary verb further in **Week 12, Lesson 2**):

	SENTENCE
WELSH	**Wneith e (SW) / o (NW) wrando?**
ENGLISH	Will he listen?
IPA	[ʷneiθ eː / oː ʷrãndo]
WELSH	**Wnân nhw ddim mynd.**
ENGLISH	They won't go.
IPA	[ʷnɑː(n) n̥uː ðɪm mɪnd]

Auxiliary verbs, like '**gwneud**' in this case, are so called because they help to form the various tenses, moods, and voices of other verbs. In the examples above, **wneith** is 'helping' the verb-nouns '**gwrando**' and '**mynd**'. The use of '**gwneud**' as an auxiliary verb is particularly prevalent in North Wales. There are no rules governing when '**gwneud**' is used in this way; it depends a lot on local custom and individual preference. There is no difference in meaning between **wnân nhw ddim mynd** [ʷnaː(n) n̥uː ðɪm mɪnd] and **ân nhw ddim** [aː(n) n̥uː ðɪm]; they both mean, 'They won't go', although the former can be more emphatic.

The polite command

The polite command 'Will you (...)?' is expressed in spoken Welsh as **Wnewch chi (...)?** [ʷnɛʊ(χ) χiː] / **Wnei di (...)?** (*fam.*) [ʷnəɪ diː]. For example:

	QUESTION
WELSH	**Wnewch chi ddod yma?**
ENGLISH	Will you come here?
IPA	[ʷnɛʊ(χ) χiː ðoːd 'əmä]
WELSH	**Wnewch chi wrando arna i?**
ENGLISH	Will you listen to me?
IPA	[ʷnɛʊ(χ) χiː ʷrändo 'ärna iː]
WELSH	**Wnei di gloi'r drws?**
ENGLISH	Will you lock the door?
IPA	[ʷnəɪ diː glɔɪr dɹuːs]
WELSH	**Wnei di symud dy liniadur di?**
ENGLISH	Will you move your laptop?
IPA	[ʷnəɪ diː 'səmɪd də lɪn'jɑˑdɪr diː]

The replies to such polite commands are **Gwnaf** 'Yes, I will' [gʷnaːv] and **Na wnaf** 'No, I won't' [na: ʷnaːv].

Vocabulary

MASCULINE NOUN	ENGLISH	IPA	PLURAL FORM	IPA
golau	light	['goˑlɛ]	**goleuadau**	[goləɪ'ɑˑdɛ]
sŵn	noise	[suːn]	**synau**	['sənɛ]
gair	word	[gaɪr]	**geiriau**	['gəɪrjɛ]
prawf	test	[praʊv]	**profion**	['prɔvjon]

FEMININE NOUN	ENGLISH	IPA
mathemateg	mathematics	[maθɛm'atɛg]

VERB-NOUN	ENGLISH	IPA	STEM	IPA
agor	to open	['ɑˑgor]	**agor-**	[a'goˑr]

estyn	to extend / to pass	[ˈɛstɪn]	**estynn-**	[ɛsˈtən]
golchi	to wash	[ˈgɔlχi]	**golch-**	[gɔlχ]
diffodd	to extinguish / to put out	[ˈdɪfoð]	**diffodd-**	[dɪfɔð]
cynnau	to switch on	[ˈkən(a)ɪ]	**cynheu-**	[kənˈhəɪ]

Below are some examples of these verb-nouns in action:

PHRASE	ENGLISH	IPA
cau'r drws	to shut the door	[kaɪr druːs]
agor y drws	to open the door	[ˈɑgor ə druːs]
cau'r ffenest(r)	to shut the window	[kaɪr ˈfɛnɛst(ɹ)]
agor y ffenest(r)	to open the window	[ˈɑgor ə ˈfɛnɛst(ɹ)]
troi'r sŵn i lawr	to turn the noise down	[trɔɪr suːn iː laʊr]
dod yma	to come here	[dod ˈəmä]
estyn y pupur	to pass the pepper	[ˈɛstɪn ə ˈpɪpɪr]
golchi'r llestri	to wash the dishes	[ˈgɔlχir ɬɛstɹi]
codi ar eich traed	to stand up	[ˈkɔdi ar əχ tɹaɪd]
diffodd y golau	to switch the light off	[ˈdɪfoð ə ˈgoˈlɛ]
cynn(a)u'r golau	to switch the light on	[ˈkən(a)ɪr ˈgoˈlɛ]

Exercise 2

Ask someone to do the things mentioned below and answer for them.

For example:

Question: Close the door.
Answer: Wnewch chi gau'r drws? Gwnaf, caea i'r drws.
(Will you close the door? Yes, I'll close the door.)

a) Open the door.

_____

b) Pass the paper.

_____

c) Wash the dishes.

_____

d) Switch on the light.

_____

e) Stand up.

_____

f) Turn the noise down.

_____

Exercise 3

Complete the following sentences by choosing an appropriate verb from the list in brackets below. Remember to mutate, as the verb will be the direct object of the simple form of the verb.

(gyrru adref, chwilio am fy waled i, dysgu'r geiriau, bwydo'r gath, brysio, dod gyda (SW) / efo (NW) fi, galw heibio, aros pum munud, cynnau'r golau, agor y ffenestr.)

1) Mae hi'n rhy boeth yn yr ystafell. Wnewch chi _____?
   (It's too hot in the room. Will you [...]?)
2) Dw i eisiau siarad â ti. Wnei di _____?
   (I want to talk to you. Will you [...]?)
3) Mae hi'n dywyll yma. Wnewch chi _____?
   (It's dark here. Will you [...]?)
4) Dw i eisiau talu'r dyn llaeth. Wnei di _____?
   (I want to pay the milkman. Will you [...]?)
5) Dw i ddim eisiau mynd wrth fy hunan. Wnewch chi _____?
   (I don't want to go by myself. Will you [...]?)
6) Dw i wedi blino. Wnei di _____?
   (I'm tired. Will you [...]?)
7) Bydda i i ffwrdd dros y penwythnos. Wnei di _____?
   (I will be away over the weekend. Will you [...]?)
8) Byddwn ni'n canu'r anthem genedlaethol. Wnei di _____?
   (We will sing the national anthem. Will you [...]?)
9) Dyn ni'n mynd i fod yn hwyr. Wnei di _____?
   (We are going to be late. Will you [...]?)
10) Mae Sioned eisiau cwmni. Wnei di _____?
    (Sioned wants company. Will you [...]?)

Dialogue

Welsh Dialogue

Ann: Wnei di ffonio Nain a dweud y gwnawn ni alw heibio bore dydd Sul? Cyrhaeddwn ni tua un ar ddeg o'r gloch os bydd y ffyrdd yn dawel. Elli di hefyd ddweud ein bod ni'n mynd i'r dref ddydd Sadwrn os bydd hi eisiau i ni gael rhywbeth iddi hi.

Tomos: Dweda i wrth Nain am fy mhrawf mathemateg i hefyd.

Ann: Syniad da, bydd hi wrth ei bodd i glywed am hynny. Awn ni â nain i'r dafarn 'na yn y bryniau, gallwn ni fynd am dro bach wedyn. Gwneith hynny'r byd o les iddi hi. Wel, i bawb.

Tomos: Wel, darllena i'r map, os bydd dad yn gwneud, awn ni i gyd ar goll eto.

Ann: Eith neb ar goll Tomos, fi fydd yn darllen y map.

English Translation

Ann: Will you phone Grandma and say that we will call by on Sunday morning? We will arrive about eleven o'clock on Sunday if the roads are quiet. Can you also say that we are going to town on Saturday – if she wants us to get something for her?

Tomos: I will tell Grandma about my maths test also.

Ann: (That's a) good idea; she will be delighted to hear about that. We will take grandma to that pub in the hills; we can go for a small walk afterwards. That will do her the world of good. Well, everyone.

Tomos: Well, I will read the map. If dad does, we will all get lost again.

Ann: No one will get lost Tomos, *I* will read the map.

Lesson 4: The simple future tense of 'cael' and asking permission

SENTENCE	ENGLISH	IPA
caf fi	I will get	[kɑː(v) viː]
cei di	you will get (*fam.*)	[kəɪ diː]
ceith e (SW)	he will get	[kəɪθ eː]
ceith o (NW)	he will get	[kəɪθ oː]
ceith hi	she will get	[kəɪθ hiː]
cawn ni	we will get	[kaʊ(n) niː]
cewch chi	you will get (*pl.*) (*sing. formal*)	[kɛʊ(χ) χiː]
cân nhw	they will get	[kɑː(n) n̥uː]

> **IMPORTANT**
> Remember that the third person singular **ceith** [kəɪθ] is used when the subject is a singular or plural noun.

As with all verbs, to express the interrogative, the initial consonant of the verb undergoes soft mutation:

SENTENCE	ENGLISH	IPA
Geith e anrheg? (SW)	Will he get a present?	[gəɪθ eː 'anɹɛg]
Geith o anrheg? (NW)	Will he get a present?	[gəɪθ oː 'anɹɛg]

To express the negative, the initial consonant of the verb '**cael**' undergoes aspirate mutation:

	SENTENCE
WELSH	**Chaf fi ddim siocledi.**
ENGLISH	I won't have any chocolates.
IPA	[χɑː(v) viː ðɪm ʃɔkˈlɛdi]

'May I?' and 'May I have?' are expressed in Welsh by **gaf fi?**

For example:

	SENTENCE
WELSH	**Gaf fi fynd?**
ENGLISH	May I go?
IPA	[gɑː(v) viː vɪnd]

WELSH	**Gaf i bwys o afalau?**
ENGLISH	May I have a pound of apples?
IPA	[gɑː(v) viː bʊɪs o avˈɑˈlɛ]

The replies to such questions are **Cewch** 'Yes, you may' [kɛʊχ] / **Cei** 'Yes, you may' (*fam.*) [kəɪ] and **Na chewch** 'No, you may not' [nɑː χɛʊχ] / **Na chei** 'No, you may not' (*fam.*) [nɑː χəɪ].

This usage of the verb '**cael**' to express permission is extended to other tenses:

QUESTION	ENGLISH	IPA
Ydyn ni'n cael mynd?	Are we allowed to go?	[ˈədɪ(n) niːn kaɪl mɪnd]
Gawsoch chi fynd?	Were you allowed to go?	[ˈgaʊso(χ) χiː vɪnd]
Fydd e'n cael mynd?	Will he be allowed to go?	[viːð eːn kaɪl mɪnd]

Exercise 1

*Complete the following using the future tense of '***cael***'.*

1) _____ i ddiffodd y golau? (May I turn the light off?)

2) _____ chi ddim aros yma. (You can't [aren't allowed] to stay here.)

3) _____ o nofio yn y môr? (Is he allowed to swim in the sea?)

4) Beth _____ ni i ginio heddiw? (What will we get for dinner today?)

5) _____ i gawod bore yfory. (I will have a shower tomorrow morning.)

6) _____ hi agor y ffenestr os ydy hi'n oer. (She may open the window if she is cold.)

7) _____ pawb ddillad newydd yn y dref. (Everyone will get new clothes in town.)

8) _____ di ddechrau unrhywbryd. (You may start anytime.)

Vocabulary

MASCULINE NOUN	ENGLISH	IPA	PLURAL FORM	IPA
peint	pint	[pəɪnt]	peintiau	['pəɪntjɛ]
bil	bill	[bɪl]	biliau	['bɪljɛ]

MISCELLANEOUS	ENGLISH	IPA
peint o gwrw	a pint of beer	[pəɪnt oː 'guːrʊ]
pwys o datws	a pound of potatoes	[pʊɪs oː 'datʊs]
bocs o fatsis	a box of matches	[bɔks oː 'vatʃɪz]
torth o fara	a loaf of bread	[tɔrθ oː 'vaːra]
tipyn o hufen	a little cream	['tɪpɪn oː 'hiːvɛn]
rhagor o laeth	more milk	['ɹaˑgor oː laɪθ]
unrhyw bryd	anytime	['ɪnɹɪʊ briːd]

Exercise 2

Ask if you may have the following items.

1) the bill
2) a pint of milk
3) more cream
4) a loaf of bread
5) box of matches
6) half a pint of beer
7) more time
8) a pound of potatoes

Vocabulary

MASCULINE NOUN	ENGLISH	IPA
llond	full	[ɬɔnd]

Llond [ɬɔnd] refers to the amount needed to completely fill something, and it is used in expressions such as **llond llaw** 'a handful' [ɬɔnd ɬaʊ], **cael llond bol** 'to have a bellyful/gutful' [kaɪl ɬɔnd bɔl].

FEMININE NOUN	ENGLISH	IPA	PLURAL FORM	IPA
troed	foot	[tɹɔɪd]	traed	[tɹaɪd]

ADVERBIAL	ENGLISH	IPA
dros nos	over night	[drɔs noːs]
yn nes ymlaen	later on	[ən neːs əmˈlaɪn]
yng nghanol	in the middle of	[ə(ŋ) ˈŋɑːnol]
bron	almost / nearly / practically	[brɔn]
draw	over	[draʊ]

ADJECTIVE	ENGLISH	IPA
bodlon	willing / satisfied	[ˈbɔdlon]
bywiog	lively	[ˈbɪʊjog]

VERB-NOUN	ENGLISH	IPA	STEM	IPA
trafod	to discuss	[ˈtrɑːvod]	**trafod-**	[trɑːvˈɔd]
addo	to promise	[ˈɑːðo]	**addaw-**	[aðˈaʊ]

PREPOSITION	ENGLISH	IPA
tan (SM)	until	[tan]

CONJUNCTION	ENGLISH	IPA
os	if	[ɔs]

Dialogue

Welsh Dialogue

Gethin: Gaf fi fynd i dŷ Garmon heno, mam? Mae ei fam e'n dweud y caf fi aros dros nos.

Ann: Wel mae'n iawn gen i. Ffonia i mam Garmon yn nes ymlaen i drafod y peth. Ceith Garmon ddod yma nos yfory os bydd ei fam o'n fodlon.

Gethin: Geith Iestyn ddod hefyd?

Ann: Na cheith! Dw i ddim eisiau llond tŷ o fechgyn yng nghanol yr wythnos. Bachgen bywiog iawn ydy Iestyn, mae ar ei draed o trwy'r nos bron! Y tro diwethaf iddo fo ddod draw wnaethoch chi ddim mynd i gysgu tan dri o'r gloch y bore.

Gethin: Awn ni i'r gwely am naw o'r gloch, a chysgwn ni tan saith o'r gloch y bore. Ddwedwn ni ddim un gair ar ôl diffodd y golau, dw i'n addo.

Ann: Cawn ni weld.

English Translation

Gethin: May I go to Garmon's house tonight, Mum? His mum says that I can stay overnight.

Ann: Well, it is all right with me. I will phone Garmon's mum later on to discuss it. Garmon can come here tomorrow night if his mum is willing.

Gethin: Can Iestyn come as well?

Ann: No, he can't! I don't want a houseful of boys in the middle of the week. Iestyn is a very lively boy; he is on his feet all night almost! The last time he came over, you didn't go to sleep until three o'clock in the morning.

Gethin: We will go to bed at nine o'clock, and we will sleep until seven o'clock in the morning. We won't say one word after turning the lights off, I promise.
Ann: We will see.

Lesson 5: The simple future tense of 'dod'

Here are the personal future forms of the irregular verb '**dod**':

SENTENCE	ENGLISH	IPA
dof fi	I will come	[doː(v) viː]
doi di	you will come (*fam.*)	[dɔi diː]
deith e (SW)	he will come	[dəɪθ eː]
deith o (NW)	he will come	[dəɪθ oː]
deith hi	she will come	[dəɪθ hiː]
down ni	we will come	[doʊ(n) niː]
dewch chi	you will come (*pl.*) (*sing. formal*)	[dɛʊ(χ) χiː]
dôn nhw	they will come	[doː(n) n̥uː]

> **IMPORTANT**
> Remember that the third person singular **deith** [dəɪθ] is used when the subject is a singular or plural noun.

As with all verbs, to express the interrogative, the initial consonant of the verb undergoes soft mutation:

	QUESTION
WELSH	**Ddewch chi ar eich pen eich hunan?**
ENGLISH	Will you come on your own?
IPA	[ðɛʊ(χ) χiː ar əχ pɛn əχ ˈhiˑnan]

To express the negative, the initial consonant undergoes soft mutation and **ddim** [ðɪm] is added after the verb:

	SENTENCE
WELSH	**Ddown ni ddim ar ein pennau ein hunain.**
ENGLISH	We won't come on our own.
IPA	[ðoʊ(n) niː ðɪm ar ən ˈpɛnɛ niː ən ˈhiˑnɛn]

Note that in the two examples above, the former is in the singular; the plural form of **pen** 'head', which is **pennau**, is used with plural pronouns. For example:

	SENTENCE
WELSH	**Ddôn nhw ddim ar eu pennau nhw eu hunain.**
ENGLISH	They won't come on their own.
IPA	[ðoː(n) n̥uː ðɪm ar iː ˈpɛnɛ n̥uː iː ˈhiːnɛn]

We saw in **Week 9, Lesson 2** that the future imperfect aspect of '**bod**' indicates a less specific intention than of the simple future tense:

	SENTENCE
WELSH	**Fydda i ddim yn dod yfory.**
ENGLISH	I won't be coming tomorrow.
IPA	[ˈvəða iː ðɪm ən doːd (ə)ˈvɔri]

WELSH	**Ddof fi ddim yfory.**
ENGLISH	I won't come tomorrow.
IPA	[ðoː(v) viː ðɪm (ə)ˈvɔri]

Vocabulary

FEMININE NOUN	ENGLISH	IPA	PLURAL FORM	IPA
traffordd	motorway	[ˈtɹafɔrð]	**traffyrdd**	[ˈtɹafɪrð]

ADJECTIVE	ENGLISH	IPA
prydlon	prompt	[ˈprədlɔn]

Exercise 1

*Replace the underlined future imperfect forms with the future tense of '**dod**'.*

For example:
Question: <u>Bydd o'n dod</u> tua wyth o'r gloch.
Answer: <u>Daw o (NW)/e (SW)</u> tua wyth o'r gloch.

1) Faint o'r gloch <u>byddwch chi'n dod</u>? _____
   (What time will you come?)

2) <u>Fyddan nhw'n dod</u> wrth eu hunain? _____
   (They won't come by themselves.)

3) <u>Fydd o ddim yn dod</u> tan bedwar o'r gloch.
   (He won't come until four o'clock.)
   _____

4) <u>Fyddi di'n dod</u> â blodau iddyn nhw? _____
   (Will you bring them flowers?)

5) <u>Bydd fy nheulu'n dod</u> gyda'i gilydd. _____

(My family will come together.)

6) <u>Fydd hi'n dod</u> yn ei gar e (SW)/o (NW)?
(She will come in his car.)

7) <u>Fyddwch chi'n dod</u> ar y draffordd?

(Will you come on the motorway?)

8) <u>Bydda i'n dod</u> yn brydlon am saith.
(I will come punctually at seven.)

Lesson 6: Dates, seasons, and months of the year

Ordinal numerals

The Welsh ordinals (words like 'first', 'ninth', etc.), which show the position of something in a list, are based on the traditional vigesimal counting system (see **Week 1, Lesson 13**). They are especially used with dates. Here are the ordinals up to 31:

ORDINAL	WELSH	ENGLISH	IPA
1st	**cynta(f)**	first	[ˈkənta(v)]
2nd	**ail** (SM)	second	[aɪl]
3rd	**trydydd**	third	[ˈtɹədɪð]
4th	**pedwerydd**	fourth	[pɛdˈwɛrɪð]
5th	**pumed**	fifth	[ˈpɪmɛd]
6th	**chweched**	sixth	[ˈχwɛχɛd]
7th	**seithfed**	seventh	[ˈsəɪθvɛd]
8th	**wythfed**	eighth	[ˈʊɪθvɛd]
9th	**nawfed**	ninth	[ˈnaʊvɛd]
10th	**degfed**	tenth	[ˈdɛgvɛd]
11th	**unfed ar ddeg**	eleventh	[ˈɪnvɛd ar ðeːg]
12th	**deuddegfed**	twelfth	[dəɪðˈɛgvɛd]
13th	**trydydd ar ddeg**	thirteenth	[ˈtɹədɪð ar ðeːg]
14th	**pedwerydd ar ddeg**	fourteenth	[pɛdˈwɛrɪð ar ðeːg]
15th	**pymthegfed**	fifteenth	[pəmˈθɛgvɛd]
16th	**unfed ar bymtheg**	sixteenth	[ˈɪnvɛd ar ˈbəmθɛg]
17th	**ail ar bymtheg**	seventeenth	[aɪl ar ˈbəmθɛg]
18th	**deunawfed**	eighteenth	[dəɪnˈaʊvɛd]
19th	**pedwerydd ar bymtheg**	nineteenth	[pɛdˈwɛrɪð ar ˈbəmθɛg]
20th	**ugeinfed**	twentieth	[ɪgˈəɪnvɛd]
21st	**unfed ar hugain**	twenty-first	[ˈɪnvɛd ar ˈhiːgɛn]
22nd	**ail ar hugain**	twenty-second	[aɪl ar ˈhiːgɛn]
23rd	**trydydd ar hugain**	twenty-third	[ˈtɹədɪð ar ˈhiːgɛn]

24th	**pedwerydd ar hugain**	twenty-fourth	[pɛdˈwɛrɪð ar ˈhiːgɛn]
25th	**pumed ar hugain**	twenty-fifth	[ˈpɪmɛd ar ˈhiːgɛn]
26th	**chweched ar hugain**	twenty-sixth	[ˈχwɛχɛd ar ˈhiːgɛn]
27th	**seithfed ar hugain**	twenty-seventh	[ˈsəɪθvɛd ar ˈhiːgɛn]
28th	**wythfed ar hugain**	twenty-eighth	[ˈʊɪθvɛd ar ˈhiːgɛn]
29th	**nawfed ar hugain**	twenty-ninth	[ˈnaʊvɛd ar ˈhiːgɛn]
30th	**degfed ar hugain**	thirtieth	[ˈdɛgvɛd ar ˈhiːgɛn]
31st	**unfed ar ddeg ar hugain**	thirty-first	[ˈɪnvɛd ar ðeːg ar ˈhiːgɛn]

There are some important rules you will need to remember about ordinals. These are:

(i) In composite ordinals (ordinals made up of more than one word, such as **nawfed ar hugain**), the noun immediately follows the first (ordinal) numeral:

	PHRASE
WELSH	yr unfed chwaraewr ar ddeg
ENGLISH	the eleventh player
IPA	[ər ˈɪnvɛd χwärəɪ.ʊr ar ðeːg]
WELSH	y nawfed noson ar hugain
ENGLISH	the twenty-ninth night
IPA	[ə ˈnaʊvɛd ˈnɔsɔn ar ˈhiːgɛn]

(ii) Note that **trydedd** 'third' [ˈtɹədɛð], and **pedwaredd** 'fourth' [pɛdˈwɑrɛð] are the forms used with feminine singular nouns.

ORDINAL	MASCULINE	FEMININE	IPA
3rd	**trydydd**	trydedd	[ˈtɹədɛð]
4th	**pedwerydd**	pedwaredd	[pɛdˈwɑrɛð]
13th	**trydydd ar ddeg**	trydedd ar ddeg	[ˈtɹədɛð ar ðeːg]
14th	**pedwerydd ar ddeg**	pedwaredd ar ddeg	[pɛdˈwɑrɛð ar ðeːg]
19th	**pedwerydd ar bymtheg**	pedwaredd ar bymtheg	[pɛdˈwɑrɛð ar ˈbəmθɛg]
23rd	**trydydd ar hugain**	trydedd ar hugain	[ˈtɹədɛð ar ˈhiːgɛn]
24th	**pedwerydd ar hugain**	pedwaredd ar hugain	[pɛdˈwɑrɛð ar ˈhiːgɛn]

For example:

PHRASE	ENGLISH	IPA
y bedwaredd anrheg	the fourth present / gift	[ə bɛdˈwɑrɛð ˈanɹɛg]

(iii) Feminine singular nouns undergo soft mutation after *all* ordinals. The definite article* **y** 'the' [ə] also causes ordinals to mutate when they are describing feminine singular nouns:

* *Remember that there is no indefinite article in Welsh.*

MUTATED PHRASE	ENGLISH	IPA	NOUN PRE-MUTATION
y drydedd <u>ferch</u>	the third girl	[ə ˈdɹədɛð vɛrχ]	merch
y ddegfed <u>wobr</u>	the tenth prize	[ə ˈðɛgvɛd ˈwoˑbor]	gwobr
y chweched <u>reilffordd</u>	the sixth railway	[ə ˈχwɛχɛd ˈrəɪlfɔrð]	rheilffordd
y nawfed <u>gath</u>	the ninth cat	[ə ˈnaʊvɛd gaːθ]	cath

Note that ordinals describing singular feminine adjectives undergo the soft mutation, whereas masculine singular nouns do not cause the ordinal to mutate.

Here is a masculine example:

PHRASE	ENGLISH	IPA
y pumed tro	the fifth time	[ə ˈpɪmɛd tɹoː]

Here is a feminine example:

PHRASE	ENGLISH	IPA
y <u>b</u>umed <u>fl</u>wyddyn	the fifth year	[ə ˈbɪmɛd ˈvlʊɪðɪn]

(iv) Dates are always masculine:

PHRASE	ENGLISH	IPA
y cyntaf o fis Mawrth	the first of March	[ə ˈkəntaˑ(v) oː viːs maʊrθ]
y trydydd o fis Gorffennaf	the third of July	[ə ˈtɹədɪð o viːs gɔrfɛnav]
y pedwerydd o fis Mai	the fourth of May	[ə pɛdˈwɛrɪð o viːs maɪ]

You will see a list of all the months of the year later in this lesson.

(v) The ordinal **cynta(f)**, unlike the other ordinals (which precede the noun they are describing), always follows the noun it is describing.

Here is a masculine example:

PHRASE	ENGLISH	IPA
y tro cynta(f)	the first time	[ˈə tɹoː ˈkəntaˑ(v)]

Here is a feminine example:

PHRASE	ENGLISH	IPA
y botel gynta(f)	the first bottle	[ˈə ˈbɔtɛl ˈgəntaˑ(v)]

Exercise 1

Write out the following as full ordinals, remembering to mutate where necessary.

For example:

Question: y 6/llyfr
Answer: y chweched llyfr

For example:
Question: yr 11/rheilffordd
Answer: yr unfed reilffordd ar ddeg

1) ei 3/pen-blwydd o (NW) _____ (his third birthday)
2) y 13/diwrnod _____ (the thirteenth day)
3) ei 2/priodas hi _____ (her second wedding)
4) y 4 /drws _____ (the fourth door)
5) y 18/gêm* _____ (the eighteenth game)
6) y 19/tŷ _____ (the nineteenth house)
7) yr 31/cerdyn _____ (the thirty first card)
8) y 27/gwers _____ (the twenty seventh lesson)
9) y 23/damwain _____ (the twenty third accident)
10) y 4/torth o fara _____ (the fourth loaf of bread)

* *Words beginning with* **g**, *which have been borrowed recently from English, never undergo the soft mutation.*

Months of the year

MONTH	ENGLISH	IPA
mis Ionawr	January	[miːs ˈjɔnaʊr]
mis Chwefror	February	[miːs ˈχwɛvrɔr]
mis Mawrth	March	[miːs maʊrθ]
mis Ebrill	April	[miːs ˈɛbrɨɫ]
mis Mai	May	[miːs maɪ]
mis Mehefin	June	[miːs mɛhˈɛvɪn]
mis Gorffennaf	July	[miːs ɡɔrˈfɛnav]
mis Awst	August	[miːs aʊst]
mis Medi	September	[miːs ˈmɛdi]
mis Hydref	October	[miːs ˈhədɹɛv]
mis Tachwedd	November	[miːs ˈtaχwɛð]
mis Rhagfyr	December	[miːs ˈr̥aɡvɪr]

February and November are also known as (**y**) **mis bach** 'the small month' [(ə) miːs baːχ] and (**y**) **mis du** 'the black month' [(ə) miːs diː] respectively, but such usage is generally confined to the older generation.

In South Wales **s** is usually pronounced **sh** /ʃ/ after the vowel **i** in words of one syllable, as well as after the last but syllable in longer words: **mis** 'month' [miːʃ], **bisi** 'busy' [ˈbiˈʃi], **meistr** 'master' [ˈmɪʃtɪr] (see **Week 1, Lesson 1**). This is not the case after **y**, which is pronunced the same way as **i** in South Wales: **bys** 'finger' [biːs], **crys** 'shirt' [ˈkriːs].

Note that **yn** 'in' [ən] becomes **ym** [əm] in front of the word **mis**: ***ym* mis Mawrth** [əm miːs ˈmaʊrθ].

Exercise 2

Write out the following dates in full. You do not need to write the Welsh name of the holiday.

For example:

Question: Saint Patrick's Day (17 March)
Answer: yr ail ar bymtheg o fis Mawrth

1) 25 January (Dydd Santes Dwynwen* [Saint Dwynwen's Day])

2) 14 February (Dydd Sant Ffolant [Saint Valentine's Day])

3) 1 March (Dydd Gŵyl Ddewi** [Saint David's Day])

4) 21 March (The first day of spring)

5) 4 July (American Independence Day)

6) 16 September (Dydd Owain Glyndŵr [Owain Glyndŵr's Day])

7) 31 October (Calan Gaeaf [Halloween])

8) 5 November (Noson Guto Ffowc [Guy Fawkes Night])

9) 26 December (Dydd Gŵyl Steffan*** [Boxing Day])

10) 31 December (Nos Galan [New Year's Eve])

*   Santes (Saint) Dwynwen is the Welsh equivalent of Saint Valentine.
** Dewi Sant, or Saint David, is the patron saint of Wales.
*** literally 'Saint Stephen's Feast Day'.

Inquiring about birthdays

Here is how to ask someone when their birthday is:

	QUESTION
WELSH	**Pryd mae'ch pen-blwydd chi?**
ENGLISH	When is your birthday?
IPA	[priːd maɪχ penˈblʊɪð χiː]

WELSH	**Pryd mae dy ben-blwydd di?**
ENGLISH	When is your birthday? (*fam.*)
IPA	[priːd maɪ də benˈblʊɪð diː]

	REPLY
WELSH	**Mae (f)y mhen-blwydd i ar y pedwerydd ar bymtheg o fis Ionawr.**
ENGLISH	My birthday is on the nineteenth of January.
IPA	[maɪ (v)ə m̥enˈblʊɪð iː ar ə pedˈwerɪð ar ˈbəmθeg oː viːs ˈjonaur]

Here are some useful phrases to use with the months of the year:

PHRASE	ENGLISH	IPA
erbyn diwedd mis Ebrill	by the end of April	[ˈerbɪn ˈdɪʊeð miːs ˈebrɪɬ]
ers mis Medi	since September	[ˈers miːs ˈmedi]
yng nghanol mis Awst	in the middle of August	[ə(ŋ) ˈŋ̊ɑnol miːs aʊst]
ar ddechrau mis Chwefror	at the beginning of February	[ar ˈðeχre miːs ˈχwevror]
ar ddiwedd mis Hydref	at the end of October	[ar ˈðɪʊeð miːs ˈhədrev]

Giving the year in Welsh

Saying the year is very straightforward:

(i) For years before 1000 CE*, you just say the number. The year 844 (the year Rhodri Mawr became King of Gwynedd) is written in full as: **wyth pedwar pedwar** [ʊɪθ ˈpedwar deːg ˈpedwar].

(ii) From 1000 until 1999, simply say **mil** 'a thousand' [miːl] and express each following digit as a number: 1588 (the year the Bible was translated into Welsh) is expressed in full as: **mil pump wyth wyth** [miːl pɪmp ʊɪθ ʊɪθ].

(iii) The years following the year 2000 begin **dwy fil** [dʊɪ viːl]. The years up to 2010 use **a** (**ac** before a vowel) before the final digit: **dwy fil ac wyth** '2008' [dʊɪ viːl äg ʊɪθ]. 2011 (the year the Welsh people voted that the Welsh Assembly should be allowed to pass laws without permission from Westminster) is written in full as: **dwy fil un deg un** [dʊɪ viːl iːn deːg iːn].

* *Common Era (corresponds to AD)*

Exercise 3

Give the following years in Welsh.

a) 1046 _____ b) 407 _____
c) 1408 _____ d) 2017 _____
e) 1485 _____ f) 1782 _____
g) 2006 _____ h) 1393 _____

The seasons of the year

SEASON	ENGLISH	IPA
y gwanwyn	the spring	[ə 'gwanwın]
yr haf	the summer	[ər hɑːv]
yr hydref	the autumn	[ər 'hədrɛv]
y gaea(f)	the winter	[ə 'gəɪa(v)]

All the seasons and months are masculine.

Vocabulary

MASCULINE NOUN	ENGLISH	IPA	PLURAL FORM	IPA
pen-blwydd	birthday	[pɛn'blʊɪð]	penblwyddi	[pɛn'blʊɪði]
y Nadolig	Christmas	[ə nad'ɔlıg]		
y Pasg	Easter	[ə pasg]		
syndod	surprise	['səndod]		

ADVERBIAL	ENGLISH	IPA
eleni	this year	[ɛ'lɛni]
os bydd rhaid	if necessary	[ɔs biːð ɹaɪd]

VERB-NOUN	ENGLISH	IPA	STEM	IPA
dathlu	to celebrate	['daθli]	dathl-	[daθl]
aros	to stay / to wait	['ɑros]	arhos-	[ar'hɔs]

ADJECTIVE	ENGLISH	IPA
agos	near / close	[ɑ'gos]

MISCELLANEOUS	ENGLISH	IPA
fel arfer	as a rule / usually	[fɛl 'arvɛr]
aml	often	['amal]
Ewrop	Europe	['ɛʊrop]

Dialogue

Welsh Dialogue

Ann: Pryd daw dy rieni di i aros?
Richard: Y mis nesaf, ar yr ail ar bymtheg.
Ann: Dyna ben-blwydd Tomos. Mae llawer o benblwyddi'n digwydd yn y teulu ym mis Mawrth. Mae'r gŵr yn cael ei ben-blwydd o ar y chweched, mae pen-blwydd Gethin ar y deunawfed, ac mae un fy mam i ar y nawfed ar hugain. Mis drud ydy mis Mawrth!
Richard: Pryd mae dy ben-blwydd di?
Ann: Dim tan fis Rhagfyr, ar yr unfed ar hugain.
Richard: Yn agos iawn at y Nadolig.
Ann: Ie, dim ond un anrheg i fi fel arfer, ar gyfer y Nadolig a fy mhen-blwydd i, ond un fawr.
Richard: Wel dyna rywbeth, ond bydda i'n siŵr o brynu dwy anrheg i ti eleni.
Ann: Diolch. Pryd mae dy ben-blwydd di Richard?
Richard: Mis Ebrill, y nawfed.
Ann: Neis, yn ystod gwyliau'r Pasg felly.
Richard: Ie, dw i'n meddwl y caf fi barti bach eleni i ddathlu fy mhen-blwydd i a phrynu fy nghartref cyntaf i. Gobeithio y doi di draw gyda'r teulu.
Ann: Down ni wrth gwrs.

English Translation

Ann: When will your parents be coming to stay?
Richard: Next month, on the seventeenth.
Ann: That is Tomos' birthday. There are lots of birthdays occurring in the family in March. My husband has his birthday on the sixth, Gethin's birthday is on the eighteenth, and my mum's is on the twenty-ninth. March is an expensive month!
Richard: When is your birthday?
Ann: Not until December, on the twenty-first.
Richard: Very close to Christmas.
Ann: Yes, only one present for me usually, for Christmas and my birthday, but a large one.
Richard: Well, that is something, but I will be sure to buy you two presents this year.
Ann: Thanks. When is your birthday, Richard?
Richard: April, the ninth.
Ann: Nice, during the Easter holidays, then.
Richard: Yes, I think I will have a small party this year to celebrate my birthday and buying my first home. I hope you will come over with the family.
Ann: Of course we will come

Lesson 7: Recap exercises

Exercise 1

Translate the following sentences using the future tense of the verb-noun **'bod'**.

For example:

Question: They won't be staying.
Answer: Fyddan nhw ddim yn aros

1) How will they be arriving?
   _____

2) Will she believe you?
   _____

3) They won't understand me.
   _____

4) The Eisteddfod will start at 8.30 p.m.
   _____

5) Everyone will be grateful.
   _____

6) Will the team be competing?
   _____

7) Will you want your sun hat? (*fam.*)
   _____

8) What will happen next?
   _____

9) What time will the match (game) begin?
   _____

10) If it's (will be) fine next week we will go to the seaside.
    _____

11) We will sell the picture if necessary.
    _____

12) When will dinner be ready?
    _____

If you have difficulty in completing this exercise, refer to **Week 9, Lesson 1**.

Exercise 2

Turn the following sentences into the negative.

1) Cofia i agor y ffenest(r).   (I will remember to open the window.)

2) Gwisgan nhw ddillad cynnes.   (They will wear warm clothes.)

3) Mwynhawn ni yrru i Gaerdydd.   (We will enjoy driving to Cardiff.)

4) Parcian nhw yn y maes parcio.   (They will park in the car park.)

5) Brysiwn ni i'r dref.   (We will hurry to town.)

6) Teithia i yn y nos.   (I will travel by night.)

7) Cysgwn ni yn y car.   (We will sleep in the car.)

8) Darllenith hi bopeth.   (She will read everything.)

9) Rhedith e / o yn y parc.   (He will run in the park.)

10) Lliwith y plant amser chwarae.   (The children will colour in at play time.)

If you have trouble completing this exercise, review **Week 9, Lesson 2**.

Exercise 3

Complete the following sentences by using the future tense of the verb in brackets.

1) Ble _____ hi ar ôl iddi hi wylio'r ffilm.   (mynd)
   (Where will she go after watching the film?)

2) Beth _____ nhw ar ôl iddyn nhw fwyta?   (gwneud)
   (What will they do after they eat?)

3) _____ i ar fy mhen fy hunan.   (dod)
   (I will come on my own.)

4) _____ hi syndod mawr ar ei phen-blwydd hi.   (cael)
   (She will have a big surprise on her birthday.)

5) Faint o'r gloch _____ di? (*fam.*)   (mynd)
   (What time will you go?)

6) _____ ni ddim nes i ni siarad â'r teulu.   (dod)
   (We won't come until we talk to the family.)

7) _____ chi ddim bwyd gwell unrhywle arall.   (cael)
   (You won't get better food anywhere.)

8) Sut _____ hi i'r parti pen-blwydd?   (mynd)
   (How will she go to the birthday party?)

9) _____ fi ddim os mai Ifan sy'n gyrru. (mynd)
   (I won't go if Ifan is driving.)

10) _____ ni frechdanau i ginio. (cael)
    (We will have sandwiches for lunch.)

If you have trouble completing this exercise, review **Week 9, Lesson 3, Lesson 4** *and* **Lesson 5**.

Exercise 4

Translate the following sentences.

1) They will be coming in spring.

2) We will get lots of rain in April.

3) Will you close the door, please?

4) He will go on his own at the end of the Easter holidays.

5) His second wife travels to Europe often.

6) She won't go to Denbigh until the twenty-ninth of February.

7) December is the twelfth month of the year.

8) Will you turn the noise down please?

9) Will you tell the police?

10) They will do nothing.

11) Will you go again in June?

12) You have to buy the tickets by the 23rd of November.

13) We used to live in the fourth house on the left.

14) Siân is my fifth grand-daughter.*

_____

* *Start the sentence with **Siân ydy**.*

*If you have trouble competing this exercise, review **Week 9, Lesson 6.***

Week 10

Lesson 1: Expressing 'ever' & 'never'

In Welsh, 'never' is expressed as **byth** [bɪθ] or **erioed** [ɛrjɔɪd]. **Erioed** is used when the action is completed, and **byth** is used when the action is ongoing or will continue*:

'Byth'

SENTENCE	ENGLISH	IPA	TENSE / ASPECT
Dw i ddim yn ennill.	I'm not winning. / I don't win.	[dwi: ðɪm ən 'ɛnɪɬ]	**PRESENT IMPERFECT** (see **Week 3, Lesson 1** to **Lesson 5**)
Dw i byth yn ennill.	I never win.	[dwi: bɪθ ən 'ɛnɪɬ]	
Fydda i ddim yn ennill.	I won't be winning. / I won't win.	['vəða i: ðɪm ən 'ɛnɪɬ]	**FUTURE IMPERFECT** (see **Week 9, Lesson 1**)
Fydda i byth yn ennill.	I will never win.	['vəða i: bɪθ ən 'ɛnɪɬ]	
Doeddwn i ddim yn ennill.	I didn't win. / I wasn't winning.	['dɔɪðʊn i: ðɪm ən 'ɛnɪɬ]	**PAST IMPERFECT** (see **Week 6, Lesson 1**)
Doeddwn i byth yn ennill.	I never won. / I was never winning.	['dɔɪðʊn i: bɪθ ən 'ɛnɪɬ]	
Allwn i ddim ennill.	I couldn't win.	['aɬʊn i: ðɪm 'ɛnɪɬ]	**CONDITIONAL** (inflected construction) (see **Week 11, Lesson 2**)
Allwn i byth ennill.	I could never win.	['aɬʊn i: bɪθ 'ɛnɪɬ]	
Fyddwn i ddim yn ennill.	I wouldn't win.	['vəðʊn i: ðɪm ən 'ɛnɪɬ]	**CONDITIONAL:** (periphrastic construction) (see **Week 11, Lesson 1** to **Lesson 3**)
Fyddwn i byth yn ennill.	I would never win.	['vəðʊn i: bɪθ ən 'ɛnɪɬ]	
Es i ddim yn ôl.	I didn't go back.	[e:s i: ðɪm ən o:l]	**SIMPLE PAST** (see **Week 7, Lesson 2** to **6**) (with a future orientation)
Es i byth yn ôl eto.	I never went back again.	[e:s i: bɪθ ən o:l 'ɛto]	

* A brief summary of the modern Welsh verbal system is given at the end of the book.

The adverb **byth** can also mean 'ever' and 'even':

	SENTENCE
WELSH	**Cymru am byth!**
ENGLISH	Wales for ever!
IPA	['kəmri am bɪθ]

	SENTENCE
WELSH	**Os byth af fi yn ôl (...)**
ENGLISH	If I ever go back (...)
IPA	[ɔs bɪθ a:(v) vi:n o:l]

WELSH	Dyn ni'n fwy penderfynol byth o ennill.
ENGLISH	We are even more determined to win.
IPA	['ðə(n) niːn vʊɪ pendɛr'vənol bɪθ oː 'ɛnɨɫ]

'Erioed'

SENTENCE	ENGLISH	IPA	TENSE
Dw i ddim wedi colli.	I haven't lost.	[dwi: ðɪm 'wɛdi 'kɔɬi]	**PRESENT PERFECT** (See **Week 5, Lesson 5**)
Dw i erioed wedi colli.	I have never lost.	[dwi: ɛrjɔɪd 'wɛdi 'kɔɬi]	
Fues i ddim yn Iwerddon.	I haven't been to (in) Ireland.	['viˑes iː ðɪm ən ɪʊ'ɛrðon]	**SIMPLE PAST TENSE OF 'BOD'** (see **Week 7, Lesson 6**)
Fues i erioed yn Iwerddon.	I have never been to (in) Ireland.	['viˑes iː ɛrjɔɪd ən ɪʊ'ɛrðon]	
Doeddwn i ddim wedi colli.	I hadn't lost.	['dɔiðʊn iː ðɪm 'wɛdi 'kɔɬi]	**PAST PERFECT** (also known as the PLUPERFECT) (see **Week 6, Lesson 2**)
Doeddwn i erioed wedi colli.	I had never lost.	['dɔiðʊn iː ɛrjɔɪd 'wɛdi 'kɔɬi]	
Chlywais i erioed dôn mor bert.	I (had) never heard a such a pretty tune.	['χlɪʊes iː ɛrjɔɪd doːn mor bert.]	**SIMPLE PAST** (see **Week 7, Lesson 2 to 6**) (with a past orientation)

Erioed can also mean 'ever' and 'always':

	SENTENCE
WELSH	Maen nhw wedi byw yma erioed.
ENGLISH	They have always lived here.
IPA	[maɪ(n) n̥uː 'wɛdi bɪʊ 'əmä ɛrjɔɪd]

WELSH	Mae'r Gweilch yn chwarae cystal ag erioed.
ENGLISH	The Ospreys are playing as good as ever.
IPA	[maɪr gwəilχ ən 'χwɑˑre 'kəstal ag ɛrjɔɪd]

Vocabulary

MASCULINE NOUN	ENGLISH	IPA	PLURAL FORM	IPA
tymor	term	['təmor]	**tymhorau**	[təm'hɔrɛ]

FEMININE NOUN	ENGLISH	IPA	PLURAL FORM	IPA
theatr	theatre	['θeˑatər]	**theatrau**	[θe'atrɛ]
gwaith	time	[gwaɪθ]	**gweithiau**	['gwəɪθjɛ]

ADVERBIAL	ENGLISH	IPA
chwaith	either	[χwaɪθ]
unwaith	once	['ɪnwaɪθ]
siŵr o fod	probably	[ʃuːr oː voːd]

VERB-NOUN	ENGLISH	IPA	STEM	IPA
ymarfer	to practise	[əm'arvɛr]	**ymarfer-**	[əmarˈvɛr]
dringo	to climb	['drɪŋo]	**dring-**	[drɪŋ]

ADJECTIVE	ENGLISH	IPA
trwchus	thick	['tʊuˈχɪs]
newydd sbon	brand new	['nɛʊɪð sbɔn]
cyfforddus	comfortable	[kəfˈɔrðɪs]
doniol	funny	['dɔnjol]
penderfynol	determined	[pɛndɛrˈvənol]

Dialogue

Welsh Dialogue

Richard: Dyma fydd y tro cyntaf dw i erioed wedi bod i weld drama Gymraeg. Dw i erioed wedi gwylio un ar y teledu chwaith. Dw i'n edrych ymlaen at fynd yn fawr iawn.

Ann: Dw i'n siŵr y byddi di'n mwynhau. Dyn ni'n mynd yn aml iawn fel teulu. Dw i hefyd yn mynd â phlant dosbarth chwech i'r theatr unwaith y tymor.

Richard: Dw i ddim yn gwybod pam dw i ddim wedi bod i'r theatr i weld drama Gymraeg o'r blaen. Yn ofni peidio deall popeth, siŵr o fod. Dw i byth yn gyfforddus os na fydda i'n deall pobl yn siarad.

Ann: Does dim rhaid deall pob gair i fwynhau'r ddrama. Mae hi'n ddrama ddoniol iawn, a dydy hi ddim yn hir iawn. Dw i'n siŵr y cei di a Rhys lawer o hwyl.

English Translation

Richard: This will be the first time I have ever been to see a Welsh language play. I have never watched one on the television, either. I am looking forward to going very much.

Ann: I am sure that you will enjoy. We go very often as a family. I also take the sixth-form children to the theatre once a term.

Richard: I don't know why I have never been to the theatre to see a Welsh play before. Afraid of not understanding everything, probably.

Ann: There is no need to understand every word to enjoy the play. It is a very funny play, and it isn't very long. I am sure you and Rhys will have lots of fun.

Exercise 1

Complete the following sentences by using either **byth** or **erioed**.

1) Dydy e (SW)/o (NW) _____ wedi anghofio ei phen-blwydd hi.
   (He has never forgotten her birthday.)
2) Chafodd e (SW)/o (NW) _____ chwarae yn nhŷ ei fam-gu e wedyn ar ôl torri'r ffenestr.
   (He was never allowed to play in his grandmother's house after breaking the window.)
3) Doedden ni _____ yn cael gwyliau pan oedden ni'n blant.
   (We never had holidays when we were children.)
4) Dyn nhw _____ yn siopa mewn archfarchnadoedd.
   (They never shop in supermarkets.)
5) Fyddwch chi _____ yn dysgu Cymraeg os na fyddwch chi'n ymarfer.
   (You will never learn Welsh if you don't practise.)
6) Welais i _____ eira mor drwchus.
   (I never saw snow so thick.)
7) Fyddwn i _____ yn prynu car newydd sbon.
   (I would never buy a brand-new car.)
8) Allwn ni _____ dringo Yr Wyddfa.
   (I could never climb Snowdon.)

Exercise 2

*Connect the questions under **A** to the correct responses under **B**.*

A
1) Fuoch chi yn Iwerddon erioed?
2) Ydy o wedi bod mewn awyren erioed?
3) Ydy'r plant wedi yfed coffi erioed?
4) Wyt ti wedi bod i gampfa erioed?
5) Ydych chi wedi gwisgo cot oren erioed?
6) Ydy hi erioed wedi canu o flaen pobl eraill?
7) Ydych chi wedi bod ar y teledu erioed?
8) Ydyn nhw wedi cael prawf mathemateg erioed?

B
a) Ydw, ond mae'n well gen i liwiau tywyll.
b) Nac ydyn, dim ond diodydd oer.
c) Do, dyn ni wedi bod yno sawl gwaith i wylio gemau rygbi.
d) Ydw, dw i'n mynd yno bob wythnos.
e) Ydyn, pan oedden nhw yn yr ysgol.
f) Ydy, hedfanodd e (SW)/gwnaeth o hedfan (NW) i Sbaen llynedd.
g) Nac ydw, ond dw i wedi siarad ar y radio.
h) Ydy, roedd hi'n arfer cystadlu'n aml iawn mewn eisteddfodau pan oedd hi'n ferch fach.

Lesson 2: Verb-nouns and related prepositions

The prepositions 'at', 'wrth', 'oddi wrth' and 'dan'

A preposition is a word governing (and usually preceding) a noun or pronoun, and expressing a relation to another word or element in the same clause. Common prepositions in Welsh are **yn** 'in' [ən], **ar** 'on' [ar], **am** 'about' / 'for' [am], **i** 'to' [iː]. Certain verb-nouns and adjectives are followed by certain prepositions. Below is a list of the most common combinations:

PHRASE	ENGLISH	IPA
siarad â	to speak to / to speak with	[ˈʃɑːrad äː]
dweud wrth	to tell	[dwəɪd ʊrθ]
gofyn i	to ask	[ˈɡɔvɪn iː]
gwrando ar	to listen to	[ˈɡʷrändo ar]
edrych ar	to look at	[ˈɛdrɪχ ar]
breuddwydio am	to dream about	[brəɪðʊɪdjo am]
ysgrifennu at	to write to	[əsɡrɪvˈɛni at]

In Welsh, as in other Celtic languages, many prepositions undergo declension, which means they change to indicate person and number. In this lesson, we will look at the prepositions **at** 'to' / 'towards' / 'from' [at], **wrth** 'by' / 'near' [ʊrθ], **oddi wrth** 'from' (a person) [ˈɔði ʊrθ], and **dan** 'under' [dan].

Declension of 'at'
At [at] means 'to' / 'towards' / 'from'. Below are examples of it in use with different people:

PHRASE	ENGLISH	IPA
ata i	to me	[ˈäta iː]
atat ti	to you (*fam.*)	[ˈäta(t) tiː]
ato fe (SW)	to him	[ˈäto veː]
ato fo (NW)	to him	[ˈäto voː]
ati hi	to her	[ˈäti hiː]
aton ni	to us	[ˈäton niː]
atoch chi	to you (*pl.*) (*sing. formal*)	[ˈäto(χ) χiː]
atyn nhw	to them	[ˈätɪ(n) n̥uː]

The preposition **at** is used after the following verb-nouns

VERB-NOUN	ENGLISH	IPA
apelio at	to appeal to	[apˈɛljo at]
cyfeirio at	to refer to	[kəvˈəɪrjo at]
cyfrannu at	to contribute to	[kəvˈrani at]
dal at	to keep at (something)	[dal at]

mynd at	to go to (a person)	[mɪnd at]
synnu at	to be surprised at	[ˈsəni at]
ychwanegu at	to add to	[əχwanˈɛgi at]

Here is an example sentence:

	SENTENCE
WELSH	**Anfonwn ni lythyr ati hi.**
ENGLISH	We will send her a letter.
IPA	[anˈvɔnʊ(n) niː ˈləθɪr ˈäti hiː]

Some phrases using **at**:

PHRASE	ENGLISH	IPA
dal ati	to keep at it	[dal ˈäti]
mynd ati	to set about	[mɪnd ˈäti]

For example:

	SENTENCE
WELSH	**Daliwch ati i ddysgu Cymraeg.**
ENGLISH	Persevere with learning Welsh.
IPA	[ˈdäljʊχ ˈäti iː ˈðəsgi kəmˈraig]

	SENTENCE
WELSH	**Mae hi wedi mynd ati i ddysgu Cymraeg.**
ENGLISH	She has set about learning Welsh.
IPA	[maɪ hiː ˈwedi mɪnd ˈäti iː ˈðəsgi kəmˈraig]

As you can see from the examples above, **at** causes the soft mutation. **At** conveys the meaning:

(i) 'towards' / 'in the direction of' / 'up to' (but not reaching):

	SENTENCE
WELSH	**Rhedodd e at y drws.**
ENGLISH	He ran to(wards) the door.
IPA	[ˈɹeˈdoð eː at ə druːs]

(ii) 'for' / 'for the purpose of':

	SENTENCE
WELSH	**Prynais i ddillad newydd at yr haf.**
ENGLISH	I bought new clothes for summer.
IPA	[ˈprənes iː ˈðɪɬad ˈnɛʊɪð at ər haːv]

(iii) 'in aid of' / 'for':

	SENTENCE
WELSH	**Codon ni arian at yr ysbyty.**
ENGLISH	We raised money for the hospital.
IPA	[ˈkɔdon niː ˈärjan at ər əsˈbəti]

(iv) 'to improve' (health):

	SENTENCE
WELSH	**Ces i foddion at fy annwyd i.**
ENGLISH	I got medicine for my cold.
IPA	[keːs i ˈvɔðjon at və ˈänʊɪd i]

Exercise 1

*Fill in the blank spaces in the sentences below with the appropriate form of **at**.*

For example:

Question: Ydych chi wedi ysgrifennu ____ hi?
(Have you written to her?)
Answer: Roeddwn i'n synnu **ati** hi.

1) Roeddwn i'n synnu _____ nhw.
   (I was surprised at them.)
2) Ydy hi wedi ysgrifennu _____ ti.
   (Has she written to you?)
3) Mae fy nghoffi i'n rhy gryf, bydd rhaid i fi ychwanegu dŵr _____ fe (SW)/fo (NW).
   (My coffee is too strong; I will have to add some water to it.)
4) Pryd penderfynoch chi fynd _____ i adeiladu eich tŷ eich hunan?
   (When did you decide to set about building your own house?)
5) Gobeithio eich bod chi'n hoffi'r anrheg, mae pawb wedi cyfrannu _____ hi.
   (I hope you like the present; everyone has contributed to it.)
6) Dwedodd e (SW)/o (NW) y bydd e'n (SW)/o 'n (NW) ysgrifennu _____ chi.
   (He said he would write to you.)
7) Mae rhaid i'r sianel deledu apelio _____ bawb.
   (The television channel has to appeal to everyone.)
8) Gallwch chi gyfeirio unrhyw gwestiynau _____ ni.
   (You can direct any questions to us.)
9) Daeth e (SW)/o (NW) _____ i neithiwr i drafod y broblem.
   (He came up to me last night to discuss the problem.)
10) Rhedodd y ci _____ hi.
    (The dog ran to her.)

The declension of 'wrth'

Wrth means 'by' / 'near' [ʊrθ]. Below are examples of it in use with different people:

PHRASE	ENGLISH	IPA
wrtha i	by / near me	['ʊrθa iː]
wrthat ti	by / near you (*fam.*)	['ʊrθat tiː]
wrtho fe (SW)	by / near him	['ʊrθo veː]
wrtho fo (NW)	by / near him	['ʊrθo voː]
wrthi hi	by / near her	['ʊrθi hiː]
wrthon ni	by / near us	['ʊrθo(n) niː]
wrthoch chi	by / near you (*pl.*) (*sing. formal*)	['ʊrθo(χ) hiː]
wrthyn nhw	by / near them	['ʊrθɪ(n) n̩uː]

SENTENCE	ENGLISH	IPA
Dwedais i wrtho fe.	I told him.	['dweˑdɛs i 'ʊrθo veː]

Remember that **wrth** causes the soft mutation (see **Week 1, Lesson 5**). Wrth can convey the following meanings:

(i) 'by':

	SENTENCE
WELSH	**Maen nhw'n sefyll wrth y drws.**
ENGLISH	They are standing by the door.
IPA	[maɪ(n) n̩uːn 'sevɨɫ ʊrθ ə drʊːs]

(ii) 'while' / 'during':

	SENTENCE
WELSH	**Gwelais i ddamwain wrth gerdded adre(f).**
ENGLISH	I saw an accident while walking home.
IPA	['gwɛlɛs iː 'ðamwaɪn ʊrθ 'gɛrðɛd 'adɹɛ(v)]

Wrth is used after some verb-nouns:

VERB-NOUN	ENGLISH	IPA
cyfadde(f) wrth	admit to	[kəv'aˑðɛ(v) ʊrθ]
dweud wrth	to say to	[dwəɪd ʊrθ]
glynu wrth	to stick to	['glənɪ ʊrθ]

Wrth is also used after some adjectives:

ADJECTIVE + WRTH	ENGLISH	IPA
caredig wrth	kind to	[karˈɛdɪg ʊrθ]
cas wrth	nasty to	[kɑːs ʊrθ]
creulon wrth	cruel to	[ˈkrəɪlon ʊrθ]
dig wrth	angry at	[diːg ʊrθ]

For example:

	SENTENCE
WELSH	**Roedd hi'n garedig iawn wrthon ni.**
ENGLISH	She was very kind to us.
IPA	[rɔɪð hiːn garˈɛdɪg jaʊn ˈʊrθo(n) niː]
WELSH	**Roedd pawb yn gas wrthyn nhw.**
ENGLISH	Everyone was nasty to them.
IPA	[rɔɪð paʊb ən gɑːs ˈʊrθɪ(n) n̥uː]
WELSH	**Roedd hi'n ddig iawn wrthyn nhw.**
ENGLISH	She was very angry at them.
IPA	[rɔɪð hiːn ðiːg jaʊn ˈʊrθɪ(n) n̥uː]
WELSH	**Maen nhw'n greulon iawn wrth eu hanifeiliaid nhw.**
ENGLISH	They are cruel to their animals.
IPA	[maɪ(n) n̥uːn ˈgrəɪlon jaʊn ʊrθ iː hanɪvˈəɪljed n̥uː]

Wrth is also used in the following expressions:

PHRASE	ENGLISH	IPA
wrth droed	at the foot of	[ʊrθ drɔɪd]
wrth law	at hand / close at hand	[ʊrθ laʊ]
wrth reswm	it stands to reason	[ʊrθ ˈrɛsʊm]

For example:

PHRASE	ENGLISH	IPA
wrth droed y mynydd	at the foot of the mountain	[ʊrθ drɔɪd ə ˈmənɪð]

'Dweud wrth' and 'dweud am'

The word for 'to tell' in Welsh is **dweud** [dwəɪd]. However, when it takes an object, the preposition **wrth** is employed:

SENTENCE	ENGLISH	IPA
Dwedais i wrth y plant.	I told the children.	[ˈdwɛˑdɛs iː ʊrθ ə plant]

After using **dweud wrth**, the preposition **am** 'about' [am] is used where in English one would have 'to':

	SENTENCE
WELSH	**Dwedais i wrth y plant am ddod.**
ENGLISH	I told the children to come. (*lit.* I told the children *about* coming.)
IPA	[ˈdweˑdes iː ʊrθ ə plant am ðoːd]

The declension of 'o'
O (see **Week 10, Lesson 5**) means 'from':

	SENTENCE
WELSH	**Dw i'n i'n dod o Gymru.**
ENGLISH	I come from Wales.
IPA	[dwiːn doːd o ˈgəmri]

When meaning 'from a person', 'from' is realised by **oddi wrth** [ˈɔði ʊrθ]. **Oddi wrth** declines in the same way as **wrth**:

PHRASE	ENGLISH	IPA
oddi wrtha i	from me	[ˈɔði ˈʊrθa iː]
oddi wrthot ti	from me (*fam.*)	[ˈɔði ˈʊrθo(t) tiː]
oddi wrtho fe (SW)	from him	[ˈɔði ˈʊrθo veː]
oddi wrtho fo (NW)	from him	[ˈɔði ˈʊrθo voː]
oddi wrthi hi	from her	[ˈɔði ˈʊrθi hiː]
oddi wrthon ni	from us	[ˈɔði ˈʊrθo(n) niː]
oddi wrthoch chi	from you (*pl.*) (*sing. formal*)	[ˈɔði ˈʊrθo(χ) χiː]
oddi wrthyn nhw	from them	[ˈɔði ˈʊrθi(n) n̥uː]

For example:

	SENTENCE
WELSH	**Cafodd e lythyr oddi wrthoch chi.**
ENGLISH	He got a letter from you.
IPA	[ˈkaˑvoð eː ˈləθɪr ˈɔði ˈʊrθo(χ) χiː]

	SENTENCE
WELSH	**Gest ti bres oddi wrtho fo?** (NW)
ENGLISH	Did you get any money from him?
IPA	[geːs(t) tiː breːs ˈɔði ˈʊrθo voː]

The declension of 'dan'
The Welsh word for 'under' is **dan** or **o dan**, which causes a soft mutation. Here is the declension of **o dan** [o dan]:

PHRASE	ENGLISH	IPA
o dana i	under me	[oː ˈdaˑna iː]

o danat ti	under you (*fam.*)	[oː ˈdaˑna(t) tiː]
o dano fe (SW)	under him	[oː ˈdaˑno veː]
o dano fo (NW)	under him	[oː ˈdaˑno voː]
o dani hi	under her	[oː ˈdaˑni hiː]
o danon ni	under us	[oː ˈdaˑno(n) niː]
o danoch chi	under you (*pl.*) (*sing. formal*)	[oː ˈdaˑno(χ) χiː]
o danyn nhw	under them	[oː ˈdaˑnɪ(n) n̥uː]

For example:

SENTENCE	
WELSH	**Gwelais i goeden gyda llawer o flodau o dani hi.**
ENGLISH	I saw a tree with many flowers under it.
IPA	[ˈgwɛlɛs iː ˈgɔiden ˈgədä ˈɬauer oː ˈvloˑde oː ˈdaˑni hiː]

The preposition 'i'

We have already seen **i** and its declension in **Week 8, Lesson 3**. The meanings conveyed by **i** are:

(i) 'for':

SENTENCE	
WELSH	**Gwnes i goffi i bawb.**
ENGLISH	I made coffee for everyone.
IPA	[gʷneːs iː ˈgɔfi iː baʊb]

(ii) 'to':

SENTENCE	
WELSH	**Cerddodd hi i'r coleg.**
ENGLISH	She walked to college.
IPA	[ˈkɛrðoð hiː iːr ˈkɔlɛg]

I is used after the following verb-nouns:

VERB-NOUN	ENGLISH	IPA
anfon i	to send to (a place)	[ˈanvon iː]
cytuno i	to agree to	[kətˈiˑno iː]
dangos i	to show to	[ˈdäŋgos iː]
dal i	to continue to	[dal iː]
disgwyl i	to expect to	[ˈdɪsgʊɪl iː]
gadael i	to let / to allow to	[ˈgaˑdɛl iː]
helpu i	to help to	[ˈhɛlpi iː]
llwyddo i	to succeed in	[ˈɬʊɪðo iː]

maddau i	to forgive	[ˈmaðɛ iː]
mynd i	to go to	[ˈmɪnd iː]
perthyn i	to belong to / to be related to	[ˈpĕrθɪn iː]
rhoi'r gorau i	to give up	[ɹɔɪr ˈgoːrɛ iː]
tueddu i	to tend to	[tiˈɛði iː]

For example:

	SENTENCE
WELSH	**Alla i ddim maddau iddi hi.**
ENGLISH	I can't forgive her.
IPA	[ˈäɬa iː ðɪm ˈmaðɛ ˈiði hiː]
WELSH	**Pryd byddan nhw'n mynd i Iwerddon?**
ENGLISH	When will they be going to Ireland?
IPA	[priːd ˈbəða(n) n̥uːn mɪnd iː ɪʊˈɛrðon]
WELSH	**Mae o'n perthyn iddyn nhw.**
ENGLISH	He is related to them.
IPA	[maɪ oːn ˈpɛrθɪn ˈiði(n) n̥uː]
WELSH	**Mae hi'n rhoi'r gorau i yfed gwin.**
ENGLISH	She's giving up drinking wine.
IPA	[maɪ hiːn ɹɔɪr ˈgoːrɛ iː ˈəvɛd gwiːn]
WELSH	**Dyn ni'n tueddu i gytuno â hi.**
ENGLISH	We tend to agree with her.
IPA	[də(n) niːn tiˈɛði iː gətˈiːno ä hiː]
WELSH	**Anfonais i'r pecyn i Aberystwyth.**
ENGLISH	I sent the package to Aberystwyth.
IPA	[anˈvɔnɛs iːr ˈpɛkɪn iː abɛrəstwɪθ]
WELSH	**Ydyn nhw wedi cytuno i gwrdd â chi?**
ENGLISH	Have they agreed to meet with you?
IPA	[ˈədɪ(n) n̥uː ˈwɛdi kətˈiːno iː gwrð ä χiː]
WELSH	**Ydw i wedi dangos y car newydd i ti?**
ENGLISH	Have I showed the new car to you?
IPA	[ˈədʊ iː ˈwɛdi ˈdäŋgos ə kar ˈnɛʊɪð iː tiː]
WELSH	**Ydy hi'n dal i fyw yn y dref?**
ENGLISH	Does she still live in town?
IPA	[ˈədi hiːn dal iː vɪʊ ən ə dɹɛː(v)]
WELSH	**Ydy o'n disgwyl i fi gredu hynny?** (NW)
ENGLISH	Does he expect me to believe that?
IPA	[ˈədi oːn ˈdɪsgʊɪl iː viː ˈgrɛdi ˈhəni]
WELSH	**Elli di adael iddo fo orffen?** (NW)
ENGLISH	Can you let him finish?

IPA	[ˈeɬi diː ˈɑˑdel ˈiðo voː ˈɔrfɛn]

WELSH	**Maen nhw'n helpu i olchi'r car.**
ENGLISH	They are helping to wash the car.
IPA	[maɪ(n) n̥uːm ˈhɛlpi iː ˈɔlχir kar]

WELSH	**Dyn ni ddim wedi llwyddo i symud tŷ.**
ENGLISH	We haven't succeeded in moving house.
IPA	[də(n) niː ðɪm ˈwedi ˈɬuɪðo iː ˈsəmɪd tiː]

As well as **rhaid i** (see **Week 8, Lesson 4**), **i** is also used in the following expressions:

PHRASE	ENGLISH	IPA
hen bryd i	high time	[heːn briːd iː]
cystal i	may as well	[ˈkəstal iː]
gwell i	better	[gweɬ iː]
i ffwrdd	away	[iː furð]

For example:

	SENTENCE
WELSH	**Mae'n hen bryd i ni adael.**
ENGLISH	It's high time for us to leave.
IPA	[maɪn heːn briːd iː niː ɑˑdɛl]

WELSH	**Cystal i chi ddod.**
ENGLISH	You may as well come.
IPA	[ˈkəstal iː χiː ðoːd]

WELSH	**Mae'n well i ti aros.**
ENGLISH	You had better stay.
IPA	[maɪn weɬ iː tiː ɑˑros]

WELSH	**Pryd byddwch chi i ffwrdd?**
ENGLISH	When will you be away?
IPA	[priːd ˈbəðʊ(χ) χiː iː furð]

Exercise 2

Complete the following sentences with the personal forms of the appropriate prepositions.

1) Ddwedoch chi _____ nhw _____ y parti?
   (Did you tell them about the party?)

2) Pryd rwyt ti'n disgwyl _____ hi gyrraedd?
   (When do you expect her to arrive?)

3) Ydych chi wedi clywed _____ fo?

(Have you heard from him?)

4) Gwnaethon nhw gyfaddef _____ i eu bod nhw wedi torri fy nrych i.
   (They admitted to me that they had broken my mirror.)

5) Pwy sy'n eistedd yn y rhes _____ chi?
   (Who is sitting in the row below you?)

6) Cystal _____ fi gael un newydd.
   (I may as well get a new one.)

7) Ydy hi'n perthyn _____ ni?
   (Is she related to us?)

8) Roedd eu mam y garedig iawn _____ ti.
   (Their mother was very kind to you.)

Lesson 3: Common prepositions

In this lesson, we will discuss more prepositions which decline in the same way as those in **Week 10, Lesson 2**. However, the group of prepositions we see here alter their stem when being declined.

The declension of 'am' (about)

Am 'about' [am] becomes **amdan-** [amˈdɑn] before the endings are added:

PHRASE	ENGLISH	IPA
amdana i	about me	[amˈdɑna iː]
amdanat ti	about you (*fam.*)	[amˈdɑna(t) tiː]
amdano fe (SW)	about him	[amˈdɑno veː]
amdano fo (NW)	about him	[amˈdɑno voː]
amdani hi	about her	[amˈdɑni hiː]
amdanon ni	about us	[amˈdɑno(n) niː]
amdanoch chi	about you (*pl.*) (*sing. formal*)	[amˈdɑno(χ) χiː]
amdanyn nhw	about them	[amˈdɑnɪ(n) n̥uː]

Am conveys the meaning:

(i) 'at' (time):

PHRASE	ENGLISH	IPA
am un o'r gloch	at one o'clock	[am iːn oːr gloːχ]

(ii) 'about':

	SENTENCE
WELSH	**Glywaist ti am Mr Jones?**
ENGLISH	Did you hear about Mr Jones?
IPA	[ˈgləʊes(t) tiː am ˈmɪstə dʒoːnz]

(iii) 'on' (clothes):

	SENTENCE
WELSH	**Mae ganddi hi fenig am eu dwylo.**
ENGLISH	She has gloves on her hands.
IPA	[maɪ 'gänddi hiː 'vɛnɪg am iː 'dʊɪlo]

(iv) 'for':

	SENTENCE
WELSH	**Cerddodd hi am filltiroedd.**
ENGLISH	She walked for miles.
IPA	['kɛrðoð hiː am vɨɬ'tiˑrɔɪð]

(v) 'what a (...)!':

	SENTENCE
WELSH	**Am ddiwrnod!**
ENGLISH	What a day!
IPA	[am 'ðɪʊrnod]

Am causes the soft mutation:

	SENTENCE
WELSH	**Dw i'n poeni am gi Mr Jones.**
ENGLISH	I am worried about Mr Jones' dog.
IPA	[dwiːn 'pɔɪni am giː 'mɪstə dʒoːnz]

Am is used after some verb-nouns:

PHRASE	ENGLISH	IPA
anghofio am	to forget about	[aŋ'hɔvjo am]
clywed am	to hear about	['kləʊɛd am]
cofio am	to remember about	['kɔvjo am]
dysgu am	to learn about	['dəsgi am]
gwybod am	to know about	['gwɨˑbod am]
meddwl am	to think about	['mɛðʊl am]
poeni am	to worry about	['pɔɪni am]
siarad am	to talk about	['ʃɑˑrad am]
ysgrifennu am	to write about	[əsgrɪ'vɛni am]

Am is used after the following adjectives:

PHRASE	ENGLISH	IPA
diolchgar am	grateful for	[diˑɔlχgar am]

hyderus am	confident about	[həd'ɛrɪs am]
parod am	ready for	['pɑ·rod am]

For example:

	SENTENCE
WELSH	**Dw i wedi clywed amdano fe.** (SW)
ENGLISH	I've heard about him.
IPA	[dwiː 'wɛdi 'kləʋɛd am'dɑ·no veː]

WELSH	**Dw i wedi clywed amdano fo.** (NW)
ENGLISH	I've heard about him.
IPA	[d̪wiː 'wɛd̪i 'kləʋɛd̪ am'd̪ɑ·no voː]

WELSH	**Mae pawb yn poeni amdanoch chi.**
ENGLISH	Everyone is worried about you.
IPA	[maɪ paʋb ən 'pɔɪni am'dɑ·no(χ) χiː]

The declension of 'trwy'

With the declension of **trwy** 'through' [trʊɪ], endings are added to the stem **trwydd-** [t̪ɹʊɪð]:

PHRASE	ENGLISH	IPA
trwydda i	through me	['t̪ɹʊɪða iː]
trwyddot ti	through you (*fam.*)	['t̪ɹʊɪðo(t) tiː]
trwyddo fe (SW)	through him	['t̪ɹʊɪðo veː]
trwyddo fo (NW)	through him	['t̪ɹʊɪðo voː]
trwyddi hi	through her	['t̪ɹʊɪði hiː]
trwyddon ni	through us	['t̪ɹʊɪðo(n) niː]
trwyddoch chi	through you (*pl.*) (*sing. formal*)	['t̪ɹʊɪðo(χ) χiː]
trwyddyn nhw	through them	['t̪ɹʊɪðɪ(n) n̪uː]

Trwy causes the soft mutation:

	SENTENCE
WELSH	**Bydd rhaid i chi yrru trwy bentre(f) Coedpoeth.**
ENGLISH	You will have to drive through the village of Coedpoeth.
IPA	[biːð ɹaɪd iː χiː 'əri t̪ɹʊɪ 'bɛnt̪ɹɛ(v) 'kɔɪdpɔɪθ]

Trwy conveys the meanings:

(i) 'through':

PHRASE	ENGLISH	IPA
trwy ddrws	through a door	[t̪ɹʊɪ ðruːs]

(ii) 'throughout':

PHRASE	ENGLISH	IPA
trwy'r nos	all night	[tɹʊɪr noːs]

(iii) 'by':

PHRASE	ENGLISH	IPA
trwy garedigrwydd	by courtesy of	[tɹʊɪ gareˈdɪgrʊɪð]
trwy ddamwain	by accident	[tɹʊɪ 'ðamwain]

Trwy is used in the following expressions:

PHRASE	ENGLISH	IPA
trwy lwc	luckily	[tɹʊɪ lʊk]
trwy drugaredd	mercifully	[tɹʊɪ drɪgˈɑreð]

For example:

	SENTENCE
WELSH	**Codon ni lawer o arian trwy werthu hen ddillad.**
ENGLISH	We raised lots of money by selling old clothes.
IPA	[ˈkɔdon niː ˈlaʊer oː ˈärjan tɹʊɪ ˈwerθi heːn ˈðɪɬad]

WELSH	**Wnei di symud, alla i ddim gweld trwyddot ti!**
ENGLISH	Will you move; I can't see through you!
IPA	[ʷnəɪ diː ˈsəmɪd ˈäɬa iː ðɪm gwɛld ˈtɹʊɪðo(t) ti]

Exercise 1

Complete the following sentences with the appropriate personal forms of the prepositions.

1) Ydych chi'n barod _____ y gwyliau?
   (Are you ready for the holidays?)

2) Gest ti'r neges _____ hi?
   (Did you get the message through her?)

3) Cofiwch _____ i!
   (Remember [about] me!)

4) Does dim rhaid i chi boeni _____ ni.
   (You don't have to worry about us.)

5) Dw i erioed wedi clywed _____ fe (SW)/fo (NW).
   (I have never heard about him.)

6) Mae'r ffenestri mor frwnt, alla i ddim gweld _____ nhw.

(The windows are so dirty, I can't see through them.)

7) Dw i'n gwybod beth dych chi'n mynd _____ fe (SW)/fo (NW).
(I know what you are going through.)

8) Anghofiwch _____ ni.
(Forget about us.)

The declension of 'yn'

With the declension of **yn** 'in' [ən], the endings are added to the stem **yndd-** ['ənð]:

PHRASE	ENGLISH	IPA
yndda i	in me	['ənða iː]
ynddot ti	in you (fam.)	['ənðo(t) tiː]
ynddo fe (SW)	in him	['ənðo veː]
ynddo fo (NW)	in him	['ənðo voː]
ynddi hi	in her	['ənði hiː]
ynddon ni	in us	['ənðo(n) niː]
ynddoch chi	in you (pl.) (sing. formal)	['ənðo(χ) χiː]
ynddyn nhw	in them	['ənðɪ(n) n̥uː]

We have already seen that **yn** causes a nasal mutation:

	SENTENCE
WELSH	**Ces i fy ngeni ym Mhentre-bach.**
ENGLISH	I was born in Pentre-bach.
IPA	[keːs iː (v)ə 'ŋeni əm 'mhɛntɹe baːχ]

Yn 'in' is used after some verb-nouns:

VERB-NOUN	ENGLISH	IPA
arbenigo yn	to specialise in	[arbenˈiˑgo ən]
credu yn	to believe in	['krɛdi ən]
cydio yn	to take hold of / to grasp	['kədjo ən]
gafael yn	to grip / to hold tight	['gɑˑvɛl ən]
ymddiried yn	to trust in	[əmˈðɪrjɛd ən]
ymffrostio yn	to boast about	[əmˈfrɔstjo ən]
ymddiddori yn	to be interested in	[əmðɪðˈɔri ən]

For example:

	SENTENCE
WELSH	**Does dim ffydd gyda fi ynddyn nhw.**
ENGLISH	I haven't got any faith in them.
IPA	[dɔɪs dɪm fiːð 'gədä viː 'ənðɪ(n) n̥uː]

> **IMPORTANT**
>
> **Mewn** 'in' [mɛʊn] is used with indefinite nouns, meaning common nouns which do not have the (definite) article **y** (**yr** before vowels and **h**) before them. This includes verb-nouns:
>
> **Dw i'n ymddiddori mewn canu gwerin.**
> I'm interested in folk music. (*lit.* folk singing)
> [dwiːn əmðɪðˈɔri mɛʊn ˈkɑˑni ˈgwɛrɪn]
>
> **Cawson ni afael mewn trydanwr.**
> We got hold of an electrician.
> [ˈkaʊso(n) niː ˈafɛl mɛʊn tɹədˈaˑnʊr]

The declension of 'dros'

With the declension of **dros** 'over' / 'on behalf of' [dɹɔs], the endings are added to the stem **drost-** [dɹɔst]:

PHRASE	ENGLISH	IPA
drosta i	over me / on my behalf	[ˈdɹɔsta iː]
drostot ti	over you / on your behalf (*fam.*)	[ˈdɹɔsto(t) tiː]
drosto fe (SW)	over him / on his behalf	[ˈdɹɔsto veː]
drosto fo (NW)	over him / on his behalf	[ˈdɹɔsto voː]
drosti hi	over her / on her behalf	[ˈdɹɔsti hiː]
droston ni	over us / on our behalf	[ˈdɹɔsto(n) niː]
drostoch chi	over you / on your behalf (*pl.*) (*sing. formal*)	[ˈdɹɔsto(χ) χiː]
drostyn nhw	over them / on their behalf	[ˈdɹɔstɪ(n) n̥uː]

Dros causes the soft mutation (see **Week 1, Lesson 5**). It conveys the meanings:

(i) 'over':

	SENTENCE
WELSH	**Gyrron ni dros y bont.**
ENGLISH	We drove over the bridge.
IPA	[ˈgəro(n) niː dɹɔs ə bɔnt]

(ii) 'on behalf of':

	SENTENCE
WELSH	**Des i yma drosto fe.**
ENGLISH	I came here on his behalf.
IPA	[deːs iː ˈəmä ˈdɹɔsto veː]

(iii) 'for':

	SENTENCE
WELSH	**Mae e'n (SW) / o'n (NW) chwarae dros Gymru.**
ENGLISH	He plays for Wales.
IPA	[maɪ eːn / oːn 'χwɑːrɛ drɔs 'gəmri]

(iv) 'in favour of':

	SENTENCE
WELSH	**Pleidleisiais i drosti hi.**
ENGLISH	I voted for her.
IPA	[pləɪd'ləɪʃes iː 'drɔsti hiː]

Dros is used after the following verb-nouns:

VERB-NOUN	ENGLISH	IPA
ateb dros	to answer for / to answer on behalf of	['atɛb drɔs]
dadlau dros	to argue for	['dadlɛ drɔs]
gweddïo dros	to pray for	[gwɛði'o drɔs]
pleidleisio dros	to vote for	[pləɪd'ləɪʃo drɔs]
ymladd dros	to fight for	['əmlað drɔs]

Dros is used after the following nouns:

NOUN	ENGLISH	IPA
esgus dros	an excuse for	['ɛsgɪs drɔs]
rheswm dros	a reason for	['r̥ɛsʊm drɔs]

For example:

	SENTENCE
WELSH	**Maen nhw eisiau penderfynu drostyn nhw eu hunain.**
ENGLISH	They want to decide for themselves.
IPA	[maɪ(n) n̥uː 'əɪʃɛ pɛndɛr'vəni 'drɔstɪ(n) n̥uː iː 'hiːnɛn]

The declension of 'heb'

With the declension of **heb** 'without' [heːb], the endings are added to the stem **hebdd-** [hɛbð]:

PHRASE	ENGLISH	IPA
hebdda i	without me	['hɛbða iː]
hebddot ti	without you (*fam.*)	['hɛbðo(t) tiː]
hebddo fe (SW)	without him	['hɛbðo veː]

hebddo fo (NW)	without him	['hɛbðo voː]
hebddi hi	without her	['hɛbði hiː]
hebddon ni	without us	['hɛbðo(n) niː]
hebddoch chi	without you (*pl.*) (*sing. formal*)	['hɛbðo(χ) χiː]
hebddyn nhw	without them	['hɛbðɪ(n) n̥uː]

Heb causes a soft mutation. It is used in the following expressions:

PHRASE	ENGLISH	IPA
heb ei ail	incomparable	[heːb iː aɪl]
heb sôn am	not to mention / never mind	[heːb soːn am]

Heb can also express the negative when used with an affirmative form of '**bod**':

	SENTENCE
WELSH	**Dw i heb orffen smwddio'r dillad heb sôn am bacio.**
ENGLISH	I haven't finished ironing the clothes never mind (about) packing.
IPA	[dwiː heːb 'ɔrfɛn 'smuðjor 'ðɪɫad heːb soːn am 'bakjo]
WELSH	**Roedden nhw heb drafod yr adroddiad.**
ENGLISH	They hadn't discussed the report.
IPA	['rɔɪðɛ(n) n̥uː heːb 'dɹaˑvod ər ad'ɹɔðjad]

The declension of 'rhwng'

With the declension of **rhwng** 'between' [ɹʊŋ], the endings are added to the stem **rhyng-** [ɹəŋ]. **Rhwng** does not cause a mutation:

PHRASE	ENGLISH	IPA
rhyngdda i	between me	['ɹəŋða iː]
rhyngddot ti	between you (*fam.*)	['ɹəŋðo(t) tiː]
rhyngddo fe (SW)	between him	['ɹəŋðo veː]
rhyngddo fo (NW)	between him	['ɹəŋðo voː]
rhyngddi hi	between her	['ɹəŋði hiː]
rhyngddon ni	between us	['ɹəŋðo(n) niː]
rhyngddoch chi	between you (*pl.*) (*sing. formal*)	['ɹəŋðo(χ) χiː]
rhyngddyn nhw	between them	['ɹəŋðɪ(n) n̥uː]

For example:

	SENTENCE
WELSH	**Does dim Cymraeg rhyngddyn nhw.**
ENGLISH	They don't talk to each other. (*lit.* There's no Welsh between them.)
IPA	Welsh [dɔɪs dɪm kəm'raɪg 'ɹəŋðɪ(n) n̥uː]

Rhwng is used in the following expressions:

PHRASE	ENGLISH	IPA
rhwng popeth	all things considered	[ɹʊŋ 'pɔpɛθ]
rhyngddot ti a fi	between you and me	['ɹəŋðɔ(t) tiː ä viː]
rhwng dau feddwl	in two minds	[ɹʊŋ daɪ 'vɛðʊl]

Exercise 2

Complete the following sentences with the personal form of the appropriate prepositions.

1) Cydia _____ fy llaw i.   (Take hold of my hand.)
2) Ewch _____ ni.   (Go without us.)
3) Roedd John yn eistedd _____ chi a fi.   (John was sitting between you and me.)
4) Wnaethoch chi bleidleisio _____ hi?   (Did you vote for her?)
5) Dyna ei char hi. Oes rhywun _____ fo?   (There is her car. Is there anyone in it?)
6) Bydd rhaid i ni fynd _____ ti.   (We will have to go without you.)
7) Roedd e'n (SW)/o'n (NW) sefyll _____ nhw.   (He was standing between them.)
8) Peidiwch ag ateb _____ i!   (Don't answer for me!)

Lesson 4: Illnesses, emotions, and idioms based on 'ar'

The declension of 'ar'
With the declension of **ar**, the endings are added to the stem **arn-** [ärn]:

PHRASE	ENGLISH	IPA
arna i	on me	['ärna iː]
arnat ti	on you (*fam.*)	['ärna(t) tiː]
arno fe (SW)	on him	['ärno veː]
arno fo (NW)	on him	['ärno voː]
arni hi	on her	['ärni hiː]
arnon ni	on us	['ärno(n) niː]
arnoch chi	on you (*pl.*) (*sing. formal*)	['ärno(χ) χiː]
arnyn nhw	on them	['ärnɪ(n) n̥uː]

Ar causes a soft mutation and is used after the following verb-nouns:

VERB-NOUN	ENGLISH	IPA
blino ar	to tire of	[ˈblɪno ar]
cefnu ar	to turn one's back on	[ˈkɛvni ar]
dibynnu ar	to depend on	[dɪbˈəni ar]
dylanwadu ar	to influence	[dəlanˈwaˑdi ar]
effeithio ar	to effect	[ɛfˈəɪθjo ar]
galw ar	to call on	[ˈgaˑlʊ ar]
gweddïo ar	to pray to	[gwɛðˈiˑo ar]
gweiddi ar	to shout at	[ˈgwəɪði ar]
gwenu ar	to smile at'	[ˈgwɛni ar]
gwrando ar	to listen to	[ˈgʷrändo ar]
lladd ar	to criticise	[ɬaːð ar]
meddu ar	to possess	[ˈmɛði ar]
rhoi bai ar	to blame	[r̥ɔi baɪ ar]
sylwi ar	to notice	[ˈsəlwi ar]
syllu ar	to stare at	[ˈsəɬi ar]
ymosod ar	to attack	[əmˈɔsod ar]

Ar precedes the following expressions:

PHRASE	ENGLISH	IPA
ar agor	open	[ar ˈaˑgor]
ar ddi-hun	awake	[ar ðiˈhiːn]
ar fin	on the point of	[ar viːn]
ar frys	in haste	[ar vriːs]
ar gau	closed	[ar gaɪ]
ar unwaith	at once	[ar ˈɪnwaɪθ]
ar y pryd	at the time	[ar ə priːd]

Ar conveys the meanings:

(i) 'on' / 'upon'

PHRASE	ENGLISH	IPA
ar y llawr	on the floor	[ar ə ɬaʊr]

(ii) 'to'

SENTENCE	ENGLISH	IPA
Gwrandewch arna i.	Listen to me.	[gʷranˈdɛʊχ ˈärna i]

(iii) 'at'

SENTENCE	ENGLISH	IPA
Edrychwch arnyn nhw.	Look at them.	[ɛdˑrəχʊχ 'ärnɪ(n) n̪uː]

(iv) 'of'

SENTENCE	ENGLISH	IPA
Dw i wedi blino arno fe / fo.	I am tired of him.	[dwiː 'wɛdi 'bliˑno 'ärno vɛː / voː]

The preposition **ar** is a very useful preposition as it occurs in a lot of idioms which denote a temporary state of mind or body.

Bodily ailments

	SENTENCE
WELSH	**Mae annwyd arna i.**
ENGLISH	I've got a cold. (*lit.* There is a cold on me.)
IPA	[maɪ 'änʊɪd 'ärna iː]

WELSH	**Mae clefyd y gwair arna i.**
ENGLISH	I've got hay fever.
IPA	[maɪ 'klɛvɪd ə gwaɪr 'ärna iː]

WELSH	**Mae brech yr ieir arna i.**
ENGLISH	I've got chicken pox.
IPA	[maɪ breːχ ər jəɪr 'ärna iː]

WELSH	**Mae'r frech goch arna i.**
ENGLISH	I've got measles.
IPA	[maɪr vreːχ goːχ 'ärna iː]

WELSH	**Mae'r ddannodd arna i.**
ENGLISH	I've got toothache.
IPA	[maɪr 'ðänoð 'ärna iː]

WELSH	**Mae'r ffliw arna i.**
ENGLISH	I've got flu.
IPA	[maɪr flɪʊ 'ärna iː]

MASCULINE NOUN	ENGLISH	IPA
gwres	temperature	[gʷreːs]
peswch	cough	['pɛsʊχ]

For example:

SENTENCE	ENGLISH	IPA
Mae gwres ar y plentyn.	The child has a temperature.	[maɪ gʷreːs ar ə ˈplɛntɪn]
Roedd peswch arna i.	I had a cough.	[rɔɪð ˈpɛsʊχ ˈärna iː]

States of mind

	SENTENCE
WELSH	**Mae ofn arna i.**
ENGLISH	I'm afraid. (*lit.* There's fear on me.)
IPA	[maɪ ɔvn̩ ˈärna iː]

WELSH	**Mae cywilydd arna i.**
ENGLISH	I'm ashamed.
IPA	[maɪ kəˈwiˈlɪð ˈärna iː]

WELSH	**Mae hiraeth arna i.**
ENGLISH	I'm homesick.
IPA	[maɪ ˈhiˑrɛθ ˈärna iː]

Other words following this pattern are:

MASCULINE NOUN	ENGLISH	IPA	PLURAL FORM	IPA
bai	blame	[baɪ]	**beiau**	[ˈbəɪe]

FEMININE NOUN	ENGLISH	IPA	PLURAL FORM	IPA
dyled	debt	[ˈdəlɛd]	**dyledion**	[dəlˈɛdjon]

Needs

	SENTENCE
WELSH	**Mae eisiau (…) arna i.**
ENGLISH	I need … (*lit.* There is a need of […] on me.)
IPA	[maɪ ˈɨˑʃɛ (…) ˈärna iː]

WELSH	**Mae eisiau bwyd arna i.**
ENGLISH	I'm hungry.
IPA	[maɪ ˈəɪˑʃɛ bʊɪd ˈärna iː]

WELSH	**Mae syched arna i.**
ENGLISH	I'm thirsty.
IPA	[maɪ ˈsəχɛd ˈärna iː]

Vocabulary

MASCULINE NOUN	ENGLISH	IPA	PLURAL FORM	IPA
pensil	pencil	['pɛnsɪl]	**pensiliau**	[pɛn'sɪljɛ]
beiro	biro	['bəɪro]	**beiros**	['bəɪrɔz]
rwber	rubber	['rʊbɛr]		
papur ysgrifennu	writing paper	['papɪr əsgrɪv'ɛni]		

FEMININE NOUN	ENGLISH	IPA	PLURAL FORM	IPA
amlen	envelope	['amlɛn]	**amlenni**	[am'lɛni]
matsien	match(stick)	['matʃɛn]	**matsys**	['matʃɪz]

MISCELLANEOUS	ENGLISH	IPA
rhagor o arian	more money	['r̥ɑ·gor o 'ärjan]

Exercise 1

Write and say that you need the following items.

1) a pencil _____
2) a biro _____

Now write and say she needs:

3) a rubber _____
4) writing paper _____

Now write and say they need:

5) envelopes _____
6) matches _____
7) more money _____

Ailments which mention a specific body part

Illnesses which mention a specific body part use the possession structure discussed in **Week 4, Lesson 2**. There are some vocabulary differences between North and South Wales. In South Welsh, to state there is something wrong with a body part (to express 'I have a sore (...)' or 'I have (...) ache', the pattern used is **Mae (...) tost gyda fi** 'I have a bad (...)' [maɪ (...) tɔst 'gədä viː]. In North Welsh, except for **cur pen** 'headache' [kiːr pɛn] and **pigyn clust** 'earache' ['pi·gɪn kɬi:st̪], the word **poen** 'pain' [pɔɪn] is placed in front of the body part.

	SOUTH WELSH	ENGLISH	NORTH WELSH
SENTENCE	Mae bola tost gyda fi.	I have a stomach ache.	Mae gen i boen bol.
IPA	[maɪ 'boˑla tɔst 'gədä viː]		[maɪ gɛn iː bɔɪn bɔl]
SENTENCE	Mae pen tost gyda fi.	I have a headache.	Mae gen i gur pen.
IPA	[maɪ pɛn tɔst 'gədä viː]		[maɪ gɛn iː gɪːr pɛn]
SENTENCE	Mae clust tost gyda fi.	I have earache.	Mae gen i bigyn clust.
IPA	[maɪ klɪst tɔst 'gədä viː]		[maɪ gɛn iː 'bɪgɪn kliːst]
SENTENCE	Mae cefn tost gyda fi.*	I have backache.	Mae gen i boen cefn.*
IPA	[maɪ 'kɛˑvɛn tɔst 'gədä viː]		[maɪ gɛn i bɔɪn 'kɛvn̩]

* In South Welsh, many words ending in two consonants are split by an epenthetic vowel: **cefn** 'back' [ˈkɛvn̩] > **cefen** [ˈkɛˑvɛn]; **ofn** 'fear' [ˈɔvn̩] > **ofon**; **trefn** 'order' [ˈtɹɛvn̩] > **trefen** [ˈtɹɛˑvɛn] (see Week 8: Lesson 1).,

The idiomatic use of 'ar' to mean 'to owe'

Another commonly used idiom with **ar** is 'to owe':

	SENTENCE	ENGLISH	IPA
	Mae arna i (...) i chi.	I owe you ...	[maɪ 'ärna iː (...) iː χiː]

For example:

	SENTENCE
WELSH	Mae arna i ddeg punt i chi.
ENGLISH	I owe you ten pounds.
IPA	[maɪ 'ärna iː ðeːg pɪnt iː χiː]

WELSH	Roedd arno fe (SW) / arno fo (NW) dipyn o arian i'r banc.
ENGLISH	He owed a bit of money to the bank.
IPA	[rɔɪð 'ärno veː / voː 'dɪpɪn o 'ärian iːr baŋk]

Here is a useful interrogative:

	SENTENCE
WELSH	Beth sy'n bod arnoch chi?
ENGLISH	What's wrong with you?
IPA	[beː(θ) siːn bɔːd 'ärno(χ) χiː]

Most of the idioms mentioned above take indefinite nouns, and therefore, **oes** [ɔɪs] and **does dim** [dɔɪs dɪm] are the respective interrogative and negative verb forms:

	SENTENCE
WELSH	Oes annwyd arnoch chi?
ENGLISH	Do you have a cold?

IPA	[ɔɪs 'änʊɪd 'ärno(χ) χiː]
WELSH	**Does dim syched arna i.**
ENGLISH	I'm not thirsty.
IPA	[dɔɪs dɪm 'səχɛd 'ärna iː]

Where definite nouns are employed, **ydy** ['ədi] and **dydy (...) ddim** [dədi (...) ðɪm] are the respective interrogative and negative forms:

	SENTENCE
WELSH	**Ydy'r ddannodd arni hi?**
ENGLISH	Has she got toothache?
IPA	['ədir 'ðänoð 'ärni hiː]

WELSH	**Dydy clefyd y gwair ddim arno fe.**
ENGLISH	He hasn't got hay fever.
IPA	[dədi 'klɛvɪd ə gwaɪr ðɪm 'ärno veː]

Vocabulary

MASCULINE NOUN	ENGLISH	IPA	PLURAL FORM	IPA
pen	head	[pɛn]	**pennau**	['pɛnɛ]
bol	belly	[bɔl]	**boliau**	['bɔljɛ]
gwddf	neck	['gʊðv]	**gyddfau**	['gəðvɛ]
arholiad	exam	[arˈhɔljad]	**arholiadau**	[arhɔlˈjaˑdɛ]

FEMININE NOUN	ENGLISH	IPA	PLURAL FORM	IPA
braich	arm	[braɪχ]	**breichiau**	['brəɪχiɛ]

ADVERBIAL	ENGLISH	IPA
o hyd	still	[oː hiːd]

VERB-NOUN	ENGLISH	IPA	STEM	IPA
gwella	to get better / to improve	['gwɛɬa]	**gwell-**	[gwɛɬ]
gwaethygu	to get worse	[gwəɪθˈəgi]	**gwaethyg-**	[gwəɪθˈəg]
dal	to catch	[dal]	**dali-**	[dalj]
paratoi	to prepare	[paratˈɔɪ]	**parato-**	[paratˈoˑ]
esbonio	to explain	[ɛsˈbɔnjo]	**esboni-**	[ɛsˈbɔnj]

ADJECTIVE	ENGLISH	IPA
ofnadwy	awful	[ɔvˈnaˑdʊɪ]
gwelw	pale	['gwɛlʊ]

Dialogue

Welsh Dialogue

Ann: Ydych chi'n dal i gymryd moddion at dy annwyd di?

Richard: Ydw, dw i ddim wedi gwella o gwbl, ac mae pen tost ofnadwy gyda fi, os rhywbeth, dw i'n gwaethygu. Mae peswch cas arna i nawr.

Ann: Mae golwg wael arnat ti, rwyt ti'n edrych yn welw iawn. Mae llawer o bobl yn yr ysgol yn sâl. Mae'n well i ti fynd adref. Dw i'n lwcus, dw i byth yn sâl. Dw i ddim yn cofio'r tro diwethaf (y) daliais i annwyd. Gobeithio fy mod i ddim yn mynd i ddal beth bynnag sydd arnat ti Richard.

Richard: Dw i'n credu mai'r ffliw sydd arna i. Mae gwddf tost gyda fi nawr hefyd.

Ann: Mae hynny'n esbonio'r sgarff drwchus am dy wddf di. Cer adref i dy wely di.

Richard: Dw i wedi siarad â'r pennaeth, dwedodd e wrtha i am fynd adref hefyd.

Ann: Pam rwyt ti yma o hyd felly?

Richard: Cafodd fy nosbarth i brawf ddydd Llun, a dw i eisiau mynd drosto fe gyda nhw. Dyn ni wrthi'n paratoi at arholiad. Dw i eisiau dangos iddyn nhw sut i gael y marciau gorau. Roeddwn i wedi anghofio amdano fe pan siaradais i â'r pennaeth.

Ann: Wel dydy hynny ddim yn rheswm da dros roi dy annwyd di i bawb arall. Dw i'n siŵr y gall dy ddosbarth di wneud hebddot ti am un prynhawn.

Richard: Dw i rhwng dau feddwl, ond cystal i fi aros nawr.

English Translation

Ann: Are you still taking medicine for your cold?

Richard: Yes, I'm not improving at all and I have an awful headache – if anything I am getting worse. I have a bad cough now.

Ann: You look bad, you look very pale. Lots of people in the school are ill. You'd better go home. I am lucky; I am never ill. I don't remember the last time I caught a cold. I hope that I'm not going to catch whatever you have, Richard.

Richard: I think it's the flu I have. I have a sore throat now as well.

Ann: That explains the thick scarf around your neck. Go home to bed.

Richard: I have spoken to the head; he told me to go home as well.

Ann: Why are you still here, then?

Richard: My class had a test on Monday; I want to go over it with them. We are preparing for an exam. I want to show them how to get the best marks. I had forgotten about it when I spoke to the head.

Ann: Well that isn't a good reason for giving your cold to everyone else. I am sure that your class can do without you for one afternoon.

Richard: I am in two minds but I may as well stay now.

Exercise 2

Have a guess in Welsh at what's wrong with the following people.

1) I haven't eaten for twelve hours.　　　_____

2) She longs to see Wales again!　　　_____

3) He feels terrible throughout June every year.

　　　_____

4) We are scared.

5) I need a drink!

6) Our teeth hurt.

7) They look guilty.

8) The red line on the thermometer is long.

Lesson 5: The use of 'mo' to negate simple past and future verb forms

We have already seen how regular verb forms are inflected:

TENSE	SENTENCE	ENGLISH	IPA
Simple past	Welais i ddim ci.	I didn't see a dog.	['wɛlɛs iː ðɪm kiː]
Simple future	Wela i ddim ci.	I won't see a dog.	['wɛla iː ðɪm kiː]

To remind yourself of the **stem + personal inflection** pattern shown in the two examples above, see **Week 7, Lesson 2** and **Week 9, Lesson 2**, respectively. The direct object **ci** is an indefinite noun, 'a dog', and to remind yourself what constitutes a definite and indefinate noun in Welsh, see **Week 1, Lesson 2**.

As we saw in **Week 8, Lesson 4**, when the direct object of an inflected verb is definite (for example: 'the dog' 'John' 'the paper', 'the papers', 'Huw'), **ddim o** [ðɪm oː] is used:

	SENTENCE
WELSH	**Welais i ddim o'r papur.**
ENGLISH	I didn't see the paper. (*lit.* I saw nothing of the paper.)
IPA	['wɛlɛs iː ðɪm oːr 'papɪr]
WELSH	**Welais i ddim o'r papurau.**
ENGLISH	I didn't see the papers. (*lit.* I saw nothing of the papers.)
IPA	['wɛlɛs iː ðɪm oːr pap'ɪrɛ]
WELSH	**Welais i ddim o Siôn.**
ENGLISH	I didn't see Siôn. (*lit.* I saw nothing of Siôn.)
IPA	['wɛlɛs iː ðɪm oː ʃoːn]

This is contracted to **mo / mo'r** in everyday spoken Welsh:

SENTENCE	IPA
Welais i mo'r papurau.	['wɛlɛs i moːr pap'ɪrɛ]
Welais i mo Siôn.	['wɛlɛs moː ʃoːn]

When pronouns like **i, ti**, etc., are the direct object of an inflected verb, the declined preposition is used:

SENTENCE	ENGLISH	IPA
Welais i ddim ohono fe (SW) / **ohono fo** (NW).	I didn't see him.	[ˈwɛlɛs iː ðɪm oˈhɔno veː / voː]
Thala i ddim ohonoch chi.	I won't pay you.	[ˈθɑˑla iː ðɪm oˈhɔno(χ) χiː]

These are shortened in speech. Here is an example of the first sentence: **Welais i ddim ohono fe** (SW) / **ohono fo** (NW).

When a verb is followed by a preposition, such as in **siarad â**, **gwrando ar**, **o** is not used in the negative as the object is no longer direct.

	SENTENCE
WELSH	**Siaradais i ddim â Mr Jones.**
ENGLISH	I didn't speak to Mr Jones.
IPA	[ʃarˈɑˑdɛs iː ðɪm ä ˈmɪstə dʒɔːnz]

WELSH	**Wrandawais i ddim arno hi.**
ENGLISH	I didn't listen to her.
IPA	[ʷränˈdaʊɛs iː ðɪm ˈärni hi]

Exercise 1

Translate the following using inflected verbs.

1) I didn't forget the water. _____

2) We won't buy a brand new laptop. _____

3) I won't send the present to her. _____

4) You didn't use the envelope. _____

5) I didn't use a pencil. _____

6) We didn't send a card. _____

7) She won't write the message. _____

8) They won't climb Snowdon. _____

Vocabulary

VERB-NOUN	ENGLISH	IPA	STEM	IPA
defnyddio	to use	[dɛvˈnəðjo]	**defnyddi-**	[dɛvˈnəðj]

The preposition **o** conveys the meaning:

(i) 'of':

PHRASE	ENGLISH	IPA
(cw)panaid o de	a cup of tea	[(kʊ)pˈaˑnɛd o de]

(ii) 'from':

PHRASE	ENGLISH	IPA
o Gymru	from Wales	[o ˈgəmri]

(iii) 'by':

PHRASE	ENGLISH	IPA
ennill o heol	win by a mile (road)	[ˈɛnɨɬ o ˈheˑol]

O causes a soft mutation (see **Week 1, Lesson 5**). It is used after these verb-nouns:

VERB-NOUN	ENGLISH	IPA
cymryd sylw o	to take notice of	[ˈkəmrɪd ˈsəlʊ oː]
deillio o	to derive from / to stem from	[ˈdəɨɬjo oː]
dioddef o*	to suffer from	[ˈdʒoˑðɛ(v) oː]

* *In spoken Welsh, the* **di** *consonant combination is usually pronounced like the English* **j** */dʒ/:* **diawl** *'devil'* [dʒaʊl]; **diogi** *'laziness'* [ˈdʒoˑgi]. *This process is called palatalization.*

O is also used after these adjectives:

ADJECTIVE	ENGLISH	IPA
bownd o	bound to	[boʊnd oː]
hoff o	fond of	[hoːf oː]
siŵr o	sure to	[ʃuːr oː]

O is also used after these expressions:

PHRASE	ENGLISH	IPA
digon o	enough	[ˈdiˑgon oː]
digon o le	enough room	[ˈdiˑgon oː le]
gormod o	too much	[ˈgɔrmod oː]
gormod o gaws	too much cheese	[ˈgɔrmod oː gaʊs]
tipyn o	a bit	[ˈtɪpɪn oː]
tipyn o laeth	a bit of milk	[ˈtɪpɪn oː laɨθ]
ychydig o	a little / a few	[əχˈədɪg oː]
ychydig o bobl	a few people	[əχˈədɪg oː ˈboˑbol]
o bell ffordd	by far	[oː beɬ fɔrð]
o bryd i'w gilydd	from time to time	[oː briːd ɪʊ ˈgiˑlɪð]
o ganlyniad	as a result	[oː ganˈlənjad]
o leia(f)	at least	[oː ˈləɪa(v)]

The preposition **o** 'of' / 'from' [oː] is a declined preposition (see **Week 10, Lesson 2**):

PHRASE	ENGLISH	IPA
ohona i	of me	[oˈhɔna iː]
ohonot ti	of you (*fam.*)	[oˈhɔno(t) tiː]
ohono fe (SW)	of him	[oˈhɔno veː]
ohono fo (NW)	of him	[oˈhɔno voː]
ohoni hi	of her	[oˈhɔni hiː]
ohonon ni	of us	[oˈhɔno(n) niː]
ohonoch chi	of you (*pl.*) (*sing. formal*)	[oˈhɔno(χ) χiː]
ohonyn nhw	of them	[oˈhɔnɪ(n) n̥uː]

For example:

	SENTENCE
WELSH	**Mae llawer ohonon ni'n mynd i siopa yng Nghaerdydd (y)fory.**
ENGLISH	Lots of us are going shopping in Cardiff tomorrow.
IPA	[maɪ ˈɬaʊɛr oh'ɔnon niːn mɪnd iː ˈʃɔpa ə(ŋ) ŋ̊aɪrˈdiːð (ə)vˈɔri]
WELSH	**Peidiwch cymryd sylw ohonyn nhw.**
ENGLISH	Don't pay any attention to them.
IPA	[ˈpəɪdjʊχ ˈkəmrɪd ˈsəlʊ ohˈɔnɪ(n) n̥uː]

Exercise 2

Complete the negative sentences below by combining the two elements in each.

For example:

Question: Welais i ddim / fe.
Answer: Welais i ddim ohono fo.

1) Phrynais i ddim / y bara.   (I didn't buy the bread.)

___

2) Wylion ni ddim / hi.   (We didn't watch her.)

___

3) Chlywais i ddim / ti.   (I didn't hear you.)

___

4) Wisgodd hi ddim / nhw.   (She didn't wear them.)

___

5) Ddefnyddiaist ti ddim / ei ffôn e (SW)/o (NW).   (You didn't use his phone.)

___

6) Thalodd o ddim / fi. (NW)   (He didn't pay me.)

___

7) Wnaethon nhw ddim / y gwaith.   (They didn't do the work.)

___

8) Enwodd o ddim / ni. (NW)   (He didn't name us.)

___

Lesson 6: Compound prepositions

Compound prepositions consist of two elements. They are declined by placing the appropriate prefixed (possessive) pronoun between them:

PHRASE	ENGLISH	IPA
yn lle	instead (*lit.* in place)	[ən ɬeː]

When declined, the above becomes:

PHRASE	ENGLISH	IPA
yn ein lle ni	instead of us	[ən ən ɬeː niː]

Here are some of the most common compound prepositions:

PHRASE	ENGLISH	IPA
yn lle	instead / in place of	[ən ɬeː]
DECLENSION	ENGLISH	
yn fy lle i*	instead of me	
yn dy le di	instead of you	
yn ei le e (SW)	instead of him	
yn ei le o (NW)	instead of him	
yn ei lle hi	instead of her	
yn ein lle ni	instead of us	
yn eich lle chi	instead of you	
yn eu lle nhw	instead of them	

PHRASE	ENGLISH	IPA
ar ôl	after / behind	[ar oːl]
DECLENSION	ENGLISH	
ar fy ôl i*	after me	
ar dy ôl di	after you (*fam.*)	
ar ei ôl e (SW)	after him	
ar ei ôl o (NW)	after him	
ar ei hôl hi	after her	
ar ein hôl ni	after us	
ar eich ôl chi	after you	
ar eu hôl nhw	after them	

PHRASE	ENGLISH	IPA
ar bwys	near	[ar bʊɪs]
DECLENSION	ENGLISH	
ar (f)y mhwys i	near me	
ar dy bwys di	near you (*fam.*)	
ar ei bwys e (SW)	near him	
ar ei bwys o (NW)	near him	
ar ei phwys hi	near her	
ar ein pwys ni	near us	

PHRASE	ENGLISH	IPA
yn erbyn	against	[ən ˈɛrbɪn]
DECLENSION	ENGLISH	
yn fy erbyn i*	against me	
yn dy erbyn di	against you (*fam.*)	
yn ei erbyn e (SW)	against him	
yn ei erbyn o (NW)	against him	
yn ei herbyn hi	against her	
yn ein herbyn ni	against us	

ar eich pwys chi	near you		yn eich erbyn chi	against you
ar eu pwys nhw	near them		yn eu herbyn nhw	against them

* In everyday speech, remember that **fy** tends to be pronounced **yn** [ən] before words beginning with a vowel and non-mutatable consonents.

PHRASE	ENGLISH	IPA
er mwyn	for sake of	[ɛr mʊɪn]
DECLENSION	**ENGLISH**	
er (f)y mwyn i	for my sake	
er dy fwyn di	for your sake (fam.)	
er ei fwyn e (SW)	for his sake	
er ei fwyn o (NW)	for his sake	
er ei mwyn hi	for her sake	
er ein mwyn ni	for our sake	
er eich mwyn chi	for your sake	
er eu mwyn nhw	for their sake	

PHRASE	ENGLISH	IPA
wrth ochr	by side of	[ʊrθ 'oːχor]
DECLENSION	**ENGLISH**	
wrth fy ochr i	by my side	
wrth dy ochr di	by your side (fam.)	
wrth ei ochr e (SW)	by his side	
wrth ei ochr o (NW)	by his side	
wrth ei hochr hi	by her side	
wrth ein hochr ni	by our side	
wrth eich ochr chi	by your side	
wrth eu hochr nhw	by their side	

PHRASE	ENGLISH	IPA
uwchben	above	[ɪʊχ'bɛn]
DECLENSION	**ENGLISH**	
uwch (f)y mhen i	above me	
uwch dy ben di	above you (fam.)	
uwch ei ben e (SW)	above him	
uwch ei ben o (NW)	above him	
uwch ei phen hi	above her	
uwch ein pennau ni	above us	
uwch eich pen(nau) chi	above you	
uwch eu pennau nhw	above them	

PHRASE	ENGLISH	IPA
ar gyfer	for	[ar 'gəvɛr]
DECLENSION	**ENGLISH**	
ar (f)y nghyfer i	for me	
ar dy gyfer di	for you (fam.)	
ar ei gyfer e (SW)	for him	
ar ei gyfer o (NW)	for him	
ar ei chyfer hi	for her	
ar ein cyfer ni	for us	
ar eich cyfer chi	for you	
ar eu cyfer nhw	for them	

PHRASE	ENGLISH	IPA
o gwmpas	around	[oː 'gʊmpas]
DECLENSION	**ENGLISH**	
o (f)y nghwmpas i	around me	
o dy gwmpas di	around you (fam.)	
o'i gwmpas e (SW)	around him	
o'i gwmpas o (NW)	around him	
o'i chwmpas hi	around her	
o'n cwmpas ni	around us	
o'ch cwmpas chi	around you	
o'u cwmpas nhw	around them	

PHRASE	ENGLISH	IPA
o flaen	in front of / before	[oː vlain]
DECLENSION	**ENGLISH**	
o (f)y mlaen i	in front of me	
o dy flaen di	in front of you (fam.)	
o'i flaen e (SW)	in front of him	
o'i flaen o (NW)	in front of him	
o'i blaen hi	in front of her	
o'n blaenau ni	in front of us	
o'ch blaenau chi	in front of you	
o'u blaenau nhw	in front of them	

PHRASE	ENGLISH	IPA
ar draws	across	[ar dɹaʊs]
DECLENSION	**ENGLISH**	
ar (f)y nhraws i	across me	
ar dy draws di	across you	
ar ei draws e (SW)	across him	
ar ei draws o (NW)	across him	
ar ei thraws hi	across her	
ar ein traws ni	across us	
ar eich traws chi	across you	
ar eu traws nhw	across them	

Here is an example sentence of how to use **ar draws** 'across' [ar dɹaʊs]:

	SENTENCE
WELSH	**Daethon nhw ar (f)y nhraws i yn y bar.**
ENGLISH	They came across me in the bar.
IPA	['dəɪθo(n) n̪uː ar (v)ə n̪ɹaʊs i ən ə bar]

IMPORTANT
Note that with **o flaen** [oː vlaɪn] and **uwchben** [ʊχ'bɛn], the plural forms **blaenau** ['blaɪnɛ] and **pennau** ['pɛnɛ] are used with the plural forms of the compound preposition

---

Exercise 1

Complete the following sentences by forming a composite preposition from the Welsh words in brackets.

For example:

Question: Roedd llawer o bobl _____. (o gwmpas + fi)
Answer: Roedd llawer o bobl o fy nghwmpas i.

1) Aeth o _____. (yn lle + ni)
   (He went in our place / instead of us.)

2) Rhedais i _____. (ar ôl + hi)
   (I ran after her.)

3) Roedden nhw'n eistedd _____. (ar bwys + fi)
   (They were sitting next to me.)

4) Roedd llawer o adar yn hedfan _____. (uwchben + nhw)
   (There were lot of birds flying above them.)

5) Pwy oedd yn sefyll _____. (o flaen + ti)?
   (Who was standing in front of you.)

6) Pwy sy _____?   (yn erbyn + fe [SW]/fo [NW])
   (Who is against him?)

7) Roeddwn i'n gweithio _____.   (wrth ochr + nhw).
   (I was working by their side.)

8) Oes pobl yn byw _____?   (o gwmpas + chi)
   (Are there people living around you?)

Vocabulary

MASCULINE NOUN	ENGLISH	IPA	PLURAL FORM	IPA
aderyn	bird	[aˈderɪn]	adar	[ˈɑːdar]

VERB-NOUN	ENGLISH	IPA	STEM	IPA
torri ar draws	to interrupt	[ˈtɔri ar draʊs]	torr-	[tɔr]

Lesson 7: Recap exercises

Exercise 1

Translate the following sentences.

1) He never drinks black coffee.

2) I never used to listen to the radio.

3) Flying has never appealed to us.

4) She never dreamed about them.

5) He was never angry at me.

6) She will never speak to him again.

7) You have never succeeded in coming between them.

8) I had never been there before.

If you have difficulty completing this execise, review **Week 10, Lesson 1, Lesson 2,** *and* **Lesson 3**.

Exercise 2

Complete the following sentences by using the personal form of the appropriate pronouns.

1) Wnaeth hi gyfeirio _____ ni pan oedd hi'n ddiolch _____ bawb?
   (Did she refer to us when she was thanking everyone?)

2) Peidiwch rhoi'r bai _____ i.
   (Don't blame me.)

3) Pwy oedd wedi gafael _____ chi?
   (Who had taken hold of you?)

4) Cytunon nhw _____ bleidleisio _____ hi.
   (They agreed to vote for her.)

5) Aeth hi _____ ti?
   (Did she go without you?)

6) Mae hi'n hen bryd _____ fe (SW)/fo (NW) roi'r gorau i smocio.
   (It is high time he gave up smoking.)

7) Oeddech chi'n poeni _____ i?
   (Were you worried/worrying about me?)

8) Beth gafodd e (SW)/o (NW) _____ nhw?
   (What did he get from them?)

9) Allwn ni ddim ymddiried _____ ti.
   (We can't trust you.)

10) Mae cywilydd _____ i.
    (I am ashamed.)

Exercise 3

Combine the two elements in the questions below to form sentences in the present tense.

For example:

Question: pen tost; fe (SW) / cur pen; fo (NW)
Answer: Mae pen tost gyda fe. (SW) / Mae ganddo fo gur pen. (NW)

1) hi; pigyn glust (NW) / hi; clust dost (SW)   _____
   (She has earache.)

2) fi; gwres   _____
   (I have a temperature.)

3) ni; annwyd
   (We have a cold.)

4) fo; brech yr ieir (NW)
   (He has chickenpox.)

5) Mr Jones; braich dost (SW)
   (Mr Jones has a sore arm.)

6) y pennaeth; bol tost (SW)
   (The chief has a stomachache.)

7) ti; peswch
   (You have a cough.)

8) nhw; ofn
   (They are afraid.)

9) ei thad; cywilydd
   (Her father is ashamed.)

10) chi; y ddannodd
    (You have toothache.)

If you have difficulty completing this exercise, review **Week 10 Lesson 4**.

Exercise 4

Translate the following sentences using the inflected form of the verb (simple past).

For example:

Question: We didn't see the man.
Answer: Welon ni ddim o'r dyn.

1) I didn't use the matches.
2) We didn't help them.
3) They didn't catch the dog.
4) He didn't drink it.
5) You didn't cross the road. (*fam.*)
6) They didn't pay her.
7) We didn't prepare the work.
8) I didn't score it (*f.*).
9) He didn't open the envelope.
10) They didn't hear me.
11) He didn't teach us.
12) I didn't see you. (*fam.*)
13) I didn't phone her.

14) He didn't understand you. _____
15) You didn't colour the picture. _____

If you have difficulty completing this exercise, review **Week 10, Lesson 5**.

Exercise 5

Complete the following sentences by translating the underlined phrase, using a compound preposition.

1) Does neb <u>against him</u>. _____
2) Pwy ddaeth <u>instead of them</u>? _____
3) Dw i'n mynd i mewn <u>after you</u>. (*fam.*) _____
4) Pwy oedd yn eistedd <u>near her</u>? _____
5) Gwnaeth o bopeth <u>for our sake</u>. _____
6) Safwch <u>in front of us</u>. _____
7) Roedd o'n dawnsio <u>by my side</u>. _____
8) Torrodd hi <u>across him.</u> (she interrupted him)
9) Roedd llun <u>above them.</u> _____
10) Roedd llawer o bethau <u>around her</u>. _____

If you have difficulty completing this execise, review **Week 10, Lesson 6**.

Week 11

Lesson 1: The subjunctive mood

In Welsh, as in English and other languages, there are special verb forms that express desire, uncertainty, supposition or unreality. These constitute a distinct mood that is known as the subjunctive. Compare the following sentences:

(i) I like learning Welsh.
(ii) I would like to learn Welsh.

The first sentence merely expresses a statement, namely that I like learning Welsh, and is said to belong to the indicative mood, whereas the second sentence expresses a desired state, and is, accordingly, placed in the subjunctive mood.*

* See the chapter entitled **A Brief Summary of the Modern Welsh Verb System** at the end of the book.

The subjunctive mood in Welsh can be classified as follows:

(i) The formulaic subjunctive
(ii) The conditional subjunctive

The formulaic subjunctive

The formulaic subjunctive is what remains of the old 'present' subjunctive, which conveys the idea that what is described is ongoing, continuous or timeless. In modern spoken Welsh, it is found in fossilized archaisms often corresponding to equivalent phrases in English:

PHRASE	ENGLISH	IPA
Da boch chi	Goodbye	[dɑː boː(χ) χiː]
Doed a ddelo	Come what may	[dɔɪd ä 'ðeˈlo]
Boed hynny fel y bo	Be that as it may	[bɔɪd 'həni vɛl ə boː]
Gorau po gynta(f)	The sooner the better	['goˑrɛ poː 'gənta(v)]
Dyn a'n helpo!	Heaven help us!	[diːn än 'hɛlpo]

They also occur in proverbs and truisms:

PHRASE	ENGLISH	IPA
Cartref yw cartref ble bynnag y bo.	Home is home wherever you are.	['kartɹɛv ɪʊ 'kartɹɛv blɛː 'bənag ə boː]
Po fwyaf y bydd dyn byw, mwyaf a wêl a mwyaf a glyw.	The more one lives the more one sees and hears.	[poː 'vʊɪav ə biːð diːn bɪʊ 'mʊɪav ä weːl ä 'mʊɪav ä glɪʊ]

The conditional subjunctive

In English, a statement such as, "I would go to the party (tomorrow), if I had something to wear," is said to express possibility because, since the party will take place in the future, and it is theoretically possible to attend it, the use of the modal 'would' implies that the speaker will not be able, or willing, to do so. In Welsh, there is a set of inflections which convey this meaning, although in spoken Welsh only a few regular verbs choose these inflections. The main ones are '**gallu**' 'can' ['gałi] and '**hoffi**' 'to like' ['hɔfi]; the majority of the rest of the verbs choose the periphrastic construction with '**bod**' (see below).

The conditional subjunctive of 'bod'

In spoken Welsh, 'I would be' can be expressed either as **byddwn i** ['bəðʊn iː] or **baswn i** ['bäsʊn iː]. The two forms are interchangable, but in North Wales the **s** forms (**baswn**) are used in the conditional, while the **dd** (**byddwn**) forms denote habituality.

Here is an example of the conditional:

	SENTENCE
WELSH	Baswn i'n mynd (pe)tasai amser gen i.
ENGLISH	I would go if I had time
IPA	['bäsʊn iːn mɪnd (pe)'täse 'ämsɛr gɛn i]

Here is an example of the habitual:

	SENTENCE
WELSH	Byddwn i'n rhedeg milltir bob dydd pan o'n i'n ifanc.
ENGLISH	I would run a mile every day when I was young.
IPA	['bəðʊn iːn 'ɹɛˑdɛg 'mɪɬtɪr boːb diːð pan ɔːðʊn iːn 'iˑvaŋk]

The **s** forms are often shortened: **'swn i** [sʊn iː], **'set ti** [sɛ̈t tiː], **'sai fe** [sɛ̈ veː], etc. Here are the personal forms in the affirmative:

PHRASE	IPA	ENGLISH	ALT. PHRASE	IPA
byddwn i	['bəðʊn iː]	I would be	**baswn i**	['bäsʊn iː]
byddet ti	['bəðɛ(t) tiː]	you would be (*fam.*)	**baset ti**	['bäsɛ(t) tiː]
byddai fe (SW)	['bəðɛ veː]	he would be	**basai fe** (SW)	['bäsɛ veː]
byddai fo (NW)	['bəðɛ voː]	he would be	**basai fo** (NW)	['bäsɛ voː]
byddai hi	['bəðɛ hiː]	she would be	**basai hi**	['bäsɛ hiː]
bydden ni	['bəðɛ(n) niː]	we would be	**basen ni**	['bäsɛ(n) niː]
byddech chi	['bəðɛ(χ) χiː]	you would be (*pl.*) (*sing. formal*)	**basech chi**	['bäsɛ(χ) χiː]
bydden nhw	['bəðɛ(n) n̥uː]	they would be	**basen nhw**	['bäsɛ(n) n̥uː]

Let us look at some examples of **byddai**. Below, it is used alongside an adjective, a noun and an adverbial respectively.

SENTENCE	ENGLISH	IPA	MUTATED ADJECTIVE
Byddwn i'n ddiolchgar.	I would be grateful.	['bəðʊn iːn ði'ɔlχgar]	diolchgar

SENTENCE	ENGLISH	IPA	MUTATED NOUN
Byddai fe'n forwr.	He would be a sailor.	['bəðɛ veːn 'fɔrʊr]	morwr

SENTENCE	ENGLISH	IPA	ADVERBIAL
Fydden nhw ddim gartre(f).	They wouldn't be home.	['vəðɛ(n) n̥uː ðɪm 'gart̬ɛ(v)]	gartre(f)

Let us look at some examples of **basai**. Below, it is used alongside an adjective, a noun, and an adverbial phrase, respectively:

SENTENCE	ENGLISH	IPA
Baswn i'n ddiolchgar.	I would be grateful.	['bäsʊn iːn ði'ɔlχgar]

SENTENCE	ENGLISH	IPA
Basai fe'n forwr.	He would be a sailor.	['bäsɛ veːn 'fɔrʊr]

SENTENCE	ENGLISH	IPA
Fasen nhw ddim gartre(f).	They wouldn't be home.	['väsɛ(n) n̥uː ðɪm 'gart̬ɛ(v)]

However, as with the indicative mood, **yn** does not cause verb-nouns to mutate (see **Week 3, Lesson 1**):

SENTENCE	ENGLISH	IPA
Byddwn i'n galw.	I would call.	['bəðʊn iːn 'gaːlʊ]
Basai fo'n talu. (NW)	He would pay.	['bäsɛ voːn 'taːłi]
Bydden nhw'n canu.	They would sing.	['bəðɛ(n) n̥uːn 'kaːni]

Questions are answered by using the appropriate personal form of the verb:

	QUESTION	AFFIRMATIVE REPLY	NEGATIVE REPLY
WELSH	Fyddech chi'n ddig?	Byddwn.	Na fyddwn.
ENGLISH	Would you be angry?	Yes, I would.	No, I wouldn't be.
IPA	['vəðɛ(χ) χiːn ðiːg]	['bəðʊn]	[na: 'vəðʊn]

As with the past imperfect and future tense of '**bod**' (see **Week 6, Lesson 1** and **Week 9, Lesson 1**), the first letter of of the interrogative conditional forms of 'bod' undergo soft mutation. Negative sentences are expressed by **soft mutation + personal verb form + ddim**. Below is an example of this in the affirmative:

SENTENCE	ENGLISH	IPA
Byddwn i'n talu.	I would pay.	['bəðʊn iːn 'taːli]

Here is an example in the interrogative:

QUESTION	ENGLISH	IPA
Fyddech chi'n talu?	Would you pay?	[ˈvəðɛ(χ) χiːn ˈtɑˑli]

Here is an example in the negative:

SENTENCE	ENGLISH	IPA
Fyddwn i ddim yn talu.	I would not pay.	[ˈvəðʊn iː ðɪm ən ˈtɑˑli]

Impossibility

A statement like, "I would have called (last night), if I hadn't been so busy," expresses impossibility because, since the aspiration expressed refers to the past, there is no possibility of fulfilling it. In the case of '**bod**', impossibility is expressed by substituting **wedi** for **yn**. Here are some examples:

SENTENCE	ENGLISH	IPA
Byddwn i wedi galw.	I would have called.	[ˈbəðʊn iː ˈwɛdi ˈgɑˑlʊ]
Basai fo wedi talu.	He would have payed.	[ˈbäsɛ voː ˈwɛdi ˈtɑˑłi]
Bydden nhw'n canu.	They would have sung.	[ˈbəðɛ(n) n̥uː ˈwɛdi ˈkɑˑni]

Compare this with the use of **wedi** as an aspectual marker (see **Week 3, Lesson 2**).

Vocabulary

MASCULINE NOUN	ENGLISH	IPA	PLURAL FORM	IPA
beic	bike	[bəɪk]	**beiciau**	[ˈbəɪkjɛ]
cigydd	butcher	[ˈkiˑgɪð]	**cigyddion**	[kiˑgˈəðjon]
cig	meat	[kiːg]	**cigoedd**	[ˈkiˑgɔɪð]

FEMININE NOUN	ENGLISH	IPA	PLURAL FORM	IPA
carafán	caravan	[karavˈan]	**carafannau**	[karavˈanɛ]

MISCELLANEOUS	ENGLISH	IPA
fel	as / like	[vɛl]
ar feic	by bike / on a bike	[ar vəɪk]

Exercise 1

Translate the following using either the **s** form (NW) or the **dd** form (SW).

For example:

Question: He would buy another one.
Answer: Basai fo'n prynu un arall. (NW) / Byddai fe'n prynu un arall. (SW)

1) I would go to work by bike.
___

2) Would he climb a tree?
___

3) She wouldn't keep a bird as a pet.
___

4) Would you live in a city?
___

5) We wouldn't go on holiday in a caravan.
___

6) I would never work as a butcher.
___

7) They wouldn't take any notice of him.
___

8) That would be very funny.
___

Exercise 2

Give the correct yes or no responses to the following questions.

For example:

Question: Fasech (NW) / Fyddech chi'n (SW) darllen yn yr eglwys? (✗)
Answer: Na faswn (NW) / Na fyddwn. (SW)

1) Fyddai'r cigydd yn gwerthu cig gwael? (SW) (✗) ___
   (Would the butcher sell bad meat?)

2) Fasen nhw'n ddig wrtho fo? (NW) (✓) ___
   (Would they be angry with him?)

3) Fyddwn i'n cael mynd? (SW) (✓) ___
   (Would I be allowed to go?)

4) Faset ti'n dweud wrthyn nhw? (NW) (✗) ___
   (Would you tell them?)

5) Fyddai fe'n gweiddi arnon ni? (SW) (✗) ___
   (Would he shout at us?)

6) Fasech chi'n gwisgo'r het 'na? (NW) (✓) ___
   (Would you wear that hat?)

7) Fyddai'r hyfforddwr yn chwarae tennis? (SW) (✓) ___

(Would the coach play tennis?)

8) Fasai hi'n disgwyl i ti dalu? (NW) (✘)
(Would she expect you to pay?)

The conditional subjunctive of 'gallu', 'hoffi' and 'caru'

PHRASE	ENGLISH	IPA
gallwn i	I could	['gäɫʊn iː]
gallet ti	you could (*fam.*)	['gäɫɛ(t) tiː]
gallai fe (SW)	he could	['gäɫɛ veː]
gallai fo (NW)	he could	['gäɫɛ voː]
gallai hi	she could	['gäɫɛ hiː]
gallen ni	we could	['gäɫɛ(n) niː]
gallech chi	you could (*pl.*) (*sing. formal*)	['gäɫɛ(χ) χiː]
gallen nhw	they could	['gäɫɛ(n) n̥uː]

PHRASE	ENGLISH	IPA
hoffwn i	I would like	['hɔfʊn iː]
hoffet ti	you would like (*fam.*)	['hɔfɛ(t) tiː]
hoffai fe (SW)	he would like	['hɔfɛ veː]
hoffai fo (NW)	he would like	['hɔfɛ voː]
hoffai hi	she would like	['hɔfɛ hiː]
hoffen ni	we would like	['hɔfɛ(n) niː]
hoffech chi	you would like (*pl.*) (*sing. formal*)	['hɔfɛ(χ) χiː]
hoffen nhw	they would like	['hɔfɛ(n) n̥uː]

PHRASE	ENGLISH	IPA
carwn i	I would love	['kaɾʊn iː]
caret ti	you would love (*fam.*)	['kaɾɛ(t) tiː]
carai fe (SW)	he would love	['kaɾɛ veː]
carai fo (NW)	he would love	['kaɾɛ voː]
carai hi	she would love	['kaɾɛ hiː]
caren ni	we would love	['kaɾɛ(n) niː]
carech chi	you would love (*pl.*) (*sing. formal*)	['kaɾɛ(χ) χiː]
caren nhw	they would love	['kaɾɛ(n) n̥uː]

IMPORTANT
Remember that the third person singular **gallai** ['gäɫɛ], **hoffai** ['hɔfɛ] and **carai** ['kaɾɛ] are used when the subject is a singular or plural noun.

The mutational rules governing the interrogative and negative forms are the same as with the simple past and simple future tenses of regular verbs (see **Week 7, Lesson 2** and **Week 9, Lesson 2**). With the interrogative, we see a soft mutation if the initial letter is subject to it (see **Week 1, Lesson 5**).

Interrogative:

	QUESTION	AFFIRMATIVE REPLY	NEGATIVE REPLY
WELSH	**Allwn i?**	**Gallech.**	**Na allech.**
ENGLISH	Could I?	Yes, you could.	No, you couldn't.
IPA	['äłʊn iː]	['gäłɛχ]	[nɑː 'äłɛχ]

	QUESTION	AFFIRMATIVE REPLY	NEGATIVE REPLY
WELSH	**Hoffet ti?**	**Hoffwn.**	**Na hoffwn.**
ENGLISH	Would you like?	Yes, I would like.	No, I wouldn't like.
IPA	['hɔfɛ(t) tiː]	['hɔfʊn]	[nɑ 'hɔfʊn]

For example:

	QUESTION	AFFIRMATIVE REPLY	NEGATIVE REPLY
WELSH	**Allwn i ddod?**	**Gallech.**	**Na allech.**
ENGLISH	Could I come?	Yes, you could.	No, you could not.
IPA	['äłʊn iː ðoːd]	['gäłɛχ]	[nɑː 'äłɛχ]

Negative:

SENTENCE	ENGLISH	IPA
Allwn i ddim.	I couldn't.	['äłʊn iː ðɪm]
Hoffwn i ddim.	I wouldn't like.	['hɔfʊn iː ðɪm]

Impossibility

In the case of '**gallu**', '**hoffi**' and '**caru**'. impossibility is expressed by inserting **bod wedi** [boːd 'wɛdi] between the personal inflected verb form and the following verb-noun.

Possibility:

SENTENCE	ENGLISH	IPA
Gallwn i fynd.	I could go.	['gäłʊn iː vɪnd]

Impossibility:

SENTENCE	ENGLISH	IPA
Gallwn i fod wedi mynd.	I could have gone.	['gäłʊn iː voːd 'wɛdi mɪnd]

The soft mutation occurs because **bod** is now the direct object of the verb (see **Week 7, Lesson 2**). For example:

	SENTENCE
WELSH	**Gallwn i fod wedi mynd.**

ENGLISH	I could have gone.
IPA	['gälʊn iː vɔːd 'wɛdi mɪnd]
WELSH	**Hoffwn i fod wedi mynd.**
ENGLISH	I would have liked to have gone.
IPA	['hɔfʊn iː vɔːd 'wɛdi mɪnd]
WELSH	**Carwn i fod wedi mynd.**
ENGLISH	I would have loved to have gone.
IPA	['kɑrʊn iː vɔːd 'wɛdi mɪnd]

Vocabulary

MASCULINE NOUN	ENGLISH	IPA	PLURAL FORM	IPA
cwrw	beer	['kuru]		
cyfarfod	meeting	[kəv'arvod]	**cyfarfodydd**	[kəvar'vɔdɪð]
bws	bus	[bəs]	**bysiau**	['bəʃɛ]

FEMININE NOUN	ENGLISH	IPA	PLURAL FORM	IPA
wats	watch	[watʃ]	**watsys**	['watʃɪs]

Exercise 3

Complete the sentences below by filling in the blanks with the appropriate verb and answer.

1) _____ chi goffi amser te? _____.
   (Would you like a coffee at tea time? Yes.)

2) _____ ei wneud e (SW)/o (NW).
   (I could have done it.)

3) _____ hi beint o gwrw? _____.
   (Would she like a pint of beer? No.)

4) _____ hedfan i ffwrdd?
   (Could they have flown away?)

5) _____ newid y llyfr 'ma.
   (We would like to change this book.)

6) _____ rhagor o bapur ysgrifennu.
   (She could buy more wrting paper.)

7. _____ bupur?
   (Would you [*fam.*] like some pepper?)

8) _____ dweud wrthon ni cyn nawr (SW)/ rŵan (NW).
   (They could have told us before now.)

Lesson 2: Conditional clauses with 'pe' and 'os'

In Welsh, there are two words which mean 'if': **os** [ɔs] and **pe** [peː].

'Os'
This form is used in the indicative mood with the following tenses:

(i) Present tense:

	SENTENCE
WELSH	**Os ydw i'n iawn, does dim diben mynd.**
ENGLISH	If I'm right, there's no point going.
IPA	[ɔs ədʊ iːn jaʊn dɔɪs dɪm ˈdiˑbɛn mɪnd]

WELSH	**Os talwch chi, gallwch chi fynd.**
ENGLISH	If you pay, you can go.
IPA	[ɔs ˈtɑˑlʊ(χ) χiː ˈgäłʊ(χ) χiː vɪnd]

(ii) Future tense:

	SENTENCE
WELSH	**Os bydd hi'n braf fory, awn ni i'r traeth.**
ENGLISH	If it's fine tomorrow, we'll go to the beach.
IPA	[ɔs biːð hiːn braːv (ə)ˈvɔri aʊ(n) niː iːr tɹaɪθ]

(iii) Simple past:

	SENTENCE
WELSH	**Os chwaraeodd tîm Cymru mor dda, sut collon nhw?**
ENGLISH	If the Wales team played so well, how did they lose?
IPA	[ɔs χwäräɪɔð tiːm ˈkəmri mɔːr ða: sɪt ˈkɔło(n) n̥uː]

(iv) Past imperfect:

	SENTENCE
WELSH	**Os oedd Gareth yn sâl, beth oedd e'n ei wneud yn y dafarn neithiwr?**
ENGLISH	If Gareth was ill, what was he doing in the pub last night?
IPA	[ɔs ɔɪð ˈgarɛθ ən saːl beːθ ɔɪð eːn (iː) ʷnəɪd ən ə ˈdavarn ˈnəɪθjʊr]

'Pe'
The phrase 'if I were' can be expressed in spoken Welsh in two ways:

(i) by putting **pe** 'if' [peː] in front of the conditional subjunctive forms of **bod**:

PHRASE	ENGLISH
pe byddwn i'n mynd. (SW)	if I went / if I were to go
pe baswn i'n mynd. (SW & NW)	if I went / if I were to go

In spoken Welsh, these forms tend to be shortened to **'ddwn i** [ðʊn iː] and **'swn i** [sʊn iː], respectively.

(ii) by using special forms:

	SOUTH WELSH	ENGLISH	NORTH WELSH
PHRASE	**petawn i**	if I were	**(pe)taswn i**
IPA	[pĕˈtaʊn i]		[(pĕ)ˈt̪asʊn i]
PHRASE	**petait ti**	if you were (*fam.*)	**(pe)taset ti**
IPA	[pĕˈtaɪ(t) tiː]		[(pĕ)ˈt̪asɛ(t) t̪iː]
PHRASE	**petai fe**	if he were	**(pe)tasai fo**
IPA	[pĕˈtaɪ veː]		[(pĕ)ˈt̪asɛ voː]
PHRASE	**petai hi**	if she were	**(pe)tasai hi**
IPA	[pĕˈtaɪ hiː]		[(pĕ)ˈt̪asɛ hiː]
PHRASE	**petaen ni**	if we were	**(pe)tasen ni**
IPA	[pĕˈtaɪ(n) niː]		[(pĕ)ˈt̪asɛ(n) niː]
PHRASE	**petaech chi**	if you were	**(pe)tasech chi**
IPA	[pĕˈtaɪ(χ) χiː]		[(pĕ)ˈt̪asɛ(χ) χiː]
PHRASE	**petaen nhw**	if they were	**(pe)tasen nhw**
IPA	[pĕˈtaɪ(n) n̥uː]		[(pĕ)ˈt̪asɛ(n) n̥uː]

IMPORTANT
Remember that the third person singular **petai** [pɛˈtaɪ] / **(pe)tasai** [(pɛ)ˈt̪asɛ] are used when the subject is a singular or plural noun.

This type of conditional clause is very common in Welsh, and you should learn the following sentence pattern thoroughly:

	SENTENCE
WELSH	**Beth fasech chi'n ei wneud (pe)tasech chi'n ennill y Loteri?** (NW)
ENGLISH	What would you do if you won the Lottery?
IPA	[beː(θ) ˈvasɛ(χ) χiːn (iː) ʷnəɪd (pĕ)ˈt̪asɛ(χ) χiːn ˈɛnɨɬ ə ˈlɔtɛri]
WELSH	**(Pe)tawn i yn eich lle chi, fyddwn i ddim yn gwneud hynny.** (SW)
ENGLISH	If I were you, I wouldn't do that. (*lit.* If I were in your place, I wouldn't do that.)
IPA	[pĕˈtaʊn iː ən əχ ɬeː χiː ˈvəðʊn i ðɪm ən gʷnəɪd ˈhəni]
WELSH	**Baswn i'n mynd (pe)taswn i'n gallu.** (NW)
ENGLISH	I would go if I could.
IPA	[ˈbasʊn iːn mɪnd (pĕ)ˈt̪asʊn iːn gaɬi]

Exercise 1

*Connect the two halves of the sentences below, taking one half from **A** and the other from **B**.*

A
1) Petawn i'n/Taswn i'n gwybod eich bod chi'n dod ... (If I knew that you were coming ...)
2) Petai/Tasai Ann yn gwybod bod yr heol ar gau ... (If Ann knew that the road was closed ...)
3) Petaen nhw/Tasen nhw wedi blino ... (If they were tired ...)
4) Petai/Tasai fy nghar i yn y garej ... (If my car was in the garage ...)
5) Petai fe'n /Tasai fo'n yfed peint o gwrw ... (If he drank a pint of beer ...)
6) Petai pen tost gyda ti/Tasai gen ti gur pen ... (If you had a headache ...)
7) Petai syched arna i/Tasai syched arna i ... (If I were thirsty ...)
8) Petawn i'n/Taswn i'n gweld damwain ... (If I saw an accident ...)
9) Petai hi'n/Tasai hi'n gwisgo wats ... (If she wore a watch ...)
10) Petai mwy o amser gyda fi/Tasai gen i fwy o amser ... (If I had more time ...)

B
a) ... byddwn i'n/baswn i'n ffonio'r heddlu.
b) ... bydddet ti'n/baset ti'n cymryd moddion ato fe (SW)/fo (NW).
c) ... byddai/basai'n well iddo fe (SW)/fo (NW) beidio â gyrru.
d) ... bydden nhw/basen nhw wedi mynd i'r gwely.
e) ... byddwn i/baswn i'n yfed dŵr.
f) ... byddai hi/basai hi wedi mynd y ffordd arall.
g) ... byddwn i'n/baswn i'n dysgu iaith arall.
h) ... byddwn i/baswn i wedi gwneud cacen.
i) ... byddwn i'n/baswn i'n mynd ar y bws.
j) ... byddai hi'n/basai hi'n gallu dweud faint o'r gloch yw hi.

Dialogue

Welsh Dialogue

Richard: Hoffet ti baned?
Ann: Hoffwn, diolch, basai'n well gen i wydraid mawr o win coch, ond cymera i banad yn ei le.
Richard: Gallwn i fod wedi dweud wrthot ti y bore 'ma fod Stryd y Farchnad ar gau petawn i wedi meddwl am y peth.
Ann: Taswn i'n gwybod bod y stryd 'na ar gau, baswn i wedi mynd y ffordd arall.
Richard: Byddet ti wedi cyrraedd hanner awr yn ôl petait ti wedi gwneud hynny.
Ann: Baswn, siŵr o fod, ond dw i yma rŵan, ac roedd rhyw sôn am baned.
Richard: Dw i newydd gofio rhywbeth. Hoffai'r pennaeth dy weld di ar ôl amser chwarae y prynhawn 'ma.
Ann: Efallai y bydd eisiau gwydraid o win arna i ar ôl y cyfarfod â fo.

English Translation

Richard: Would you like a cuppa?
Ann: Yes, thanks; I would prefer a large glass of red wine, but I'll take a cuppa in its place.

Richard: I could have told you this morning that Market Street was closed if I had thought about it.
Ann: If I had known that street was closed I would have gone the other way.
Richard: You would have arrived half an hour ago if you had done that.
Ann: Yes, probably, but I'm here now, and there was some talk of a cuppa.
Richard: I have just remembered something. The head woud like to see you after playtime this afternoon.
Ann: Perhaps I will need a glass of wine after the meeting with him.

Lesson 3: Expressing 'should' and 'ought to'

'I should' is expressed in Welsh as **dylwn i** [ˈdəlʊn iː], which is formed by adding the conditional subjunctive personal inflection **-wn i** to the verb stem **dyl-**. Here are the personal forms:

PHRASE	ENGLISH	IPA
dylwn i	I should	[ˈdəlʊn iː]
dylet ti	you should (*fam.*)	[ˈdəlɛ(t) tiː]
dylai fe (SW)	he should	[ˈdəlɛ vɛː]
dylai fo (NW)	he should	[ˈdəlɛ voː]
dylai hi	she should	[ˈdəlɛ hiː]
dylen ni	we should	[ˈdəlɛ(n) niː]
dylech chi	you should (*pl.*) (*sing. formal*)	[ˈdəlɛ(χ) χiː]
dylen nhw	they should	[ˈdəlɛ(n) n̥uː]

> **IMPORTANT**
> Remember that the third person singular **dylai** [ˈdəlɛ] is used when the subject is a singular or plural noun.

For example:

	QUESTION	AFFIRMATIVE REPLY	NEGATIVE REPLY
WELSH	**Ddylwn i fynd?**	**Dylech.**	**Na ddylech.**
ENGLISH	Should I go?	Yes, you should.	No, you shouldn't.
IPA	[ˈðəlʊn iː vɪnd]	[ˈdəlɛχ]	[nɑː ˈðəlɛχ]

SENTENCE	ENGLISH	IPA
Dylech chi fynd adre(f).	You should go home.	[ˈdəlɛː(χ) χiː vɪnd ˈadɹɛ(v)]

Vocabulary

VERB-NOUN	ENGLISH	IPA	STEM	IPA
cadw	to keep	[ˈkaˑdʊ]	cadw-	[kaˑdw]
cwyno	to complain	[ˈkʊɪno]	cwyn-	[kʊɪn]

Exercise 1

Translate the following.

1) I should have gone to hospital.
2) Should you do that? (*fam.*)
3) He shouldn't have kept her money.
4) We should complain.
5) Should you switch the light on? Yes (I should).
6) Should he hurry? No (he shouldn't).
7) They should have told her.
8) We shouldn't criticise you. (*fam.*)
9) You shouldn't blame him.
10) Should I turn my back on them? Yes (you should).

Lesson 4: The passive voice

In Welsh, a passive phrase like 'the house was built' can be expressed in two ways:

(i) by the use of the the auxiliary verb **cael** 'to get' [kaɪl] + **prefixed possesive pronoun + infinitive**:

	SENTENCE
WELSH	**Cafodd y tŷ ei godi.**
ENGLISH	The house was built. (*lit.* The house got its building.)
IPA	[ˈkaˑvoð ə tiː iː ˈgɔdi]

(ii) by the use of special impersonal forms (see **Week 12, Lesson 5**):

	SENTENCE
WELSH	**Codwyd y tŷ.**
ENGLISH	The house was built.
IP	[ˈkɔdʊɪd ə tiː]

The latter is mostly used in newspapers and other media, whereas the former is the usual construction in spoken Welsh and is used in periphrastic (long) sentences with '**bod**', as well as with inflected forms of '**cael**':

	SENTENCE
WELSH	**Mae'r tŷ'n cael ei godi.**
ENGLISH	The house is being / getting built.
IPA	[maɪr tiːn kaɪl iː 'gɔdi]
WELSH	**Roedd y tŷ yn cael ei godi.**
ENGLISH	The house was being / getting built.
IPA	[rɔɪð ə tiːn kaɪl iː 'gɔdi]

Here are the past inflected personal forms, using the infinitive **dal** 'to catch':

SENTENCE	ENGLISH	IPA
Ces i fy nal.	I was caught.	[keːs iː (v)ə nal]
Cest ti dy ddal.	You were caught. (*fam.*)	[keːs(t) tiː də ðal]
Cafodd e ei ddal. (SW)	He was caught.	['kavoð eː iː ðal]
Cafodd o ei ddal. (NW)	He was caught.	['kavoð oː iː ðal]
Cafodd hi ei dal.	She was caught.	['kavoð hiː iː dal]
Cawson ni ein dal.	We were caught.	['kaʊso(n) niː ən dal]
Cawsoch chi eich dal.	You were caught. (*pl.*) (*sing. formal*)	['kaʊso(χ) χiː əχ dal]
Cawson nhw eu dal.	They were caught.	['kaʊso(n) n̥u iː dal]

> **IMPORTANT**
> In the passive construction there is no affixed pronoun after the verb-noun, cf. **ei dad e** [iː dad eː] 'his father', but **cafodd ei ei ddal** 'he was caught' ['kavoð eː iː ðal].

Interrogatives follow the the same pattern as other past inflected verbs (see **Week 7, Lesson 3**):

QUESTION	ENGLISH	IPA
Gest ti dy ddal?	Were you caught? (*fam.*)	[geːs(t) tiː də ðal]

Here are some interrogatives you will find useful (remember that *any* verb-noun can be substituted for the ones used here):

QUESTION	ENGLISH	IPA
Pwy gafodd ei ladd?	Who was killed?	[pʊɪ 'gavoð iː laːð]
Beth gafodd ei ddweud?	What was said?	[beː(θ) 'gavoð iː ðwəɪd]
Ble cawsoch chi eich geni?	Where were you born?	[bleː 'kaʊso(χ) χiː əχ 'geni]
Pryd cawsoch chi eich geni?	When were you born?	[priːd 'kaʊso(χ) χiː əχ 'geni]

Since phrases containing a prefixed possessive pronoun, like 'my car', 'his bike', etc., are definite, the negative forms of the inflected passive contain **ddim o** (see **Week 10, Lesson 4**):

SENTENCE	ENGLISH	IPA
Ches i ddim o (fy) nal.	I wasn't caught.	[ˈχeːs i ðɪm oː (v)ə nal]
Chest ti ddim o dy ddal.	You weren't caught. (*fam.*)	[ˈχeːs(t) ti ðɪm oː də ðal]
Chafodd e ddim o'i ddal. (SW)	He wasn't caught.	[ˈχaˑvoð eː ðɪm ɔi ðal]
Chafodd o ddim o'i ddal. (NW)	He wasn't caught.	[ˈχaˑvoð oː ðɪm ɔi ðal]
Chafodd hi ddim o'i dal.	She wasn't caught.	[ˈχaˑvoð hiː ðɪm ɔi dal]
Chawson ni ddim o'n dal.	We weren't caught.	[ˈχausо(n) niː ðɪm oːn dal]
Chawsoch chi ddim o'ch dal.	You weren't caught. (*pl.*) (*sing. formal*)	[ˈχausо(χ) χiː ðɪm oːχ dal]
Chawson nhw ddim o'u dal.	They weren't caught.	[ˈχausо(n) n̥uː ðɪm ɔi dal]

> **IMPORTANT**
> The third person singular **chafodd (...) ddim o'i (...)** [ˈχaˑvoð (...) ðɪm ɔi (...)] is used when the subject is a singular or plural noun:
>
> **Chafodd Siôn ddim o'i ddal.**
> [ˈχaˑvoð ʃoːn ðɪm ɔi ðal]
>
> **Chafodd y plant ddim o'u ddal.**
> [ˈχaˑvoð ə plant ðɪm ɔi dal]

Vocabulary

MASCULINE NOUN	ENGLISH	IPA	PLURAL FORM	IPA
gofid	worry / sorrow	[ˈgɔvɪd]	**gofidiau**	[gɔˈvɪdjɛ]
cyfarfod	meeting	[kəˈvarvod]	**cyfarfodydd**	[kəvarˈvɔdɪð]

ADJECTIVE	ENGLISH	IPA
trist	sad	[tɹɪst]

VERB-NOUN	ENGLISH	IPA	STEM	IPA
lladd	to kill	[ɬaːð]	**lladd-**	[ɬaˑð]
anafu	to injure	[anˈɑvi]	**anaf-**	[anˈɑv]

PREPOSITION	ENGLISH	IPA
hyd nes	until	[hiːd nɛs]

ADVERBIAL	ENGLISH	IPA
yn syth	straightaway / straight	[ən siːθ]

Dialogue

Welsh Dialogue

Ann: Pam mae Stryd y Farchad ar gau?
Richard: Buodd ddamwain gas yno y bore 'ma. Cafodd dyn ei ladd, a chafodd dau o bobl eu hanafu. Clywais i'r newyddion ar y radio. Cafodd yr heol ei chau bron yn syth ar ôl i'r heddlu gyrraedd.
Ann: Am newyddion trist! Ydy'r bobl wedi cael eu henwi eto?
Richard: Nac ydyn. Chân nhw mo'u henwi hyd nes i'r heddlu ddweud wrth eu teulu.
Ann: Mae ein gofidiau ni'n fach, Richard.
Richard: Ydyn, wir.

English Translation

Ann: Why is Market Street closed?
Richard: There was a nasty accident there this morning. A man was killed, and two people were injured. I heard the news on the radio. The road was closed almost straight after the police arrived.
Ann: What sad news! Have the people been named yet?
Richard: No. They won't be named until the police tell their families.
Ann: Our sorrows are small, Richard.
Richard: Yes, indeed.

Exercise 1

Complete the following sentences with the appropriate prefixed possessive pronoun and verb-noun.

For example:

Question: Cafodd y siop _____ (The shop was opened.)
Answer: Cafodd y siop ei hagor.

1) Mae'r golau'n cael _____. (The fire is being lit.)
2) Mae'r cyfarfod yn cael _____. (The meeting is being held.)
3) Cawson nhw _____. (They were accepted.)
4) Gawsoch chi _____? (Were you chosen?)
5) Chaiff o ddim _____. (It won't get done.)
6) Cafodd y tân _____. (The fire was lit.)
7) Cafodd y plant _____. (The children were taught.)
8) Cawson nhw _____. (They were excused.)
9) Cawson ni _____. (We were named.)
10) Ces i _____ ar gyfer y swydd. (I was turned down for the job.)

Lesson 5: The relative clause

We have already come across the relative forms of the irregular verb '**bod**' (see **Week 8, Lesson 2**). In the case of regular verbs, the relative clause is formed as follows:

	ANTECEDENT (SUBJECT)	RELATIVE PARTICLE (+ SOFT MUTATION)	RELATIVE CLAUSE
WELSH	y tîm	a	enillodd
ENGLISH	the team	that	won
IPA	[ə tiːm]	(ä)	ɛnˈɬoð]

Compare this example with:

	MUTATED PHRASE	VERB PRE-MUTATION
WELSH	(...) y bachgen a bwdodd	pwdu
ENGLISH	(...) the boy who sulked	to sulk
IPA	[ə ˈbaχgɛn ä ˈbʊdoð]	[ˈpʊdi]
WELSH	(...) y merched a ganodd	canu
ENGLISH	(...) the girls who sang	to sing
IPA	[ə ˈmɛrχɛd ä ˈgɑˈnoð]	[ˈkɑˈni]
WELSH	(...) y tîm a fydd yn ennill	bydd
ENGLISH	(...) the team that will win	to be (future)
IPA	[ə tiːm ä viːð ən ˈɛnɪɬ]	[biːð]

The relative particle **a** [ä] is usually omitted in spoken Welsh, but the mutation it causes remains. This is true when the antecedent of the relative clause is either the subject or the object of the verb:

(i) In the case of the subject:

	VERB	SUBJECT	RELATIVE PARTICLE	RELATIVE CLAUSE
WELSH	Cyrhaeddodd	y tîm	a	enillodd y cwpan.
IPA	[kərˈhəɪðoð	ə tiːm	ä	ɛnˈɬoð ə ˈkʊpan]

The above translates to: 'The team who won the cup arrived.'

(ii) In the case of the object:

	VERB	SUBJECT	RELATIVE PARTICLE	RELATIVE CLAUSE
WELSH	Gwelais i	'r dyn	a	enillodd y wobr.
IPA	[ˈgwɛlɛs iː	r diːn	ä	ɛnˈɬoð ə ˈwoˈbor]

The above translates to: 'I saw the man who won the prize.'

Vocabulary

ADVERBIAL	ENGLISH	IPA
llynedd	last year	[ˈɬənɛð]
yn barod	already	[ən ˈbɑrod]

MISCELLANEOUS	ENGLISH	IPA
p'un	which one (shortened form of **pa un**)	[piːn]

Exercise 1

Complete the following sentences by translating the underlined English text.

1) P'un ydy'r ferch <u>who specialises</u> mewn gwneud bara?

2) Dyna'r fenyw <u>who used to ring</u> 'r gloch ar gyfer cinio.

3) Ydych chi wedi cwrdd â fy nghyfnither <u>who had an accident</u> llynedd?

4) Beth ydy enw'r eli haul <u>which they used</u> ar eu gwyliau llynedd?

5) Bwytodd hi'r gacen <u>which her mother made</u>.

6) Oedden nhw'n cofio'r ffermwr <u>who would drive</u> ei dractor trwy'r dref?

7) Roedden ni'n credu'r stori <u>which they told everyone</u>.

8) Mae'r dillad <u>which you washed</u> yn y cwpwrdd.

9) Beth oedd y cwestiwn <u>which he asked you</u>?

10) Mae'r cwpanau <u>which I bought</u> yn y farchnad wedi torri yn barod.

Lesson 6: The oblique relative clause

The oblique relative clause is really an independent sentence joined to the main clause by the relative particle (link word) **y** [ə], which does *not* cause mutation. Below is an example of two sentences without the link word **y**:

	SENTENCE	SENTENCE
WELSH	Dyma'r dyn.	Mae pawb yn hoffi'r dyn.
ENGLISH	Here is the man.	Everyone likes the man.
IPA	['dəmär di:n]	[maɪ paʊb ən 'hɔfir di:n]

Now we connect them with **y**:

	MAIN CLAUSE	RELATIVE PARTICLE	RELATIVE CLAUSE
WELSH	Dyma'r dyn	y	mae pawb yn ei hoffi
ENGLISH	Here is the man	who	everyone likes
IPA	['dəmär di:n]		[maɪ paʊb yn i: 'hɔfi]

Above, **dyn** is the antecedent of the relative clause, and is represented in the relative clause by the prefixed possesive pronoun **ei**. The sentence can be translated as 'Here's the man who everyone likes'.

The oblique relative clause is used in the following contexts:

(i) where the antecedent takes the place of an adverbial phrase (usually words denoting time, place or reason):

CLAUSE	ENGLISH	IPA
y diwrnod y cyrhaeddais i	the day I arrived	[ə 'dɪʊrnod ə kər'haɪðɛs i:]
y lle y gadawon nhw	where (the place) they left	[ə ɬe: ə gad'aʊo(n) n̥u:]
y rheswm y ffonion nhw	the reason they telephoned	[ə 'r̥ɛsʊm ə 'fɔnjo(n) n̥u:]

Compare the above with:

CLAUSE	ENGLISH	IPA
y dyn a welodd y gêm	the man (subject) who saw the game	[ə di:n ä 'wɛloð ə ge:m]
y dyn a welais i	the man (object) I (subject) saw	[ə di:n ä 'wɛlɛs i:]

(ii) when a preposition ('on which', 'in which', etc.) is part of the relative clause:

	CLAUSE
WELSH	**y car y gweithiais i arno (fe)**
ENGLISH	the car on which I worked
IPA	[ə kar ə 'gwəɪθjes i: 'arno (ve:)]
WELSH	**yr ysgol y dysgon nhw ynddi (hi)**
ENGLISH	the school in which they taught/learnt.
IPA	[ər 'əsgol ə 'dəsgo(n) n̥u: 'ənði (hi:)]

(iii) when the relative clause is in the genitive state (corresponds to the English 'whose'):

	CLAUSE
WELSH	y dyn y gwelais i <u>ei frawd</u> e
ENGLISH	the man **whose brother** I saw (*lit.* the man I saw his brother)
IPA	[ə diːn ə ˈgwɛlɛs iː iː vraʊd eː]

WELSH	y rhieni y priododd <u>eu merch</u>
ENGLISH	the parents **whose daughter** got married (*lit.* the parents their daughter got married)
IPA	[ə r̥ˈjɛni ə priˈɔdɔð iː mɛrχ n̥uː]

> **IMPORTANT**
>
> In the examples above, **brawd** 'brother' [braʊd] and **merch** 'daughter' [mɛrχ] are nouns. In Welsh, verb-nouns like **eistedd** 'to sit' [ˈəɪstɛð], **cadeirio** 'to chair' [kadˈəɪrjo] and **coroni** 'to crown' [kɔrˈɔni], etc., can also behave like nouns:
>
> **y bardd y gwelais i ei goroni**
> the bard whose chairing I saw (*lit.* the bard I saw his chairing)
> [ə barð ə ˈgwɛlɛs iː iː gadˈəɪrjo]
>
> With the verb '**bod**', such relative clauses are expressed as below. Don't forget to include one of the aspectual markers, **yn** or **wedi** (see **Week 3, Lesson 2**):
>
> **y llyfr y mae Lowri yn ei ddarllen**   the book Lowri is reading
> [ə ɬəvr̩ ə maɪ ˈloʊri ən iː ˈðar̥ɬɛn]
>
> **y llyfr y mae Lowri wedi ei ddarllen**   the book Lowri has read
> [ə ɬəvr̩ ə maɪ ˈloʊri ˈwɛdi iː ˈðar̥ɬɛn]
>
> **y llyfr yr oedd Lowri yn ei ddarllen**   the book Lowri was reading
> [ə ɬəvr̩ ər ɔɪð ˈloʊri ən iː ˈðar̥ɬɛn]
>
> **y llyfr yr oedd Lowri wedi ei ddarllen**   the book Lowri had read
> [ə ɬəvr̩ ər ɔɪð ˈloʊri ˈwɛdi iː ˈðar̥ɬɛn]
>
> **y llyfr y bydd Lowri yn ei ddarllen**   the book Lowri will read
> [ə ɬəvr̩ ə biːð ˈloʊri ən iː ˈðar̥ɬɛn]
>
> **y llyfr y bydd Lowri wedi ei ddarllen**   the book Lowri will have read
> [ə ɬəvr̩ ə biːð ˈloʊri ˈwɛdi iː ˈðar̥ɬɛn]

In the examples above, the prefixed possessive pronoun **ei** [iː] refers back to the antecedent (**llyfr** in this case) and agrees with it with respect to number and gender; **llyfr** is a masculine singular noun, and so the pronoun is also masculine and singular – **ei** 'his', which causes the soft mutation. If the antecedent were a feminine singular noun, such as **ystafell** 'room' [əsˈtɑvɛɬ], the pronoun would also be feminine and singular – **ei** 'her', which causes the aspirate mutation:

	MUTATED PHRASE	VERB-NOUN PRE-MUTATION
WELSH	yr ystafell y mae Lowri yn ei **phaentio**	paentio
ENGLISH	the room Lowri is painting	painting
IPA	[ər əsˈtɑːvɛɬ ə maɪ ˈlouri ən iː ˈfəɪntjo]	[ˈpəɪntjo]

If the antecedent were a plural noun, the corresponding prefixed possessive pronoun would also be plural – **eu** 'their' [iː]:

	PHRASE
WELSH	y llyfrau y mae Lowri yn eu darllen
ENGLISH	the books Lowri is reading
IPA	[ə ɬəvrɛ ə maɪ ˈlouri ən iː ˈdarɬen]

WELSH	yr ystafelloedd y mae Lowri yn eu paentio
ENGLISH	the rooms Lowri is painting
IPA	[ər əstavˈɛɬɔɪð ə maɪ ˈlouri ən iː ˈpəɪntjo]

The same oblique construction is used in questions like:

	QUESTION
WELSH	Beth yr ydych chi'n ei wneud?
ENGLISH	What are you doing?
IPA	[beːθ ər ˈədɪ(χ) χiːn iː ʷnəɪd]

WELSH	Pwy y maen nhw'n ei gefnogi?
ENGLISH	Who do they support?
IPA	[pʊɪ ə maɪ(n) ņuːn iː gɛvˈnɔgi]

In spoken Welsh, the relative particle **y** and the prefixed possessive pronoun **ei** are not usually pronounced, but the mutations they cause are:

QUESTION	IPA
Be(th) dych chi'n (ei) (w)neud?	[beː(θ) də(χ) χiːn (iː) (ʷ)nəɪd]
Pwy (y) maen nhw'n (ei) gefnogi?	[pʊɪ (ə) maɪ(n) ņuːn (iː) gɛvˈnɔgi]

IMPORANT

The relative particle **a** is used with personal inflected forms of **cael** in the passive voice:

y dyn a gafodd ei eni ym Mangor   the man who was born in Bangor
[ə diːn a ˈgɑvoð iː ˈɛni əm ˈmaŋgor]
y parti a gaiff ei gynnal heno   the party that will be held tonight
[ə ˈparti a ˈgaɪf iː ˈgənal ˈhɛno]

Vocabulary

VERB-NOUN	ENGLISH	IPA	STEM	IPA
arbenigo	to specialise	[arbɛnˈigo]	**arbenig-**	[arbɛnˈig]
gyrru	to drive	[ˈgəri]	**gyrr-**	[gər]
golchi	to wash	[ˈgɔlχi]	**golch-**	[gɔlχ]

Exercise 1

Complete the following sentences by translating the underlined text from English to Welsh.

1) Mae'r dyn <u>whose sister lives in Egypt</u> yn mynd i siarad am y wlad honno heno.

2) Ydych chi'n cofio <u>the reason that they left</u>.

3) Mae'r ffilm <u>that you were talking about</u> yn cael ei dangos yn y sinema dros y penwythnos.

4) Cafodd e (SW)/o (NW) ei eni <u>the year that the rugby team won the cup</u>.

5) Ble mae'r esgidiau <u>that you were wearing</u>?

6) Mae'r dyn <u>that they attacked has died</u>.

7) Mae eisiau golchi'r dillad <u>which you were wearing</u>.

8) Mae'r dyn <u>whom you were smiling at</u> eisiau prynu diod i ti. (*fam.*)

9) Cafodd ei brawd hi ei anafu <u>the week she went on holiday</u>.

10) Roedd y gerddoriaeth <u>which you were listening to</u> yn uchel iawn.

11) Mae'r bobl <u>whose children were searching for their dog</u> wedi cynnig gwobr os bydd rhywun yn dod o hyd iddo fe (SW)/fo (NW).

12) Mae'r fenyw <u>whose husband painted the hall</u> wedi gofyn am ddau gan punt am y gwaith.

Vocabulary

MASCULINE NOUN	ENGLISH	IPA	PLURAL FORM	IPA
morgais	mortgage	['mɔrgaɪs]	morgeisi	[mɔr'gəɪsi]
trên	train	[tɹeːn]	trenau	['tɹeˑnɛ]
cwrs	course	[kʊrs]	cyrsiau (*llu.*)	['kərʃɛ]

FEMININE NOUN	ENGLISH	IPA	PLURAL FORM	IPA
cerddoriaeth	music	[kɛrð'ɔrjeθ]		
selsigen	sausage	[sɛl'siˑgɛn]	selsig	['sɛlsɪg]
coes	leg	[kɔɪs]	coesau	['kɔɪsɛ]
ras	race	[rɑːs]	rasys	['rasɪs]
Yr Aifft	Egypt	[ər aɪft]		

VERB-NOUN	ENGLISH	IPA	STEM	IPA
geni	to be born	['gɛni]		
(ad)nabod	to recognise (a person or place)	[(ad)'nɑˑbod]		
ymddiheuro	to apologise	[əmði'həɪro]	ymddiheur-	[əmði'həɪr]

ADJECTIVE	ENGLISH	IPA
clir	clear	[kliːr]

ADVERBIAL	ENGLISH	IPA
lle	where*	[ɬeː]

* *There are two words in Welsh for 'where':* **ble** [blɛː] *is used to ask a question, such as in* '**Ble aeth hi?**'; **lle** [ɬeː] *is used when you are not asking a question:*

	SENTENCE
WELSH	**Dyna'r tŷ lle maen nhw'n byw.**
ENGLISH	That's the house where they live.
IPA	['dənar tiː ɬeː maɪ(n) n̥uːn bɪʊ]

Lesson 7: Recap exercises

Exercise 1

Translate the following sentences.

1) I would be very sad if you left.

2) Would you (*fam.*) consider retiring?

3) He could have sent them an email.

4) They wouldn't like the weather in Egypt.

5) Would he be lonely?

6) I could have drunk another bottle(ful).

7) They would like to practise more before the exam.

8) The butcher could have made the sausages.

9) You could have told us yesterday.

10) You would blame us again.

If you have any problems completing this exercise, review **Week 11, Lesson 1** *and* **Lesson 2**.

Exercise 2

Mark the correct form of 'if' in the following sentences. The answers are lettered.

For example:

Question: Bydden nhw (SW)/Basen nhw (NW) wedi cwyno [(a) petai (SW)/tasai (NW); (b) os oedd] rhywbeth yn bod ar y bwyd.
Answer: (a)

1) Byddet ti (SW) /Baset ti (NW) wedi cyrraedd y rhestr fer [(a) petaech chi (SW)/tasech chi (NW); (b) os oeddet ti] wedi cynnig.
2) Af fi am dro y prynhawn 'ma [(a) petai hi'n (SW)/tasai hi'n (NW); (b) os bydd hi'n] braf.
3) Ewch â'r siwt yn ôl i'r siop [(a) pe na hoffech y; (b) os dych chi ddim yn hoffi'r] patrwm.
4) Byddwn i'n (SW)/Baswn i'n (NW) sylwi [(a) petai fe (SW)/tasai fo'n (NW); (b) os oedd o'n] torri ei wallt.
5) Bydden ni'n gyfoethog hefyd [(a) petaen ni'n (SW)/tasen ni'n (NW); (b) os oedden ni'n] perthyn iddyn nhw.

6) Pryna i gar newydd [(a) petawn i'n (SW)/taswn i'n (NW); (b) os bydda i'n llwyddo] yn fy mrawf gyrru i.
7) Byddwn i'n (SW)/Baswn i'n (NW) ymddeol [(a) petai dim morgais gyda fi (SW)/tasai gen i ddim morgais (NW); (b) os nad oedd morgais gyda fi (SW)/os nad oedd gen i forgais (NW).]
8) Byddwn i'n (SW)/Baswn i'n (NW) rhedeg yn y ras [(a) petawn i/taswn i ddim; (b) os doeddwn i ddim] wedi torri fy nghoes i.
9) Gallech chi weld arfordir Iwerddon [(a) petai hi'n (SW)/tasai hi'n; b) os oedd hi'n ddiwrnod clir].
10) Bydden ni'n (SW)/Basen ni'n (NW) gwneud ymarfer bob wythnos [(a) petai (SW)/tasai (NW); (b) os oedd] campfa yn y pentref.

Exercise 3

*Connect the problems under **A** with the advice under **B**.*

A
1) Mae cefn tost gyda fi (SW)/mae gen i boen cefn (NW).
2) Dydy hi ddim yn deall ei acen e (SW)/o (NW).
3) Dydy'r bara dw i newydd ei brynu ddim yn ffres.
4) Mae hi'n meddwl ei bod hi'n rhy gynnes yn yr ystafell.
5) Roedd y daith ar y trên yn hir iawn.
6) Mae ein plentyn ni ar goll.
7) Does dim arian gyda nhw (SW)/Does ganddyn nhw ddim pres (NW) ar ôl.
8) Mae'r bws yn hwyr.
9) Bydd hi'n bwrw glaw trwy'r dydd yfory.
10) Mae cywilydd arnyn nhw.
11) Mae eu blodau nhw'n marw.
12) Mae plant drwg yn dylanwadu ar ein merch ni.
13) Mae ei gefn e'n (SW)/o'n (NW) goch iawn.
14) Mae eu hesgidiau'n dyn iawn.
15) Mae o'n meddwl bod y diodydd yn y theatr yn ddrud iawn.

B
a) Dylet ti fod wedi hedfan.
b) Dylai hi newid ysgol.
c) Dylet ti fynd ag ymbarél.
d) Dylet ti fynd at y meddyg.
e) Dylen nhw ymddiheuro.
f) Dylen nhw gael pâr arall.
g) Dylen nhw fynd i'r banc.
h) Dylet ti gerdded.
i) Dylai fo fynd â fflasg.
j) Dylen nhw roi dŵr iddyn nhw.
k) Dylai hi agor y ffenestr.
l) Dylai fe (SW)/fo (NW) wedi gwisgo eli haul.
m) Dylech chi ffonio 999 ar unwaith.

n) Dylech chi fynd â fe (SW)/fo (NW) yn ôl i'r siop lle prynoch chi fe (SW)/fo (NW).
o) Dylai hi ofyn iddo siarad yn arafach.

If you have any difficulty completing this exercise, review **Week 11, Lesson 3**.

Exercise 4

Translate the following sentences.

1) The trainer was injured at the game. _____
2) The milk was spilt. _____
3) They were changed. _____
4) I was moved by the police. _____
5) Were you stopped? _____
6) She will be paid tomorrow. _____
7) Was he discussed in the meeting? _____
8) I wasn't considered. _____
9) The bottle was filled. _____
10) We weren't recognised. _____

Exercise 5

Give a 'yes' or 'no' response to the following questions / statements.

1) Hoffech chi gacen? (✓)*
   (Would you like a cake.)
   _____

2) Allai hi ganu'r anthem petai'r geiriau gyda hi/petasai ganddi hi'r geiriau? (✓)
   (Could she sing the anthem if she had the words?)
   _____

3) Fydden nhw'n (SW)/Fasen nhw'n (NW) apelio atoch chi? (✗)
   (Would they appeal to you?)
   _____

4) Gawsoch chi eich geni yng Nghymru? (✗)
   (Were you born in Wales?)
   _____

5) Allen ni fod wedi gwella'r llun? (✗)*
   (Could we have improved the picture?)
   _____

6) Hoffet ti deithio'r byd? (✗)
   (Would you like to travel the world?)
   _____

7) Ddylwn i ofyn iddyn nhw? (✗)*

(Should I ask them?)

8) Dylech chi roi'r gorau i smocio. (✓)
(Should you give up smoking?)

* Each of these questions has two possible answers.

If you have any difficulty completing this exercise, review **Week 11, Lesson 1** *to* **Lesson 5**.

Exercise 6

Translate the following sentences.

1) Did you know the man whose grand-daughter won the first prize?

2) The bedroom he had painted looks lovely.

3) My children still play with the toys my grandfather made for them.

4) I met them the day we moved to the village.

5) The clothes which he bought suit him.

6) The railway which he worked on has closed now.

7) That is something that I should have done.

8) The man whose car was in the accident has to do a driving course.

If you have any difficulty completing this exercise, review **Week 11, Lesson 5** *to* **Lesson 6**.

Week 12

Lesson 1: Defective verbs

Defective verbs are those which do not possess the full range of tenses and / or personal forms. We have already come across 'should' / 'ought to' (see **Week 11, Lesson 4**), which is restricted to the subjunctive mood. There are a number of verbs in Welsh which are even more restricted:

'Meddai' (said)
Meddai means 'said' and is used in quotative, or reported, speech:

	REPORTED SPEECH
WELSH	"Dw i'n mynd nawr," meddai fe.
ENGLISH	"I'm going now," he said.
IPA	[dwiːn mɪnd naʊr 'meˑðɛ veː]
WELSH	"Fi oedd e (SW) / o (NW)," meddwn i.
ENGLISH	"It was me," I said.
IPA	[viː ɔɪð eː 'meˑðʊn iː]

Here are the personal forms of '**meddai**':

PHRASE	ENGLISH	IPA
meddwn i	I said	['meˑðʊn iː]
meddet ti	you said (*fam.*)	['meˑðɛ(t) tiː]
meddai fe (SW)	he said	['meˑðɛ veː]
meddai fo (NW)	he said	['meˑðɛ voː]
meddai hi	she said	['meˑðɛ hiː]
medden ni	we said	['meˑðɛ(n) niː]
meddech chi	you said (*pl.*) (*sing. formal*)	['meˑðɛ(χ) χiː]
medden nhw	they said	['meˑðɛ(n) n̥uː]

> **IMPORTANT**
> Remember the third person singular **meddai** ['meˑðɛ] is used when the subject is a singular or plural noun.

'Geni' (to be born)
The verb '**geni**' 'to be born' ['gɛni] only occurs in impersonal forms like **ganwyd** 'was born' ['ganʊɪd] (see **Week 12, Lesson 5**), and in the passive construction (see **Week 11, Lesson 4**).

For example:

	SENTENCE
WELSH	**Ces i (f)y ngeni yn Ne Cymru.**
ENGLISH	I was born in South Wales.
IPA	[keːs iː (v)ə 'ŋeni ən neː 'kəmri]

WELSH	**Cafodd Dafydd ei eni yng Ngogledd Cymru.**
ENGLISH	Dafydd was born in North Wales.
IPA	['kaˑvoð 'daˑvɪð iː 'ɛni ə(ŋ) 'ŋɔglɛð 'kəmri]

Exercise 1

Change the following sentences from reported speech to quotative speech.

For example:

Question: Dwedodd e (SW)/o (NW) ein bod ni ar goll.
Answer: "Dyn ni ar goll," meddai fe (SW) / fo (NW).

1) Dwedais i fy mod i'n trïo ymlacio.
   (I said I was trying to relax.)
   _____

2) Dwedon nhw y bydden nhw'n (SW)/basen nhw'n (NW) ymddiheuro wrthon ni.
   (They said that they would apologise to us.)
   _____

3) Dwedodd ei chymar hi fod eisiau bwyd arno fe (SW) / fo (NW).
   (Her partner said that he was hungry.)
   _____

4) Dwedaist ti ei fod e (SW) / o (NW) wedi gafael ynddot ti.
   (He said that he had grabbed you.)
   _____

5) Dwedon ni dy fod ti'n poeni gormod.
   (We said that you worry too much.)
   _____

6) Dwedodd hi y ceith hi selsig a wyau i frecwast.
   (She said that she will have sausages and eggs for breakfast.)
   _____

7) Dwedoch chi fod ganddi hi gariad newydd.
   (You said that she had a new boyfriend.)
   _____

8) Dwedodd y meddyg y bydda i'n gwella.
   (The doctor said that I will get better.)
   _____

Vocabulary

MASCULINE NOUN	ENGLISH	IPA	PLURAL FORM	IPA
cariad	boyfriend / girlfriend / sweetheart	['karjad]	cariadon	[karˈjɑˑdon]

Lesson 2: 'Gwneud' as an auxiliary verb

As we saw in **Week 9, Lesson 3**, **'gwneud'** 'to do' / 'to make' [gʷnəɪd] is often used as an auxiliary verb in the future tense, especially with interrogatives and negatives:

SENTENCE	ENGLISH	IPA
Wneith e (SW) / o (NW) wrando?	Will he listen?	[ʷnəɪθ eː / oː ʷrändo]
Wnân nhw ddim mynd.	They won't go.	[ʷnɑː(n) n̥uː ðɪm mɪnd]

'Gwneud' can, in fact, be used as an auxiliary verb to form the past tense also. This is particularly true in North Wales.

Here are examples of the past tense:

SENTENCE	ENGLISH	IPA
Gwnes i alw.	I called. (*lit.* I did call.)	[gʷneːs i ˈɑˑlʊ]
Gwnaethon nhw ateb.	They answered.	[ˈgʷnəɪθo(n) n̥uː ˈatɛb]

Here are examples of the future tense:

	SENTENCE
WELSH	**Gwnaf fi barcio'r car.**
ENGLISH	I will park the car.
IPA	[gʷnɑː(v) viː ˈbarkjor kar]

WELSH	**Gwnân nhw sylwi arni hi.**
ENGLISH	They will notice her.
IPA	[gʷnɑː(n) n̥uː ˈsəlwi ˈärni hiː]

The use of **'gwneud'** as an auxiliary verb in this way is down to personal preference, and there is no difference in meaning between structures such as **gwneith e** (SW) / **o** (NW) **deithio** 'he will travel' [gʷnəɪθ eː / oː ˈdəɪθjo] and **teithith e** (SW) / **o** (NW) 'he will travel' [ˈtəɪθɪθ eː / oː].

Exercise 1

*Rewrite the following sentences by substituting the underlined words for a verb form which uses **gwneud** as an auxiliary verb.*

For example:

Question: Wisgodd hi ddim gwregys.
Answer: Wnaeth hi ddim gwisgo gwregys.

For example:

Question: Wela i mo'r gêm heno.
Answer: Wna i ddim gweld y gêm heno.

1) Ymwelais i ddim â fy nhad-cu/nhaid i.
   (I didn't visit my grandfather.)

2) Ddarllenodd hi mo'r nofel.
   (She didn't read the novel.)

3) Cyrhaeddwn ni yn brydlon.
   (We won't arrive punctually.)

4) Neidiaist ti dros y ffens.
   (You jumped over the fence.)

5) Golchoch chi'r ffenest(r).
   (You washed the window.)

6) Dderbynith o ddim byd. (NW)
   (He won't accept anything.)

7) Thorrodd o mo'i goes. (NW)
   (He didn't break his leg.)

8) Welith neb mo'r ddrama.
   (No-one will see the play.)

Vocabulary

FEMININE NOUN	ENGLISH	IPA	PLURAL FORM	IPA
nofel	novel	[ˈnɔvɛl]	**nofelau**	[nɔvˈɛlɛ]
ffens	fence	[fɛns]	**ffensys**	[ˈfɛnsɪs]

VERB-NOUN	ENGLISH	IPA	STEM	IPA
ymweld â	to visit	[ˈəmwɛld ä]	**ymwel- â** (AM)	[əmˈwɛl ä]

The use of 'gwneud' to emphasise verb-nouns

'**Gwneud**' can also be used to emphasise a verb-noun, as in the examples below:

	SENTENCE WITHOUT EMPHASIS	SENTENCE WITH EMPHASIS
WELSH	**Nofiodd e** (SW) / **o** (NW). **Gwnaeth e** (SW) / **o** (NW) **nofio.**	*Nofio* **wnaeth e** (SW) / **o** (NW).
ENGLISH	He swam.	He *swam*.

	IPA	['nɔvjoð eː / ɔː] / [gʷnaɪθ eː / ɔː 'nɔvjo]	['nɔvjo ʷnaɪθ eː / ɔː]
	WELSH	**Cysga i. / Gwnaf fi gysgu.**	***Cysgu* wnaf fi.**
	ENGLISH	I will sleep.	I will *sleep*.
	IPA	['kəsga iː] [gʷnaː(v) viː 'gəsgi]	['kəsgi ʷna(v) viː]

		QUESTION WITHOUT EMPHASIS	REPLY WITH EMPHASIS
	WELSH	**Arhosodd Gareth?**	**Naddo, *gadael* wnaeth e** (SW) / **o** (NW).
	ENGLISH	Did Gareth stay?	No, he *left*. (*lit.* left he did.)
	IPA	[arˈhɔsoð 'gareθ]	['naˑðo 'gadɛl ʷnaɪθ eː / ɔː]
	WELSH	**Beth wnaeth Ross?**	***Cwyno* wnaeth e** (SW) / **o** (NW).
	ENGLISH	What did Ross do?	He *complained*.
	IPA	[beːθ ʷnaɪθ rɔs]	['kʊɪno ʷnaɪθ eː / ɔː]

You may find it helpful to think of **nofio wnaeth e** (SW) / **o** (NW) as translating to 'swam he did'. In English, it is usual to emphasise by raising the tone of the voice, whereas in Welsh whatever you wish to emphasise comes first in the sentence.

Exercise 2

Rewrite the following sentences to imply emphasis.

For example:

Question: Cwynais i.
Answer: Cwyno wnes i.

1) Breuddwydiais i.
   (I dreamt.)

2) Dadleuodd e (SW)/o (NW).
   (He argued.)

3) Yfwn ni.
   (We will drink.)

4) Gwaeddon nhw.
   (They shouted.)

5) Llwyddaist ti.
   (You succeeded.)

6) Symudodd hi.
   (She moved.)

7) Gofynnais i.
   (I asked.)

8) Safoch chi.
   (You stood.)

Lesson 3: Emphatic sentences

As we have seen, sentences in Welsh generally start with a verb (See **Week 3, Lesson 1**).

SENTENCE	ENGLISH	IPA
Dw i ar y trên.	I am on the train.	[dwiː ar y tɹeːn]
Roedd hi'n canu.	She was singing.	[rɔið hiːn ˈkɑni]

However, the order of a sentence changes when the speaker wishes to emphasise a word or words; the emphasised words come first (see **Week 12, Lesson 2**):

SENTENCE	ENGLISH	IPA
Ar y trên dw i.	I am <u>on the train</u>.	[ar ə tɹeːn dwiː]
Canu roedd hi.	She was <u>singing</u>.	[ˈkɑni rɔið hi]

In Welsh, any part of the sentence can be placed first in order to emphasise it. Sentences in which a stressed element comes first are called emphatic sentences.

Here is an example using an adjective:

	NEUTRAL SENTENCE	EMPHATIC SENTENCE
WELSH	**Maen nhw'n flasus.**	**Blasus ydyn nhw.**
ENGLISH	They are tasty.	They are <u>tasty</u>.
IPA	[maɪ(n) n̥uːn ˈvlasɪs]	[ˈblasɪs ˈədɪ(n) n̥uː]

Here is an example using a noun

	NEUTRAL SENTENCE	EMPHATIC SENTENCE
WELSH	**Mae Iwan yn blismon.**	**Plismon ydy Iwan.**
ENGLISH	Iwan is a policeman.	Iwan is a <u>policeman</u>..
IPA	[maɪ ˈɪʊan ən ˈblɪsmon]	[ˈplɪsmon ydy ˈɪʊan]

Even though these sentences are emphatic, they follow the pattern of identification sentences (see **Week 2, Lesson 4**)

Here is an example using an adverbial which which begins with a preposition (**wrth**):

	NEUTRAL SENTENCE	EMPHATIC SENTENCE
WELSH	**Bydd hi wrth y drws.**	**Wrth y drws (y) bydd hi.**
ENGLISH	She will be by the door.	She will be <u>by the door</u>.
IPA	[biːð hiː ʊrθ ə dɹuːs]	[ʊrθ ə dɹuːs (ə) biːð hiː]

Here is an example using a verb-noun:

	NEUTRAL SENTENCE	EMPHATIC SENTENCE
WELSH	Byddan nhw'n cwyno.	Cwyno (y) byddan nhw.
ENGLISH	They will complain.	They will <u>complain</u>.
IPA	[ˈbəða(n) n̥uːn ˈkʊɪno]	[ˈkʊɪno (ə) ˈbəða(n) n̥u]

Here is an example using an adverb:

	NEUTRAL SENTENCE	EMPTHATIC SENTENCE
WELSH	Mae'r cyfarfod yfory.	Yfory (y) mae'r cyfarfod.
ENGLISH	The meeting is tomorrow.	The meeting is <u>tomorrow</u>.
IPA	[maɪr kəvˈarvod (ə)vˈɔri]	[(ə)vˈɔri (ə) maɪr kəvˈarvod]

These sentences follow the pattern of the oblique relative clause (see **Week 11, Lesson 6**) and so the oblique relative particle **y** comes between the part of the sentence which is emphasised and the rest of the sentence:

	PART OF THE SENTENCE WHICH IS EMPHASISED	RELATIVE PARTICLE	REST OF THE SENTENCE
WELSH	**Wrth y drws**	y	bydd hi.
ENGLISH	by the door		She will be.
IPA	[ʊrθ ə dɹuːs]	ə	biːð hi]

However, the relative particle is rarely heard in everyday speech, and so it appears in brackets in the examples given above.

Vocabulary

ADJECTIVE	ENGLISH	IPA
diflas	miserable	[ˈdɪvlas]

ADVERBIAL	ENGLISH	IPA
ganol nos	at midnight	[ˈgɑˑnol noːs]

Exercise 1

Translate the following sentences, emphasising the element underlined.

1) She is <u>glad/proud</u>. _____
2) They went <u>last year</u>. _____
3) She is <u>locking the door</u>. _____
4) They arrived home <u>at midnight</u>. _____
5) They were <u>feeding the cat</u>. _____
6) They are <u>under the table</u>. _____

7) It's <u>miserable</u>. _____

8) I saw them <u>every day</u>. _____

In formal, written contexts, the emphasised element is followed by the oblique relative particle **y** (**yr** before vowels):

	SENTENCE
WELSH	**Ddydd Llun yr aethon ni.**
ENGLISH	We went *on* <u>Monday</u>.
IPA	[ði:ð ɬi:n ər 'əɪθon ni]

WELSH	**Llynedd y cawson ni eira mawr.**
ENGLISH	We had a lot of snow <u>last year</u>.
IPA	['ɬəneð ə 'kaʊso(n) ni: 'əɪrä maʊr]

Emphasising the subject or object of a sentence

When emphasising the subject (the person or thing doing the action of a verb) or object (the person or thing receiving the action of a verb) of a sentence, the subject / object comes first. When emphasising the subject, the verb is always in the third person singular (the form used with **e** [SW] / **o** [NW] and **hi**). In formal written contexts, the direct relative particle **a** [ä] (which causes the soft mutation) is used. This is not usually pronounced in everyday speech, but the soft mutation it causes remains. The affixed pronouns **i** and **e** (SW) / o (NW) become the independent pronouns **fi** and **fe** (SW) / **fo** (NW).

In the examples below, the subject is emphasised:

	SENTENCE	EMPTHATIC SENTENCE
WELSH	**Cyrhaeddais i'n hwyr.**	<u>Fi</u> (a) gyrhaeddodd yn hwyr.
ENGLISH	I arrived late.	<u>I</u> arrived late.
IPA	[kər'həɪðes i:n hʊɪr]	[vi: (ä) gər'həɪðoð ən hʊɪr]

WELSH	**Byddwn ni gartre(f).**	<u>Ni</u> (a) fydd gartre(f).
ENGLISH	We will be at home.	<u>We</u> will be at home.
IPA	['bəðʊ(n) ni: 'gartɹe(v)]	[ni: ä vi:ð 'gartɹe(v)]

WELSH	**Roeddet ti'n astudio.**	<u>Ti</u> (a) oedd yn astudio.
ENGLISH	You were studying. (*fam.*)	<u>You</u> were studying. (*fam.*)
IPA	['rɔɪðe(t) ti:n as'tɪdjo]	[ti: (ä) ɔɪð ən as'tɪdjo]

WELSH	**Enillodd yr hyfforddwr.**	<u>Yr hyfforddwr</u> (a) enillodd.
ENGLISH	The trainer won.	<u>The trainer</u> won.
IPA	[en'ɬoð ər həfɔrðʊr]	[ər həfɔrðʊr (ä) ɛn'ɬoð]

In the examples below, the object is emphasised:

	SENTENCE	EMPHATIC SENTENCE
WELSH	Prynon nhw bapur.	Papur (a) brynon nhw.
ENGLISH	They bought a paper.	They bought a paper.
IPA	['prəno(n) ṇuː 'bapɪr]	['papɪr (ä) 'brəno(n) ṇuː]
WELSH	Dalia i bysgodyn mawr.	Pysgodyn mawr (a) ddalia i.
ENGLISH	I will catch a big fish.	I will catch a big fish.
IPA	['dalja i bəs'gɔdɪn maʊr]	[pəs'gɔdɪn maʊr (ä) 'ðalja i]
WELSH	Cawson nhw wydraid o win.	Gwydraid o win (a) gawson nhw.
ENGLISH	They had a glass of wine.	They had a glass of wine.
IPA	['kaʊso(n) ṇuː 'wɪdrɛd oː wiːn]	['gwɪdrɛd oː wiːn (a) 'gaʊso(n) ṇuː]

When emphasising the subject in the present tense, the relative present form of '**bod**', namely **sy'** [siː] **is used** before a consonant and **sydd** [siːð] before a vowel (see **Week 4, Lesson 4**).

	SENTENCE	EMPHATIC SENTENCE
WELSH	Dw i'n rhedeg.	Fi sy'n rhedeg.
ENGLISH	I am running.	I am running.
IPA	[dwiːn 'ɹɛdɛg]	[viː siːn 'ɹɛdɛg]
WELSH	Maen nhw ar bwys y ddesg.	Nhw sydd ar bwys y desg.
ENGLISH	They are near the desk.	They are near the desk.
IPA	[maɪ(n) ṇuː ar bʊɪs ə ðɛsg]	[ṇuː siːð ar bʊɪs ə ðɛsg]

Negating an emphatic sentence

Emphatic sentences are negated by placing the negative particle **nid** [nɪd] in front of the emphasised element:

	SENTENCE	EMPHATIC SENTENCE
WELSH	Fi (a) ddaeth yn hwyr.	Nid fi (a) ddaeth yn hwyr.
ENGLISH	I came late.	I didn't come late.
IPA	[viː (ä) ðaɪθ ən hʊɪr]	[nɪd viː (ä) ðaɪθ ən hʊɪr]
WELSH	Ar y bwrdd (y) mae'r deisen.	Nid ar y bwrdd (y) mae'r deisen.
ENGLISH	The cake isn't on the table.	The cake isn't on the table.
IPA	[ar ə bʊrð (ə) maɪr 'gakɛn]	[nɪd ar ə bʊrð (ə) maɪr 'gakɛn]
WELSH	Chwerthin (a) wnaeth e (SW) / o (NW).	Nid chwerthin (a) wnaeth e (SW) / o (NW).
ENGLISH	He laughed.	He didn't laugh.
IPA	['χwɛrθɪn (ä) ʷnaɪθ eː / oː]	[nɪd 'χwɛrθɪn (ä) ʷnaɪθ eː / oː]

Vocabulary

FEMININE NOUN	ENGLISH	IPA	PLURAL FORM	IPA
wal	wall	[wal]	**welydd**	['wɛlɪð]

VERB-NOUN	ENGLISH	IPA	STEM	IPA
chwerthin	to laugh	['χwɛrθɪn]	**chwardd-**	[χwarð]

Exercise 2

Rewrite the following sentences, emphasising the underlined element.

1) Darllenais i nofel.
   (I read a novel.)

2) Darllenais i ddim nofel.
   (I didn't read a novel.)

3) Maen nhw'n fywiog.
   (They are lively.)

4) Byddwn ni'n yfed dŵr.
   (We will be drinking water.)

5) Roeddech chi'n dadlau.
   (You were arguing.)

6) Dydy'r gadair ddim yn erbyn y wal.
   (The chair isn't against the door.)

7) Gwnaf fi frechdan.
   (I will make a sandwich.)

8) Byddan nhw'n hyderus am ennill.
   (They will be confident about winning.)

9) Rwyt ti'n yfed cwrw.
   (You are drinking beer.)

10) Ciciodd yr hyfforddwr bêl.
    (The trainer kicked a ball.)

11) Cytunon ni i faddau iddyn nhw.
    (They agreed to forgive them.)

12) Newidiais i ddim sianel.
    (I didn't switch channels.)

Lesson 4: The use of 'piau' to indicate possession

Piau ['pi·aɪ] is only used in emphatic sentences like:

SENTENCE	ENGLISH	IPA
Pwy sy' biau'r llyfr (y)ma?	Who owns this book?	[pʊɪ siː ˈbiˑaɪr ˈləvr̩ (ə)mä]
Fi sy' biau fe.	It's mine.	[viː siː ˈbiˑaɪ veː]
Fo oedd biau'r moddion. (NW)	He owned the medicine.	[voː ɔið ˈbiˑaɪr ˈmɔðjon]
Hi fydd biau'r tŷ.	She will own the house.	[hiː viːð ˈbiˑaɪr tiː]

Piau functions as a means of identifying who owns something. To ask a question using **piau** in everyday speech, one only needs to inflect the sentence to make it sound like a question:

	SENTENCE
WELSH	**Ti sy' biau popeth?**
ENGLISH	Do you own everything? / Is it you who owns everything?
IPA	[tiː siː ˈbiˑaɪ ˈpɔpɛθ]

In formal written contexts, **ai** is used:

QUESTION	ENGLISH	IPA
Ai ti sy' biau popeth?	Do *you* own everything?	[aɪ tiː siː ˈbiˑaɪ ˈpɔpɛθ]
Ai fe (SW) / fo (NW) sy' biau'r radio?	Does *he* own the radio?	[aɪ veː siː ˈbiˑaɪr ˈradjo]

Vocabulary

FEMININE NOUN	ENGLISH	IPA	PLURAL FORM	IPA
fan	van	[van]	**faniau**	[ˈvanjɛ]

Exercise 1

*Rewrite the following sentences to use **piau**.*

For example:

Question: Mae'r bwyd yn perthyn iddyn nhw.
(The food belongs to them.)
Answer: Nhw sy' biau'r bwyd.
(They own the food.)

1) Roedd y radio yn perthyn i ti.
(The radio belonged to you.)

_____

2) Doedd yr oergell ddim yn perthyn iddo fe (SW)/fo (NW).
(The fridge didn't belong to him.)

_____

3) Bydd yr adeiladau'n perthyn i'r cwmni.
   (The buildings will belong to the company.)

4) Mae'r garafán yn perthyn i fy rhieni i.
   (The caravan belongs to my parents.)

5) Mae'r fan yn perthyn i'r swyddfa bost.
   (The van belongs to the post office.)

6) Fydd y traeth ddim yn perthyn i'r gwesty.
   (The beach won't belong to the hotel.)

7) Mae'r ymbarél yn perthyn i ni.
   (The umbrella belongs to us.)

8) Mae'r maes parcio'n perthyn i'r capel.
   (The car park belongs to the chapel.)

9) Dyn nhw ddim yn perthyn i ni.
   (They don't belong to us.)

10) Mae'r esgidiau'r perthyn iddyn nhw.
    (The shoes belong to them.)

Lesson 5: Impersonal forms of the verb

Throughout this course, we have listed all the inflected verb forms except one – the impersonal inflection. The reason for this is that impersonal forms of the verb are not common in everyday speech (with the notable exception of the past impersonal form). However, they occur very frequently in written Welsh, and are used quite extensively in the mass media of television and radio. Below are the different impersonal inflections using **canu** 'to sing' [ˈkaˑni], the stem of which is **can-** [kaˑn].

These deal with the indicative mood:

SENTENCE	ENGLISH	IPA	TENSE / ASPECT
Cenir y gân.	The song is sung / will be sung.	[ˈkɛnɪr ə gaːn]	present / future
Canwyd y gân.	The song was sung.	[ˈkaˑnʊɪd ə gaːn]	simple past
Cenid y gân.*	The song would be sung.	[ˈkɛnɪd ə gaːn]	past habitual
Canasid y gân.*	The song had been sung.	[kanˈasɪd ə gaːn]	past perfect

* *The past habitual and the past perfect are purely literary forms and are almost <u>never</u> heard in everyday speech.*

Here is an example of the conditional, which again is vary rarely heard in everyday speech:

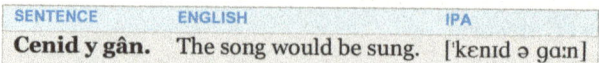

SENTENCE	ENGLISH	IPA
Cenid y gân.	The song would be sung.	[ˈkɛnɪd ə gɑːn]

The **i** in the present / future and past habitual / conditional inflections causes the **a** in the stem of the verb to become **e**. This change is known as affection.

Here is a list of the impersonal forms of irregular verbs. You should always remember that these are *written* rather than spoken forms:

	VERB-NOUN	PRESENT / FUTURE	PAST	PAST HABITUAL / CONDITIONAL
WELSH	bod	ydys	buwyd	byddid
IPA	[boːd]	[ˈədɪs]	[ˈbɪʊɪd]	[ˈbəðɪd]
WELSH	mynd	eir	aethpwyd	eid
IPA	[mɪnd]	[əɪr]	[ˈəɪθpʊɪd]	[əɪd]
WELSH	dod	deuir	daethpwyd	deuid
IPA	[doːd]	[ˈdəɪ.ɪr]	[ˈdəɪθpʊɪd]	[ˈdəɪ.ɪd]
WELSH	gwneud	gwneir	gwnaethpwyd	gwneid
IPA	[gʷnəɪd]	[gʷnəɪr]	[ˈgʷnəɪθpʊɪd]	[gʷnəɪd]
WELSH	cael	ceir	cafwyd	ceid
IPA	[kaɪl]	[kəɪr]	[ˈkɑˑvʊɪd]	[kəɪd]
WELSH	gwybod	gwyddys	gwybuwyd	gwybyddid
IPA	[ˈgwɪˑbod]	[ˈgwədɪs]	[gwəˈbɪʊɪd]	[gwəˈbəðɪd]
WELSH	adnabod	adwaenir	adnabuwyd	adweinid
IPA	[adˈnabod]	[adˈwəɪnɪr]	[adnaˈbɪʊɪd]	[adˈwəɪnɪd]
WELSH	dylai*			dylid
IPA	[ˈdəlai]			[ˈdəlɪd]

* '*Dylai*' is in fact the 3. pers. sing. form; there is no verb-noun in modern Welsh that corresponds to 'should'.

The direct object of the impersonal form of the verb is *not* mutated:

	SENTENCE
WELSH	Cyhoeddwyd llyfr ar hanes Cymru.
ENGLISH	A book was published on Welsh history.
IPA	[kəˈhɔɪðʊɪd ɬəvr̩ ar ˈhanɛs ˈkəmri]

WELSH	Anafwyd bachgen mewn damwain car.
ENGLISH	A boy was injured in a car accident.
IPA	[anˈɑvʊɪd ˈbäχgɛn mɛʊn ˈdamwɛn kar]

In the exercises, we will concentrate on the present / future and past forms, as they are the ones most widely used.

Present and future tense

As you can see from the tables above, in the present and future tense **-ir** [ɪr] is added to the stem. The impersonal forms can be considered as a more literary way of expressing the passive voice (see **Week 11, Lesson 4**):

Ysgrifennir adroddiad. = **Mae adroddiad yn cael ei ysgrifennu.**
A report is being written.   A report is being written.
[əsgrɪvˈɛnɪr adˈrɔðjad]   [maɪ adˈrɔðjad ən kaɪl iː əsgrɪvˈɛni]

Ysgrifennir adroddiad. = **Bydd adroddiad yn cael ei ysgrifennu.**
A report will be written.   A report will be written.
[əsgrɪvˈɛnɪr adˈrɔðjad]   [biːð adˈrɔðjad ən kaɪl iː əsgrɪvˈɛni]

Ysgrifennir adroddiad. = **Ceith adroddiad ei ysgrifennu.**
A report will be written.   A report will be written.
[əsgrɪvˈɛnɪr adˈrɔðjad]   [kəɪθ adˈrɔðjad iː əsgrɪvˈɛni]

Vocabulary

FEMININE NOUN	ENGLISH	IPA	PLURAL FORM	IPA
cân	song	[kɑːn]	**caneuon**	[kanˈəɪon]

VERB-NOUN	ENGLISH	IPA	STEM	IPA
gwario	to spend (money)	[ˈgwarjo]	**gwari-**	[gwarj]
treulio	to spend (time)	[ˈtɹəɪljo]	**treuli-**	[tɹəɪlj]
perfformio	to perform	[pɛrˈfɔrmjo]	**perfformi-**	[pɛrˈfɔrmj]

Exercise 1

Rewrite the following sentences using an impersonal verb.

1) Ceith archfarchnad newydd ei hagor. _____
   (A new supermarket will be opened.)

2) Mae petrol yn cael ei werthu yma. _____

(Petrol is sold here.)

3) Bydd y goleuadau'n cael eu diffodd. _____
   (The lights will be switched off.)

4) Bydd coeden yn cael ei thorri i lawr. _____
   (A tree will be cut down.)

5) Mae drama'n cael ei pherfformio. _____
   (A play will be performed.)

6) Ceith y bobl eu henwi. _____
   (The people will be named.)

7) Bydd y welydd yn cael eu paentio. _____
   (The walls will be painted.)

8) Mae'r problemau'n cael eu trafod. _____
   (The problems will be discussed.)

Past tense

The ending **-wyd** [ʊɪd] is added to the stem of a verb to form the impersonal:

	SENTENCE	IMPERSONAL SENTENCE
WELSH	**Cafodd y problemau eu hanghofio.**	**Anghofiwyd y problemau.**
ENGLISH	The problems were forgotten.	The problems were forgotten.
IPA	[ˈkɑːvoð ə prɔbˈlɛmɛ iː hanˈhɔvjo]	[aŋˈhɔvjʊɪd ə prɔbˈlɛmɛ]
WELSH	**Cafodd y nodyn ei anfon.**	**Anfonwyd y nodyn.**
ENGLISH	The note was sent.	The note was sent.
IPA	[ˈkɑːvoð ə ˈnɔdɪn iː ˈanvon]	[anˈvɔnʊɪd ə ˈnɔdɪn]

Exercise 2

Change the following passive sentences into ones containing a past impersonal verb.

1) Cafodd yr anrheg ei phrynu. _____
   (The present was bought.)

2) Cafodd llawer o arian (SW)/bres (NW) ei wario. _____

   (A lot of money was spent.)

3) Cafodd y caneuon eu canu. _____
   (The songs were sung.)

4) Cafodd y digwyddiad ei gynnal. _____
   (The event was held.)

5) Cafodd y ras ei dechrau. _____
   (The race was started.)

6) Cafodd y drws ei gau. _____
   (The door was closed.)

7) Cafodd y dynion eu holi.
   (The men were questioned.)

8) Cafodd amser ei dreulio.
   (The time was spent.)

The impersonal negative

The preverbial negative particle **ni** [niː] (**nid** [nɪd] before a vowel) is used to negate impersonal forms. **Ni** causes the aspirate mutation in verbs which begin with **p, t** and **c**; and the soft mutation occurs in verbs which begin with **b, d, g, m, ll, rh** (see **Week 1, Lesson 5**).

SENTENCE	ENGLISH	IPA
Ni chaniateir ysmygu.	Smoking isn't allowed.	[ni χanjatˈəɪr əsˈməgi]
Ni laddwyd neb.	No-one was killed.	[ni ˈlɑðʊɪd neːb]
Nid ysgrifennwyd y llyfr.	The book was not written.	[nɪd əsgrɪvˈɛnʊɪd neːb]

Exercise 3

Turn the following sentences into negative ones.

1) Gwnaethpwyd y gwaith.
   (The work was done.)

2) Gwelwyd damwain.
   (An accident was seen.)

3) Cafwyd hwyl.
   (Fun was had.)

4) Lliwir y lluniau.
   (The pictures were coloured.)

5) Enillwyd y ras.
   (The race was won.)

6) Telir y biliau.
   (The bills will be paid.)

7) Maddeuwyd i bawb.
   (Everyone was forgiven.)

8) Sgoriwyd gôl.
   (A goal was scored.)

9) Cedwir arian/pres yn y neuadd.
   (The money is kept at the hall.)

10) Aethpwyd â nhw i'r ysbyty.
    (They were taken to hospital.)

The impersonal imperative

The impersonal imperative inflection is **-er** [ɛr]. An impersonal imperative verb is negated by placing the preverbial negative particle **na** [nɑː] in front of a word beginning with a consonant and **nac** [nɑːg] in front of a verb beginning with a vowel. The same mutations are caused by **na** [nɑː] as **ni** [niː]. The impersonal negative can be seen on public signs and notices and in examination booklets.

Here are some examples of the negative impersonal:

PHRASE	ENGLISH	IPA
Na nofier.	Do not swim.	[nɑː 'nɔvjɛr]
Nac ysmyger.	Do not smoke.	[nɑː 'nɔvjɛr]
Na thwyller.	Do not cheat.	[nɑː 'θʊɬɛr]
Na phoener.	Do not worry.	[nɑː 'fɔɪnɛr]

In uninflected commands such as 'no smoking', 'no' is expressed by **dim** [dɪm] (which translates as 'zero' or 'nothing' in modern Welsh), and 'smoking' by the infinitive of the verb concerned:

PHRASE	ENGLISH	IPA
Dim ysmygu.	No smoking.	[dɪm ysˈməgi]
Dim parcio.	No parking.	[dɪm 'parkjo]
Dim stopio.	No stopping.	[dɪm 'stɔpjo]
Dim nofio.	No swimming.	[dɪm 'nɔvjo]

Lesson 6: Useful phrases

These questions below will help you to communicate while learning Welsh:

QUESTION	ENGLISH	IPA
Beth ydy (...) yn Saesneg?	What is (...) in English?	[beːθ ədi (...) ən 'səɪsnɛg]
Beth ydy (...) yn Gymraeg?	What is (...) in Welsh?	[beːθ ədi (...) ən gəmˈraɪg]
Allwch chi ddweud hynny eto?	Can you say that again?	['äɬʊχ χi ðwəɪd 'həni 'ɛto]
Beth ddwedoch chi?	What did you say?	[beː(θ) ðwɛˈdɔχ χi]
Beth ydy hwn? (*m.*)	What is this?	[beː(θ) 'ədi hʊn]
Beth ydy hon? (*f.*)	What is this?	[beː(θ) 'ədi hɔn]
Beth ydy hwnna? (*m.*)	What is that?	[beː(θ) 'ədi 'hʊna]
Beth ydy honna? (*f.*)	What is that?	[beː(θ) 'ədi 'hɔna]

The following is easy to remember, and it may come in useful if someone is speaking too quickly:

PHRASE	ENGLISH	IPA
yn arafach	slower	[ən arˈɑvaχ]

Below are some more useful phrases:

GREETING	ENGLISH	IPA
Pen-blwydd Hapus	Happy Birthday	[pɛnˈblʊɪð ˈhapɪs]
Nadolig Llawen	Merry Christmas	[nadˈɔlɪg ˈɬaʊɛn]
Pasg Hapus	Happy Easter	[pasg ˈhapɪs]
Blwyddyn Newydd Dda	Happy New Year	[ˈblʊɪðɪn ˈnɛʊɪð ðɑː]

WISH	ENGLISH	IPA
Pob lwc!	Good luck!	[poːb lʊk]
Iechyd da!	Good health! / Cheers!	[ˈjɛχɪd dɑː]
Brysiwch wella!	Get well soon!	[ˈbrəʃʊχ ˈwɛɬa]
Llongyfarchiadau	Congratulations	[ɬɔŋɡəvarχˈjɑˑdɛ]
Llongyfarchiadau ar (...)	Congratulations on (...)	[ɬɔŋɡəvarχˈjɑˑdɛ ar]
Croeso	Welcome	[ˈkrɔɪso]

EXPRESSION	ENGLISH	IPA
Dw i'n dy garu di.	I love you.	[dwiːn də ˈgɑˑri diː]
Bechod!	Pity! / That's a shame!	[ˈbɛχod]
Dyna drueni.	That's a pity.	[ˈdəna drɪˈɛni]
Chwarae teg.	Fair play.	[ˈχwɑˑrɛ teːg]

The following will help while speaking on the phone:

EXPRESSION	ENGLISH	IPA
(...) sy'n siarad.	[Name] speaking.	[(...) siːn ˈʃɑˑrad]
Pwy sy'n siarad?	Who is speaking?	[pʊɪ siːn ˈʃɑˑrad]
Gaf fi siarad â (...)?	Can I speak to [Name]?	[gaː(v) viː ˈʃɑˑrad ä (...)]

The following will help in writing a letter:

PHRASE	ENGLISH
Annwyl (...) (SM)	Dear [Name]
Oddi wrth	From
Gyda chariad	With love
Cofion	Regards
Yr eiddoch yn gywir	Yours faithfully
Yn gywir	Yours faithfully (less formal than above)
Yr eiddoch yn ddiffuant	Yours sincerely
Yn ddiffuant	Yours sincerely (less formal than above)
Diolch am eich cydweithrediad	Thanks for your cooperation
Gyda phob dymuniad da	With every good wish

	SENTENCE
WELSH	**Mae'n ddrwg gen i glywed hynny.**
ENGLISH	I'm sorry to hear that.
IPA	[maɪn ðruːg gɛn iː 'gləʊɛd 'həni]
WELSH	**Rydym yn meddwl amdanoch chi.**
ENGLISH	We are thinking about you
IPA	['rədɪm ən 'mɛðʊl amˈdɑˑno(χ) χiː]
WELSH	**Mae'n ddrwg gen i glywed am eich profedigaeth / colled.**
ENGLISH	I'm sorry to hear of your bereavement / loss.
IPA	[maɪn ðruːg gɛn iː 'gləʊɛd am əɪχ ˌprɔvɛdˈiˑgaɪθ / 'kɔɬɛd]

PHRASE	ENGLISH	IPA
Byddai'n / basai'n well gen i beidio.	I would prefer not to.	['bəðɛn / 'bäsɛn wɛɬ gɛn i 'beɪdjo]
Does dim ots.	It doesn't matter.	[dɔɪs dɪm ɔts]
Dim problem.	No problem.	[dɪm 'prɔblɛm]
Hwyl am y tro.	Bye for now.	[hʊɪl am ə tɹ̥oː]

Exercise 1

Write a response for each event below.

1) Mae hi newydd gael baban.
   (She has just had a baby.)

2) Mae ei chariad newydd gael ei ladd mewn damwain.
   (Her boyfried has just been killed in an accident.)

3) Dych chi newydd godi'r ffôn.
   (You have just picked up the phone.)

4) Rhagfyr y pumed ar hugain ydy hi.
   (It's December the twenty fifth.)

5) Mae eich ffrind chi wedi llwyddo yn ei arholiadau.
   (Your friend has succeeded in his exams.)

6) Dych chi'n dechrau ysgrifennu llythyr.
   (You are starting to write a letter.)

7) Dych chi'n ffonio swyddfa Mr Williams.

(You are phoning Mr Williams' office.)

8) Ionawr y cyntaf ydy hi.
   (It's the first of January.)

Vocabulary

MASCULINE NOUN	ENGLISH	IPA	PLURAL FORM	IPA
tsieina	china	[ˈtʃəɪna]		
corff	body	[kɔrf]	**cyrff**	[kɪrf]
darn	piece	[darn]	**darnau**	[ˈdarnɛ]
baban	baby	[ˈbaban]	**babanod**	[babˈɑˑnod]

FEMININE NOUN	ENGLISH	IPA	PLURAL FORM	IPA
gwe	web	[gweː]		
swyddfa	office	[ˈsʊɪðva]	**swyddfeydd**	[sʊɪðˈvəɪð]

ADVERBIAL	ENGLISH	IPA
bellach	any more / any longer	[ˈbeɬaχ]

ADJECTIVE	ENGLISH	IPA
frifol	[kəvˈriˑvol]	responsible

Dialogue

Welsh Dialogue

Ann: Pwy sydd wedi torri fy ngheffyl tsieina i? Roedd hi mewn un darn y tro diwethaf (y) gwelais i fo, dim ond ei goesau sydd ar ôl yn sefyll rŵan, mae'r corff mewn darnau ar y llawr.

Gethin: Nid fi dorrodd o. Nid arna i mae'r bai. Dwedais i wrtho fo am beidio cicio pêl yn y tŷ. Garmon wnaeth gicio'r bêl. Fo dorrodd y ceffyl.

Ann: Y ceffyl 'na oedd fy hoff ddarn i o tsiena. Un drud oedd o hefyd. Dyn nhw ddim yn cael eu gwneud bellach. Bydd rhaid i fi chwilio am un ar y we. A ti gaiff dalu amdano fo allan o dy bres poced di.

Gethin: Beth! Dwedais i wrthoch chi mai Garmon oedd wedi torri'r ceffyl, nid fi. Fo sy'n gyfrifol. Fo ddylai dalu!

Ann: Ti sy'n gyfrifol am beth fydd dy ffrindiau di'n ei wneud pan fyddan nhw yn y tŷ felly ti gaiff dalu.

Gethin: Dydy hynny ddim yn deg.

English Translation

Ann: Who has broken my china horse? It was in one piece the last time I saw it. Only his legs are left standing now; the body is in pieces on the floor.

Gethin: *I* didn't break it. It's not my fault. I told him not to kick a ball in the house. *Garmon* kicked the ball. *He* broke the horse.

Ann: That horse was my favourite piece of china. It was *an expensive one* as well. They aren't made any more. I will have to search for one on the web. And *you* will pay for it out of your pocket money.

Gethin: What! I told you that (it was) Garmon who had broken the horse, not me. He is resposible. *He* should pay!

Ann: *You* are responsible for what your friends do when they are in the house so (it is) *you* who will pay.

Gethin: That isn't fair.

Lesson 7: Recap exercises

Exercise 1

Translate the following sentences.

1) "Congratulations," he said.
2) They were born in West Wales.
3) "It doesn't matter," we said.
4) What is 'pet' in Welsh?*
5) Get well soon.
6) Where were you born?
7) Cheers!
8) Can I speak to a policeman?
9) I love you.
10) "I'm sorry to hear that," I said.

* Do not translate 'pet'.

If you have any difficulty completing this exercise, review **Week 12, Lesson 1, Lesson 2,** *and* **Lesson 6**.

Exercise 2

Rewrite the following sentences emphaising the underlined element.

For example:

Question: Gofynnais i iddyn nhw.
Answer: Fi ofynnodd iddyn nhw.

For example:

Question: Mae hi'n sefyll.

Answer: Hi sy'n sefyll.

For example:

Question: Dyn ni'n perthyn <u>iddi hi.</u>
Answer: Iddi hi dyn ni'n perthyn.

1) Canon <u>nhw</u>'r anthem genedlaethol.
   (They sang the national anthem.)

2) Cawson nhw eu geni <u>yn yr ardal 'na</u>.
   (They were born in that region.)

3) Est <u>ti</u> i'r banc ddoe.
   (You went to the bank yesterday.)

4) Defnyddiodd hi <u>fy meiro i</u>.
   (She used my biro.)

5) Doedden nhw ddim yn <u>brysio</u>.
   (They weren't hurrying.)

6) Chwarddodd e (SW)/<u>o</u> (NW).
   (He laughed.)

7) Maen <u>nhw</u>'n gas wrthon ni.
   (They are nasty to us.)

8) Bydd ei gariad e'n (SW)/o'n (NW) <u>paratoi'r gerddoriaeth</u>.
   (His girlfriend will prepare the music.)

9) Byddai hi <u>wrth ei bodd</u>.
   (She would be delighted.)

10) Roedd hi'n <u>noson stormus</u>.
    (It was a stormy night.)

11) Mae e'n (SW)/o'n (NW) <u>disgwyl colli</u>.
    (He is expecting to lose.)

12) Rwyt ti'n perthyn <u>i ni</u>.
    (You belong to us.)

If you have any difficulty completing this exercise, review **Week 12, Lesson 3.**

Exercise 3

*Translate the following sentences using **piau**.*

1) Who owns this ball? _____
2) We own the fridge and television.
   _____
3) I own this dress. _____
4) Garmon owns that ball. _____
5) The teacher (f.) owns those books.
   _____
6) Does he own this hotel? _____
7) Who owned the mirror which he broke?
   _____
8) You own this garage? (*fam.*) _____
9) Her uncle owns the walking stick.
   _____
10) Do they own this picture? _____

*If you have any difficulty completing this exercise, review **Week 12, Lesson 4**.*

Exercise 4

Translate the following sentences using the impersonal:

1) When was the church built?
   _____
2) The shop was not opened after the fire.
   _____
3) The clock will not be changed.
   _____
4) The baby was washed.
   _____
5) Breakfast was made in the kitchen.
   _____
6) The words will be sung in Welsh.
   _____
7) A body was found on the beach yesterday morning.
   _____
8) The door was not closed.
   _____

9) The alarm will not be heard.
   _____

10) Everyone was woken up.
    _____

If you have any difficulty completing this exercise, review **Week 12, Lesson 5**.

Taking It Further

USEFUL WEBSITES FOR WELSH LEARNERS

If you live in Wales, you will find that there are many opportunities to practise your Welsh locally and online. A good place to start would be the website of *Canolfan Dysgu Cymraeg Genedlaethol* (the National Centre for Teaching Welsh): https://learnwelsh.cymru/.

The Centre is responsible for the provision of adult Welsh classes throughout Wales, and also funds extra-curricular activities whereby learners come into contact with fluent Welsh speakers. There are also numerous websites, some interactive, aimed at helping Welsh learners and fluent Welsh-speakers to improve their spoken and written skills in the language.

The levels adopted below are based on the CEFR system. CEFR, which stands for the 'Common European Framework of Reference for Languages', is a guideline used to describe achievements of learners of foreign languages across Europe and in other countries. Its main aim is to provide a method of learning, teaching and assessing which applies to all languages in Europe. There are six reference levels:

LEVEL GROUP	LEVEL GROUP NAME	LEVEL	LEVEL NAME	CQFW LEVEL*
A	Basic User	A1	Beginner	Entry
		A2	Elementary	Foundation
B	Independent User	B1	Intermediate	Intermediate
		B2	Upper Intermediate	Advanced
C	Proficient User	C1	Advanced	Proficiency
		C2	Proficiency	Proficiency

* *The equivalent CQFW (Credit and Qualifications Framework for Wales) levels are shown in the right hand column.*

Below is a list of some of the most useful websites. All are live at the time of publication.

A1 & A2 LEVELS

www.duolingo.com/course/cy/en/Learn-Welsh-Online
Duolingo is an app with online support dedicated to helping people learn Welsh.

https://learnwelsh.cymru/
The website of the National Centre for Learning Welsh. It includes information about courses and an online registration system, together with online teaching resources that compliment national courses.

www.memrise.com/courses/english/welsh/
Memrise is an online vocabulary learning tool with 'courses' created by its users.

www.saysomethingin.com/welsh//
An online Welsh course using podcasts.

B1, B2 & C1 LEVELS
www.colegcymraeg.ac.uk/en/study/languageskills/languageskillscertificate/
Presentations for *Coleg Cymraeg Cenedlaethol*'s Language Skills Certificate explaining grammatical points that can cause difficulties when writing Welsh (C1 Level).

http://resources.hwb.wales.gov.uk/VTC/2012-13/22032013/sglein-ar-lein/index.html
An interactive website for Upper Intermediate and Advanced Level students.

ALL LEVELS
www.gwales.com
The online bookstore of the Welsh Books Council. Also available as an app.

www.wjec.co.uk/qualifications/welsh-for-adults-qualification-suite/#tab_overview
Specifications, exemplary papers, together with videos of exemplary interviews for A1, A2, B1 and B2 level examinations.

ONLINE DICTIONARIES
www.geiriadur.net
The University of Wales Trinity St David's Welsh/English and English/Welsh dictionary.

http://geiriadur.bangor.ac.uk/
Bangor University's Welsh/English and English/Welsh dictionary.

www.geiriaduracademi.org/
The Welsh Academy's English/Welsh dictionary.

www.gweiadur.com/
A project to create a dictionary and multimedia resources for learners of Welsh.

If you have a smartphone, the English/Welsh dictionary *Ap Geiriaduron* is very useful:
https://itunes.apple.com/gb/app/ap-geiriaduron/id570171569?mt=8.

OTHER USEFUL WEBSITES
www.bbc.co.uk/cymru/
News and general information.

www.bbc.co.uk/cymru/cymraeg/dysgu/
Lots of resources for learners, including tools such as a dictionary, mutation and spelling checker.

www.bbc.co.uk/wales/catchphrase/
Welsh course and resources.

www.bbc.co.uk/cymrufyw/cylchgrawn
BBC online Welsh-language magazine.

www.golwg360.com/
Online national newspaper.

www.iclanguage.com/welsh
Online resources to help children and young adults learn Welsh.

https://parallel.cymru/
Bilingual online magazine.

www.s4c.cymru/en/
S4C website.

Reading Practice

Reading practice 1
The extract below is taken from *DeltaNet*, by Andras Millward. It set in the world of Information Technology, with the main character facing great risks as he tries to unravel what secrets his employers are trying to hide from their customers. *DeltaNet* as part of the series: *Nofelau Nawr* aimed at B1 and B2 level learners. It was published in 1999 by Gwasg Gomer, Llandysul.

Welsh Reading

Canodd y ffôn. Rhoddodd Ben y papur newydd roedd yn ei ddarllen i un ochr. Cododd e a chroesi ei ystafell fyw i'w ateb.

"Helo?"

"Ben, Alan sydd yma. Sut rwyt ti?"

Roedd Ben yn eistedd ar y gadair freichiau agosaf. "Dw i'n iawn, mwy neu lai. Mae popeth yn dipyn o sioc o hyd. Glywaist ti unrhyw beth?"

"Do. Ces i sgwrs â Rodgers. Wel, ces i alwad i ddod i'w swyddfa fe tua hanner awr ar ôl i ti adael ddoe. Maen nhw wedi dy gyhuddo di o ladrata syniadau DeltaNet er mwyn eu gwerthu nhw i'n cystadleuwyr ni, Ben."

Ochneidiodd Ben. Roedd hi'n dechrau bwrw glaw yn drwm. Syllodd e am funud ar y dafnau mawr yn taro'r ffenestr cyn dweud unrhyw beth.

"Ben? Wyt ti yna?"

"Ydw. Alan, gelli di fy ngalw i'n baranoiaidd unwaith eto, ond dw i'n credu bod hyn i gyd yn dangos bod rhywbeth o'i le ar y Connect. Damio ... Ddwedodd Rodgers unrhyw beth am dystiolaeth yn fy erbyn i?"

"Na, dim felly. Rwyt ti wedi rhoi cynlluniau'r Connect i 'un o'n prif gystadleuwyr ni', ac wedi bod yn gwneud hynny ers misoedd, ac mae'r dystiolaeth yn bendant a chlir, yn ôl Rodgers. Mae'n debyg y bydd rhywun yn cysylltu â ti heddiw."

"Dyna beth ddwedodd y Pennaeth Diogelwch ddoe wrth i fi gael fy nhaflu ma's. Dw i wedi siarad â fy nghyfreithiwr. Mae e'n aros i glywed y manylion a'r cyhuddiad swyddogol gan DeltaNet neu'r heddlu. Dw i wedi cael gorchmynion gan yr heddlu i aros gartref am y tro." Oedodd Ben am eiliad cyn siarad eto. "Wyt ti'n credu Rodgers?" Chwarddodd Alan. "Ddim am eiliad! Ben, dw i'n dy adnabod di'n dda, efallai'n well na neb, a dw i'n hollol sicr nad dyna dy steil di. Ac ar ben hynny, dyn ni ddim wedi treulio mwy nag awr ar ein pennau ein hunain yn y labordy uffernol hwn."
"Diolch."

English Translation

The phone rang. Ben put the newspaper he was reading to one side. He got up and crossed his living room to answer.

"Hello?"

"Ben, it's Alan here. How are you?"

Ben was sat on the nearest armchair. I'm fine, more or less. Everything is still a bit of a shock. "Did you hear anything?"

"Yes. I had a chat with Rodgers. Well, I got a call to come to his office about half an hour after you left yesterday. They've accused you of stealing DeltaNet's ideas to sell them to our competitors, Ben."

Ben sighed. It was starting to rain heavily. He stared for a minute at the big drops hitting the window before saying anything.

"Ben? Are you there?"

"Yes. Alan, you can call me paranoid again, but I think it all shows that there is something wrong with the Connect. Damn ... Did Rodgers say anything about evidence against me?"

"No, not as such. You've given the Connect plans to 'one of our main competitors', and have been doing so for months, and the evidence is clear and clear, according to Rodgers. You are likely to be contacted today."

"That's what the Head of Security said yesterday as I was thrown here. I've spoken to my solicitor. He is waiting to hear the details and the official allegation from DeltaNet or the police. I've got orders from the police to stay home for the time being." Ben paused for a moment before speaking again. "Do you believe Rodgers?"

Alan laughed. "Not for a moment! Ben, I know you well, maybe better than anyone, and I'm sure that's not your style. And besides, we have not spent more than an hour alone in this hell lab."

"Thank you."

Reading practice 2

Below is an adapted article from *Golwg360*, the online Welsh-language daily newspaper sponsored by the Welsh Government. It was published on 05/02/2017. A translation has been provided to help with your studies.

Ffilm am Gymru yn Ewro 2016 yn 'stori am wlad yn darganfod ei lle yn y byd'

Daeth cyhoeddiad ddoe y byddai'r ffilm am brofiadau tîm pêl-droed Cymru yng nghystadleuaeth Ewro 2016 yn cael ei dangos am y tro cyntaf fis nesaf.

Bydd hi'n bosib gweld *Don't Take Me Home* o Ddydd Gŵyl Dewi ymlaen.

"Stori am lwyddiant annisgwyl ydy'r ffilm, a hefyd, mae hi'n stori am wlad yn darganfod ei lle yn y byd," meddai Jonny Owen.

"Ni yw'r wlad leiaf i i fynd mor bell mewn prif gystadleuaeth. Curon ni'r wlad fwyaf y byd, sef Rwsia, a churon ni ffefrynnau'r gystadleuaeth, sef Gwlad Belg, hefyd. Felly, roeddwn i'n meddwl ei bod hi'n ffilm brydferth i'w gwneud."

Stori'r cefnogwyr
Er mwyn casglu deunydd ar gyfer y ffilm, buodd Jonny Owen yn cyfweld â'r holl chwaraewyr, ac roedd e'n ddigon ffodus i dderbyn deunydd gan Gymdeithas Bêl-droed Cymru, ond roedd y cefnogwyr yn bwysig iddo hefyd.

"Fy nghynllun i oedd cael deunydd gan y cefnogwyr fel fy mod i'n gallu dangos eu stori nhw a'u cyffro yn Bordeaux a Toulouse," meddai Jonny. "Dw i'n credu mai dyma'r defnydd mwyaf o ddeunydd ffonau symudol sydd erioed wedi bod mewn ffilm."

Mae'r cyfarwyddwr yn pwysleisio pwysigrwydd y cefnogwyr yn y ffilm gan nodi, "roedden ni'n wych, nid yn unig ar y cae ond i ffwrdd o'r cae hefyd."

Chris Coleman a'i dîm
Mae e'n cyfeirio at gyfweliad â rheolwr Cymru, Chris Coleman fel "un o'r cyfweliadau gorau dw i erioed wedi ei gael," gan nodi ei fod e'n "siarad yn arbennig, dych chi'n gallu gweld sut mae e'n cael ymateb mor dda gan y chwaraewyr."

Er gwaethaf cryfder y rheolwr, mae e hefyd yn cymeradwyo'r chwaraewyr, gan dynnu sylw at eu cyfraniad nhw at apêl y stori gan ddweud, "Mae'r tîm i gyd yn hoffus, erbyn diwedd y gystadleuaeth, roedd llwythi o bobl oedd yn cefnogi'r tîm oedd â dim diddordeb mewn pêl-droed."

Mae e'n sôn am olygfa yn y ffilm lle mae'r tîm yn chwarae tennis bwrdd – golygfa sy'n pwysleisio pa mor agos oedd y chwaraewyr at ei gilydd, a chymaint roedden nhw'n mwynhau.

Y da a'r drwg
Er mai awyrgylch cadarnhaol sydd i'r ffilm, caiff agweddau da a drwg ar daith tîm Cymru sylw, gan gynnwys "gwrth-Gymreictod yn y cyfryngau Seisnig" a methiant y tîm yn erbyn Portiwgal.

Mae e'n gorffen trwy ddweud, "Aethon ni, a cheision ni ein gorau."

English Translation

A film about Wales in Euro 2016 is 'a story about a country discovering its place in the world'

An announcement came yesterday that a film about the Welsh football team's experiences in the Euro 2016 competition will be shown for the first time next month.

It will be possible to see *Don't Take Me Home* from St David's Day onwards.

"The film is the story of unexpected success, and it's also the story of a country finding its place in the world," said Jonny Owen.

"We are the smallest country to go so far in a major competition. We beat the world's largest country, Russia, and we also beat the competition favourites, Belgium. So, I thought that it was a beautiful film to make."

The fans' story
In order to gather material for the film, Jonny Owen interviewed all the players, and he was fortunate enough to receive material from the Football Association of Wales, but the fans were important to him as well.

"My plan was to get material from the fans so I would be able to show their story and their excitement in Bordeaux and Toulouse," he said. "I think that this is the greatest use of mobile phones that has ever been in a film."

The director stresses the importance of the fans in the film, stating, "We were brilliant, not only on the field but off the field as well."

Chris Coleman and his team
He refers to an interview with the manager of Wales, Chris Coleman, as "one of the best interviews I've ever had," noting that he "spoke wonderfully; you can see how he gets such a good response from the players."

Despite the strength of the manager, he also praises the players, highlighting their contribution to the appeal of the story by saying, "The team are all amiable. By the end of the competition, there were loads of people who supported the team but who had no interest in football."

He talks about a scene in the film where the team plays table tennis – a scene that emphasizes how close the players were to each other, and how much they enjoyed [the experience].

The good and the bad
Although there is a positive atmosphere to the film, both good and bad aspects of the Welsh team's tour get attention, including the "anti-Welshness in the English media" and the failure of the team against Portugal.

He concludes by saying, "We went and we tried our best."

Key to Exercises

Week 1, Lesson 2
Exercise 1: 1 – e 2 – g 3 – d 4 – h
5 – c 6 – a 7 – f 8 – b

Exercise 2:
1) a girl/a daughter
2) a man
3) dogs
4) shoes
5) a shop
6) a dog/dog
7) a village/village
8) a house/house

Exercise 3:
1) ci
2) dynion
3) tŷ
4) tre(f)
5) siopau
6) esgidiau
7) merch
8) pentre(f)

Exercise 4:
1) tai
2) siopau
3) dynion
4) trefi
5) esgidiau
6) pentrefi
7) cŵn
8) merched

Exercise 5:
1) tŷ
2) pentre(f)
3) merch
4) esgid
5) ci
6) dyn
7) tre(f)
8) siop

Exercise 6: 1) f 2) m 3) f 4) f 5) m
6) m 7) m 8) f 9) m 10) f

Week 1, Lesson 3
Exercise 1:
1) tŷ mawr
2) merched tal
3) pentrefi bach
4) dynion da
5) esgidiau mawr
6) siopau da
7) dyn tal
8) cŵn da
9) trefi bach
10) tarw mawr

Week 1, Lesson 4
Exercise 1:
1) y tarw
2) i'r siop
3) yr oren
4) y merched
5) o'r pentre(f)
6) yr hufen
7) y ci
8) y trefi

Week 1, Lesson 5
Exercise 1:
a) Bore da
b) Prynhawn da
c) Noswaith dda
d) Bore da
e) Noswaith dda
f) Prynhawn da
g) Noswaith dda

Exercise 2:
1) pentre(f) prysur
2) esgidiau gwyrdd
3) gwlad fawr
4) tref leol
5) mam falch
6) tarw da
7) cath ddu
8) cadair rad
9) bachgen cryf
10) mamau balch

Exercise 3:
1) y fam
2) y bont
3) y wlad
4) y blodyn
5) y merched
6) y ddesg
7) y ffenestr
8) y gadair
9) y llaw
10) y tad

Week 1, Lesson 6
Exercise 1:
1) wyth ci
2) un pentre(f)
3) tri bore
4) dau enw
5) tri blodyn
6) deg cath
7) saith tad
8) pedwar dyn
9) pum pont
10) naw gwlad

Exercise 2: a) dau ddeg pump b) wyth deg chwech c) tri deg saith
d) naw deg un e) chwe deg pump f) dau ddeg pedwar

Week 1, Lesson 7
Exercise 1: 1) cŵn 2) siopau 3) merched 4) pentrefi 5) cathod
6) desgiau 7) tai 8) dynion 9) trefi 10) esgidiau.

Exercise 2: a) tarw mawr b) dyn tal c) gwlad fach d) cath ddrwg
e) merch brysur f) cegin rad g) ffenest gryf h) caseg ddu
i) blodyn melyn j) pont dda.

Exercise 3: a) y siop b) y bore c) yr afal d) yr oren e) yr esgidiau
f) yr un g) y gadair h) y ddesg i) y llaw j) yr enw.

Exercise 4: 1 – g 2 – j 3 – f 4 – a 5 – b
6 – c 7 – i 8 – d 9 – e 10 – h

Exercise 5: a) tri deg un b) pedwar deg naw c) wyth deg chwech
ch) dau ddeg saith d) pum deg wyth.

Week 2, Lesson 1
Exercise 1: 1) ydyn 2) i 3) ni 4) ydy
5) wyt 6) hi 7) e (SW)/o (NW) 8) ydych.

Exercise 2: 1) Athro/athrawes ydw i. 2) Tad ydy e (SW)/o (NW).
3) Meddyg ydy hi. 4) Gareth ydw i.
5) Meddygon ydyn ni. 6) Cymry ydych chi.
7) Pentref ydy e (SW)/o (NW). 8) Merched ydyn nhw.
9) Mam wyt ti. 10) Gwlad fach ydy hi.

Week 2, Lesson 2
Exercise 1: 1) Nid athro/athrawes ydw i. 2) Nid cathod ydyn nhw.
3) Nid tref ydy Caerdydd. 4) Nid plant ydyn nhw.
5) Nid meddygon ydyn ni. 6) Nid cath ydy Meg.
7) Nid meddyg ydy hi. 8) Nid gwlad fach ydy hi.
9) Nid pobl brysur ydyn ni. 10) Nid nyrs ydy e (SW)/o (NW).

Week 2, Lesson 3
Exercise 1: 1) (Ai) nyrs wyt ti?
2) (Ai) postmon ydy e (SW)/o (NW)?
3) (Ai) Saeson ydyn nhw?
4) (Ai) Ffrancwyr ydyn nhw?
5) (Ai) athro da/athrawes dda ydw i?
6) (Ai) pobl dda ydyn ni?
7) (Ai) Almaenwr enwog ydy e (SW) / o (NW)?
8) (Ai) gwas sifil ydych chi?
9) (Ai) cadeiriau rhad ydyn nhw?
10) (Ai) Albanes ydy hi?

Exercise 2: 1) Ie, siop dda ydy hi.
2) Nage, nid blodyn melyn ydy e (SW)/o (NW).
3) Nage, nid meddygon ydyn nhw.
4) Ie, Mr a Mrs Williams ydyn nhw.
5) Nage, nid merch enwog ydw i.
Alternative answer: Nage, nid merch enwog wyt ti/ydych chi.
6) Ie, Almaenwyr ydyn ni.
Alternative answer: Ie, Almaenwyr ydych chi.
7) Ie, nyrs dda ydy e (SW)/o (NW).
8) Ie, Albanes wyt ti/ydw i.
9) Nage, nid plentyn tal ydy e (SW)/o (NW).
10) Ie, pobl leol ydyn nhw.

Week 2, Lesson 4
Exercise 1: 1) ydyn 2) ydy 3) wyt 4) ydy 5) ydy
6) ydy 7) ydy 8) ydych 9) ydy

Week 2, Lesson 5
Exercise 1: 1) dau Sais 2) tair nyrs 3) pedwar blodyn
4) tair gwlad 5) pedair tref 6) tri meddyg
7) dau fynydd 8) tair pont 9) pedair cadair
10) dwy Gymraes.

Week 2, Lesson 6
Exercise 1: 1) y dyn yma 2) y ferch yna 3) y merched yma
4) y wers yma 5) y llyfr yna 6) y tŷ yma
7) y papurau yna 8) y pethau yma 9) y teimlad yma.

Week 2, Lesson 7
Exercise 1: 1) Cymro ydw i. 2) Bechgyn da ydyn ni.
3) Pobl enwog ydyn nhw. 4) Albanes ydy hi.
5) Gwlad fach ydy Cymru. 6) Dinas brysur ydy Caerdydd.
7) Athro ydy e (SW)/o (NW). 8) Plentyn wyt ti.
9) Nyrsys ydyn ni. 10) Americanwyr ydyn nhw.

Exercise 2: 1) Nid Siôn ydy e (SW)/o (NW). 2) Nid athrawon ydyn nhw.
3) Nid plismon ydy Gareth. 4) Nid Albanwr ydw i.
5) Nid ci ydy Ffido. 6) Nid pobl leol ydyn ni.
7) Nid nyrs wyt ti. 8) Nid Ffrancwyr ydych chi.
9) Nid gwas sifil ydy hi. 10) Nid problem fawr ydy hi.

Exercise 3: 1) (Ai) Cymro ydw i? 2) (Ai) Rhiannon ydych chi?
3) (Ai) pobl enwog ydyn ni? 4) (Ai) meddyg wyt ti?
5) (Ai) Almaenwyr ydy'r plant? 6) (Ai) Cymry ydyn nhw?
7) (Ai) myfyrwraig ydy hi? 8) (Ai) Ffrancwr ydy e (SW)/o (NW)?

Exercise 4: 1) Ie, Alun ydw i.
2) Nage, nid Siôn ydy e (SW)/o (NW).
3) Nage, nid dinas ydy Aberystwyth.

4) Ie, Ffrancwr ydy Pierre.
5) Nage, nid Albanwyr ydyn nhw?
6) Ie, Hufen ydy o.
7) Nage, nid gweision sifil ydyn ni/ydych chi.
8) Ie, meddygon ydy'r dynion yna/'na.

Exercise 5: 1) Faint o'r gloch ydy hi? 2) Faint ydy'r gadair yma?
3) Pwy ydyn nhw? 4) Pwy ydy'r meddygon?
5) Pwy ydy e (SW) / o (NW)? 6) Beth ydy'r teimlad?
7) Beth ydy'r broblem? 8) Faint ydy'r ffenestri yna?

Exercise 6: 1) tair chwaer 2) dau ddeg naw o bobl
3) deg o blant 4) pedair pont
5) dau ddeg tri Ffrancwr/o Ffrancwyr 6) cant o ddoleri
7) tair mil o bunnoedd 8) pum deg o dai
9) dau gant o wledydd 10) y ddwy ferch yna

Exercise 7: 1) y dyn yma 2) y ferch yna 3) y merched yma
4) y broblem yma 5) y llyfr yna 6) y tŷ yma
7) y pethau yna 8) y pethau yma 9) y teimlad yma

Week 3, Lesson 1

Exercise 1: 1) Mae Gareth yn rhedeg. 2) Mae'r meddygon yn gweithio.
3) Mae Tom yn dysgu Cymraeg. 4) Mae Ann yn dysgu.
5) Mae'r cŵn yn rhedeg. 6) Mae Gareth a Siân yn gweithio.
7) Mae Tom yn gyrru. 8) Mae'r bachgen yn chwarae.
9) Mae Gareth yn chwarae. 10) Mae Siân yn gweithio.

Exercise 2: 1 – h 2 – f 3 – i 4 – g 5 – b
6 – d 7 – a 8 – j 9 – e 10 – c

Exercise 3: 1) Dw 2) Dyn 3) Maen 4) Rwyt 5) Mae
6) Dyn 7) Dw i 8) Mae 9) Mae 10) Dych.

Exercise 4: 1) Mae'r bechgyn yn chwarae gartref heddiw.
2) Dw i'n gweithio yn y tŷ yn y bore.
3) Mae hi'n gyrru i'r dref heddiw.
4) Maen nhw'n darllen yn y nos.
5) Dyn ni'n siarad Cymraeg.
6) Mae e'n (SW)/o'n (NW) mynd allan heno.
7) Rwyt ti'n paentio gartref heddiw.
8) Mae'r plant yn gwisgo.
9) Dw i'n cerdded i'r dre(f) bob bore.
10) Dych chi'n rhedeg yn y prynhawn.

Exercise 5: 1) Gymru 2) weithio 3) Fangor 4) ddarllen 5) baentio
6) Faesteg 7) Ros 8) Lanelli 9) Dremadog 10) ddosbarth

Exercise 6: 1) Dw i'n sâl. 2) Mae e'n (SW)/o'n (NW) dal.
3) Maen nhw'n fyr. 4) Mae Siân yn brysur.
5) Mae hi'n gynnes (NW)/dwym (SW). 6) Dyn ni'n ddiflas.

7) Mae'r plant yn ddrwg.
9) Mae'r merched yn drist.
8) Rwyt ti'n/dych chi'n siriol.
10) Dw i'n hapus.

Week 3, Lesson 2
Exercise 1: 1 – e 2 – c 3 – f
4 – a 5 – b 6 – d

Exercise 2: 1) yn 2) mewn 3) mewn 4) mewn
5) mewn 6) yn 7) yn 8) mewn

Week 3, Lesson 3
Exercise 1: 1) Ydyn ni'n cerdded i'r dre(f)?
2) Ydych chi'n darllen?
3) Ydw i'n enwog?
4) Ydy'r athro (*m.*)/athrawes (*f.*) arall yn gweithio?
5) Ydy'r blodau yn y gegin?
6) Ydy hi mewn dosbarth Cymraeg?
7) Ydy e'n (SW)/o'n (NW) byw mewn pentref?
8) Wyt ti'n canu bob bore?
9) Ydy'r plant yn gwisgo?
10) Ydy hi'n chwarae rygbi yn y prynhawn?

Exercise 2: 1 – f 2 – a 3 – h 4 – b
5 – g 6 – d 7 – c 8 – e

Exercise 3: 1) Ydy. Mae'r ci'n breuddwydio.
2) Ydyn. Mae'r plant yn ysgrifennu yn yr ysgol.
3) Ydw. Dw i'n ymolchi bob bore.
4) Ydyn. Dyn ni'n rhedeg tair milltir.
Alternative Answer: Ydych, dych chi'n rhedeg tair milltir.
5) Ydy. Mae Richard yn dysgu Cymraeg.
6) Ydw. Dw i'n gwisgo het.
7) Ydy. Mae hi'n siarad â'r postmon.
8) Ydw, dw i'n hoffi llaeth
Alternative Answer: Ydyn, dyn ni'n hoffi llaeth.
9) Wyt. Rwyt ti'n gwisgo esgidiau gwyrdd.
Alternative Answer: Ydych, dych chi'n gwisgo esgidiau gwyrdd.
10) Ydyn. Maen nhw'n ymlacio nawr.

Exercise 4: 1) Ydw i'n gweithio heddiw?
2) Ydyn nhw'n cerdded i'r ysgol?
3) Ydych chi'n canu yn y cawod?
4) Ydy hi'n chwarae rygbi bob dydd?
5) Ydych chi'n codi nawr (SW)/rŵan (NW)?
6) Ydw i'n dysgu heddiw?
7) Ydy'r fenyw'n meddwl?
8) Ydyn ni'n mynd i siarad â phlismon?
9) Ydych chi'n darllen y papur?
10) Ydy e'n (SW)/o'n (NW) rhedeg?

Week 3, Lesson 4

Exercise 1: 1) Nac ydy. Dydy hi ddim yn gwylio'r gêm.
2) Nac ydy. Dydy o ddim yn ysgrifennu llyfr.
3) Nac ydyn. Dyn ni ddim yn chwarae rygbi heno.
4) Nac ydyn. Dydy'r plant ddim yn bwyta yn y gegin.
5) Nac ydw. Dw i ddim yn hoffi'r nyrs.
Alternative Answer: Nac ydyn. Dyn ni ddim yn hoffi'r nyrs.
6) Nac ydw. Dw i ddim yn parcio'r car.
7) Nac ydyn, dyn nhw ddim yn darllen y papur.
8) Nac wyt, dwyt ti ddim yn mynd i Fangor gyda (SW)/efo (NW) fi.
Alternative Answer: Nac ydych, dych chi ddim yn mynd i Fangor gyda (SW)/efo (NW) fi.

Exercise 2: 1) Dwyt ti ddim yn gwylio'r gêm.
2) Dydy hi ddim yn enwog.
3) Dw i ddim yn bwyta brechdan.
4) Dyn ni ddim yn gweithio mewn siop.
5) Dydy'r athro ddim yn dysgu heddiw.
6) Dw i ddim yn parcio'r car yn y maes parcio.
7) Dydy e ddim yn breuddwydio.
8) Dych chi ddim yn darllen llyfr.
9) Dydy'r ceffyl ddim yn cicio.
10) Dydy'r plant ddim yn canu yn yr ysgol.

Exercise 3: 1) Dw i ddim yn y maes parcio.
2) Dyn ni ddim yn hoffi brechdanau.
3) Dydy'r bachgen ddim yn gwisgo.
4) Dydy hi ddim yn gwylio'r gêm rygbi.
5) Dych chi (*formal*)/Dwyt ti (*fam.*) ddim yn mynd bob dydd.
6) Dw i ddim yn siarad Cymraeg.
7) Dych chi (*formal*)/Dwyt ti (*fam.*) ddim yn codi.
8) Mae'r athrawon yn hapus.
9) Dyn nhw ddim yn cwrdd (SW)/cyfarfod (NW) â'r dosbarth y prynhawn 'ma.
10) Dydy o ddim yn hoffi'r bont newydd.

Week 3, Lesson 5

Exercise 1: 1) flodau 2) geffyl 3) lyfr da 4) ffenest[r] fach 5) dŷ mawr 6) faes parcio prysur 7) ddesg fawr 8) bentref bach 9) reilffordd 10) waith da

Exercise 2: 1) Dyna gryf. 2) Dyna ddiddorol. 3) Dyna ddyn!
4) Dyna fore! 5) Dyna ddrwg. 6) Dyna newydd.
7) Dyna bobl! 8) Dyna fach. 9) Dyna broblem.

Exercise 3: 1) Ai dyna'r rheswm? 2) Nage, nid dacw Fangor.
3) Ie, dyma'r gwir. 4) Nage, nid dyna'r llwy.
5) Ie, dyma'r fenyw (SW)/ddynes (NW). 6) Nid dyma'r mynydd.
7) Ai dyma'r ddinas? 8) Nid dyna'r rheswm.
9) Nage, nid dyna'r teimlad. 10) Ai dacw'r tŷ?

Week 3, Lesson 6

Exercise 1: 1) Nac ydy, dydy hi ddim yn braf.
2) Mae hi'n mynd i fod yn wyntog y prynhawn 'ma.
3) Dydy hi ddim yn dwym (SW)/gynnes (NW).
4) Mae hi'n stormus.
5) Mae hi'n niwlog.
6) Ydy hi'n dwym (SW)/gynnes (NW)?
7) Mae hi'n gymylog.
8) Ydy, mae hi'n gymylog.
9) Ydy hi'n wlyb?
10) Dydy hi ddim yn niwlog heddiw, mae hi'n hyfryd.

Exercise 2: 1) gymylog   2) gynnes   3) bwrw eirlaw
4) wyntog   5) braf   6) dwym
7) wlyb   8) rhewi

Exercise 3: 1) Mae e'n (SW)/o'n (NW) brysur iawn.
2) Maen nhw'n gynnes (NW)/dwym (SW) iawn.
3) Dw i'n gryf iawn.
4) Dydy e (SW)/o (NW) ddim yn ddrwg iawn.
5) Mae'r gadair yn fach iawn.
6) Dw i ddim yn dal iawn.
7) Dydy hi ddim yn gynnes (NW)/dwym (SW) iawn.
8) Ydyn nhw'n fawr iawn?
9) Mae hi'n rhad iawn.
10) Ydyn ni'n dda iawn?

Week 3, Lesson 7

Exercise 1: 1) e (SW)/o (NW)   2) ti   3) nhw   4) chi
5) ni   6) hi   7) i   8) e (SW)/o (NW)

Exercise 2: 1) Mae'r plant wedi canu.
2) Mae o wedi paentio'r ffenestr.
3) Rwyt ti wedi gwisgo.
4) Dyn ni wedi ymlacio.
5) Dych chi ddim wedi cwrdd (SW)/cyfarfod (NW) â'r athro.
6) Dw i wedi gyrru tractor gwyrdd.
7) Maen nhw wedi parcio'r car.
8) Ydych chi wedi ysgrifennu at yr athrawes?
9) Dw i wedi gwylio'r gêm.
10) Mae hi wedi dysgu Cymraeg.

Exercise 3: 1) Dw   2) Maen   3) Ydyn   4) Dydy   5) Rwyt
6) Mae   7) Ydych   8) Ydyn   9) Dyn   10) Ydy

Exercise 4: 1) Dw i ddim yn hoffi cerdded a dw i ddim yn hapus.
2) Dim syniad.
3) Ble maen nhw'n byw? Dyn nhw ddim yn byw yn y gogledd.
4) Ydy hi'n dwym (SW)/gynnes (NW)?
5) Pryd dych chi'n codi?
6) Ydyn nhw'n meddwl am fynd i'r gwaith?

7) Dyn ni'n hoffi ceffylau.
8) Diolch yn fawr.
9) Sut dych chi'n mynd i'r gwaith.
10) Ydyn ni'n cwrdd (SW)/cyfarfod (NW) yfory?

Exercise 5: 1 – h   2 – d   3 – i   4 – b   5 – g
6 – c   7 – e   8 – a   9 – j   10 – f

Exercise 6: 1) Fetws Garmon   2) Ddinas Powys   3) Langollen   4) Bontypridd
5) Orseinon   6) Ruthun   7) Faesteg   8) Ffwrnais
9) Donypandy   10) Gaernarfon.

Exercise 7: 1) yn   2) mewn   3) mewn   4) yn   5) mewn
6) yn   7) mewn   8) mewn   9) mewn   10) yn

Exercise 8: 1) Ydy
2) Wyt
Alternative Answer: Ydych
3) Nac ydy
4) Nac ydyn
5) Ydw
Alternative Answer: Ydyn
6) Nac ydy
7) Nac ydyn
Alternative Answer: Nac ydych
8) Ie
9) Ydyn
10) Nac ydw.

Exercise 9: 1) Dyma'r bobl leol.   2) Dacw'r bont newydd.   3) Dyna bris!
4) Dyma raw dda.   5) Ai dyma'r ffordd?   6) Dyna'r pecyn.
7) Nid dyna'r rheswm.   8) Ai dyna'r gwir?   9) Dyna'r broblem.
10) Dyna lyfr da.

Exercise 10:   dry – sych   misty – niwlog   sleet – fwrw eirlaw
west – gorllewin   wet – wlyb   snow – fwrw eira
wet – wlyb   rain – glaw   freeze – rewi
windy – gwyntog   stormy – stormus

Week 4, Lesson 1
Exercise 1: 1) blant   2) gadair   3) wlad   4) wers   5) ddafad
6) broblem   7) reswm   8) ffenestr   9) deimladau   10) newyddion

Exercise 2: 1) merch unig   2) hen lyfrau   3) gwir ogledd
4) yr unig lwy   5) yr unig fachgen   6) y prif faes parcio
7) yr hen wlad   8) prif ffordd

Week 4, Lesson 2
Exercise 1: 1) Mae coffi cryf yn y fflasg.   2) Mae pobl yn darllen yn y llyfrgell.
3) Mae cath yn cysgu yn y gadair.   4) Mae dosbarthiadau y prynhawn 'ma.
5) Mae Richard ar y ffôn.

Exercise 2: 1) Oes Almaenwr yn y dosbarth? 2) Oes tarw yn y cae?
3) Oes desgiau yn y llyfrgell? 4) Oes llyfr yn yr ystafell?
5) Oes llawer o geir yn y maes parcio?

Exercise 3: 1) Ydy Mr Williams yn y dosbarth? 2) Ydy'r tarw yn y cae?
3) Ydy'r desgiau yn y llyfrgell? 4) Ydy'r llyfr yn yr ystafell?
5) Ydy'r ceir yn y maes parcio.

Exercise 4: 1) Does dim lorïau yn y maes parcio.
2) Does dim llaeth (SW)/llefrith (NW) yn yr oergell.
3) Does dim llwyau glân.
4) Does dim mynydd yn y wlad.
5) Does dim prisiau ar y pethau yn y siop.

Exercise 5: 1) Dydy'r lorïau ddim yn y maes parcio.
2) Dydy'r llaeth (SW)/llefrith (NW) ddim yn yr oergell.
3) Dydy'r llwyau ddim yn lân.
4) Dydy Mr Williams ddim yn y wlad.
5) Dydy'r bwyd ddim yn rhad.

Exercise 6: 1) Oes 2) Does 3) Ydy 4) Oes 5) Oes
6) Does 7) Dydy

Exercise 7: 1) Nac oes, does dim newyddion yn y papur.
2) Oes, mae buwch yn y cae.
3) Oes, mae llyfrau yn y llyfrgell.
4) Nac oes, does dim Cymry yn yr ysgol.
5) Oes, mae meddyg yn yr ystafell.
6) Nac oes, does dim esgidiau ar y bwrdd.
7) Nac oes, does dim cath yn y ffenestr.
8) Oes, mae gêm ar y teledu heno.

Exercise 8: 1) Mae arian gyda fi. 2) Mae llawer o amser gyda ni.
3) Mae cawod newydd gyda fe. 4) Mae hufen gyda'r gath.
5) Mae ci mawr gyda chi. 6) Mae maes parcio mawr gyda'r dref.
7) Mae ffenestri glân gyda'r lorri. 8) Mae ffrindiau da gyda hi.
9) Mae tŷ hyfryd gyda ti. 10) Mae hen raw gyda nhw.

Exercise 9: 1) Mae gen i bres. 2) Mae ganddon ni lawer o amser.
3) Mae ganddo fo gawod newydd. 4) Mae gan y gath hufen.
5) Mae ganddoch chi gi mawr. 6) Mae gan y dref faes parcio mawr.
7) Mae gan y lorri ffenestri glân. 8) Mae ganddi hi ffrindiau da.
9) Mae gen ti dŷ hyfryd. 10) Mae ganddyn nhw hen raw.

Exercise 10: *Below are the answers in South Welsh:*

1) Oes coffi cryf gyda ti? 2) Oes digon o amser gyda fi?
3) Oes llaeth gyda'r gath? 4) Oes fflasg gyda hi?
5) Oes plant gyda fe? 6) Oes pecyn gyda'r postmon i ni?
7) Oes digon o fwyd gyda chi? 8) Oes llwyau glân gyda ni?

9) Oes anifeiliaid anwes gyda nhw? 10) Oes newid gyda chi?

Below are the answers in North Welsh:

1) Oes gen ti goffi cryf?
2) Oes gen i ddigon o amser?
3) Oes gan y gath lefrith?
4) Oes ganddi hi fflasg?
5) Oes ganddo fo blant?
6) Oes gan y postmon becyn i ni?
7) Oes ganddoch chi ddigon o fwyd?
8) Oes ganddon ni lwyau glân?
9) Oes ganddyn nhw anifeiliaid anwes?
10) Oes ganddoch chi newid?

Exercise 11: *Below are the answers in South Welsh:*

1) Ydy'r pethau gyda hi? Ydyn.
2) Ydy'r amser gyda chi? Ydy.
3) Ydy'r arian gyda nhw? Ydy.
4) Ydy'r pecyn gyda'r postmon? Nac ydy.
5) Ydy'r fflasg gyda ni? Nac ydy.
6) Ydy'r llwy gyda fo? Nac ydy.
7) Ydy'r newid gyda chi? Ydy.
8) Ydy'r rhaw gyda fe? Nac ydy.
9) Ydy'r blodau gyda nhw? Ydyn.
10) Ydy'r ddesg gyda chi? Nac ydy.

Below are the answers in North Welsh:

1) Ydy'r pethau ganddi hi? Ydyn.
2) Ydy'r amser ganddoch chi? Ydy.
3) Ydy'r arian ganddyn nhw? Ydy.
4) Ydy'r pecyn gan y postmon? Nac ydy.
5) Ydy'r fflasg ganddon ni? Nac ydy.
6) Ydy'r llwy ganddo fo? Nac ydy.
7) Ydy'r newid ganddoch chi? Ydy.
8) Ydy'r rhaw ganddo fo? Nac ydy.
9) Ydy'r blodau ganddyn nhw? Ydyn.
10) Ydy'r ddesg ganddoch chi? Nac ydy.

Exercise 12: *Below are the answers in South Welsh:*

1) Dydy'r arian ddim gyda fi.
2) Does dim rheswm da gyda ti.
3) Dydy'r teledu ddim gyda Mr Jones.
4) Dydy'r blodau ddim gyda ni.
5) Does dim flasg dda gyda hi.
6) Does dim ffôn newydd gyda nhw.
7) Does dim cwpan mawr gyda chi.
8) Does dim llawer o fwyd gyda'r ci.
9) Dydy'r newid ddim gyda hi.
10) Does dim hen gar gyda fe.

Below are the answers in North Welsh:

1) Dydy'r pres ddim gen i.
2) Does gen ti ddim rheswm da.
3) Dydy'r teledu ddim gan Mr Jones.
4) Dydy'r blodau ddim ganddon ni.
5) Does ganddi hi ddim fflasg dda.
6) Does ganddyn nhw ddim ffôn newydd.
7) Does ganddoch chi ddim cwpan mawr.
8) Does gan y ci ddim llawer o fwyd.
9) Dydy'r newid ddim ganddi hi.
10) Does ganddo fo ddim hen gar.

Week 4: Lesson 3
Exercise 1: 1) ar nos Wener 2) ddydd Sul 3) nos Iau
4) ar ddydd Sadwrn 5) bob dydd Sul 6) bob prynhawn dydd Gwener
7) ar ddydd Mawrth 8) ddydd Mercher 9) bob dydd Llun
10) ar ddydd Sadwrn

Exercise 2 1) Mae e'n (SW)/o'n (NW) siopa prynhawn dydd Mercher.
2) Ydych chi'n rhedeg ar ddydd Gwener?
3) Ydych chi'n mynd i'r dref nos Fawrth?
4) Dw i'n disgwyl gweithio nos Fercher.
5) Maen nhw'n bwyta sglodion yn y parc.
6) Dyn ni'n cael cawod bob dydd.
7) Dw i'n mynd i'r pwll nofio bore dydd Llun.
8) Dyn ni ddim yn cerdded i'r ysgol dydd Mawrth.
9) Mae hi'n mynd i fwrw eira trwy'r nos dydd Sadwrn.
10) Maen nhw'n mynd i'r capel ar ddydd Sul.

Week 4, Lesson 4
Exercise 1: 1) sy'n mynd i Fangor.
2) sy'n ysgrifennu llyfr am Gymru.
3) sydd wedi adeiladu tŷ yn y pentref?
4) sy'n byw yn y gorllewin?
5) sy'n cerdded saith milltir i'r gwaith.
6) sy'n gwneud y blodau yn yr eglwys bob dydd Sul?
7) sy'n gweithio ar ddydd Sadwrn.
8) sy'n cerdded i'r ysgol.

Exercise 2: 1 – d 2 – g 3 – h 4 – f
5 – a 6 – b 7 – c 8 – e

Exercise 3: 1) Beth sydd wedi digwydd?
2) Pwy sy'n cael coffi gyda fi?
3) Pa fath o gar sydd gyda fe (SW)/ganddo fo (NW)?
4) Pwy sydd wedi gwylio'r gêm?
5) Pwy sydd yn yr ysbyty?
6) Faint sydd wedi cyrraedd?
7) Pwy sy'n barod?
8) Faint o'r bobl yna sy'n Albanwyr?

Exercise 4: 1) sydd ddim wedi ennill   2) sydd ddim yn mynd i'r parti

3) sydd ddim ar y ddesg   4) sydd ddim yn ffonio

Exercise 5: 1) Dyna'r hen ddyn sy'n nofio bob dydd.
2) Mae pawb sy'n ennill yn cael arian (SW)/pres (NW).
3) Mae ffrind gyda fe sy'n ficer. (SW)
Alternative Answer: Mae ganddo fo ffrind sy'n ficer. (NW)
4) Faint o bobl sy'n bwyta bara gwyn?
5) Mae'n well gyda fi (SW)/gen i (NW) anifeiliaid anwes sy'n cysgu trwy'r nos.
6) Pwy sy'n ddig (SW)/flin (NW)?
7) Dw i'n adnabod rhywun sy'n gwneud bara bob dydd.
8) Mae hi'n ysgrifennu llyfr i blant sy'n dechrau darllen.
9) Faint o newid sydd gyda (SW)/ganddoch chi (NW)?
10) Dyn ni'n siarad â'r fenyw (SW)/ddynes (NW) sy'n cerdded o Land's End i John O'Groats.

Week 4, Lesson 5
Exercise 1: 1) dinas Caerdydd   2) ystyr y gair 'mynydd'   3) pris bara
4) ffrind Gareth   5) anthem Cymru   6) ci ffrind Gareth
7) llyfrgell yr ysgol   8) sŵn y môr   9) te Ifan
10) pennaeth yr ysgol

Exercise 2: 1) Megan ydy chwaer Sam.   2) Tomos ydy cefnder Sam.
3) Catrin ydy chwaer Bryn.   4) Bryn ydy mab Ioan.
5) Catrin ydy merch Meri.   6) Bryn ydy brawd Catrin.
7) Tomos a Bethan ydy plant Ifan.   8) Bryn ydy ewythr Bethan.

Exercise 3: 1) Ie, Siân ydy gwraig Bryn.   2) Nage, Ifan ydy tad Tomos.
3) Ie, Tomos ydy brawd Bethan.   4) Nage, Siân ydy mam Megan.
5) Ie, Ioan ydy taid Tomos.   6) Ie, Meri ydy nain Sam.
7) Nage, Catrin ydy chwaer Bryn.   8) Ie, Ifan ydy gŵr Catrin.

Week 4, Lesson 6
Exercise 1: 1) fy mhrif reswm i   2) fy nheledu i   3) fy mwyd i
4) fy ffrindiau i   5) fy mhres i   6) fy nghwpan i
7) fy nheimladau i   8) fy nesg i   9) fy ystafell i
10) fy ngwely i

Exercise 2: 1) Ym Mhorthmadog   2) Ym Mrymbo   3) Yng Ngwynedd
4) Yn Nhregaron   5) Yn Rhiwabon   6) Yn Nolgellau
7) Yng Nghaernarfon   8) Ym Mhentre Bach

Week 4, Lesson 7
Exercise 1: *Below are the answers in South Welsh:*

1) Oes, mae hen gar gyda fi.
2) Nac oes, does dim ffenestri mawr gyda'r tŷ.
3) Oes, mae cawod gyda fe yn y tŷ.
4) Oes, mae digon o arian gyda hi.
5) Nac oes, does dim brawd gyda fi.

6) Oes, mae digon o amser gyda ni.
Alternative answer: Oes, mae digon o amser gyda chi.
7) Nac oes, does dim hoff lyfr gyda fi.
8) Oes, mae teulu gyda fi/ni sy'n byw yng ngogledd Cymru.

Below are the answers in North Welsh:

1) Oes, mae gen i hen gar.
2) Nac oes, does gan y tŷ ddim ffenestri mawr.
3) Oes, mae ganddo fo gawod yn y tŷ.
4) Oes, mae ganddi hi ddigon o arian.
5) Nac oes, does gen i ddim brawd.
6) Oes, mae ganddon ni ddigon o amser.
Alternative answer: Oes, mae ganddoch chi ddigon o amser.
7) Nac oes, does gen i ddim hoff lyfr.
8) Oes, mae ganddon ni/gen i deulu sy'n byw yng Ngogledd Cymru.

Exercise 2: 1) Mae brawd gyda fi (SW)/ gen i frawd (NW) sy'n adeiladu tai.
2) Mae e'n (SW)/o'n (NW) dysgu Cymraeg am wahanol resymau.
3) Ydyn nhw'n mynd ddydd Mawrth?
4) Mae'n gas gyda hi (SW)/ganddi (NW) hi smocio tu allan i siopau.
5) Dw i'n cael car newydd ddydd Gwener.
6) Mae hi'n mynd i'r pwll nofio ar nos Fercher.
7) Mae'n well gyda ni (SW)/ganddon (NW) ni fwyta sglodion.
8) Beth ydy'r wir broblem?
9) Ydych chi'n gweithio dros y penwythnos?
10) Beth sy'n digwydd yn yr ysgol?

Exercise 3:

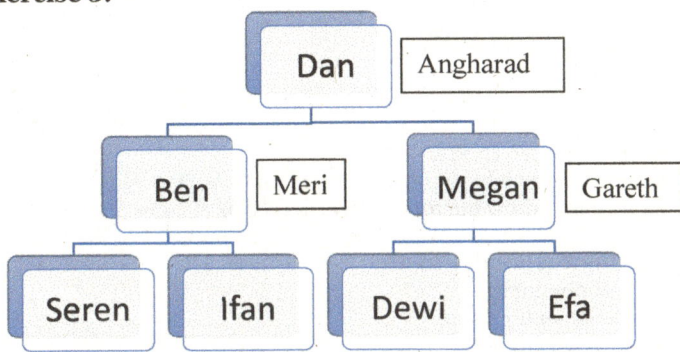

Exercise 4: 1) Ydych chi'n gwybod beth ydy pris bara?
2) Mae capeli'r pentref yn hen iawn.
3) Beth ydy prif iaith y wlad?
4) Pryd mae parti'r plant?
5) Pwy ydy ficer yr eglwys?
6) Mae ffenestri'r tŷ'n frwnt (SW)/fudr (NW) iawn.

Exercise 5: 1 – g 2 – h 3 – a 4 – c 5 – f 6 – e 7 – i 8 – b 9 – d

Week 5, Lesson 1
Exercise 1: 1) fy ffonio i   2) fy helpu i   3) fy nhalu i
4) fy neall i   5) fy nghicio i   6) fy adnabod i
7) fy nghodi i   8) fy nisgwyl i   9) fy mwrw i
10) fy nysgu i

Exercise 2: 1) Oes teulu gyda'ch cymar/partner chi yng Ngogledd Cymru? (SW)
Alternative Answer: Oes gan eich cymar/partner chi deulu yng Ngogledd Cymru? (NW)
2) Dyn ni ddim yn gallu eich ffonio chi heno.
3) Ydyn nhw wedi'ch talu chi?
4) Ble mae'ch mab chi'n gweithio nawr (SW)/rŵan (NW)?
5) Mae e (SW)/o (NW) eisiau eich clywed chi'n canu.
6) Ydw i'n gallu'ch gweld chi?
7) Mae'ch gwallt chi'n wahanol heddiw.
8) Dw i'n ceisio'ch deall chi.
9) Sut mae'ch dant chi?
10) Mae pawb yn eich disgwyl chi.

Exercise 3: 1) Gwyn ydy lliw fy nghar i.
2) Gwyrdd ydy fy hoff liw i.
3) Siôn ydy enw fy mrawd i.
4) Un deg saith ydy rhif fy nhŷ i.
5) Chwech ac wyth ydy oedran fy mhlant i.
6) Cymru ydy fy hoff wlad i.

Week 5, Lesson 2
Exercise 1: 1) Dy waith di.
2) Ei ford e (SW)/ei fwrdd o (NW).
3) Dy broblem di.
4) Ei gwpanau e (SW)/o (NW).
5) Dy fodryb di.
6) Ei wely e (SW)/o (NW).
7 Dy bartner/gymar di.
8) Ei wraig e (SW)/o (NW).
9) Dyn ni eisiau dy dalu di nawr (SW)/rŵan (NW)?
10) Pwy sy'n mynd i'w baentio e (SW)/o (NW)?

Exercise 2: 1) Ydych chi wedi ei chlywed hi?
2) Ydw i'n ei phoeni hi?
3) Dw i'n ceisio ei helpu hi.
4) Ble mae ei harian hi?
5) Pwy sy'n mynd i'w heglwys hi?
6) Mae ei chadeiriau hi'n frwnt (SW)/fudr (NW).
7) Mae ei thad-cu (SW)/thaid (NW) hi'n ysgrifennu i'r papur.
8) Mae ei chŵn hi a'i chathod hi'n gyfeillgar iawn.

Exercise 3: 1) Mae ein bordydd (SW)/ byrddau (NW) ni a'n cadeiriau ni yn eu garej nhw.
2) Dw i ddim yn deall eu hiaith nhw o gwbl.
3) Mae e (SW)/o (NW) eisiau ein gweld ni heddiw.

4) Ydych chi'n gallu eu codi nhw?
5) Pwy sy'n siarad â'u teulu nhw?
6) Pwy sy'n ein disgwyl ni?
7) Dw i ddim yn gallu eu bwyta nhw.
8) Mae ein hesgidiau'n lân.

Week 5, Lesson 3
Exercise 1: 1) Maen nhw'n cerdded wrth eu hunain.
2) Dyn ni'n mynd yn ein ceir ein hunain.
3) Mae'n well gyda fi (SW)/ganddo fo (NW) ei gwmni ei hunan.
4) Mae eu ffordd eu hunain o wneud pethau gyda nhw. (SW)
Alternative Answer: Mae ganddyn nhw eu ffordd eu hunain o wneud pethau. (NW)
5) Mae hi'n adeiladu ei thŷ hi wrth ei hunan.

Week 5, Lesson 4
Exercise 1: 1) ers 2) am 3) at 4) heb 5) wrth ochr
6) tua 7) ar draws 8) yn lle 9) i

Week 5, Lesson 5
Exercise 1: 1) Ydy hi wedi bwrw glaw heddiw?
2) Dyn nhw ddim wedi ceisio siarad â'u tad-cu (SW)/taid (NW) nhw.
3) Ydy hi wedi cwrdd â fe (SW)/ cyfarfod â fo (NW)?
4) Dyn ni wedi cyrraedd Abertawe.
5) Pwy sydd wedi dechrau gwneud brecwast?
6) Dw i wedi anfon e-bost at fy nhad i.
7) Beth sydd wedi digwydd yn ei ystafell wely e (SW)/ ei lofft o (NW)?
8) Dydy e (SW)/o (NW) ddim wedi gweld y ffilm yna.
9) Ydy hi wedi paentio ei hystafell hi eto?
10) Ydych chi wedi cael brecwast eto?

Week 5, Lesson 6
Exercise 1: a) chwarter i ddeg y nos
b) chwarter wedi deg y bore
c) pum munud wedi chwech y nos
d) pum munud ar hugain i bedwar y prynhawn
e) deg munud i dri y bore f. ugain munud wedi un y prynhawn
g) ugain munud i bump y bore
h) pum munud i ddeg y nos

Week 5, Lesson 7
Exercise 1: 1) adael 2) ateb 3) chwestiwn 4) mhennaeth
5) weld 6) deulu 7) henw 8) dillad
9) hoergell 10) helpu

Exercise 2: 1) ers 2) rhwng 3) tua 4) heblaw 5) â
6) heb 7) ar ôl 8) trwy 9) yn lle 10) ar draws

Exercise 3: 1) Maen nhw wedi dod i'r dref wrth eu hunain.
2) Ydy e (SW) / o (NW) wedi gadael ar ei ben ei hunan?

3) Mae hi wedi torri ei gwallt ei hunan.
4) Ydych chi wedi cofio cael caws a llaeth (SW)/llefrith (NW)?
5) Dyn ni wedi gadael ein hwyres ni gyda'i thad hi.
6) Pwy sydd wedi ei fwyta e (SW)/o (NW)?
7) Mae hi wedi anfon llythyr a cherdyn at ei brawd hi.
8) Dw i ddim wedi cerdded i fyny'r bryn eto a dw i wedi blino.

Exercise 4: 1) Mae Mair/hi'n cael brecwast am wyth o'r gloch.
2) Mae Mair/hi'n cyrraedd y gwaith am naw o'r gloch.
3) Mae Mair/hi'n cael coffi am hanner awr wedi deg.
4) Mae Mair/hi'n cael cinio am bum munud ar hugain wedi deuddeg.
5) Mae Mair hi'n mynd adref am chwarter i bump.

Week 6, Lesson 1
Exercise 1: 1) Roedd e'n (SW)/o'n (NW) gobeithio rhedeg yn y marathon.
2) Roedd e'n (SW)/o'n (NW) ysgrifennu llythyr yn ei ystafell wely.
3) Roedden ni'n siarad trwy'r nos.
4) Roeddwn i'n arfer gweithio mewn sinema brysur.
5) Roedd pobl yn dechrau gadael.
6) Roedd hi'n niwlog iawn.
7) Roedd fy modryb yn (arfer) byw yn Llandegla.
8) Roedden nhw'n sefyll rhwng fy rhieni.
9) Roeddwn i'n gwybod y ffordd.
10) Roedd hi'n arfer mynd i'r gampfa bob nos.

Exercise 2: 1) Oedd y llaeth (SW)/llefrith (NW) yn oer?
2) Oeddet ti'n ei gredu e (SW)/o (NW)?
3) Oedden nhw'n deall?
4) Oedd hi'n gymylog ddoe?
5) Oeddech chi'n arfer byw gyda'i rhieni hi?
6) Oedd y llythyr yn hir?
7) Oedd e'n (SW)/o'n (NW) deall fy nghwestiwn i?
8) Oeddech chi'n gobeithio cyrraedd neithiwr?
9) Oedden nhw'n disgwyl ein gweld ni?
10) Oedd hi'n ddig (NW)/flin (SW) iawn?

Exercise 3: 1) Doeddwn i ddim yn sefyll am amser hir.
2) Doedden ni ddim yn ei hadnabod hi.
3) Oedden nhw'n hoffi hanes yn yr ysgol?
4) Doedd y blodau ddim yn yr ystafell.
5) Doedd e (SW)/o (NW) ddim (yn arfer) bwyta cig.
6) Doedden nhw ddim yn gyfeillgar.
7) Doedden ni ddim yn dysgu Cymraeg yn yr ysgol.
8) Doedd fy ewythr i ddim yn enwog.
9) Doedd y dosbarth ddim yn ddiddorol iawn.
10) Doedd hi ddim yn bwrw eirlaw; roedd hi'n bwrw eira.

Exercise 4: 1) Oeddech. Roeddech chi'n meddwl am adael.
　　　　　Alternative Answer: Oedden. Roedden ni'n meddwl am adael.
2) Nac oedd, doedd hi ddim yn oer ddoe.
3) Oedden, roedden nhw eisiau gweithio heno.

4) Nac oedd, doedd Gareth ddim yn gwybod y ffordd.
5) Nac oedd, doedd y wers ddim yn ddiddorol.
6) Oeddwn, roeddwn i'n arfer gyrru lorri.
7) Oedd, roedd llawer o bobl yn y llyfrgell.
8) Nac oedden, doedd y plant ddim yn deall.
9) Oeddwn, roeddwn i'n meddwl am fy nhad i.
10) Nac oedden, doedden nhw ddim yn arfer chwarae rygbi yn yr ysgol.

Week 6, Lesson 2
Exercise 1: 1) Doeddwn i ddim wedi ysgrifennu'r llythyr at fy rhieni erbyn pump o'r gloch.
2) Oedd e (SW)/o (NW) wedi darllen y llyfrau?
3) Doedd e (SW)/o (NW) ddim wedi meddwl am y newyddion o gwbl.
4) Roedden ni wedi newid ein car.
5) Oedd hi wedi nofio yn y môr?
6) Oeddech chi wedi rhoi'r llaeth (SW)/llefrith (NW) yn yr oergell?
7) Roeddwn i wedi rhoi'r teledu i'r plant.
8) Roedd fy mam wedi paentio'r gadair yn wydd.
9) Roedd y plismon wedi gweld y ddamwain.
10) Oedd rhywun wedi bwyta'r bara i gyd?

Week 6, Lesson 3
Exercise 1: 1) bod   2) fod   3) bod   4) bod   5) bod
6) bod   7) fod   8) mod   9) bod   10) bod

Exercise 2: 1) Mae e'n gwybod ei fod e'n iawn. (SW)
Alternative Answer: Mae o'n gwybod ei fod o'n iawn. (NW)
2) Dw i'n credu ei fod e'n (SW)/o'n (NW) gwybod.
3) Dyn ni'n gobeithio bod y tŷ'n barod.
4) Dw i'n credu bod pawb yn dod.
5) Maen nhw'n gwybod eu bod nhw yn y ffordd.
6) Dyn ni'n credu eich bod chi'n iawn.
7) Mae pawb yn gwybod ei bod hi'n cystadlu.
8) Dw i'n deall bod y rheilffordd yn hen iawn.

Week 6, Lesson 4
Exercise 1: 1) Wrth gwrs fy mod i'n falch.
2) Mae'n drueni eu bod nhw ddim yn cofio eu tad-cu (SW)/taid (NW)
3) Efallai ei fod e'n cysgu. (SW)
Alternative Answer: Hwyrach ei fod o'n cysgu. (NW)
4) Er ei bod hi'n rhewi dyn ni'n mynd.
5) Dw i'n astudio yng Nghaernarfon achos bod cefnder gyda fi (SW) / gen i (NW) gefnder sy'n byw yno.
6) Dw i ddim yn mynd gan ei bod hi'n stormus iawn.

Week 6, Lesson 5
Exercise 1: 1) bod   2) mai   3) bod   4) bod
5) mai   6) bod   7) mai   8) bod

Week 6, Lesson 6
Exercise 1: a) flynedd b) mlynedd c) mlynedd d) mlynedd e) blynedd
f) mlynedd g) blynedd h) blynedd i) mlynedd j) mlynedd
k) mlynedd l) mlynedd

Week 6, Lesson 7
Exercise 1: 1) Roeddwn 2) Roedd 3) Oeddech
4) Doeddet 5) Roedden 6) Doedden
7) Doedd 8) Roeddwn 9) Doedd
10) Oeddech

Exercise 2: 1) Roedd hi'n wyntog ddoe.
2) Doedden nhw dddim eisiau mynd allan.
3) Roeddwn i wedi gyrru.
4) Roedd pawb wedi ein deall ni.
5) Oedd hi wedi cynnig?
6) Roeddwn i'n meddwl ei bod hi'n wir.
7) Wrth gwrs ei fod e (SW)/o (NW) wedi ei chredu hi.
8) Roedden nhw wedi symud tŷ.
9) Oeddech chi wedi bwyta'ch brecwast chi?
10) Doeddwn i ddim wedi gweld y ddamwain.

Exercise 3: 1) Mae e'n (SW)/o'n (NW) dweud ein bod ni'n wirion.
2) Wrth gwrs fy mod i'n gwrando.
3) Dw i'n meddwl ein bod ni'n gynnar.
4) Roeddwn i wedi clywed bod Eisteddfod yr wythnos nesaf.
5) Maen nhw'n dweud ei bod hi wedi ysgrifennu llythyr arall.
6) Trueni ei bod hi mor wyntog.
7) Roedden ni'n meddwl mai plismon oedd e (SW)/o (NW).
8) Er ei bod hi'n bwrw eira, dyn ni'n mynd i gerdded.

Exercise 4: 1) mlynedd 2) mlwydd 3) blynedd
4) flynedd 5) flwyddyn 6) flwyddyn.

Week 7, Lesson 1
Exercise 1: 1) Cwyd 2) Ysgrifenna 3) Siarad 4) Bydd
5) Meddylia 6) Saf 7) Cofia 8) Cer (SW)/Dos (NW)
9) Eistedd 10) Paid.

Exercise 2: 1) Byddwch 2) Gwnewch 3) Cysgwch 4) Cerwch/Ewch
5) Safwch 6) Rhedwch 7) Dewch 8) Symudwch
9) Yfwch 10) Caewch.

Week 7, Lesson 2
Exercise 1: 1) Bwytais 2) Canodd 3) Gwrandawodd 4) Gadawaist
5) Cyrhaeddodd 6) Nofion 7) Cerddon 8) Darllenoch

Week 7, Lesson 3
Exercise 1: 1) Wylioch 2) Brynodd 3) Symudaist 4) Gysgodd
5) Glywon 6) Ddysgon 7) Siaradodd 8) Redodd

Week 7, Lesson 4
Exercise 1: 1) Ysgrifennais i ddim llythyr at yr heddlu.
2) Yrron nhw ddim i Ddinbych.
3) Cherddon ni ddim adref.
4) Ddigwyddodd ddim byd.
5) Yfais i ddim coffi.
6) Theithion ni ddim gyda'n gilydd.
7) Phrynoch chi ddim dillad.
8) Ffonion nhw ddim ddoe.

Exercise 2: 1) Canodd y ffôn. 2) Ddarllenais i ddim o'r papur.
3) Enillodd Siôn wobr? 4) Rhedon ni adref.
5) Ysgrifennoch chi lythyr? 6) Olchoch chi ddim o'r carped.
7) Gadawodd e'r (SW)/o'r (NW) clwb. 8) Chollodd hi ddim o'r trên.
9) Alwodd Mair? 10) Glywoch chi'r newyddion?

Week 7, Lesson 5
Exercise 1: 1) Des i i'r gampfa yn y car.
2) Beth gawsoch chi am eich pen-blwydd chi?
3) Wnaeth e'r (SW)/o'r (NW) bara?
4) Ble cafodd hi fwyd?
5) Gwnaethon ni goffi yn y gegin.
6) Wnaethoch chi'r gwely?
7) Daethon ni bore ddoe.
8) Wnaethi hi ei gwaith hi?
9) Ddaethon ni â chotiau?
10) Aethon nhw ddim â'r arian (SW)/pres (NW).

Week 7, Lesson 6
Exercise 1: 1) Fues 2) Buodd 3) Fuest 4) Buodd
5) Fuodd 6) Fuon 7) Fues 8) Doedd

Week 7, Lesson 7
Exercise 1: 1) Cerwch (SW)/Ewch (NW) â'r ci am dro.
2) Saf ar y gornel.
3) Dihunwch.
4) Paid â phoeni.
5) Newidiwch y sianel.
6) Gwnewch rywbeth
7) Dewch â'ch dillad brwnt (SW)/budr (NW).
8) Cerwch (SW)/Ewch (NW) â moddion at eich annwyd.
9) Gofynnwch am y tywydd.
10) Bydd yn dawel.

Exercise 2: 1) Do, canodd o'r anthem genedlaethol.
2) Naddo, ofynnon nhw ddim cwestiwn.
3) Do, newidiais i fy meddwl.
4) Naddo, ddihunon ni ddim yn gynnar.
Alternative answer: Naddo, ddihunoch chi ddim yn gynnar.
5) Naddo, phrynon nhw ddim car newydd.
6) Naddo, weithiodd pawb ddim yn galed.

7) Do, gadawais i'r gwaith yn gynnar.
Alternative Answer: Do, gadawon ni'r gwaith yn gynnar.
8) Do, bwyton ni'r caws i gyd.
Alternative Answer: Do, bwytoch chi'r caws i gyd.

Exercise 3: 1) Beth wnaethon ni?
2) Ddaeth hi â chyllell?
3) Es i ddim i'r archfarchnad.
4) Wnest ti ddigon o frechdanau?
5) Gwnaethon nhw eu dillad eu hunain.
6) Aeth e (SW)/o (NW) â'r ci am dro.
7) Aethoch chi am bythefnos?
8) Faint o'r gloch aeth hi?
9) Pwy wnaeth y cacennau?
10) Wnaethon ni ddim llanast.

Exercise 4: 1) Fuon nhw'n hwylio'r penwythnos diwethaf?
2) Ble roedd e (SW)/o (NW) neithiwr?
3) Roeddwn i yn y capel.
4) Doedd hi ddim yn y digwyddiad.
5) Fuest ti yng Nghaerdydd dros y penwythnos?
6) Roedden ni'n gwylio'r ddrama.
7) Doedden nhw ddim yn yr ysgol.
8) Oeddech chi yn y ddinas?

Week 8, Lesson 1
Exercise 1: 1) Gawsoch chi afalau o'r siop?
2) Cafodd yr ysgol garpedi newydd.
3) Faint o'r gloch cawson ni goffi?
4) Cafodd e (SW)/o (NW) ddamwain neithiwr.
5) Gafodd hi gawod y bore 'ma?
6) Gest ti ddillad newydd?
7) Chawson nhw ddim bwyd.
8) Gawsoch chi got newydd yn y dref.
9) Cafodd y dosbarth Cymraeg amser da yn Ffrainc.
10) Ches i ddim pwdin.

Week 8, Lesson 2
Exercise 1: 1) a adeiladodd
2) a oedd yn eich credu chi
3) a ysgrifennodd lythyr
4) a oedd wedi gadael
5) a ganodd
6) a oedd yn gwylio
7) a aeth i'r ddrama
8) a ddaeth
9) a oedd eisiau
10) a gafodd ddamwain.

Week 8, Lesson 3
Exercise 1: 1) Mae'n well i fi brynu tocyn.
2) Mae'n well iddi hi ganu'r anthem genedlaethol. Mae hi'n canu'n well na fi.
3) Mae'n well i ni beidio aros yn rhy hir.
4) Mae'n well iddyn nhw benderfynu nawr (SW)/rŵan (NW).
5) Mae'n well i chi fod yn dawel.
6) Mae'n well iddo fe (SW)/fo (NW) beidio nofio yn y môr.

7) Mae'n well i fi beidio siarad â nhw.
8) Mae'n well i'r teulu deithio mewn awyren.

Exercise 2: 1) Mae'n well gyda fi (SW)/gen i (NW) beidio dweud.
2) Mae'n well gyda (SW)/ganddon ni (NW) brynu ein tocynnau mewn siop leol.
3) Mae'n well gyda fe (SW)/ganddo fo (NW) siopa yn yr archfarchnad fawr.
4) Oes well gyda (SW)/gandddoch chi (NW) dywydd poeth?
5) Mae'n well gyda hi/ ganddi hi'r carped coch.
6) Mae'n well gyda nhw (SW)/ganddyn nhw (NW)'r cwmni arall.
7) Mae well gyda (SW)/gan (NW) y myfyrwyr astudio yn y llyfrgell.
8) Oes well gyda fe (SW)/ganddo fo (NW) gerdded?

Week 8, Lesson 4
Exercise 1: 1) Mae rhaid i fi fynd i'r archfarchnad ar y ffordd adref.
2) Oes rhaid iddo fe (SW)/fo (NW) aros yn y gwesty?
3) Mae rhaid iddo fo beidio yfed gormod.
4) Does dim rhaid i ni dderbyn y wobr.
5) Mae rhaid i chi beidio smocio.
6) Mae rhaid i bawb benderfynu.
7) Mae rhaid iddyn nhw fod wedi clywed erbyn hyn.
8) Mae rhaid iddi hi godi'n gynnar.
9) Mae rhaid i chi yrru'n ofalus.
10) Does dim rhaid i fi fynd mewn awyren.

Exercise 2: 1) Rhaid eich bod chi'n cofio.
2) Rhaid ei fod e'n dwym. (SW)
Alternative Answer: Rhaid ei fod o'n gynnes. (NW)
3) Rhaid bod pawb yn ddig (SW)/flin (NW).
4) Rhaid eu bod nhw'n enwog.
5) Rhaid fy mod i'n clywed pethau.

Exercise 3: 1) Mae'n well i ni fynd cyn iddi hi fwrw eira.
2) Mae hi wedi dysgu Cymraeg ers iddi hi symud i Gymru.
3) Roedden nhw wedi gadael erbyn i ni gyrraedd.
4) Ewch ag ymbarél rhag ofn iddi hi fwrw glaw.
5) Wrth i ni eistedd ar y gadael torrodd hi.
6) Cyn iddo fe barcio'r car edrychodd e yn y drych. (SW)
Alternative Answer: Cyn iddo fo barcio'r car edrychodd o yn y drych. (NW)
7) Daethon nhw ar ôl i ni gyrraedd.
8) Mae e eisiau mynd i'r Aifft cyn iddo fe ymddeol. (SW)
Alternative Answer: Mae o eisiau mynd i'r Aifft cyn iddo fo ymddeol. (NW)

Week 8, Lesson 5
Exercise 1: 1) Dydy Twm ddim mor dal ag Ifan.
2) Dydy Abertawe ddim mor fawr (cymaint) â Chaerdydd.
3) Dydy e (SW)/o (NW) ddim yn rhedeg mor araf ag Elen.
4) Dydy fy nghot i ddim mor dwym (SW)/gynnes (NW) â'i chot hi.

5) Dydy Siôn ddim mor gryf â Cheri.
6) Dydy hi ddim mor wyntog heddiw.
7) Dydy'r llyfr dw i'n ei ddarllen ddim mor ddiddorol â'r un a ddarllenais i'r wythnos diwethaf.
8) Mae hi mor ddrwg/cynddrwg â fe (SW)/fo (NW).

Exercise 2: 1) gryfach 2) fwy gofalus 3) rhatach
4) hapusach 5) well 6) fwy stormus
7) fwy cyfeillgar 8) gwaeth 9) decach
10) drymach

Week 8, Lesson 6
Exercise 1: 1) hira(f) 2) enwoca(f) 3) fwya(f) stormus
4) deca(f) 5) tryma(f) 6) cyflyma(f)
7) tala(f) 8) gorau 9) gwlypa(f)
10) waetha(f)

Week 8, Lesson 7
Exercise 1: 1) Gawsoch 2) Cawson; ces; Cafodd; Chawson
3) gafodd 4) Cafodd; Cawson
5) gest 6) Ces; Cafodd; chafodd

Exercise 2: 1) Ble mae'r dyn a oedd yn ystyried prynu ei thŷ hi?
2) Siaradon ni â rhywun a oedd yn adnabod y meddyg yn dda.
3) Ydych chi'n adnabod yr athro (*m*.)/athrawes (*f*.) a oedd yn arfer chwarae rygbi rhyngwladol?
4) Cwrddais i â'r bobl a gollodd yr arian i gyd.
5) Ydyn nhw wedi enwi'r fenyw (SW)/ddynes (NW) a yrrodd ei char hi i fyny Yr Wyddfa?
6) Gadawodd pawb a oedd wedi clywed y larwm yr adeilad.
7) Roedd pawb a oedd wedi bwyta'r selsig yn teimlo'n sâl wedyn.
8) Roedd y plant oedd wedi cael cawod cynnar yn lwcus iawn. Roedd y dŵr yn boeth.

Exercise 3: 1) Mae'n well iddo fe benderfynu nawr. (SW)
Alternative Answer: Mae'n well iddo fo benderfynu rŵan. (NW)
2) Mae'n well i ti beidio cymryd y papur i gyd.
3) Mae'n well gyda hi (SW)/ganddi hi (NW) sglodion.
4) Ydy'n well gyda nhw (SW)/ganddyn nhw (NW) roi arian neu brynu anrheg?
5) Mae'n well i fi fod yn barod mewn pryd.
6) Ydy'n well gyda chi (SW)/ganddoch chi (NW) fynd i fyny yn y lifft?
7) Mae'n well i ni beidio poeni am y ddamwain.
8) Mae'n well i fi beidio torri'r bara nawr (SW)/rŵan (NW).

Exercise 4: 1) Mae rhaid iddi hi ddewis
2) ar ôl i fi wylio'r ffilm
3) wrth i fi adael
4) Oes rhaid iddyn nhw ofyn
5) Mae rhaid i ni
6) cyn i ti gael

7) Does dim rhaid iddo fe (SW)/fo (NW) gyrraedd
8) rhag ofn i fi anghofio
9) ers iddi hi ymddeol
10) Erbyn i Marc gyrraedd

Exercise 5: 1) Dydy'r ardal yma ddim mor bert â Gorllewin Cymru.
2) Dw i mor dal â fy nhad i.
3) Dydy Siwan ddim mor brydlon â Megan.
4) Mae'r ffilm mor wirion (NW)/ dwp (SW) â'r ddrama.
5) Mae hi mor denau â'i gŵr hi.

Exercise 6: 1) Dw i'n mynd i Gaerdydd yn fwy aml/amlach na fy rhieni.
2) Gobeithio bod y pysgod yn fwy ffres heddiw.
3) Mae'r tywydd yn fwy heulog yn y De.
4) Mae bwyd yn rhatach heddiw.
5) Mae ei siwt hi'n fwy tywyll na'r ffrog.

Exercise 7: 1) Meri yw'r decaf.
2) Fe (SW)/Fo (NW) yw'r athro gwaethaf.
3) Anthony Hopkins yw'r enwocaf.
4) Blaenau Ffestiniog yw'r pentref gwlypaf.
5) Hi yw'r fyrraf.

Week 9, Lesson 1

Exercise 1: 1) byddwch 2) bydda 3) bydd 4) byddan
5) byddwn 6) bydd 7) bydd 8) byddi

Exercise 2: 1) Fydd 2) Fyddwch 3) Fydd 4) Fyddi
5) Fyddwn 6) Fydda 7) Fyddan 8) Fydd

Exercise 3: 1) Bydd, bydd o'n cytuno â fi.
2) Na fyddan, fydd y plant ddim yn cloi'r drws.
3) Bydda, bydda i'n cwrdd â fe yfory. (SW)
Alternative Answer: Bydda, bydda i'n cyfarfod â fo yfory. (NW)
4) Byddi, byddi di'n cerdded yno.
Alternative Answer: Byddwch, byddwch chi'n cerdded yno.
5) Na fydd, fydd hi ddim yn stormus yfory.
6) Byddan, byddan nhw'n credu'r meddyg.
7) Na fydda, fydda i ddim yn galw heibio.
Alternative Answer: Na fyddwn, fyddwn ni ddim yn galw heibio.
8) Na fyddwch, fyddwch chi ddim yn cael brecwast cyn mynd.
Alternative Answer: Na fyddwn, fyddwn ni ddim yn cael brecwast cyn mynd.

Week 9, Lesson 2

Exercise 1: 1) Paentia 2) Newidiwn 3) Nofian 4) siaradwn
5) Clywith 6) Bwytwn 7) Prynwn 8) Ceisith
9) Dwedith 10) Cytunwn

Exercise 2: 1) Wela i chi yfory?
2) Allith hi weld y môr o'i ffenestr hi?

3) Fydd y meddyg yn galw?
4) Fyddan nhw'n gwerthu'r tŷ?
5) Allan nhw helpu?
6) Fyddan nhw'n darllen yr adroddiad?
7) Fydd Emyr yn gwylio'r gêm heno?
8) Gymerwch chi un arall?
9) Pwy welwn ni nesaf?
10) Gymeri di baned?

Exercise 3: 1 – e   2 – d   3 – g   4 – h   5 – f
6 – i   7 – b   8 – a   9 – c

Exercise 4: 1) llwyaid o siwgr   2) bagaid o lyfrau   3) potelaid o win
4) basgedaid o flodau   5) cwpanaid o siocled poeth   6) bocsaid o siocledi

Exercise 5: 1 – b   2 – d, e   3 – d, e   4 – f
5 – a   6 – d, e   7 – b   8 – a

Exercise 6: 1) Ddysgi di ddim.   2) Chlywa i ddim.
3) Wylith hi ddim o'r gêm.   4) Ddealla i ddim.
5) Redwch chi ddim.   6) Chysgwn ni ddim yn y car.
7) Adawith e (SW)/o (NW) ddim. 8) Weithith y meddygon ddim yfory.
9) Ofynnwn ni ddim.   10) Liwith y plant ddim amser
                                   chwarae.

Week 9, Lesson 3
Exercise 1: 1) ewch   2) Eith   3) Wnân   4) wnawn   5) Af
6) Ei   7) Awn   8) Wneith   9) Wnaf   10) Wneith

Exercise 2: a) Wnewch chi agor y drws? Gwnaf, agora i'r drws.
b) Wnewch chi estyn y papur? Gwnaf, estynna i'r papur.
c) Wnewch chi olchi'r llestri? Gwnaf, golcha i'r llestri.
d) Wnewch chi gynnau'r golau? Gwnaf, cynheua i'r golau.
e) Wnewch chi godi ar eich traed? Gwnaf, coda i ar fy nhraed
f) Wnewch chi droi'r sŵn i lawr? Gwnaf, troa i'r sŵn i lawr.

Exercise 3: 1) agor y ffenestr   2) aros pum munud
3) gynnau'r golau   4) chwilio am fy waled i
5) ddod gyda (SW)/efo (NW) fi 6) yrru adref
7) fwydo'r gath   8) ddysgu'r geiriau
9) frysio   10) alw heibio

Week 9, Lesson 4
Exercise 1: 1) Gaf   2) Chewch   3) Geith   4) gawn
5) Caf   6) Ceith   7) Ceith   8) Cei

Exercise 2: 1) Gaf fi'r bil?   2) Gaf i beint o laeth (SW)/lefrith (NW)?
3) Gaf fi ragor o hufen?   4) Gaf i dorth o fara?
5) Gaf fi focsaid o fatsis.   6) Gaf i hanner peint o gwrw.
7) Gaf fi ragor o amser.   8) Gaf fi bwys o datws.

Week 9, Lesson 5
Exercise 1: 1) dewch chi   2) Ddôn nhw   3) Ddeith o ddim   4) Ddoi di
5) Deith fy nheulu   6) Ddeith hi   7) Ddewch chi   8) Dof fi

Week 9, Lesson 6
Exercise 1: 1) ei drydydd ben-blwydd o
2) y trydydd diwrnod ar ddeg
3) ei hail briodas hi
4) y pedwerydd drws
5) y ddeunawfed gêm
6) y pedwerydd tŷ ar bymtheg
7) yr unfed cerdyn ar ddeg ar hugain
8) y seithfed wers ar hugain
9) y drydedd ddamwain ar hugain
10) y bedwaredd dorth o fara.

Exercise 2: 1) y pumed ar hugain o fis Ionawr
2) y pedwerydd ar ddeg o fis Chwefror
3) y cyntaf o fis Mawrth
4) yr unfed ar hugain o fis Mawrth
5) y pedwerydd o fis Gorffennaf
6) yr unfed ar bymtheg o fis Medi
7) yr unfed ar ddeg ar hugain o fis Hydref
8) y pumed o fis Tachwedd
9) y chweched ar hugain o fis Rhagfyr
10) yr unfed ar ddeg ar hugain o fis Rhagfyr

Exercise 3: a) mil dim pedwar chwech   b) pedwar dim saith
c) mil pedwar dim wyth   d) dwy fil ac un deg saith
e) mil pedwar wyth pump   f) mil saith wyth dau
g) dwy fil a chwech   h) mil tri nawr tri.

Week 9, Lesson 7
Exercise 1: 1) Sut byddan nhw'n cyrraedd?
2) Fydd hi'n eich credu chi?
3) Fyddan nhw ddim yn fy neall i.
4) Bydd yr Eisteddfod yn cychwyn am hanner awr wedi wyth yn y nos.
5) Bydd pawb yn ddiolchgar.
6) Fydd y tîm y cystadlu?
7) Fyddi di eisiau dy het haul di?
8) Beth fydd yn digwydd nesaf?
9) Faint o'r gloch bydd y gêm yn cychwyn?
10) Os bydd hi'n braf yr wythnos nesaf byddwn ni'n mynd i lan y môr.
11) Byddwn ni'n gwerthu'r llun os bydd rhaid.
12) Pryd bydd cinio'n barod?

Exercise 2: 1) Chofia i ddim agor y ffenest.
2) Wisgan nhw ddim dillad cynnes.
3) Fwynhawn ni ddim gyrru i Gaerdydd.
4) Pharcian nhw ddim yn y maes parcio.
5) Frysiwn ni ddim i'r dref.
6) Theithia i ddim yn y nos.
7) Chysgwn ni ddim yn y car.
8) Ddarllenith hi ddim popeth.
9) Redith e (SW)/o (NW) ddim yn y parc.

10) Liwith y plant ddim amser chwarae.

Exercise 3: 1) eith 2) wnân 3) dof 4) ceith 5) ei
6) ddown 7) chewch 8) eith 9) af 10) cawn

Exercise 4: 1) Byddan nhw'n dod yn y gwanwyn.
2) Cawn ni lawer o law ym mis Ebrill.
3) Wnewch chi gau'r drws os gwelwch yn dda?
4) Eith e (SW)/o (NW) ar ei ben ei hunan ar ddiwedd gwyliau'r Pasg.
5) Mae ei ail wraig e (SW)/o (NW) yn teithio i Ewrop yn aml.
6) Eith hi ddim i Ddinbych tan y nawfed ar hugain o fis Chwefror.
7) Mis Rhagfyr ydy'r deuddegfed mis o'r flwyddyn.
8) Wnewch chi droi'r sŵn i lawr os gwelwch yn dda.
9) Ddwedwch chi wrth yr heddlu?
10) Wnân nhw ddim byd.
11) Ewch chi eto ym mis Mehefin?
12) Mae rhaid i chi brynu'r tocynnau erbyn y trydydd ar hugain o fis Tachwedd.
13) Roedden ni'n arfer byw yn y pedwerydd tŷ ar y chwith.
14) Siân ydy fy mumed wyres i.

Week 10, Lesson 1
Exercise 1: 1) erioed 2) byth 3) byth 4) byth
5) byth 6) erioed 7) byth 8) byth

Exercise 2: 1 – c 2 – f 3 – b 4 – d
5 – a 6 – h 7 – g 8 – e

Week 10, Lesson 2
Exercise 1: 1) atyn 2) atat 3) ato 4) ati 5) ati
6) atoch 7) at 8) aton 9) ata 10) ati

Exercise 2: 1) wrthyn; am 2) iddi 3) oddi wrtho 4) wrtha
5) o danoch 6) i 7) i 8) wrthot

Week 10, Lesson 3
Exercise 1: 1) am 2) trwyddi 3) amdana 4) amdanon
5) amdano 6) trwyddyn 7) trwyddo 8) amdanon

Exercise 2: 1) yn 2) hebddon 3) rhyngddoch 4) drosti
5) ynddo 6) hebddot 7) rhyngddyn 8) drosta

Week 10, Lesson 4
Exercise 1: 1) Mae eisiau pensil arna i.
2) Mae eisiau beiro arna i.
3) Mae eisiau rwber arni hi.
4) Mae eisiau papur ysgrifennu arni hi.
5) Mae eisiau amlenni arnyn nhw.
6) Mae eisiau matsis arnyn nhw.
7) Mae eisiau rhagor o arian (SW)/bres (NW) arnyn nhw.

Exercise 2: 1) Mae eisiau bwyd arna i 2) Mae hiraeth arni hi.
3) Mae clefyd y gwair arno fe (SW)/fo (NW) 4) Mae ofn arnon ni.
5) Mae syched arna i. 6) Mae'r ddannodd arnon ni.
7) Mae bai arnyn nhw. 8) Mae gwres arna i.

Week 10, Lesson 5
Exercise 1: 1) Anghofiais i ddim o'r dŵr.
2) Phrynwn ni ddim gliniadur newydd sbon.
3) Anfona i ddim o'r anrheg ati hi.
4) Ddefnyddioch chi ddim o'r amlen.
5) Ddefnyddiais i ddim pensil.
6) Anfonon ni ddim cerdyn.
7) Ysgrifennith hi ddim o'r neges.
8) Ddringan nhw ddim o'r Wyddfa

Exercise 2: 1) Phrynais i ddim o'r bara.
2) Wylion ni ddim ohoni.
3) Chlywais i ddim ohonot ti.
4) Wisgodd hi ddim ohonyn nhw.
5) Ddefnyddiaist ti ddim o'i ffôn e (SW)/o (NW).
6) Thalodd o ddim ohona i. (NW)
7) Wnaethon nhw ddim o'r gwaith.
8) Enwodd o ddim ohonon ni. (NW)

Week 10, Lesson 6
Exercise 1: 1) yn ein lle ni 2) ar ei hôl hi
3) ar fy mhwys i 4) uwch eu pennau nhw
5) o dy flaen di 6) yn ei erbyn e (SW)/o (NW)
7) wrth eu hochr nhw 8) o'ch cwmpas chi

Week 10, Lesson 7
Exercise 1: 1) Dydy e (SW)/o (NW) byth yn yfed coffi du.
2) Doeddwn i byth yn arfer gwrando ar y radio.
3) Dydy hedfan byth wedi apelio aton ni.
4) Freuddwydiodd hi erioed amdanyn nhw.
5) Doedd e (SW)/o (NW) byth yn ddig wrtha i.
6) Fydd hi byth yn siarad â fe (SW)/fo (NW) eto.
7) Dych chi byth wedi llwyddo i ddod rhyngddyn nhw.
8) Doeddwn i erioed wedi bod yno o'r blaen.

Exercise 2: 1) aton; i   2) arna   3) ynddoch   4) i; drosti
5) hebddot   6) iddo   7) amdana   8) oddi wrthyn
9) ynddot   10) arna

Exercise 3: 1) Mae ganddi hi bigyn clust, mae clust dost gyda hi.
2) Mae gwres arna i.
3) Mae annwyd arnon ni.
4) Mae ganddo fo frech yr ieir.

5) Mae braich dost gyda Mr Jones. (SW)
6) Mae bol tost gyda'r pennaeth. (SW)
7) Mae peswch arnat ti.
8) Mae ofn arnyn nhw.
9) Mae cywilydd ar ei thad hi.
10) Mae'r ddannodd arnoch chi.

Exercise 4: 1) Ddefnyddiais i ddim o'r matsis.
2) Helpon ni ddim ohonyn nhw.
3) Ddalion nhw ddim o'r ci.
4) Yfodd e ddim ohono fe. (SW)
   Yfodd o ddim ohono fo. (NW)
5) Chroesaist ti ddim o'r heol.
6) Thalon nhw ddim ohoni hi.
7) Pharatôn ni ddim o'r gwaith.
8) Sgoriais i ddim ohoni hi.
9) Agorodd e (SW)/ o (NW) ddim o'r amlen.
10) Chlywon nhw ddim ohona i.
11) Ddysgodd e (SW)/ o (NW) ddim ohonon ni.
12) Welais i ddim ohonot ti.
13) Ffoniais i ddim ohoni hi.
14) Ddeallodd o ddim ohonoch chi.
15) Liwioch chi ddim o'r llun.

Exercise 5: 1) yn ei erbyn e (SW)/o (NW) 2) yn eu lle nhw
3) ar dy ôl di 4) ar ei phwys hi
5) er ein mwyn ni 6) o'n baenau ni
7) wrth fy ochr 8) ar ei draws e (SW) / o (NW)
9) uwch eu pennau nhw 10) o'i chwmpas hi

Week 11, Lesson 1
Exercise 1: 1) Byddwn i'n (SW)/Baswn i'n (NW) mynd i'r gwaith ar feic.
2) Fyddai fe'n (SW)/Fasai fo'n (NW) dringo coeden?
3) Fyddai (SW)/Fasai hi ddim (NW) yn cadw aderyn fel anifail anwes.
4) Fyddech (SW)/Fasech chi'n (NW) byw mewn dinas?
5) Fydden (SW)/Fasen ni ddim (NW) yn mynd ar wyliau mewn carafán.
6) Fyddwn (SW)/Faswn i byth (NW) yn gweithio fel cigydd.
7) Fydden nhw ddim yn cymryd sylw ohono fe. (SW)
Alternative Answer: Fasen nhw ddim yn cymryd sylw ohono fo. (NW)
8) Byddai (SW)/Basai (NW) hynny'n ddoniol iawn.

Exercise 2: 1) Na fasai.
2) Basen.
3) Byddet. (*fam.*)/Byddech.
4) Na faswn.
5) Na fyddai.
6) Baswn./Basen.
7) Byddai.
8) Na fasai.

Alternative Answer: Na fyddai (SW)

Exercise 3: 1) Hoffech; Hoffwn. 2) Gallwn i fod wedi
3) Hoffai; Na hoffai. 4) Allen nhw fod wedi
5) Hoffen ni 6) Gallai hi brynu
7) Hoffet ti 8) Gallen nhw fod wedi

Week 11, Lesson 2
Exercise 1: 1 – h 2 – f 3 – d 4 – i 5 – c
6 – b 7 – e 8 – a 9 – j 10 – g

Exercise 1: 1) Dylwn i fod wedi mynd i'r ysbyty.
2) Ddylet ti wneud hynny?
3) Ddylai fe ddim bod wedi cadw ei harian hi. (SW)
Alternative Answer: Ddylai fo ddim bod wedi cadw ei phres hi. (NW)
4) Dylen ni gwyno.
5) Ddylech chi gynnau'r golau? Dylwn.
6) Ddylai fe (SW)/fo (NW) frysio? Na ddylai.
7) Dylen nhw fod wedi dweud wrthi hi.
8) Ddylen ni ddim lladd arnat ti.
9) Ddylech chi ddim rhoi'r bai arno fe (SW)/fo (NW).
10) Ddylwn i gefnu arnyn nhw? Dylet/Dylech.

Week 11, Lesson 4
Exercise 1: 1) ei gynnau 2) ei gynnal 3) eu derbyn 4) eich dewis
5) o'i wneud 6) ei gynnau 7) eu dysgu 8) eu hesgusodi
9) ein henwi 10) fy nhroi i lawr

Week 11, Lesson 5
Exercise 1: 1) sy'n arbenigo 2) a oedd yn arfer canu
3) a gafodd ddamwain 4) a ddefnyddion nhw
5) a wnaeth ei mam hi 6) a fyddai'n gyrru/oedd yn gyrru
7) a ddwedon nhw wrth bawb 8) a olchoch chi
9) a ofynnodd e (SW)/o (NW) i chi 10) a brynais i

Week 11, Lesson 6
Exercise 1: 1) y mae ei chwaer e'n (SW)/o'n (NW) yn byw yn Yr Aifft.
2) y rheswm y gadawon nhw.
3) yr oeddech chi'n siarad amdani hi.
4) y flwyddyn yr enillodd y tîm rygbi'r cwpan.
5) yr oeddech chi'n eu gwisgo.
6) yr ymosodon nhw arno fe (SW)/fo (NW).
7) yr oeddech chi'n eu gwisgo.
8) yr oeddet ti'n gwenu arno fe (SW)/fo (NW).
9) yr wythnos yr aeth hi ar wyliau.
10) yr oeddech chi'n gwrando arni hi.
11) yr oedd eu plant yn chwilio am eu ci nhw.
12) y paentiodd ei gŵr y neuadd.

Week 11, Lesson 7

Exercise 1: 1) Byddwn i'n (SW) /Baswn i'n (NW) drist iawn petaech chi'n (SW)/ tasech chi'n (NW) gadael.
2) Fyddet ti'n (SW) /Faset ti'n (NW) ystyried ymddeol?
3) Gallai fe (SW)/fo (NW) fod wedi anfon e-bost atyn nhw.
4) Fydden nhw (SW)/Fasen (NW) nhw ddim yn hoffi'r tywydd yn Yr Aifft.
5) Fyddai fe'n (SW)/Fasai fo'n (NW) unig?
6) Gallwn i fod wedi yfed potelaid arall.
7) Hoffen nhw ymarfer mwy cyn yr arholiad.
8) Gallai'r cigydd fod wedi gwneud y selsig.
9) Gallech chi fod wedi dweud wrthon ni ddoe.
10) Byddech chi'n (SW)/Basech chi'n (NW) rhoi bai arnon ni eto.

Exercise 2: 1 – a 2 – b 3 – b 4 – a 5 – a
6 – b 7 – a 8 – a 9 – a 10 – a

Exercise 3: 1 – d 2 – o 3 – n 4 – k 5 – a 6 – m 7 – g 8 – h
9 – c 10 – e 11 – j 12 – b 13 – l 14 – f 15 – i

Exercise 4: 1) Cafodd yr hyfforddwr ei anafu yn y gêm.
2) Cafodd y llaeth (SW)/llefrith (NW) ei golli.
3) Cawson nhw eu newid.
4) Ces i fy symud gan yr heddlu.
5) Gawsoch chi eich stopio?
6) Caiff hi ei thalu yfory.
7) Gafodd e (SW)/o (NW) ei drafod yn y cyfarfod?
8) Ches i ddim o fy ystyried.
9) Cafodd y botel ei llenwi.
10) Chawson ni ddim o'n hadnabod.

Exercise 5: 1) Hoffwn/Hoffen.
2) Gallai.
3) Na fydden. (SW)
Alternative Answer: Na fasen. (NW)
4) Naddo.
5) Na allech.
Alternative answer: Na allen.
6) Na hoffwn.
Alternative answer: Na hoffen.
7) Na ddylet.
Alternative answer: Na ddylech.
8) Dylwn.

Exercise 6: 1) Ydych chi'n adnabod y dyn yr enillodd ei wyres y wobr gyntaf?
2) Mae'r ystafell wely a beintiodd e'n (SW)/o'n (NW) edrych yn hyfryd.
3) Mae fy mhlant i'n dal i chwarae gyda'r teganau y gwnaeth fy nhad-cu (SW)/nhaid (NW) iddyn nhw.
4) Cwrddais i â nhw y diwrnod y symudon ni i'r pentref. (SW)
Alternative answer: Gwnes i gyfarfod â nhw y diwrnod y symudon ni i'r pentref. (NW)
5) Mae'r dillad a brynodd e'n ei siwtio e. (SW)

Alternative answer: Mae'r dillad a brynodd o'n ei siwtio o. (NW)
6) Mae'r rheilffordd y gweithiodd e (SW)/o (NW) arni hi wedi cau nawr (SW)/rŵan (NW).
7) Dyna rywbeth y dylwn i fod wedi ei wneud.
8) Mae rhaid i'r dyn yr oedd ei gar e (SW)/o (NW) yn y ddamwain wneud cwrs gyrru.

Week 12, Lesson 1
Exercise 1: 1) "Dw i'n trïo ymlacio," meddwn i.
2) "Byddwn ni'n ymddiheuro wrthoch chi," medden nhw.
3) "Mae eisiau bwyd arna i," meddai ei chymar hi.
4) "Mae o wedi gafael yndda i," meddet ti.
5) "Rwyt ti'n poeni gormod," medden ni.
6) "Caf fi selsig ac wyau i frecwast," meddai hi.
7) "Mae ganddi hi gariad newydd," meddech chi.
8) "Byddwch chi'n gwella," meddai'r meddyg.

Week 12, Lesson 2
Exercise 1: 1) Wnes i ddim ymweld 2) Wnaeth hi ddim darllen y nofel
3) Gwnawn ni gyrraedd 4) Gwnest ti neidio
5) Gwnaethoch chi olchi 6) Wneith o derbyn ddim byd
7) Wnaeth o ddim torri 8) Wneith neb weld y

Exercise 2: 1) Breuddwydio wnes i. 2) Dadlau wnaeth e (SW)/ o (NW).
3) Yfed wnawn ni. 4) Gweiddi wnaethon nhw.
5) Llwyddo wnest ti. 6) Symud wnaeth hi.
7) Gofyn wnes i. 8) Sefyll wnaethoch chi.

Week 12, Lesson 3
Exercise 1: 1) Balch ydy hi. 2) Llynedd (yr) aethon nhw.
3) Cloi'r drws (y) mae hi. 4) Ganol nos (y) cyrhaeddon nhw adref.
5) Bwydo'r gath (yr) oedden nhw. 6) O dan y bwrdd (y) maen nhw.
7) Diflas ydy hi. 8) Bob dydd (y) gwelais i nhw.

Exercise 2: 1) Fi (a) ddarllenodd nofel.
2) Nid nofel (a) ddarllenais i.
3) Nhw sy'n fywiog.
4) Dŵr (y) byddwn ni'n ei yfed.
5) Chi oedd yn dadlau.
6) Nid yn erbyn y wal mae'r gadair.
7) Brechdan (a) wnaf i.
8) Nhw fydd yn hyderus am ennill.
9) Ti sy'n yfed cwrw.
10) Pêl (a) giciodd yr hyfforddwr.
11) Ni (a) gytunodd i faddau iddyn nhw.
12) Nid fi (a) newidiodd sianel.

Week 12, Lesson 4
Exercise 1: 1) Ti oedd biau'r radio.
2) Nid fe (SW)/fo (NW) oedd biau'r oergell.

3) Y cwmni fydd biau'r adeiladau.
4) Fy rheini sy' biau'r carafán.
5) Y swyddfa'r bost sy' biau'r fan.
6) Nid y gwesty fydd biau'r traeth.
7) Ni sy' biau'r ymbarél.
8) Y capel sy' biau'r maes parcio.
9) Nid ni sy' biau nhw.
10) Nhw sy' biau'r esgidiau.

Week 12, Lesson 5
Exercise 1: 1) Agorir archfarchnad newydd. 2) Gwerthir petrol yma. 3) Diffoddir y goleuadau. 4) Torrir coeden i lawr. 5) Perfformir drama. 6) Enwir y bobl. 7) Paentir y welydd. 8) Trafodir y problemau.

Exercise 2: 1) Prynwyd yr anrheg. 2) Gwariwyd llawer o arian (SW)/bres (NW). 3) Canwyd y caneuon. 4) Cynhaliwyd y digwyddiad. 5) Dechreuwyd y ras. 6) Caewyd y drws. 7) Holwyd y dynion. 8) Treuliwyd amser.

Exercise 3:
1) Ni wnaethpwyd y gwaith.
2) Ni welwyd damwain.
3) Ni chafwyd hwyl.
4) Ni liwir y lluniau.
5) Nid enillwyd y ras.
6) Ni thelir y biliau.
7) Ni faddeuwyd i bawb.
8) Ni sgoriwyd gôl.
9) Ni chedwir arian (SW)/pres (NW) yn y neuadd.
10) Nid aethpwyd â nhw i'r ysbyty.

Week 12, Lesson 6
Exercise 1:
1) Llongyfarchiadau!
2) Mae'n ddrwg gyda fi (SW)/gen i (NW) glywed am eich profedigaeth/colled.
3) Pwy sy'n siarad?
4) Nadolig Llawen!
5) Llongyfarchiadau!
6) Annwyl (...)
7) Gaf i siarad â Mr Williams os gwelwch yn dda.
8) Blwyddyn Newydd Dda!

Week 12, Lesson 7
Exercise 1:
1) "Llongyfarchiadau," meddai fe (SW)/ fo (NW).
2) Cawson nhw eu geni yng Ngorllewin Cymru.
3) "Does dim ots," medden ni.
4) Beth ydy 'pet' yn Gymraeg?
5) Brysiwch wella!
6) Ble cawsoch chi eich geni?

7) Iechyd da!
8) Gaf fi siarad â phlismon?
9) Dw i'n dy garu di.
10) "Mae'n ddrwg gyda fi (SW)/gen i (NW) glywed hynny," meddwn i.

Exercise 2: 1) Nhw (a) ganodd yr anthem genedlaethol.
2) Yn yr ardal yna (y) cawson nhw eu geni.
3) Ti (a) aeth i'r banc ddoe.
4) Fy meirio i (a) ddefnyddiodd hi.
5) Nid brysio (yr) oedden nhw.
6) Chwerthin (a) wnaeth o.
7) Nhw sy'n gas wrthon ni.
8) Paratoi'r gerddoriaeth (y) bydd ei gariad e (SW)/o (NW).
9) Wrth ei bodd (y) byddai hi.
10) Noson stormus oedd hi.
11) Disgwyl colli (y) mae e (SW)/o (NW).
12) I ni (yr) wyt ti'n perthyn.

Exercise 3: 1) Pwy sy' biau'r bêl 'ma?
2) Ni sy' biau'r oergell a'r teledu.
3) Fi sy' biau'r wisg/ffrog 'ma.
4) Garmon sy' biau'r bêl 'na.
5) Yr athrawes sy' biau'r llyfrau 'na.
6) Ai fe (SW)/fo (NW) sy' biau'r gwesty 'ma?
7) Pwy oedd biau'r drych (a) dorrodd e (SW)/o (NW)?
8) Ai ti sy' biau'r garej 'ma?
9) Ei hewythr sy' biau'r ffon gerdded.
10) Ai nhw sy' biau'r llun 'ma?

Exercise 4: 1) Pryd adeiladwyd yr eglwys?
2) Nid agorwyd y siop ar ôl y tân.
3) Ni newidir y cloc.
4) Golchwyd y baban.
5) Gwnaethpwyd brecwast yn y gegin.
6) Cenir y geiriau yn Gymraeg.
7) Daethpwyd o hyd i gorff ar y traeth bore ddoe.
8) Ni chaewyd y drws.
9) Ni chlywir y larwm.
10) Dihunwyd pawb.

A Brief Summary of the Modern Welsh Verb System

The verb system of most languages can be classified according to:

- Mood
- Tense
- Aspect

In grammar, 'mood' is the term used to categorise verbs according to what they express. It is generally agreed that Welsh possesses three such moods:

1. The indicative mood
2. The subjunctive mood
3. The imperative mood

1. THE INDICATIVE MOOD

The indicative mood is used to express factual statements. It is further divided into tenses and aspects.

Modern spoken Welsh possesses two simple tenses:

a) Past
b) Future

TENSE	WELSH	ENGLISH
Past	**Dysgais i.**	I learnt.
Future	**Dysga i.**	I will learn.

These are formed by combining the stem of the verb and a personal inflection. For example:

VERB-NOUN	STEM	PERSONAL INFLECTION
dysgu	dysg-	-ais i
to learn		I learnt

As we have learnt, there are irregular simple verb forms usually based on '**mynd**'. For example:

VERB-NOUN	IRREGULAR PERSONAL ENDING
mynd	es i
to go	I went

In order to show other tenses and aspects, Welsh uses the periphrastic construction based on '**bod**'. These can be classified as follows:

TENSE	ASPECT	WELSH	ENGLISH
Present	Imperfect	Dw i'n dysgu.	I am learning. / I learn.
	Perfect	Dw i wedi dysgu.	I have learnt.
Past	Imperfect	Roeddwn i'n dysgu.	I was learning. / I learnt.
	Perfect	Roeddwn i wedi dysgu.	I had learnt.
Future	Imperfect	Bydda i'n dysgu.	I will be learning. / I will learn.
	Perfect	Bydda i wedi dysgu.	I will have learnt.

2. THE SUBJUNCTIVE MOOD

As we saw in **Week 11, Lesson 1**, the subjunctive mood expresses a wish, desire, uncertainty, possibility and unreality. In modern spoken Welsh, the subjunctive mood can be divided into:

i.) The formulaic subjunctive
ii.) The conditional

The formulaic subjunctive
The formulaic conveys the idea that what is described is ongoing, continuous or timeless. In modern spoken Welsh, it is found in fossilized archaisms often corresponding to equivalent phrases in English:

WELSH	ENGLISH
Duw a'th fendithio!	(God) bless you!
A fo ben bid bont!	He who would be chief be a bridge!*
Tra bo dau	As long as there are two

From Pedair Cainc Mabinogi 'The Four Branches of the Mabinogi'.

However, modern literary Welsh still possesses the following full range of personal forms for the subjunctive 'present' tense:

THE SUBJUNCTIVE MOOD	
Literary Welsh	
'Present' subjunctive	
Sing.	*Plu.*
1. -wyf	-om
2. -ych	-och
3. -o	-ont

For example:

WELSH	ENGLISH	SOURCE
Un funud fach cyn <u>elo</u>'r haul o'r wybren	One small minute before the sun goes from the sky	From 'Cofio' by Waldo Williams.
Pan <u>rodiwyf</u> ddaear Ystrad Fflur o'm dolur ymdawelaf.	When I wander Strata Florida's ground I am content with my pain.	From 'Ystrad Fflur' by T. Gwynn Jones.

The conditional subjunctive

In spoken Welsh, there is a set of personal verb inflections to indicate that an action or state depends on some other desired or unreal condition. The verbs involved are '**gallu**', '**hoffi**', '**caru**' a '**dylai**'. These, in turn, can be divided into two categories:

1. the **possible conditional** – where the desired or unreal event has yet to occur
2. the **impossible conditional** – where the desired or unreal event has already occurred

CONDITIONAL	WELSH	ENGLISH
Possibility	Gallwn i fynd.	I could go.
Impossibility	Gallwn i fod wedi mynd.	I could have gone.

The conditional structure of 'bod'

In the case of other verbs, Welsh uses periphrastic based on '**bod**'. For example:

CONDITIONAL	WELSH	ENGLISH
Possibility	Byddwn / Baswn i'n mynd. (SW) Baswn i'n mynd (NW)	I would go.
Impossibility	Byddwn / Baswn i wedi mynd. (SW) Baswn i'n mynd (NW)	I would have gone.

3. THE IMPERATIVE

As we saw in **Week 7, Lesson 1**, the imperative is a grammatical mood which is used to express commands, instructions or requests. We learnt that Welsh differentiates between five types of imperative based on person. There is also the impersonal imperative, so, strictly speaking, there are six types of imperative:

	PERSON	ENGLISH FORM	WELSH COMMAND	ENGLISH EQUIVALENT
i)	second person singular	you (*fam.*)	**Paid!**	Don't!
ii)	second person plural	you	**Peidiwch!**	Don't!
iii)	third person singular	he, she	**Peidied (rhag)!**	Let him / her / it refrain (from)!
iv)	first person plural	we	**Peidiwn (rhag)!**	Let us refrain (from)!
v)	third person plural	they	**Peidient (rhag)!**	Let them refrain (from)!
vi)	Impersonal		**Peidier (rhag)!**	Let everyone refrain from!

Only i) and iii) and iv) are used regularly in modern spoken Welsh; iii) is heard occasionally – usually by the older generation, whilst v) and vi) are purely literary forms.

Mini Dictionary

Welsh-English

A

a (*cnj.*) (AM) and
â (*prp.*) (AM) with (by means of)
Abertawe Swansea
acen (*f.*) accent, **acenion** (*pl.*)
(o) achos (*prp.*) because
adeilad (*m.*) building, **adeiladau** (*pl.*)
adeiladu (*vb*) build, **adeilad-** (*stem*)
aderyn (*m.*) bird, **adar** (*pl.*)
(ad)nabod (*vb*) know (a person, place), to recognise (*periph.*)
adref (*adv.*) home(wards)
adroddiad (*m.*) report, **adroddiadau** (*pl.*)
addo (*vb*) promise, **addaw-** (*stem*)
afal (*m.*) apple, **afalau** (*pl.*)
agor (*vb*) to open, **agor-** (*stem*)
agos (*adj.*) near, close
anghofio am (SM) (*vb*) forget about, **anghofi-** (*stem*)
anghytuno (*vb*) disagree, **anghytun-** (*stem*)
Albanes (*f.*) Scottish (woman) **Albanesau** (*pl.*)
Albanwr (*m.*) Scottish (man) **Albanwyr** (*pl.*)
Almaenes (*f.*) German (woman) **Almaenesau**
Almaenwr (*m.*) German (man) **Almaenwyr** (*pl.*)
allan (*ad.*) out
am (*prp.*) (SM) for, because, about, at, on, what a
am faint for how long
Americanes (*f.*) American (woman) **Americanesau** (*pl.*)
Americanwr American (man) (*m.*) **Americanwyr** (*pl.*)
aml (*adj.*) often
amlen (*f.*) envelope, **amlenni** (*pl.*)
amlwg (*adj.*) obvious
amser (*m.*) time, **amserau** (*pl.*)
anafu (*vb*) injure, **anaf-** (*stem*)
anfon (*vb*) send, **anfon-** (*stem*)
  anfon at (SM) send to (a person)
  anfon i (SM) send to (a place)
anifail (*m.*) animal, **anifeiliaid** (*pl.*)
anifail anwes (*m.*) pet, **anifeiliaid anwes** (*pl.*)
annisgwyl (*adj.*) unexpected
annwyd (*m.*) cold, **anwydau** (*pl.*)
annwyl (*adj.*) dear
anodd (*adj.*) difficult, hard
anrheg (*f.*) present, gift, **anrhegion** (*pl.*)
anthem (*f.*) anthem, **anthemau** (*pl.*)
  anthem genedlaethol, national anthem
apelio (*vb*) appeal, **apeli-** (*stem*)
  apelio (at) (SM) (*vb*) appeal (to), **apeli-** (*stem*)
ar (*prp.*) (SM) on
  ar agor open
  ar bwys near
  ar draws across
  ar droed on foot
  ar ddi-hun awake
  ar ei ben exactly
  ar ei ben ei hunan on his own
  ar fin about to, on the point of
  ar frys in haste, in a hurry
  ar gau closed
  ar goll lost
  ar gyfer for
  ar hyn o bryd (*adv.*) at the moment
  ar ôl (*prp.*) after, behind
  ar unwaith at once
  ar y chwith on the left
  ar y dde on the right
  ar y pryd at the time
ar-lein (*adv.*) online
araf (*adj.*) slow
arall (*adj.*) other
arbenigo (yn (NM)/**mewn)** (*vb*) to specialise (in)
arbennig (*adj.*) special, particular
archfarchnad (*f.*) hypermarket, supermarket, **archfarchnadoedd** (*pl.*)
ardal (*f.*) district, region, area, **ardaloedd** (*pl.*)
arfer (*vb*) get used to, used to (*periph.*)

arholiad (*m.*) exam, **arholiadau** (*pl.*)
arian (*pl.*) money
arogl (*m.*) scent, smell, **aroglau** (*pl.*)
aros (*vb*) stay, wait, **arhos-** (*stem*)
astudio (*vb*) study, **astudi-** (*stem*)
at (*prp.*) to, towards, at
ateb (*vb*) answer, **ateb-** (*stem*)
  ateb dros (SM) to answer on behalf of
atgoffa (*vb*) remind, **atgoff-** (*stem*)
athrawes (*f.*) teacher, **athrawesau** (*pl.*)
athro (*m.*) teacher, **athrawon** (*pl.*)
awr (*f.*) hour, **oriau** (*pl.*)
awyren (*f.*) aeroplane, **awyrennau** (*pl.*)
awyrgylch (*m.*) atmosphere

B

baban (*m.*) baby, **babanod** (*pl.*)
bach (*adj.*) small, little
bachgen (*m.*) boy, **bechgyn** (*pl.*)
bai (*m.*) fault, **beiau** (*pl.*)
bag (*m.*) bag, **bagiau** (*pl.*)
balch (*adj.*) glad, proud
banc (*m.*) bank, **banciau** (*pl.*)
bara (*m.*) bread
beic (*m.*) bike, **beiciau** (*pl.*)
  ar feic by bike
beiro (*m.*) biro, **beiros** (*pl.*)
bellach any more
bendigedig (*adj.*) splendid, brilliant
benyw (*f.*) woman, **benywod** (*pl.*)
beth (*pn*) (SM) what
bil (*m.*) bill, **biliau** (*pl.*)
blasus (*adj.*) tasty, delicious
ble (*adv.*) where
blin (NW) (*adj.*) angry
blino (*vb*) tire, **blin-** (*stem*)
  blino ar (SM) (*vb*) tire of, **blin-** (*stem*)
blodyn (*m.*) flower, **blodau** (*pl.*)
blwydd (*f.*) year (with age)
blwyddyn (*f.*) year, **blynyddoedd** (*pl.*)
blynedd (*pl.*) years (after numerals)
bob (*adv.*) every
  bob bore every morning
  bob dydd everyday
bocs (*m.*) box, **bocsys** (*pl.*)

bod (*vb*) be (*irreg.*)
bodlon (*adj.*) willing, satisfied
bol (*m.*) tummy, belly, **bolau** (*pl.*)
bore (*m.*) morning, **boreau** (*pl.*)
bownd o (SM) bound to
braf (*adj.*) fine
braich (*f.*) arm, **breichiau** (*pl.*)
brawd (*m.*) brother, **brodyr** (*pl.*)
brecwast (*m.*) breakfast, **brecwastau** (*pl.*)
brech (*f.*) pox
  brech goch measles
  brech yr ieir chicken pox
brechdan (*f.*) sandwich, **brechdanau** (*pl.*)
breuddwydio (*vb*) dream, **breuddwydi-** (*stem*)
  breuddwydio am (SM) (*vb*) dream about, **breuddwydi-** (*stem*)
bron (*adv.*) almost, nearly, practically
brown (*m.*) brown
brwnt (SW) (*adj.*) dirty
bryn (*m.*) hill, **bryniau** (*pl.*)
brysio (*vb*) to hurry, **brysi-** (*stem*)
budr (NW) (*adj.*) dirty
buwch (*f.*) cow, **buchod** (*pl.*)
bwrdd (NW) (*m.*) table, **byrddau** (*pl.*)
bwrw (*vb*) hit, **bwrw-** (*stem*)
  bwrw cesair hail (*vb*)
  bwrw eira snow (*vb*)
  bwrw eirlaw sleet (*vb*)
  bwrw (glaw) rain (*vb*)
bws (*m.*) bus, **bysiau** (*pl.*)
bwyd (*m.*) food, **bwydydd** (*pl.*)
bwydo (*vb*) feed, **bwyd-** (*stem*)
bwyta (*vb*) eat, **bwyt-** (*stem*)
byd (*m.*) world, **bydoedd** (*pl.*)
byr (*adj.*) short
byth (*adv.*) ever, never, even
byw (*vb*) live (*periph.*)
bywiog lively (*adj.*)

C

cacen (*f.*) cake, **cacennau** (*pl.*)
cadair (*f.*) chair, **cadeiriau** (*pl.*)
  cadair freichiau armchair
cadw (*vb*) keep, **cadw-** (*stem*)
cae (*m.*) field, **caeau**
cael (*vb*) have, get, obtain, receive (*irreg.*)

Caerdydd Cardiff
Caerfyrddin Carmarthen
caled (*adj.*) hard
camera (*m.*) camera, **camerâu** (*pl.*)
camel camel (*m.*), **camelod** (*pl.*)
campfa (*f.*) gym, **campfeydd** (*pl.*)
cân (*f.*) song, **caneuon** (*pl.*)
canol (*m.*) middle, mid
  canol nos midnight
cant (*adv.*) hundred, **cannoedd** (*pl.*)
canu (*vb*) sing, ring, **can-** (*stem*)
  canu gwerin folk singing
capel (*m.*) chapel, **capeli** (*pl.*)
car (*m.*) car, **ceir** (*pl.*)
carafán (*f.*) caravan, **carafannau** (*pl.*)
caredig (*adj.*) kind
  caredig wrth (SM) kind to
cariad (*m.*) love, sweetheart, **cariadon** (*pl.*)
carped (*m.*) carpet, **carpedi** (*pl.*)
caru (*vb*) love, **car-** (*stem*)
cas (*adj.*) nasty
  cas wrth (SM) nasty to
cath (*f.*) cat, **cathod** (*pl.*)
cau (*vb*) shut, close, **cae-** (*stem*)
cawod (*f.*) shower, **cawodydd** (*pl.*)
cefn (*m.*) back (of the body), **cefnau** (*pl.*)
cefnder (*m.*) cousin, **cefnderoedd** (*pl.*)
cefnogwr (*m.*) supporter, **cefnogwyr** (*pl.*)
cefnu ar (SM) (*vb*) turn one's back on, **cefn-** (*stem*)
cegin (*f.*) kitchen, **ceginau** (*pl.*)
ceisio (*vb*) try, **ceisi-** (*stem*)
cenedlaethol (*adj.*) national
cerdyn (*m.*) card, **cardiau**
cerdded (*vb*) walk, stroll, **cerdd-** (*stem*)
cerddoriaeth (*f.*) music
cesair (*m.*) hail(stones)
ci (*m.*) dog, **cŵn** (*p*)
cig (*m.*) meat, **cigoedd** (*pl.*)
cigydd (*m.*) butcher, **cigyddion** (*pl.*)
cinio (*m.*) dinner, lunch
clefyd y gwair (*m.*) hayfever
clir (*adj.*) clear
cloc (*m.*) clock, **clociau** (*pl.*)
cloch (*f.*) bell, **clychau** (*pl.*)
cloi (*vb*) lock, **cloi-** (*stem*)
clust (*f.*) ear, **clustiau** (*pl.*)
clwb (*m.*) club, **clybiau** (*pl.*)
clywed (*vb*) hear, **clyw-** (*stem*)
  clywed am (SM) hear about
coch (*adj.*) red
codi (*vb*) get up, build, lift, raise, **cod-** (*stem*)
  codi ar eich traed to get to your feet, to stand up
  codi arian to raise money
coeden (*f.*) tree, **coed**
  coeden achau (*f.*) family tree, **coed achau** (*pl.*)
coes (*f.*) leg, **coesau** (*pl.*)
cofio (*vb*) remember, **cofi-** (*stem*)
  cofio am (SM) (*vb*) remember about
coffi (*m.*) coffee
coleg (*m.*) college, **colegau** (*pl.*)
colled (*f.*) loss, **colledion** (*pl.*)
colli (*vb*) lose, miss, spill, **coll-** (*stem*)
côr (*m.*) choir, **corau** (*pl.*)
corff (*m.*) body, **cyrff** (*pl.*)
cornel (*f.*) corner, **corneli** (*pl.*)
cost (*f.*) cost, **costau** (*pl.*)
cot (*f.*) coat, **cotiau** (*pl.*)
credu (*vb*) believe
  credu yn (NM)/**mewn** to believe in
creulon (*adj.*) cruel
  creulon wrth (SM) cruel to
croesawu (*vb*) to welcome, **croesaw-** (*stem*)
croesfan (*f.*) pedestrian crossing, **croesfannau** (*pl.*)
croesffordd (*f.*) crossroads, **croesffyrdd** (*pl.*)
croesi (*vb*) to cross, **croes-** (*stem*)
croeso (*m.*) welcome
cryf (*adj.*) strong
cur pen (NW) (*m.*) headache
cwestiwn (*m.*) question, **cwestiynau** (*pl.*)
cwmni (*m.*) company, **cmwnïau** (*pl.*)
cwpan (*m.*) cup, **cwpanau** (*pl.*)
cwpanaid (*m.*) cupful, **cwpaneidi** (*pl.*)
cwpwrdd (*m.*) cupboard, **cypyrddau** (*pl.*)
cwrdd (â) (*vb*) meet (with), **cwrdd-** (*stem*)

cwrs (*m.*) course, **cyrsiau** (*pl.*)
cwrw (*m.*) beer
cwsg (*m.*) sleep
cwyno (*vb*) complain, **cwyn-** (*stem*)
cychwyn (*vb*) set out, start, **cychwynn-** (*stem*)
cydio yn (NM)/**mewn** (*vb*) take hold of, **cydi-** (*stem*)
cydymdeimlo (*vb*) sympathise **cydymdeiml-** (*stem*)
cyfaddef (**wrth**) (SM) (*vb*) admit (to), **cyfaddef-** (*stem*)
cyfarfod (*m.*) meeting, **cyfarfodydd** (*pl.*); (*vb*) meet
cyfeillgar (*adj.*) friendly
cyfeiriad (*m.*) direction, address, **cyfeiriadau** (*pl.*)
i gyfeiriad in the direction of
cyfeirio (**at**) (SM) (*vb*) refer (to), **cyfeiri-** (*stem*)
cyfleus (*adj.*) convenient
cyfnither (*f.*) cousin, **cyfnitheroedd** (*pl.*)
cyfnod (*m.*) period, **cyfnodau** (*pl.*)
cyfrannu (**at**) (SM) (*vb*) contribute (towards), **cyfrann-** (*stem*)
cyfrifol (*adj.*) responsible
cyfweliad (*m.*) interview, **cyfweliadau** (*pl.*)
cyfforddus (*adj.*) comfortable
cyngor (*m.*) council, **cynghorau** (*pl.*)
cyngor (*m.*) advice, **cynghorion** (*pl.*)
cymar (*m.*) partner, **cymheiriaid** (*pl.*)
cyhoeddiad (*m.*) announcement, **cyhoeddiadau**
cymdeithas (*f.*) society, **cymdeithasau** (*pl.*)
Cymraeg (*f.*) Welsh (language)
Cymraes (*f.*) Welshwoman, **Cymraesau** (*pl.*)
Cymreig (*adj.*) Welsh (country)
Cymro (*m.*) Welshman, **Cymry** (*pl.*)
Cymru (*f.*) Wales
cymryd (*vb*) take (medicine, etc.), **cymer-** (*stem*)
cymryd sylw o take notice of
cymylog (*adj.*) cloudy
cyn (*prp.*) before
cyn bo hir before long
cynllun (*m.*) plan, **cynlluniau** (*pl.*)

cynnal (*vb*) hold (an event, etc.), **cynhali-** (*stem*)
cynnar (*adj.*) early
cynnau (*vb*) light (fire), switch on (light), **cynheu-** (*stem*)
cynnau'r golau to switch the light on
cynnes (*adj.*) warm
cynnig (*vb*) to try, to apply, **cynigi-** (*stem*)
cyntaf (*adj.*) first
cyrraedd (*vb*) arrive, reach, **cyrhaedd-** (*stem*)
cysgu (*vb*) sleep, **cysg-** (*stem*)
cystadlu (*vb*) compete, **cystadleu-** (*stem*)
cystadleuaeth (*f.*) competition, **cystadlaethau**
cystadleuydd (*m.*) competitor, **cystadleuwyr**
cystal (*ans.*) as good; so good
cystal i (**fi**) (SM) (I) may as well
cysylltu â (AM) contact, **cysyllt-** (*stem*)
cytuno (**â**) (AM), (**i**) (SM) (*vb*) agree (with), (to), **cytun-** (*stem*)
cywilydd (*m.*) shame

Ch

chi (*pn*) you (*formal*) (*pl.*)
chwaer (*f.*) sister, **chwiorydd** (*pl.*)
chwaith (*adv.*) either
chwarae (*vb*) play, **chwarae-** (*stem*)
chwarae teg fair play
chwech (*adj.*) six
chwerthin (*vb*) laugh, **chwardd-** (*stem*)
chwilio (**am**) (*vb*) look, search (for), **chwili-** (*stem*)
chwith (*m.*) left

D

da (*adj.*) good
yn dda well
dacw (SM) (*adv.*) yonder is/are
dadlau (**dros**) (SM) (*vb*) argue (for), **dadleu-** (*stem*)
dangos (**i**) (SM) (vb) show (to), **dangos-** (*stem*)
dal (*vb*) catch, **dali-** (*stem*)

dal at (SM) keep at (something), **dali-** (*stem*)
dal i (SM) (*vb*) continue to, **dali-** (*stem*)
damwain (*f.*) accident, **damweiniau** (*pl.*)
(**o**) **dan** (*prp.*) (SM) under
dannodd (*f.*) toothache
dant (*f.*) tooth, **dannedd** (*pl.*)
darllen (*vb*) read, **darllen-** (*stem*)
darn (*m.*) piece, **darnau** (*pl.*)
dathlu (*vb*) celebrate, **dathl-** (*stem*)
dau (*m.*) (SM) two
de (*m.*) south
de (*f.*) right
deall (*vb*) understand, **deall-** (*stem*)
dechrau (*vb*) begin, start, **dechreu-** (*stem*)
defnyddio (*vb*) use, **defnyddi-** (*stem*)
deg (*adj.*) ten
deillio (**o**) (SM) (*vb*) derive (from), stem (from), **deilli-** (*stem*)
del (NW) (*adj.*) pretty
derbyn (*vb*) receive, accept, **derbyni-** (*stem*)
desg (*f.*) desk, **desgiau** (*pl.*)
deuddeg (*adj.*) twelve
deunydd (*m.*) material, **deunyddiau** (*pl.*)
dewis (*m.*) choice, **dewisiadau** (*pl.*)
dewis (*vb*) choose, **dewis-** (*stem*)
dibynnu (**ar**) (SM) (*vb*) depend (on), **dibynn-** (*stem*)
diddordeb (*m.*) interest, **diddordebau** (*pl.*)
diddorol (*adv.*) interesting
diffodd (*vb*) put out (fire), extinguish, to switch off (light), **diffodd-** (*stem*)
diflas (*adj.*) miserable
dig (**wrth**) (SM) (NW) (*adj.*) angry (at)
dig (NW) (*adj.*) angry
digon (*adv.*) enough
  digon o (SM) enough of
digwydd (*vb*) happen, **digwydd-** (*stem*)
digwyddiad (*m.*) event, **digwyddiadau** (*pl.*)
dihuno (*vb*) wake up, **dihun-** (*stem*)
gardd (*f.*) garden, **gerddi** (*pl.*)

dim (**byd**) (*m.*) nothing, no, zero, not
  dim ond only
dinas (*f.*) city, **dinasoedd** (*pl.*)
Dinbych Denbigh
diod (*f.*) drink, **diodydd** (*pl.*)
dioddef (**o**) (SM) (*vb*) suffer (from), **dioddef-** (*stem*)
diolch (*m.*) thanks, **diolchiadau** (*pl.*)
  diolch am (SM) thanks for
  diolch yn fawr iawn thank you very much
diolchgar (**am**) (*adj.*) grateful (for)
diogelwch (*m.*) safety
  pennaeth diogelwch head of safety
disgwyl (*vb*) expect (to), **disgwyli-** (*stem*)
  disgwyl i (SM) expect for (someone to/something to)
distaw (*adj.*) quiet
diwedd (*m.*) end
diwethaf (*adj.*) last (in a series), previous
diwrnod (*m.*) day, day's length
  diwrnodau (*pl.*)
dod (*vb*) come (*irreg.*)
  dod â (AM) (*vb*) bring (*irreg.*)
  dod draw (*vb*) to come over
  dod o hyd i to find, to come across, find (*vb*) (*irreg.*)
doniol (*adj.*) funny
dosbarth (*m.*) class, **dosbarthiadau** (*pl.*)
drama (*f.*) play, **dramâu** (*pl.*)
draw (*adv.*) over there, yonder
dringo (*vb*) climb, **dring-** (*stem*)
dros (*prp.*) (SM) over, for, in favour of, on behalf of
  dros nos over night
drud (*adj.*) expensive
drwg (*adj.*) bad, naughty
drws (*m.*) door, **drysau** (*pl.*)
drych (*m.*) mirror, **drychau** (*pl.*)
du (*adj.*) black
dweud wrth (*vb*) tell, say (to), **dwed-** (*stem*)
dŵr (*m.*) water, **dyfroedd** (*pl.*)
dwy (*adj.*) (SM) two (*f.*)
dwyrain (*m.*) east
dydd (*m.*) day, **dyddiau** (*pl.*)

Dydd Gŵyl Dewi Saint David's Day
dylanwadu ar (SM) (*vb*) influence, **dylanwad-** (*stem*)
dyled (*f.*) debt, **dyledion** (*pl.*)
dyma (*adv.*) (SM) here is/are
dymuno (*vb*) wish, **dymun-** (*stem*)
dyn (*m.*) man, **dynion** (*pl.*)
dyna (*adv.*) (SM) there is/are
  dyna i gyd that's all
dysgu (**am**) (*vb*) learn, teach, (about), **dysg-** (*stem*)

Dd
ddoe (*adv.*) yesterday

E
e-bost (*m.*) email, **e-byst** (*pl.*)
echdoe (*adv.*) the day before yesterday
echnos (*adv.*) the night before last
edrych (**ar**) (SM) (*vb*) look (at), **edrych-** (*stem*)
  edrych ymlaen at (SM) to look forward to
efallai (*adv.*) perhaps
efo (*prp.*) (NW) with
effeithio ar (SM) (*vb*) effect, **effeithi-** (*stem*)
eglwys (*f.*) church, **eglwysi** (*pl.*)
eiliad (*f.*) second, **eiliadau** (*pl.*)
eira (*m.*) snow
eirlaw (*m.*) sleet
eisiau (*m.*) need, want
  eisiau bwyd (*m.*) hunger
eistedd (*vb*) sit, **eistedd-** (*stem*)
eisteddfod (*f.*) eisteddfod, **eisteddfodau** (*pl.*) a Welsh literary and musical festival
eithaf (*adv.*) quite
eleni (*adv.*) this year
eli haul (*m.*) sun cream
ennill (*vb*) win, gain, **enill-** (*stem*)
enw (*m.*) name, **enwau** (*pl.*)
enwi (*vb*) name, **enw-** (*stem*)
enwog (*adj.*) famous
er (*prp.*) although
  er gwaethaf inspite
  er mwyn (in order) to, for the sake of
erbyn (*prp.*) by (time)

  erbyn hyn by now
  yn erbyn against
ers (*prp.*) since
  ers faint for how long
  ers hynny since then
esbonio (*vb*) to explain, **esboni-** (*stem*)
esgid (*f.*) shoe, **esgidiau** (*pl.*)
esgus (*m.*) excuse, **esgusodion** (*pl.*)
esgusodi (*vb*) to excuse, **esgusod-** (*stem*)
  esgusodwch fi excuse me
estyn (*vb*) pass, extend **estynn-** (*stem*)
eto (*adv.*) again, yet
Ewrop (*f.*) Europe
ewyrth (*m.*) uncle, **ewyrthod** (*pl.*)

F
faint (*adv.*) how much, how many
  faint o (SM) how much, how many
  faint o'r gloch (*adv.*) what time
fan (*f.*) van, **faniau** (*pl.*)
fel (*prp.*) like, as
  fel arfer usually, as a rule
felly (*adv.*) therefore
ficer (*m.*) vicar, **ficeriaid** (*pl.*)

Ff
ffa pob (*pl.*) baked beans
ffarwél farewell
ffenestr (*f.*) window, **ffenestri** (*pl.*)
ffens (*f.*) fence, **ffensys**
ffermwr (*m.*) farmer, **ffermwyr** (*pl.*)
ffilm (*f.*) film, **ffilmiau** (*pl.*)
fflasg (*f.*) flask, **fflasgiau** (*pl.*)
ffliw (*m.*) influenza
ffon (*f.*) stick, **ffyn** (*pl.*)
  ffon gerdded walking stick
ffôn (*m.*) telephone, **ffonau** (*pl.*)
ffôn clyfar (*m.*) smart phone, **ffonau clyfar** (*pl.*)
ffonio (*vb*) telephone, **ffoni-** (*stem*)
ffordd (*f.*) way, road, **ffyrdd** (*pl.*)
Ffrances (*f.*) French (woman), **Ffrancesau** (*pl.*)
Ffrancwr (*m.*) French (man), **Ffrancwyr** (*pl.*)
ffres (*adj.*) fresh
ffrind (*m.*) friend, **ffrindiau** (*pl.*)
ffrog (*f.*) dress, frock, **ffrogiau** (*pl.*)

G

gadael (*vb*) leave, **gadaw-** (*stem*)
  gadael i (SM) let, allow to
(y) gaeaf (*m.*) winter, **gaeafau** (*pl.*)
gafael (**yn** (NM)/**mewn**) (*vb*) grip, hold tight, **gafael-** (*stem*)
gair (*m.*) word, **geiriau** (*pl.*)
galw (**ar**) (*vb*) call (on), **galw-** (*stem*)
  galw heibio (*vb*) call by, **galw-** (*stem*)
gallu (*vb*) can, **gall-** (*stem*)
gan (*prp.*) (SM) by, since (because)
gardd (*f.*) garden, **gerddi** (*pl.*)
garej (*f.*) garage, **garejys** (*pl.*)
gartref (*adv.*) (at) home
gêm (*f.*) game, **gemau** (*pl.*)
geni (*vb*) to be born, **gan-** (*stem*)
glan y môr seaside
glân (*adj.*) clean
glas (*m.*) blue, **gleision** (*pl.*)
glaw (*m.*) rain, **glawogydd** (*pl.*)
gliniadur (*m.*) laptop, **gliniaduron** (*pl.*)
glynu wrth (SM) (*vb*) stick to, **glyn-** (*stem*)
gobeithio (*vb*) hope, **gobeithi-** (*stem*)
gofid (*m.*) worry, sorrow, **gofidiau** (*pl.*)
gofyn (**i**) (SM) (*vb*) ask, **gofynn-** (*stem*)
gogledd (*m.*) north
gôl (*f.*) goal, **goliau** (*pl.*)
golau (*m.*) light, **goleuadau** (*pl.*)
golau (*m.*), (*adj.*) light
golchi (*vb*) wash, **golch-** (*stem*)
golygfa (*f.*) view, **golygfeydd** (*pl.*)
gorau (*adj.*) best
gorffen (*vb*) finish, end, **gorffen-** (*stem*)
gorllewin (*m.*) west
gormod (**o**) (SM) (*adv.*) too much (of)
gwael (*adj.*) bad, poor (quality)
gwaelod (*m.*) bottom, **gwaelodion** (*pl.*)
gwaethygu (vb) get worse, worsen, **gwaethyg-** (*stem*)
gwahanol (*adj.*) different
gwaith (*m.*) work, **gweithfeydd** (*pl.*)
gwaith (*f.*) time, **gweithiau** (*pl.*)
gwallt (*m.*) hair, **gwalltiau** (*pl.*)
(y) gwanwyn (*m.*) spring
gwario (*vb*) spend (money), **gwari-** (*stem*)
gwas sifil (*m.*) civil servant, **gweision sifil** (*pl.*)
gwddf (*m.*) neck, **gyddfau** (*pl.*)
gwe (*f.*) web, **gweoedd** (*pl.*)
gweddïo (**ar**); (**dros**) (SM) (*vb*) pray (to); (for), **gweddï-** (*stem*)
gweiddi (**ar**) (SM) (*vb*) shout (at), **gweiddi-** (*stem*)
gweithio (*vb*) work, **gweithi-** (*stem*)
gweld (*vb*) see, **gwel-** (*stem*)
gwelw (*adj.*) pale
gwell (*adj.*) better
  mae'n well i (TM) it's better
gwella (*vb*) improve, get better, **gwell-** (*stem*)
gwely (*m.*) bed, **gwelyau** (*pl.*)
gwenu (**ar**) (SM) (*vb*) smile (at), **gwen-** (*stem*)
gwerin (*f.*) folk
gwers (*f.*) lesson, **gwersi** (*pl.*)
gwerthu (*vb*) sell, **gwerth-** (*stem*)
gwesty (*m.*) hotel, **gwestai** (*pl.*)
gwin (*m.*) wine, **gwinoedd** (*pl.*)
gwir (*m.*) truth; (*adj.*) true
gwirion (*adj.*) silly
gwisgo (*vb*) dress, wear, put on, **gwisg-** (*stem*)
gwlad (*f.*) country, **gwledydd** (*pl.*)
  Gwlad Belg Belgium
gwlyb (*adj.*) wet
gwneud (*vb*) do, make (*irreg.*)
gwobr (*f.*), prize, reward, **gwobrau** (*pl.*)
gŵr (*m.*) husband, **gwŷr** (*pl.*)
gwraig (*f.*) wife, **gwragedd** (*pl.*)
gwrando (**ar**) (*vb*) listen (to), **gwrandaw-** (*stem*)
gwregys (*m.*) belt, **gwregysau**
gwybod (**am**) (*vb*) know (a fact) (about) (*periph.*)
gwych (*adj.*) excellent, brilliant
gwydraid (*m.*) glassful, **gwydreidiau** (*pl.*)
gwyliau (*pl.*) holidays
gwylio (*vb*) to watch, **gwyli-** (*stem*)
gwyn (*adj.*) white

gwynt (*m.*) wind, **gwyntoedd**
gwyntog (*adj.*) windy
gwyrdd (*adj.*) green
gyda (*prp.*) (AM) with
  gyda'n gilydd together (us)
gynnau fach (*adv.*) just now
gyrru (*vb*) drive, **gyrr-** (*stem*)

H

(**yr**) **haf** (*m.*) summer
hanes (*m.*) history, **hanesion** (*pl.*)
hanner (*m.*) half, **haneri** (*pl.*)
  hanner dydd midday
hapus (*adj.*) happy
haul (*m.*) sun
heb (*prp.*) without
  heb sôn am (SM) not to mention, never mind
heblaw (*prp.*) besides
hedfan (*vb*) fly, **hedfan-** (*stem*)
heddiw (*adv.*) today
heddlu (*m.*) police(force), **heddluoedd** (*pl.*)S
hefyd (*adv.*) as well, also, too
heibio (*adv.*) by, past
helpu (**i**) (SM) (*vb*) help (to), **help-** (*stem*)
hen (*adj.*) old
  hen bryd i (SM) high time to
hen dad-cu (SW) (*m.*) great grandfather
hen daid (NW) (*m.*) great grandfather, **hen deidiau** (*pl.*)
hen fam-gu (SW) (*f.*) great grandmother
hen nain (NW) (*f.*) great grandmother, **hen neiniau** (*pl.*)
heno (*adv.*) tonight
heol (*f.*) road, **heolydd** (*pl.*)
het (*f.*) hat, **hetiau** (*pl.*)
heulog (*adj.*) sunny
hir (*adj.*) long
hiraeth (*m.*) homesickness, longing
hoff (*adj.*) favourite
hoff o (SM) fond of
hoffi (*vb*) like, **hoff-** (*stem*)
hoffus (*adj.*) amiable
holi (**am**) (SM) (*vb*) ask, inquire (about), **hol-** (*stem*)
holl (SM) (*adj.*) all
hon (*pn*) (*f.*) this

honna (*pn*) (*f.*) that one
hufen (*m.*) cream
hunan (*pn*) self, **hunain** (*pl.*)
hwyl bye
hwyl (*f.*) fun
  hwyl am y tro bye for now
  hwyl fawr good bye
hwylio (*vb*) sail, **hwylio-** (*stem*)
hwn (*pn*) (*m.*) this
hwnna (*pn*) (*m.*) that one
hwyrach (NW) (*adv.*) perhaps
hyd (*m.*) length; (*prp.*) until
  hyd nes (*prp.*) until
  hyd yn hyn (*adv.*) so far
hyderus (**am**) (SM) (*adj.*), confident (about)
(**yr**) **hydref** (*m.*) autumn
hyfryd (*adj.*) pleasant, nice
hyfforddwr (*m.*) trainer, **hyfforddwyr** (*pl.*)
hynny (*pn*) that (*abstract*)

I

i (*prp.*) (SM) to (a place); for
 i fyny up
 i ffwrdd away
 i gyfeiriad in the direction of
 i gyd all
 i lawr down
 i'r to the
iach (*adj.*) healthy
iaith (*f.*) language, **ieithoedd** (*pl.*)
iawn (*adj.*) right, correct; (*adv.*) very, all right
iechyd (*m.*) health
  iechyd da cheers, good health
ifanc (*adj.*) young, **ifainc** (*pl.*)
isel (*adj.*) low
Iwerddon Ireland

J

jam (*m.*) jam, **jamiau** (*pl.*)

L

labordy (*m.*) laboratory, **labordai** (*pl.*)
larwm (*m.*) alarm, **larymau** (*pl.*)
lifft (*m.*) lift, **lifftiau** (*pl.*)
lorri (*f.*) lorry, **lorïau** (*pl.*)
lwc (*f.*) luck

pob lwc good luck
lwcus (*adj.*) lucky

Ll

lladrata (*vb*) to steal
lladd (*vb*) kill, **lladd-** (*stem*)
  lladd ar (SM) (*vb*) criticise, **lladd-** (*stem*)
llaeth (*m.*) milk
llanastr (*m.*) mess (The final **r** is dropped in speech.)
llaw (*f.*) hand, **dwylo** (*pl.*)
llawer (o) (SM) (*m.*) a lot (of), lots of, many
llawn (*adj.*) full
lle (*m.*) place, **llefydd** (*pl.*)
lle (*adv.*) where
lledr (*m.*) leather, **lledrau** (*pl.*)
llenwi (*vb*) fill, **llenw-** (*stem*)
lles (*m.*) benefit, good
llestri (*pl.*) dishes
lleol (*adj.*) local
lliw (*m.*) colour, **lliwiau** (*pl.*)
lliwgar (*adj.*) colourful
lliwio (*vb*) to colour in, **lliwi-** (*stem*)
Lloegr England
llofft (NW) (*f.*) bedroom, **llofftydd** (*pl.*)
llond (*m.*) full
llongyfarchiadau (*pl.*) congratulations
llun (*m.*) picture, **lluniau** (*pl.*)
llwy (*f.*) spoon, **llwyau** (*pl.*)
llwyd (*adj.*) grey
llwyddiant (*m.*) success, **llwyddiannau**
llwyddo (i) (SM) (*vb*) succeed (in), **llwydd-** (*stem*)
llwyth (*m.*) load, **llwythi** (*pl.*)
llyfr (*m.*) book, **llyfrau** (*pl.*)
llyfrgell (*f.*) library, **llyfrgelloedd** (*pl.*)
llynedd (*adv.*) last year
llysfab (*m.*) stepson, **llysfeibion** (*pl.*)
llysfam (*f.*) stepmother, **llysfamau** (*pl.*)
llysferch (*f.*) stepdaughter, **llysferched** (*pl.*)
llysieuyn (*m.*) vegetable, **llysiau** (*pl.*)
llystad (*m.*) stepfather, **llystadau** (*pl.*)
llythyr (*m.*) letter, **llythyron** (*pl.*)

M

mab (*m.*) son, **meibion** (*pl.*)
maddau i (SM) (*vb*) forgive, **maddeu-**(*stem*)
maes parcio (*m.*) car park. **meysydd parcio** (*pl.*)
mam (*f.*) mother, **mamau** (*pl.*)
mam-gu (SW) (*f.*) grandmother
marchnad (*f.*) market, **marchnadoedd** (*pl.*)
mans (*m.*) manse, **mansys** (*pl.*)
marw (*vb*) die (*periph*)
matsien (*f.*) match(stick), **matsys** (*pl.*)
math (*m.*) type, kind **mathau** (*pl.*)
mathemateg (*f.*) mathematics
mawr (*adj.*) big, **mawrion** (*pl.*)
meddu ar (SM) (*vb*) own, possess
meddwl (*m.*) mind, thought, **meddyliau** (*pl.*)
meddwl (**am**) (SM) (*vb*) think (about), **meddyli-** (*stem*)
meddyg (*m.*) doctor, **meddygon** (*pl.*)
melyn (*adj.*) yellow, **melen** (*f.*)
mentro (*vb*) to venture, **mentr-**(*stem*)
merch (*f.*) girl, daughter, **merched** (*pl.*)
mewn (*prp.*) in (with an indefinite noun or verb-noun)
  mewn golwg in mind
  mewn pryd in time
mil (*f.*) thousand, **miloedd** (*pl.*)
mis (*m.*) month, **misoedd** (*pl.*)
modryb (*f.*) aunt, **modrybod** (*pl.*)
moddion (*pl.*) medicine
mor (SM) (*adv.*) so, as
môr (*m.*) sea, **moroedd** (*pl.*)
morgais (*f.*) mortgage, **morgeisi** (*pl.*)
munud (*f.*) (SW), (*m.*) (NW) minute, **munudau** (*pl.*)
mwy (*adj.*) bigger, greater, more
mwynhau (*vb*) enjoy, **mwynha-**(*stem*)
myfyriwr (*m.*) student, **myfyrwyr** (*pl.*)
myfyrwraig (*f.*) student, **myfyrwragedd** (*pl.*)

mynd (*vb*) go (*irreg.*)
  mynd â (*vb*) take
  mynd am dro go for a walk
  mynd at (SM) (*vb*) go to (a person)
  mynd i (SM) (*vb*) go to (a place)
mynydd (*m.*) mountain, **mynyddoedd** (*pl.*)

N

na (*cnj.*) nor, than
  na'r disgwyl than expected
(Y) Nadolig (*m.*) Christmas, **Nadoligau** (*pl.*)
nai (*m.*) nephew, **neiant** (*pl.*)
nain (NW) (*f.*) grandmother, **neiniau** (*pl.*)
naw (*adj.*) nine
nawr (*adv.*) now
neb (*m.*) no one, nobody
neges (*f.*) message, **negeseuon** (*pl.*)
neidio (*vb*) jump, **neidi-** (*stem*)
neis (*adj.*) nice
neithiwr (*adv.*) last night
(yn) nes ymlaen later on
nesaf (*adv.*) next
neu (*cnj.*) (SM) or
neuadd (*f.*) hall, **neuaddau** (*pl.*)
newid (*m.*) change, **newidiadau** (*pl.*)
newid (*vb*) change, **newidi-** (*stem*)
newydd (*adj.*) (SM) new
  newydd droi just turned
  newydd sbon brand new
newyddion (*pl.*) news
nith (*f.*) niece, **nithod** (*pl.*)
niwlog (*adj.*) foggy, misty
nodyn (*m.*) note, **nodiadau** (*pl.*)
nofel (*f.*) novel, **nofelau** (*pl.*)
nofio (*vb*) swim, **nofi-** (*stem*)
nos (*f.*) night, **nosau** (*pl.*)
  nos Lun Monday night
  nos da good night
noson (*f.*) night's length; evening
  noson dda o gwsg a good night's sleep
  noson lawen an evening of light entertainment in Welsh, *cf.* the *ceilidh* in Gaelic culture
noswaith (*f.*) evening, **nosweithiau** (*pl.*)
  noswaith dda good evening
nyrs (*f./m.*) nurse, **nyrsys** (*pl.*)

O

o (*prp.*) (SM) from; of; by
  o amgylch, o gwmpas (*prp.*) around
  o bell ffordd by a long way
  o bryd i'w gilydd from time to time
  o dan (SM) under
  o flaen in front of
  o ganlyniad i (SM) as a result of, consequently
  o gwbl at all
  o gwmpas around
  o heol by a mile
  o hyd still
  o hyn ymlaen from now on
  o leiaf at least
  o'r blaen before
  o'r diwedd at last
  o'r gloch o'clock
oddi wrth (SM) from (a person)
oed (*m.*) age, **oedrannau** (*pl.*)
oer (*adj.*) cold
oergell (*f.*) fridge, **oergelloedd** (*pl.*)
ofn (*m.*) fear, **ofnau** (*pl.*)
ofnadwy (*adj.*) awful
  ofnadwy o (SM) awfully
ofni (*vb*) be afraid of, fear, **ofn-** (*stem*)
ond (*cnj.*) but
oni bai (*cnj.*) unless
oren (*adj.*) orange
os (*cnj*) if (indicative mood)

P

pa (*pn*) (SM) which
  pa fath o (SM) what type of
paentio (*vb*) paint, **paenti-** (*stem*)
pam (*adv.*) why
papur (*m.*) paper, **papurau** (*pl.*)
  papur newydd newspaper
  papur ysgrifennu writing paper
paratoi (*vb*) prepare, **parato-** (*stem*)
pâr (*m.*) pair, **parau** (*pl.*)
paranoiaidd (*adj.*) paranoid
parc (*m.*) park, **parciau**
parcio (*vb*) park, **parci-** (*pl.*)
parod (**am**) (SM) (*adj.*) ready (for)
parti (*m.*) party, **partïon** (*pl.*)
partner (*m.*) partner, **partneriaid** (*pl.*)

(Y) Pasg (*m.*) Easter
patrwm (*m.*) pattern, **patrymau** (*pl.*)
pawb (*pn*) everyone
pecyn (*m.*) package, **pecynnau** (*pl.*)
pedair (*adj.*) (*f.*) four
pedwar (*adj.*) (*m.*) four
peidio (**â**) (AM) (*vb*) don't, **peidi-** (*stem*) (the **â** is often dropped in speech and can be left out when writing)
peint (*m.*) pint, **peintiau** (*pl.*)
pêl (*f.*) ball, **peli** (*pl.*)
pell (*adj.*) far
pen (*m.*) head, end, **pennau** (*pl.*)
pen-blwydd (*m.*) birthday, **penblwyddi** (*pl.*)
penderfynol (**o**) (**SM**) (*adj.*) determined (to)
penderfynu (*vb*) decide, **penderfyn-**(*stem*)
Penfro Pembroke
pennaeth (*m.*) head, chief, **penaethiaid** (*pl.*)
pensil pencil, **pensiliau** (*pl.*)
pentref (*m.*) village, **pentrefi** (*pl.*)
penwythnos (*m.*) weekend **penwythnosau** (*pl.*)
  dros y penwythnos over the weekend
perffaith (*adj.*) perfect
perfformio (*vb*) perform, **perfformi-** (*stem-*)
persawr (*m.*) perfume, **persawrau** (*pl.*)
pert (*adj.*) pretty
perthyn (**i**) (*vb*) belong (to), to be related (to)
peswch (*m.*) cough
peth (*m.*) thing, **pethau** (*pl.*)
pigyn clust (NW) (*m.*) earache
pinc (*adj.*) pink
pleidleisio dros (SM) (*vb*) vote for, **pleidleisi-** (*stem*)
plentyn (*m.*) child, **plant** (*pl.*)
plismon (*m.*) policeman, **plismyn** (*pl.*)
plismones (*f.*) policewoman, **plismonesau** (*pl.*)
pob (*adj.*) every, each (**pob** mutates to **bob** when it begins an adverbial phrase)
pob hwyl all the best
pob lwc good luck
pobl (*f.*) people, **pobloedd** (*pl.*)
poced (*f.*) pocket, **pocedi** (*pl.*)
poeni (**am**) (SM) (*vb*) worry (about), bother, **poen-** (*pl.*)
poeth (*adj.*) hot
pont (*f.*) bridge, **pontydd** (*pl.*)
popeth everything
porffor (*adj.*) purple
posib (*adj.*) possible
postmon (*m.*) postman, **postmyn** (*pl.*)
postmones (*f.*) postwoman, **postmonesau** (*pl.*)
potel (*f.*) bottle, **poteli** (*pl.*)
potelaid (*f.*) bottle(ful), **poteleidiau** (*pl.*)
prawf (*m.*) test, **profion** (*pl.*)
pren (*adj.*) wood(en)
pres (NW) (*m.*) money
prif (*adj.*) (SM) main, chief, head
  prif weinidog prime/first minister
prifddinas (*f.*) capital city, **prifddinasoedd** (*pl.*)
priodas (*f.*) wedding, marriage, **priodasau** (*pl.*)
priodfab (*m.*) bridegroom, **priodfeibion** (*pl.*)
pris (*m.*) price, **prisiau** (*pl.*)
problem (*m.*) (NW), (*f.*) (SW) problem, **problemau** (*pl.*)
profiad (*m.*) experience, **profiadau** (*pl.*)
prosiect (*m.*) project, **prosiectau** (*pl.*)
pryd (*adv.*) when
prydferth (*adj.*) beautiful
prydlon (*adj.*) punctual
prynhawn (*m.*) afternoon, **prynhawniau** (*pl.*)
prynu (*vb*) buy, **pryn-** (*pl.*)
prysur (*adj.*) busy
pump (*adj.*) five
punt (*f.*) pound (£), **punnoedd** (*pl.*)
pupur (*m.*) pepper, **puprau** (*pl.*)
pwdin (*m.*) dessert, pudding, **pwdinau** (*pl.*)
pwdu (*vb*) sulk, **pwd-** (*stem*)
pwll nofio (*m.*) swimming pool, **pyllau nofio** (*pl.*)
pwy (*pn*) who

pwys (*f.*) pound (lb), **pwysi** (*pl.*)
pysgodyn (*m.*) fish, **pysgod** (*pl.*)
pythefnos (*m.*) fortnight, **pythefnosau** (*pl.*)

R
radio (*m.*) radio, **radios** (*pl.*)
ras (*f.*) race, **rasys** (*pl.*)
rŵan (*adv.*) (NW) now
rwber (*m.*) rubber
rygbi (*m.*) rugby

Rh
rhad (*adj.*) cheap
rhag ofn in case
rhagor (**o**) (SM) (*adv.*) more
rhai some; ones
rhaid (*m.*) necessity
rhaw (*f.*) shovel, spade **rhawiau** (*pl.*)
rhedeg (*vb*) run, **rhed-** (*stem*)
rheilffordd (*f.*) railway, **rheilffyrdd** (*pl.*)
(**y**) **rheiny** (*pn*) those
rheolwr (*m.*) manager, **rheolwyr**
rhestr (*f.*) list, **rhestrau**
  rhestr fer short list
rheswm (*m.*) reason, **rhesymau** (*pl.*)
rhesymol (*adj.*) reasonable
rhewi (*vb*) freeze, **rhew-** (*stem*)
rhiant (*m.*) parent, **rhieni** (*pl.*)
rhif ffôn (*m.*) telephone number, **rhifau ffôn** (*pl.*)
rhoi (*vb*) give; put, **rho-** (*stem*)
  rhoi bai ar (SM) (*vb*) blame
  rhoi'r gorau i (SM) (*vb*) give up
rhwng (*prp.*) between
  rhwng dau feddwl in two minds
  rhwng popeth all things considered
rhy (*adv.*) (SM) too
rhyngwladol (*adj.*) international
rhyw (*pn*) some
  rhywbeth something
  rhywbryd sometime
  rhywle somewhere
  rhywsut somehow
  rhywun someone, **rhywrai** (*pl.*)

S
sach (*f.*) sack, **sachau** (*pl.*)
Saesnes (*f.*) English (woman), **Saesnesau** (*pl.*)
Saesneg (*f.*) English (language)
Sais (*m.*) Englishman, **Saeson** (*pl.*)
saith (*adj.*) seven
sâl (*adj.*) ill
sawl (*adj.*) several
sefyll (*vb*) stand, **saf-** (*stem*)
Seisnig (*adj.*) English (country)
selsigen (*f.*) sausage, **selsig** (*pl.*)
sêt (*f.*) seat, **seti** (*pl.*)
sgert (*f.*) skirt, **sgertiau** (*pl.*)
sglodyn (*m.*) chip, **sglodion** (*pl.*)
sgorio (*vb*) score, **sgori-** (*stem*)
sianel (*f.*) channel, **sianeli** (*pl.*)
siarad (**â**) (*vb*) speak (to), **siarad-** (*stem*)
siarad am (SM) (*vb*) talk about
sinema (*f.*) cinema, **sinemâu** (*pl.*)
siocled (*m.*) chocolate, **siocledi** (*pl.*)
siop (*f.*) shop, **siopau** (*pl.*)
  siop fara bakery, bread shop
siopa (*vb*) shop, go shopping, **siop-** (*stem*)
siriol (*adj.*) cheerful
siwgr (*m.*) sugar
siwmper (*f.*) jumper, **siwmperi** (*pl.*)
siŵr (*adj.*) sure, certain
  siŵr o (SM) sure to
  siŵr o fod probably
siwt (*f.*) suit, **siwtiau** (*pl.*)
siwtio (*vb*) suit, **siwti-** (*stem*)
smocio (*vb*) smoke (*informal*), **smoci-** (*stem*)
staff (*m.*) staff
stamp (*m.*) stamp, **stampiau** (*pl.*)
stopio (*vb*) stop, **stopi-** (*stem*)
stormus (*adj.*) stormy
stryd (*f.*) street, **strydoedd** (*pl.*)
sut (*adv.*) how
sŵn (*m.*) noise, sound, **synau** (*pl.*)
swper (*m.*) supper, **swperau** (*pl.*)
swydd (*f.*) job, **swyddi** (*pl.*)
swyddfa (*f.*) office, **swyddfeydd** (*pl.*)
  swyddfa bost post office
syched (*m.*) thirst, dryness
sylwi ar (SM) (*vb*) notice, **sylw-** (*stem*)
syllu (**ar**) (*vb*) stare (at), **syll-** (*stem*)
symud (*vb*) move, **symud-** (*stem*)

syndod (*m.*) surprise (*m.*), **syndodau** (*pl.*)
syniad (*m.*) idea, **syniadau** (*pl.*)
synnu (**at**) (SM) (*vb*) be surprised (at), **synn-** (*stem*)
syth (*adj.*) straight
  yn syth straightaway

T

tad (*m.*) father, **tadau** (*pl.*)
tad-cu (*m.*) grandfather
tafarn (*f.*) pub, **tafarnau** (*pl.*)
taid (NW) (*m.*) grandfather, **teidiau** (*pl.*)
tair (*adj.*) (*f.*) three
taith (*f.*) journey, trip, **teithiau** (*pl.*)
tal (*adj.*) tall
talu (*vb*) pay, **tal-** (*stem*)
tan (*prp.*) (SM) until
tân (*m.*) fire, **tanau** (*pl.*)
tarw (*m.*) bull, **teirw** (*pl.*)
tawel (*adj.*) quiet
te (*m.*) tea
teg (*adj.*) fair
tegan (*m.*) toy, **teganau** (*pl.*)
teimlad (*m.*) feeling, **teimladau** (*pl.*)
teithio (*vb*) travel, **teithi-** (*stem*)
teledu (*m.*) television
tennis (*m.*) tennis
  tennis bwrdd table tennis
teulu (*m.*) family, **teuluoedd** (*pl.*)
ti (*pn*) you (*informal*)
tîm (*m.*) team, **timau** (*pl.*)
tipyn (*m.*) a little
  tipyn o (SM) a bit of
tocyn (*m.*) ticket, **tocynnau** (*pl.*)
torri (*vb*) cut, break, **torr-** (*stem*)
  torri ar draws interrupt
  torri i lawr break down
torth (*f.*) loaf, **torthau** (*pl.*)
traeth (*m.*) beach, **traethau** (*pl.*)
trafod (*vb*) to discuss, **trafod-** (*stem*)
traffordd (*f.*) motorway, **traffyrdd** (*pl.*)
tref (*f.*) town, **trefi** (*pl.*)
trên (*m.*) train, **trenau** (*pl.*)
treulio (*vb*) spend (time), **treuli-** (*stem*)
tri (*adj.*) (*m.*) three
trïo (*vb*) try, **trï-** (*stem*)
trist (*adj.*) sad

tro (*m.*) time, turning, occasion, **troeon** (*pl.*)
troed (*f.*) foot, **traed** (*pl.*)
troi (*vb*) turn, **tro-** (*stem*)
  troi i lawr turn down
trueni (*m.*) pity
trwchus (*adj.*) thick
trwm (*adj.*) heavy
trwy (*prp.*) (SM) through, throughout, by
  trwy drugaredd mercifully
  trwy lwc luckily
  trwy'r dydd all day
trydanwr (*m.*) electrician, **trydanwyr**
tsieina (*m.*) china
tua (*prp.*) (AM) about, approximately
tu allan (*adv.*) outside
  tu allan (i) (SM) outside of
tueddu (i) (SM) (*vb*) tend (to), **tuedd-** (*stem*)
tu mewn (*adv.*) inside
  tu mewn (i) (SM) inside of
twp (*adj.*) stupid
twym (*adj.*) warm
tŷ (*m.*) house, **tai** (*pl.*)
Tyddewi St David's
tymor (*m.*) term, season, **tymhorau** (*pl.*)
tyn (*adj.*) tight ([t]**ynn** when mutated)
tynnu (*vb*) pull, draw, **tynn-** (*stem*)
tywod (*m.*) sand
tywydd (*m.*) weather
tywyll (*adj.*) dark

Th

theatr (*f.*) theatre, **theatrau** (*pl.*)

U

uchel (*adj.*) high, loud
uffernol (*adj.*) infernal
un (*adj.*) one
unig (*adj.*) lonely; only (SM)
  plentyn unig lonely child
  unig blentyn only child
unrhyw (*adj.*) (SM) any
  unrhyw bryd anytime
unwaith (*adv.*) once
uwchben (*prp.*) above, over

W

wal (*f.*) wall, **welydd** (*pl.*)
wats (*f.*) watch, **watshys** (*pl.*)
wedi (*prp.*) after
  wedi blino tired
  wedi ymddeol retired
wedyn (*adv.*) then, afterwards
wrth (*prp.*) (SM) by, near
  wrth fodd delighted
  wrth law at hand, close at hand
  wrth ochr by the side of
  wrth reswm it stands to reason
  wrth gwrs of course
wy (*m.*) egg, **wyau** (*pl.*)
wyneb (*m.*) face, **wynebau** (*pl.*)
ŵyr (*m.*) grandson, **wyrion** (*pl.*)
wyres (*f.*) grand-daughter, **wyresau** (*pl.*)
wyth (*adj.*) eight
wythnos (*f.*) week, **wythnosau** (*pl.*)
  yr wythnos diwethaf last week
  yr wythnos nesaf next week

Y

y (*adj.*) the (<yr> before vowels and <'r> after vowels); that (preverbial particle: future and conditional)
ychwanegu (**at**) (SM) (*vb*) add (to), **ychwaneg-**(*stem*)
ychydig (**o**) (SM) a little/few (of)
yfed (*vb*) drink, **yf-** (*stem*)
yfory (*adv.*) tomorrow
ynghylch (*prp.*) about, concerning
yma (*adv.*) here
ymarfer (*m.*) exercise, practice, **ymarferion** (*pl.*)
ymarfer (*vb*) practise, **ymarfer-** (*stem*)
ymbarél (*f.*) umbrella, **ymbareli** (*pl.*)
ymddeol (*vb*) retire, **ymddeol-** (*stem*)
ymddiddori yn (NM)/**mewn** (*vb*) be interested in, take an interest in, **ymddiddor-** (*stem*)
ymddiheuro (*vb*) apologise, **ymddiheur-** (*stem*)
ymddiried yn (NM)/**mewn** (*vb*) trust, **ymddiri-** (*stem*)
ymffrostio yn (NM)/**mewn** (*vb*) boast, **ymffrosti-** (*stem*)

ymhen (*prp.*) within (time)
ymlacio (*vb*) relax, ymlaci- (*stem*)
ymladd (**dros**) (SM) (*vb*) fight (for), **ymladd-** (*stem*)
ymolchi (*vb*) wash oneself, **ymolch-** (*stem*)
ymosod ar (SM) (*vb*) attack, **ymosod-** (*stem*)
ymweld â (AM) (*vb*) visit, **ymwel-** (*stem*)
ymysg (*prp.*) amongst
yn (*prp.*) (NM) in (with definite nouns)
yn lle (*prp.*) instead of
yn ymyl (see **ar bwys**)
yn ôl according to; back(wards); ago
yn (*adv.*) (TM) adverbial and predicative marker:
  yn anffodus unfortunately
  yn barod already
  yn fawr iawn very much
  yn syth straightaway, straight
yno (*adv.*) there (not in sight)
yr (*adj.*) the (before a vowel)
  Yr Aifft Egypt
  yr un the same
  Yr Wyddfa Mount Snowdon
ysbyty (*m.*) hospital, **ysbytai** (*pl.*)
ysgol (*f.*) school, **ysgolion** (*pl.*)
  ysgol gynradd primary school
  ysgol uwchradd secondary school
ysgrifennu (*vb*) write, **ysgrifenn-** (*stem*)
  ysgrifennu at (SM) write to
  ysgrifennu am (SM) write about
ysmygu (*vb*) smoke (*formal*), **ysmyg-** (*stem*)
ystafell (*f.*) room, **ystafelloedd** (*pl.*)
ystafell wely (*f.*) (SW) bedroom, **ystafelloedd gwely** (*pl.*)
ystyr (*m.*) meaning, **ystyron** (*pl.*)
ystyried (*vb*) consider, **ystyri-**(*stem*)

English-Welsh

A

able (to be) (see **be able**)
about am (*prp.*) (SM), ynghylch (*prp.*), tua (*prp.*) (AM)
  about to ar fin
above uwchben

accent acen (*f.*)
accept derbyn (*vb*)
accident damwain (*f.*)
according to yn ôl
across (*prp.*) ar draws
accusation cyhuddiad (*m.*)
add (**to**) ychwanegu (at) (SM) (*vb*)
address cyfeiriad (*m.*)
admit (**to** [someone]) cyfaddef (wrth) (SM) (*vb*)
advice cyngor (*m.*)
aeroplane awyren
(**to be**) **afraid** ofni (*vb*)
after ar ôl (*cnj.*), wedi
afternoon prynhawn (*m.*)
afterwards wedyn (*adv.*)
again eto (*adv.*)
against yn erbyn (*prp.*)
age oed (*m.*), oedrannau
ago yn ôl (*adv.*)
agree with (*vb*) cytuno â (AM)
alarm (*m.*) larwm
almost bron (*prp.*)
all holl (SM) (*adj.*), i gyd
  all day trwy'r dydd
  all the best pob hwyl
  all right iawn
allow (**to**) gadael (i) (SM) (*vb*)
also hefyd (*adv.*)
although er (*prp.*)
American (**man**) Americanwr (*m.*)
American (**woman**) Americanes (*f.*)
amiable hoffus (*adj.*)
amongst ymysg (*prp.*)
and a (*cnj.*) (AM) ('ac' before a vowel)
angry dig, blin (NW) (*adj.*)
animal anifail (*m.*)
announcement cyhoeddiad (*m.*)
answer ateb (*vb*)
anthem anthem (*f.*)
any unrhyw (*adj.*) (SM)
  any longer bellach
  any more bellach
  anytime unrhyw bryd
apologise ymddiheuro (vb)
appeal (**to**) apelio (*vb*) (at) (SM)
apple afal (*f.*)
apply cynnig (*vb*)
approximately tua (*prp.*) (AM)
area ardal (*f.*)

argue (**for**) dadlau (dros) (SM) (vb)
arm braich (*f.*)
around o amgylch, o gwmpas (*prp.*)
arrive cyrraedd (*vb*)
as mor (SM), wrth (SM), fel
  as well hefyd
ask gofyn i (SM) (*vb*), holi (*vb*)
at at (*prp.*) (SM), am (*prp.*) (SM), ar (SM) (*prp.*)
  at all o gwbl
  at home gartref
  at least o leiaf
  at seven o'clock am saith o'r gloch
  at the moment ar hyn o bryd
atmosphere awyrgylch (*m.*)
attack ymosod ar (SM) (*vb*)
aunt modryb (*f.*)
autumn hydref (*m.*) (yr)
awake ar ddi-hun
away i (*adv.*) ffwrdd
awful ofnadwy (*adj.*)
  awfully ofnadwy o

B

baby baban (*m.*)
back(wards) yn ôl (*adv.*)
back (**of body**) cefn (*m.*)
bad drwg (*adj.*), gwael (*adj.*)
bag bag (*m.*)
baked beans ffa pob (*pl.*)
bakery siop fara (*f.*)
ball pêl (*f.*)
bank banc (*m.*)
be bod (*vb*) (*irreg.*)
  be able gallu (*vb*)
beach traeth (*m.*)
beautiful prydferth (*adj.*)
because (o) achos, am (SM) (*prp.*)
bed gwely (*m.*)
bedroom (*f.*) llofft (NW), ystafell wely (SW)
beer cwrw (*m.*)
before cyn (*prp.*), o'r blaen
  before long cyn bo hir
begin dechrau (*vb*)
behind ar ôl (*prp.*)
Belgium Gwlad Belg
believe (**in**) credu (yn [SM]/mewn) (*vb*)
bell cloch (*f.*)
belly bol (*m.*)

belong (to) perthyn (i) (SM) (*vb*)
belt gwregys (*m.*)
benefit lles (*m.*)
besides heblaw (*prp.*)
best gorau (*adj.*)
  all the best pob hwyl
better gwell (*adj.*)
  get better gwella (*vb*)
  it's better mae'n well (i)
between rhwng (*prp.*)
big mawr (*adj.*)
bigger mwy (*adj.*)
bike beic (*m.*)
  by bike ar y beic
bill bil (*m.*)
bird aderyn (*m.*)
biro beiro (*m.*)
birthday pen-blwydd (*m.*)
bit tipyn (*m.*)
  bit of tipyn o (SM)
black du (*adj.*)
blame rhoi bai ar (SM) (*vb*)
blue glas (*m.*)
boast ymffrostio (*vb*)
body corff (*m.*)
book llyfr (*m.*)
(be) born (cael eich) geni (*vb*)
bother poeni (*vb*)
bottle potel (*f.*)
bottle(ful) potelaid (*f.*)
bottom gwaelod (*m.*)
bound to bownd o (SM)
box bocs (*m.*)
boy bachgen (*m.*)
bread bara (*m.*)
  bakery, bread shop siop fara
break torri (*vb*)
  break down torri i lawr
breakfast brecwast (*m.*)
bridegroom priodfab (*m.*)
bridge pont (*f.*)
brilliant gwych (*adj.*), bendigedig (*adj.*)
bring dod â (AM) (*vb*) (*irreg.*)
brother brawd (*m.*)
build adeiladu (*vb*), codi (*vb*)
building adeilad (*m.*)
bull tarw (*m.*)
bus bws (*m.*)
busy prysur (*adj.*)
but (*cjn*) ond

butcher cigydd (*m.*)
buy prynu (*vb*)
by (time) erbyn (*prp.*)
by gan, wrth (*prp.*) (SM), heibio (*adv.*), trwy (*prp.*) (SM), o (SM)
  by all means ar bob cyfrif
  by now erbyn hyn (*adv.*)
  by the side of wrth ochr
bye hwyl
  bye for now hwyl am y tro

C

cake cacen (*f.*)
call galw (*vb*)
  call by galw heibio (*vb*)
camel camel (*m.*)
camera camera (*m.*)
can gallu (*vb*)
capital (city) prifddinas (*f.*)
car car (*m.*)
  car park maes parcio
caravan carafán (*f.*)
Cardiff Caerdydd
Carmarthen Caerfyrddin
card cerdyn (*m.*)
carpet carped (*m.*)
cat cath (*f.*)
catch dal (*vb*)
celebrate dathlu (*vb*)
certain siŵr (*adj.*)
chair cadair (*f.*)
  armchair cadair freichiau
change newid (*m.*); newid (*vb*)
channel sianel (*f.*)
chapel capel (*m.*)
cheap rhad (*adj.*)
cheerful siriol (*adj.*)
cheers iechyd da (*pl.*), (*interj.*)
chicken pox brech yr ieir (*f.*)
chief prif (*adj.*), pennaeth (*m.*)
child plentyn (*m.*)
china tsieina (*adj.*)
chip sglodyn (*m.*)
chocolate siocled (*m.*)
choice dewis (*m.*)
choir côr (*m.*)
choose dewis (*vb*)
Christmas Nadolig (*m.*)
church eglwys (*f.*)
cinema sinema (*f.*)
city dinas (*f.*)

civil servant gwas sifil (*m.*)
class dosbarth (*m.*)
clean glân (*adj.*)
clear clir (*adj.*)
climb dringo (*vb*)
clock cloc (*m.*)
close cau (*vb*)
close agos (*adj.*)
  close at hand wrth law
  closed ar gau
clothes dillad (*pl.*)
cloudy cymylog (*adj.*)
club clwb (*m.*)
coat cot (*f.*)
coffee coffi (*m.*)
cold oer (*adj.*)
cold (ailment) annwyd (*m.*)
college coleg (*m.*)
colour lliw (*m.*)
colour in lliwio (*vb*)
colourful lliwgar (*adj.*)
come dod (*vb*) (*irreg.*)
  come across dod ar draws
  come over dod draw
comfortable cyfforddus (*adj.*)
company cwmni (*m.*)
compete cystadlu (*vb*)
complain cwyno (*vb*)
concerning ynghylch (*prp.*)
consider ystyried (*vb*)
  all things considered rhwng popeth
confident (about) hyderus am (SM) (*adj.*)
congratulations llongyfarchiadau (*pl. & interj.*)
consequently o ganlyniad (*adv.*)
contact cysylltu â (AM) contact
continue (to) dal (i) (SM) (*vb*)
contribute (to) cyfrannu (at) (SM) (*vb*)
convenient cyfleus (*adj.*)
compete cystadlu (*v.*)
competition cystadleuaeth (*f.*)
competitor cystadleuydd (*m.*)
corner cornel (*f.*)
correct cywir, iawn (*adj.*)
cost cost (*f.*)
cough peswch (*m.*)
country gwlad (*f.*)
course cwrs (*m.*)

cousin cefnder (*m.*), cyfnither (*f.*)
cow buwch (*f.*)
cream hufen (*m.*)
criticise lladd ar (SM) (*vb*)
cross croesi (vb)
crossroads croesffordd (*f.*)
cruel (to/towards) creulon (wrth) (SM) (*adj.*)
cup cwpan (*m.*)
cupboard cwpwrdd (*m.*)
cupful cwpanaid (*m.*)
cut torri (*vb*)

D

dark tywyll (*ans.*)
daughter merch (*f.*)
day dydd (*m.*)
  all day trwy'r dydd
  day before yesterday echdoe (*adv.*)
  day's length diwrnod (*m.*)
  Saint David's Day Dydd Gŵyl Dewi
dear annwyl (*adj.*), drud
debt dyled (*f.*)
decide penderfynu (*vb*)
delicious blasus (*adj.*)
delighted wrth fodd (*adj.*)
Denbigh Dinbych
depend (on) dibynnu (ar) (SM) (*vb*)
derive (from) deillio o (SM) (*vb*)
desk desg (*f.*)
dessert pwdin (*m.*)
determined to penderfynol o (SM) (*adj.*)
die marw (*vb*) (*periph.*)
different gwahanol (*adj.*) (SM)
difficult anodd (*adj.*)
dinner cinio (*m.*)
direction cyfeiriad (*m.*)
  in the direction of i gyfeiriad
dirty brwnt (*adj.*) (SW), budr (*adj.*) (NW)
disagree (with) anghytuno (â) (AM) (*vb*)
discuss trafod (*vb*)
dishes llestri (*pl.*)
district ardal (*f.*)
do gwneud (*vb*) (*irreg.*)
doctor meddyg (*m.*)
dog ci (*m.*)

don't peidio (â) (AM) (*vb*) (the **â** is often dropped in speech and can be left out when writing)
door drws (*m.*)
down i lawr (*adv.*)
draw tynnu (*vb*)
dream (about) breuddwydio (am) (SM) (*vb*)
dress gwisgo (*vb*)
dress ffrog (*f.*)
drink diod (*f.*)
drink yfed (*vb*)
drive gyrru (*vb*)
dryness sryched (*m.*)

E

email e-bost (*m.*)
each pob (*adj.*)
ear clust (*f.*)
earache clust dost (SW), pigyn clust (NW)
early cynnar (*adj.*)
east dwyrain (*m.*)
Easter (Y) Pasg (*m.*)
eat bwyta (*vb*)
effect effeithio ar (SM) (*vb*)
egg wy (*m.*)
Egypt Yr Aifft
eight wyth (*adj.*)
either chwaith (*adv.*)
electrician trydanwr (*m.*)
end diwedd (*m.*), pen, (*m.*) gorffen (*vb*)
England Lloegr
English Saesneg (language) (*f.*); Seisnig (*ans.*) (country)
Englishman Sais (*m.*)
Englishwoman Saesnes (*f.*)
enjoy mwynhau (*vb*)
enough digon (*adv.*), digon o (SM)
Europe Ewrop (*f.*)
envelope amlen (*f.*)
evening noson (*f.*); noswaith (*f.*)
even hyd yn oed, byth (*adv.*)
event digwyddiad (*m.*)
ever byth, erioed (*adv.*)
every pob (*adj.*) (mutates to **bob** when used adverbially)
  every morning bob bore
  every time bob tro
  everyday bob dydd

everyone pawb
everything popeth
exactly ar ei ben (*adv.*)
exam arholiad (*m.*)
excuse esgusodi (*vb*)
  excuse me esgusodwch fi
excellent gwych (*adj.*)
exercise ymarfer (*m.*) (*vb*)
expect disgwyl (*vb*)
expensive drud (*adj.*)
experience profiad (*m.*)
explain esbonio (*vb*)
extend estyn (*vb*)
extinguish diffodd (*vb*)

F

face wyneb (*m.*) (*pl.*)
fair teg (*adj.*)
  fair play chwarae teg
famous enwog (*adj.*)
family teulu (*m.*)
  family tree coeden achau
famous enwog (*adj.*)
far pell (*adj.*)
farmer ffermwr (*m.*)
father tad (*m.*)
fault bai (*m.*)
(in) favour of dros (*prp.*) (SM)
favourite hoff (*adj.*) (SM)
fear ofni (*vb*), ofn (*m.*)
feed bwydo (*vb*)
feeling teimlad (*m.*)
fence ffens (*f.*)
few ychydig (o)
field cae (*m.*)
fight (for) ymladd (dros) (SM) (*vb*)
fill llenwi (*vb*)
film, ffilm (*f.*)
find dod o hyd i (SM)
fine braf (*adj.*)
finish gorffen (*vb*)
fire tân (*m.*)
first cyntaf (*adj.*)
fish pysgodyn (*m.*)
five (*adj.*) pump ('pum' before noun)
flask fflasg (*f.*)
flower blodyn (*m.*)
fly hedfan (*vb*)
foggy niwlog (*adj.*)
folk gwerin (*f.*)
  folk singing canu gwerin

fond of hoff o (SM)
food bwyd (*m.*)
foot troed (*f.*), traed (*pl.*)
  on foot ar droed
  to get to one's feet codi ar eich traed
for am (*prp*) (SM); i (*prp*) (SM); ar gyfer (*prp*); dros (SM) (*prp.*)
  for the sake of er mwyn
forget (about) anghofio (am) (SM) (*vb*)
forgive maddau i (SM) (*vb*)
fortnight pythefnos (*m.*)
four (*ans.*) pedwar (*m.*), pedair (*f.*) (language) (*f.*)
freeze rhewi (*vb*)
French Ffrangeg (language) (*f.*); Ffrengig (country) (*ans.*)
French(man) Ffrancwr (*m.*)
French (woman) Ffrances (*f.*)
fresh ffres (*adj.*)
fridge oergell (*f.*)
friend ffrind (*m.*)
friendly cyfeillgar (*adj.*)
frock ffrog (*f.*)
from (a place) o (*prp.*)
from (a person) oddi wrth (*prp.*)
  from now on o hyn ymlaen
front blaen (*m.*)
  in front of o flaen
full llond (*m.*), llawn (*adj.*)
fun hwyl (*f.*)
funny (doniol) (*adj.*)

G

gain ennill (*vb*)
game gêm (*f.*)
garage garej (*f.*)
garden gardd (*f.*)
garment dilledyn (*m.*), dillad (*pl.*)
German Almaeneg (language) (*f.*); Almanaidd (country) (*ans.*)
German Almaenwr (*m.*)
German (woman) Almaenes (*f.*)
get cael (*vb*) (*irreg.*)
get dressed gwisgo (*vb*)
get up codi (*vb*)
girl merch (*f.*)
gift anrheg (*f.*)
give rhoi (*vb*)
  give up rhoi'r gorau i (SM)

glad balch (*adj.*)
  I'm glad mae'n dda gyda fi (SW)
  I'm glad mae'n dda gen i (NW)
glassful gwydraid (*m.*)
go mynd (*vb*) (*irreg.*)
  go to (person) mynd at (SM)
  go to (place) mynd i (SM)
goal gôl (*f.*)
good da (*adj.*)
goodbye hwyl fawr (*interj.*)
grand-daughter wyres (*f.*)
grandfather tad-cu (*m.*) (SW), taid (NW)
grandmother mam-gu (*f.*) (SW), nain (NW)
grandson ŵyr (*m.*)
grateful diolchgar (*adj.*)
great grandfather hen dad-cu (*m.*) (SW), hen daid (*m.*) (NW)
great grandmother hen fam-gu (*f.*) (SW), hen nain (*f.*) (NW)
greater mwy (*adj.*)
green gwyrdd (*adj.*)
grey llwyd (*adj.*)
grip gafael yn (NM)/mewn (*vb*)
gym campfa (*f.*)

H

hail (stones) cesair (*pl.*); bwrw cesair (*vb*)
hair gwallt (*m.*)
half hanner (*m.*)
hall neuadd (*f.*)
hand llaw (*f.*)
  at hand wrth law
happen digwydd (*vb*)
happy hapus (*adj.*)
hard caled (*adj.*), anodd (*adj.*)
haste brys (*m.*)
  (in) haste, in a hurry ar frys
hat het (*f.*)
hate casáu (*vb*)
  I hate mae'n gas gyda fi (SW)
  I hate mae'n gas gen i (NW)
have cael (obtain) (*vb*) (*irreg.*); bod ... gyda (SW)/gan (NW) (possession) (*prp.*)
hay gwair (*m.*)
  hay fever clefyd y gwair (*m.*)
head pen (body) (*m.*); pennaeth (institution) (*m.*); prif (*adj.*) (SM)

headache cur pen (*m.*) (NW), pen tost (SW)
health iechyd (*m.*)
  good health, cheers iechyd da
healthy iach (*adj.*)
hear (about) clywed (am) (SM)
heavy trwm (*adj.*)
help help (*m.*); helpu (*vb*)
here yma (*adv.*)
  here (is/are) dyma (SM)
high uchel (*adj.*)
  high time (to) hen bryd (i) (SM)
hill bryn (*m.*)
history hanes (*m.*)
hit bwrw (*vb*)
  bwrw cesair to hail
  bwrw eira to snow
  bwrw glaw to rain
hold dal (something) (*vb*); cynnal (event) (*vb*)
holidays gwyliau (*pl.*)
home(wards) adre(f) (*adv.*)
  at home gartref (*adv.*)
homesickness hiraeth (*m.*)
hope gobaith (*m.*); gobeithio (*vb*)
hospital ysbyty (*m.*)
hot poeth (*adj.*)
hotel gwesty (*m.*)
hour awr (*f.*)
house tŷ (*m.*)
how (*adv.*) sut
  how many faint
  how much faint o (SM)
hundred cant (*adj.*)
hunger eisiau bwyd (*m.*)
hurry brys (*m.*) brysio (*vb*)
  in a hurry ar frys
husband gŵr (*m.*)
hypermarket archfarchnad (*f.*)

I

idea syniad (*m.*)
if os (indicative) (*cjn*), pe (subjunctive) (*cjn*)
ill sâl (*adj.*)
improve gwella (*vb*)
in yn (NM) (*prp.*); mewn (with indefinite nouns)
  in case rhag ofn
  in order to er mwyn
  inspite er gwaethaf

infernal uffernol (*adj.*)
influence dylanwadu ar (SM) (*vb*)
influenza ffliw (*m.*)
injure anafu (*vb*)
inside (*adv.*) tu mewn
  inside of tu mewn i (SM)
instead of yn lle (*prp.*)
interest diddordeb (*m.*)
  be interested in, take an interest in ymddiddori yn (NM)/mewn (*vb*)
interesting diddorol (*adj.*)
interview cyfweliad (*m.*)
international rhyngwladol (*adj.*)
interrupt torri ar draws (*vb*)
Ireland Iwerddon

J

jam (*m.*) jam
job swydd (*f.*)
journey taith (*f.*)
jump neidio (*vb*)
jumper siwmper (*f.*)
just (at this minute) newydd (*adv.*)
  just now gynnau fach (*adv.*)
  just turned newydd droi

K

keep cadw (*vb*)
  keep at (something) dal at (SM) (*vb*)
kill lladd (*vb*)
kind math (*m.*)
kind (to) caredig (wrth) (SM) (*adj.*)
kitchen cegin (*f.*), ceginau (*pl.*)
know (a fact) gwybod (*vb*) (*periph.*)
know (a person, place) adnabod (*vb*) (*periph.*)

L

laboratory labordy (*m.*)
language iaith (*f.*)
laptop gliniadur (*m.*)
large mawr (*adj.*)
last (previous) diwethaf (*adj.*)
  at last o'r diwedd
  last night neithiwr
later on (yn) nes ymlaen
laugh chwerthin (*vb*)
learn dysgu (*vb*)
least lleiaf

at least o leiaf
leather lledr (*m.*)
leave gadael (*vb*)
left chwith (*adj.*)
leg coes (*f.*)
lesson gwers (*f.*)
let (allow) gadael i (SM) (*vb*)
letter llythyr (*m.*)
library llyfrgell (*f.*)
lift codi (*vb*), llfft (*m.*)
light (a fire) cynnau (*vb*)
light golau (*m.*), golau (*adj.*)
like hoffi (*vb*), fel (*prp.*)
list rhestr (*f.*)
  rhestr fer short list
listen (to) gwrando (ar) (SM) (*vb*)
little bach (*adj.*); tipyn (*m.*); ychydig (*ans.*)
live byw (*vb*) (*periph.*); byw (*ans.*)
lively bywiog (*adj.*)
load llwyth (*m.*)
loaf torth (*f.*)
local lleol (*adj.*)
lock cloi (*vb*)
lonely unig (*adj.*)
long hir (*adj.*)
  by a long way o bell ffordd
  for how long ers faint
longing hiraeth (*m.*)
look (at) edrych (ar) (*vb*),
  look for chwilio am (SM)
  look forward to edrych ymlaen at (SM)
lorry lorri (*f.*)
lose colli (*vb*)
loss colled (*f.*)
lost ar goll (*adj.*)
lot (of), lots of llawer (o) (SM) (*m.*)
loud uchel (*adj.*)
love cariad (*m.*); caru (*vb*)
low isel (*adj.*)
lovely hyfryd (*adj.*)
luck lwc (*f.*)
  good luck pob lwc
lucky lwcus (*adj.*)
  luckily trwy lwc
lunch cinio (*m.*)

M

main prif (*adj.*)
make (see **do**)

man dyn (*m.*)
manse mans (*m.*)
manager rheolwr (*m.*)
many llawer (*m.*)
market marchnad (*f.*)
marriage priodas (*f.*)
match(stick) matsien (*f.*)
material deunydd (*m.*)
mathematics mathemateg (*f.*)
may gallu (*vb*)
  may as well cystal i (SM) (*adv.*)
mean golygu (*vb*)
meaning ystyr (*m.*)
measles y frech goch (*f.*)
meat cig (*m.*)
medicine moddion (*pl.*)
meet (with) cwrdd (â) (AM) (*vb*) (SW), cyfarfod â (AM) (NW)
meeting cyfarfod (*m.*)
mess llanastr (*m.*)
message neges (*f.*)
mid canol (*m.*)
  midday hanner dydd
  midnight canol nos
milk llaeth (*m.*)
middle canol (*m.*)
mind meddwl (*m.*)
  in mind mewn golwg
  in two minds rhwng dau feddwl
minute munud (*f.*) (SW), (*m.*) (NW)
mirror drych (*m.*)
miserable diflas (*adj.*)
miss colli (*vb*)
misty niwlog (*adj.*)
money arian (SW), pres (NW) (*pl.*)
month mis (*m.*)
more rhagor (o) (SM) (*m.*), mwy (*adj.*)
morning bore (*m.*)
mortgage morgais (*m.*)
mother mam (*f.*)
motorway traffordd (*f.*)
mountain mynydd (*m.*)
move symud (*vb*)
music cerddoriaeth (*f.*)

N

name enw (*m.*); enwi (*vb*)
nasty (to) cas (wrth) (SM) (*adj.*)
national cenedlaethol (*adj.*)
naughty drwg (*adj.*)

near ar bwys (SW), yn ymyl (NW), wrth (SM) (*prp.*); agos (*adj.*)
nearly bron (*adv.*)
necessity rhaid (*m.*)
need eisiau (*m.*)
nephew nai (*m.*)
never (*adv.*) byth, erioed
  never mind heb sôn am (SM)
new newydd (*adj.*)
  brand new newydd sbon
news newyddion (*pl.*)
next nesaf (*adj.*)
nice hyfryd, neis (*adj.*)
niece nith (*f.*)
night nos (*f.*); noson (night's length; evening) (*f.*)
  a good night's sleep noson dda o gwsg
  good night nos da
  Monday night nos Lun
  the night before last echnos
nine naw (*adj.*)
nobody, no one neb (*pn*)
noise sŵn (*m.*)
nor na (AM) (*cnj.*)
north gogledd (*m.*)
not dim (*m.*)
  not to mention heb sôn am (SM)
  not yet dim eto
note nodyn (*m.*)
nothing dim (byd) (*m.*)
notice sylwi (*vb*)
  take notice of cymryd sylw o (SM) (*vb*)
novel nofel (*f.*)
now nawr (SW), rŵan (NW) (*adv.*)
  from now on o hyn ymlaen
number rhif (*m.*)
  phone number rhif ffôn (*m.*)
nurse nyrs (*f.*)

O

o'clock o'r gloch (*adj.*)
obtain cael (*vb*) (*irreg.*)
obvious amlwg (*adj.*)
occasion tro (*m.*)
of o (SM) (*prp.*)
  of course wrth gwrs
office swyddfa (*f*)
often aml (*adj.*)
old hen (*adj.*) (SM)

on ar (SM) (*prp.*)
  on behalf of dros (SM)
  on the left ar y chwith
  on the right ar y dde
once unwaith (*adv.*)
  at once ar unwaith
one un (*adj.*)
  ones rhai
online ar-lein (*adj.*)
only (see **lonely**), dim ond (*adv.*)
open agor (*vb*); ar agor (*adj.*)
or neu (*cnj.*) (SM)
orange oren (*adj.*)
order gorchymyn (*m.*) (*vb*)
other arall (*adj.*), eraill (*pl.*)
out allan (*adv.*)
outside tu allan (*adv.*)
  outside of tu allan i (SM)
over dros (SM) (*prp.*), uwchben
  overnight dros nos
  over there dacw, draw
  over the weekend dros y penwythnos
owe bod + ar (*vb*):
  I owe mae arna i
own meddu ar (SM) (*vb*); hunan (*adj.*)
  I own a cat Dw i'n meddu ar gath.
  on his own ar ei ben ei hunan

P

package pecyn (*m.*)
paint peintio (*vb*)
pair pâr (*m.*)
pale gwelw (*adj.*)
paper papur (*m.*)
  newspaper papur newyddion
  writing paper papur ysgrifennu
paranoid paranoiaidd (*adj.*)
parent rhiant (*m.*)
park parc (*m.*),
park parcio (*vb*)
particular arbennig (*adj.*)
partner partner (*m.*), cymar (*m.*)
party parti (*m.*)
pass estyn (*vb*)
past heibio (*adv.*)
pattern patrwm (*m.*)
pay talu (*vb*)
pedestrian crossing croesfan
Pembroke Penfro
pencil pensil

people pobl (*f.*)
pepper pupur (*m.*)
perfect perffaith (*adj.*)
perform perfformio (*vb*)
perfume persawr (*m.*)
perhaps efallai (SW), hwyrach (NW) (*adv.*)
period cyfnod (*m.*)
pet anifail anwes (*m.*)
phone (see **telephone**)
picture llun (*m.*)
piece darn (*m.*)
pink pinc (*adj.*)
pint peint (*m.*)
pity trueni (*m.*)
place lle (*m.*)
plan cynllun (*m.*)
play chwarae (*vb*); drama (*f.*)
pleasant hyfryd (*adj.*)
pocket poced (*f.*)
police(force) heddlu
policeman plismon (*m.*)
policewoman plismones (*f.*)
point pwynt (*m.*)
  on the point of ar fin
poor (quality) gwael (*adj.*)
possible posib (*adj.*)
post office swyddfa bost (*f.*)
postman postmon (*m.*)
postwoman postmones (*f.*)
pound (£) punt (*f.*)
pound (lb) pwys (*f.*)
practically bron (*adv.*)
practice ymarfer (*m.*)
practise ymarfer (*vb*)
pray gweddïo (*vb*)
  pray to gweddïo ar (SM)
  pray for gweddïo dros (SM)
prepare paratoi (*vb*)
present anrheg (*f.*)
pretty del (NW), pert (SW) (*adj.*)
price pris (*m.*)
prize gwobr (*f.*)
probably siŵr o fod (*adv.*)
problem problem (*f.*)
project prosiect (*m.*)
promise addo (*vb*)
proud balch (*adj.*)
pub tafarn (*f.*)
pudding pwdin (*m.*)
pull tynnu (*vb*)

punctual prydlon (*adj.*)
purple porffor (*adj.*)
put rhoi (*vb*)
  put on gwisgo (*vb*)
  put out (**fire**) diffodd (*vb*)

Q

question cwestiwn (*m.*)
quiet distaw, tawel (*adj.*)
quite eithaf (*adv.*)

R

race ras (*f.*)
radio radio (*m.*)
railway rheilffordd (*f.*)
rain bwrw (glaw) (*vb*), glaw (*m.*)
raise codi (*vb*)
  raise money codi arian
reach cyrraedd (*vb*)
read darllen (*vb*)
ready parod (*adj.*)
real gwir (*adj.*)
reason rheswm (*m.*)
  stands to reason wrth reswm
  reason for rheswm dros (SM)
reasonable rhesymol (*adj.*)
receive derbyn (*vb*)
recognise adnabod (*vb*) (*periph.*)
red coch (*adj.*)
refer to cyfeirio at (SM) (*vb*)
region ardal (*f.*)
(to be) related to perthyn i (SM) (*vb*)
relax ymlacio (*vb*)
remember (about) cofio (am) (SM) (*vb*)
remind atgoffa (*vb*)
report adroddiad (*m.*)
responsible cyfrifol (*adj.*)
result canlyniad (*m.*)
  as a result of o ganlyniad i (SM)
retire ymddeol (*vb*)
reward gwobr (*f.*)
right de (*f.*); iawn (*adj.*)
ring canu (*vb*)
road heol (*f.*) (SW), ffordd (*f.*) (NW)
room ystafell (*f.*)
rubber rwber (*m.*)
rugby rygbi (*m.*)
rule rheol (*f.*)
  as a rule fel rheol
run rhedeg (*vb*)

S

sad trist (*adj.*)
sack sach (*f.*)
safety diogelwch (*m.*)
  head of safety pennaeth diogelwch
sail hwylio (*vb*)
(the) same yr un
sand tywod (*m.*)
sandwich brechdan (*f.*)
satisfied bodlon (*adj.*)
sausage selsigen (*f.*)
say (to) dweud (wrth) (SM) (*vb*)
scene golygfa (*f.*)
scent arogl (*m.*)
school ysgol (*f.*)
  primary school ysgol gynradd (*f.*)
  secondary school ysgol uwchradd (*f.*)
score sgorio (*vb*)
Scotland Yr Alban
Scotsman Albanwr (*m.*)
Scotswoman Albanes (*f.*)
sea môr (*m.*)
search (for) chwilio am (SM)
seaside glan y môr
season tymor (*m.*)
seat sêt (*f.*)
second eiliad (*f.*)
see gweld (*vb*)
seem ymddangos (*vb*)
  it seems mae'n debyg
self hunan (*pn*), hunain (*pl.*)
sell gwerthu (*vb*)
send anfon (*vb*)
  send to (person) anfon at (SM)
  send to (place) anfon i (SM)
set out cychwyn (*vb*)
seven saith (*adj.*)
several sawl (*adj.*)
shame cywilydd (*m.*)
shoe esgid (*f.*)
shop siop (*f.*), siopa (*vb*)
  go shopping siopa
short byr (*adj.*)
shout (at) gweiddi (ar) (SM) (*vb*)
shovel rhaw (*f.*)
show (to) dangos (i) (SM) (*vb*)
shower cawod (*f.*)
shut cau (*vb*)
side ochr (*f.*)

by the side of wrth ochr
silly gwirion (*adj.*)
since (because) gan (*prp.*) (SM); ers (*prp.*)
since then ers hynny
sing canu (*vb*)
sister chwaer (*f.*)
sit eistedd (*vb*)
six chwech (*adj.*)
skirt sgert (*f.*)
sleep cysgu (*vb*), cwsg (*m.*)
sleet eirlaw (*m.*), bwrw eirlaw (*vb*)
slow araf (*adj.*)
small bach (*adj.*)
smartphone ffôn clyfar (*m.*)
smell arogl (*m.*)
smile gwenu (ar) (*vb*)
smoke smocio, ysmygu (*vb*)
snow eira (*m.*), bwrw eira (*vb*)
(Mount) Snowdon Yr Wyddfa
society cymdeithas (*f.*)
so felly (*adv.*); mor (SM) (*adv.*)
  so far hyd yn hyn
some rhyw (SM) (*pn*), rhai (*pl.*)
  somehow rhywsut
  someone rhywun, rhywrai (*pl.*)
  something rhywbeth
  sometime rhywbryd
  somewhere rhywle
son mab (*m.*)
song cân (*f.*)
sorrow gofid (*m.*)
sorry blin (*adj.*)
  I'm sorry mae'n flin 'da fi (SW)
  I'm sorry mae'n ddrwg gen i (NW)
south de (*m.*)
spade rhaw (*f.*)
speak (to) siarad (â) (AM) (*vb*)
special arbennig (*adj.*)
specialise (in) arbenigo (yn [NM]/mewn) (*vb*)
spend (money) gwario (*vb*)
spend (time) treulio (*vb*)
spill colli (*vb*)
splendid bendigedig (*adj.*)
spoon llwy (*f.*)
spring (y) gwanwyn (*m.*)
St David's Tyddewi
staff staff (*m.*)
stamp stamp (*m.*)
stand sefyll (*vb*)

stand up codi ar eich traed (*vb*)
stare syllu (ar) (SM) (*vb*)
start dechrau (*vb*), cychwyn (*vb*)
stay aros (*vb*)
steal lladrata (*vb*)
stem from deillio o (SM) (*vb*)
stepdaughter llysferch (*f.*)
stepfather llystad (*m.*)
stepmother llysfam (*f.*)
stepson llysfab (*m.*)
stick ffon (*f.*)
  ffon gerdded walking stick
stick to glynu wrth (SM) (*vb*)
still o hyd (*adv.*)
stop stopio (*vb*)
stormy stormus (*adj.*)
story hanes (*m.*)
straight syth (*adj.*)
  straight away yn syth
street stryd (*f.*)
stroll cerdded (*vb*)
strong cryf (*adj.*)
student myfyriwr (*m.*), myfyrwraig (*f.*)
study astudio (*vb*)
stupid twp (*adj.*)
succeed (in) llwyddo (i) (SM) (*vb*)
success (*m.*) llwyddiant
suffer (from) dioddef (o) (SM) (*vb*)
sugar siwgr (*m.*)
suit siwt (*f.*), siwtio (*vb*)
sulk pwdu (*vb*)
summer haf (*m.*)
sun haul (*m.*)
sun cream eli haul (*m.*)
sunny heulog (*adj.*)
supermarket archfarchnad (*f.*)
supper swper (*m.*)
support cefnogi (*vb*)
supporter cefnogwr (*m.*)
sure siŵr (*adj.*)
  sure to siŵr o (SM)
surprise syndod (*m.*)
  be surprised (at) synnu (at) (SM) (*vb*)
Swansea Abertawe
sweetheart cariad (*m.*)
swim nofio (*vb*)
swimming pool pwll nofio (*m.*)
  switch off (light) diffodd (*vb*)
  switch on cynnau (*vb*)

sympathise with cydymdeimlo â (AM) (*vb*)

T

table bord (*f.*) (SW), bwrdd (*m.*) (NW)
take mynd â (*vb*); cymryd (*vb*)
  take an interest in cymryd diddordeb yn (NM)/mewn
  take hold of cydio yn (NM)/mewn (*vb*)
talk about siarad am (SM) (*vb*)
tall tal (*adj.*)
tasty blasus (*adj.*)
tea te (*m.*)
teach dysgu (*vb*)
teacher athro (*m.*), athrawes (*f.*)
team tîm (*m.*)
telephone ffôn (*m.*); ffonio (*vb*)
  telephone number rhif ffôn
television teledu (*m.*)
tell (*vb*) dweud (wrth) (SM)
ten deg (*adj.*)
tend (to) tueddu (i) (SM) (*vb*)
tennis tennis (*m.*)
  tennis bwrdd table tennis
term tymor (*m.*)
test prawf (*m.*)
than na (AM) (*conj.*)
  than expected na'r disgwyl
thanks diolch (*m.*)
  thanks for diolch am (SM)
  thank you very much diolch yn fawr iawn
that hynny (*pn*) (*abstract*); bod (present and past imperfect) (*vb*), y (future and conditional) (preverbial particle)
  that one hwnna (*pn*) (*m.*), honna (*pn*) (*f.*)
the y (<yr> before vowels and <'r> after vowels)
theatre theatr (*f.*)
then wedyn (*adv.*)
there (not in sight) yno (*adv.*)
there (is/are) dyna (SM) (*adv.*)
therefore felly (*adv.*)
thick trwchus (*adj.*)
thing peth (*m.*)
think (about) meddwl (am) (SM) (*vb*)
thirst syched (*m.*)

thirsty sychedig (*adj.*)
this hwn (*m.*), hon (*f.*) (*pn*)
those y rheiny (*pn*)
thought meddwl (*m.*)
thousand mil (*f.*)
three tri (*m.*), tair (*f.*)
through trwy (*prp.*) (SM)
throughout trwy (*prp.*) (SM)
ticket tocyn (*m.*)
tight tyn (*adj.*)
time amser (*m.*), gwaith (*f.*), tro (*m.*)
  at the time ar y pryd
  from time to time o bryd i'w gilydd
  four times pedair gwaith
  in time mewn pryd
tire blino (*vb*)
  tired wedi blino
  tire of blino ar (SM)
to (a person) at (*prp.*) (SM), (a place) i (SM)
  to the i'r
today heddiw (*adv.*)
together (us) gyda'n gilydd
tomorrow yfory (*adv.*)
tonight heno (*adv.*)
too hefyd (*adv.*); rhy (SM) (*adv.*)
  too much (of) gormod (o) (SM)
tooth dant (*f.*)
toothache y ddannodd (*f.*)
towards at (*prp.*) (SM)
town tref (*f.*)
toy tegan (*m.*)
train trên (*m.*)
trainer hyfforddwr (*m.*)
travel teithio (*vb*)
tree coeden (*f.*)
trip taith (*f.*)
trust in ymddiried yn (NM)/mewn (*vb*)
true gwir (*adj.*)
truth gwir (*m.*)
try ceisio, trïo (*vb*)
tummy bol (*m.*)
turn troi (*vb*)
  turn down troi i lawr
  turn one's back cefnu ar (SM)
turning tro (*m.*)
twelve deuddeg (*adj.*)
two dau (SM) (*m.*), dwy (*adj.*) (SM) (*f.*)
type math (*m.*) mathau (*pl.*)

what type of pa fath o (SM)

U

umbrella ymbarél (*f.*)
uncle ewyrth (*m.*)
under (o) dan (*prp.*) (SM)
understand deall (*vb*)
unexpected annisgwyl (*adj.*)
unfortunately yn anffodus (*adv.*)
unless oni bai (*conj.*)
until tan (SM) (*prp.*), hyd nes
up i fyny (*adv.*), ar (SM) (*prp.*)
use defnyddio (*vb*)
(get) used to arfer (*vb*) (*periph.*)
usually fel arfer (*adv.*)

V

van fan (*f.*)
vegetable llysieuyn (*m.*), llysiau (*pl.*)
venture mentro (*vb*)
very (*adv.*) iawn
  very much yn fawr iawn
vicar ficer (*m.*)
village pentref (*m.*)
visit ymweld (â) (AM) (*vb*)
voice llais (*m.*)
vote for pleidleisio dros (SM) (*vb*)

W

wait aros (*vb*)
wake (up) dihuno (*vb*)
Wales Cymru
walk cerdded (*vb*)
  go for a walk mynd am dro
walking stick (see **stick**)
wall wal (*f.*)
want eisiau (*m.*)
warm twym (*adj.*) (SW), cynnes (*adj.*) (NW)
wash golchi (*vb*)
  wash (oneself) ymolchi (*vb*)
watch gwylio (*vb*), wats (*f.*)
water dŵr (*m.*)
way ffordd (*f.*)
  by a long way o bell ffordd
wear gwisgo (*vb*)
weather tywydd (*m.*)
web gwe (*f.*)
wedding priodas (*f.*)
week wythnos (*f.*)

next week yr wythnos nesaf
weekend penwythnos (*m.*)
  over the weekend dros y penwythnos
welcome croeso (*m.*)
welcome croesawu (*vb*)
Welsh (*f.*) Cymraeg (language); Cymreig (country)
Welshman Cymro (*m.*), **Cymry** (*pl.*)
Welshwoman Cymraes (*f.*), **Cymraesau** (*pl.*)
well yn dda (*adv.*)
west gorllewin (*m.*)
wet gwlyb (*adj.*)
what beth (*pn*) (SM)
  what time faint o'r gloch
  what type of pa fath o (SM)
when pryd (*adv.*)
where ble (*adv.*), lle (*cnj.*)
white gwyn (*adj.*)
who pwy (*pn*)
why pam (*adv.*)
wife gwraig (*f.*)
willing bodlon (*adj.*)
win ennill (*vb*)
wind gwynt (*m.*)
window ffenestr (*f.*)
windy gwyntog (*adj.*)
wine gwin (*m.*)
winter (y) gaeaf (*m.*)
wish dymuno (*vb*)

with â (AM) (*prp.*); gyda (AM) (SW), efo (NW) (*prp.*)
within (**time**) ymhen (*prp.*)
without heb (SM) (*prp.*)
woman benyw (*f.*)
wooden pren (*adj.*)
word gair (*m.*)
work gwaith (*m.*)
work gweithio (*vb*)
world byd (*m.*)
worry poeni (*vb*), gofid (*m.*)
worse gwaeth (*adj.*)
worsen gwaethygu (*vb*)
write to ysgrifennu at (SM) (*vb*)

Y

year blwyddyn (*f.*), blwydd (with age), blynedd (after numerals) (*pl.*)
  last year llynedd (*adv.*)
  this year eleni (*adv.*)
yellow melyn (*adj.*), melen (*f.*)
yesterday ddoe (*adv.*)
yet eto (*adv.*)
yonder (**is/are**) dacw (SM) (*adv.*)
you chi (*pn*) (*formal*), ti (*informal*)
young ifanc (*adj.*), ifainc (*pl.*)

Z

zero (*m.*) dim

Index

adjective, 8, 9, 11, 12, 18, 19, 20, 45, 60, 62, 71, 72, 97, 137, 165, 208, 212, 215, 216, 218, 309, 310, 340
adverbial, 20, 45, 86, 92, 107, 109, 155, 309, 310, 326, 340, 412
affixed pronouns, 124, 171
alphabet, 1, 5
antecedent, 197, 198, 324, 326, 327, 328
asking permission, 250
aspectual marker, 36, 38, 44, 114, 131, 190, 311
aspirate mutation, 10, 11, 27, 121, 129, 177, 182, 195, 199, 213, 216, 242, 250, 327, 350
auxiliary verbs, 247
Breton, 10
Canolfan Dysgu Cymraeg Genedlaethol (the National Centre for Teaching Welsh), 359
Common European Framework of Reference for Languages, 359
compound prepositions, 301
conditional clause, 317
conditional clauses, 316
consonant, 2, 3, 4, 177, 181, 182, 186, 188, 232, 237, 242, 245, 246, 250, 254, 299, 343, 351
consonants, 1, 2, 9, 10, 105, 106, 182, 195, 199, 242, 294
copula, 20
Cornish, 10
decimal counting system, 17
declension, 271, 274, 276, 277, 280, 282, 284, 285, 286, 287, 288, 300, 301
defective verbs, 335
definite article, 9, 14, 15, 48, 72, 91, 221
definite noun, 48, 73, 75, 82, 83, 84
demonstrative phrases, 30, 31, 35
diacritical marks, 5
diacritics, 2
diaeresis, 5
digraphs, 1
diphthong, 4, 5
eisteddfodau, 271, 407
emphatic conjunction, 156
emphatic sentences, 340, 343, 344
equative comparison of adjectives, 212
expressing 'ever' & 'never', 268
expressing a preference, 202
expressing obligation, 206
formulaic subjunctive, 308, 400
gender, 6, 21, 203, 241, 327

genitive noun phrase, 48, 73
habituality, 309
identification sentences, 20, 23, 24, 25, 340
identification structure, 219
imperative, 36, 164, 172, 351, 399, 401
imperfect aspectual marker, 36
impersonal inflection, 346
impossibility, 311
indefinite article, 7, 9, 257
indefinite noun, 56, 73, 75, 81, 83, 84, 96, 297
independent pronouns, 80, 126
indicative mood, 36, 308, 310, 316, 346, 399
inflected verbs, 36, 172, 235, 298, 321
inflection, 36, 100, 171, 180, 297, 319, 351
interrogative adverb, 46
interrogative identification sentence, 24
interrogative pronoun, 94
Irish, 10
labialization, 3
locative adverbs, 30, 56
Manx, 10
monophthong, 3
must be, 126, 207, 208, 209, 217
mutation, 10, 119
nasal mutation, 10, 11, 45, 105, 106, 107, 108, 114, 285
negative identification sentence, 23
negative particle, 153, 231, 343, 350
nominative clauses, 156
North Welsh, 2, 4, 7, 80, 82, 83, 84, 85, 87, 213, 216, 293, 375, 378
noun plural, 6
nouns, 6, 7, 8, 10, 12, 14, 16, 18, 28, 29, 30, 39, 48, 49, 60, 62, 71, 73, 74, 75, 76, 77, 126, 142, 164, 165, 166, 190, 221, 228, 247, 248, 257, 258, 272, 275, 278, 282, 285, 286, 287, 289, 294, 295, 299, 310, 327, 338
numerals, 11, 15, 16, 17, 19, 28, 29, 106, 108, 133, 158, 159, 256, 403, 428
object, 20, 36, 79, 100, 167, 172, 177, 178, 249, 276, 297, 298, 314, 324, 326, 342, 347
oblique relative clause, 325, 326
ordinals, 158, 256, 257, 258
palatalization, 299
parenthesis, 86
partitive genitive, 104

passive voice, 320, 328, 348
past imperfect aspect, 141, 143, 190, 197, 230
past perfect aspect, 149
perfect aspect, 65, 130, 131, 149
perfect aspectual marker, 38
points of the compass, 59, 63
polite command, 247
possession, 73, 78, 79, 80, 81, 86, 293, 344
predicate, 20, 156
predicative marker, 44, 60
prefixed possessive pronouns, 114, 118, 119, 120, 121, 124, 126, 128, 150, 151, , 216301, 322, 323, 327
prepositional clauses, 210
prepositions, 11, 38, 45, 48, 80, 81, 92, 97, 107, 120, 122, 123, 124, 126, 127, 129, 130, 138, 143, 153179, 200, 201, 202, 206, 213, 272, 276, 278, 291, 297, 298, 299, 303, 307, 326, 340 200, 272, 280, 281, 284, 289, 301
present habitual, 39
present tense, 20, 21, 36, 37, 38, 39, 40, 49, 51, 53, 66, 73, 79, 81, 115, 131, 149, 197, 228, 244, 305, 343
preverbal particle, 172, 173
proverbs and truisms, 308
relative clause, 197, 198, 324, 326, 341
relative particle, 197, 324, 325, 328, 341, 342
Romance languages, 87
S4C, 361
Scots Gaelic, 2, 10
semivowel, 4, 5
simple future tense, 36, 235, 236, 239, 255
simple past tense, 36, 141, 171, 174, 177, 180, 181, 182, 185, 186, 188, 190, 194, 198, 199, 235, 237, 245

soft mutation, 10, 11, 12, 14, 17, 19, 29, 44, 45, 56, 57, 60, 71, 80, 86, 87, 88, 119, 120, 129, 134, 137, 167, 172, 177, 181, 182, 190, 194, 197, 199, 201, 205, 213, 214, 221, 230, 231, 237, 242, 243, 245, 250, 254, 257, 258, 259, 273, 275, 277, 282, 283, 286, 288, 289, 299, 310, 314, 327, 342, 350
South Welsh, 2, 4, 79, 82, 83, 84, 85, 195, 211, 293, 294, 374, 375, 377
stress accent, 1, 2, 3, 5
subject, 20, 21, 22, 23, 25, 36, 39, 45, 49, 81, 83, 84, 142, 145, 146, 156, 172, 175, 177, 181, 185, 186, 188, 194, 228, 230, 232, 235, 237, 250, 254, 313, 314, 317, 319, 322, 324, 326, 335, 342, 343
subjunctive mood, 36, 308, 335, 399, 400
superlative form of adjectives, 218
that-clause, 150
verb, 20, 21, 27, 28, 36, 38, 39, 51, 62, 66, 79, 80, 96, 114, 115, 124, 130, 137, 142, 143, 150, 164, 165, 166, 167, 168, 169, 171, 172, 173, 174, 176, 177, 178, 181, 182, 183, 188, 190, 194, 195, 201, 206, 207, 219, 222, 228, 230, 232, 235, 236, 237, 240, 242, 245, 246, 247, 248, 249, 250, 251, 254, 263, 265, 272, 275, 278, 282, 285, 286, 287, 289, 294, 297, 298, 299, 306, 308, 310, 314, 315, 319, 320, 321, 323, 324, 327, 335, 337, 338, 340, 342, 346, 347, 348, 349, 351, 399, 401
verb-nouns, 36, 38, 96, 114, 115, 143, 164, 165, 167, 171, 173, 176, 201, 206, 207, 222, 235, 236, 263, 272, 286, 314, 321, 323, 327338, 340, 347
verbs of mental state, 143, 171
vigesimal counting system, 17, 256